CW01335904

RIGHTS OF WAY

a guide to law and practice

Second edition
by John Riddall and John Trevelyan

THE OPEN SPACES SOCIETY

The Ramblers

First edition by Paul Clayden and John Trevelyan published 1983
Second edition published 1992

Cover Design by DP Press Ltd, St Julians, Sevenoaks, Kent TN15 0RX

© 1992 by Commons, Open Spaces and Footpaths Preservation Society and Ramblers' Association

Extracts from Acts of Parliament, Statutory Instruments and Government Circulars are Parliamentary or Crown Copyright and are included with the permission of the Controller of Her Majesty's Stationery Office or the issuing department.

British Library Cataloguing in Publication Data
A catalogue record for this book is available from the British Library

ISBN 0 946574 04 9
ISBN 0 900613 73 4 (Ramblers' Association)

Typeset, printed and bound in Great Britain by H Charlesworth and Co. Ltd., Huddersfield HD2 1JJ

Preface

Major changes to rights-of-way legislation contained in the Wildlife and Countryside Act 1981 provided the spur to the production of the first edition of this book. It incorporated material previously published elsewhere by the RA, and by the OSS under its full title of the Commons, Open Spaces and Footpaths Preservation Society, and we are grateful to Mr J J Pearlman LLB, Honorary Solicitor to the RA, and to Mr Ian Campbell LLB and Mrs Mary McArevey, both of whom formerly worked for the OSS, for their permission to use material previously published over their names.

Since the first edition in 1983, there have been several important court cases on the provisions of the 1981 Act. These, together with other relevant cases, have been included.

There have also been changes to the legislative provisions included in the second part of the book, with, in particular, consolidation of the legislation now in the Road Traffic Regulation Act 1984, the Road Traffic Act 1988 and the Town and Country Planning Act 1990. Other new legislation of importance includes the Cycle Tracks Act 1984, the Local Government Act 1985, the Local Government (Access to Information) Act 1985, the Environmental Protection Act 1990 and the Rights of Way Act 1990. Associated regulations and circulars have also been included. The legislation is stated as at *1 April 1991*.

The structure of the first part of the book has been revised, with the former appendices included in chapters, and with legal action on obstructions and maintenance included in chapters 6 and 7 on those subjects. Chapters 2 and 4 have also been substantially rewritten, with a new chapter 3 on how rights of way come into existence. Chapter 5 has been amended in the light of experience with the Wildlife and Countryside Act 1981. Further text has been added, in chapter 9, giving an outline of ways in which a right to roam, as distinct from a right of way, may arise. The index has been revised and expanded.

Thanks are due to all who assisted us with this second edition, whether by commenting on draft material, suggesting additional topics or drawing our attention to deficiencies in the first edition. Particular thanks are due to Paul Clayden, now Deputy Secretary of the National Association of Local Councils, and to J J Pearlman LLB, on whose extensive practical experience of rights-of-way law we have drawn widely.

John Riddall
Hills View Cottage
Bradwell
Derbyshire S30 2HR

John Trevelyan
Ramblers' Association
1/5 Wandsworth Road
London SW8 2XX

Contents

Table of cases   12
Table of statutes (Acts of Parliament)   16
Table of statutory instruments (Regulations)   23
Table of circulars issued by government departments   25
Abbreviations used   26

1 : Introduction
1.1 The value of public rights of way   29
1.2 Definitions in this book   31
    1.2.1 *Rights of way and highways*
    1.2.2 *Local authorities*
    1.2.3 *Other definitions*
1.3 Rights of way, local authorities and central government   33
    1.3.1 *Highway authorities*
    1.3.2 *Surveying authorities*
    1.3.3 *District councils and planning boards*
    1.3.4 *National parks and the Broads Authority*
    1.3.5 *Greater London*
    1.3.6 *Local councils*
    1.3.7 *Access to local authority meetings and information*
    1.3.8 *Crown land*
    1.3.9 *The Parliamentary Commissioner for Administration*
1.4 Rights of way and the legal system   39
    1.4.1 *Sources of law*
    1.4.2 *Criminal law and civil law*
    1.4.3 *The courts*
    1.4.4 *Law reports*

2 : Public rights of way
2.1 What is a public right of way?   43
2.2 'Once a highway, always a highway'   43
2.3 The public's rights   43
    2.3.1 *Extent of the rights*
    2.3.2 *Dogs*
2.4 Trespass   46
    2.4.1 *Nature of trespass*
    2.4.2 *Deviation from a right of way*
    2.4.3 *Trespass as a crime*
2.5 Who owns a highway?   48
    2.5.1 *The subsoil*

      2.5.2   *The surface of a publicly-maintainable highway*
      2.5.3   *Transfer of land*
2.6   Liability for injury to the user of a right of way   50
      2.6.1   *Injury caused by failure to repair the way*
      2.6.2   *Injury caused by a defective stile or gate*
      2.6.3   *When deviating with the owner's permission*
      2.6.4   *When deviating to avoid an obstruction*
      2.6.5   *When trespassing*
      2.6.6   *The Occupiers' Liability Act 1957*
2.7   Who can use which highways?   53
      2.7.1   *Pedal cyclists*
      2.7.2   *Horse-riders*
      2.7.3   *Motor vehicles*
      2.7.4   *Public nuisance*
      2.7.5   *Processions*
2.8   Certain special types of way   56
      2.8.1   *Permissive paths*
      2.8.2   *Paths across railway lines*
      2.8.3   *Tow-paths*
      2.8.4   *The sea-shore*
      2.8.5   *Ferries*

3 : How rights of way come into being
3.1   Express dedication   61
3.2   Presumed dedication — at common law   62
3.3   Presumed dedication — under section 31 of the Highways Act 1980   62
      3.3.1   *A summary of the provisions*
      3.3.2   *Nature of the way*
      3.3.3   *Nature of the public's use*
      3.3.4   *Evidence of an intention not to dedicate*
      3.3.5   *Calculation of the 20-year period*
      3.3.6   *Presumed dedication of one highway over another*
      3.3.7   *Ancient ways*
      3.3.8   *Other matters*
3.4   Statute   71
      3.4.1   *Creation orders*
      3.4.2   *Creation agreements by local authorities*
      3.4.3   *Creation agreements by local councils*
      3.4.4   *Maintenance of a dedicated way*
      3.4.5   *Other statutory creation*

4 : Definitive maps and other records
4.1   Introduction   73
4.2   The initial survey under the National Parks Act 1949   74
      4.2.1   *The preliminary work and consultations*

CONTENTS

    4.2.2   The geographical extent of the survey
    4.2.3   Publishing the draft map
    4.2.4   The relevant date
    4.2.5   The statement
    4.2.6   Modifying the draft map and statement
    4.2.7   Objections dealt with by the Secretary of State
    4.2.8   The provisional map and statement
    4.2.9   The definitive map and statement
    4.2.10 Surveys following the Countryside Act 1968
4.3 Reviews under the National Parks Act 1949   82
    4.3.1   Introduction
    4.3.2   The events to be considered
    4.3.3   Timing and procedure
4.4 Reviews under the Countryside Act 1968   83
    4.4.1   The two-stage procedure
    4.4.2   Timing of reviews
    4.4.3   Deletion of paths on review
    4.4.4   Reclassification of roads used as public paths
4.5 Changes made by the Local Government Act 1972   88
4.6 The Wildlife and Countryside Act 1981   89
    4.6.1   The changes summarised
    4.6.2   Existing surveys and reviews
    4.6.3   Areas previously excluded from the survey
    4.6.4   Bringing and keeping existing maps up to date
    4.6.5   Procedure for making and confirming orders
    4.6.6   Deletion and downgrading of paths
    4.6.7   Reclassification of roads used as public paths
    4.6.8   How to apply for a modification order
    4.6.9   Conclusive evidence
    4.6.10 Supplementary provisions
4.7 The 'relevant date' of a path on the definitive map   105
4.8 The progress of the survey and reviews   105
    4.8.1   The position at 31 March 1974
    4.8.2   The position at 28 February 1983
    4.8.3   Progress since 28 February 1983
4.9 Evidence of right-of-way status   108
    4.9.1   Documentary evidence
    4.9.2   User evidence
4.10 Lists of streets   117
4.11 Rights of way on Ordnance Survey maps   118

5 : Changes to the network
5.1 How can changes come about?   121
    5.1.1   Introduction
    5.1.2   Use of the powers
    5.1.3   Summary list of powers for changing the network

RIGHTS OF WAY

5.2 Administrative procedure for public path orders   125
    5.2.1 Introduction
    5.2.2 Consultation
    5.2.3 Making the order and publishing the notice
    5.2.4 Dealing with objections
    5.2.5 Procedure at public inquiries
    5.2.6 Decision and confirmation
    5.2.7 Modification
    5.2.8 Coming into operation
    5.2.9 Application to the High Court
    5.2.10 Subsequent variation or revocation
    5.2.11 Charging applicants
    5.2.12 Compensation
    5.2.13 Procedure for Secretary of State's orders
5.3 Changes using the administrative procedure   137
    5.3.1 Public path extinguishment orders
    5.3.2 Public path diversion orders
    5.3.3 Public path creation orders
    5.3.4 Concurrent orders under the Highways Act 1980
    5.3.5 Rights of way affected by development
    5.3.6 Orders under the Town and Country Planning Act 1990
    5.3.7 Other development : roads, reservoirs, mines and airports
    5.3.8 Land held for housing and planning purposes
5.4 Changes using other procedures   153
    5.4.1 Applications to the magistrates' court
    5.4.2 Private and Local Acts of Parliament
    5.4.3 Rights of way over military land
5.5 Changes to permit or restrict vehicular use   158
    5.5.1 Traffic regulation orders
    5.5.2 Cycle Tracks Act conversion orders
    5.5.3 Extinguishment of vehicular rights
5.6 How to oppose a path order   162
5.7 Temporary changes   165
    5.7.1 Major development
    5.7.2 Maintenance
    5.7.3 Animal and plant diseases
    5.7.4 Disturbance of a public path over agricultural land
5.8 Major changes to the network   167
    5.8.1 Rationalisation schemes in Nottinghamshire and West Sussex
    5.8.2 'Changing the Rights of Way Network'

6 : Obstructions and other nuisances
6.1 What is an obstruction?   169
6.2 The highway authority's duty to prevent obstructions   170
6.3 The highway authority's powers of enforcement   172

CONTENTS

- 6.4 Ploughing and other disturbance or damage — 173
  - 6.4.1 Introduction
  - 6.4.2 Common law right to plough
  - 6.4.3 Statutory right to plough
  - 6.4.4 Making good and marking the line
  - 6.4.5 The minimum width
  - 6.4.6 Enforcement and default powers
  - 6.4.7 Other disturbance of the surface
  - 6.4.8 Damaging the surface of a highway
- 6.5 Crops and overhanging vegetation — 180
  - 6.5.1 Crops as an obstruction
  - 6.5.2 Section 137A of the Highways Act 1980
  - 6.5.3 Overhanging vegetation
- 6.6 Bulls, dogs and other animals — 184
  - 6.6.1 Bulls
  - 6.6.2 Dogs
  - 6.6.3 Horses
  - 6.6.4 Animals generally
- 6.7 Other forms of obstruction or nuisance — 186
  - 6.7.1 Statutory nuisances
  - 6.7.2 Stiles, gates and barriers
  - 6.7.3 Unauthorised or misleading notices and signs
  - 6.7.4 Intimidation
  - 6.7.5 Motor vehicles
  - 6.7.6 Firearms and fires
  - 6.7.7 Dangerous excavations and erections
  - 6.7.8 Barbed wire at the side of highways
  - 6.7.9 Pesticides
  - 6.7.10 Miscellaneous nuisances
- 6.8 Getting an obstruction removed — 195
  - 6.8.1 Self-help — the remedy of abatement
  - 6.8.2 Reporting problems
- 6.9 Action in the magistrates' court — 198
  - 6.9.1 Introduction
  - 6.9.2 Before starting proceedings
  - 6.9.3 Proof of highway status
  - 6.9.4 Anticipate the defence
  - 6.9.5 Laying the complaint
  - 6.9.6 The hearing
  - 6.9.7 Appeals
- 6.10 Prosecutions for obstruction under the Highways Act 1980 — 204
  - 6.10.1 'Without lawful authority or excuse'
  - 6.10.2 'Wilfully'
  - 6.10.3 'Obstructs the free passage'
  - 6.10.4 A continuing offence

RIGHTS OF WAY

     6.10.5 The penalty
     6.10.6 Before starting proceedings
     6.10.7 The wording of the complaint
     6.10.8 Particular points
6.11 Prosecutions for crop interference under the Highways Act 1980   210
     6.11.1 Before starting proceedings
     6.11.2 The wording of the complaint
     6.11.3 Particular points
6.12 Application for an order to abate a nuisance   214
     6.12.1 Before starting proceedings
     6.12.2 The wording of the complaint
     6.12.3 Particular points
6.13 Other legal action   218
     6.13.1 Applications for judicial review
     6.13.2 Prosecutions for obstruction under the common law
     6.13.3 Civil proceedings for an injunction

7 : Maintenance and improvement
7.1 What constitutes maintenance?   219
7.2 Whose job is it?   221
     7.2.1 Privately- and publicly-maintainable highways
     7.2.2 The duties of highway authorities
     7.2.3 The powers of non-metropolitan district councils
     7.2.4 The powers of local councils
     7.2.5 Waterside paths
7.3 How wide should a path be?   227
7.4 Stiles and gates   228
7.5 The civil liability of highway authorities   229
7.6 Enforcing the duty to maintain   230
     7.6.1 Introduction
     7.6.2 Outline of the procedure
     7.6.3 The preliminary steps
     7.6.4 Serving the notice
     7.6.5 Applying to the magistrates' court
     7.6.6 Applying to the Crown Court
     7.6.7 Further application to the magistrates' court
7.7 Improving rights of way   236
     7.7.1 Introduction
     7.7.2 Signposting and waymarking
     7.7.3 Widening
     7.7.4 Aids to passage
     7.7.5 Footways, subways and bridges over carriageways
     7.7.6 Margins for horse-riders
     7.7.7 Other specific improvement powers

CONTENTS

    7.7.8   *The general power of highway authorities*
    7.7.9   *Powers of local councils*

8 : Things you can do
8.1   Introduction   242
8.2   Getting problems dealt with   243
    8.2.1   *Reporting problems*
    8.2.2   *Inducing a highway authority to act*
8.3   Path surveys   249
8.4   Producing a path guide or map   253
8.5   Waymarking   257
    8.5.1   *Introduction*
    8.5.2   *The recommended arrow*
    8.5.3   *Materials and equipment for painting waymarks*
8.6   Stile building   261
    8.6.1   *Introduction*
    8.6.2   *Dimensions*
    8.6.3   *Construction and erection*
8.7   Path clearance   265

9 : Further information
9.1   A right to roam : access to open country and commons   270
    9.1.1   *By permission of the landowner*
    9.1.2   *Access agreements*
    9.1.3   *Access orders*
    9.1.4   *Common land under Law of Property Act 1925 s 193*
    9.1.5   *Common land owned by the National Trust*
    9.1.6   *Common law — acquisition by long usage?*
    9.1.7   *Information about rights of access to land*
9.2   Statistics of recreational activity   275
9.3   Long-distance routes   276
9.4   Further reading   278
9.5   Useful addresses   281

Acts, Regulations and Circulars
Introduction   285
Acts of Parliament (table on p 16)   286
Regulations (table on p 23)   445
Circulars (table on p 25)   480

Index   517

RIGHTS OF WAY
TABLE OF CASES

Abel v Stone (1969) (unreported)	207, 210
Absalom v Martin [1974] RTR 145	207
A-G v Antrobus [1905] 2 Ch 188	273
A-G v Benyon [1969] 2 All ER 273	227
A-G v Brotherton (1991) Times 10 December 1991	63
A-G v Colchester Corporation [1955] 2 QB 207	60
A-G v Harris [1961] 1 QB 74	208
A-G v Sharpness New Docks Co [1914] 3 KB 1	223
A-G v Staffordshire CC [1905] 1 Ch 336	226
A-G v Watford Rural District [1912] 1 Ch 417	223
Arrowsmith v Jenkins [1963] 2 QB 561	205
Ashby & Dalby v Secretary of State for the Environment [1980] 1 All ER 508	148
Bagshaw v Buxton Local Board of Health (1875) 1 Ch D 220	170
Bateman v Burge (1834) 6 C & P 391	169, 194
Bishop Auckland Local Board v Bishop Auckland Iron Co (1882) 10 QBD 138	187
Blake, see R v Secretary of State for the Environment, ex p Blake	
Braim, see R v Doncaster Metropolitan Borough Council ex p Braim	
British Railways Board v Herrington [1972] AC 877	51
British Transport Commission v Westmorland CC [1958] AC 126	58, 62
Burgess v Northwich Local Board (1880) 6 QBD 264	219
Burns v Ellicott (1969) 113 SJ 490	239
Burrows, see R v Secretary of State for the Environment, ex parte Burrows & Simms	
Campodonic v Evans (1966) 200 EG 857	205
Cheshire CC, see R v Secretary of State for the Environment, ex p Cheshire CC	
Colchester Corporation v Brooke (1845) 7 QBD 339	195
De Rothschild v Buckinghamshire CC (1957) 55 LGR 595	67
Devon CC v Gateway Foodmarkets Ltd (1990) Daily Telegraph 22 March 1990	169
Dimes v Petley (1850) 15 QBD 276	196
Dollman v Hillman [1941] 1 All ER 355	194
Durham CC v Scott [1991] JPL 362	169, 205
Dyfed CC v Secretary of State for Wales (1988) (unreported)	96
Dyfed CC v Secretary of State for Wales (1989) 58 P & CR 68	64
Fairey v Southampton CC [1956] 2 QB 439	63, 65, 67
Fowler, see R v Devon CC, ex p Fowler	
Gloucestershire CC v Farrow [1985] 1 WLR 741	69
Grampian Regional Council v City of Aberdeen District Council [1984] 47 P & CR 633	146

CONTENTS

Grand Junction Canal Co v Petty (1881) 21 QB 373	58
Gravesham Borough Council v Wilson and Straight [1983] JPL 607	155, 156
Greenhalgh v British Railways Board [1969] 2 All ER 114	53, 58
Griesley's case (1669) 1 Vent 4	173
Gully v Smith (1883) 12 QB 21	206, 207, 210
Guyer, see R v Lancashire CC, ex p Guyer	
Harrison v Duke of Rutland [1893] 1 QB 145	44
Harvey v Truro Rural District Council [1903] 2 Ch 638	43
Haydon v Kent CC [1978] 2 WLR 485	229
Hereford & Worcester CC v Newman [1975] 1 WLR 901	219, 230
Hickman v Maisey [1900] 1 QB 752	44
Hood, see R v Secretary of State for the Environment, ex p Hood	
Hue v Whiteley [1929] 1 Ch 440	64
Hunt v Broome [1974] 2 WLR 58	205
James v Hayward (1630) Cro Car 184	194
Johnson, see R v West Sussex Quarter Sessions, ex p Albert and Maud Johnson Trust	
Jones v Bates [1938] 2 All ER 237	29, 65, 121
K C Holdings Ltd v Secretary of State for Wales [1990] JPL 353	147
King v Page (1970) 114 SJ 355	205
G & K Ladenbau Ltd v Crawley & de Reya [1978] 1 WLR 266	49
League against Cruel Sports v Scott [1985] 2 All ER 489	45
Lewis v Thomas [1950] 1 KB 438	65
London Borough of Redbridge v Jacques [1971] 1 All ER 260	170, 205
Mayor of Tunbridge Wells v Baird [1896] AC 434	48
Mercer v Woodgate (1869) 5 QB 26	174
Merstham Manor v Coulsdon & Purley Urban District Council [1937] 2 KB 77	64
Mint v Good [1951] 1 KB 517	194
Monmouthshire Canal Co v Hill (1859) 4 H & N 421	58
Morgan v Herts CC (1965) 63 LGR 456	80
Nagy v Weston [1965] 1 WLR 280	170
New Windsor Corporation v Mellor [1975] 3 All ER 44	273
O'Keefe, see R v Isle of Wight CC, ex p O'Keefe	
Overland and Howard v Secretary of State for the Environment and Norfolk CC (1987) (unreported)	65
Owen v Buckinghamshire CC (1957) 8 P & CR 312	67
Pearson v Secretary of State for the Environment (1981) 42 P & CR 40	86, 93, 218
Pridham v Hemel Hempstead Corporation (1969) 114 SJ 92	229
Pugh v Pigden (1987) 151 JP 644	170

Puttnam v Colvin [1984] RTR 150   194

Ramblers' Association v Kent CC (1990) JP 716   153, 154, 155
R v Dart (1865) 29 JP 359   186
R v Devon CC, ex p Fowler [1991] JPL 520   81, 87
R v Doncaster Metropolitan Borough Council ex p Braim (1987)
   85 LGR 233   273
R v Greenhow (1876) 1 QBD 703   226
R v High Halden (1859) 1 F & F 678   219
R v Isle of Wight CC, ex p O'Keefe [1989] JPL 934   94
R v Lancashire CC, ex p Guyer [1980] 2 All ER 520   172, 248
R v Matthias (1861) 2 F & F 570   44, 55, 169, 193
R v Ogden, ex p Long Ashton Rural District Council [1963]
   1 All ER 574   200
R v Petrie (1855) 4 El & Bl 737   62
R v Richmond upon Thames BC, ex parte McCarthy & Stone
   (1991) Times 15 November 1991   136
R v Secretary of State for the Environment, ex p Blake [1984] JPL 101   65
R v Secretary of State for the Environment, ex parte Burrows &
   Simms [1990] 3 All ER 490   97, 99, 103
R v Secretary of State for the Environment, ex p Cheshire CC
   [1991] JPL 537   136, 138, 140
R v Secretary of State for the Environment, ex p Hood [1975]
   3 WLR 172   86, 89, 98, 218
R v Secretary of State for the Environment, ex p Riley [1989]
   JPL 921   87, 99, 103
R v Secretary of State for the Environment, ex p Barry Stewart
   [1980] JPL 175   136, 138, 148
R v Southampton (1852) 18 QBD 74   223
R v Surrey CC, ex p Send Parish Council (1979) 40 P & CR 390   171, 248
R v Thames Justices, ex p London Borough of Tower Hamlets
   (1982) (unreported)   148
R v United Kingdom Telegraph Co Ltd (1862) 3 F & F 73   194
R v West Sussex Quarter Sessions, ex p Albert and Maud Johnson
   Trust [1973] 3 WLR 149   79
Re Hadden [1932] 1 Ch 133   273, 274
Remet Co Ltd v London Borough of Newham [1981] RTR 502   194
Riley, see R v Secretary of State for the Environment, ex p Riley
Rubinstein v Secretary of State for the Environment [1988] JPL 485   97, 99
Rugby Charity Trustees v Merryweather (1790) 11 East 375n   62

Sandgate Urban District Council v Kent CC (1898) 79 LT 425   226
Seaton v Slama (1932) 31 LGR 41   195
Seekings v Clarke (1961) 59 LGR 268   169, 206
Send, see R v Surrey CC, ex p Send Parish Council
Simms, see R v Secretary of State for the Environment, ex parte
   Burrows & Simms
Shears Court (West Mersea) Management Co Ltd v Essex CC (1987)
   85 LGR 497   70
Stacey v Sherrin (1913) 29 TLR 555   47

CONTENTS

Stewart, see R v Secretary of State for the Environment, ex p Barry Stewart
Stewart v Wright (1893) 9 TLR 480   193
Stone v Bolton [1949] 2 All ER 851   194
Suffolk CC v Mason [1979] 2 WLR 571   80, 81, 90, 218

Taylor v Whitehead (1781) 2 Doug KB 745   47
Thomas v British Railways Board [1976] 2 WLR 761   57
Tomkins v Padfield (1973) (unreported)   206, 210
Tower Hamlets, see R v Thames Justices, ex p London Borough of Tower Hamlets
Trevett v Lee (1955) 1 All ER 406   187

Vasiliou v Secretary of State for Transport (1990) Times 16 July 1990   147

Waite v Taylor (1985) 149 JP 551   44
Walker v Horner (1875) 1 QBD 4   183
Welsh Aggregates Ltd v Clwyd CC (1988) 57 P & C R 166   170
Whiting v Hillingdon LBC (1970) 68 LGR 437   229
Williams-Ellis v Cobb [1935] 1 KB 310   59
Wiltshire CC v Frazer (1984) 82 LGR 313   48, 191
Wolverton Urban District Council v Wills [1962] 1 All ER 243   206
Worcestershire CC v Newman [1974] 1 WLR 938   172

RIGHTS OF WAY
TABLE OF STATUTES

Alphabetical

For the page references for legislation in an Act in this list see the chronological list on p 17.

Acquisition of Land Act 1981
Agriculture Act 1947
Airports Act 1986
Animal Health Act 1981
Animals Act 1971

British Transport Commission Act 1949

Chronically Sick and Disabled Persons Act 1970
Civil Aviation Act 1982
Coast Protection Act 1949
Commons Act 1899
Commons Registration Act 1965
Companies Act 1985
Copyright, Designs and Patents Act 1988
Countryside Act 1968
Criminal Damage Act 1971
Criminal Justice Act 1982
Criminal Justice Act 1988
Criminal Justice Act 1991
Criminal Law Act 1977
Cycle Tracks Act 1984

Dangerous Dogs Act 1989
Defence Act 1842
Defence Act 1860
Dogs Act 1871
Dogs (Protection of Livestock) Act 1953

Environmental Protection Act 1990

Finance Act 1910
Firearms Act 1968
Food and Environment Protection Act 1985
Forestry Act 1967

Guard Dogs Act 1975

Health and Safety at Work Act 1974
Highways Act 1835
Highways Act 1862
Highways Act 1959
Highways Act 1980
Highways (Miscellaneous Provisions) Act 1961
Housing Act 1937
Housing Act 1985
Housing Act 1988
Housing and Planning Act 1986

Industrial Relations Act 1971

Justice of the Peace Act 1361

Land Powers (Defence) Act 1958
Land Registration Act 1987
Law of Property Act 1925
Legal Aid Act 1974
Local Government Act 1929
Local Government Act 1972
Local Government Act 1974
Local Government Act 1985
Local Government (Access to Information) Act 1985
Local Government (Miscellaneous Provisions) Act 1976
Local Government Finance Act 1982
Local Government, Planning and Land Act 1980
Local Government and Housing Act 1989

Magistrates' Court Act 1980
Military Lands Act 1892
Mines and Quarries Act 1954

National Parks and Access to the Countryside Act 1949
National Trust Act 1907
National Trust Act 1971
New Towns Act 1981

CONTENTS

Norfolk and Suffolk Broads Act 1988

Occupiers' Liability Act 1957
Occupiers' Liability Act 1984
Open Spaces Act 1906
Opencast Coal Act 1958

Parish Councils Act 1957
Public Health Act 1875
Public Health Act 1936
Public Order Act 1986

Railway Clauses Consolidation Act 1845
Requisitioned Land and War Works Act 1945
Requisitioned Land and War Works Act 1948
Rights of Way Act 1932

Rights of Way Act 1990
Road Traffic Act 1988
Road Traffic Regulation Act 1984
Road Traffic (Temporary Restrictions) Act 1991

Statutory Declarations Act 1835

Town and Country Planning Act 1971
Town and Country Planning Act 1990
Town Police Clauses Act 1847
Transport Act 1968

Unfair Contract Terms Act 1977

Water Act 1989
Wildlife and Countryside Act 1981

Chronological

In this table a reference in **bold** type is a reference to the text of the statute.

1361 Justice of the Peace Act	190
1835 Highways Act	
s 23	222
s 72	53, 183, 191, 206
1835 Statutory Declarations Act	116
1842 Defence Act	
s 16	158, **286**
s 17	158, **286**
1845 Railway Clauses Consolidation Act	
s 61	57, **286**
s 65	57, **286**
s 68	58, 192
1847 Town Police Clauses Act	
s 3	185, **287**
s 28	185, 190, 191, **287**
1860 Defence Act	
s 40	158, **287**
1862 Highways Act	111
1871 Dogs Act	
s 2	185, **287**
1875 Public Health Act	
s 171	192
1892 Military Lands Act	
s 13	158, **288**
1899 Commons Act	
s 1	270
s 10	270
1906 Open Spaces Act	
s 15	270
1907 National Trust Act	270, 272
1910 Finance Act	110
1925 Law of Property Act	
s 193	272

17

1929 Local Government Act 118
1930 Road Traffic Act 69
1932 Rights of Way Act
  62, 63, 64, 110

1937 Housing Act
s 46 153

1945 Requisitioned Land and War Works Act 112

1947 Agriculture Act
s 11 175

1948 Requisitioned Land and War Works Act 112

1949 British Transport Commission Act
s 57 64, **288**

1949 Coast Protection Act
s 34 59

1949 National Parks and Access to the Countryside Act
s 27 74, 77, 85
s 28 74, 89
s 29 77, 78, 81, 82
s 30 78
s 31 79
s 32 80, 81, 85, 86, 98, 103, 104
s 33 82, 83, 84, 85, 88
s 34 83
s 35 75, 76
s 47 221, 222
s 50A **288**
s 51 276, **289**
s 52 276, **289**
s 53 60, 276, **289**
s 54 276, **290**
s 55 276, **291**
s 57 189, **291**
s 59 272
s 70 272
s 76 274
s 77 274

s 78 274
s 87 270
s 90 270
s 101 38, 74, **292**
Sch 1 80
Sch 2 271

1953 Dogs (Protection of Livestock) Act
s 1 45, **292**
s 2 45, **293**
s 3 45, **293**

1954 Mines and Quarries Act
s 151 187, 192, **294**

1957 Housing Act
s 64 153

1957 Occupiers' Liability Act
s 1 52, **294**
s 2 52, 185, **295**

1957 Parish Councils Act
s 1 240, **296**
s 3 240, **296**
s 5 240, **296**
s 7 240, **296**

1958 Land Powers (Defence) Act
s 8 158, **297**
s 25 158, **297**

1958 Opencast Coal Act
s 15 150, **297**
s 15A 150, **298**

1959 Highways Act
s 34 62
s 44 229
s 59 219
s 110 139
s 116 171, 218
s 117 180
s 121 200, 205, 207
s 124 171
s 129 230
s 269 200

CONTENTS

1961 Highways (Miscellaneous Provisions) Act		1972 Local Government Act	
s 1	229	s 100A	37, **305**
		s 100B	37, **306**
1965 Commons Registration Act		s 100C	37, **307**
s 1	274	s 100D	38, **307**
		s 100E	38, **308**
1967 Forestry Act	270	s 100G	38, 126, **308**
		s 100H	38, **309**
1968 Countryside Act		s 101	35, 172, 224
s 27	195, 236, **300**	s 111	136
s 30	54, **300**	s 112	34, **309**
s 41	270	s 123	273
s 49	53, **301**	s 137	240
Sch 3	83, 84, 86, 87, 222	s 187	189, **309**
		s 222	172, **309**
1968 Firearms Act		s 225	109, **310**
s 19	192, **301**	s 228	109, **310**
s 20	192, **301**	s 235	53, 54
s 57	192, **301**	s 250	129, **311**
		s 262	157
1968 Transport Act		s 270	**311**
s 105	225	Sch 12	37
		Sch 14	192
1970 Chronically Sick and Disabled Persons Act		Sch 17	88
s 20	55	1974 Health and Safety at Work Act	
		s 3	184, 191, 193, **312**
1971 Animals Act		s 33	184, **312**
s 2	185, 186, **302**		
s 5	186, **302**	1974 Local Government Act	
s 6	186, **302**	s 9	60
s 9	46, **303**		
s 11	186, **303**	1975 Guard Dogs Act	
		s 1	185, **312**
1971 Criminal Damage Act		s 5	185, **313**
s 1	55, 180, 196, **304**	s 7	185, **313**
s 5	196, **304**		
s 10	196, **304**	1976 Local Government (Miscellaneous Provisions) Act	
1971 Industrial Relations Act		s 16	173, **313**
s 134	205	s 44	173, **314**
1971 National Trust Act	270, 272	1977 Criminal Law Act	
		s 6	267, **314**
1971 Town and Country Planning Act		s 12	267, **314**
s 209	122, 147		
s 210	122		
s 290	273	1977 Unfair Contract Terms Act	52

19

RIGHTS OF WAY

1980 Highways Act		s 130	170, **339**
s 1	32, **315**	s 131	180, 195, **340**
s 3	34, **315**	s 131A	178, **341**
s 14	149, **316**	s 132	189, **341**
s 18	149, **316**	s 134	81, 175, **341**
s 25	71, **317**	s 135	166, 179, **342**
s 26	142, **318**	s 137	170, 204, **343**
s 27	134, **319**	s 137A	181, 210, **343**
s 28	136, **320**	s 143	173, **344**
s 29	71, 142, **320**	s 145	188, 228, **345**
s 30	71, **320**	s 146	50, 228, **345**
s 31	56, 62–71, **321**	s 147	188, **346**
s 32	108, **322**	s 148	194, **346**
s 33	**322**	s 149	173, **347**
s 36	71, 117, **322**	s 150	172, 230, 248, **347**
s 37	72, **324**	s 154	56, 183, **348**
s 38	72, **324**	s 160A	**349**
s 41	223, **325**	s 161	191, 193, 194, **349**
s 42	224, **325**	s 161A	191, **350**
s 43	225, **326**	s 162	195, **350**
s 49	223, **326**	s 164	193, **350**
s 50	225, **326**	s 165	192, **351**
s 56	230, **327**	s 175A	189, 220, 236, **351**
s 57	221, **328**	s 263	48, 180, **352**
s 58	229, **329**	s 293	126, **352**
s 61	225, **329**	s 297	173, **352**
s 62	239, 240, **330**	s 300	46, 55, **353**
s 66	189, 239, **330**	s 302	129
s 69	239	s 307	137, **353**
s 70	239	s 311	**353**
s 71	239, **331**	s 315	**354**
s 72	238, **331**	s 316	**354**
s 76	240, **331**	s 317	235, **354**
s 77	240, **332**	s 318	**354**
s 82	170, 240	s 320	232, **354**
s 91	240, **332**	s 322	232, **355**
s 92	240, **332**	s 323	**355**
s 96	240	s 326	136, **356**
s 99	240	s 327	38, 70, **356**
s 100	240, **332**	s 328	223, **357**
s 102	240, **332**	s 329	
s 104	240		55, 58, 81, 117, 179, 200, 219, **357**
s 116	153, **333**	s 333	172, 194, **358**
s 117	153, **334**	Sch 1	149, **359**
s 118	81, 137, **335**	Sch 2	136, 149, **362**
s 119	59, 81, 140, **335**	Sch 6	126, **363**
s 120	126, **337**	Sch 7	224, **368**
s 121	136, 137, **338**	Sch 12	153, **370**
s 122	165, **339**	Sch 12A	176, **371**
s 123	**339**	Sch 23	**373**

CONTENTS

1980 Local Government, Planning
and Land Act
Sch 28 152, **374**

1980 Magistrates' Court Act
s 1 212, 213, 216

1981 Acquisition of Land Act
s 32 152, **375**
s 33 152, **376**

1981 Animal Health Act
s 23 166, **377**
s 27 166, **377**

1981 New Towns Act
s 23 152, **377**
Sch 8 152, **378**

1981 Wildlife and Countryside Act
s 53 91, 99, 222, **379**
s 54 87, 98, 222, **380**
s 55 90, **381**
s 56 81, 90, 174, **381**
s 57 104, 135, **382**
s 58 36, 91, **383**
s 59 184, **384**
s 62 44, **384**
s 66 81, 200, **384**
s 70A **385**
s 71 **385**
Sch 14 99, **385**
Sch 15 91, 94–7, **387**

1982 Civil Aviation Act
s 48 151, **392**

1982 Criminal Justice Act 285

1982 Local Government Finance Act
s 15 247

1984 Cycle Tracks Act
s 3 161, **393**
s 4 161, **395**
s 5 161, **396**
s 6 161, **396**
s 8 161, **396**

1984 Occupiers' Liability Act
s 1 51, **396**

1984 Road Traffic Regulation Act
s 1 158, **397**
s 2 159, **398**
s 3 159, **399**
s 4 159, **399**
s 5 159, **399**
s 14 160, **399**
s 15 160, **400**
s 16 160, **400**
s 22 159, **401**
s 65 237
s 69 189, **402**
s 71 237, **402**
s 72 240, **402**
s 122 159, **403**
s 127 159, **403**
s 142 46, 159, **404**
Sch 3 160, **404**

1985 Companies Act 61

1985 Housing Act
s 294 153, **405**

1985 Food and Environment
Protection Act 193

1985 Local Government Act 33

1985 Local Government (Access to
Information) Act 37

1986 Airports Act
s 59 151, **405**

1986 Housing and Planning Act
s 42 132, **406**

1986 Public Order Act
s 4 190, **407**
s 5 190, **407**
s 6 190, **408**
s 11 55, **408**
s 16 55, **409**
s 39 47, **409**

1988 Copyrights, Designs and
  Patents Act
s 46   129
s 47   38

1988 Criminal Justice Act
s 139   196, 266, **410**

1988 Housing Act
Sch 10   152, **411**

1988 Land Registration Act 101, 197

1988 Norfolk and Suffolk Broads Act
Sch 3   35, **412**

1988 Road Traffic Act
s 2   190, **412**
s 3   190, **412**
s 12   191, **413**
s 13   191, **413**
s 21   55, **413**
s 27   45, **414**
s 28   54, **415**
s 29   54, **415**
s 30   454
s 31   54, **415**
s 33   81, 191, **416**
s 34   54, 69, 81, 190, **416**
s 185   54, **417**
s 191   54, **417**
s 192   54, 191, **417**

1989 Dangerous Dogs Act
s 1   185, **418**

1989 Local Government and
  Housing Act
s 151   136

1989 Water Act
s 8   226
s 10   226
s 155   150, **419**

Sch 20   150, **419**

1990 Environmental Protection Act
s 79   187, **423**
s 80   188, **424**
s 81   188, **425**
s 82   188, 214–7, **426**
Sch 3   187, **427**
Sch 11   278, **429**

1990 Rights of Way Act
        166, 175, 178, 180, 181, 227

1990 Town and Country Planning
  Act
s 55   144, **430**
s 57   144
s 59   144
s 69   144
s 246   151
s 247   146, **430**
s 248   150, **431**
s 249   161, **432**
s 251   151, **432**
s 252   137, 146, 161, **433**
s 253   147, **434**
s 257   146, **435**
s 258   151, **436**
s 259   **436**
s 261   150, **436**
s 287   135, **437**
s 320   129, **438**
s 321   129, **438**
s 322   132, **438**
s 329   **439**
s 333   136, **439**
s 336   **439**
Sch 14   126, 135, **440**

1991 Criminal Justice Act
s 17   285

1991 Road Traffic (Temporary
  Restrictions) Act   160

CONTENTS
TABLE OF STATUTORY INSTRUMENTS

Church Property (Miscellaneous Provisions) Measure 1960 s 11   72, **445**

SR&O 1937 No 79 Housing Act (Extinguishment of Public Right of Way) Regulations 1937   153

Defence (General) Regulations 1939   112, 175

SI 1950 No 1066 National Parks and Access to the Countryside Regulations 1950   76, 274

SI 1962 No 2340 Control of Dogs on Roads Orders (Procedure) (England and Wales) Regulations 1962   45

SI 1963 No 2126 Vehicles (Conditions of Use on Footpaths) Regulations 1963   54

SI 1971 No 1292 Crown Court Rules 1971   156

SI 1981 No 859 Traffic Signs and General Directions 1981   237

SI 1983 No 20 The Wildlife and Countryside Act (Commencement No 6) Order 1983   92, 106

SI 1983 No 21 Wildlife and Countryside (Definitive Maps and Statements) Regulations 1983   94, **445**

SI 1983 No 22 Town and Country Planning (Public Path Orders) Regulations 1983   126, 146, **453**

SI 1983 No 23 Public Path Orders and Extinguishment of Public Right of Way Orders Regulations 1983   126, 137, 140, 142, **460**

SI 1983 No 512 Wildlife and Countryside (Isles of Scilly) Order 1983   91

SI 1983 No 1950 Foot and Mouth Disease Order 1983   166, **471**

SI 1984 No 1431 Cycle Tracks Regulations 1984   161, **472**

SI 1986 No 854 Local Government (Inspection of Documents) (Summary of Rights) Order 1986   38, 105

SI 1987 No 1758 Plant Health (Great Britain) Order 1987   166

SI 1987 No 1915 Opencast Coal (Compulsory Rights and Rights of Way) (Forms) Regulations 1987   150, **475**

SI 1989 No 553 Plant Health (Great Britain) Amendment Order 1989   166

RIGHTS OF WAY

SI 1989 No 1120 Local Authorities' Traffic Orders (Procedure)
(England and Wales) Regulations 1989 159

SI 1991 No 1409 Water (Compulsory Works Powers) (Notice)
Regulations 1991 150

CONTENTS
TABLE OF CIRCULARS

DOE Circular 44/68: Countryside Act 1968   85, 86

Department of Transport Circular Roads 13/71 : Pedestrianisation   162

DOE Circular 123/77: Roads Used as Public Paths   87

DOE Circular 32/81, Welsh Office Circular 50/81:
Wildlife and Countryside Act 1981   185, **480**

DOE Circular 1/83, Welsh Office Circular 1/83: Public Rights of Way
90, 92-6, 103-5, 120, 125, 126, 128, 133,
137-8, 140-2, 145, 146, 156, 172, 219, **481**

DOE Circular 1/85, Welsh Office Circular 1/85: The use of
conditions in planning permission   146, **496**

Department of Transport Circular Roads 1/86, Welsh
Office Circular 3/86: Cycle Tracks Act 1984 The Cycle Tracks
Regulations 1984   161, **497**

DOE Circular 2/87, Welsh Office Circular 2/87: Award of Costs
Incurred in Planning and Compulsory Purchase Order Proceedings
132, **507**

DOE Circular 25/87, Welsh Office Circular 50/87: Housing
and Planning Act 1986: Town and Country Planning:
Simplified Planning Zones   147, **508**

Department of Transport Circular 2/89, Welsh Office
Circular 49/89: New Procedures for Traffic Orders   160

Home Office Circular 63/89: Dangerous Dogs Act 1989 and
Dogs Act 1871   185, **509**

DOE Circular 18/90, Welsh Office Circular 45/90: Modifications
to the Definitive Map: Wildlife and Countryside Act 1981   98, **510**

Public rights of way and development: Letter dated August
1987 from DOE and Welsh Office   146, **511**

Proposed changes to rights of way and definitive maps: a code of
practice on consultation for local authorities in England and
Wales (prepared by the Rights of Way Review Committee)
126, 137, 140, 142, **512**

RIGHTS OF WAY
ABBREVIATIONS USED

In general the masculine includes the feminine, the singular the plural and vice versa

Acts of Parliament

NPACA 49	National Parks and Access to the Countryside Act 1949
CA 68	Countryside Act 1968
LGA 72	Local Government Act 1972
HA 80	Highways Act 1980
WCA 81	Wildlife and Countryside Act 1981
LGA 85	Local Government Act 1985
RTA 88	Road Traffic Act 1988
EPA 90	Environmental Protection Act 1990
RWA 90	Rights of Way Act 1990
TCPA 90	Town and Country Planning Act 1990
s	section of an Act; s 31(6) means subsection 6 of section 31
ss	sections of an Act
Sch	Schedule to an Act
para	paragraph
SI	Statutory Instrument

Examples

HA 80 s 1	section 1 of the Highways Act 1980
HA 80 Sch 3 para 6(1)	sub-paragraph 1 of paragraph 6 of Schedule 3 to the Highways Act 1980

CONTENTS

Other abbreviations

CC	County Council
LBC	London borough council
BC	Borough council
DC	District council
p	page
DOE	Department of the Environment
RUPP	road used as public path

1
Introduction

1.1 The value of public rights of way

Walking is the most popular active recreation in England and Wales. Analysis of the government's 1986 General Household Survey shows that the adult population spent about 750 million days in 1986 taking walks over two miles or more. This figure, to be appreciated fully, needs to be compared with the figure of about 650 million days participation in all other outdoor sports, including activities generally regarded as mass activities, such as swimming, fishing, football and golf. Horse-riding accounted for some 22 million days participation per year. Further details of these and other statistics are given in chapter 9.2.

To the walker and rider in the countryside, the single most important way of gaining access is through the 140,000-mile network of footpaths, bridleways and certain other tracks, collectively known as public rights of way. The value of legal protection of the network for recreational purposes was recognised over 50 years ago by Lord Justice Scott in *Jones v Bates* (1938): 'In these days, when motor buses, motor cars and motor cycles transport so many into the countryside both for business and for pleasure, and when practically all agricultural workers, and indeed most of the rural population, have their bicycles, long footpaths, which 50 years ago meant so much for ease of communication, are infinitely less frequented, and it becomes easier and easier for real public rights of way to disappear, just because they become unprovable. Yet the rambler — sometimes called the 'hiker' — needs the footpath more than ever. The movement represented by the ramblers' societies is of national importance, and to the real lover of the country, who knows that to see it properly he must go on foot, but who is driven off all main roads and a good many others by the din and bustle of motor traffic, the footpath is everything. In short, it is of real public moment that no genuine public footpath should be lost, without statutory action to close it.'

The closing sentence neatly makes the point that, in walking or riding over public rights of way in the countryside, members of the public are exercising rights protected by law, not enjoying privileges granted by landowners. It is the purpose of this book to explain the law on the origin, recording and protection of public rights of way in England and Wales, and to suggest how a walker or rider, when faced with obstacles such as ploughed-up paths, barbed wire or missing bridges, may seek remedies.

That there is a need for remedies is shown by the results of the first-ever national survey of the condition of rights of way, conducted by the Countryside Commission in 1988. The survey found that more than half of all rights of way were effectively unavailable to those without the skill to use a map and the confidence to assert their rights. Moreover, on a typical two-mile walk, walkers faced a two-in-three chance of meeting an impassable obstruction on a walk on a route randomly selected from paths shown on an OS map.

The Commission has set a target, endorsed by the government in its 1990 White Paper *This Common Inheritance*, of having the full 140,000-mile network legally defined, properly maintained and kept free from obstruction and well publicised by the year 2000.

The development of the law Rights-of-way law has been substantially amended, and improved, since 1938, due largely to the efforts of the 'movement represented by the ramblers' societies', notably the Open Spaces Society (OSS) and the Ramblers' Association (RA).

It is a mixture of common law (law defined by judgments in court cases) and statute law, contained in Acts of Parliament and subordinate regulations (see p 39). Five such Acts in the last 50 years have made substantial changes to the law of public rights of way.

The National Parks and Access to the Countryside Act 1949 introduced procedures for recording the public's rights on definitive maps, so called because they can be produced in court as conclusive evidence of those rights, and for creating, diverting and extinguishing footpaths and bridleways by orders whose merits are argued at public inquiries rather than in the courts. It also made footpaths and bridleways maintainable at public expense, and authorised the ploughing of footpaths and bridleways subject to their restoration for public use.

The Highways Act 1959, now consolidated into the Highways Act 1980, introduced a new procedure for enforcing a highway authority's duty to keep paths in good repair.

The Countryside Act 1968 revised the arrangements made in the 1949 Act for updating definitive maps, gave cyclists the right to ride on bridleways and required paths to be signposted and waymarked.

The Wildlife and Countryside Act 1981 made further substantial changes to definitive map procedures and also introduced legislation about the pasturing of bulls in fields crossed by public rights of way.

The Rights of Way Act 1990 amended the duties and powers of farmers on ploughing and disturbing rights of way and introduced new duties to prevent crops inconveniencing users.

Associated with each of these Acts was a committee which sat before, and in some cases during, the passage of the Bill, and whose recommendations influenced its contents. The respective committees, with the dates of their reports, were as follows:

1 : INTRODUCTION

Committee on Footpaths and Access to the Countryside (Chairman: Sir Arthur Hobhouse) (September 1947) (Cmd 7207)

Committee on the Consolidation of Highway Law (Chairman: The Marquess of Reading) (January 1959) (Cmnd 630)

Footpaths Committee (Chairman: Sir Arthur Gosling) (March 1968)

Rights of Way Review Committee (Chairman: Mr Michael Spicer MP) (June 1982)

Report of the working party of the Rights of Way Review Committee on ploughing and cropping (Chairman: Mr Roy Hickey) (December 1989)

The Spicer Committee, unlike the others, was not set up by the government. It was formed initially by the RA, the Country Landowners Association and the National Farmers Union, and later expanded to include representatives of other users, local authorities, the Countryside Commission and the Sports Council. In addition it has observers from the Departments of the Environment and Transport and the Ministry of Agriculture. It continued in existence after the passage of the 1981 Act and is currently chaired by Mr Alan Haselhurst MP.

1.2 Definitions in this book

1.2.1 Rights of way and highways

'Public right of way' and 'highway' — these terms both mean a way over which the public have a right to pass and repass, though by convention the former term excludes roads normally used by motor vehicles. Strictly, there is a distinction in that the right is an abstract thing and the highway a strip of land. The nature of the right determines the type of way, which under common law can be either:

a **footpath**, over which the right of way is on foot only;

a **bridleway**, over which the right of way is on foot and on horseback, possibly with an additional right to drive animals;

a **carriageway**, over which there is a right of way on foot, on horseback, and in or on a vehicle.

Parliament has introduced some statutory amendments to the three common law definitions. Bicycles are vehicles within the common law, and thereby only entitled at common law to use carriageways, but Parliament granted cyclists the right to use bridleways in 1968. It has also introduced the concept of a **cycle track**, which is a way over which there is a right to cycle, and possibly also to walk. At the other extreme, a **motorway** is a way normally restricted to certain kinds of motor traffic. Further restrictions can be placed on the public's rights by means of traffic regulation orders (p 158).

A **road used as a public path (RUPP)** is a particular category of way recorded on definitive maps. See chapters 4.4.4 and 4.6.7.

RIGHTS OF WAY

A **byway open to all traffic** is also a special category of way recorded on definitive maps. It is a carriageway and thus a right of way for vehicular traffic, but one which is used mainly for the purposes for which footpaths and bridleways are used, ie by walkers and horse-riders.

It is important to note that the depiction of a right of way on a definitive map is a record only of the existence of those rights. Other rights may exist, but not be recorded, eg a way shown on a definitive map as a footpath may be a bridleway or even a carriageway (see p 81), or a right of way may exist which is not recorded at all.

A **road** is usually defined in statutes as including any highway and any other road to which the public has access. This is a very wide definition, including not only footpaths and bridleways but also ways to which the public has access by permission of the landowner, not by right.

A **street** is usually defined in statutes as including any highway (eg by HA 80 s 329), and therefore includes footpaths and bridleways.

A **footway** is a way set aside for pedestrians at the edge of a carriageway, commonly known as a pavement. Most statutory definitions of footpath make it clear that footpaths and footways are to be regarded as different, although both provide a public right of way on foot only.

A **green lane** is a term with no legal meaning. It is a physical description of an unsurfaced track, normally hedged, and often, but not always, of some antiquity. It may be a footpath, bridleway or carriageway or may carry no public rights of way at all.

1.2.2 Local authorities

A **highway authority** is the local government body responsible for public rights of way. In London, the highway authorities are the London borough councils; in the metropolitan counties (Greater Manchester, Merseyside, South Yorkshire, Tyne and Wear, West Midlands, West Yorkshire) they are the metropolitan district councils; elsewhere, including throughout Wales, they are the county councils.

A **surveying authority** is the body responsible for the preparation and upkeep of the definitive map. The councils which are highway authorities are also surveying authorities.

A **local authority** means in Greater London the London borough council, in the metropolitan counties the metropolitan district council and elsewhere the county or district council. The term also includes the Lake District and Peak District national park planning boards and, for most purposes, the Broads Authority set up in 1989 to administer the Norfolk and Suffolk Broads.

A **local council** means, in England, a parish council, and in Wales, a community council.

Some district councils, both metropolitan and non-metropolitan, have

1 : INTRODUCTION

adopted the title 'borough' or 'city', and some local councils have similarly adopted 'town' or 'city' as their title.

1.2.3 Other definitions

A landholder means the owner of the land, or, where the land is leased, the tenant.

The functions of a Secretary of State, eg Secretary of State for Environment, are, in Wales, undertaken by the Secretary of State for Wales.

The functions of the Countryside Commission in Wales became functions of the Countryside Council for Wales on 1 April 1991.

1.3 Rights of way, local authorities and central government

The Local Government Act 1972 abolished from 1 April 1974 all the then county, urban and rural district and borough councils in England and Wales outside Greater London and created new county and district councils. The Local Government Act 1985 abolished from 1 April 1986 the Greater London Council and the metropolitan county councils; it transferred relevant functions to the London borough and metropolitan district councils respectively.

1.3.1 Highway authorities

The bodies to which all the duties for public rights of way are assigned have been designated as highway authorities (HA 80 s 1) and surveying authorities (WCA 81 s 66). Highway authorities are county councils, metropolitan district councils and London borough councils. The principal rights-of-way duties of highway authorities are as follows:

(a) To maintain publicly-maintainable highways or to reimburse the district council for its maintenance of publicly-maintainable footpaths and bridleways (p 223) (HA 80 ss 41 & 42).

(b) To keep an up-to-date list of publicly-maintainable highways available for public inspection in each district (p 117) (HA 80 s 36).

(c) To assert and protect the rights of the public to the use and enjoyment of, and to prevent so far as possible the stopping up or obstruction of, all their highways (p 170) (HA 80 s 130).

(d) To enforce the restoration of footpaths and bridleways lawfully ploughed or disturbed (p 177) (HA 80 s 134).

(e) To take action if the ploughing or disturbance of a highway was unlawful (p 178) (HA 80 s 131A).

(f) To enforce the duty of an occupier to ensure that crops do not inconvenience users of footpaths, bridleways and unmetalled carriageways (p 181) (HA 80 s 137A).

RIGHTS OF WAY

(g) To signpost and waymark footpaths, bridleways and byways (p 236) (CA 68 s 27 as amended by WCA 81 s 65).
(h) To prosecute anyone responsible for a misleading notice on or near a footpath, bridleway or RUPP shown on a definitive map (p 189) (NPACA 49 s 57).

If a highway crosses a bridge joining two counties, HA 80 s 3 (p 316) sets out the procedure for determining which CC is to be the highway authority for the bridge.

1.3.2 Surveying authorities

Highway authorities are also surveying authorities. As such, their principal duties are:

(a) To keep the definitive map under continuous review (p 91) (WCA 81 s 53).
(b) To make modification orders to take account of events requiring the map to be modified (p 91) (WCA 81 s 53).
(c) To make reclassification orders for any RUPPs on the definitive map (p 98) (WCA 81 s 54).
(d) To prepare definitive maps for any areas not previously surveyed (p 91) (WCA 81 ss 55).
(e) To keep copies of the definitive map and statement, together with copies of any subsequent modification and reclassification orders, available for public inspection in every district (p 104) (WCA 81 s 57).
(f) To draw the attention of the public to this availability and to the right to apply for modification orders to be made (p 104) (WCA 81 s 57).

An authority is required, by LGA 72 s 112 (p 309), to appoint such staff as are necessary to carry out its functions, including its duties as highway and surveying authority.

1.3.3 District councils and planning boards

Metropolitan and non-metropolitan district councils A distinction has to be drawn between the *metropolitan district councils*, which are the highway and surveying (and planning) authorities in the metropolitan counties (p 32), and the *non-metropolitan district councils* in the shire counties in England and Wales.

Powers of the non-metropolitan district councils These latter have no duties for rights of way, although they do have certain powers.

Claiming maintenance powers In particular, they have the right to take over from the county council the maintenance of footpaths and bridleways (HA 80 s 42). If this right is exercised the district council acquires additional powers. These are as follows:

1 : INTRODUCTION

- (a) Removal of structures from highways (p 173) (HA 80 s 143).
- (b) Repairing and making good stiles and gates (p 228) (HA 80 s 146).
- (c) Authorising the erection of stiles and gates (p 188) (HA 80 s 147).
- (d) Making good the surface of a right of way made inconvenient by disturbance (p 177) (HA 80 Sch 12A para 3).
- (e) Making good the surface of a footpath or bridleway, or defining its route, after authorised ploughing or other disturbance (p 177) (HA 80 Sch 12A para 4).
- (f) Removal of crops inconveniencing use of a right of way, or defining the line of a way through crops (p 182) (HA 80 Sch 12A para 4).
- (g) Carrying out work to comply with conditions attached to a licence to disturb the surface for agricultural purposes (p 179) (HA 80 Sch 12A para 5).

Acting as the county council's agent Any function of the county council can be exercised on its behalf by the district council if an agreement is made under LGA 72 s 101, although such an agreement does not relieve the county council of its duties. See chapter 7.2.3 for details of these powers and procedures.

Making public path orders Non-metropolitan district councils have the same powers as county councils to make public path orders under HA 80 ss 26, 118 and 119.

Planning authorities In the shire counties most planning applications are dealt with by the district councils. As a result they make most orders needed for enabling development to take place (p 146).

1.3.4 National parks and the Broads Authority

Planning boards have been established for only two of the ten national parks in England and Wales, the Lake District and Peak District. The boards are planning authorities within their areas, and have power to make public path orders. They can also take over rights-of-way functions from the county or district councils by agreement.

In the other eight national parks, which are run by committees of county councils, certain functions may have been delegated to the committee by the council, but the committee cannot make orders under its own name.

The Broads Authority established in 1989 under the Norfolk and Suffolk Broads Act 1988 has similar powers to those of a planning board. See Sch 3 to the 1988 Act (p 412).

1.3.5 Greater London

In Greater London the London borough councils act as highway authorities and (except in Inner London) as surveying authorities. Within

RIGHTS OF WAY

Inner London they can resolve to become surveying authorities for part or all of their area (WCA 81 s 58 — p 383). The LBCs are also planning authorities.

1.3.6 Local councils

Local councils (p 32) have no duties for rights of way, but they are given certain rights and powers which can contribute greatly to the public's ability to enjoy the rights of way in the parish or community. These are as follows:

(a) To undertake the maintenance of any footpath or bridleway (p 225) (HA 80 ss 43 and 50).

(b) To erect lighting on any footpath or bridleway (p 240) (Parish Councils Act 1957 s 3).

(c) To erect notices on footpaths and bridleways warning of local dangers (p 240) (Road Traffic Regulation Act 1984 s 72).

(d) To make representations to the highway authority that a highway has been unlawfully stopped up or obstructed. The authority must act unless satisfied that the representations are incorrect (p 171) (HA 80 s 130(6)).

(e) To prosecute anyone who wilfully obstructs the free passage along any highway (p 204) (HA 80 s 137).

(f) To prosecute an occupier who fails to ensure that crops do not inconvenience users of footpaths, bridleways and unmetalled carriageways (p 210) (HA 80 s 137A).

(g) To prosecute if a footpath or bridleway has been lawfully ploughed or disturbed, but not restored, or if any highway has been unlawfully ploughed or disturbed (p 178) (HA 80 ss 131A and 134).

(h) To insist that a particular footpath, bridleway or byway should be signposted where it meets a metalled road (p 236) (CA 68 s 27).

(i) To veto a proposal by a highway authority to apply to a magistrates' court for an order stopping-up or diverting a highway (p 154) (HA 80 s 116).

(j) To hold for public inspection a copy of the definitive map for the parish or community, and copies of orders made to modify it (p 104) (WCA 81 s 57(5)).

(k) To be consulted by a surveying authority on every application for a definitive map modification order (p 102) (WCA 81 Sch 14).

(l) To be consulted by a surveying authority before a definitive map modification or reclassification order is made (p 94) (WCA 81 Sch 15).

(m) To object to a public path order or a definitive map modification or reclassification order. A copy of every such order, both when made and when confirmed, must be served upon the council (p 90, 127) (HA 80 Sch 6 para 1(3)(b)(ii), WCA 81 Sch 15 para 3(2)(b)(ii) & TCPA 90 Sch 14 para 1(2)(b)(ii)).

1 : INTRODUCTION

(n) To signpost and waymark footpaths, bridleways and byways on behalf of, and with the consent of, the highway authority (p 238) (CA 68 s 27).

(o) To create new footpaths and bridleways by agreement with the landowner over land in their own and adjoining parishes (p 71) (HA 80 s 30).

Parish meetings in those parishes where there is no council have the same rights and powers as a council under (d),(i),(j),(k),(l) and (m) above. The powers at (d) and (j) apply also to a community meeting where there is no council. Every parish and community must hold a meeting between 1 March and 1 June each year, and, where there is no council, at least one other meeting must be held during the year. Additionally any six local government electors in the parish can cause a meeting to be held. (LGA 72 Sch 12 Pts 3 and 5).

The RA publishes a leaflet *Paths for People* for members of local councils.

1.3.7 *Access to local authority meetings and information*

The public's rights of access to meetings of local authorities and to the information given to members of local authorities for those meetings are to be found in sections 100A to 100H of the Local Government Act 1972 (p 305–309), added by the Local Government (Access to Information) Act 1985.

Meetings Notice of meetings must be given at least three days before the date of the meeting, or, when the meeting is convened at shorter notice, as soon as it is convened (s 100A(6)).

Meetings must normally be open to the public (s 100A(1)). The exception is if confidential information or exempt information would be disclosed to the public if they were present (s 100A(3)&(4)).

Papers The agenda and reports for a meeting must be available to the public (s 100B(1)), except to the extent that they refer to business from which the public is likely to be excluded (s 100B(2)). They must be available for as long before the meeting as notice is required to be given (s 100B(3)). Copies of the agenda and reports must also be available at the meeting (s 100B(6)).

After the meeting, the agenda and reports, as above, together with the minutes and a summary of any proceedings from which the public was excluded must be available for 6 years from the date of the meeting (s 100C).

In addition a list of background papers for each report and copies of those papers must be available for four years from the date of the meeting (s 100D(1)&(2)). For what are 'background papers' see s 100D(5).

Committees and subcommittees The provisions above apply to committees and subcommittees as they do to meetings of the full council (s 100E).

Additional information Authorities must also maintain a register of the names and addresses of the members of the council and of the members of committees and subcommittees (s 100G(1)). There must also be a register of the powers delegated to officers, except for temporary delegation for up to 6 months (s 100G(2)).

In addition the authority must keep a written summary of the public's rights to attend meetings and inspect documents conferred by the 1972 Act and by such other enactments as may be prescribed by regulations made by the Secretary of State. The regulations, the Local Government (Inspection of Documents) (Summary of Rights) Order 1986, list, among other rights, the right to inspect the list of streets prepared under HA 80 s 36 and the right, under WCA 81 s 57(5), to inspect a definitive map and statement.

The copying of material open to public inspection by virtue of a statutory provision is not normally a breach of copyright. (Copyright, Designs and Patents Act 1988 s 47.)

1.3.8 Crown land

What is Crown land? 'Crown land' comprises land owned directly by the royal family and land held by the government. It thus includes land held by government departments such as the Ministry of Defence and the Forestry Commission. But it does not include land owned by local authorities or nationalised industries such as British Coal and British Rail.

Application of the law to Crown land The general principle is that legislation applies to Crown land only if that application is specified in the legislation. Thus rights of way over Crown land are recorded on definitive maps because the provisions in the 1949 National Parks and Access to the Countryside Act and the 1981 Wildlife and Countryside Act do apply to the Crown.

But the Crown does not need planning permission for development on Crown land, nor may it normally be prosecuted if there is an obstruction of a right of way on its land, because the relevant Acts (the Town and Country Planning Act 1990 and the Highways Act 1980) do not bind the Crown. See, for example, HA 80 s 327 (p 356).

1.3.9 The Parliamentary Commissioner for Administration

The Parliamentary Commissioner for Administration, also known as the Ombudsman, investigates complaints of maladministration by

1 : INTRODUCTION

government departments and other public bodies such as the Countryside Commission. He is not to be confused with the Commissioners for Local Administration, or Local Ombudsmen (see chapter 8.2.2). The Ombudsman can act only if asked to do so by a MP or a member of the House of Lords.

He could be asked to investigate, for instance, alleged maladministration by the Secretary of State in carrying out his responsibilities for public path orders.

In 1983 the Ombudsman found maladministration causing injustice to the applicant for a public path diversion order which the Department had refused to confirm. In 1986 he criticised the DOE for its handling of appeal cases arising out of the provisions of the Wildlife and Countryside Act 1981. In 1989 he was critical of a lapse in procedures which had denied the RA the right to be heard in pursuance of its objection to a public path diversion order.

1.4 Rights of way and the legal system

This section is intended to provide a brief layman's guide to the legal system and to which courts hear which cases on rights-of-way matters.

1.4.1 Sources of law

British law has two sources. The older source is the body of principles inherent in the judgments of the courts. These principles, which have evolved down the centuries, form what is known as the *common law*. Once a principle has been established it remains in force until overturned by a later decision of a higher court or by an Act of Parliament.

The second source is legislation — Acts of Parliament or legislation made under the authority of an Act, eg regulations made by a Minister or byelaws made by a local authority. Law that stems from Act of Parliament, whether made directly or under regulated powers, is termed *statute law*.

A particular branch of law may be governed by both common law and statute, common law providing the framework and statute making provision for particular circumstances or modifying or superseding a common law principle. An example is the law of trespass: statute has intervened to modify the common law (see chapter 2.4).

1.4.2 Criminal law and civil law

A breach of the criminal law is primarily an offence against the state. In its origins the offence consisted of a breach of the King's Peace: murder was not, and indeed still is not, a wrong against the person killed. The wrong is the failure to obey the sovereign's command not to kill. In criminal law, serious cases are decided by a jury at a Crown Court. If the accused is found guilty, the sanction is punishment in the form of imprisonment, fine or other sanction, eg disqualification from driving.

In civil law the action is by one person against another: a plaintiff sues a defendant. Unless the action is for defamation, it is decided not by a jury but by a judge (or, in the Divisional Court, the Court of Appeal and the House of Lords, by a panel of judges). If the decision goes against the defendant he is found to be 'liable'. The sanction is an award that he should pay damages to the plaintiff or the granting of an order, eg an *injunction*, an order by the court requiring the defendant to refrain from specified action.

A particular incident may give rise to an action in both criminal law and civil law. For example, if a car driver knocks down a pedestrian, the driver may be prosecuted for the criminal offence of dangerous driving and sued by the injured person in civil law for damages for negligence.

1.4.3 The courts

At the lowest level is the magistrates' court. Most magistrates, or justices of the peace, are unpaid and are not legally qualified; in a large city court there may be a stipendiary (paid) magistrate who is a lawyer. A court usually consists of at least two magistrates. Each magistrates' court has a clerk who is normally a solicitor or a barrister.

Anyone alleged to have committed a statutory offence in relation to a right of way (eg obstruction or ploughing) will have his case heard in a magistrates' court. These courts also handle two other important aspects of rights-of-way work: applications for closure and diversion orders under HA 80 s 116 (p 153) and most applications for orders under HA 80 s 56 requiring highways to be put in proper repair (p 230).

The next level is the Crown Court. In this court there is a circuit judge, who is normally a barrister, and who, on rights-of-way cases, sits with two magistrates. For rights of way, Crown Courts handle only appeals against convictions in the magistrates' court, appeals against decisions of the magistrates' court on applications made under s 56 and s 116, and certain initial applications under the s 56 procedure.

The next level, and the lowest level at which decisions set a precedent, is the Queen's Bench Division of the High Court. There is a special part of the Queen's Bench Division, known as the Divisional Court. This Court hears, *inter alia*, appeals against the confirmation of definitive map and public path orders. It is also in this Court that applications are made for judicial review of the decisions and actions of authorities (p 218), and where appeals, by way of case stated, against decisions of the magistrates' and Crown Courts are heard.

Most appeals against decisions of the High Court are made to the Court of Appeal. Its decisions are also binding on lower courts.

Appeals against decisions of the Court of Appeal, and sometimes

1 : INTRODUCTION

against decisions of the High Court, are made to the House of Lords, presided over by the Lord Chancellor. Any member of the House of Lords may take part in the House's deliberations on such appeals; in practice they are considered only by the Lord Chancellor and the law lords, who are life peers appointed from the judiciary.

1.4.4 Law reports

The references in the list of cases on p 12 are explained below. Some cases appear in more than one report. For example, many cases are reported both in the All England Law Reports and in the Weekly Law Reports, and all cases in the WLR are also published in the annual volume(s) for the appropriate division of the High Court.

The availability of reports to the general public varies. Current and fairly recent cases in the All ER, WLR, LGR and P & CR series and in journals such as the Solicitors' Journal and the Estates Gazette, can be obtained from the publishers. Most larger reference libraries subscribe to the All ER or the WLR reports or both, and to one or more of the journals. They usually have the bound volumes of cases going back over a number of years. It should be possible to borrow report volumes through the British Library lending service, details of which can be obtained from public libraries. Complete sets of law reports are held by Bar libraries, the Law Society's library and by many university law faculty libraries: these libraries are not open to the general public.

Where a case is shown as 'unreported', no report has appeared in a law report series or other publicly available source. A transcript of a judgment in the Supreme Court (High Court, Court of Appeal, House of Lords) can be obtained through the Supreme Court Office, Royal Courts of Justice, Strand, London WC2A 2KK. Transcripts are prepared by an official transcriber to whom a fee is payable, based on the length of the transcript.

Decisions by Crown Courts, county courts and magistrates' courts are rarely reported. Transcripts of Crown and county court decisions can be obtained: enquiries should be directed to the local court office.

'AC' Appeal Court Reports; reports of cases heard in the Court of Appeal and the House of Lords. Published in the same way as QB reports.
'All ER' All England Law Reports, published by Butterworth & Co..
'C & P' Carrington and Payne's Reports, Nisi Prius, 1823-41.
'Ch' Chancery reports; reports of cases heard in the Chancery
(or 'Ch D') division of the High court. Published in the same way as QB reports.
'COD' Crown Office Digest; published by Sweet & Maxwell.
'Cro Car' Croke's Reports, time of Charles 1, King's Bench and Common Pleas, 1625-41.

'Doug KB'	Douglas's King's Bench Reports.
'East'	East's Term Reports.
'EG'	Case reports in a weekly journal, *Estates Gazette*.
'El & Bl'	Ellis and Blackburn's Queen's Bench Reports.
'F & F'	Foster and Finlason's Reports, Nisi Prius, 1856-67.
'H & N'	Hurlston and Norman's Reports, Exchequer, 1856-62.
'JP'	Justice of the Peace.
'JPL'	Journal of Planning and Environment Law, (formerly the Journal of Planning Law) (see 'Further Reading').
'KB'	King's Bench; reports of cases heard in the King's Bench Division of the High Court.
'LGR'	Local Government Reports.
'LT'	Law Times reports 1877-1949.
'P & CR'	Property and Compensation Reports, published by Butterworths.
'QB'	Queen's Bench; reports of cases heard in the Queen's Bench division of the High Court. ('QBD' appears for earlier reports (Queen's Bench Division).)
'RTR'	Road Traffic Reports.
'SJ'	Solicitors' Journal.
'Times'	Law reports published in *The Times* newspaper.
'TLR'	Times Law Reports. A series of volumes of cases reported in *The Times* newspaper 1884-1950.
'Vent'	Ventris' reports, King's Bench and Common Pleas, 1668-91.
'WLR'	The Weekly Law Reports, published by the Incorporated Council of Law Reporting for England and Wales.

2
Public rights of way

2.1 What is a public right of way?

As noted in the last chapter (p 31), a public right of way is a way over which all members of the public have a right of passage. A right of way on foot constitutes a footpath, a right of way on horseback constitutes a bridleway, a right of way for vehicles constitutes a carriageway.

A right of way for an individual or any group other than the public at large is a private right of way. (A private right of way annexed to, and for the benefit of, a particular piece of land is termed an 'easement'.)

The term 'way' is useful. A way is a route along which people go. It is an omnibus term that can refer to a footpath, a bridleway or a carriageway. It can refer to use that is private or public (or permissive, see p 56). Since the word carries no legal connotation, its use is convenient when the legal status of a route is uncertain or disputed.

2.2 'Once a highway, always a highway'

Failure to exercise a private right of way over a period of time may, if the disuse is held to constitute evidence of an intention to abandon the right, lead to the right being held to have become extinguished. This principle has no application in the case of a public right of way. Once such a right has come into existence, by whatever means, it continues indefinitely. It can only be brought to an end by use of a statutory provision.

This is the meaning of the maxim 'Once a highway, always a highway'. In *Harvey v Truro Rural District Council* (1903) Mr Justice Joyce said (at p 644) 'Mere disuse of a highway cannot deprive the public of their rights. Where there has once been a highway no length of time during which it may not have been used would preclude the public from resuming the exercise of the right to use it if and when they think proper.'

2.3 The public's rights

2.3.1 Extent of the rights

The public's right over a highway is a right of passage for the purpose of passing and repassing and for purposes reasonably incidental thereto. On a footpath the latter phrase would include such things as stopping

RIGHTS OF WAY

to look at a view, to talk to a passer-by, to take a photograph or to sit down to rest.

If there is use other than for passing and repassing or a purpose reasonably incidental thereto, the user exceeds his entitlement to be on the land and becomes a trespasser. For example, in *Harrison v Duke of Rutland* (1893), Harrison went on to a public carriageway on the Duke's land, walked up and down and shouted and waved flags so as to disturb grouse and interfere with a shooting party. The Duke ordered his gamekeepers to restrain Harrison. They did so and he sued for assault. The Court held that Harrison had exceeded his right of passage and was a trespasser. The Duke had therefore been entitled to have him restrained.

In *Hickman v Maisey* (1900) Hickman let his land to a trainer of racehorses. Maisey, a journalist, walked backwards and forwards over about 15 yards of a public highway for an hour and a half taking notes of the horses' performance. The Court of Appeal held that Maisey had exceeded his right and was a trespasser. Lord Justice Smith summarised his view of the extent of the public's right in his judgment: 'If a man, while using a highway for passage, sat down for a time to rest himself, to call that a trespass would be unreasonable. Similarly, if a man took a sketch from a highway, I should say that no reasonable person would treat that as an act of trespass.' The motive for a person's journey is irrelevant, provided that his use of the way is for passage.

If the use exceeds what is legally permitted and has the effect of obstructing the free passage along the way for other users, the offence of obstruction under HA 80 s 137 may be committed. An example was juggling in a pedestrian precinct for the purpose of collecting money. *(Waite v Taylor* (1985).) Obstruction is considered in chapter 6.

Can the path-user take anything with him? It was held in *R v Matthias* (1861) that the owner of land over which a path runs could remove 'anything that encumbers the close, except such things as are usual accompaniments of a large class of foot passengers, being so small and light, as neither to be a nuisance to other passengers nor injurious to the soil.' The case was about a 'perambulator' 18 inches wide and weighing 14 pounds, which in current terms is more like a pushchair than a pram. The jury decided that such a 'perambulator' was a 'usual accompaniment'. There is no exhaustive list of 'usual accompaniments'. Whether any particular item comes within this term is a matter for a court to decide.

A local authority may appoint wardens to 'advise and assist' the public in connection with the use of footpaths, bridleways and byways in its countryside. (WCA 81 s 62 — p 384.)

2.3.2 Dogs

A 'usual accompaniment' As dogs have since time immemorial been taken on footpaths it seems that a court would hold that they are a usual accompaniment of a foot passenger. For a walker to take a dog is therefore no trespass.

But the entitlement to take a dog on a public right of way is confined to the line of the path, and exists while the dog is accompanying its owner or keeper. Thus if a dog is allowed to run around off the path, trespass is committed against the holder of the land. (*League against Cruel Sports v Scott* (1985), injunction granted against master of hounds to stop hounds going on land closed to hunt.)

Chapter 9.1 deals with dogs on land to which the public has a right of access.

Must the dog be on a lead? There is no rule requiring that on a right of way a dog must be kept on a lead. But a highway authority has power under s 27 of the Road Traffic Act 1988 (p 414) to make an order requiring dogs to be kept on a lead on specified rights of way. Failure to comply is an offence.

The Control of Dogs on Roads Orders (Procedure) (England and Wales) Regulations 1962 set out the way in which such orders are to be made. Before making an order, the authority must consult the police and representative organisations, and either publish notice in the local paper and on or near the paths affected by the proposed order or hold a public inquiry. An inquiry may also be held if a notice is published, in which case it must also be advertised by notice in the local press and on the rights of way. Notice of the inquiry must also be given to objectors.

If the authority decides to make an order, it must tell the objectors and give its reasons for so doing. It must also publish notice of the order in the local press, keep a copy of the order available for public inspection and erect on the affected ways signs in such positions as it considers requisite to ensure that users of the ways are aware of the effect of the order.

Dogs and sheep Under the Dogs (Protection of Livestock) Act 1953 s 1(2)(c) (p 293), it is an offence to allow a dog to be at large in a field or enclosure in which there are sheep. '*At large*' is defined as not on a lead or otherwise under close control. '*Field or enclosure*' is not defined, but is generally considered not to include open country such as unenclosed mountain or moorland. However, this particular offence does not apply to a dog owned or controlled by the occupier of the field, the owner of the sheep or a person authorised by either of them, nor does it apply to a police dog, a trained sheepdog, or working gun-dog or a pack of hounds (s 1(2A)).

Dogs which attack or chase livestock Section 1(2) of the 1953 Act makes it an offence to allow a dog to attack or chase livestock (as defined in s 3), and s 9 of the Animals Act 1971 (p 303) enables a farmer to shoot a dog which is attacking or chasing livestock without being liable to compensate the dog's owner.

These provisions add legal weight to the advice in the Countryside Commission's Country Code 'Keep your dogs under close control'.

Dogs which deter or prevent people from using a right of way are considered in chapter 6.6.2.

Can dogs be banned from rights of way? Because it seems that dogs are 'usual accompaniments', it would be outside the scope of a byelaw to seek to restrict their being taken on a right of way. But it may be possible for a traffic regulation order to be made. Section 142 of the Road Traffic Regulation Act 1984 (p 404) provides that 'traffic' may be defined or described by reference to any characteristics of the traffic or to any other circumstances whatever. It is submitted that this may allow 'traffic' consisting of pedestrians accompanied by dogs to be restricted from using a right of way.

2.4 Trespass

2.4.1 Nature of trespass

A person who enters or remains on land without lawful authority commits trespass against the holder of the land. 'Lawful authority' can be any of the following:

(a) Permission granted by the landholder (for example, where he invites the use of an alternative route by signposts or notices).

(b) The common law right of the public to follow a public right of way.

(c) Authority granted by statute. For example, HA 1980 s 300 (p 353) permits a local authority to take a vehicle on to a footpath or bridleway for certain purposes. (See p 54.)

A person who strays from a right of way or uses it other than for passing and repassing commits trespass.

Trespass is a civil wrong, actionable by the landholder in the civil courts. The courts can award damages or grant an injunction prohibiting future trespass, or both.

If a person commits trespass and refuses to comply with a request by the landholder or his agent to leave the land, reasonable force may be used to compel him to do so. The use of force unnecessarily, or the use of more force than is reasonably necessary, constitutes the civil wrong of battery actionable by the trespasser against the person who applied the force.

2 : PUBLIC RIGHTS OF WAY

2.4.2 Deviation from a right of way

What if the right of way is blocked and cannot be followed? If the obstruction is by the holder of the land crossed by the way, there is undoubtedly a right to deviate on to other land belonging to the same landholder in order to get round the obstruction. (*Stacey v Sherrin* (1913).) Thus, if a cross-field path has been ploughed or disturbed and not reinstated within the prescribed period (see chapter 6.4), and a walker goes round the edge of the field to avoid mud and furrows making its use unreasonably inconvenient, he commits no trespass.

If crops are of a kind or of a height that makes it difficult to follow the line of a cross-field path, they constitute an obstacle that entitles the walker to deviate (eg by going round the edge of the field). It is, however, the view of the RA and the OSS that unless crops present a severe obstacle, the legal line of a path across a field should be followed. See chapter 6.5.2 for details of the duty of the occupier to keep paths through or adjacent to crops convenient to use and to follow.

What if the obstruction was not wilful, eg if it was due to natural causes such as a fall of rock? In *Taylor v Whitehead* (1781) Lord Mansfield said '[Highways] ... are for the public service, and if the usual track is impassable, it is for the general good that people should be entitled to pass into another line'. It is submitted that this means that there is a right to deviate in such circumstances.

Whether the right to deviate entitles a user to go on to land belonging to an (adjoining) landholder to avoid an obstruction has not been decided by the courts. Because a user cannot be certain who holds any particular land, special care should be taken to avoid causing damage if a deviation is made.

2.4.3 Trespass as a crime

At common law trespass is a civil wrong, not a crime. Thus a notice 'Trespassers will be prosecuted' states an intention that cannot normally be carried out. (A notice that stated 'Trespassers will be sued' would, on the other hand, have legal meaning.)

In certain circumstances, statute has made trespass a crime. For example, it is an offence wilfully to trespass on any railway or any of the stations or premises connected with it.

Following complaints about the behaviour of 'hippy convoys', Parliament enacted s 39 of the Public Order Act 1986 (p 409). Several conditions have all to be met before an offence is committed under this section. Firstly, someone has to have entered land as a trespasser with at least one other person; they must be there together with the common purpose of residing on the land. Secondly, reasonable steps must have been taken by the occupier to ask them to leave. Thirdly, one of those present must have caused damage or used threatening or abusive words or behaviour towards the occupier, or, alternatively, between them they must have brought at least 12 vehicles onto the land. Finally, the most senior police officer present at the scene must have ordered them to leave the land, and they must have failed to do so. A police constable in uniform who reasonably suspects a person of committing the offence may arrest him without warrant.

The government stated in 1986 that it had no intention of making trespass a criminal offence, and that walkers have no need to fear section 39. For members of a party to commit the offence they would have to enter land to camp, refuse to leave when requested to do so by the occupier of the land and ordered to do so by the police, and behave in an abusive or threatening way.

2.5 Who owns a highway?

2.5.1 The subsoil

The land over which some highways run is owned by the local highway authority, or by the Crown on behalf of the Department of Transport. For example, when a new motorway is constructed, the land over which it runs is purchased, if necessary compulsorily, from the landowners concerned.

Generally, however, a right of way runs over land that is in private ownership, eg a footpath across a field. Where a highway runs between land owned by two different owners, the presumption is that their ownership boundary runs along the centre line of the highway.

2.5.2 The surface of a publicly-maintainable highway

If (as will normally be the case — see chapter 7.2) a highway is maintainable at public expense, it is owned by the highway authority (HA 80 s 263 — p 352).

The extent of the authority's ownership This provision gives the authority ownership of the surface of the highway, and so much of the soil below, and of the air above, as is 'necessary for its control, protection and maintenance as a [highway] for the use of the public' (Lord Herschell, *Mayor of Tunbridge Wells v Baird* (1896)). In the same case Lord Macnaghten said that ownership entitles the authority 'to sue and be sued as occasion may require in the course of such control and management'.

In *Wiltshire County Council v Frazer* (1984) it was held that the highway authority's ownership of the surface entitled it to succeed in an action for recovery of possession of the highway (under Order 113 of the Rules of the Supreme Court) from a group that had pitched tents and parked vehicles and caravans on a stretch of the highway verge.

2 : PUBLIC RIGHTS OF WAY

(The nature of the ownership was held to be a fee simple determinable in certain events.) A highway authority is thus entitled to bring proceedings in civil law to obtain an injunction against anyone who obstructs a publicly-maintainable highway, requiring the removal of the obstruction.

It follows that any disturbance of the surface is a trespass against the authority's interest, unless it is carried out with statutory authority, eg agricultural disturbance of a cross-field path (p 175). So, if seed is planted in the surface of a highway causing a crop to grow there, the authority is entitled by its ownership to remove the crop if its presence interferes with the public's use of the highway. Indeed the authority's permission would need to be sought and obtained before such a crop was planted or sown.

The remaining rights of the owner of the subsoil The provision does not otherwise affect the property rights of the landowner. Thus the subsoil of the highway together with minerals beneath the surface remains the property of the owner, who can maintain an action for trespass if his rights are infringed.

2.5.3 Transfer of land

A new owner may sometimes be unaware of the existence of a right of way across his land. The solicitor who acted for him in the purchase of the land may have failed to take advantage of the search procedure that will reveal the existence of certain public rights of way.

When acting for a purchaser, a solicitor makes (or ought to make) an official search of the local land-charges register maintained by the district or London borough council. With the search application he also submits (or should submit) a form asking for information on matters which will not be revealed by the official search (eg whether the land is served by main drainage).

The form, known as CON 29, is in two parts. The information requested in Part I will be supplied automatically (if available) but that in Part II will be provided only if the relevant question is ticked and an extra fee paid. One of the Part II questions is as follows: 'Has any public path, or road used as a public path, bridleway or byway which abuts on or crosses the property been shown in a definitive map or revised definitive map prepared under Part IV of the National Parks and Access to the Countryside Act 1949 or Part III of the Wildlife and Countryside Act 1981? If so, please mark its approximate route on the attached plan.' If this question is not ticked the purchaser may be unaware of any rights of way over the land. (Not many purchasers examine the definitive map.)

Moves by the RA and other bodies to have this question put into Part I of the form have been resisted by the Law Society and the local authority associations, which jointly decide on the form's contents. It is possible that a solicitor who fails to discover the existence of a right of way would be held to be liable for any loss suffered by his client as a result. (*G & K Ladenbau Ltd v Crawley and de Reya* (1978), solicitors who failed to search the register of common land on behalf of a purchaser held to be negligent.)

2.6 Liability for injury to the user of a right of way

If a walker is injured, or suffers damage to his property, eg if his clothing is torn, does he have a right of action for his loss? And, if so, against whom does his action lie?

2.6.1 Injury caused by failure to repair the way

If the injury is caused by a defect in the surface of the highway which arises out of a failure by the highway authority to keep the way in a proper state of repair, the authority will be liable. The nature of the authority's duty is considered in chapter 7.2.2, and the civil liability of authorities in chapter 7.5. The landowner will not be liable. Surface defects could include pot-holes, slippery paving-stones, or a tree-stump in the line of the path.

2.6.2 Injury caused by a defective stile or gate

If the injury is caused by the condition of a stile or gate (eg if a wooden step is rotten and breaks, or if there is barbed wire round the post of a 'squeezer' stile), there are two grounds for maintaining that the landowner is liable.

By virtue of the statutory duty under HA 80 s 146 This section (p 345) imposes a duty on the landowner to maintain any 'stile, gate or other similar structure' across a footpath or bridleway in a safe condition. It is submitted that the section gives a right of action for damages (for the civil wrong of breach of statutory duty) if damage or injury is caused by the failure to maintain the structure in a safe condition.

By virtue of occupier's liability Since a stile or gate, although on a highway, is not part of it (being for the advantage of, owned by, and maintainable by, the landowner) liability rests with the landowner (and is governed by the Occupiers' Liability Act 1957, see chapter 2.6.6 below).

2.6.3 When deviating with the owner's permission

If the incident that caused the injury occurred off the right of way, the walker having left the legal line with the express permission of the

2 : PUBLIC RIGHTS OF WAY

owner (eg if he says, 'Go round by the house, you'll avoid the mud in the yard that way') or his implied permission (eg if he has provided and signposted a concessionary path as an alternative to the legal line), the injured person ranks in law as a visitor, and liability is regulated by the Occupiers' Liability Act 1957, see chapter 2.6.6 below.

2.6.4 When deviating to avoid an obstruction

If a walker deviates onto land to avoid an obstruction and is injured while so doing, it seems that the walker will be deemed to have received the implied permission of the landowner to deviate, provided that the injury occurs on land in the same ownership and that the landowner was responsible for the obstruction. The injured walker ranks in law as a visitor, and liability is regulated by the Occupiers' Liability Act 1957, see chapter 2.6.6 below. See chapter 2.4.2 on the right to deviate.

2.6.5 When trespassing

If the injury occurred when the walker was off a highway without the permission, express or implied, of the landowner (eg if he leaves a path to examine a plant, to take a short cut, to follow a more attractive route, or because he is lost), he is a trespasser and liable accordingly (see chapter 2.4 above).

At common law a landowner originally owed no duty of care to a trespasser. Indeed, he was not liable even if the injury was caused intentionally, eg as the result of his setting mantraps or spring guns. But, in the course of time, the common law came to regard him as owing at least a minimum duty of care to a trespasser. (The setting of traps was made illegal by statute in the last century.) Many of the cases that illustrate the development of the law concern children. A special duty of care came to be regarded as being owed to them because of their age and the likelihood of their being attracted to 'allurements' on land.

The development of the common law culminated in the case of *British Railways Board v Herrington* (1972). A child who had climbed through a broken stile on to a railway line was hit by a passing train (see chapter 2.8.2). The House of Lords held that the Board, having been aware of the broken fence, and of the fact that children played on the line, was under a duty to take reasonable steps to mitigate the risk of injury. Having been in breach of the duty by failing to repair the fence, the Board was liable. The case illustrated the uncertainties that existed about the nature of the duty owed to a trespasser and in 1984 legislation was enacted with the aim of making the law more certain.

This statute, the Occupiers' Liability Act 1984 (p 396), lays down, s 1, that if (a) an occupier of premises is aware of a danger or has reasonable grounds to believe that it exists; and (b) the occupier knows that a person other than a visitor is in the vicinity of the danger or that he may come into the vicinity; and (c) the risk posed by the danger is one against which, in all the circumstances of the case, he may reasonably be expected to offer some protection, he owes a duty to take such care as is reasonable in all the circumstances of the case to see that the person does not suffer injury on the premises. The Act provides that any duty owed may be discharged by giving appropriate warning of the danger, that no duty is owed in respect of risks willingly accepted, and that no duty is owed by virtue of the Act to persons using a highway. The liability relates to personal injury, not to property. (In *White v St Albans City and District Council* (1990) it was held that the fact that an occupier erects a fence to keep out trespassers is not of itself to be treated as evidence that he knew that trespassers might come into the vicinity.)

2.6.6 The Occupiers' Liability Act 1957

The duty of care Section 2(2) of the 1957 Act (p 295) provides that a person who is in occupation or control of premises owes a duty to a visitor 'to take such care as in all the circumstances of the case is reasonable to see that the visitor will be reasonably safe in using the premises for the purposes for which he is invited or permitted by the occupier to be there'. The duty applies to property as well as personal injury.

A 'visitor' is a person who is on the premises by the express or implied permission of the person occupying or having control of the premises. 'Premises' includes land, fixed or moveable structures, and a vehicle, aircraft or vessel. The occupier will not necessarily be the owner of the land.

Standard of the duty On the duty owed to a visitor, the Act provides that an occupier must be prepared for children to be less careful than adults; that no duty is owned in respect of risks willingly accepted by a visitor; and that the duty may be discharged by giving warning (eg by a notice) of a danger, provided that the warning is 'enough to enable the visitor to be reasonably safe'.

Exemption from liability Can an occupier exempt himself from liability, eg by erecting a notice with wording to this effect? Under the Unfair Contract Terms Act 1977, if a person enters premises for the 'business purposes' of the occupier (eg if a walker leaves a public path to enter a shop), the duty imposed by the 1957 Act cannot be excluded, ie any purported exclusion is void. Otherwise there is no legal bar to an occupier excluding himself by such a notice from the liability imposed by the 1957 Act. But for the exclusion to be effective he must show that the notice was brought sufficiently to the attention of the visitor.

Duty not applying to highway users The Act also provides (s 2(5)) that 'persons who enter for any purpose in the exercise of a right conferred by law are to be treated as permitted by the occupier to be there for that purpose, whether they in fact have his permission or not'. It might be thought that this brings a user of a highway within the duty of care, since such a person is one who is on land in exercise of a right of law. However, it was held in *Greenhalgh v British Railways Board* (1969) that although a person exercising a public right of way was exercising a right conferred by law, he was not a visitor within the meaning of the 1957 Act. The reasoning was that at common law the owner or occupier of land was not responsible for the safety of members of the public using the highway and the 1957 Act was not intended to change the law in this respect. In other words, since the landowner has no power to control the use of the highway by the public, he is not to be burdened with responsibility for defects in the highway.

2.7 Who can use which highways?

The rule at common law is that a walker may walk on a footpath, a bridleway or a carriageway; a horse-rider may ride (or lead) a horse on a bridleway or a carriageway; a vehicle may be driven on a carriageway. By statute a pedal cyclist may ride on a bridleway (see below).

What is the position if these rules are infringed, for example if a motorcyclist rides on a footpath? In answering this and similar questions it is necessary to bear in mind the distinction between a civil wrong and a crime explained in chapter 1.4: a particular act may be a civil wrong but not a crime, or a crime but not a civil wrong, or it may be both.

2.7.1 Pedal cyclists

On footpaths A cyclist who rides on a *footpath* commits trespass against the holder of the land over which the path runs. District and London borough councils have powers to make byelaws under LGA 72 s 235 to restrict or prohibit cycling on specified footpaths or bridleways, and county, metropolitan district and London borough councils have powers under the Road Traffic Regulation Act 1984 to make orders to the same effect (p 158). Infringement of such byelaws or orders is a criminal offence.

It is submitted that a bicycle is not a 'natural accompaniment' of a user of a footpath, and that to push one along a footpath is to commit trespass against the landholder, even if there is no infringement of a byelaw or traffic order.

RIGHTS OF WAY

Under the Highways Act 1835 s 72, it is an offence to ride a bicycle on a *footway* (a pavement at the side of a carriageway).

On bridleways At common law a cyclist who rode over a *bridleway* committed trespass against the holder of the land. The position was changed by CA 68 s 30 (p 300). This gives the public the right to ride bicycles on bridleways, provided that they give way to walkers and horse-riders. The right conferred by the 1968 Act is subject to any order or byelaw that prohibits riding on a particular bridleway (see above).

The Road Traffic Act 1988 contains other provisions governing the behaviour of cyclists. Section 28 (p 415) makes it an offence to cycle on a bridleway recklessly, s 29 (p 415) an offence to do so without due care and attention, or without reasonable consideration for other users, and s 30 an offence to do so while unfit to ride through drink or drugs.

Section 31 of the 1988 Act (p 415) makes it an offence to promote or take part in an unauthorised race or trial of speed between cycles on a public way, which is defined in the section as including a bridleway but not a footpath. Races or trials of speed may, under subsection (2), be authorised on a road but not on a bridleway or footpath.

'Mountain' or 'all-terrain' bikes come within the definition of 'cycle' in the 1988 Act — see s 192 (p 418).

2.7.2 Horse-riders

If a person rides (or leads) a horse over a footpath he commits trespass against the holder of the land. District and London borough councils have powers to make byelaws under LGA 72 s 235 to restrict or prohibit horse-riding on specified footpaths or bridleways, and county, metropolitan district and London borough councils have powers under the Road Traffic Regulation Act 1984 to make orders to the same effect (p 158). Infringement of such byelaws or orders is a criminal offence.

2.7.3 Motor vehicles

A person who drives a vehicle over any private land, including any footpath or bridleway on that land, commits trespass against the holder of the land.

In addition, RTA 88 s 34 (p 416) makes it an offence to drive a motor vehicle without lawful authority over any footpath or bridleway (or upon any common land, moorland or other land not being land forming part of a road). (But see below about driving within 15 yards of a carriageway.) 'Motor vehicle' is defined in s 185 (p 417), and such a vehicle is deemed, by s 191 (p 417), to be a carriage for the purpose of any Act of Parliament. A motor vehicle may thus lawfully be used on a carriageway.

2 : PUBLIC RIGHTS OF WAY

Under s 34 the possession of 'lawful authority' avoids the offence. For example, s 300 of the Highways Act 1980 (p 353) authorises local authorities and local councils to take appliances or vehicles on to footpaths or bridleways in order to maintain or clean these ways and also structures or other works on them. That use is subject to the Vehicles (Conditions of Use on Footpaths) Regulations 1963. These require, among other matters, observance of a speed limit of 5 mph. The Chronically Sick and Disabled Persons Act 1970, s 20, by providing that an invalid carriage shall not be treated as a vehicle for the purposes of RTA 88, means that its use on a footpath or bridleway is not a crime. It is not clear whether it still remains trespass.

'Lawful authority' can also take the form of permission by the holder of the land over which the way passes. Permission can be express or implied. But mere acquiescence in vehicular use cannot be taken as implied permission unless it is clear that the owner knew that the path was being so used. If a footpath or bridleway is publicly maintainable the surface belongs to the highway authority. It is submitted that, for lawful authority to exist, permission is required from the authority in addition to the owner of the subsoil. (See chapter 2.5.2 above.)

The offence created by s 34 of the Road Traffic Act 1988 is not committed if the vehicle is driven on to land not more than 15 yards from a road which is a public carriageway for the purpose of parking the vehicle on that land. This exception does not confer a *right* to drive this distance off a road to park. It merely provides a defence to the offence introduced by s 34. A person who drives a vehicle off a carriageway commits trespass. In addition, if damage is caused, an offence under the Criminal Damage Act 1971 (p 304) may have been committed.

It is an offence under RTA 88 s 21 (p 413) to drive or park a motor vehicle on a cycle track. 'Cycle track' is defined by reference to HA 80 s 329 (p 357): that definition includes, but is not limited to, cycle tracks converted from footpaths under the Cycle Tracks Act 1984 (see chapter 5.5.2).

2.7.4 Public nuisance

As well as the civil or criminal wrongs noted above, use of pedal cycles, horses and motor vehicles on a footpath (or use of vehicles on a bridleway) may also constitute the criminal offence of public nuisance if the use 'prevents the convenient use of the way by passengers' (Mr Justice Byles, *R v Matthias* (1861)), eg by causing walkers to have to jump out of the way, or by churning up the path. Use of motor vehicles on footpaths and public nuisance are considered further in chapter 6.

2.7.5 Processions

Section 11 of the Public Order Act 1986 (p 408) provides that written notice must be given to the police of any proposed public procession intended to demonstrate support for, or opposition to, the views or actions of any person or body of persons, to publicise a cause or campaign, or to mark or commemorate an event. Failure by the person organising the procession to give notice is an offence. There is a defence that it was not reasonably practicable to give advance notice of the procession.

The provision does not apply to a static gathering. But if a walk is used to gain publicity in some campaign, eg to press for increased access to a particular area or to oppose the use of attractive countryside for military training, the organisers are likely to need to give notice.

2.8 Certain special types of way

2.8.1 Permissive paths

A permissive path (sometimes termed a 'concessionary path') is a path which the landowner permits the public to use, with the intention that it should not become a public right of way. He may erect notices to that effect and, perhaps, close the path once a year. To ensure that the public does not acquire a right of way, as might happen if a notice was removed and not replaced, the owner can take advantage of the alternative procedures laid down in HA 80 s 31(5) (p 321). Unofficial diversions of public rights of way made by landowners can be regarded as permissive paths, though if the above procedures are not used, the new route may in time become a public right of way. (See chapter 3.)

A permissive path may be no more than a way, the use of which is not normally objected to by the landholder. But it may also be a way which has been the subject of a formal agreement between the landowner and a local authority. Such a way is sometimes referred to as a 'licenced' path: the agreement or licence might provide for the way to remain available to the public for a stated period, eg five years.

Because a permissive path is not a public right of way, it is not in general subject to rights-of-way law. By way of exception, HA 80 s 154 (p 348), under which overhanging vegetation may be required to be cut back, applies to 'any road or footpath to which the public has access', and specifically to 'a road or footpath that is not a highway' (subsection 1(c)). In addition, certain provisions in the Road Traffic Act 1988, eg ss 2 & 3, apply to a 'road'. This is defined (s 192) as 'any highway and any other road to which the public has access' and thus applies to permissive paths.

A user of a permissive path will be a visitor for the purposes of the Occupiers' Liability Act 1957, and will be owed a duty of care by the occupier accordingly (see chapter 2.6.6).

Where the existence of a permissive footpath (or bridleway) has been notified to the Ordnance Survey, these are indicated (on certain maps)

2 : PUBLIC RIGHTS OF WAY

by short brown dashes for footpaths and long brown dashes for bridleways.

Although not substitutes for rights of way, permissive paths can be a useful supplement to the public path network.

2.8.2 Paths across railway lines

Paths crossing on the level Numerous rights of way cross railway lines, either on the level or above or below. The British Railways Board inherited from the former railway companies the power to dedicate, either expressly or impliedly, rights of way across its lines. For most public rights of way which cross a railway line on the level, the Board's obligations are set out in s 61 of the Railway Clauses Consolidation Act 1845 (p 286). These are to make and maintain convenient approaches to the line and good and sufficient gates and stiles in the lineside fences.

The duties can be enforced by application to a magistrates' court using the procedure set out in s 65 of the same Act (p 286). However, they apply only if the 1845 Act was itself applied by the statute authorising the construction of the line. In some such statutes alternative or additional duties may have been imposed on the Board.

The Board also has a civil liability. It was held by the Court of Appeal in *Thomas v British Railways Board* (1976) that if a railway undertaking allows a public right of way to come into existence across a railway line, it is under a duty at common law, quite apart from s 61, to provide proper safeguards, particularly where the crossing is almost as old as the railway. In the case a line had been built in 1861 and by 1876 a public right of way had been established over it. In 1968 the local authority built a housing estate on one side of the line with a stile to provide access over the line along the right of way. On 1 April 1969 a new stile was erected. By 13 April the stile was so broken that small children could walk straight through on to the line. On 17 April the two-year-old plaintiff, who lived on the estate, lost her legs when hit by a train while she was sitting on the line. The court held the Board responsible both under the common law and for breach of its duty under s 61.

Private Acts of Parliament promoted by the Board often contain provisions extinguishing some or all of the public's rights of way over a particular crossing (which may be a bridge or a tunnel). The path may continue to exist on the ground but, if it is no longer a public right of way, the statutory and common law obligations described above do not apply. If the Board still permits the public to use such a crossing it may incur liability under the Occupiers' Liability Act 1957 (see chapter 2.6.6).

Crossings above or below the line Sections 61 and 65 do not apply to crossings above or below a railway line. If the bridge or underpass was provided as part of the construction of the line the authorising Act may have made the Board liable for its maintenance (although it may also be maintainable at public expense — chapter 7.2.1).

The Board has a statutory responsibility under s 68 of the 1845 Act to maintain works provided for the benefit of owners and occupiers of lands adjoining the railway, commonly known as 'accommodation works'. In many instances, the public have acquired a right of way over bridges or through underpasses but that acquisition does not impose a liability for maintenance on the Board so far as the public is concerned: that liability will normally fall on the highway authority (see chapter 7.2). Thus in *Greenhalgh v British Railways Board* (1969) it was held that the Board was not liable to a member of the public who stepped into a pothole on a bridge which had originally been provided as an accommodation work.

In *British Transport Commission v Westmorland CC* (1958) the CC showed on its provisional map of rights of way a public footpath over an accommodation bridge on the Windermere branch line in Cumbria. The Commission, predecessors of the British Railways Board, appealed on the ground that the dedication of the right of way would be incompatible with the purposes of their railway undertaking. The House of Lords decided that there was nothing to prevent dedication, provided that the use by the public of the right of way so dedicated was not incompatible with those purposes.

Private railway companies Private railway companies operating railway lines will be under the same obligations as the Board.

2.8.3 Tow-paths

A tow-path is legally a part of the navigation of a canal or navigable river. *(Monmouthshire Canal Co v Hill* (1859).) It may or may not also be a public right of way. A tow-path is capable of being dedicated as a public right of way. (HA 80 s 329(2) — p 359.) If it is so dedicated, the public takes it subject to the primary needs of navigation. (*Grand Junction Canal Co v Petty* (1881).) In that case Lord Esher, Master of the Rolls, said: 'The public must be taken to accept it as a limited dedication and cannot set up a right to prevent or limit the user of the towing-path. If the horse or the tow-rope and the foot passengers are in one another's way, the foot-passenger must look out for himself and get out of the way.'

The definitive map must be consulted to find if a particular tow-path has been recorded as a public right of way. On the Thames, for example, most of the tow-path along the river is a public footpath, but along the 'cuts' it is not, for there the Thames Water Authority and its predecessors maintained notices to prevent presumption of dedication.

There is no right to ride a horse on a tow-path except for pulling

2 : PUBLIC RIGHTS OF WAY

boats, unless the tow-path is also a bridleway; but this is rare, for most canal companies took steps to prevent dedication of their tow-paths for riding.

It has been the policy of the British Waterways Board not to dedicate tow-paths along its canals as public rights of way, although it generally allows the public to use them. The Board is likely to have taken appropriate steps, under HA 80 s 31 (see chapter 3.3.4), to prevent a public right of way arising by presumed dedication. Nonetheless, many miles of tow-paths alongside canals are recorded as public rights of way (normally footpaths) on definitive maps, eg the Kennet and Avon canal tow-path from Bath to Reading.

2.8.4 The sea-shore

The foreshore (land between medium high and medium low water) There is no right of way for the public over the foreshore unless such a right has been dedicated, expressly or by presumption. The foreshore is generally owned by the Crown, but in some cases the Crown has granted or sold it to another person or body. In the past this is likely to have been the Lord of the Manor, but more recently a local authority or other public body, or a private body such as the National Trust, is likely to be the grantee or purchaser. As owner of the soil, the Crown may dedicate a right of way expressly or by presumption. However, HA 80 s 31 (chapter 3.3) does not bind the Crown, so presumed dedication can only be claimed at common law (chapter 3.2). Any other owner of the foreshore is subject to s 31.

In practice, it is virtually impossible to acquire a right of way over the foreshore by presumed dedication because of the practical difficulty in establishing the right over a defined track. The sea covers the foreshore twice a day throughout most of the year and will almost invariably wash away any tracks. However it would be lawful, though not necessarily desirable, for a right of way to be created over the foreshore, eg by means of a creation or diversion order.

A public right of way may, however, lawfully have its terminus at the edge of the foreshore. (*Williams-Ellis v Cobb* (1935).) If it does, that terminus may not be moved by a public path diversion order made under HA 80, since it is not on a highway. (s 119(2)(a) — p 335.) Even if the public has no right of way, it is usually difficult for the owner to prevent public use of the foreshore as a means of passage. The reason is that there is a public right of navigation over the foreshore when it is covered with water and the erection of fences which would interfere with that right would be unlawful without statutory authority. Further, section 34 of the Coast Protection Act 1949 makes it an offence to erect fencing on the foreshore without the consent of the Secretary of State for Trade and Industry.

Land above medium high water There is no presumption that the land immediately above medium high water mark belongs to the Crown, even if it is not physically distinguishable from the foreshore. Such land is subject to the normal rules as to dedication. However if, as frequently happens, the high water mark moves, the land forming the foreshore also moves. It may thus be difficult to establish sufficient use of a defined track on or near the sea-shore to presume dedication of a right of way.

2.8.5 Ferries

In places a ferry is an important link in a path network. For many centuries ferries were profitable, and the right to operate one was jealously guarded. The existence, past or present, of a ferry may be useful evidence to support a claim that paths leading to it are public rights of way.

The remedy at common law if a ferryman did not operate properly was an action to remove the franchise and give it to someone else, but this is likely to be of little worth when the ferry is unprofitable. The courts have refused to grant a mandatory injunction to compel a ferry operator to continue working at a loss. (*A-G v Colchester Corporation* (1955).)

The Countryside Commission can make grants under s 9 of the Local Government Act 1974 to a private individual to help keep a ferry open if the ferry is important in securing access to the countryside. Furthermore, ferries may be provided and operated as part of a long-distance route (p 276) under the powers contained in s 53 of the 1949 Act (p 290).

3

How rights of way come into being

3.1 Express dedication

A right of way may come into existence by a landowner giving the public the right to use a way over his land. In so doing he is said to dedicate it as a public right of way. Dedication may be as a footpath, a bridleway or a carriageway. For example, a local authority, having purchased land over which a concessionary path exists, may decide to dedicate the route as a public footpath. Or the developer of an estate may dedicate roads on the estate as public carriageways.

In order to show that a right of way has come into existence by express dedication certain conditions must be satisfied.

Intention to dedicate The landowner must be shown to have had an intention to dedicate the way as a public right of way. This will be a matter of fact to be decided on the evidence. The question may sometimes turn on the construction placed on certain words in a deed.

Acceptance by the public The dedication must be accepted by the public. This means that the way must come into use.

For the public at large The dedication must be for the public at large (not merely, for example, for the inhabitants of a particular parish).

For all time The dedication must be for all time. So dedication of a way for, say, 100 years, creates no right of way but merely constitutes permission, revocable by the landowner, for the public to use the way while he holds the land.

Capacity to dedicate Only the person who holds the freehold in land has the legal capacity to dedicate. It follows that a tenant under a lease cannot dedicate unless he does so with the concurrence of the freeholder.

The freeholder may be an individual or a statutory corporation (ie a company registered under the Companies Act 1985 or earlier Companies Acts). Exceptions exist in the case of certain corporations incorporated under special statutes. For example, some nineteenth-century railway and canal Acts prevent dedication of rights of way. Statutory undertakers can dedicate, provided that the dedication does not conflict with their statutory purposes. (*British Transport Commission v Westmorland CC* (1958) — see p 58.)

3.2 Presumed dedication — at common law

Relatively few highways can be shown to have been expressly dedicated. The great majority have been accepted as being public since beyond memory. In order to explain the legal basis of such ways, the law presumes that at some time in the past the landowner dedicated the way to the public, either expressly, the evidence of the dedication having since been lost, or impliedly, by making no objection to the use by the public of the way.

Early in the development of highway law, it was established that proof of public use of a way for a certain period created a presumption of implied dedication as a right of way. Each case turned on whether the facts indicated an intention to dedicate. No minimum period was required to be shown. In some cases, because of the particular circumstances (eg heavy use) relatively short periods were accepted as sufficient; for example, in *R v Petrie* (1855) eight years and in *Rugby Charity Trustees v Merryweather* (1790) six.

Uncertainty as to what period would be treated as sufficient to raise the presumption caused difficulty for those wishing to claim that a certain way, hitherto used by the public but not challenged by the landowner, was a public right of way. For many decades governments were urged to introduce legislation that would lay down a specific period after which a presumption of dedication would arise. Private members' bills were introduced into the Commons (the first in 1906) to effect the change. Opposition by landowning interests defeated successive attempts, but, after long campaigning (by the OSS in particular), the reform was made by the Rights of Way Act 1932.

3.3 Presumed dedication — under section 31 of the Highways Act 1980

3.3.1 A summary of the provisions

The Rights of Way Act 1932 was repealed and its provisions (including amendments made by NPACA 49) were replaced by s 34 of the Highways Act 1959. With the consolidation of the 1959 Act and later legislation by the Highways Act 1980, the provisions now appear in s 31 of that Act (p 321). (Notices erected to prevent the acquisition of a right of way may be seen quoting any of these three Acts.)

The effect of s 31 is, very broadly, that after 20 years' use a way is deemed to have been dedicated as a highway unless there is evidence

3 : HOW RIGHTS OF WAY COME INTO BEING

of a contrary intention. To understand the operation of the section it is necessary to examine its precise wording. This begins as follows:

'(1) Where a way over any land other than a way of such a character that use of it by the public could not give rise at common law to any presumption of dedication has been actually enjoyed by the public as of right and without interruption for a full period of 20 years, the way is to be deemed to have been dedicated as a highway unless there is sufficient evidence that there was no intention during that period to dedicate it.

(2) The period of 20 years referred to in subsection (1) above is to be calculated retrospectively from the date when the right of the public to use the way is brought into question whether by a notice ... or otherwise.'

To establish the presumed dedication of a right of way under s 31 it is necessary to show that the following all apply:

(a) The nature of the way was not such that dedication could not be presumed at common law (p 64).
(b) The public at large must have used the way (p 64).
(c) The use must have been over a period of at least 20 years without effective interruption (p 65).
(d) That 20-year period must have ended with an act that brought into question the public's right to use the way (p 67).
(e) The landowner must not be able to prove that he had no intention to dedicate the way (p 65).

Retrospective effect of the 1932 Act The 1932 Act had retrospective effect. Thus the date when the public's right to use a way is brought into question can be before the 1932 Act came into operation in 1934. In *Fairey v Southampton CC* (1956) a landowner objected to the inclusion of a footpath on a definitive map. He was able to show that he had objected to use of the way by the public in 1931. However, there was evidence of public use of the path for 20 years prior to 1931 and the inclusion of the path on the definitive map was therefore upheld.

Section 31 of the 1980 Act also has retrospective effect. Its provisions thus apply to use of a way before 1980 just as they do to use since that date.

3.3.2 Nature of the way

'a way over land' The section applies to any way, ie a footpath, a bridleway or a carriageway. 'Land' is defined (s 31(11)) as including land covered by water. Thus the section can apply to the acquisition of a right of way through a ford or along a causeway covered in water at some stage of the tide. In *A-G v Brotherton* (1991) it was held that the section did not extend to the acquisition of a right of navigation along the course of a river. The section can apply to the acquisition of bridleway rights over an existing footpath — see chapter 3.3.6.

RIGHTS OF WAY

'**other than a way of such a character that its use could not give rise at common law to any presumption of dedication**' An example would be a way the use of which was a criminal offence, eg to walk along a motorway except for the purpose of obtaining assistance.

Similarly, in the case of land owned by the British Railways Board on which it is by statute an offence to trespass, long usage of a way, eg across or alongside a railway line, cannot give rise to the acquisition of a right of way by presumed dedication.

Statutory presumption ousted by other legislation The section can be overruled by other legislation if that provides that no right of way shall be acquired over certain land by use, eg under section 57 of the British Transport Commission Act 1949 (p 288) in respect of certain land owned by the Commission. Such statutory exclusion also ousts any presumption of dedication at common law.

Limitations or conditions The public's right to use a way may be subject to limitations or conditions. For example, the landowner may have a right to erect and maintain a stile or gate to prevent movement of stock. If the public freely uses a way subject to such a limitation during the qualifying period, the right of way is held to have been dedicated subject to the limitation. But once the way has been dedicated, no further limitation can be imposed other than by statutory means such as the authorisation of a stile under HA 80 s 146 (see chapter 7.4).

3.3.3 Nature of the public's use

'**actually enjoyed**' There must have been sufficient use of the way for the required period. This will be a matter of fact to be determined in each case. The motive in using the way is irrelevant. It will accordingly be sufficient if the sole purpose of the use was recreation. (*Hue v Whiteley* (1929); *Dyfed CC v Secretary of State for Wales* (1989).)

'**by the public**' Use must be by the public at large. It is not sufficient if the use has been merely by a class of the public, such as the employees of a particular employer, customers of a particular business or tenants of a particular landlord.

'**as of right**' This means that the use must have been *as if* a right of way existed. In *Merstham Manor v Coulsdon and Purley UDC* (1937) Mr Justice Hilbery said '... where the words "as of right" are used in the Rights of Way Act 1932 ... they are satisfied if the evidence shows that the actual enjoyment has been open, not by force and not by permission from time to time given'. Thus there will be no deemed dedication if the landowner can show that the use was by his permission, or that the use had entailed force. And it must be 'open', ie it must

3 : HOW RIGHTS OF WAY COME INTO BEING

have been such that the landowner could have challenged it if he wished. (But provided the use was of a kind that was capable of being challenged it will be immaterial that the reason why the user was not challenged was that the landowner believed that the way was public. ((*Jones v Bates* (1938).)

Inherent within the requirement of use as of right is the notion that there must have been acquiescence by the landowner. (Clearly there can have been no acquiescence if the user was by force or if it was undetectable.) But the onus is not on the user to show that the landowner acquiesced; it is on the landowner to show that he did not. *(Overland and Howard v Secretary of State for the Environment and Norfolk CC* (1987).)

'without interruption' 'Interruption' means 'actual and physical stopping of the enjoyment' of the public's use of the way (*Merstham Manor*, above) by the landowner or someone acting lawfully on his behalf, eg an employee acting in the course of his employment. The words do not refer to interruption of *use*: there is no requirement that the use must have been constant, although it must have been sufficient to satisfy the requirement that the way was 'actually enjoyed'.

The interruption must be with intent to prevent public use of the way. (*Lewis v Thomas* (1950).) It will not be sufficient if the interruption is shown to have been for some other purpose, eg to prevent cattle straying. (*Jones v Bates* (1938).) If a gate across a way is locked, but people continue to use the way by going round the side of the gate, there is an interruption within the meaning of the section. If it were not so, 'it would ... be impossible ever for a landowner to prevent the acquisition of a right of way over land ... by the erection of a gate across any part, because given the nature of the terrain it would always be possible for persons wishing to use the path to find a way round and then ... claim that they were using the way ...', Mr Justice Walton, *R v The Secretary of State for the Environment, ex p Blake* (1984).

3.3.4 Evidence of an intention not to dedicate

'deemed to have been dedicated as a highway unless there is sufficient evidence that there was no intention during that period to dedicate it' It is therefore *presumed* to have become a highway, the class of highway (footpath, bridleway or carriageway) depending on the use made of the way. However, the words emphasise that the section creates no more than a presumption rebuttable by evidence of a contrary intention.

The landowner must take overt action to disabuse the public at large of any belief that the way is public. It will not be sufficient for him to produce evidence (eg correspondence with his solicitor) that he had made up his mind that the way was not public, or evidence that he had told a stranger to the locality that he had had no intention to dedicate the way. (*Fairey*, above.)

The customary means of showing a contrary intention is by a notice with such words as 'Private road [or Private path]. No public right of way' sometimes followed by a reference to the legislation current when the notice was erected (ie the Act of 1932, 1959 or 1980, see chapter 3.3.1 above). Section 31(3) confirms that such a notice, erected so as to be visible to users of the way, will be sufficient evidence of an intention that the way is not intended to be dedicated.

Wording of the notice For a notice to be effective its wording must clearly deny a public right of way. Words such as 'Close the gate' or 'Dangerous bull' would not be sufficient. The words 'Private road' are of doubtful adequacy because of their ambiguity: the words could be interpreted as showing an intention to deny the existence of a carriageway, but not that of a right of way on foot.

Notice to the authority if the notice on the path is torn down or defaced A landowner who has put up a notice on a way indicating that he has no intention to dedicate it as public may find that it is subsequently torn down or defaced. Section 31(5) provides that he may then give notice to the surveying authority (or Inner London borough council) of his intention that the way should not be dedicated. This notice will be sufficient evidence of his intention.

Deposit of maps and declarations with the authority There is a further provision in s 31(6) enabling a landowner to deposit with the authority a map and statement showing the ways (if any) which he admits are dedicated as highways.

If he then, within six years, deposits a statutory declaration that no additional ways have been dedicated since the deposit of the map, this is sufficient, in the absence of proof of the contrary, to establish that no additional ways have in fact been dedicated. The landowner may continue to deposit similar declarations at intervals of six years or fewer, with the same effect. These procedures are little used.

But the deposit of the map does not establish that the rights of way shown on it were the only ones then in existence, nor does the subsequent deposit of statutory declarations affect any rights which existed then, but were not shown on the map. On the other hand, the deposited maps and statements provide one of the strongest proofs available of the existence of the rights of way shown on them. The maps should be inspected by organisations concerned with rights of way, since there is no guarantee that the admitted rights of way will have been put on the definitive map. See chapter 4.9.1.

3 : HOW RIGHTS OF WAY COME INTO BEING

3.3.5 Calculation of the 20-year period

'The period of 20 years..is to be calculated retrospectively from the date when the right of the public to use the way is brought into question' It might be thought that the 20-year period would start when use began, but this is not how the Act operates. The period is 20 years calculated backwards from the date when the right of the public to use the way is 'brought into question' by the landowner (or his agent) doing some act that challenges the public's right to use the way. So the 20-year period of use has no fixed starting point, only a fixed finishing point. (*Fairey v Southampton CC* (1956).)

This was illustrated by *De Rothschild v Buckinghamshire CC* (1957). The public used a path across De Rothschild's land for a period of 26 years, from 1914 to 1940. From 1940 to 1947 the land was requisitioned for war purposes and there was no evidence of public use. Prior to 1914 and again in 1948 the public's right to use the way was challenged by the padlocking of a gate. It was held that, since there had been no use by the public of the path for 20 years immediately preceding the dates when the use of the path was brought into question, no presumption of dedication arose.

Bringing the right to use the way into question Acts that would bring the public's right to use the way into question include the following:
(a) Locking a gate.
(b) Putting up a notice denying the existence of a right of way.
(c) Physically preventing a walker from proceeding along a path.
(d) Bringing an action for trespass (for damages or for an injunction to prohibit future use).
(e) Seeking a declaration from the court that the way is not public.
(f) Opposing an application for a definitive map modification order that adds the way to the definitive map or lodging an objection to such an order.

In *Owen v Buckinghamshire CC* (1957) it was held that the ploughing-up of a path was not sufficient to bring the right of the public to use the path into question.

The effect of a notice denying right-of-way status should be noted. If after, say, 10 years' use of a path a landowner puts up such a notice, this rebuts any presumption of dedication and even if the public uses the path for a further ten years, no right of way will arise by virtue of the Act.

Suppose, on the other hand, that the public uses a way for 21 years before the landowner puts up the notice. The erection of the notice constitutes an act bringing into question the public's right of passage. Since 20 years' use can be shown prior to this act, the requirements of the section are satisfied, and dedication will be presumed (assuming that no evidence of an earlier contrary intention can be produced by the landowner).

Retrospective effect Once it is established that a way is public, the determination is retrospective. Suppose that the public's right to use the way is brought into question when the owner of the land uses reasonable force physically to prevent a walker from using the way. It is subsequently determined that the way is public. An action by the walker will lie against the landowner for damages for the civil wrong of battery, since the landowner had no justification in law for his action (the walker not having been a trespasser).

Determining the existence of a right of way in practice Although the Act provides that a right of way is deemed to have been dedicated after 20 years' use prior to the right being brought into question, its existence can in practice be established only when the 'question' has been determined in favour of the existence of a public right of way. Examples would be a court ruling that an action by the landowner for trespass failed (on the ground that the path is a right of way) or the confirmation of a definitive map modification order adding a path to the definitive map.

It may happen that the date when the public's right to use a way was called into question is not known. Consider this example. In 1984 a notice saying 'Private. Concessionary footpath only. X Ltd' is observed, but there is no evidence when the notice was erected, and the company declines to give this information. There is evidence that the present owner acquired the property sometime in 1962. Thus the earliest that the notice could have been put up and the right of the public called into question is 1 January 1962.

If evidence of public use can be shown for 20 years prior to this date, the statutory presumption arises. Evidence of use since at least as early as 1 January 1942 is collected and in 1986 a claim is submitted to the surveying authority for an order modifying the definitive map by the addition of the path. The authority makes the order in 1986. The order is opposed, and in 1988 a public inquiry is held. The decision letter confirming the order is issued on 1 January 1989. It is only at this point that it can be said conclusively that a right of way exists over the path — 47 years after the date from which, under the Act, evidence of public use was required to be shown.

3.3.6 Presumed dedication of one highway over another

Acquisition of additional rights over existing highway The principle of presumed dedication can give rise to a right of way on horseback being acquired over a footpath, thus producing a change in the status of the way to bridleway.

3 : HOW RIGHTS OF WAY COME INTO BEING

Can use by motor vehicles of a footpath or bridleway result in the creation of a carriageway? The Road Traffic Act 1988 s 34 (p 416) makes it an offence to drive a motor vehicle without lawful authority on any footpath or bridleway. This provision was originally introduced in the Road Traffic Act 1930. Use since 1930 by motor vehicles of a way which was then, or has since become, a footpath or bridleway does not give rise to the acquisition of a vehicular right of way, since such use, being a criminal offence, cannot be 'as of right'.

Rededication free from limitations or conditions If a way originally dedicated subject to a limitation or condition (see p 64) is subsequently used for a 20-year period during which time it is free from that limitation or condition, the highway is presumed to have been rededicated free from the limitation or condition. *(Gloucestershire CC v Farrow* (1985).) For example, a footpath may have been dedicated subject to the landowner's right to erect a stile at a field boundary, but the stile disappears or is removed. The public then walks the path for 20 years without having to climb the stile. The path will thus be presumed to have been rededicated free from the limitation, ie the landowner will have lost his right to erect a stile. However, if the original limitation was recorded in the statement accompanying the definitive map, a definitive map modification order will be needed to amend the statement to reflect the change.

3.3.7 Ancient ways

Suppose that evidence exists that in the past packhorses followed a certain route over the moors, the evidence being tracks worn in the ground by horses' hooves and references by contemporary diarists to use of the way. The way is not shown on the definitive map as a public right of way.

Does this evidence of use by the public means that the way can today be claimed as a public right of way, even if it has not been used for many years?

If there is documentary evidence that the way was accepted as a public highway (see chapter 4.9.1), under the maxim 'once a highway, always a highway', it continues to be a highway and its use can be resumed.

In the absence of such evidence, a presumption of dedication could not be shown to have arisen (either under s 31 or at common law) since no legally *admissible* evidence (ie witnesses) would be produced.

The only way in which a claim could be made would be if there was *fresh* use of the way in modern times, ending in an act that called into question the right to use the way.

3.3.8 Other matters

Application to the Crown Section 31 does not apply to Crown land, which includes land owned by the Crown, the Duchies of Lancaster and Cornwall, government departments and the Forestry Commission. (HA 80 s 327 — p 356.)

Dedication at common law The provisions of section 31 of the 1980 Act do not supersede the principles of implied dedication that existed at common law before 1932. These principles are expressly preserved. (s 31(9) — p 322.) Thus if evidence of use for the full 20-year period required by the Act is not available, a claim may still be made, based on the presumption at common law. In considering a claim for a modification order adding a path to the definitive map, it is generally the practice of surveying authorities to consider evidence of use both for periods of 20 years and above, treating these as relating to the presumption under the statute, and also for periods of less than 20 years, treating these as being capable of giving rise to a presumption of dedication at common law.

Using section 31 — the Wildlife and Countryside Act 1981 and the courts If a user is prevented from using a way, and there is sufficient evidence of use to satisfy section 31, he may apply for an order modifying the definitive map by the addition of the way (see chapter 4.6.8). The order, if confirmed, will prove that a public right of way exists. The process, however, might take longer than the user believes should be allowed to elapse before the issue is resolved. He might, for example, not be content to see walkers prevented for several years from using a path he considers to be public. In such a case, it is open to him (in addition to, or instead of, applying for a modification order) to apply to the court for a declaration of the legal status of the way.

Similarly, a landowner is entitled to apply to the court for a declaration that a way is not public. In *Shears Court (West Mersea) Management Co Ltd v Essex CC* (1986) the plaintiff company sought a declaration from the court that a certain path across its land was not a public right of way. The application to the court was made after a definitive map modification order had been made by the CC, but not confirmed.

The council contended that the company was seeking to circumvent and frustrate the procedure laid down by Parliament for the resolution of questions relating to rights of way. It argued that the company's action should be stayed on the ground that it should be allowed to continue with its highway duties without threat of legal proceedings for a declaration every time it did so.

The court held that, in issuing its writ against the council, the

3 : HOW RIGHTS OF WAY COME INTO BEING

company was relying on a fundamental right that existed under law. The right to go to court for a ruling on a matter was not to be defeated unless Parliament had specifically taken away that right. There was nothing in the 1981 Act, nor in decided cases, which expressly, or by implication, prohibited a person interested from applying to the court for a ruling as to a right of way.

However, in pursuit of common sense, it was necessary to consider whether in the circumstances the two sets of proceedings should be allowed to continue or whether one ought to be stayed, and if so which. The court concluded that, as the 1981 Act procedure had been properly set in motion, and as this procedure would result in the determination of the status of the way, it would be vexatious and harassing for the company to be allowed to continue with its action. The company's action was accordingly ordered to be stayed. The order was subsequently confirmed by the Secretary of State in January 1988.

3.4 Statute

3.4.1 Creation orders

Local authorities may make public path creation orders for the creation of a new footpath or bridleway. This power, in HA 80 s 26, is considered in chapter 5.3.3.

3.4.2 Creation agreements by local authorities

Under HA 80 s 25 (p 317) a local authority has power to enter into an agreement with any person having the capacity to dedicate a footpath or bridleway in its area. Before making such an agreement, an authority must consult any other authority in the area, but need not consult the parish or community council or the public. The authority must, under HA 80 s 29 (p 71), have regard to the needs of agriculture and forestry.

The agreement may provide for compensation to be paid, and may also provide for the new path to be subject to limitations and conditions. When an agreement is made, the authority must ensure that the path is created physically (s 25(5)) and must also give notice to the public in at least one local newspaper (s 25(6)). A way created under an agreement automatically becomes maintainable at public expense. (HA 80 s 36(2)(d) — p 323.)

3.4.3 Creation agreements by local councils

Local councils have their own separate power under s 30 of the 1980 Act (p 320) to enter into agreements to create new highways, including footpaths and bridleways, if satisfied that the creation would be beneficial to the inhabitants of all, or any part of, the parish or community. Such agreements may only be made for land within the council's own parish or community or in an adjoining one.

The power differs from an authority's power under s 25 in a number of ways.

Firstly, there is no provision to place limitations or conditions on any right of way created under such an agreement.

Secondly, the local council is not under any obligation either to see that the new path is created physically or to publicise the fact of its existence.

Thirdly, the council is not subject to the s 29 duty to have regard to the needs of agriculture and forestry.

Fourthly, the way so created does not automatically become maintainable at public expense.

Finally, there is no power to pay compensation.

3.4.4 Maintenance of a dedicated way

As seen earlier (p 61), there is nothing in law to prevent anyone with the necessary capacity from dedicating a way as a highway. There are, however, restrictions if he wants it to be publicly maintainable. HA 80 s 37 (p 324) requires him to give notice to the highway authority, and to repair the way for at least 12 months before it can become publicly maintainable, and the authority may, if it considers that the way will not be of sufficient utility to the public to justify its being maintained at public expense, take the issue to a magistrates' court.

There is also provision in s 38 of the 1980 Act (p 324) for a highway authority to agree to take over a way as a highway maintainable at public expense. This is the section normally used by developers entering into agreements for estate roads to become publicly maintainable.

3.4.5 Other statutory creation

Powers enabling highways to be created in connection with works are contained in the Civil Aviation Act 1982 s 48, and the Water Act 1989 s 155. See chapter 5.3.7.

The Church Property (Miscellaneous Provisions) Measure 1960 s 11 (p 445) empowers the incumbent of a Church of England benefice to dedicate land belonging to the benefice and forming part of the glebe or the residence of the benefice as a highway, subject to the consent of, *inter alia*, the bishop and the Church Commissioners.

New rights of way may also be created by Private Act of Parliament, see chapter 5.4.2.

4
Definitive maps and other records

4.1 Introduction

In September 1947 the Report of the Committee on Footpaths and Access to the Countryside was published. It recommended that all public rights of way should be surveyed and recorded on maps, the work to be the responsibility of county and county borough councils. The recommendation was put into effect through the enactment of sections 27 to 38 of the National Parks and Access to the Countryside Act 1949. Under these provisions all county councils in England and Wales were given the duty of surveying and mapping all public rights of way in their area, classifying them as bridleways, footpaths or roads used as public paths (RUPPs).

The survey had to be undertaken in three stages: draft, provisional and definitive. The showing of a path on the definitive map was, and is, conclusive evidence that it was a public right of way at the date the map was prepared (the 'relevant date') (p 105). The survey was optional in London and in the county boroughs; county councils were also empowered to exclude built-up areas from the otherwise compulsory survey (p 76).

Early hopes of a swift completion of the initial task of surveying and preparing maps were not realised as insufficient resources were made available by many councils. The compulsory survey in the counties was finally completed with the publication of the definitive map of North Bedfordshire in May 1982.

An attempt to speed up matters was made by CA 68 Sch 3, particularly with regard to the reviews which were supposed to be carried out once the initial (definitive) maps had been prepared. However, by requiring all disputes to be determined by the Secretary of State, central government took on a task to which it was not prepared to devote sufficient resources. Coupled with complications introduced by local government reorganisation in 1974, this led to a virtual breakdown of the system by the late 1970s, with thousands of objections awaiting determination by the Secretary of State, and some definitive maps, which had never been reviewed, still reflecting the position at the date of the original survey in the early 1950s.

The approach adopted in the Wildlife and Countryside Act 1981 to tackle these problems was to replace the procedure for county-wide surveys and reviews with a system of continuous amendments to the definitive maps existing at the commencement date of the Act (28 February 1983), and the gradual compilation of definitive maps in all areas (except Inner London) not previously surveyed.

However, where a survey or review was in progress at the commencement date, the new continuous amendment procedure did not begin to operate until that survey or review had been completed or abandoned. In such areas the procedures under NPACA 49 and CA 68 remained in force. Because of their historical importance, and the frequency with which reference is in practice made to them, these procedures are described fully in this chapter, although the text of the legislation is not included in the second part of the book.

The working of the 1981 Act procedures has been monitored by the Countryside Commission through a research contract awarded to the RA (see 'Further Reading'). The findings showed that while the Act has been effective in breaking the log-jam caused by the 1968 Act procedures and the inactivity of the Department of the Environment in its handling of them, the resources devoted by most surveying authorities to bringing definitive maps up to date have been inadequate and insufficient for there to be any prospect of all claims for modifications to definitive maps and statements being dealt with in the near future. The 1981 Act is considered further in chapter 4.6.

4.2 The initial survey under the National Parks Act 1949

4.2.1 The preliminary work and consultations

Section 27 of the 1949 Act required every county council to carry out a survey and prepare a draft map, showing on it footpaths, bridleways and roads used as public paths which, in the opinion of the county council as surveying authority, were reasonably alleged to be public rights of way at the relevant date of the survey.

The three categories were defined in s 27(6): footpaths, bridleways and roads used as public paths (see chapter 4.4.4). Although the survey had to be carried out for the whole of the county, s 27(5) allowed a surveying authority to divide its area and produce separate draft, provisional and definitive maps at different times for the separate parts. The survey applied to land which was Crown land (S 101 — p 292.)

While the surveying authority had a duty to prepare the map, it clearly could not do this without information from other sources. Section 28 required the authority to consult district and parish councils about the arrangements to be made for the provision of information. Section 28(3) provided that a parish council must call a parish meeting to consider the information to be provided.

4 : DEFINITIVE MAPS AND OTHER RECORDS

In a parish with no council, the chairman of the parish meeting, or any person representing the parish on the district council, had to call a meeting to consider the information to be supplied to the district council (which passed it on to the surveying authority).

Properly carried out, the survey entailed an immense amount of work. Documentary evidence such as inclosure awards, old Ordnance Survey maps, tithe maps, parish maps, local histories and guidebooks, maps of admitted rights of way and local authority minutes had to be consulted. Such documentary evidence had to be supplemented by local knowledge, eg an old Ordnance Survey map might show the physical existence of a track on the ground, but evidence of use by the public as of right would have to be collected to show public status.

It was also necessary to consider all those paths which could be presumed to have been dedicated to the public because of use over a period of at least twenty years (chapter 3.3), even though there was no documentary evidence of status.

Much evidence, both documentary and user, was provided to surveying authorities by local representatives of the OSS and RA, which worked jointly with other bodies at national level, through the Central Rights of Way Committee, to ensure that all draft maps were checked and the provisions in the Act generally monitored.

4.2.2 The geographical extent of the survey

As noted above, the survey was not compulsory throughout England and Wales, with some densely-populated areas being excluded.

London In London, NPACA 49 s 35 provided that the then London County Council (LCC) was not under a duty to undertake a survey, but that it could, if it wished, adopt the survey provisions for any part of its area. The LCC was abolished in March 1965, without having adopted the provisions, and its area, together with parts of the adjoining counties, was taken over by a new authority, the Greater London Council. The GLC had no powers in relation to the survey; instead the 32 newly-created London boroughs were made surveying authorities.

In the 12 inner London boroughs which comprised the former LCC area, the survey remained optional. In the 20 outer London boroughs the new borough council was in the same position as its predecessor authorities. So, if the survey provisions already applied to all or part of the borough by virtue of having been part of a county, the borough council was required to continue with the procedures. However, if any part had either been in a county borough or had been excluded as being fully developed (see below), the adoption of the provisions remained optional.

County boroughs Although the former county boroughs were excluded from the compulsory survey, their councils were empowered, under NPACA 49 s 35, to adopt its provisions; a list of those that did not do so is at p 107.

Fully-developed areas Section 35 also empowered a county council to exclude by resolution from the survey provisions any part of the county which appeared to the council to be so fully developed that a survey would be inexpedient. The resolution had to be approved by the Secretary of State, and could be later amended or revoked.

Isles of Scilly The Isles of Scilly were also excluded from the compulsory survey and no definitive map was produced under the 1949 Act.

4.2.3 Publishing the draft map

In the light of the information it collected the surveying authority prepared the draft map and statement. It had to publish notice of its preparation in the *London Gazette* and one or more local newspapers circulating in the area of the authority (s 29(1)). These notices stated where the draft map and statement could be inspected, and the time (not less than four months) within which representation and objection as to paths shown or omitted, or as to matters contained in, or omitted from, the statement, could be made to the surveying authority. There was no provision for notification to be given to individual owners and occupiers that rights of way were shown over their land on the draft map.

Authorities were required by the National Parks and Access to the Countryside Regulations 1950 to prepare the map on a scale of not less than 2½" to the mile, and to show footpaths by means of a purple line, bridleways by a green line and roads used as public paths by a broken green line. As these methods of marking do not show up in black-and-white reproduction, later amendments to the Regulations allowed for varying forms of notation.

4.2.4 The relevant date

The 'relevant date' referred to above was a date fixed by the authority not more than six months before the date on which notices of the preparation of the draft map were published in the press. The surveying authority therefore had up to six months from the relevant date to complete its consideration of the information obtained from many sources, map the paths and prepare copies of the draft map and statement for inspection.

4.2.5 The statement

As the draft map was prepared an accompanying statement was also produced. This contained the relevant date (see above) and 'such par-

4 : DEFINITIVE MAPS AND OTHER RECORDS

ticulars appearing to the authority to be reasonably alleged as to position and width (of paths) or as to any limitations or conditions affecting the public right of way, as in the opinion of the authority it is expedient to record' (s 27(4)).

Surveying authorities interpreted this in a variety of ways: some gave full information as to when paths narrowed or widened, the position of stiles, gates, footbridges, conditions of surface or existence of a common law right to plough. However, others considered that practically no fact was expedient to record. The fuller a statement is, the more helpful it is for users to find their way and the better for settling a dispute whether a path has been obstructed. For subsequent changes to statements see pp 82 & 91.

It appears to have been common for authorities to have put into the statement the report compiled in the parish council's survey. Thus, if that survey found that a path was obstructed by a barbed-wire fence, the statement might well record the fact. But does this mean that the right of way is recorded as being subject to a right of the owner to obstruct it with barbed wire? It is submitted that a limitation or condition affecting a right of way must be clearly identified as such in the statement, eg in a separate column. If it is not so identified, reference in the statement to, eg, a barbed-wire fence is no more than a record of the fact that there was an unlawful obstruction of the path at the time of the survey in, say, 1951.

4.2.6 Modifying the draft map and statement

The purpose of the public notice of the preparation of the draft map and statement was to give the public an opportunity to inspect them and see whether the information they contained appeared correct, eg whether all the paths believed to be public had been included and whether the information in the statement was accurate, and also to give landowners and occupiers an opportunity to see if paths they regarded as private were shown as public. Anyone could object to what was included in, or omitted from, the map and statement.

If any representation or objection was so made, the authority had, under s 29(3), to consider the objection or representation, appoint a person to hear the objector and then determine whether any modification of the map or statement should be made. The result of this determination had to be notified to the person making the representation or objection. If the authority determined to modify the map by the deletion or addition of a path, notice of its determination had to be published in the *London Gazette* and local newspapers, giving 28 days for objections.

If any representation or objection was then made to the determination, the authority had, under s 29(4), to notify the original objector, and, after hearing both parties, decide whether to maintain or revoke the determination. It had to serve notice of its decision on both parties.

RIGHTS OF WAY

4.2.7 Objections dealt with by the Secretary of State

If the authority determined not to give effect to a claim to add a path or amend the statement, or decided to maintain a determination to modify a map by the deletion of a path, or decided to revoke a determination to add a path, anyone aggrieved by its decision could serve appeal to the Secretary of State (s 29(5)). The appeal had to be lodged within 28 days after the service of the surveying authority's decision.

The Secretary of State was required to appoint a person to hear the appellant, the original objector (if not the appellant) and the surveying authority (s 29(6)). Having considered that person's report, he then either dismissed the appeal or directed the authority to modify the particulars in the draft map and statement.

However, no appeal could be made to the Secretary of State against a decision of a surveying authority not to downgrade a way shown on the draft map, eg where ramblers objected without success to the authority that a way shown as a bridleway should have been shown as a footpath.

By way of illustration of the procedures, the following might have occurred. The Barsetshire CC, as surveying authority, showed on its draft map a footpath in the parish of St Julian, running from Farthing Lane across the fields of farmer G to join another path. Farmer G objected under s 29(3) to the inclusion of the path. After hearing farmer G, who stated that the path was not a public right of way but a track made by one of his tenants coming to work, the authority determined to delete the path, and published a notice to that effect in the press.

The local footpath society objected under s 29(4) to the deletion. The authority heard both the society and farmer G. The society produced evidence of many years' use of the path by the public, but, following the hearing, the authority decided to maintain its determination to modify the map by deleting the path. The society appealed under s 29(5) to the Secretary of State. He appointed someone to hear the appeal, and thereafter decided whether to direct the authority to keep the path on the map.

4.2.8 The provisional map and statement

Following the determination of any appeals to the Secretary of State the authority then prepared, under s 30, a provisional map and statement. This was the draft map and statement modified by the various decisions made by the authority and the Secretary of State, and had the same relevant date.

Notice of preparation of the provisional map and statement was given in the *London Gazette* and the local press as before. Section 31 gave a right to any owner, lessee or occupier of land over which the map showed a public right of way to apply to the Crown Court (formerly

4 : DEFINITIVE MAPS AND OTHER RECORDS

Quarter Sessions) for a declaration that, at the relevant date of the map, one of the following applied:

(a) There was no public right of way over the land.
(b) The rights of the public were those specified in the application and not those specified in the map and statement.
(c) The position or width of the right of way were as indicated in the application and not as indicated in the map and statement.
(d) The public right of way was subject to limitations or conditions other than those recorded in the statement or that those so recorded were incorrect.

The public had no right to apply to the Crown Court. The provisional stage thus placed owners, lessees and occupiers of land in the privileged position of having a further chance to object. If an application was made, the surveying authority defended the case and could call the public as witnesses. On hearing the application the Court had to decide whether to make the declaration sought. It had power to decide that the route shown on the map was the wrong one and that the path should instead go across other land. In such a case it then made not only the declaration applied for but also a further one showing the correct line of the path.

Section 31(8) provided that, subject to any further appeal to the High Court on a point of law only and to section 32 (below), a declaration by the Court was conclusive evidence of the matters stated therein. In *R v West Sussex Quarter Sessions ex parte Albert and Maud Johnson Trust Ltd* (1973) the appellants sought to have a declaration, by the West Sussex Quarter Sessions that a certain right of way existed, quashed on the ground that they had later found evidence which would have been relevant to their contention that no right of way existed. The Court of Appeal rejected their claim; they were trying to reopen matters of fact, whereas an appeal could only be on points of law.

The effect of a declaration by the Court that no right of way existed at the relevant date was to prevent a new claim for a right of way over the same path based on evidence which could have been available at that date. However, a later claim based on use after that date would not be defeated by such a declaration, nor would a claim for a right of way for a different type of use (eg a claim that a way which had been declared not to be a footpath did in fact have the status of bridleway).

4.2.9 The definitive map and statement

If no applications were made to the Crown Court within 28 days of publication of the provisional map, or when any such applications had been determined, s 32(1) required the surveying authority to prepare a definitive map and statement. Notice of its preparation had to be given in the same way as for the draft and provisional maps.

The particulars in the definitive map and statement were those contained in the provisional map and statement modified by any declarations made at provisional stage. The relevant date was again the same as in the statement accompanying the draft map.

Within six weeks of the notice of publication of the definitive map an application could be made to the High Court under Sch 1 para 9 on the grounds that the map, or any part of it, was not within the powers of the Act, or that the Act or regulations had not been complied with. If the Court was satisfied that this was so, it could make an order declaring that the definitive map or statement was not conclusive evidence of something which had been shown, but it had no power to add a path. It was, and is, possible to challenge the content of the definitive map by means of judicial review; the case of *Suffolk CC v Mason* below is an example.

Conclusive evidence Section 32(4) provided that the definitive map and statement were conclusive evidence in law of the particulars they contained. This was the fundamental provision which, by providing a record of the public's rights which could be used as evidence in court, made the compilation of definitive maps so valuable. In the case of *Morgan v Herts CC* (1965) the Court of Appeal decided that, even if a path had been included in error, the map still provided conclusive evidence of the public's rights over it.

However, although the map provided conclusive evidence of the existence of rights, the reverse was not true: a way not shown on the map could still be a public right of way, although its status would need to be proved. The possible addition to the map of such paths, or the proof of additional rights by depicting as bridleways ways shown previously as footpaths, was one of the reasons for reviewing the maps (see chapter 4.3). The only instance where evidence could arise through the survey procedure of the non-existence of public rights was if a declaration was made by the Crown Court at provisional stage (p 78) that there was, in a particular case, no public right of way (either at all or of a particular type, eg bridleway).

Section 32(4)(a) provided that the inclusion in a definitive map of a way as a footpath was conclusive evidence of the existence at the relevant date of a footpath, ie a way over which there was a public right of way on foot.

Section 32(4)(b) provided that the showing of a way on the map as a bridleway or RUPP was conclusive evidence of the existence of public rights of way on foot and on horseback, with a right to lead a horse, but was without prejudice to the possible existence of other rights.

Section 32(4)(c) provided that if the map showed a footpath, bridleway or RUPP, and was thus conclusive evidence of the existence of rights of way, any particulars in the statement of position or width of the right of way were also conclusive evidence. It also provided that if

4 : DEFINITIVE MAPS AND OTHER RECORDS

the statement listed limitations or conditions affecting the public's rights, that was likewise conclusive evidence of the limitations or conditions to which the right of way was subject at the relevant date, but it was without prejudice to the possible existence of other limitations or conditions.

In the case of *Suffolk CC v Mason* (1979) the House of Lords considered the absence from s 32(4)(a) of any reference to the depiction of a footpath being without prejudice to the possible existence of other rights, such a reference being contained in s 32(4)(b). It held that the omission meant that a way shown as a footpath could be only that, and in effect provided conclusive evidence of the non-existence of higher rights. This decision was overruled by WCA 81 s 56(1)(a) (p 381), so that the definitive map now provides in all cases conclusive evidence only of what is shown. In *R v Devon CC, ex parte Fowler* (1990) it was held that the showing of a way as a footpath under s 32(4)(a) had not had the effect of extinguishing higher rights. The decision was upheld by the Court of Appeal in 1991.

This is an important point, since it means that a way that is shown on the definitive map as a footpath may nevertheless be a bridleway or even a carriageway within the definitions in HA 80 s 329 (p 359) and WCA 81 s 66 (p 384), or likewise that a way shown on the map as a bridleway could in fact be a carriageway. Several important provisions apply to footpaths and bridleways, but not to carriageways, eg HA 80 s 118 (p 335), s 119 (p 335) & s 134(1) (p 341) and RTA 88 ss 33 & 34 (p 416). So, if there is evidence that the status of a way shown on the map may be incorrect, it is important that this should be tested by way of a modification order (see chapter 4.6.5), and the map amended if necessary.

Conflict between the map and statement There is no provision in either NPACA 49 or WCA 81 for deciding whether, in the case of conflict, the map or statement takes precedence. However NPACA 49 s 32(4)(c) provided, as does WCA 81 s 56(4), that the statement is conclusive evidence of the position and width of a way only if it is shown on the map. If a path has been left off the map, the inclusion of its particulars in the statement will not provide conclusive evidence of its existence, let alone its width. However, a modification order under WCA 81 s 53 may modify not only the definitive map but also the particulars contained in the statement (see subsection (4) in particular), so the map and statement can be reconciled.

4.2.10 Surveys following the Countryside Act 1968

The 1968 Act made two changes to the procedure for an initial survey. When dealing with an appeal under NPACA 49 s 29(6), the Secretary of State was required to allow a hearing not only to the appellant, the original objector and the surveying authority but also to any other person appearing to him to have an interest in the subject matter of the appeal. Following such an appeal the Secretary of State was given power to vary, rather than either revoke or maintain, a determination made under s 29(4).

4.3 Reviews under the National Parks Act 1949

4.3.1 Introduction

Section 33 of the 1949 Act provided for a periodic review of the definitive map and statement by a surveying authority, having regard to the events which had occurred since the relevant date of the survey, or the date of a previous review. The object of a review was to enable the surveying authority to produce a revised map by adding any rights of way omitted from the previous map and by showing changes (creations, diversions, extinguishments) arising from the coming into operation of agreements or orders.

Although a county council was allowed to publish its first definitive map on a piecemeal basis, the review had, under s 34(3), to be undertaken for the whole county at the same time. The authority determined the 'date of review' as it did the relevant date in the survey.

4.3.2 The events to be considered

Section 33(1) & (2) required events which had occurred between the relevant date or date of previous review and the date of the review in question to be taken into consideration when the particulars contained in a definitive map were reviewed. The events were as follows:

(a) The coming into operation of a statutory order made or confirmed by the Secretary of State or confirmed by a local authority, or made by a magistrates' court, extinguishing, diverting, widening or extending a path shown on the definitive map.

(b) The change of status of a path shown on the previous definitive map (eg by a landowner dedicating a footpath as a bridleway).

(c) The coming into operation of a creation agreement or order for a new path.

(d) The lapse of a sufficient period of time (at least 20 years) of use of a path by the public freely and as of right as to raise a presumption of dedication of the path as a public right of way. (This would cover rights of way which at the relevant date or previous date of review could not be shown to have sufficient length of use.)

(e) The discovery of new evidence that a path should be shown as a public right of way. (This would cover paths which were public but which were omitted from the previous map or were shown in a lesser category. The evidence could relate to a period earlier

4 : DEFINITIVE MAPS AND OTHER RECORDS

than the date of that map, but the discovery had to have occurred during the period under review.)

There was therefore no power to close or divert rights of way under the review procedure.

4.3.3 Timing and procedure

Section 33(3) required the surveying authority to review the definitive map at intervals not exceeding five years — a provision almost universally ignored. Section 34 required the review to be carried out in three stages — draft, provisional and definitive (corresponding to the stages of the initial preparation of the definitive map). The procedure for the initial survey was applied to the review, with the appropriate changes of nomenclature. As mentioned above, the review had to cover the whole of the area mapped by the surveying authority.

4.4 Reviews under the Countryside Act 1968

4.4.1 The two-stage procedure

CA 68 Sch 3 Pt II amended NPACA 49 to shorten considerably the stages for all reviews begun after 3 August 1968 (the date on which CA 68 came into force). It did not alter the requirements for consultation with district and parish councils and, save in one respect noted below (see chapter 4.4.3), did not alter the list of events set out in NPACA 49 s 33 to be considered at a review.

When the authority had taken into consideration all events occurring since the relevant or review date of the previous map and statement, the preparation of the revised draft map was advertised in the *London Gazette* and one or more local newspapers circulating in the area.

The notice stated:

(a) Where copies of the revised draft map could be inspected at all reasonable hours.

(b) When and how representations or objections about alterations made by the revised draft map, or about anything omitted from it, had to be made direct to the Secretary of State. If a review was a Special or Limited Special Review (see chapter 4.4.4), the objection period remained at four months: for other reviews it was reduced to 28 days.

The effect of this change was to cut out both the provisional stage and the determination by surveying authorities of certain objections at draft stage, and to require all objections to be made directly to the Secretary of State. These included objections by members of the public, concerned at an authority's failure to add to the map a path believed to be public, and objections by landowners when such a path was added by the authority.

If any representation or objection was made to the Secretary of State and not withdrawn, an inspector appointed by him held a local inquiry at which all interested parties could be represented. The date and place of such inquiries were notified to the local authorities, to objectors, landowners and occupiers. Notices were normally placed in the local press and on public notice-boards; these included both the path numbers involved and a short note as to what was in dispute.

After considering the inspector's report, the Secretary of State decided whether to direct the surveying authority to modify the draft map. Thus, if a local society objected that a path not on the revised map should be added because it was a public right of way, and the Secretary of State agreed with the objection, he would direct the surveying authority to add it.

If he considered such a modification might adversely affect persons other than those who made the representation, he was required to give those persons an opportunity of being heard before directing the authority to modify the map.

After the inquiries and the Secretary of State's decisions, the surveying authority published and advertised the revised definitive map. This was the revised draft map modified as directed by the Secretary of State.

4.4.2 Timing of reviews

The timing of reviews under CA 68 was governed by Sch 3 Pt IV para 14, which substituted a new s 33(3) in NPACA 49 for reviews begun after 3 August 1968. Those begun, but not completed, before that date were governed by the original s 33(3). Under the substituted s 33(3) the timing of reviews was as follows:

(a) The period covered by a review (ie from the relevant or review date of the previous definitive map to the date fixed for the current review) should not be longer than five years.

(b) The interval between the end of the period covered by a review and the publication of the revised draft map was to be not more than two years for a Special Review and not more than six months for any subsequent review.

(c) If a Limited Special Review was undertaken (see chapter 4.4.4), the next review had to cover the period since the relevant or review date of the previous map. This was because the Limited Special Review dealt only with reclassification of RUPPs, and thus did not include consideration of all the events listed in NPACA 49 s 33(2).

4.4.3 Deletion of paths on review

Under NPACA 49 no machinery existed for removing a path at review from a definitive map unless it had been closed by a statutory order.

4 : DEFINITIVE MAPS AND OTHER RECORDS

CA 68 added s 33(2)(e) to the 1949 Act. It gave the surveying authority power to take into account the discovery, in the period under review, of new evidence that no public right of way existed over a way shown on the definitive map or that other amendment to the map was required (eg to change the line of a path).

However, this evidence could not be considered if the landowner or his predecessor could have produced it at the relevant date of the previous survey, and had no reasonable grounds for not so doing.

Paragraph 74 of Ministry of Housing and Local Government Circular 44/68 requested surveying authorities to include in the notice of preparation of the revised draft map the reference numbers of any public rights of way deleted from the definitive map as a result of this new provision. This was to alert the public to the possible deletion and to allow objections to be made and further evidence brought to show that such a way was indeed public.

Before an authority could remove a path on the previous definitive map it had to be convinced that there was no public right of way. As the previous definitive map was evidence of the existence of a path, it was thought that the proof that no way did exist had to be very strong, and that the onus of proof lay with the landowner and not with the authority.

However the working of the legislation showed that the proviso about evidence was so badly drafted as to be almost useless. Two bridleways at Brewood, Staffordshire, shown on the definitive map were omitted on the revised draft map. Objectors claimed that the evidence for deletion was inadmissible because it could have been produced at a previous stage. The CC replied that the paths had been added to the original draft map as the result of an objection; they were not therefore on the map at the relevant date and the landowner had no reason to produce his evidence then. The Secretary of State accepted the argument and dismissed the objection.

But in practice the delays in the 1968 Act reviews meant that very few rights of way were deleted from definitive maps as a consequence of the provision.

4.4.4 Reclassification of roads used as public paths

The category 'road used as public path' — often shown on a definitive map as CRB (carriage-road used mainly as a bridleway) or CRF (carriage-road used mainly as a footpath), although these terms had no legal significance — did not in practice prove to be satisfactory.

Part of the problem was caused by the failure of NPACA 49 to make it clear whether RUPPs were subject to vehicular rights. Section 27(6) defined a RUPP as a way other than a footpath or bridleway and therefore implied that such a way was subject to vehicular rights, but s 32(4)(b) provided that the showing of a way as a RUPP on a definitive map was conclusive evidence only of the public's rights to use it on foot or on horseback.

The Gosling Committee (p 31) recommended that each RUPP should be reclassified either as an unclassified road, a bridleway or a footpath. This recommendation was given legislative effect in CA 68 Sch 3 Pt III, which required each RUPP to be reclassified either as a byway open to all traffic (over which there were vehicular rights), a bridleway or a footpath.

The aim was to simplify matters for the public, landowners and occupiers and highway authorities. However, owing partly to the very large numbers of RUPPs in some areas, partly to the difficulty in deciding into which category a way should go and partly to the decision in the *Hood* case (below), confusion rather than simplification resulted.

The tests for reclassification CA 68 Sch 3 para 10 listed the considerations to be taken into account in deciding in which class a RUPP should be placed:
(a) Whether any vehicular right of way had been shown to exist.
(b) Whether it was suitable for vehicles having regard to its position and width, its condition and state of repair, and the nature of the soil.
(c) If it had been used by vehicular traffic, whether the extinguishment of vehicular rights would cause undue hardship.

In paragraph 76 of Circular 44/68 the Ministry of Housing and Local Government said 'The intention of the Special Review is to establish in the first instance what public rights exist over these roads ... the fact that a road may not be suitable for all traffic need not deter the authority from an initial classification as a "byway open to all traffic"'.

It is, however, difficult to reconcile this statement with para 10(b) and (c) of Sch 3 quoted above, from which it appears that current use and state of repair were important considerations. It is clear from Sch 3 Pt III generally that reclassification of RUPPs was not to be based solely on legal status. Indeed, in *Pearson v Secretary of State for the Environment* (1981) the Court of Appeal specifically disapproved the quoted statement; in the case the court quashed a decision to reclassify a RUPP as a byway open to all traffic because the surveying authority had failed to consider the hardship test in Sch 3 para 10(c).

The test for reclassification in para 10 was considered by the Court of Appeal in *R v Secretary of State for the Environment, ex parte Hood* (1975). The Court held that NPACA 49 s 32(4)(b) provided conclusive evidence of the existence of a public right of way on horseback over a way shown on a definitive map as a RUPP. Therefore, in the absence of new evidence, or of evidence not previously considered by the surveying authority, a RUPP could not be reclassified as a footpath. Naturally, the decision caused confusion among surveying authorities. A number

4 : DEFINITIVE MAPS AND OTHER RECORDS

of RUPPs had already been reclassified as footpaths other than on the basis of new evidence. Was their status retrospectively changed to bridleway by the decision or not?

The Department of the Environment and the Welsh Office issued a circular (DOE 123/77) in an attempt to guide surveying authorities. The circular recognised that anomalies would arise and said that legislation would be considered if they could not be satisfactorily dealt with under existing procedures. That proved to be the case: amending legislation can be found in WCA 81 s 54 (p 380), although this applies only to RUPPs not reclassified under the 1968 Act. Section 53 of the 1981 Act allows further consideration of the status of former RUPPs which were so reclassified.

Did reclassification as bridleway or footpath extinguish any vehicular rights? The 1968 Act also failed to make clear what was the effect of reclassifying as a bridleway a RUPP over which vehicular rights had been shown to exist. Were those rights extinguished by the reclassification or not? The arguments in favour of extinguishment are that reclassification as bridleway would otherwise be pointless, the resulting way being no different from a way reclassified to byway, and the specific reference in paragraph 10(c) to the extinguishment of vehicular rights.

But against that is the rule that 'the general attitude of the common law to establish rights of way is such that it would need express statutory words to destroy them' (Mr Justice Kennedy, *R v Devon CC, ex parte Fowler* (1990)). No such words are to be found in the 1968 Act.

In the case of *R v Secretary of State for the Environment, ex parte Riley* (1989) the judge declined to make any conclusion on the question. He inclined to the view that the Act did not have the effect of extinguishing vehicular rights, but, as the Secretary of State had chosen not to argue the point, he was not obliged to reach a conclusion. The matter therefore remains undecided.

The Special Review The reclassification of RUPPs was to be carried out by means of a Special Review of the definitive map. Sch 3 para 8 instructed surveying authorities to act as follows:

(a) To abandon any review begun before 3 August 1968 (the date CA 68 came into force) if the revised draft map and statement had not been published.
(b) If no review had been begun by that date, or if any review so begun was abandoned under (a), to publish a Special revised draft map by 3 August 1971.
(c) If a review had been begun before 3 August 1968, and was not abandoned under (a), to complete that review and then publish a Special revised draft map within one year of the completion of the review, or by 3 August 1971 if that would be later.

(d) If they considered it unnecessary to do more than reclassify RUPPs, to make the Special Review a Limited Special Review. This only reclassified RUPPs: consideration of the events in NPACA 49 s 33(2) had to wait until the next full review, which had to cover the period from the previous definitive map (p 82).

Special and Limited Special Reviews were carried out under the two-stage CA 68 procedure (see chapter 4.4.1) except that the objection period was four months and the notice advertising the preparation of the revised draft map had to state that the review reclassified RUPPs.

Ways to be reclassified Under either a Special Review or a Limited Special Review, reclassification could be considered for ways shown on the definitive map as RUPPs and for ways shown as footpaths and bridleways which the authority considered should have been shown as RUPPs.

Under a Special Review only, ways not previously shown at all, but which the authority considered would have been added to the map as RUPPs but for reclassification, could also be considered.

4.5 Changes made by the Local Government Act 1972

County boroughs were abolished by the Local Government Act 1972 and their areas were absorbed into counties, thereby making county councils the surveying authorities for those areas. The county councils were given the same powers as the former authorities, ie the survey was optional, but once begun, it had to be continued. The Act also reorganised many county boundaries. LGA 72 Sch 17 Pt II modified the survey and review provisions as a consequence. A list showing the position reached in the survey by each former authority on 31 March 1974 is on p 105.

The new county councils were required to continue any survey or review in progress on 1 April 1974 with the following exceptions:

(a) They were allowed (but not required) to abandon and start again a survey in which a draft map, but not a provisional map, had been published by 1 April 1974 (Sch 17 para 24).

(b) They were required to abandon and start again any review for which no revised draft map had been published by 1 April 1974 (para 25).

(c) They were allowed (but not required) to abandon and start again a review in which a revised draft map but not a revised provisional or definitive map, had been published by 1 April 1974 (para 26).

It was open to the Secretary of State to modify the above provisions in any particular case.

Because of reorganisation, many new county councils found that different parts of their areas had reached different stages of the survey. These separate areas were required, by Sch 17 para 29, to be reviewed

4 : DEFINITIVE MAPS AND OTHER RECORDS

at one and the same time. The relevant date for review was the earliest of the various maps, unless, following an application by a county council, the Secretary of State directed otherwise. One further, minor, change was that the provision in NPACA 49 s 28(3) requiring a parish meeting to be held (see chapter 4.2.1) ceased to apply to Wales as from 1 April 1974 (LGA 72 Sch 17 Para 32), although a community meeting could be held if the community council wished.

4.6 The Wildlife and Countryside Act 1981

4.6.1 The changes summarised

As noted on p 83, all objections and representations arising out of a review of the definitive map under CA 68 were made to the Secretary of State, and he was required to hold a public inquiry before coming to a decision. The Department of the Environment never kept pace with the objections, and surveying authorities were therefore unable to keep to the timetable laid down in the Act (p 83).

By mid-1980, some 15,000 objections were outstanding, many of which had been with the Department for five years or more. The 1981 Act sought to deal with this problem, and in addition made numerous other changes to definitive map procedures. These amounted to a complete revision of NPACA 49 procedures. The principal changes were as follows:

(a) The system of countywide reviews at intervals was abolished and replaced by modification orders which could be made at any time. Surveying authorities have a duty to bring the map and statement up to date, and then keep them up to date as changes occur.

(b) A new power enabled anyone to apply for a modification order to amend the map by way of upgrading, downgrading, addition or deletion or other change, or to amend particulars contained in the statement.

(c) A new power enabled ways to be added directly to the definitive map as byways open to all traffic.

(d) The previous tests for the reclassification of RUPPs were abolished and replaced by a test which considers only the existence or otherwise of vehicular rights. An attempt was made to enshrine the principle of the *Hood* case (p 86) in statute law.

(e) The Secretary of State was empowered to direct a surveying authority to complete or abandon, wholly or partially, any survey or review in progress at the commencement date (28 February 1983). In such an area the introduction of the new continuous review procedure was deferred until the survey or review had been completed or abandoned.

(f) The coverage of the compulsory survey was extended to the whole of England and Wales, except Inner London and the Isles of

Scilly, where it remained optional. Definitive maps must now be produced, through the making of modification orders, for any area previously excluded.

(g) The decision in *Suffolk CC v Mason* (p 81) was overruled by the addition of a proviso to the conclusive evidence provisions relating to the showing of a way on the map as a footpath. (S 56(1)(a) — p 381.)

The provisions in the Act generally came into effect on 28 February 1983, with the exception noted in (e) above, and a Circular (1/83) was issued by DOE and the Welsh Office. This part of the book should be read with paragraphs 4-6 of and Annex A to that Circular (p 481).

4.6.2 Existing surveys and reviews

Section 55 of the 1981 Act (p 381) prevented any survey or review under the 1949 Act from being begun after 28 February 1983. If a survey or review had been begun, but had not been completed, by that date the Secretary of State had power, after consulting the surveying authority, to order that it be either completed or partially or wholly abandoned. A survey or review which was not abandoned continued to completion under the provisions under which it had been begun.

However, if a survey or review was abandoned, the Secretary of State had to give notice of its abandonment (s 55(2)). This notice consisted of one or more announcements in a local paper, and direct notification to objectors whose objections sought to add paths not previously shown (Circular 1/83, Annex A, para 62). When abandonment took place after the end of the period for objections, the surveying authority had to act as follows:

(a) For a draft map (ie a survey), to prepare a definitive map showing those paths:
  (i) for which a decision or determination had been made under NPACA 49 s 29(3) or (4) and no appeal had been or could be lodged;
  (ii) for which a decision had been made by the Secretary of State under s 29(6);
  (iii) shown on the draft map to which there had been no objection (or to which any objection had been withdrawn).

(b) For a revised draft map (ie a review), to modify the definitive map to give effect to:
  (i) any decision by the Secretary of State under CA 68 Sch 3 Pt II para 4(4);
  (ii) any changes made by the revised draft map to which there had been no objection (or to which any objections had been withdrawn).

Where numerous ways not hitherto recorded had been shown on the revised draft map, and had not attracted any objection, the s 55(5) order

4 : DEFINITIVE MAPS AND OTHER RECORDS

made under (b)(ii) above therefore added to the definitive map many ways of which the public were probably previously unaware.

Objections which were not preserved under the above provisions were not wholly lost. Sch 15 para 4 provides that if, subsequently, a modification order is made which revives either a proposal to show a path on a draft or revised draft map, or a proposal to omit from a revised draft map a path previously shown (ie to delete a path), any objection made to that draft or revised draft map is treated as an objection to the order. Thus an objection by a landowner to the addition of a path or an objection to the deletion of a path would be revived.

However, para 4 does not cover an objection to the omission of a path from the draft review map where none had been shown before (ie a claim for a new path). Such a claim has to be the subject of a separate order.

4.6.3 Areas previously excluded from the survey

The surveying authority no longer has the option of excluding built-up areas. Definitive maps therefore have to be produced for those areas excluded under the 1949 Act.

In addition the requirement to produce a map has been extended to former county boroughs where the survey was never adopted, such as Bath and Plymouth.

In such an area where no survey had been begun, or in an area where the provisions applied or had been adopted but where a survey had been abandoned before the end of the period for objections to the draft map, the authority must prepare a new map and statement. This will be a plain base-map and blank statement, since no survey has taken place, to which rights of way will be added by means of modification orders made by the authority as required under s 53. As soon as the first order is made and, if necessary, confirmed, the map and statement become definitive, even if further orders are subsequently made.

The 1981 Act was applied to the Isles of Scilly by the Wildlife and Countryside (Isles of Scilly) Order 1983. As a consequence, only the 12 Inner London boroughs are now excluded from the compulsory survey (s 58(1)).

4.6.4 Bringing and keeping existing maps up to date

Section 53(2) of the 1981 Act (p 379) places two duties on every surveying authority:

(a) As soon as reasonably practicable after the commencement date (see below), it must make the modifications to the definitive map necessary to take account of the 'events' which occurred before the commencement date. This must be done by modification orders under the procedure described in chapter 4.6.5 so that, for example, all diversions and extinguishments confirmed and brought into operation prior to the commencement date are recorded on, and form part of, the definitive map and statement.

The 'events' are virtually the same as in NPACA 49 s 33: thus the duty imposed by subsection (2) is to carry out a full review of the definitive map. However there is an important difference: there is no starting point to the period under the 1981 Act, as there was under s 33 of the 1949 Act. An event which occurred prior to the relevant date of the first definitive map can therefore be the subject of a modification order.

(b) It must then keep the map and statement under continuous review. This means modifying the map and statement to take account of an event as soon as reasonably practicable after it occurs.

Definition of 'definitive map and statement' The term 'definitive map and statement' for an area is defined by s 53(1) as follows:

(a) The latest revised definitive map and statement prepared under s 33 of the 1949 Act.

(b) If no review had taken place, the original definitive map and statement.

(c) If no map had been prepared, the map to be prepared under s 55(3) of the 1981 Act (see chapter 4.6.3).

A surveying authority may have several different definitive maps for its area. There is no clearly-expressed power in the 1981 Act for those maps to be combined or divided where administratively convenient for the purposes of producing consolidated maps and statements under s 57(3) (see chapter 4.6.10).

The commencement date The *commencement date* was, by virtue of the Wildlife and Countryside Act (Commencement No 6) Order 1983, 28 February 1983 unless a survey or review was in progress. In such areas the commencement date was when the survey or review was completed or abandoned. Surveying authorities were asked to advertise such a commencement in the local press (Circular 1/83, Annex A, para 5).

The events which give rise to modification of the map and statement Section 53(3) sets out the 'events' which give rise to modification of the definitive map. These are as follows:

(a) If, under statutory powers:
  (i) a public right of way shown on the definitive map has been extinguished, diverted, widened or extended;
  (ii) a way shown on the map as a public right of way of a particular description has ceased to be a right of way of that description, eg a bridleway has been made up into a carriageway;

4 : DEFINITIVE MAPS AND OTHER RECORDS

    (iii) a new footpath or bridleway has been created, whether by agreement or by order.

(b) If a path has been long enough in public use to give rise to a presumption of its dedication as a right of way (see chapter 3).

(c) If the surveying authority discovers evidence which, when considered with all other relevant evidence available to it, shows:
- (i) that a right of way (ie a footpath, bridleway or byway open to all traffic) exists, but is not shown on the definitive map;
- (ii) that a right of way shown on the map in a particular class ought to be shown in a different class, eg a bridleway as a footpath, or vice versa;
- (iii) that there is no right of way over a path shown on the map, or that any other particulars contained in the map and statement need modification. Under subsection (4) a modification order may add to, or amend, the statement to include or vary details of the position or width of a path shown on the map, or may amend details already contained in the statement.

Events listed under (a) above are often referred to as 'legal events'; those under (b) and (c) as 'evidential events'.

Statements of priorities The task of bringing definitive maps up to date was recognised by Circular 1/83 (para 6) to be a considerable one. In some counties hundreds of 'legal' events, eg public path orders confirmed and brought into operation, have had to be taken into account, as well as numerous claims for 'evidential event' orders, eg for paths to be added to the map. The Circular recommends that surveying authorities publish periodic statements of their priorities for bringing and keeping the map up to date, and that potential applicants for orders be guided by such statements.

Such statements may be useful, provided that they show an adequate determination by the surveying authority to get on with the work. The Act imposes a clear duty on authorities to do so, and the courts take little notice of a government circular which appears to them to contradict the wording of an Act, as was demonstrated in *Pearson's* case (p 86). An authority which tries to use para 6 of the Circular as an excuse for ignoring its duty may therefore have to justify its position to the Divisional Court.

In decisions on applications to the Secretary of State for directions to be given to surveying authorities to decide modification order applications under WCA 81 Sch 14 para 3(2), he has indicated that the factors he takes into account include any statement of priorities adopted by the authority, the reasonableness of such priorities, action taken by the authority or expressed intention of further action on the application and the importance of the case compared to others.

RIGHTS OF WAY

4.6.5 Procedure for making and confirming orders

The form of orders is prescribed in the Wildlife and Countryside (Definitive Maps and Statements) Regulations 1983 (p 445).

'Legal event' orders Modification orders under s 53(2) which are consequential on events listed in s 53(3)(a) take effect on being made, and cannot be the subject of objections or representations. Such orders reflect the conclusion of statutory procedures which allow some form of objection (see chapter 5) and are therefore purely administrative in nature. However, they take the same form as other modification orders.

'Evidential event' orders Orders to give effect to all other events of the kind described in s 53(3)(b) and (c), and reclassification orders made under s 54 to reclassify RUPPs, are made under the procedure in Sch 15 (p 387), set out below.

Consultation Before making the order, the authority must consult every local authority or local council (p 32) for the area (para 1).

Considering the evidence The authority must consider all the relevant evidence available to it (s 53(3)) and must be advised by its officers on the correct application of the law to that evidence. (*R v Isle of Wight CC, ex parte O'Keefe* (1989).)

Making the order The order must be in the form prescribed by the regulations (Sch 2 to the Regulations (p 447) for modification orders, Sch 3 (p 448) for reclassifications). It must contain a plan, on a scale of not less than 1:25,000. Since the order, once confirmed, becomes part of the definitive map and statement, Circular 1/83 advises authorities to take care to ensure its accuracy (Annex A, para 24).

Giving notice of the making of the order On making the order, the authority must give notice (Sch 15 para 3(1)) in the form prescribed in Sch 5 to the Regulations (p 450). The notice must describe the general effect of the order and say where a copy may be inspected free of charge, and copies purchased at a reasonable charge, at all reasonable hours. It must also specify when (not less than 42 days from the first publication of the notice) and how representations or objections may be made.

The notice must be published in at least one local newspaper. A copy must be served on (ie sent to):
(a) Every owner and occupier of any of the land affected by the order.
(b) Every other local authority and local council for the area.
(c) Every person on whom notice is required to be served under Sch 15 sub-para 3(3) (see below).

4 : DEFINITIVE MAPS AND OTHER RECORDS

(d) The bodies prescribed in Sch 6 to the Regulations (p 451) and such other persons or bodies as the authority considers appropriate.

It must also be prominently displayed at council offices in the locality and at such other places as the authority considers appropriate. The notice must also be displayed at the ends of the ends of every path or way affected by the order; this notice must be accompanied by a plan showing the effect of the order on the path or way concerned. (Sch 15 para 3(7).)

Sub-para 3(3) of Sch 15 enables any person to require the authority, on payment of a reasonable charge, to give him notice of all orders of a specified description made during a specified period and covering a specified area. This is a useful provision enabling, for example, a local rambling club to place a standing order for notification of all orders within a district, or certain specified parishes.

However, it would be cheaper to persuade the surveying authority that such a club is an 'appropriate body' to be sent notices free of charge under Sch 15 sub-para 3(2)(c)(iii). Such an arrangement has the advantage that copies of the orders come with the notices, and do not have to be bought separately. Circular 1/83, Annex A, para 29, recommends that the 'appropriate' bodies be the county and other local organisations which are recognised as representative of path-user interests.

In any particular case the Secretary of State may allow notification of an owner or occupier to be impersonal by affixing a copy of the notice to a conspicuous object on the land. (Sch 15 para 3(4).)

The notice served on an owner or occupier of land, or on a local authority, must be accompanied by a copy of so much of the order as relates to the land or to the area of the authority. A notice served on a prescribed or 'appropriate' person or body must be accompanied by a copy of the whole order. (Sch 15 para 3(6).)

What evidence did the authority take into account? During the period allowed for representations or objections any person may require the authority to inform him what documents (if any) were taken into account when the order was prepared. (Sch 15 para 3(8).) If they are in the authority's possession, the documents must be made available for inspection and copying within 14 days of the requirement being made. If the documents are not in the authority's possession, the authority must say where they are, again within the 14-day period. This is a valuable opportunity to examine the evidence behind the authority's decision to make the order. However the authority is not prevented from bringing forward other evidence at an inquiry. (Sch 15 para 3(9).)

Objections If an order is unopposed, or if the objections are subsequently withdrawn, the authority may confirm the order, but it must not make any modification to it. If there are any objections, or if the authority wants modifications made to the order even though there are no objections, the order must be submitted to the Secretary of State. Paragraphs 38 and 39 of Annex A to Circular 1/83 tell an authority what to send.

If only some of the modifications made by an order are opposed, the authority may, on giving notice to the Secretary of State, divide it so that the unopposed modifications are separated from those which are opposed. (Sch 15 para 5(1).) The authority can then confirm the unopposed part.

The Secretary of State normally delegates his power to make a decision on an order submitted to him to an inspector, although he has power to recover jurisdiction. (Sch 15 para 10.) The objections may be heard by arranging a public inquiry, or by arranging a hearing (at which only the objectors and their witnesses may be heard), or, with the agreement of the objectors, by an exchange of written representations. The DOE's normal practice has been to arrange a public inquiry. The procedure at an inquiry is essentially the same as that for public path order inquiries (see chapter 5.2.5).

Modifications There are restrictions on the power of the Secretary of State (and thus on an inspector) to modify orders. Without further notice, he cannot modify an order in the following ways:

(a) To affect land not affected by the order.
(b) To omit a path from, or add a path to, the order.
(c) To alter the description of a path from that shown on the order (eg by changing it from a bridleway to a footpath).

If he gives notice of the proposed modification (Sch 15 para 8) and there are objections he must hold a public inquiry or hearing or allow written representations about the proposed modification. However in *Dyfed CC v Secretary of State for Wales* (1988) Mr Justice Macpherson held that the failure of the Secretary of State's inspector to advertise a proposed modification to omit a path from an order was insufficient to justify quashing of the decision, since he considered that there was no prospect of a different decision being reached if a further inquiry was to be held.

The power to modify is nonetheless a wide-ranging one. If, for example, an authority makes an order to delete a right of way from the map, and objectors claim that the order should have also added a right of way but in a slightly different position (ie that the right of way was rightly on the map, but in the wrong place) the inspector appears to have power, under (b) above, to modify the order to give effect to their claim.

Notice of confirmation Once the decision to confirm an order has been made the authority must, as soon as practicable thereafter, give

4 : DEFINITIVE MAPS AND OTHER RECORDS

notice of confirmation. The notice must be published, served and displayed (Sch 15 para 11(2)) in the same way as notice was given when the order was made (p 94). It must describe the general effect of the order as confirmed, state whether it has been confirmed with or without modifications and give the date on which it took effect.

However, because the words 'in the prescribed form' do not appear in para 11, the Regulations cannot prescribe the wording of the confirmation notice. If either the Secretary of State or the authority decides not to confirm an order, notice must be served by the authority on those who were served with notice of the making of the order (Sch 15 para 11(4)), but no announcement has to be made in a local paper nor need a copy of the notice be placed on the path. Again, there is no prescribed form of notice, but the notice would clearly need to indicate which order it is that has not been confirmed, and it would be helpful if it also indicated whether the authority or the Secretary of State had made the decision.

High Court challenge Within 42 days of publication of the notice of final decision on an order which has taken effect, ie been confirmed, an application may be made to the High Court (Sch 15 para 12) by a person aggrieved by the order to question its validity on the ground that it is not within the powers of the Act or that any procedural requirements have not been complied with. This power was used by the RA to challenge the inspector's decision in the *Rubinstein* case (below). It is also open to anyone to challenge decisions made by an inspector, or by an authority, by way of judicial review. This route has to be followed in cases where an order is not confirmed, since the provisions of Sch 15 para 12 do not apply in such cases.

4.6.6 Deletion and downgrading of paths

The provision in s 53(3)(c)(iii) for the deletion or downgrading of paths shown on the map caused a great deal of concern to user organisations when the Act was going through Parliament in 1981 because it places no limits on the evidence which is admissible to support deletion or downgrading.

Those concerns were justified when some surveying authorities made modification orders to delete or downgrade. In *Rubinstein v Secretary of State for the Environment* (1987) the RA challenged the Secretary of State's confirmation of an order to delete Kirkby Underwood FP 7 in Lincolnshire. The argument advanced for the RA was that the review provisions of s 53 were subject to the conclusive evidence provisions in s 56. This argument was accepted by Mr Justice Taylor, who quashed the confirmation of the order.

However his decision was overturned by the Court of Appeal in *R v Secretary of State for the Environment, ex parte Burrows and Simms*

(1990). The Court held that sections 53 and 56 could be reconciled once the purpose of the legislation as a whole was understood, namely the preparation and maintenance of an authoritative record of ways over which there were public rights.

DOE Circular 18/90 (p 510) sets out the Department's current view of modification orders to delete and downgrade ways shown on the definitive map and statement. It puts the onus of proof firmly on those seeking to demonstrate that the map is wrong (para 4). It also takes a firmer line than did Circular 1/83 about the conclusiveness of the map and statement if disputes arise. Paragraphs 6 and 10 of the 1990 circular give clear advice to authorities to treat the map and statement as correct unless and until it is proved otherwise by the confirmation of a modification order.

4.6.7 Reclassification of roads used as public paths

The problems of the reclassification of RUPPs under CA 68 were considered in chapter 4.4.4. WCA 81 s 54 (p 380) attempts to solve those problems.

Section 54(1) requires every surveying authority to review all the RUPPs shown on its definitive map and make one or more reclassification orders to give effect to the requirements of subsections (2) and (3). The form of order is specified in the Regulations, particularly in Sch 3 (p 448). The duty is to carry out the review as soon as reasonably practicable after the commencement date.

Section 54(2) requires every RUPP to be reclassified as a byway open to all traffic, as a bridleway, or as a footpath. The choice of three categories is as in CA 68, but the test, in subsection (3), for deciding into which category a RUPP should be placed is not, being based simply on the existence or otherwise of rights.

If a public right of way for vehicular traffic is shown to exist, reclassification must be as a byway open to all traffic. However a traffic regulation order (see chapter 5.5.1) may be made if the way is thought unsuitable for use by vehicles, or if use by vehicles will cause problems for other users. Vehicular rights may be extinguished by order of the magistrates' court under HA 80 s 116 (see chapter 5.4.1).

If no vehicular rights exist, and bridleway rights have not been disproved, reclassification is as a bridleway. This provision, in subsection 3(b), is intended to give effect to the decision in the *Hood* case (p 86), but it does not clearly do so. Instead it creates a presumption that bridleway rights exist which must be disproved before a RUPP can be reclassified as a footpath.

Since by virtue of NPACA 49 s 32(4) and WCA 81 s 56(1) the depiction of a way as a RUPP on the definitive map is conclusive evidence of the existence of bridleway rights, it is difficult to see how one can ever be properly reclassified as a footpath under s 54. If evidence

4 : DEFINITIVE MAPS AND OTHER RECORDS

exists that a way shown as a RUPP should have been shown as a footpath, or indeed should not have been shown at all, it should be tested by way of a modification order under s 53(3)(c), which requires all the relevant evidence to be taken into account.

Following the decision in the *Rubinstein* case (above), the British Horse Society applied by way of judicial review for the quashing of the decision of the Secretary of State to confirm an order under s 54 reclassifying a RUPP in Leicestershire as a footpath. Late in 1988, the Secretary of State decided to submit to judgment and allow the decision and order to be quashed, thereby accepting that a RUPP could not be reclassified as a footpath. But following the *Burrows and Simms* case, the Secretary of State reverted to his original view. (Circular 18/90 para 9 — p 511.)

Ways reclassified from RUPP under the Countryside Act 1968
Anyone seeking a change in the status (eg from footpath to bridleway) of a RUPP reclassified under the provisions of CA 68 will have to pursue his case by means of a modification order, and if necessary application, under s 53 for two reasons:
(a) Section 54 applies only to ways shown as RUPPs on the definitive map.
(b) The application procedure (see below) applies only to modification orders under s 53(3)(b) and (c), and not to reclassification orders under s 54.

This was the action taken by Mr Bill Riley. Two ways had been reclassified from RUPP to bridleway by Wiltshire CC under the 1968 Act. Mr Riley applied to the CC under WCA 81 Sch 14 for modification orders to be made to show them as byways. The CC refused the applications, and, on appeal under Sch 14, the Secretary of State supported the CC. Mr Riley applied for judicial review of the Secretary of State's decision.

Mr Justice Macpherson held that, as there had been discovery of evidence since the original consideration by Wiltshire CC under the 1968 Act, the matter came within the provisions of s 53(3)(c), and that, as it was agreed that there was ancient evidence of vehicular rights, Mr Riley's challenge had to succeed. (*R v Secretary of State for the Environment, ex parte Riley* (1989).)

4.6.8 How to apply for a modification order

The definitive map and statement are modified by orders made by the surveying authority. Section 53(5) enables any person to apply to the authority for an order to give effect to one or more of the events set out in s 53(3)(b) and (c) (p 380).

The procedure for making such an application is set out in WCA 81 Sch 14 (p 385) and is as follows.

RIGHTS OF WAY

Application to the surveying authority The application is made in the form set out in Sch 7 to the Regulations (p 452), of which a specimen is set out below. It must be accompanied by a map drawn to a scale of 1:25,000 or larger (eg 1:10,000) and by copies of any documentary evidence which the applicant wishes to submit in support of the application. For a claim under s 53(3)(b), the evidence will be primarily, if not exclusively, evidence of use; for a claim under s 53(3)(c)(i) documentary evidence may also be relevant. See chapter 4.9 for evidence generally.

Specimen form for application for modification order

Wildlife and Countryside Act 1981
Definitive map and statement for the county of Barset

To: Barset County Council
Of: County Hall, West Street, Barchester

I, Janet Smith, of 24 Whiteacre Lane, Hightown, Barset, hereby apply for an order under section 53(2) of the Wildlife and Countryside Act 1981 modifying the definitive map and statement for the county of Barset by adding the footpath from Barchester Road, Hightown, (grid reference 701472) to Marshvale Lane, Hightown (grid reference 705469) with a width of two metres and shown on the map annexed hereto.

I attach copies of the following documentary evidence (including statements of witnesses) in support of this application:

Extracts from the Deposited Plan and Book of Reference of the East Barset Railway Act 1874.

Minutes of the Hightown Urban District Council Highways Committee referring to the condition of the path on various occasions between 1947 and 1968.

Ordnance Survey six-inch map dated 1934 showing the path as a physical feature.

32 evidence forms completed by witnesses showing use of the path over a period from 1930 to 1982.

Dated 10 April 1991   *Signed* Janet Smith

4 : DEFINITIVE MAPS AND OTHER RECORDS

Notice to landowners and occupiers The applicant must notify every owner and occupier of land affected by the application that it has been made. The form of notice is prescribed by Sch 8 to the Regulations (p 452); a specimen is set out below. If, after reasonable enquiry has been made, the surveying authority is satisfied by the applicant that it is not practicable to ascertain the name or address of an owner or occupier, the authority may allow the applicant to serve the notice by affixing it to some conspicuous object(s) on the land. In such a case, the notice may be addressed impersonally to the 'owner' or 'occupier'.

Specimen form of notice to landowners and occupiers

Wildlife and Countryside Act 1981
Definitive map and statement for the county of Barset

To: Mr P Lucas
Of: Mill Farm, Marshvale Lane, Hightown

Notice is hereby given that on 10 April 1991 I, Janet Smith, of 24 Whiteacre Lane, Hightown, made application to the Barset County Council of County Hall, West Street, Barchester that the definitive map and statement for the county of Barset be modified by adding the footpath from Barchester Road, Hightown (grid reference 701472) to Marshvale Lane, Hightown (grid reference 705469).

Dated 11 April 1991   *Signed* Janet Smith

The requirement for an applicant to notify landowners and occupiers of his application has no precedent in rights-of-way legislation, and is an onerous burden on applicants wishing to add to the record of the public's rights constituted by the definitive map and statement. It was strongly opposed by user organisations during the Act's passage through Parliament, but defended by the government partly by analogy with planning applications (which, it should be noted, are for private gain, not to record public rights) and partly on the ground that such consultation was desirable but was too great a burden to impose on surveying authorities.

The provisions of the Land Registration Act 1988 ease matters a little by giving the public access to the Land Register. However, much rural land remains unregistered. Furthermore, only when the lease is for over 21 years does the Register gives the name of a tenant. Information is obtained first by applying to inspect the Public Index Map. If this inspection reveals that a property is registered details of ownership can be obtained by further application (see 'Further Reading').

Certifying service of notice on landowners and occupiers The applicant must give a certificate to the surveying authority that notice has been served on owners and occupiers. The certificate must be in the form prescribed by Sch 9 (p 453) to the Regulations, a specimen of which is set out below.

Specimen certificate of service of notice of application for modification order

---

Wildlife and Countryside Act 1981
Definitive map and statement for the county of Barset

Certificate of service of notice of application for modification order

To: Barset County Council
Of: County Hall, West Street, Barchester

I, Janet Smith, of 24 Whiteacre Lane, Hightown Barset, hereby certify that the requirements of paragraph 2 of Schedule 14 to the Wildlife and Countryside Act 1981 have been complied with in connection with my application to you dated 10 April 1991 for the modification of the definitive map and statement for the county of Barset by the addition of a footpath from Barchester Road to Marshvale Lane, Hightown.

Dated 15 April 1991   *Signed* Janet Smith

Action by the surveying authority As soon as reasonably practicable after receiving the certificate the authority must investigate the application and consult every local authority or council for that area (ie district council in non-metropolitan counties, parish or community council, or parish meeting where there is no parish council) before deciding whether to make the order.

Failure to make a decision If the authority has not made a decision within 12 months of receiving the certificate the applicant may, under Sch 14 para 3(2), make representations to the Secretary of State (in England via the regional offices of the Department of the Environment). The Secretary of State may, after consulting the authority, direct that the application be determined within a specified period. He is not

4 : DEFINITIVE MAPS AND OTHER RECORDS

obliged to give such a direction. An indication of his attitude was given in para 6 of Circular 1/83 (p 481). Decisions made by him up to the end of 1987 on applications for directions are summarised in the digest of decisions published by the Countryside Commission (see 'Further Reading').

If the Secretary of State decides not to give a direction, it is open to the applicant to make a further application for a direction at a later date if the authority continues to fail to make a decision on the application.

Appeal against refusal to make an order If the authority decides not to make an order, the applicant may, under Sch 14 para 4, serve notice of appeal on the Secretary of State and the authority. This must be done within 28 days after service of notice of the decision on the applicant.

If the Secretary of State allows the appeal, he will direct the authority to make the necessary order. Decisions on appeals made up to the end of 1987 are also included in the digest of decisions referred to above. The Secretary of State's decision on an appeal may be challenged by application for judicial review: the *Riley* and *Burrows and Simms* cases are examples of such applications.

The authority may make an order of its own volition, in which case Schedule 14 does not apply. Since such a decision involves the authority in less work than a decision made following an application, it is in the interests of the authority, as well of the applicant, to avoid applications wherever possible. We therefore suggest that those with evidence which, in their view, justifies the making of a modification order present it to the authority, which may be persuaded to make an order. The formal application procedure can be used if this course of action fails.

If the authority makes, or is directed to make, an order following an application, the applicant has no special rights: he will not necessarily be notified that the order has been made, nor will he be automatically informed that an inquiry is to be held into objections to it.

4.6.9 Conclusive evidence

Section 56(1) of the 1981 Act replaced NPACA 49 s 32(4) with effect from 28 February 1983. It provides that the depiction of a path on the definitive map is conclusive evidence that, at the relevant date, a public right of way existed over that path to the following extent:

(a) Where the map shows a footpath, there was a right of way on foot, but without prejudice to the possible existence of other rights.
(b) Where the map shows a bridleway or a RUPP, there was a right of way on foot and on horseback, again without prejudice to the possible existence of other rights.
(c) Where the map shows a byway open to all traffic, there was a right of way for vehicular and all other kinds of traffic.

RIGHTS OF WAY

The subsection also provides, as did NPACA 49 s 32(4)(c), that where the statement contains particulars of the position or width of a path shown on the map, or of any conditions or limitations affecting the public right over such a path, it is conclusive evidence of the position or width, or of the conditions or limitations, at the relevant date but without prejudice to the possible existence of other limitations or conditions at that date.

In common with the 1949 Act (see chapter 4.2.9), the 1981 Act does not give precedence to either the map or the statement, although differences may be reconciled by the making of a modification order.

4.6.10 Supplementary provisions

Section 57 (p 382) contains a number of important supplementary provisions.

Regulations Subsections (1) and (2) empower the Secretary of State to make regulations prescribing the form of orders and the method of showing paths on the map. He has made the Wildlife and Countryside (Definitive Maps and Statements) Regulations 1983 (p 445) under this power. Definitive maps must be on a scale of not less than 1:25,000 and must show rights of way in the notation shown in Sch 1 to the Regulations.

Preparing a new map and statement Sections 57(3) and (4) enable a surveying authority to prepare an updated definitive map from time to time, incorporating any modifications made by order since the previous map was published. The new map has its own relevant date (not earlier than six months before the map is prepared), which has the effect of updating the evidential provisions in s 56(1). Circular 1/83, Annex A, para 67 recommends that public notice be given of the preparation of such a consolidated map. A copy of any earlier map and statement must be kept available for public inspection (s 57(6)).

The new map and statement are not put on public deposit for comment: they are assumed to be correct. If errors of transcription come to light they have to be corrected by the making of further modification orders under s 53(3)(c). As indicated above, there is no clear power in the Act to merge or divide the definitive maps covering an authority's area when the consolidating power in s 57 is exercised.

Keeping maps and statements available for public inspection Subsection (5) requires a surveying authority to keep a copy of the definitive map and statement, together with copies of all modification and reclassification orders which have caused it to be modified, available for free inspection at all reasonable hours at one or more places in each district, and, where practicable, in each parish or community. District

4 : DEFINITIVE MAPS AND OTHER RECORDS

and parish copies need comprise only that part of the map and statement for the district or parish. Circular 1/83, Annex A, para 69 also recommends that maps be sold to the public.

The public's right to inspect the map and statement is one of the rights prescribed for the purposes of LGA 72 s 100G(3), added by the Local Government (Access to Information) Act 1985.

4.7 The 'relevant date' of a path on the definitive map

The relevant date of a particular path shown on the map will, under s 56(2) and (3), be one of the following:

(a) The relevant date or date of review of the definitive map prepared under NPACA 49.

(b) The relevant date of a consolidated map prepared under WCA 81 s 57(3). If a new map is produced under the provisions of s 57(3), all the ways shown on it have to be given the same relevant date. By virtue of s 57(4) this must be no earlier than six months before the preparation of the map and statement.

(c) The date specified in a modification order modifying the map. This date must not be more than six months before the making of the order (s 56(3)).

If a map has been amended by modification orders it will thus be subject to more than one relevant date. As the conclusive evidence of the map and statement is proof of the existence of rights only at the relevant date, anyone wishing to rely on those provisions should check carefully the relevant date applicable to the path in question.

4.8 The progress of the survey and reviews

4.8.1 The position at 31 March 1974

This list sets out the position in the former counties immediately before local government reorganisation on 1 April 1974. The number describes the number of definitive maps produced, eg 1 = initial definitive map completed but no revised map completed, 2 = one revised map completed, and the letters show the position reached with the initial survey or the review. 'D' means draft or revised draft, 'P' provisional or revised provisional, and 'SRD' and 'LSRD' special revised draft and limited special revised draft respectively. In four counties the initial survey was only partly complete; these are indicated by 'OD/1' meaning that in part of the county a definitive map was available and in part the initial survey had reached draft stage. County boroughs are not covered by this list.

English counties Bedfordshire OD/1; Berkshire 1; Buckinghamshire 2P; Cambridgeshire and Isle of Ely 1/3SRD; Cheshire 1; Cornwall

1LSRD; Cumberland 1P; Derbyshire OD/1; Devon 1LSRD; Dorset 1; Durham 4LSRD; East Suffolk 2SRD; East Sussex 2SRD; Essex 2SRD; Gloucestershire OD/1; Hampshire 3; Herefordshire 1SRD; Hertfordshire 1; Huntingdon and Peterborough 2SRD; Isle of Wight 1D; Kent 1SRD; Lancashire 1P; Leicestershire 2; Lincolnshire-Holland 2SRD; Lincolnshire-Kesteven 1D; Lincolnshire-Lindsey OP/1; Norfolk 1D; Northamptonshire 3SRD; Northumberland 2; Nottinghamshire 1LSRD; Oxfordshire 1D; Rutland 2; Shropshire 2D; Somerset 1; Staffordshire 1SRD; Surrey 2D; Warwickshire 1; Westmorland 1LSRD; West Suffolk 1SRD; West Sussex 1; Wiltshire 2SRD; Worcestershire 4; Yorkshire-East Riding 1SRD; Yorkshire-North Riding 1; Yorkshire-West Riding 1.

Welsh counties Anglesey 2; Breconshire 1P; Caernarvonshire OP; Cardiganshire 1; Carmarthenshire 1LSRD; Denbighshire 1; Flintshire 2SRD; Glamorgan 1SRD; Merioneth 1; Monmouthshire 1SRD; Montgomeryshire 1; Pembrokeshire 1; Radnorshire 1SRD.

4.8.2 The position at 28 February 1983

A commencement order, the Wildlife and Countryside Act (Commencement No 6) Order 1983, brought sections 53 and 54 of the 1981 Act into effect on 28 February 1983. But it provided that the sections did not apply to any definitive map for which a review was in progress until that review had been either completed or abandoned.

The Secretary of State gave the following directions for reviews in progress at 28 February 1983:

Direction to complete review *England:* Cleveland, Cornwall, Cumbria, Durham, Humberside (former East Riding), Northamptonshire, Staffordshire, North Yorkshire (former East Riding), plus the London boroughs of Bexley and Richmond. *Wales:* Clwyd, Dyfed (former Carmarthenshire), Mid Glamorgan, West Glamorgan, Powys (former Breconshire and Radnorshire)

Direction to abandon review *England:* Berkshire, Buckinghamshire, Cambridgeshire (former Cambridgeshire and Isle of Ely), Derbyshire, Devon, Dorset*, East Sussex, Essex*, Hereford and Worcester (former Herefordshire), Hertfordshire, Kent, Leicestershire, Northumberland, Nottinghamshire, Oxfordshire (part formerly in Berkshire), Somerset, Suffolk, Warwickshire, West Sussex (part formerly in East Sussex), West Yorkshire, Wiltshire*. *Wales:* Gwynedd

* these reviews were abandoned subject to the Secretary of State agreeing to issue decisions in respect of inquiries which had already been held.

4 : DEFINITIVE MAPS AND OTHER RECORDS

Former county borough areas where no survey begun In former county boroughs and areas excluded as fully developed (p 76) the position was different. Listed below are the former county boroughs where, to the best of our knowledge, no survey was ever begun, and to which s 55(3) now applies. In the other former county borough areas the position varied between the possession of a definitive map and having a survey at draft or provisional stage. In some of those boroughs the survey covered only part of the area. Circular 1/83, Annex A, paras 56–58 indicated that most such surveys were likely to be completed. Any areas excluded from the original survey became subject to s 55(3) on 28 February 1983.

England: Bath; Barnsley; Birkenhead; Bootle; Brighton; Burton-upon-Trent; Chester; Coventry; Derby; Great Yarmouth; Grimsby; Ipswich; Kingston-upon-Hull; Leicester; Liverpool; Northampton; Norwich; Nottingham; Plymouth; Portsmouth; Rotherham; Salford; Southampton; Southport; Wakefield; Wallasey; Warley; Warrington; West Bromwich; Wigan; Wolverhampton; Worcester; York.
Wales: Cardiff; Merthyr Tydfil; Swansea.
Outer London Borough: Newham.

4.8.3 Progress since 28 February 1983

Progress with updating definitive maps and statements since 28 February 1983 has been mixed. In general, progress has been much slower than authorities, users and landowners alike would have wished. The path-by-path nature of the present system, as opposed to the previous review of the whole map, has tended to focus attention on individual cases and thereby cause delay. Against that, it is undoubtedly true that the log-jam which had occurred under the 1968 Act has been broken — a substantial part of the task of bringing maps up to date to reflect the 'legal' events which have occurred since the relevant date or date of review of the map has now been undertaken. But in many counties there is still a very long way to go before the maps can be said to provide a complete record of the public's rights.

The powers in ss 53 & 54 to make modification orders under the provisions of Sch 15 to reflect 'evidential' events or to reclassify RUPPs have been used in recent years as follows (figures for events in orders with closing dates for objections in 1988, 1989 and 1990):

Modification order 'evidential event'	1988	1989	1990
Addition of footpath	224	248	292
Addition of bridleway	36	58	46
Addition of byway	44	46	50
Upgrade footpath to bridleway	22	57	47

Upgrade footpath or bridleway to byway	7	25	9
Downgrade way shown on the map	8	1	3
Delete way shown on the map	35	0	24
Amend statement or map but not status	63	10	5
Total of modification order events	439	445	476
Reclassification of RUPPs			
Reclassify RUPP as footpath	8	0	0
Reclassify RUPP as bridleway	66	38	25
Reclassify RUPP as byway	19	173	156
Total of reclassifications	193	211	181

Note The figures are for orders *made*; not all these have been, or will be, confirmed.

4.9 Evidence of right-of-way status

Evidence for the status of a particular way, ie whether it is a footpath, bridleway or carriageway, or indeed whether it is a public right of way at all, can be either documentary evidence or user evidence.

4.9.1 Documentary evidence

This is evidence recorded at some time in the past of the status then attributed to the way concerned. HA 80 s 32 (p 322) specifically permits it to be presented to a court or inquiry considering the status of a way. The list below indicates where such evidence may be found. The list needs to be supplemented by local research and contact with the local record office to discover what documents are available locally.

Much of the evidence contained in the documents is open to interpretation and its strength will often be vigorously contested by landowners and highway authorities. In relatively few cases will it be considered so conclusive as to amount to proof. Perhaps the greatest value of most documents is that they very often support each other or can be used to supplement user evidence and thus form an important element of the case being presented.

As a rough guide, the items which appear at the beginning of the list are those whose legal 'weight' is normally greatest and some of these may be sufficient in their own right to prove a point. It is important to realise that some earlier items may have been invalidated by later enactments such as inclosure awards or highway orders. The majority of the items referred to are likely to be available for inspection in a county record office. Some may be in the keeping of parish councils. Public authorities and statutory undertakers such as water authorities

4 : DEFINITIVE MAPS AND OTHER RECORDS

may have copies of local and private Acts of Parliament. The Public Record Office and the Record Office of the House of Lords also hold important sources.

Under LGA 72 s 228 (p 310) documents in the custody of a local authority may be inspected by local government electors for the area or, in some cases, by interested members of the public. Minutes (including minutes of a committee which have been placed before the council of the authority for approval), orders for payment and accounts may be inspected, free of charge, by a local government elector for the area. It is unlikely that an authority would refuse to allow any other person to inspect these documents since in practice such a person could easily get an elector to obtain the information instead.

Documents which are required by law to be deposited with a local authority (LGA 72 s 225 — p 310) may be inspected by any interested person. Such documents include the definitive map and statement, public path and definitive map orders and historical records such as inclosure awards and quarter sessions records. Unless the statute requiring a document to be deposited provides that public inspection is to be free of charge, eg the definitive map and associated orders (WCA 81 s 57), a fee may be payable. (LGA 72 s 228(5).)

It should not be assumed that, because authorities such as county councils are the custodians of records, the records will have been studied by their highway departments. Experience has shown that important documents may be in the hands of the county surveyor and yet be ignored. One such issue concerns the status of roads and the nature of a highway authority's schedule of maintainable roads. Many roads — mostly 'green lanes' — which ought to be recorded in lists of streets (see chapter 4.10) have not been included in them. An inquiry addressed to the county surveyor about a green lane not listed in his schedule or on the definitive map will probably elicit the response that it is private. The truth may be that he has never yet been compelled to look at the evidence or that the matter is in some doubt. The procedure for the addition of 'discovered' public roads to the list of streets is not set out in HA 80 and may well vary from authority to authority.

Highway orders These may be found dating from well before 1800. Until 1949 the diversion or extinguishment of public roads and paths could only be carried out by application to the justices of the peace. Diversion orders may be of greater interest than those for the extinguishment of public rights of way, but the latter should not be ignored. Both varieties often refer, either in the text or on the plans, to connecting public roads or paths. It is not unusual to discover that the order affects a path starting on a green lane and thereby provides clear evidence that the lane itself was a public highway.

Orders made during the present century may be held in the county

RIGHTS OF WAY

surveyor's department rather than the record office. In counties which were subject to boundary changes in 1974 there may be some difficulty in locating these and other documents.

Rights of Way Act 1932 Although parts of this Act were altered by later legislation, one section which remains in existence (now HA 80 s 31(6)) enabled landowners to deposit with the county council a map of the admitted rights of way on their land (see chapter 3.3.4). Where a map has been deposited it will be very strong evidence of the status of any way shown on it as an admitted right of way. Local authorities were also urged to draw up registers of rights of way following the coming into force of the Act, but these did not have any legal status. However they could provide useful supporting evidence.

Deposited plans The significance of the heading is that there were and still remain statutory requirements that plans of undertakings such as railways, major roads and canals and drainage channels be deposited with the appropriate public authorities. Where the works were authorised by Private Act of Parliament, as was normally the case, the Acts, plans and books of reference can be inspected (by appointment) at the House of Lords Record Office. All three documents must be considered together in each case. It is worth noting that some works were authorised but not constructed: the evidence for right-of-way status will be just as good.

Increment value duty The 1910 Finance Act created the increment value duty tax on land. Owners could apply for a reduction of the tax if they admitted the existence of a public right of way across a particular plot of land. The registers and maps (they are always the OS 25-inch series) are now in the Public Record Office which has produced an information sheet about them (see 'Further Reading'). In some cases registers or maps (or both) are also available in county record offices. However, as rights of way are not recorded as such on the maps, evidence of the route would also be needed. In some cases the register lists the numbers of the fields crossed by the rights of way for which tax reduction was claimed.

Inclosure awards These are some of the most important historical documents available, but they do not exist for every parish, nor do they normally cover the whole of a parish area. The name reveals their primary purpose, but the Inclosure Commissioners were also empowered to stop-up or divert existing highways and set out new highways of any category.

An inclosure award will probably include a schedule of new roads and paths to be set out, but it is important also to read other sections

4 : DEFINITIVE MAPS AND OTHER RECORDS

of the text. There was quite often a provision that private roads were to include the status of a public bridleway or footpath. There may well be important references in the lengthy description of the boundaries of the parish or the boundaries of individual plots of land.

Difficulties can arise about new roads or paths set out or others partially realigned by the award. In some cases there may be no physical evidence that the proposals were put into effect, although legally authorised. Is it necessary to have supporting evidence that the new route was physically laid out and came into public use? It might be a useful precaution to consult the provisions of the relevant Act, where it may have been laid down that none of the ways scheduled to be extinguished could be 'stopped' until all the new ones had been properly set out. If the Act so provides, then if it is argued that the 'new' paths were never properly laid out, it can be argued in response that the 'old' paths were never stopped up, and remain in existence. See also 'Further Reading'.

Highway maintenance records: (i) Parish records The survival rate of these does not appear to have been very high and it is rare to find maps among them. However useful evidence can be gleaned, notably from the account books of the parish highway surveyors who were responsible for the upkeep of the roads until late in the nineteenth century. These detail the payments made to labourers of the parish for their work in 'mending' the roads and some specify the names of the roads upon which they worked on a given day. One snag which may be difficult to overcome is that the names of the roads may not be those still in use or shown on maps, and local opinion may be at variance about these or not completely reliable.

Highway maintenance records: (ii) highway districts In some parts of the country there may be records of the highway districts which were set up under the Highways Act 1862. In some counties it appears that the requirements of the Act were ignored because the parishes refused to give up their responsibilities to the new authorities. In West Suffolk, for example, five highway boards were set up to run the county's roads, but in East Suffolk, nothing of the kind seems to have occurred.

One of the most valuable documents to have survived is a detailed survey of the complete network of roads in the 55 parishes of a West Suffolk highway district. Here again a copy was found to be in the keeping of the county's highway department, but until recent years it seems not to have been referred to.

Tithe apportionments Around the early 1840s the majority of parishes were surveyed by the tithe commissioners. These were appointed by statute to commute tithes in kind to a money rent. They produced detailed, large-scale parish maps and accompanying schedules. These were concerned solely with identifying titheable lands, and not with roads or their status, so cannot be used as definitive evidence about public roads, but the maps do mark roads quite accurately and, taken in conjunction with the schedules, the tithe award, as it is called, can provide useful supporting evidence. As tithes were not payable on public highways, these are often shown in a special colouring on the plans.

Records of war-time stopping up or diversion and ploughing authorisation During the Second World War the Defence (General) Regulations 1939 empowered the temporary stopping-up or diversion of highways, and the authorisation by County Agricultural Executive Committees of the ploughing of others, subject to restoration and the provision of diversions. These orders should have been deposited with local authorities, but it is far from clear how many have survived. There appears to be no extant national collection.

After the war the Requisitioned Land and War Works Acts 1945 and 1948 allowed orders to be made to stop-up or divert permanently highways which had been, or could have been, stopped-up or diverted under the Regulations. Objections to such orders were heard by the War Works Commission.

The orders made under the Acts are held by the Public Record Office at Kew, class MT78; class T180 contains the Commission's papers. They may also be held in local record offices. These orders may be of interest insofar as they provided for new highways to be created. They also record the highways that were extinguished on land which may now be no longer in use for military purposes. That change of use will not re-create the paths automatically, but the record of what was taken away may be of assistance to those arguing for the creation of new paths in their place.

Ordnance Survey books of reference In certain areas the first edition of the Ordnance Survey 1:2,500 (25-inch) map was accompanied by a published 'Book of Reference' for each parish. In areas where the first edition was published before 1880, constituting about a quarter of England and Wales (broadly speaking, Cumberland, Durham, Northumberland, Westmorland, Cheshire, Denbighshire, Flintshire, Glamorgan, Cornwall, the Isle of Wight, Hampshire, Sussex and London and its adjoining counties), the Book of Reference gives the land use of each separately numbered parcel on the map. One of the categories is 'Public Road' (or simply 'Road' in some of the later books).

It is not known whether this description was based on the appearance of the way or on local enquiries. The information is clearly not defini-

4 : DEFINITIVE MAPS AND OTHER RECORDS

tive, but could well be useful supporting evidence. The maps and books of reference are available in the Map Department of the British Library, from which photocopies may be obtained for a fee. Further details of the Books of Reference are given in *The Ordnance Survey and Land-Use Mapping* — see 'Further Reading'.

Parish records Apart from the records of the parish highway surveyor which were mentioned in a previous section, a variety of documents have survived, though they may prove difficult to locate if they are not in a county record office. Minute books and other miscellaneous books and papers may contain references to dealings over public rights of way. In earlier days boundary disputes between parishes and landowners seem to have cropped up from time to time and, as may also be discovered in the inclosure awards, descriptions of land bounded by the public road or bridle-road may be of some significance.

Evidence forms Over the years many hundreds of these have been completed and forwarded to highway authorities particularly in the years following NPACA 49 when the first definitive maps were being created.

It may prove difficult to try to discover the whereabouts of forms sent to a county council in the early 1950s but it could be worth the effort if there is new evidence for ways which may have been claimed then. The minutes of parish meetings or parish councils may give an idea of when these were collected.

Local history and records of use The works of historians and of leisured travellers may be useful as well as interesting. Journal accounts of journeys made or even fairly detailed personal surveys of a network of roads and lanes used may be found.

Some information may be extracted from the large holdings of copies of old newspapers. This is being made more accessible by such technical aids as microfilm, but the discovery of evidence from this kind of source is likely to be rather a matter of chance. Perhaps the newspaper featured the reports of natural historians, ramblers and others who described their wanderings through the countryside, in which case the chances are clearly greater. Many rambling clubs and other organisations representing users of rights of way keep records of the paths they have used, and in some cases these records have been kept for many years.

Local archives may contain records of property sales, solicitors' files or old title deeds, which sometimes refer to rights of way.

Maps Maps produced simply to portray the landscape as it was found without any consideration of rights of way, or of ownership, will some-

RIGHTS OF WAY

times be useful. These include the attractive county maps of the eighteenth and early nineteenth centuries and of course the whole range of Ordnance Survey maps in pre-definitive map days. The greatest practical use to rights-of-way researchers is likely to be in confirming the route or mere physical existence of a road or path at the time of survey. Just occasionally, however, a note is added, eg the marking of a 'Bridle' Road on one of Bryant's maps of Suffolk.

Estate maps County record offices will probably include in their holdings maps of private estates or of portions of estates. These may range from rough pencil sketches to detailed large-scale plans of high technical and artistic quality. Such maps can be valuable evidence about roads. Many of them are however on deposit from private owners. Access to them to research for rights-of-way status may be a matter for the owner's agreement.

4.9.2 User evidence

This evidence can be used in two ways:
(a) Submission to a surveying authority with an application for a modification order under WCA 81 Sch 14.
(b) Production at a public inquiry into a modification or reclassification order made by an authority under that Act.

Evidence can be collected and submitted in one of two ways. The easier way is to ask people to fill in answers to the questions on a form such as that set out below.

Public right of way evidence form

Name

Address

Date of birth   Occupation

Description of path
From   Grid reference

To   Grid reference

Believed status of path (eg footpath)

---

4 : DEFINITIVE MAPS AND OTHER RECORDS

If necessary, continue your answers on an additional sheet of paper

1. (a) Have you regarded the above way as a public right of way?
   (b) If so, for how many years?
2. Have you used the above way?

   If so: (a) During which years?
   (b) Where were you going to and from?
   (c) For what purpose?
   (d) How many times a year?
   (e) By what means (eg on foot, on horseback)?

3. Has the way always run over the same route? If not, give details and dates of any changes.

4. Have there to your knowledge ever been any stiles or gates on the way? If so, state (with details of location) where the stiles or gates stood.

5. If you were working for any owner or occupier of land crossed by the way at the time when you used it, or were then a tenant of any such owner, give particulars and dates. If not, write 'No'.

6. If so, did you ever receive any instructions from him as to the use of the way by the public? If so, what were they?

7. Have you ever been stopped or turned back when using this way, or do you know or have you heard of anyone else having been stopped or turned back? If so, state when the interruption took place and give particulars.

8. Were you ever told by any owner or tenant of the land crossed by the way, or by anyone in their employment, that the way was not public? If so, state when and give particulars and dates.

9. Have you ever known any locked gates or other obstruction to the way? If so, state when and give particulars.

10. Have you ever seen notices such as 'Private', 'No Road', 'No Thoroughfare' or 'Trespassers will be Prosecuted' on or near the way? If so, what did the notices say?

> 11. Have you ever asked permission to use the way?
>
> 12. Please give any other information that you think is relevant overleaf.
>
> I hereby certify that to the best of my knowledge and belief the facts that I have stated are true.
>
> I am/am not willing to attend a hearing, public inquiry or court to give evidence on this matter, if this should prove to be necessary.
>
> Signature   Date

If the person giving the evidence seems to be unwilling or unlikely to attend a public inquiry, at which he can be cross-examined so that his evidence can be tested to the satisfaction of the other parties and the inspector, he can be asked to agree to make a statutory declaration. There are two ways in which this can be done. One is that the statement should be taken as provided for in the Statutory Declarations Act 1835. The requirements are that the document starts by saying:

> I AB do solemnly and sincerely declare that: (here would appear the evidence in statement form, preferably by numbered paragraphs).
>
> AND I MAKE this solemn declaration conscientiously believing the same to be true and by virtue of the Statutory Declarations Act 1835.
>
> DECLARED before me this ... day of ... 199 .
>
> A commissioner for oaths/solicitor.

The other is to have the original on one sheet of paper and mark it with the initials of the witness, for instance 'AB' and then have a separate sheet to which the first would be attached. The separate sheet should contain the declaration in the following terms:

4 : DEFINITIVE MAPS AND OTHER RECORDS

> I AB do solemnly and sincerely declare that the contents of my statement attached hereto and marked 'AB' are to the best of my knowledge recollection and belief true and correct in every respect.
>
> AND I MAKE this solemn declaration conscientiously believing the same to be true, and by virtue of the provisions of the Statutory Declarations Act 1835.
>
> DECLARED before me this ... day of ... 199 .
>
> A commissioner for oaths/solicitor.

At one time a solicitor who had been in practice for more than a specified number of years could be appointed a commissioner for oaths and he alone (as opposed to any other solicitor) could take oaths and statutory declarations. Now all practising solicitors can take oaths or statutory declarations. The fee is currently £3.50 for the declaration or oath and £1.50 for each exhibit.

The person making the declaration is asked by the solicitor or commissioner 'Do you declare that the contents of this your declaration are true?' and upon a reply being given in the affirmative the declaration is deemed to have been made and the commissioner or solicitor signs to that effect.

4.10 Lists of streets

Section 36(6) of the Highways Act 1980 (p 323) requires every highway authority to make, and keep up-to-date, a list of streets within its area which are highways maintainable at public expense. The list must be available for inspection free of charge at the council's offices. A county council must also supply each district council in its area with a list of the publicly-maintainable streets in the district; that list must also be available for free inspection at district council offices. However there is no requirement for the list to be accompanied by a map and no specification of the detail to be included in the list, eg location, status, width.

'Street' is defined in HA 80 s 329 (p 357) as including any highway. The list must therefore contain all footpaths, bridleways and carriageways which are maintainable at public expense, whether or not they are shown on the definitive map. It ought to be possible, by comparing the list with the definitive map, to find out which rights of way shown on the map are not publicly maintainable.

The reverse can also apply, in that there will be streets shown in the list which do not appear on the map. In some cases these will be carriageways which, because they are not used mainly by walkers and riders, do not qualify for addition to the definitive map as byways open to all traffic. The list may well provide strong, though not conclusive, evidence of the public's rights. However it cannot be relied upon as evidence of the nature of those rights, ie whether the way should be shown on the definitive map as a footpath, bridleway or byway.

This is particularly true of a way shown in the list as an 'unclassified county road'. Although the use of the word 'road' implies vehicular rights, all that can in fact be deduced from the term, which was created by the Local Government Act 1929 and abolished by LGA 72, is that the way concerned was a highway maintainable at public expense, other than a way such as an A road classified by the Minister of Transport. Further evidence from other sources would be needed to establish conclusively the existence of vehicular rights.

Some authorities have taken the view that the list of streets and the definitive map are in some way mutually exclusive: a way should not be included in both. This view is clearly mistaken. The definitive map records only the public's rights; the list of streets records only the highway authority's maintenance liability. Since most rights of way shown on definitive maps are also maintainable at public expense (see chapter 7.2), it follows that there should be a considerable overlap between the contents of the two documents. But the entries on the two will not be identical.

4.11 Rights of way on Ordnance Survey maps

It has long been a feature of Ordnance Survey maps that the representation on the map of a path, track or way as a topographical feature is not evidence that it is (or is not) a public right of way. When the Hobhouse Committee recommended in 1947 that there should be a survey of public rights of way leading to the compilation of what became definitive maps, it also recommended (paragraph 45 of its report) that the information contained in those maps should also be shown on OS maps.

Although that recommendation was accepted in 1958 by OS the relatively slow rate at which definitive maps were produced meant that rights-of-way information was equally slow in appearing on OS maps. However, with the completion of the original survey of rights of way in 1982 (through the publication of the remaining parts of the definitive map for Bedfordshire), the areas left without definitive maps — namely the Isles of Scilly, a large part of Greater London and many former county boroughs — formed only a small part of the total area of England and Wales. This will be still further reduced now that the provisions

4 : DEFINITIVE MAPS AND OTHER RECORDS

in WCA 1981 have made the survey compulsory everywhere except Inner London (see chapter 4.6.3).

Rights-of-way information is not shown on OS maps of Scotland, as there is no equivalent to the definitive maps produced in England and Wales. Long-distance routes are, however, shown. For the Isle of Man a definitive map was produced by the Isle of Man government following the passage of a Rights of Way Act in 1961. Rights-of-way information taken from that map appears on OS Landranger sheet 95, and on the 1:25,000 scale Public Rights of Way and Outdoor Leisure Map for the Island, published by the Island's Highway and Transport Board.

OS maps at three scales show rights of way: 1:25,000 *(Pathfinder and Outdoor Leisure)*, 1:50,000 *(Landranger and some Tourist)* and one-inch to the mile or 1:63,360 *(Tourist)*. The 1:25,000 scale is the most useful, not simply because it is the largest of the three, but because it alone shows field boundaries. The Pathfinder and Outdoor Leisure Maps are thus the only ones which show both field boundaries *and* public rights of way, a most valuable combination. The Pathfinder series covers the whole of England and Wales except where Outdoor Leisure Maps have been published. Each sheet normally covers an area of 20 km by 10 km. There are now 28 Outdoor Leisure Maps in England and Wales. All, except that for the Isle of Scilly, show rights of way. Sheets normally cover an area of 26 km by 21 km: some are produced back to back. Although Outdoor Leisure maps use the same base (reduced from the 1:10,000 map) as Pathfinder maps, they contain additional information by way of depiction of national trails and other long-distance paths, some permissive paths and tourist information, and are often printed in different colours.

The 1:50,000 Landranger series is the metric successor to the old one-inch maps. 123 sheets, each covering an area of 40 km by 40 km, cover England and Wales and, except in the most rural areas, are frequently revised. Rights of way are shown in red and national trails highlighted.

Tourist maps at a scale of 1:50,000 or 1:63,360 (one-inch to the mile) are produced for the Broads, Cotswold, Dartmoor, Exmoor, the Lake District, New Forest, North York Moors and Peak District. Rights of way are shown in red.

The RA's journal, *Rambling Today*, contains information on OS developments, including details of new and revised maps showing rights of way.

The information shown on OS maps is derived from definitive, or revised definitive, maps supplied by surveying authorities as amended by subsequent changes notified by order-making authorities. However, subsequent changes have not always been notified, either through oversight of the authority concerned or because no requirement or request

RIGHTS OF WAY

has ever been made that they be sent to OS. The provisions in WCA 1981 requiring the definitive maps to be brought, and maintained, up to date should lead to the information held by OS being equally accurate, so long as OS receives copies of all confirmed public path, modification and reclassification orders. (See Circular 1/83, Annex A paras 40 and 47 and Annex B para 8.)

5
Changes to the network

5.1 How can changes come about?

5.1.1 Introduction

This chapter is concerned with the procedures whereby a public right of way may be legally created, diverted or extinguished. A diversion or extinguishment can only come about through one of the procedures described in this chapter, for, as Lord Justice Scott pointed out in *Jones v Bates* (1938): 'It is of real public moment that no genuine public footpath should be lost, without statutory action to close it'. The creation of new public rights of way by order is considered in chapter 5.3.3. Other means whereby new rights of way come into being are considered in chapter 3.

With few exceptions, the procedures for diverting or extinguishing public rights of way require public notice of the proposed change to be placed on the path, published in the local press and either given directly to national organisations such as the RA and OSS or published in the *London Gazette*. They also allow objectors to the proposal to have their objections heard and determined by a person or body other than the body putting forward the proposal.

The most common procedure is for an order to be made and advertised by a county, district or London borough council. At this stage objections may be made. If the council receives any objections, it has to forward these to the Secretary of State. He in turn normally delegates the consideration of objections and the making of the decision to an inspector from the Lord Chancellor's Panel. If the inspector approves the order then he confirms it: otherwise the terminology is that he decides not to confirm it. If there are no objections, the council may itself confirm the order as an unopposed order.

5.1.2 Use of the powers

Some idea of the extent to which the powers are used can be gained from the following statistics, which are of notices of orders sent to the RA or published in the *London Gazette* with closing dates for objections in the three years from 1 January 1988 to 31 December 1990. More detailed statistics for the period commencing 28 February 1983 are to be found in the monitoring reports published by the Countryside Commission (see 'Further Reading').

RIGHTS OF WAY

	1988	1989	1990
Highways Act 1980 *(Note 1)*			
Creation agreements (s 25) *(Note 2)*	44	40	46
Creation orders (s 26)	64	57	67
Diversion orders (s 119)	689	766	926
Extinguishment orders (s 118)	164	117	184
Town and Country Planning Act 1990 *(Note 3)*			
Diversion orders (s 247)	363	398	345
Extinguishment orders (s 257)	113	107	92
Highways Act 1980 ss 14 & 18			
Side roads orders *(Note 4)*	82	85	73
Highways Act 1980 s 116 *(Note 5)*			
Diversion order applications	14	23	15
Extinguishment order applications	68	53	72
Other orders *(Note 6)*	75	74	79
Total of proposed changes	1676	1720	1899

Notes
1. Some orders may be concurrent, eg a creation order may seek to create a path to replace one being closed by an extinguishment order.
2. Allocated to year by the date of the agreement.
3. Includes orders made under the predecessor legislation — sections 209 and 210 of the Town and Country Planning Act 1971.
4. Only those applications which affected, or appeared to affect, footpaths, bridleways and byways have been counted.
5. Only those applications which affected, or appeared to affect, footpaths, bridleways and byways have been counted. An application to extinguish may have been to extinguish only certain rights, eg to extinguish vehicular rights whilst retaining bridleway rights.
6. Includes joint orders under the Highways and Town and Country Planning Acts, orders connected with land acquired or held for planning purposes and New Towns, orders made under the Opencast Coal and Mineral Workings Acts and those made under defence legislation.

5.1.3 Summary list of powers for changing the network

This list is chronological by year of Act. In the second column 'SOS' means that the power is exercisable by a Secretary of State, 'LA' by a county or district council. In the third column 'C' means creation, 'D'

5 : CHANGES TO THE NETWORK

diversion, 'E' extinguishment (which can include provision of an alternative route) and 'FB' that the power may be used only on footpaths and bridleways, ie cannot affect vehicular rights. In the fifth column 'Standard' procedure is that described in chapters 5.2.1 to 5.2.12 below. 'SOS' procedure is the procedure for an order made by the Secretary of State: this is described in chapter 5.2.13.

Reference in chapter	Statutory provision	Type	Grounds for making change	Procedure
5.4.3	Defence Act 1842 s 16 (p 286) SOS	D/E FB	None.	No notice required
5.4.3	Defence Act 1860 s 40 (p 287) SOS	D/E	Applies to land taken under or affected by the Act.	No notice required
5.4.3	Military Lands Act 1892 s 13 (p 288) LA	D/E	Applies HA 80 s 116 where footpath crosses dangerously or inconveniently near to land leased under the Act.	Magistrates' court
5.4.3	Land Powers (Defence) Act 1958 s 8 (p 297) SOS	D/E	Applies TCPA 47 s 49 where land used for defence purposes.	SOS
5.3.7	Opencast Coal Act 1958 s 15 (p 297) SOS	E FB	Where authorisation has been given for opencast coal mining.	SOS
5.3.7	HA 80 s 14 (p 316) SOS/LA	D/E	Affected by construction or improvement of trunk or classified road.	SOS
5.3.7	HA 80 s 18 (p 316) SOS/LA	D/E	Affected by construction or improvement or special road.	SOS
5.3.3	HA 80 s 26 (p 318) SOS/LA	C FB	Path would add to the convenience or enjoyment of substantial section of the public or of local residents.	Standard
5.4.1	HA 80 s 116 (p 333) LA	D	New path will be nearer or more commodious to the public.	Magistrates' court
5.4.1	HA 80 s 116 (p 333) LA	E	Path is unnecessary.	Magistrates' court
5.3.1	HA 80 s 118 (p 335) SOS/LA	E FB	Path is not needed for public use.	Standard
5.3.2	HA 80 s 119 (p 335) SOS/LA	D FB	In interests of the owner, occupier or lessee of land crossed by the path or of the public.	Standard

RIGHTS OF WAY

Reference in chapter	Statutory provision	Type	Grounds for making change	Procedure
5.3.8	Local Government, Planning and Land Act 1980 Sch 28 (p 374) SOS	E	Where land acquired by or vested in highway authority or urban development corporation.	SOS
5.3.8	Acquisition of Land Act 1981 s 32 (p 375) LA	E FB	Where land has been, could have been or will be acquired by compulsory purchase.	Standard
5.3.8	New Towns Act 1981 s 32 (p 377) SOS	E	Where land acquired by or vested in highway authority or new town development corporation.	SOS
5.3.7	Civil Aviation Act 1982 s 48 (p 392) SOS	D/E	For safe and efficient use for civil aviation purposes of land owned by SOS or Civil Aviation Authority.	SOS plus special parliamentary procedure
5.5.2	Cycle Tracks Act 1984 s 3 (p 393) LA	C	To convert a footpath into a cycle track.	See text of chapter
5.3.8	Housing Act 1985 s 294 (p 405) LA	E	Where land acquired for slum clearance.	See text of chapter
5.3.7	Airports Act 1986 s 59 (p 405) SOS	D/E	Applies Civil Aviation Act 1982 where land owned by a relevant airport operator.	SOS plus special parliamentary procedure
5.3.8	Housing Act 1988 Sch 10 (p 411) SOS	E	Where land acquired by or vested in housing action trust.	SOS
5.3.7	Water Act 1989 s 155 (p 419) SOS	D/E	To facilitate works by water undertakers.	SOS
5.3.6	TCPA 90 s 247 (p 430) SOS	D/E	To enable development to take place.	SOS
5.3.7	TCPA 90 s 248 (p 431) SOS	D/E	In interests of safety of users or movement of traffic on new highway for which planning permission has been granted.	SOS
5.5.3	TCPA 90 s 249 (p 432) SOS	E	To convert a carriageway into a footpath or bridleway for planning purposes.	SOS
5.3.8	TCPA 90 s 251 (p 432) SOS	E	Where land acquired or held for planning purposes.	As for s 247

5 : CHANGES TO THE NETWORK

Reference in chapter	Statutory provision	Type	Grounds for making change	Procedure
5.3.6	TCPA 90 s 257 (p 435) LA	D/E FB	To enable development to take place.	Standard
5.3.8	TCPA 90 s 258 (p 436) LA	E	Where land acquired or held for planning purposes.	As for s 257
5.3.7	TCPA 90 s 261 (p 436) SOS/LA	D/E	Applies TCPA 90 s 247 (SOS) and s 257 (LA) where highway can be restored after surface working of minerals.	As for s 247 or s 257
5.4.2	Private and Local Act of Parliament	C/D /E	Change cannot be effected without the authority of Parliament.	See text of chapter

5.2 Administrative procedure for public path orders

5.2.1 Introduction

This description is of the procedure which applies, under HA 80 Sch 6, to public path creation, diversion and extinguishment orders and, under TCPA 90 Sch 14, to public path orders made under TCPA 90 s 257 to enable development to take place. It should be read in conjunction with Annex B of DOE Circular 1/83 (p 493).

5.2.2 Consultation

Orders under the Highways Act 1980 Before any order can be made under HA 80 ss 26, 118 or 119, and notice of its making published, there must be consultation. A non-metropolitan district council must consult a county council, and vice versa, and if a diversion or extinguishment is proposed in a national park, there must also be consultation with the Countryside Commission or Countryside Council for Wales.

In the Lake District and Peak District national parks, where there are joint planning boards, the boards have power to make orders. They must consult the county and district councils. In turn county and district councils must consult the boards before they make orders. The same requirements apply in the area defined as the Norfolk and Suffolk Broads by the Norfolk and Suffolk Broads Act 1988, where the Broads Authority must consult, or be consulted by, the county and district councils before an order is made.

In the metropolitan counties and Greater London, where there is now only one tier of local authority, there is thus no statutory requirement to consult (the only exception being those parts of the Peak District national park within metropolitan counties).

The Secretary of State also has power to make orders. If he is contemplating making a creation order, he must consult every local authority concerned (see s 26(2) — p 318). But if he has in mind a diversion or extinguishment order under HA 80, the Act requires him to consult only the 'appropriate authority'. (S 120(2) — p 337.) In practice he exercises only exceptionally his powers to make orders which could have been made by local authorities. (Circular 1/83 paras 15 and 16 — p 483.)

Orders under the Town and Country Planning Act 1990 There is no requirement for any consultation over the order. Consultation may take place between local authorities over a planning application which, if approved, will give rise to an order under the 1990 Act.

Consultation with users, landowners and local councils There is no statutory requirement for users, landowners or even local councils to be consulted, but in practice they often are. Many authorities have found such action not only to be good public relations, but also helpful in discovering whether the order, if made, is likely to attract opposition, and, if so, whether the proposal can be modified to meet that opposition. The Rights of Way Review Committee (p 31) has published a Code of Practice on consultation for proposed changes (p 512). This code has the backing of the local authority associations.

5.2.3 Making the order and publishing the notice

When the consultations are complete, there must be a formal decision by the authority at some level to make the order. The decision may be made by the full council, or it may be made by a committee or even by an officer under delegated powers. (The authority must maintain a list of powers delegated to officers: LGA 72 s 100G(2) — p 308.)

The order must be prepared in the form prescribed by regulations, and must contain a plan on a scale of not less than 1:2500. The regulations are the Town and Country Planning (Public Path Orders) Regulations 1983 (p 453) and the Public Path Orders and Extinguishment of Public Right of Way Orders Regulations 1983 (p 460). The description in the schedule should 'if possible' include details of the width of the path or way. (Circular 1/83, Annex B, para 12.)

Section 293 of the 1980 Act (p 352) gives a power to enter on land to survey it in connection with an order or a claim for compensation.

If the order is a creation or diversion order, it must allow sufficient time for any new right of way to be created on the ground before the existing path, if any, is closed. (Circular 1/83, Annex B, paras 3 and 7.) This important matter is often given inadequate attention when the order is drafted, and we consider it further in chapter 5.2.8.

Notice of making of the order must then be given in accordance with

5 : CHANGES TO THE NETWORK

the requirements of HA 80 Sch 6 para 1 (p 363) and TCPA 90 Sch 14 para 1 (p 440).

The notice must include the following information:
 (a) A description of the general effect of the order.
 (b) That it will be confirmed by the authority if it is unopposed and submitted to the Secretary of State if there are objections.
 (c) Where a copy of the order and the map can be inspected free of charge and where it may be purchased.
 (d) How and by when objections and representations may be made. At least 28 days must be allowed from the date of the first publication of the notice.

The notice must appear in at least one local newspaper. The DOE takes the controversial view that placing a notice in a 'free newspaper' may be sufficient to satisfy the requirement. In such a case the DOE has also said that, if the use of a paper which cannot be purchased is challenged, the onus would be on the order-making authority to produce evidence that the paper was one 'circulating in the area in which the land to which the order relates is situated'.

The notice must also be served, together with a copy of the order, on every owner, occupier and lessee of any of the land affected by the order and every other local authority. These include parish and community councils and parish meetings where there is no parish council.

Copies of the notice, again with a copy of the order, must also go to such persons as may be prescribed by the Secretary of State or as the authority may consider appropriate. The persons prescribed to receive notices and orders are listed in the regulations (p 459 & 471). Any other person may, by advance notice and payment, place an order for notices of any particular description and relating to any particular area. (See p 95 for further details of this procedure.)

The notice must also be displayed prominently in the following places:
 (a) At the ends of any length of path affected by the order. This notice must be accompanied by a plan showing the effect of the order on that path.
 (b) At council offices in the locality. These can include offices owned or provided by a parish or community council or parish meeting.
 (c) At such other places as the authority consider appropriate.

All the service and display of notices must be carried out not less than 28 days before the closing date for objections specified in the notice.

5.2.4 Dealing with objections

At the end of the objection period the authority may itself confirm the order if no objections have been received, but not otherwise. If objections have been received the authority has three options:

RIGHTS OF WAY

(a) It can decide not to confirm the order.
(b) It can seek the withdrawal of objections.
(c) It can submit the order with the objections to the Secretary of State for confirmation.

Deciding not to confirm the order Although there is no specific power in the Act for orders to be withdrawn by an authority, the DOE takes the view that an authority may make a formal resolution not to proceed with an order. (Circular 1/83, Annex B, para 4.) Alternatively, the order may be submitted to the Secretary of State with a request that he refuse to confirm it.

Any decision not to confirm an order, whether made by an authority or by the Secretary of State, must be notified to every person on whom a copy of the notice of the making of the order was served. (HA 80 Sch 6 para 4(3); TCPA 90 Sch 14 para 7(4).)

Seeking withdrawal of objections Since an authority's power to confirm unopposed orders extends to orders the objections to which have been withdrawn, it is clearly in the authority's interest to secure the withdrawal of the objections if possible. In any event, it is customary for there to be an exchange of views between the order-making authority and the objectors before an order is submitted to the Secretary of State. Such an exchange may lead to the authority agreeing to ask the Secretary of State to modify the order.

In such a case, objectors would be well advised not to withdraw their objections, as there is no guarantee that the modification will prove acceptable to the Secretary of State. However objectors can send a letter to the authority indicating that the order will be acceptable if modified as proposed, but that, if the modification is not acceptable to the Secretary of State, they would wish to be heard in opposition to the order.

Submitting the order to the Secretary of State for confirmation
Once the order and objections are submitted to the Secretary of State the power of decision passes to him. If a county or district council enters an objection to an order, the Secretary of State is obliged to hold a public inquiry. (HA 80 Sch 6 para 2(2); TCPA 90 Sch 14 para 3(2).) In other cases he may deal with the order by holding a public inquiry, by arranging a hearing or by written representations.

If he chooses to deal with it by written representations each party is invited to comment on the other's case, and an inspector makes a site inspection before a decision is made.

Proceedings at public inquiries are dealt with in chapter 5.2.5 below. Hearings are similar to public inquiries, but are more restricted in that no public notice is given and the right to be heard is normally limited

5 : CHANGES TO THE NETWORK

to the authority and anyone who lodged an objection during the objection period. However, witnesses may be called, so an objector may be able to call as witnesses at a hearing people who would have spoken at a public inquiry if one had been held. See also chapter 5.6.

5.2.5 Procedure at public inquiries

The legal background Under HA 80 s 302 the Secretary of State may cause such inquiries to be held as he may consider necessary or desirable for the purposes of his functions under the Act. In certain cases, normally when a local authority objects to a proposal, an inquiry is obligatory. Any inquiry, whether obligatory or discretionary, is governed by LGA 72 s 250 (p 311). That section does not prescribe the publicity to be given to inquiries, which is at the discretion of the Secretary of State. In practice, he normally gives the inquiry the same publicity as was given to the making of the order.

Similar powers to hold inquiries are contained in other Acts, for example in TCPA 90 s 320 (p 438). The provisions of LGA 72 s 250 normally apply also to such inquiries. For inquiries held under TCPA 90 additional provisions apply: see TCPA 90 s 321 (p 438).

There are no rules for most inquiries into orders that affect rights of way; the inspector has complete discretion in his conduct of the inquiry, so long as it follows the rules of natural justice. In practice most inquiries follow the order set out below.

Copyright is not infringed by anything done for the purposes of the proceedings of an inquiry. (Copyright, Designs and Patents Act 1988 s 46.)

Location and timing The location and date of an inquiry is decided by the Department of the Environment. Although the Department will normally notify an objector in advance that it has decided that an inquiry will be held, it does not consult the objector to ensure that the date will be one on which he may conveniently attend. If, therefore, an objector is notified of an inquiry to be held on which he will be unable to attend he should make immediate representations to the Department for a change of date.

In choosing a location the Department is normally advised by the local authority. Normally a local village hall is used if one is available. Again if the chosen location appears unreasonably remote from the order path or inconvenient for objectors or their witnesses representations should be made to the Department.

Those representations should not be left until the opening of the inquiry; once an inspector has opened an inquiry he will wish to complete it expeditiously, and he is in any case not responsible for prior arrangements. The arrangements for a public inquiry have to meet the needs of all parties; attempts to alter them should therefore be made only when there is good reason for so doing.

The inspector The inspector is appointed by the Secretary of State to make an independent assessment of the merits of the order in question. Currently most are drawn from the Lord Chancellor's Panel of Independent Inspectors.

It is the inspector's job to conduct the inquiry or hearing and to ensure that all those who wish to be heard are heard, to make a site visit, with or without the objectors present, and thereafter, unless the order is one for which the Secretary of State has retained jurisdiction, to issue a decision letter (see chapter 5.2.6 below). Inspectors are given general guidance by the Secretary of State: a handbook for inspectors has been deposited in the House of Commons Library.

When the Secretary of State is exercising jurisdiction, the inspector will submit a report to him. This will include conclusions and a recommendation in place of the decision in the above list. The Secretary of State then issues a separate decision letter, which includes the inspector's conclusions and recommendation, and indicates whether the Secretary of State has decided to accept the recommendation.

Inspector's introduction and appearances The inspector introduces himself and cites his authority. He then asks who wishes to be heard and makes a list of their names and the organisations (if any) which they represent. Any objectors wishing to speak at the inquiry should say so at this point. The order of appearances will then be determined. If an objector has to leave early, he can ask to be heard out of turn; such requests are normally given sympathetic consideration. The inspector will also ask if the press are present and take details of any representatives.

Seating arrangements Inspectors are required to ensure that all parties to an inquiry have equal facilities. If those that have been provided appear unequal, or unsatisfactory to, say, objectors, the inspector's attention should be drawn to this, and a remedy sought, before the inquiry proper commences.

The case for the order-making authority The inquiry proper begins with the authority which has made the order stating its case. The authority's representative, usually a solicitor, will introduce the order and explain the authority's reasons for making it. He will then call and examine a witness from the authority, and may call others such as the owner or occupier of the land crossed by the path.

These witnesses may well make statements, copies of which should be made available to objectors. If they are, they should be obtained. If they are not made available, the inspector should be asked to tell the authority to produce copies, as they will prove useful to objectors conducting cross-examination.

5 : CHANGES TO THE NETWORK

Objectors are entitled to cross-examine any witness. This power should be used. It can be a very useful way for the objector to make his points, since the witness has to reply. If the reply is unconvincing, it will help considerably to make the objector's case. Cross-examination must be undertaken by asking questions of the witness.

If there have been problems on the path, eg obstructions or no maintenance, and these have been reported to the council with no effect, then its representative can be asked why this was so. If the authority claims that there has been little or no use of the path, it should produce evidence in support of its claim.

The advocate for the authority cannot be cross-examined, but the inspector can be asked to put a question to him if a remark he made, eg in introduction, has not been covered in the evidence of witnesses and needs to be challenged. When an objector presents his case, he is entitled to refer to remarks made by the authority's advocate.

The case for supporters of the order Individuals or organisations wishing to express support for the order are normally heard after the order-making authority has presented its case. Witnesses, or anyone giving evidence, may be cross-examined by objectors.

The case for the objectors Guidance on how to prepare and present a case is given in chapter 5.6. If an objector calls a witness, the witness should make a statement. It is preferable if this can be in writing, with copies provided for the inspector and the authority; if the inspector does not have to make notes he will be able to concentrate better on the evidence. The objector can ask questions of the witness, for example to reinforce points made in the statements or to draw out any matters which may have been overlooked, and which have arisen during the presentation of the authority's case.

The authority (and any supporters of the order) may cross-examine any witnesses called by an objector. It may not question an objector directly as advocate, but if he himself gives evidence, he may be cross-examined on it. The inspector is entitled to ask him questions about anything he has said. An objector may re-examine a witness about matters raised in cross-examination, but may not introduce any new matter when re-examining.

Closing statement by the order-making authority After the objectors have presented their cases, the authority makes a closing statement. This may refer, and reply, to points made by the objectors, but no new material may be introduced, since the objectors would have no opportunity to comment on it.

Closing of the inquiry and the site visit The inspector then closes the inquiry and announces that he will be issuing a decision letter or writing a report for submission to the Secretary of State. He also fixes a time (normally later that day) and meeting place for the site visit with the parties concerned. He will normally travel to and from the site on his own or with representatives of both sides. The site visit is worth attending, since it affords an opportunity to show the inspector points raised at the inquiry. No new matter may be raised by any party on a site visit. Inspectors often make an unaccompanied site visit before an inquiry.

Application for costs There is a power in LGA 72 s 250(5) for the Secretary of State to make an award of costs against any party to an inquiry. This power is, in practice, exercised only when there is an application by one of the parties, and then only when the Secretary of State is satisfied that the party against whom the award is sought has behaved unreasonably, vexatiously or frivolously. If one of the parties wishes to make an application for costs, it should do so before the formal close of the inquiry. A party other than the order-making authority should refer to its intention to apply when making its case for, or against, the order; the inspector may ask that the formal application be presented at the end of the inquiry. Any party against whom costs are sought will have the right of reply to the application. The power to recover costs was extended by s 42 of the Housing and Planning Act 1986 (p 406) and by TCPA 90 s 322 (p 438). A landowner who objects successfully to a public path creation order will normally be awarded costs. (DOE Circular 2/87 — p 507.)

The Secretary of State's decision on an application for an award of costs is conveyed to the parties in a decision letter.

5.2.6 Decision and confirmation

Once the inspector or Secretary of State has made his decision, his decision letter is sent to the order-making authority and to the objectors. For most cases handled by an inspector the decision letter is issued within two months of the inquiry, hearing or site visit.

A typical decision letter issued by an inspector will include the following headings:
General description of the order path and surroundings
The case for the order-making authority
The case for the objectors
Findings of fact
Conclusions
Decision

The authority must then publish and serve notice of the outcome. It must also publish and serve notices when it makes a decision on an unopposed order.

5 : CHANGES TO THE NETWORK

If the order is confirmed without modification The authority must serve notice on every person on whom a copy of the notice of the making of the order was served. Notices need not be sent if the person concerned has not asked for notice of confirmation and indicated the address to which such notice should be sent. Notices sent to owners and occupiers, and to other councils, must be accompanied by a copy of the confirmed order. Notice must also be published in the local press and put on site.

If the order is confirmed with modification Notice must be published and served as when the order is confirmed without modification, but in addition persons or organisations other than owners and occupiers who were sent a copy of the made order have to receive a copy of the confirmed order. Thus a prescribed body such as the RA has to be sent a confirmed order only if it has been confirmed with modifications: in other cases the order will be unchanged from that which was sent with the notice of making of the order.

If the order is not confirmed Notice must be served on all those on whom notice of the making of the order was served (the proviso does not apply), but need not be published in the press or put on site.

5.2.7 Modification

Modifications made by the Secretary of State to orders fall into two classes: those which affect land not affected by the made order (and these require special notice — see below), and those which do not.

What constitutes 'land not affected by the order as submitted' has not been considered by the courts, but is normally considered to be anything other than a minor alteration of a proposed diversion. The Secretary of State may not modify an order so as to divert or close any part of a path not affected by the order as made. He may, however, modify an order so that it diverts or extinguishes a lesser length of a path. In such a case he need not give notice of the proposed modification, since it does not affect other land.

He also takes the view that he has no power to modify an order so as to correct defects in its wording. (Circular 1/83, Annex B, para 9.)

Modifications requiring notice to be given If it is necessary for the Secretary of State to give notice, how he does so is left to his discretion. In practice, he issues a first decision letter giving advance warning of the proposal and also sends the formal notice of the proposed modification to everyone receiving the letter. In addition, he gives notice in the press, on the path and on council notice-boards, just as notice was given of the made order. A period of 28 days is normally allowed for objections.

RIGHTS OF WAY

Before making a decision on the proposed modification, the Secretary of State is required to consider any objections. He does so as he considers objections to orders, ie by holding an inquiry or hearing, or by written representations.

After hearing the objections he may decide that his proposed modification itself needs modifying, in which case the process is repeated, although this is a rare occurrence. He may also decide that the modification should not after all be made, and that the order should be either confirmed without modification or not confirmed.

When he makes his decision on the proposed modification, he issues a decision letter. The procedures for giving notice described in chapter 5.2.6 above then apply.

5.2.8 Coming into operation

There is a difference between the way changes which involve the creation of a new right of way (eg creations and diversions), are implemented in practice according to whether they are made under the Highways Act or the Town and Country Planning Act.

Under the Highways Act The highway authority must carry out any works necessary for the physical creation of the new path, or to arrange with the order-making authority to do so. This duty is contained in HA 80 s 27 (p 319), and is applied to new paths created by diversion orders by virtue of s 119(9).

The highway authority has no power to enter on land before the right of way exists legally, hence the provision in s 119(3) for the date on which the existing path is extinguished to follow the date on which the new path is created so as to allow time for the works to be carried out.

Two legal rights of way therefore exist during the overlapping period, even though in practice only one may be usable. At the end of the period the existing path will cease to be a right of way, and the owner of the land over which it runs will be free to exclude the public from it. It is thus essential that the newly-created path is available for public use by that date.

An order under the Highways Act is so worded that the period within which the new path must be made usable starts on confirmation of the order. If the order is unopposed, the order-making authority can choose when to confirm the order, and can, if it wishes, time that so as to be convenient for the works. But if the order is opposed, the date of confirmation will be that of the inspector's decision letter, a date which may not be convenient to the authority. It is thus important that the order provides ample time for any necessary works to be undertaken.

Under the Town and Country Planning Act Construction of the new path will be part of, and therefore linked to, the process of carrying

5 : CHANGES TO THE NETWORK

out the associated development. The developer is expected to carry out the physical construction of the new path, after which either the order-making authority or the highway authority has to certify that the new path has been constructed to a satisfactory standard. Upon that certification the order comes into operation.

Thus, if the certificate is never issued, whether because the construction is unsatisfactory or because the development has not been proceeded with, there is no legal change to the right of way, even though there is a confirmed order.

If the notice of confirmation does not give a specific date on which the order will become operative, the authority must publish a notice in at least one local paper when it does come into operation. (TCPA 90 Sch 14 para 8 — p 444.) The need for this further notice is that instances have occurred where an order has been confirmed, but the works needed to create the new path have never been carried out. The order has therefore never come into operation, although the public notice (of confirmation) would have given the impression that a legal change to the right of way had taken place.

Amending the definitive map and statement It is important to remember that the 'event' connected with an order which gives rise to the need to modify a definitive map and statement is its coming into operation, not its confirmation. As soon as reasonably practicable after an order has come into operation the surveying authority must make a modification order to amend the map and statement to show the change which has taken place. (WCA 81 s 53(2) & 53(3)(a) — p 379.)

The need for a separate modification order arises because the description needed in a path order for a change to a path will not be the same as the amendment needed to the definitive map and statement. Copies of any such modification orders must be kept with the definitive map for public inspection. (WCA 81 s 57(7) — p 383.)

5.2.9 Application to the High Court

Once a decision has been made to confirm an order, either by an authority or by the Secretary of State, the only way in which its implementation can be prevented is by an order of the High Court.

Application for such orders can arise through either of two different processes. The first is an application for judicial review of a decision of the Secretary of State to confirm the order. Such application has to be made not later than three months after the date of the decision letter: further details of the procedure are given in chapter 6.13.1.

The other course of action arises from the statutory provision of a six-week period following publication of the notice of confirmation, during which time application may be made to the High Court for the order to be quashed on the grounds that it is not within the powers of the relevant section of the Act or that the prescribed procedures have not been followed. Provision for such application is made in HA 80 Sch 2, as applied by Sch 6 para 5 (p 362), and also in TCPA 90 s 287 (p 437).

This procedure was used by the RA in 1981 when Newbury DC published notice of confirmation of a public path extinguishment order without having previously published notice of its making and thereby invited objections. As the RA had indicated in earlier consultations that it would object if an order was made, the only way closure of the path could be prevented was by application to the High Court. This was done; the DC agreed that the order should be quashed and that it should pay a proportion of the RA's costs. If action is not taken within the six-week period, the order becomes immune from legal challenge.

If the authority or the Secretary of State decides not to confirm the order, judicial review may be sought of that decision. This was the course followed in the *Stewart (Dorset)* and *Cheshire CC* cases (see chapter 5.3.1 below).

5.2.10 Subsequent variation or revocation

Orders may subsequently be varied or revoked by further orders made under the same procedures, with the same rights of objection. (HA 80 s 326 — p 356; TCPA 90 s 333(7) — p 439.) The powers are used only rarely. An order revoking a diversion order under HA 80 s 119 or extinguishment order under HA 80 s 118 would have the effect of re-creating the former path — presumably compensation would be payable under s 28 as applied by s 121(2) as if the path were being created where none had previously existed.

5.2.11 Charging applicants

The 1980 and 1990 Acts do not specifically provide for such an applicant to be obliged to pay the costs of making and publicising the order and of any subsequent public inquiry. There is a general power in LGA 72 s 111(1) for an authority to do anything calculated to facilitate, or be conducive or incidental to, the discharge of any of its functions, but this has been held by the House of Lords not to permit a planning authority to charge a developer a fee for a consultation meeting to discuss a possible planning application. *(R v London Borough of Richmond upon Thames, ex parte McCarthy & Stone* (1991).) It therefore appears that this power may not permit charging of applicants for public path orders. In practice many authorities do charge applicants a fee.

The Local Government and Housing Act 1989, section 151, empowers the Secretary of State to make regulations to prescribe charges for local authority services. In late 1990 the Department of the Environment issued a consultation paper on proposals to require charges to be levied on most applicants for public path orders, but at the time of writing no regulations had been laid before Parliament.

5 : CHANGES TO THE NETWORK

5.2.12 Compensation

There is provision in HA 80 s 28 for the payment of compensation to anyone who is able to show that the value of his interest in land is depreciated, or that he has suffered damage by being disturbed in his enjoyment of land as a consequence of a creation order. Compensation may also be payable consequent on the coming into operation of diversion and extinguishment orders, to which the provisions of s 28 are also applied by s 121(2). Applicants for diversion orders may be required to agree to defray any compensation which becomes payable.

Claims for compensation must be submitted within six months of the coming into operation of an order (s 28(2) and Regulation 16 of the Public Path Orders Regulations) and any dispute as to the amount of compensation payable is adjudged by the Lands Tribunal (s 307(1) — p 353).

There is no provision for compensation for orders under TCPA 90 s 257. As noted in chapter 5.2.8 above, the section provides for a developer to construct the new path — he is therefore assumed to own or control the land over which it will run.

5.2.13 Procedure for Secretary of State's orders

There are certain variations to the above when the Secretary of State makes an order, ie for those orders referred to by 'SOS' in the list in chapter 5.1.3.

Firstly, the terminology is different. When an authority *makes* an order a decision is then made either to *confirm* or not to confirm, whether that decision is made either by the authority or by the Secretary of State. But if the initiative comes from the Secretary of State, he *proposes to make* an order, at which stage notice is given and objections invited, and then *makes*, or decides not to make, the order.

Secondly, notification to prescribed bodies does not occur, except where the Secretary of State uses his power under HA 80 s 120 to make a public path order. Instead, notice of the proposal is normally published in the *London Gazette* as well as in the local press, although for certain orders (see chapter 5.3.8) publicity is entirely at the Secretary of State's discretion.

5.3 Changes using the administrative procedure

5.3.1 Public path extinguishment orders

Legislation
Grounds — HA 80 s 118 (p 335)
Procedure — HA 80 Sch 6 (p 363)
Compensation — HA 80 s 28 (as applied by s 121(2)) (p 320)
Regulations — Public Path Orders Regulations (p 460)

RIGHTS OF WAY

Advice
Circular 1/83, Annex B, paras 31-33 (p 495)
Consultation Code of Practice (p 512)

A council can have only one reason in law under s 118 for making a public path extinguishment order, and that is that it appears to it expedient on the ground that the path or way is not needed for public use. However, a slightly different test of expediency has to be applied, both by the council and by the Secretary of State, when considering the confirmation of an order, namely that it is expedient to do so having regard to the extent to which it appears that the path or way would, apart from the order, be likely to be used by the public and having regard to the effect which the extinguishment would have on the land crossed by the path.

Circular 1/83, Annex B, para 31 advises authorities making orders which entail the closure of part only of a path or way to take care to avoid creating a cul-de-sac in the remaining part of the path or way.

The tests to be considered These two tests, and the distinction between them, were considered by Mr Justice Phillips in *R v Secretary of State for the Environment, ex parte Barry Stewart* (1980). In this case Mr Stewart was the owner of a property through which ran a footpath shown on the definitive map, although he disputed that it should be so shown. He persuaded his local Borough Council to make an extinguishment order, but the Secretary of State refused to confirm it. Mr Stewart then applied to the High Court for an order of *certiorari* (p 218) to quash the Secretary of State's decision.

The first ground on which he sought to quash the order was that the Secretary of State had said in his decision that he could not be satisfied that the path was not needed for public use, which was the test to be applied by the authority making the order, not by the Secretary of State. Mr Justice Phillips said that the correct test was that contained in subsection (2); he interpreted it to mean that confirmation was not necessarily ruled out by the fact that the path was, or was going to be, used to something more than a minimal extent. The Secretary of State could therefore confirm an order if he thought that, despite the fact that a path was likely to be used, it was not needed, as for example, there was an equally convenient path nearby. However, the test concentrated on use as being the prime consideration, although the use of the word 'expedient' meant that, to some extent, other considerations could be taken into account. His approach to the interpretation of subsection (2) was adopted by Mr Justice Auld in *R v Secretary of State for the Environment, ex parte Cheshire CC* (1990).

'Temporary circumstances' affecting use of the way The other ground on which relief was sought was that the Secretary of State and

5 : CHANGES TO THE NETWORK

the inspector had erred in law in holding that an electricity substation, a pine tree with a trunk girth of approximately 2ft 6ins at its base and a laurel hedge 4ft wide and 12ft high were capable of constituting 'temporary circumstances' preventing or diminishing the use of the path and which they were therefore required to disregard (subsection (6)). Mr Justice Phillips dealt with this matter at considerable length; extracts from his judgment are set out below:

'The expression "temporary circumstances" entitles one to have regard to a wide variety of considerations, but obviously the prime question is, in the case of an obstruction, whether it is likely to endure. Now it may, by its nature, be temporary, or it may, by its nature, seem to be permanent; but if it appeared, in the case of what seemed to be a permanent obstruction, that it was likely to be removed, I ... see no reason why it could not be regarded as temporary ... It seems to me that it would be quite intolerable in the case of an admitted highway in the form of a public path for it to be accepted as a good ground for stopping it up that encroachments and obstructions had made it difficult to say precisely to within a yard or so where it ran. It seems to me the objections are those which I have mentioned earlier, that is to say, that to allow such a ground would be an encouragement to those who improperly obstruct the highways.

'Well now, what is the situation where you have an obstruction? It seems to me that shrubs and the hedge and the tree are really "temporary circumstances". There is a highway there; either they obstruct it or they do not. If they do not, it is nothing to the point. If they do, it seems to me that determined members of the public, or relevant associations, will have no problem in taking the correct steps to have them removed.

'Well, what about the substation? The information is sparse. There is no reason to suppose that it is very large and no doubt it is of the ordinary kind that one sees in such positions. Again, the situation is that it is either obstructing the line of the path or not. If it is not, it does not matter. If it is, it seems to me to be impossible for there to be any justification for it remaining where it is. Then again, while I do not go so far as to say that these matters are irrelevant when considering section 110, I would have thought that they could be of only the most marginal importance.'

The appeal was dismissed, and no order for *certiorari* granted. The reference to section 110 in the judgment is a reference to section 110 of the Highways Act 1959, which was superseded by HA 80 s 118.

It is submitted that, following this judgment, virtually all obstructions should be regarded as temporary, and should be disregarded, for the purposes of s 118. The problem facing an inspector conducting an inquiry is how to assess what the use of the path or way would be if the obstructions were removed. The problem facing objectors in such a case is how to persuade the inspector that the use would be such as to justify refusal to confirm the order. The more people who can be persuaded to indicate, either by appearance at the inquiry, by writing a letter or by signing a petition, that they would use the path or way if it were freely available, the stronger the case that can be mounted.

Effect of the extinguishment on land served by the right of way
In *R v Secretary of State for the Environment, ex parte Cheshire CC* (1990) Mr Justice Auld held that the reference in subsection (2) to the effect which the extinguishment would have as respects land served by the right of way was 'clearly directed to the consideration of adverse effects from extinguishment on nearby landowners who derive a benefit of one sort of another from the use of the footpath'.

5.3.2 Public path diversion orders

Legislation
Grounds — HA 80 s 119 (p 335)
Procedure — HA 80 Sch 6 (p 363)
Making-up of new path — HA 80 s 27 (as applied by s 119(9)) (p 319)
Compensation — HA 80 s 28 (as applied by s 121(2)) (p 320)
Regulations — Public Path Orders Regulations (p 460)

Advice
Circular 1/83, Annex B, paras 34–36 (p 495)
Consultation Code of Practice (p 512)

A council may make an order to divert a public path if satisfied that it is expedient to do so either in the interests of the owner, lessee or occupier of the land crossed by the path or way in question or that it is expedient in the interests of the public. However, that apparently simple test of expediency is, rightly, complicated by other considerations and restrictions contained in s 119.

Diversion of the ends of the path The first of these concerns the ends of the path which is being diverted. Subsection (2) prevents the diversion of the end of a path if it is not on a highway (eg when a path leads to the top of a mountain or to the sea-shore). If the path does end on a highway, it may be diverted only to a point which is on the same, or a connected, highway and which is substantially as convenient to the public.

It is submitted that this means that, if a path terminates on a main road and another path leads off nearby on the other side of the road, the termination of the first path should not be moved further away from it by a diversion.

5 : CHANGES TO THE NETWORK

Other tests The second is that, by virtue of subsection (6), a diversion order may not be confirmed, either by the Secretary of State or by an authority, unless he or they, as the case may be, is satisfied that the path or way will not be substantially less convenient to the public as a result of the diversion and that confirmation is expedient having regard to the effect of the diversion on public enjoyment of the path or way as a whole, and on land crossed by the existing path or to be crossed by the new one. (See also Circular 1/83, Annex B, para 35.)

Although these tests are, according to the Act, to be applied only at the confirmation stage, it would clearly be nonsensical for a council not to take them into account before deciding whether to make the order in the first place. It is submitted that, therefore, diversion orders should seek to ensure a balance between, on the one hand, the interests of the public, as users and, on the other, the interests of the owner, lessee or occupier of the land.

This does not mean that orders can only be made where there is a clear advantage to the owner etc, and not too much disadvantage to the public; orders can be made in the interests of the public, and can and should be made where the public will benefit. The owner, lessee or occupier of the land crossed by the existing path or that crossed by the proposed path has the right to object, and also to claim compensation if injuriously affected by the new path, just as if it were a creation order (s 28 applied by s 121(2)); but he has no power of veto.

It is further submitted that the 'substantially as convenient' test in this subsection and the 'not substantially less convenient' test in subsection (6) differ materially, in that the former test requires the new point of termination to be at most only marginally less convenient, whereas the latter allows a greater degree of inconvenience, albeit not a substantial one.

Conditions and limitations Subsection (4) of section 119 allows conditions or limitations to be placed on the public's rights over the new right of way being created by the order, even if no such limitations or conditions apply to the existing right of way. If the new path or way is to pass over a stile or through a gate, the landowner's right to erect that stile or gate is a limitation on the public's right and should be recorded in the order. If it is not recorded, the limitation does not exist, and any stile or gate will be an obstruction unless separately authorised under s 147 (see chapter 6.7.2).

Costs and compensation The legislation on diversion orders differs from that on creation and extinguishment orders in providing for orders to be made on the representations of an owner, lessee or occupier, and for him to be required to agree to pay the expenses of the physical works needed to create the new path, and also any compensation which may be claimed.

RIGHTS OF WAY

What if the existing path is obstructed? A criterion laid down in s 118 (see above) is that temporary circumstances preventing or diminishing the use of path by the public shall be disregarded when assessing whether or not the path is needed for public use. Such a criterion does not appear in s 119, but the issue nonetheless often arises, in a case where the existing path cannot be used because of obstructions and, often, where the proposed new line of the path has already been made available. How does one assess the relative convenience to the public of the two alternatives when the issue has apparently been prejudiced in this way?

It is submitted that the highway authority should be assumed to have carried out its duties to maintain the existing path and keep it free from obstruction, and that therefore the 'temporary circumstances' criterion can be read into s 119. Some authorities require rights of way to be free from obstruction before they will make diversion orders, so that the public can judge properly the merits of the proposed change.

5.3.3 Public path creation orders

Legislation
Grounds — HA 80 s 26 (p 318)
Procedure — HA 80 Sch 6 (p 363)
Making-up of new path — HA 80 s 27 (p 319)
Compensation — HA 80 s 28 (p 320)
Regulations — Public Path Orders Regulations (p 460)

Advice
Circular 1/83, Annex B, para 30
Consultation Code of Practice (p 512)

In addition to having powers to create public paths by agreement (see chapter 3.4.2), local authorities also have power, under s 26, to do so by creation order. It is not a prerequisite for the making of such an order that an authority should have sought, and failed, to make an agreement.

Before making an order, the authority must consult the other local authorities, but there is no requirement to consult anyone else. In particular there is no requirement to consult the owners and occupiers of the land.

The authority must be satisfied that it is expedient that a path should be created. In considering the matter it must have regard to the extent to which the path or way would add to the convenience or enjoyment of a substantial section of the public, or to the convenience of persons resident in the area. It must also have regard to the effect which the creation would have on the rights of persons interested in the land, and in so doing should take into account the provisions in s 28 under which

5 : CHANGES TO THE NETWORK

compensation may be payable. It must also have regard, by virtue of HA 80 s 29 (p 320), to the needs of agriculture and forestry.

If the authority wishes to impose any limitations or conditions on the right of way to be created, it must specify these in the order, as it must for diversion orders.

As the statistics on p 122 show, the power to make creation orders is not as widely used as the corresponding powers to divert or close paths. The statistics also suggest that relatively few new paths are created by agreement, but, as there is no requirement to notify the RA and OSS of such agreements, as distinct from orders, the statistics may not be comprehensive.

Provision is made in s 27 for ensuring that paths created by agreement or order are created physically as well as legally (and see chapter 5.2.8 above). For compensation which may be payable see chapter 5.2.12 above.

5.3.4 Concurrent orders under the Highways Act 1980

Section 118(5) and Sch 6 para 3(2) allow extinguishment orders to be considered concurrently with creation or diversion orders. They also allow regulations to be made to set out the procedure to be followed (see Regulation 11 of the Public Path Orders Regulations — p 461).

These provisions may allow a change to be made if the other order-making powers on their own are insufficient. For example, if the proposed alternative to a path fails to satisfy the criteria in section 119(2) for the terminal points of a diversion, concurrent creation and extinguishment orders may be made. Or, if an authority wishes to try to divert two paths on to the same new line, it could make concurrent diversion and extinguishment orders, diverting one path on to the new line and closing the other.

The legislation does not require one order to be dependent upon the other. If they are not so drafted, there is the possibility that, say, a creation order might be objected to, but not the concurrent extinguishment order. The latter could be confirmed as unopposed, leaving the public with no path. If orders are not worded so as to make confirmation of one dependent upon confirmation of the other, an objection should be lodged.

A further use to which concurrent orders have been put is in downgrading bridleways to footpaths. Although this can be achieved by an application to a magistrates' court for an order under s 116 (see chapter 5.4.1), there is no equivalent power to downgrade in s 118. The only way of bringing about such a change by orders which can be considered at a public inquiry is to make an extinguishment order for the bridleway and a concurrent creation order for a new footpath over the same line. There is no need to make concurrent bridleway creation and footpath extinguishment orders in order to convert a footpath into a bridleway;

either a creation order or an agreement to create a bridleway on the line of the path will suffice, with the former being preferred since it allows the public to object.

Section 118(5) provides that where an extinguishment order is being considered concurrently with a creation or diversion order, then, in considering the extent to which the path the subject of the order would be likely to be used by the public (s 118(2)), the Secretary of State (or his inspector) may (but not must) have regard to the extent to which the creation or diversion order would provide an alternative path or way.

It is submitted that, in such a case, the wording of the section means that the inspector must first consider the creation or diversion order on its own merits, ie ignoring the extinguishment order, and, if he is satisfied that it should be confirmed, take its prospective confirmation into account in his consideration of the extinguishment order. The reference in subsection (5) to subsection (1) means that the order-making authority should undertake a similar consideration of the proposals before it decides to make the order.

5.3.5 Rights of way affected by development

In this section we consider paths affected by development, but not where the development is the construction of a new road (see chapter 5.3.7). For development on defence land there is separate legislation (see chapter 5.4.3), although the provisions of TCPA 90 ss 247 and 257 can be, and sometimes are, used in such cases.

Development and planning permission Development is defined by TCPA 90 s 55 (p 430) as 'the carrying out of building, engineering, mining or other operations in, on, over or under land, or the making of any material change in the use of any buildings or other land' subject to a number of exclusions detailed elsewhere in the section. Section 57 requires, again subject to certain exceptions, that planning permission must be obtained before development can be carried out. However s 59 empowers the Secretary of State to make orders either to permit classes of development without the need to apply for planning permission (a General Development Order), or to grant permission for specific development (a Special Development Order).

An application for planning permission is made to the district or London borough council. After the application for planning permission has been made, it is entered in the authority's planning register (TCPA 90 s 69): this is open for public inspection. Some authorities also publish lists of applications in the local press.

The application is sent by the authority to other relevant authorities for their comments, and sometimes also to voluntary organisations. In such cases only a short period, eg 14 days, is normally allowed for

5 : CHANGES TO THE NETWORK

comments, as planning authorities are expected to decide applications within eight weeks.

Although all applications in non-metropolitan counties are made to district councils, some (principally those seeking permission for mineral working) are decided by the county council. In a national park, the park authority acts as the planning authority and therefore decides planning applications. Urban development corporations, enterprise zone authorities and housing action trusts can also be planning authorities with power to grant planning permission and make consequential orders under the 1990 Act.

A planning application may seek permission in one of two forms: outline or detailed. Outline permission means permission granted with the reservation that certain matters not included in the outline permission (referred to as 'reserved matters') must be approved at a later date before development can start. The approval of the reserved matters is the same as the granting of detailed planning permission.

'Reserved matters' are commonly access to the proposed development, its design and the materials to be used. An application for outline permission usually contains as a minimum the proposed use (eg housing development, golf course, quarry), the location of the site and the proposed density; it often also includes a layout and the proposed access. If the application contains all the necessary information the authority may grant detailed permission.

The effect of planning permission on rights of way The granting of outline or detailed permission or approval of reserved matters does not constitute permission to close or divert a public right of way affected by the development. Some authorities have taken the step of including a standard note to this effect on the form notifying an applicant that permission has been granted.

The authority for such closure or diversion of a right of way is granted by an order under s 247 or 257 of the 1990 Act — see chapter 5.3.6 below. Most orders under sections 247 and 257 arise from planning permission granted by the local planning authority. But the granting of planning permission does nevertheless have an impact, even if indirect, on the right of way, since the permission will be prayed in aid in support of any proposed closure or diversion.

Anyone learning of proposals to develop land crossed by a public right of way should therefore inspect the planning application, consider what effect the development will have on the right of way and make appropriate representations to the planning authority.

Planning authorities are, however, encouraged by the DOE (in para 14 of Circular 1/83) to consider giving publicity to such applications. In February 1992 the government announced that from 4 May 1992 local planning authorities woud have to publicise such applications by means of newspaper advertisements and site notices.

RIGHTS OF WAY

Conditions on planning permission In some cases authorities have sought to prevent the carrying out of the development affecting a right of way before it has been legally diverted or extinguished. In Circular 1/83, paragraph 14, the Secretary of State took the view that such a condition was both unnecessary and unreasonable.

However, in *Grampian Regional Council v City of Aberdeen District Council* (1984), the House of Lords decided that a condition requiring the stopping up of a highway (under the Scottish equivalent of TCPA 90 s 247) before development could proceed was reasonable, Lord Keith of Kinkel expressing the view that the relevant section was 'entirely general and apt to favour strongly the reasonableness of negative conditions relating to the closure of highways in all appropriate cases'. The issue in the case was safety at a junction some distance from the development, not a right of way across the site.

As a result of the case the DOE issued Circular 1/85, paragraph 34 of which (p 496) accepts that a condition prohibiting development until a right of way has been diverted or extinguished (a 'Grampian condition') may in some cases be appropriate. Although the circular refers to action by the highway authority, orders under s 257 are normally made by the planning authority, which in the non-metropolitan counties is not normally the highway authority. In the absence of a Grampian condition, a planning authority will have to rely on the exercise by the highway authority of its powers to deal with nuisances and obstructions (see chapter 6). The new power given in 1990 by the Rights of Way Act to highway authorities to deal with unauthorised disturbance of the surface of rights of way (HA 80 s 131A and Sch 12A) should be useful in taking action against developers who interfere with rights of way.

The interference by development with rights of way and the failure by planning authorities and developers to consider them properly in relation to development proposals, have caused continuing concern. These problems are referred to in DOE Circular 1/83 para 14 (p 483) and in a letter sent by DOE to planning authorities in 1987 (p 511). In 1989 the RA published a leaflet *Who needs a hole in the wall?* aimed at persuading developers to take proper account of rights of way in preparing their proposals.

5.3.6 Orders under the Town and Country Planning Act 1990

Legislation
Grounds — s 247 (p 430), s 257 (p 435)
Procedure — s 252 (p 433), Sch 14 (p 440)
Regulations — Town and Country Planning (Public Path Orders) Regulations (p 453)

Advice
Circular 1/83, Annex B, paras 23-25 (p 494)
Consultation Code of Practice (p 512)

5 : CHANGES TO THE NETWORK

As noted above, the granting of planning permission for development of land over which there is a public right of way does not itself constitute authority for interference with the right of way or for its closure or diversion. This applies equally to development authorised by a special planning zone. (DOE Circular 25/87 — p 508.)

Powers are, however, granted to planning authorities (in respect of footpaths and bridleways) and the Secretary of State (in respect of all highways, including footpaths and bridleways) to make orders under TCPA 90 ss 247 and 257 to stop up or divert highways affected by development which is permitted under the General Development Order or for which planning permission has been granted, or is not needed, eg for development by a government department or in an enterprise zone. The Secretary of State may, in certain circumstances, publish notice of a draft order before planning permission has been granted. (S 253 — p 434.)

Procedure Orders under s 257 follow the procedure described in chapter 5.2 above. Orders under s 247 follow the broadly similar procedure in s 252. The orders may provide for the stopping-up of a footpath or bridleway without replacement, for the diversion of a path or way to a new line, or for the stopping up of the path or way subject to the provision of an alternative path. An alternative path, unlike a diversion, does not have a terminus on the original path.

The test to be applied As has been confirmed in recent cases (see below), the power of confirmation is discretionary: it is not obligatory to confirm an order even if the development affects the line of the path or way. Circumstances in which non-confirmation might be justified include those in which a path or way proposed for stopping-up could instead be diverted, or in which a proposed diversion is not the most suitable and modification of the order is not possible.

The Secretary of State has no power to amend a planning permission so as to facilitate what the objectors to an order claim to be a preferable diversion, and inspectors are advised not to allow objectors to seek to re-argue the merits of a development for which planning permission has been granted.

In *K C Holdings (Rhyl) Ltd v Secretary of State for Wales* (1989) it was held that under s 209 of the 1971 Act (now TCPA 90 s 247) there was a discretion to consider the merits and demerits of the proposed closure of a footpath in relation to the particular facts that obtain. The judge, Sir Graham Eyre QC, rejected the contention that once the Secretary of State was satisfied that the development could be carried out only if the footpath was stopped-up he was obliged to confirm the order.

In *Vasiliou v Secretary of State for Transport* (1990) the Court of

Appeal held that the Secretary of State had to take into account the effect that an order would have on those entitled to the rights which would be extinguished by the order, especially as the section contained no provision for compensating those so affected.

What if the path has already been built over? Although, as noted above, the granting of planning permission does not authorise interference with rights of way, such interference does occur from time to time. A question that then arises is whether the making of an order under ss 247 or 257 has been precluded. This was considered by the Court of Appeal in *Ashby & Dalby v Secretary of State for the Environment* (1980), a case brought by the RA. The Court held that orders could be made so long as some of the authorised development remained to be carried out, but if it had been completed, the powers in the 1971 Town and Country Planning Act corresponding to those in TCPA 90 sections 247 and 257 could not be used.

If an order is made under HA 80 s 118 to deal with the problem, the *Stewart* case (p 138) will apply, and the obstruction caused by the development must be disregarded in assessing whether the path is needed for public use.

If an order is sought in the magistrates' court under HA 80 s 116 (see chapter 5.4.1), the case of *R v Thames Justices, ex parte London Borough of Tower Hamlets* (1982) will apply. In that case Mr Justice Forbes said that a magistrates' court's jurisdiction to hear an application for an extinguishment or diversion order under s 116 was not ousted by the fact that development of the land over which the highway ran had been completed. But, in considering whether to make an order, the magistrates would have to look at the situation prevailing at the time of the hearing and decide, in the light of circumstances as they then existed, whether the old highway was unnecessary. Such circumstances would include the extent to which, if any, the old highway was already blocked up and the extent to which, if any, adequate alternative highways had been provided.

5.3.7 Other developments: roads, reservoirs, mines and airports

Roads New roads are proposed either by the Secretary of State, if a trunk road, or by the highway authority. Outline proposals for new roads are to be found in their respective published plans. There is usually extensive consultation about the route of a new road before its line is fixed: this consultation gives an opportunity to consider the effect the proposals will have on rights of way, and to make representations if necessary.

On roads other than motorways, pedestrians and horse-riders are allowed, although they may be excluded by a traffic regulation order; the plans for a new or improved road often propose that walkers and

5 : CHANGES TO THE NETWORK

riders should cross on the level, with stiles or gates in the road-side fencing. Although this may appear preferable to the closure of the path, the safety problems in crossing a road designed for fast-moving traffic may mean that in practice users will be deterred, and a bridge or underpass should be pressed for.

On motorways, pedestrians and horse-riders are not allowed, and footpaths and bridleways which cross their line have to be either closed or taken above or below by a bridge or underpass. Often a path or way is proposed for diversion alongside the motorway to cross it at a point where a road or accommodation crossing is already being provided. Such a diversion can be both circuitous and unpleasantly noisy, but users may find that they have to argue strongly for a separate crossing on or close to the line of the existing rights of way. Similar problems also arise with proposals for new roads which are not motorways.

Side roads orders Most orders stopping-up or diverting paths in connection with road schemes are made under HA 80. Section 18 (p 316) allows for a side roads order to be made for a special road (motorway), and s 14 allows (p 316) for similar orders to be made for a trunk or classified road. Orders for most motorways and all trunk roads are made by the Secretary of State: a few motorways are promoted by highway authorities who, in such cases, make orders under s 18. They also make orders under s 14 for schemes affecting classified roads. If a highway authority makes an order under either section, it has to be confirmed by the Secretary of State. The procedure is in HA 80 Schs 1 and 2 (p 359 & 362).

Side roads orders can stop-up, divert, raise, lower, or otherwise alter any highway that crosses or enters the route of the new road, or will be otherwise affected by its construction or improvement. But no order which stops up a highway may be made or confirmed by the Minister unless he is satisfied that another reasonably convenient route is available or will be provided before the highway is stopped up.

The meaning of 'reasonably convenient' in this context has not been considered by the courts. It is submitted that the convenience is that of the users of the highway proposed for stopping-up, not that of the authority proposing the new road, and that cost is therefore not a relevant issue. It is also submitted that factors to be taken into account in assessing the convenience of a proposed alternative include its length (and therefore the time taken to use it) and the prospective enjoyment of its users. For example, if, as is often the case, the proposed alternative runs alongside what will be a busy road, the impact on people out for a country walk of the noise, fumes and visual intrusion of the traffic are relevant factors.

Use of the powers in TCPA 90 New roads may also be constructed, or existing roads improved, under planning powers. In such cases

TCPA 90 s 248 (p 431) provides for orders to be made by the Secretary of State to authorise the stopping up or diversion of any highway which crosses or enters the route of the highway which is being constructed or improved, or which is, or will be, otherwise affected by the construction or improvement of a highway.

The Secretary of State has to be satisfied that it is expedient to make the order in the interests of the safety of users of the highway which is to be constructed or improved or to facilitate the movement of traffic along that highway. The provisions which govern the procedures for orders under s 247 apply also to orders under this section.

Reservoirs Section 155 of the Water Act 1989 (p 419) allows the Secretary of State to make orders on behalf of water undertakers and the National Rivers Authority to enable them to carry out works and, incidental to those works, to stop-up or divert public rights of way. Public notice of the proposal has to be given as set out in Sch 20 to the Act, including a plan showing the effect the order sought would have on any footpath or bridleway, and inquiries may be held by the Secretary of State into objections.

The Water (Compulsory Works Powers) (Notice) Regulations 1991 require notice of any application for a draft order which would authorise the stopping-up or diversion of a footpath or bridleway to be given to the bodies prescribed in them: these are the same bodies as are listed in Sch 5 to the Public Path Orders Regulations 1983 (p 471). By virtue of Sch 20 para 5(1)(b)(i) to the 1989 Act notice of any made order will also have to be served on the prescribed bodies.

Mines Major developments for mining and quarrying are approved through the planning procedure, and orders to close or divert paths permanently are made under TCPA 90 ss 247 or 257. However, a temporary order may be made under TCPA 90 s 261 (p 436) if minerals (including coal, sand and gravel) are to be obtained by surface working and if the highways can be restored after the working to a condition not substantially less convenient to the public. An order under s 261 may stop-up or divert a highway for a considerable period of time.

For opencast coal mining carried out by British Coal, special provision is made in the Opencast Coal Act 1958. Sections 15 and 15A of the Act (p 297) allow the Secretary of State to suspend a non-vehicular right of way (ie a footpath or bridleway) if planning permission has been granted for opencast mining in the land over which the path or way runs and if he is satisfied that a suitable alternative will be made available by British Coal or that such an alternative is not required.

The Opencast Coal Regulations 1987 (p 475) prescribe the notices to be given when orders are applied for and made.

5 : CHANGES TO THE NETWORK

Airports Section 48 of the Civil Aviation Act 1982 (p 392) empowers the Secretary of State for Transport to stop-up or divert any highway if satisfied that this is necessary in order to secure the safe and efficient use of land for civil aviation purposes. The land has to be owned or proposed to be acquired by the Secretary of State or the Civil Aviation Authority. Orders under this section are subject to special parliamentary procedure, which gives objectors a chance to take their case to a parliamentary committee, rather as with Private Bills (see chapter 5.4.2), provided that they can prove *locus standi* (right of audience) if necessary. But the usual process of giving notice of the proposal, allowing objections, and possibly holding an inquiry into those, still applies (Statutory Orders (Special Procedure) Act 1945, as amended); only when that has been completed does the Parliamentary process begin.

Section 59 of the Airports Act 1986 (p 405) applies section 48 of the 1982 Act to land vested in, or proposed to be acquired by, any 'relevant airport operator' to whom the other provisions in the Act apply.

The existence of these sections does not mean that all proposals to close and divert highways as a result of proposed airport development are made under them. The proposal to develop Stansted Airport as the third London airport was made by way of an ordinary planning application; associated with it were draft orders made by the Secretary of State under the predecessor section to TCPA 90 s 247 to stop-up and divert various highways.

5.3.8 Land held for housing and planning purposes

Generally Two statutes provide for the extinguishment of rights of way over land held by local authorities for purposes connected with development. TCPA 90 s 251 (p 432) allows the Secretary of State to extinguish any public right of way, and s 258 (p 436) allows a local authority to extinguish any footpath or bridleway, over land which has been acquired or appropriated for planning purposes and is for the time being held by the authority for those purposes. The procedure for an order under s 251 is as for s 247 and for an order under s 258 the same as under s 257 (see chapter 5.3.6 above).

But before making an order the Secretary of State or the local authority, as the case may be, must be satisfied that an alternative right of way has been or will be provided or that such an alternative is not required. Since the local authority owns the land it has power to dedicate an alternative right of way if it wishes. 'Planning purposes' are defined by reference to s 246(1)(b) of the Act, which in turn refers to an authority's power of acquisition under other provisions of Part IX of the Act. Essentially that power is to acquire land in its area which is suitable for, and is required in order to secure, development, re-development or improvement, or which is required for a necessary purpose in the interests of the proper planning of the area.

RIGHTS OF WAY

Under s 32 of the Acquisition of Land Act 1981 (p 375) an authority acquiring land by compulsory purchase order may make an order extinguishing any footpath or bridleway across that land, but it must be satisfied that an alternative right of way has been or will be provided or that such a way is not required. The section also applies to land which the authority is proposing to acquire by compulsory purchase and to land acquired by agreement but which could have been acquired by compulsory purchase. Section 32(7) precludes the use of s 32 orders where TCPA 90 s 251 or 258 can be used.

The procedure to be followed in the making of such orders is that set out in HA 80 Sch 6 (p 363) for public path orders under HA 80, ie it is the administrative procedure described in chapter 5.2. The form for orders and notices under s 32 is prescribed in the Public Path Orders Regulations (p 460): see in particular regulations 17 to 20 and Sch 3.

Urban development corporations and new towns The Secretary of State also has power to make orders to extinguish any highway over land vested in, or acquired by, an urban development corporation or highway authority for the purposes associated with such a corporation. (Local Government, Planning and Land Act 1980 Sch 28 para 11 — p 374.) He has a similar power in respect of land vested in, or acquired by, a new town development corporation. (New Towns Act 1981 s 23 — p 377.) Public notice of the Secretary of State's proposal to make an order under either of these sections is given in whatever manner he deems requisite. (Sch 28 para 11(2) to the 1980 Act; s 23(2) of the 1981 Act.) In practice he gives a notice similar to that for other orders he might propose to make, ie in the local press, on the paths concerned, and in the *London Gazette*.

The sections provide only for the extinguishment of rights of way. There is no power to make diversions, although in practice orders often mention alternative routes. However, the Secretary of State has no power under s 23 to require a development corporation to dedicate and provide these physically. Since the only ground needed to justify making an order is that the land is owned by the development corporation or highway authority and is being held for new town or urban development corporation purposes, the public is given little scope to argue the merits of retaining the right of way. In practice, the Secretary of State will normally allow a development corporation's proposals to be examined at an inquiry, but successful objections to such proposals are rare.

Housing action trusts Similar powers are contained in Schedule 10 to the Housing Act 1988 (p 411), under which a housing action trust may apply to the Secretary of State for an order extinguishing a right of way.

5 : CHANGES TO THE NETWORK

Slum clearance areas Finally, s 294 of the Housing Act 1985 (p 405) empowers a housing authority (district or London borough council) to extinguish any public right of way over land acquired or proposed to be acquired by the authority for the purpose of slum clearance, subject to approval by the Secretary of State. The procedures to be followed are specified by regulations. As none have been made under the 1985 Act, nor were any made under its predecessor (s 64 of the Housing Act 1957), those made under the original section (s 46 of the Housing Act 1937) remain in force. These, the Housing Act (Extinguishment of Public Right of Way) Regulations 1937, require notices in the local paper and on site, and a period of at least six weeks for objections.

5.4 Changes using other procedures

5.4.1 Applications to the magistrates' court

Section 116 of the Highways Act 1980 (p 333) allows application to be made by a highway authority to a magistrates' court for an order to stop-up or divert any highway other than a trunk road or special road.

An order under s 116 may stop-up a highway either completely or subject to the reservation of a footpath or bridleway. It can thus be used to remove vehicular rights from a way while keeping it open for riders and walkers. It can also be used to downgrade a bridleway to a footpath, but this can also be achieved by concurrent creation and extinguishment orders — see chapter 5.3.4. It is possible for an order both to downgrade a way by extinguishing some of the rights and to divert it to a new line.

Section 117 (p 334) empowers anyone to apply to the highway authority for it to make application to the magistrates' court. The authority may require such an applicant to agree to meet some or all of the costs of the court application.

The notice that must be given Notice of any proposed application to a court must be given, under HA 80 Sch 12 (p 370), in the *London Gazette*, in a local paper and on the path or way concerned. It must also be served on adjoining landowners.

Subsection (6) obliges the magistrates to be satisfied that there has been compliance with these requirements. In *Ramblers' Association v Kent CC* (1990) this obligation, and the requirements, were considered in detail. It was held that the obligation was mandatory, and that the court therefore had no power to dispense with it.

It was held further that the requirement to place a notice on the path or way concerned meant that the notice had to be placed at the ends of that part of the path of way affected by the application. If no such notice was placed, that was sufficient to deprive the court of its jurisdiction to hear the application, but if there was physical difficulty in placing the notice precisely at the required location, it was sufficient for there to have been substantial compliance with the requirement.

It was also held that the notice must be accurate. A reference to an application for 'stopping-up and diversion' when no alternative right of way was to be provided was sufficient to deprive the magistrates of their jurisdiction.

The notice on the path or way must 'embody' a plan showing the effect of the order which is being applied for (Sch 12 para 1). The meaning of 'embody', in relation to s 116, has not been considered by the High Court, but on three occasions (Worcester in July 1978, Winchester in July 1980 and St Albans in May 1981) Crown Courts have held that it means that a plan should be displayed on the site, and that simply to refer in the site notice to the availability of a plan for inspection in council offices did not satisfy the requirements of the Act.

The meaning of the requirement that the plan must show 'the effect of the order' has not been considered by the courts. Clearly, if the order applied for is a diversion order, the plan should show the line of both the existing highway and the new one, and, if part of the new line is along an existing highway, the status of that highway should be shown, eg if the diversion of a footpath would necessitate extra road walking, that fact should be evident from the plan. But what of an extinguishment order? It is submitted that the effect of the order is to require anyone who would have used the highway in question to use an alternative route, and that alternative ought to be shown on the plan, so that anyone inspecting the plan can judge whether the existence of the alternative could be said to render unnecessary the highway threatened with closure.

The local and district councils' powers of veto Before making an application for an unclassified road, bridleway or footpath, the authority must, under subsection (3), give notice of the proposed application to the district council, and to the parish or community council or chairman of the parish council. Any person or council receiving such a notice may, within two months of the date of service of the notice, veto the proposed application.

This veto is a powerful weapon in the hands of parish and community councils. Its potential use may encourage an authority to use s 118 or 119 rather than s 116.

Grounds for extinguishment The ground under which applications and orders may be made to extinguish is that the way is unnecessary. The meaning of 'unnecessary' was considered by the High Court in *Ramblers' Association v Kent CC* (1990). It was held that the magistrates would need to bear in mind that the way had to be unnecessary for the

5 : CHANGES TO THE NETWORK

public; the convenience of the landowner was not a relevant factor. It was held further that the absence of the test of expediency to be found in s 118 was relevant, Lord Justice Woolf saying that where there was evidence of use, it would be difficult for the magistrates properly to come to the conclusion that a way was unnecessary unless the public were, or were going to be, provided with a reasonably suitable alternative way.

In deciding whether an alternative way was reasonable, it had to be a way which was suitable, or reasonably suitable, for the purpose for which the public were using the existing way. Mr Justice Pill added that it was not open to the magistrates to decide that a way was unnecessary because they held the view that it was in the public interest that the highway should be closed.

Grounds for diversion The ground under which applications and orders may be made to divert is that the new route will be nearer or more commodious to the public. Whether it is nearer is a straightforward matter of fact. In the case of *Gravesham BC v Wilson and Straight* (1983) Mr Justice Woolf held that 'commodious' in s 116 had to be given its ordinary and natural meaning: 'a flavour of convenience, roominess and spaciousness' which also included a flavour of utility. The commodiousness is that of the public; the convenience of landowners is not relevant.

The hearing in the magistrates' court Objection to an application has to be made at the hearing, the time, date and place of which must be specified in the public notice of the application. This requires attendance in court, which in itself is sufficient to deter some people who would be prepared to attend a public inquiry. In addition magistrates' courts appear to have discretion to refuse to allow organisations to be represented by someone who is not legally qualified, so if a local society wishes to oppose an application in the magistrates' court, it is advisable that the person representing it should be prepared to do so as an individual objector if the court will not allow him to appear on behalf of the society. However, such practice is by no means universal, and courts can be, and often are, helpful to the objector who is not, or is not represented by, a lawyer. Witnesses may be called both by the applicants and by the objectors; they will be subject to cross-examination.

The court is not obliged to explain its decision on the application; it is rare for reasons to be given in the detail to be found in a decision letter following a public inquiry. However, in *Ramblers' Association v Kent CC* (1990), Mr Justice Pill said that where magistrates held that a way was unnecessary he would expect them to give reasons for their finding upon a case being stated for the opinion of the High Court. It is submitted that a similar reasoning would apply to a decision on an application for a diversion order.

Appeal to Crown Court Section 317 of the 1980 Act (p 354) gives a right of appeal to the Crown Court against the decision of the magistrates' court to anyone who was, or claimed to be, entitled to be heard at that court. A right of appeal is also given to the authority applying for the order, so a successful objector may find himself faced with an appeal by the highway authority to the Crown Court.

Even if he then takes no part in the Crown Court proceedings, which are essentially a rehearing of the case, he may still be liable to costs in that Court. No specific rule applies to such costs, but the Court may find a parallel in rule 10(3)(b) of the Crown Court Rules 1971, which provides that in a liquor licensing case no order for costs shall be made against a person who appeared before the licensing justices and opposed the grant of the licence, unless he also appeared at the hearing of the appeal in the Crown Court and opposed it.

Appeal to the High Court There is a right of appeal to the High Court from a decision of the magistrates' court by way of case stated, but only on a point of law. This was the action taken by Gravesham BC in the *Gravesham* case and by the RA in the *Kent CC* case. If the authority chooses to question the magistrates' decision by appeal to the High Court by way of case stated, it is again the successful objectors rather than the magistrates who are faced with a potential bill for costs, as Mrs Wilson and Mrs Straight found in the *Gravesham* case in 1983. Fortunately for them, they had appeared in the magistrates' court on behalf of the RA, which organisation naturally backed their (successful) defence of the council's challenge.

An outmoded relic from the past? The RA and OSS have long considered that the involvement of the magistrates' courts in decisions of changes to the rights-of-way network is a historical anomaly which should be removed. The government proposed in 1985 a reform of the law which would have excluded footpaths and bridleways from s 116, but this has been neither pursued nor officially abandoned.

Although the Secretary of State has advised authorities that they should employ powers that are available other than under section 116 unless there are good reasons for not doing so (DOE Circular 1/83, para 21), his advice is not binding on authorities.

The procedure has several defects. The prospect of appearing in court is a deterrent to potential witnesses; the prospect of facing costs if an objection is lodged to a s 116 application is very worrying to small and relatively impoverished organisations concerned about the proposals of a highway authority backed by public funds; there is no requirement on magistrates to give reasons for their decision. All these are reasons why the use of the powers should be kept to a minimum, and why district and local councils should be willing to use their power of veto.

5 : CHANGES TO THE NETWORK

5.4.2 Private and Local Acts of Parliament

Changes to the rights-of-way network may also be brought about by Acts of Parliament. These can be either Private Acts, promoted by a body such as British Rail, or Local Acts promoted by and applying to the area of a local authority. A Private Act is likely to affect specified paths, whereas a Local Act could, for instance, introduce special local procedures for closing and diverting paths.

Outside Greater London, all the local legislation inherited by the new county councils in 1974 expired at the end of 1986 (LGA 72 s 262 as amended) unless the provisions had been re-enacted by a new Act in the meantime. This provision required the new county councils to look at their local legislation and modernise any that was still needed. No county now has any local power to close or divert rights of way permanently, although in Greater Manchester there is a power to do so temporarily for land-reclamation purposes. A similar power exists in Lancashire for the purposes of land-reclamation and associated waste-disposal.

Since many authorities inherited powers, mainly acquired in the nineteenth century, for closures and diversions with little or no scope for the public to object, the present situation is a considerable improvement, brought about by the activities of the OSS and RA.

All Private and Local Bills have to be deposited in Parliament at the same time in the year (late November). There is a formal process of objecting to such Bills by way of petition against them, but a petitioner needs *locus standi* (right of audience). The promoter of a Bill may challenge a petitioner's *locus*. The Standing Orders of the Houses of Parliament grant a right of audience on a petition to societies, associations or other bodies sufficiently representing amenity, educational, travel or recreational interests whose petition alleges that the interests they represent will be adversely affected to a material extent by the provisions contained in the Bill. The RA, OSS and other bodies have used this provision to enter petitions against Private Bills in recent years; their right to do so has not been challenged.

The Standing Orders also require (through an amendment made after representations by the RA) that notice of any Bill that seeks to stop-up or divert a specific path or way be posted in a prominent position at the ends of the part of the path or way concerned not later than 20 November in the year of the Bill's introduction. But the Standing Orders do not require notice to be posted on the path or given to the surveying authority when a power in a Private Act to change a right of way is exercised.

In November 1991 the government introduced in Parliament the Transport and Works Bill, a measure to create new order-making procedures to remove the need for Private Bills in most cases where such Bills at present affect specified rights of way.

RIGHTS OF WAY

5.4.3 Rights of way over military land

Defence Act 1842 and Defence Act 1860 The only power to close paths without anyone being given an opportunity to object belongs, perhaps not surprisingly, with the Secretary of State for Defence under s 16 of the Defence Act 1842 (p 286) and s 40 of the Defence Act 1860 (p 287). It is compulsory under the former provision (see s 17), but merely optional under the latter, for an alternative path or way to be provided.

As there is no requirement in either section to give public notice of the change, it is possible that we not are aware of all the use made of these powers. But as far as we know, only the 1842 Act has been used in recent times. It was used in February 1985 to divert a bridleway along the perimeter of the Molesworth airfield, Cambridgeshire, when the airfield was extended to site cruise missiles, in October 1985 to divert a footpath which ran across the USA government's communications base at Menwith Hill, North Yorkshire, and in 1990 to divert the end of a cul-de-sac bridleway at RAF Upper Heyford, Oxfordshire.

Military Lands Act 1892 The other statutes enabling changes to paths on military land are s 13 of the Military Lands Act 1892 (p 288) and s 8 of the Land Powers (Defence) Act 1958 (p 297). The 1892 Act applies the magistrates' court procedure in HA 80 s 116 (see chapter 5.4.1) to footpaths (but not bridleways) which cross or run inconveniently or dangerously near to any land leased under the Act. Although the magistrates' court must be satisfied that a convenient new path will be made, no appeal may be made to the Crown Court on this point.

Land Powers (Defence) Act 1958 The 1958 Act applies TCPA 90 powers (see chapter 5.3.6) if land is, or is to be, used by a Secretary of State for defence purposes, or used by a manufacturer of aircraft wholly or mainly for defence purposes. 'Defence purposes' are defined in s 25 (p 297). The Secretary of State has to be satisfied that the highway must be stopped up or diverted to allow the land to be used efficiently without danger to the public. The 1958 Act was used in 1984 to close many rights of way across the Larkhill ranges in Wiltshire. A temporary order may be made under the 1958 Act.

5.5 Changes to permit or restrict vehicular use

5.5.1 Traffic regulation orders

Permanent orders County and metropolitan district councils have power, under s 1 of the Road Traffic Regulation Act 1984 (p 397), to

5 : CHANGES TO THE NETWORK

make traffic regulation orders. These orders are normally used to regulate motor traffic, eg through restrictions on parking, imposition of a speed limit or prescription of the direction in which traffic must go (one-way streets). However they can be applied to any road. 'Road' is defined by s 142 of the Act (p 404) as including any highway; it thus covers footpaths and bridleways.

Section 122 of the Act (p 403) places a duty on these authorities so to exercise their powers to make traffic regulation orders, both permanent and temporary, as to secure the expeditious, convenient and safe movement of all traffic, including walkers, cyclists and horse-riders.

By s 2 (p 398) orders may restrict, prohibit or regulate the use of roads by traffic, which includes cyclists and walkers. But an order must not prevent access to premises by pedestrians (s 3 — p 399). If the road is a footpath, bridleway or byway open to all traffic (as defined in WCA 81 s 66), orders may, under s 127 of the 1984 Act (p 403), also regulate or prohibit use by horse-riders.

Contravention of an order is an offence (s 5 — p 399). This could produce a curious situation on a field-path where, if a traffic regulation order was in operation, use of the line of the right of way could render the user liable to a fine of up to £400, whereas to walk or ride a few yards away would be merely to risk an action for damages for trespass.

The grounds under which an order may be made are extensive, and are set out in subsections (1)(a)-(f). Orders are often made to prohibit cycling on footpaths, but only rarely for other purposes on rights of way. Section 22 of the Act (p 401) extends the grounds in certain areas of countryside.

The procedure for making orders is set out in the Local Authorities' Traffic Orders (Procedure) (England and Wales) Regulations 1989. For a traffic regulation order likely to be made on a footpath, bridleway or byway, this is as follows:

(a) The authority must consult with one or more organisations representing users of the road (unless it considers there are none) before making the order.

(b) Notice of the proposal to make the order must be published in a local paper and in the *London Gazette*, sent to consultees and, if the authority considers it desirable in the interests of giving adequate publicity to the order, placed on site.

(c) The order, a map showing its effect and the alternative routes for diverted traffic, and a statement of the authority's reasons for proposing to make it must be made available for public inspection during the objection period. That period must be at least 21 days after all the notices have been displayed.

(d) The authority must consider all the objections received and may hold an inquiry, although it is not obliged to do so. On making the order, it must notify objectors and publish further notices as

in (b), and make available documents as in (c), together with the report of the inspector if an inquiry was held, for six weeks from the date of the order.

Advice on the procedure was given to authorities in Department of Transport Circular 2/89.

Temporary orders Section 14 of the 1984 Act (p 399) empowers highway authorities temporarily to restrict or prohibit the use of any road (defined as above) either because of works being executed on or near the road or because of the likelihood of danger to the public. The classes of users who may be restricted or prohibited by a temporary order are the same as for permanent orders.

If the authority knows in advance of the need for the order, it must publish, under Sch 3 to the 1984 Act (p 404), notice of its intention in the local press not less than seven days before making the order, and must also within seven days of its making give notice of that fact. There is no specified procedure for objections, but this does not preclude anyone aggrieved by the first notice making representations to the authority, or his councillor. The notice must contain a statement of the effect of the order and give details of the alternative route to be followed.

Such an order may last only for three months (s 15(1) — p 400), unless the Secretary of State agrees to an extension, when it may be continued for as long as he sees fit. There is no set procedure for making application to the Secretary of State, and no requirement for the public to be notified of the application, nor for the Secretary of State to consult the public before making a decision.

A restriction or prohibition may be imposed at any time, without warning, if it appears necessary to the highway authority (s 14(3)), but such a notice can last only for two weeks. (S 15(5).) An emergency notice posted under s 14(3) can be converted into an ordinary temporary restriction without a published notice of the intention to do so. (Sch 3 para 3(2).)

In either case notices must also be put on the road concerned, and must be kept there in a conspicuous position while the prohibition lasts. The requirement to keep notices posted is essential, since to contravene such a temporary restriction is an offence. (S 16 — p 400.)

The powers in s 14 have been used on a number of occasions where the RA has felt that the grounds in the section did not justify it, eg during droughts, mock battles and golf tournaments. However we know of no case where a walker or rider has been prosecuted for contravention of a temporary closure order.

The Road Traffic (Temporary Restrictions) Act 1991 will, when brought into operation, amend s 14 to extend to six months the period for which a temporary traffic regulation order may be made for a footpath, bridleway, byway open to all traffic or cycle track. Any exten-

5 : CHANGES TO THE NETWORK

sion to that period will, as at present, require the approval of the Secretary of State. Prescription by regulations of the procedural requirements will replace Sch 3 to the Act.

5.5.2 Cycle Tracks Act conversion orders

A footpath (a right of way on foot only) may be converted into a cycle track (a right of way on foot and on a pedal cycle) by means of a conversion order made under s 3 of the Cycle Tracks Act 1984 (p 393). A right to use a pedal cycle on a footpath may also be conferred by converting it into a bridleway by means of a creation agreement or order under ss 25 or 26 of the Highways Act 1980, but this would also give equestrians the right to use it.

The Cycle Tracks Regulations 1984 (p 472) specify the procedure to be followed when conversion orders are made. It is essentially the standard procedure (see chapter 5.2 above), though without notification to prescribed bodies. However, there is a requirement to consult (Reg 3) and anyone so consulted must be notified of the making of the order (Reg 4(d)). Department of Transport Circular Roads 1/86 (p 497) describes the provisions of the Act and Regulations in detail, and advises local authorities on use of the powers.

Widespread conversion of footpaths to cycle tracks was not envisaged when the Act was passed by Parliament, and has not occurred. The requirement to obtain consent for conversion of any path across agricultural land gives landowners a right to veto conversion of rural paths. (S 4 — p 395.) Compensation is payable if damage is caused by conversion work, or if there is depreciation in the value of land as a result of a confirmed order. (S 5 — p 395.)

5.5.3 Extinguishment of vehicular rights

Section 249 of the Town and Country Planning Act 1990 (p 432) permits the Secretary of State to make an order extinguishing vehicular rights over a highway on application by a local planning authority. Before applying to the Secretary of State the authority must both adopt by resolution a proposal for improving the amenity of that part of its area which includes the highway, and consult the highway authority (if different) and any other authority which is also a local planning authority for the area.

The procedure to be followed by the Secretary of State is set out in s 252 (p 433), and is described in chapter 5.2.13 above.

This section contains three special features. Firstly, there is a specific power (ss (6)) to revoke an order, such revocation to have the effect of re-creating the vehicular right of way. In other words, the effect of an order is to suspend vehicular rights for an indefinite period rather than extinguish them permanently. Nevertheless it is submitted that any way converted by a s 249 order will have become a footpath or bridleway as defined by WCA 81 s 66 and, as such, should be added to the definitive map and statement by means of a modification order made under s 53(3)(a) of the 1981 Act.

Secondly, subsection (1) refers to the public 'ceasing to have a right of way with vehicles'. Before conversion, the way will be a right of way for vehicular and all other kinds of traffic, including those using the way on horseback. Extinguishing vehicular rights will not affect the equestrian rights, and it is therefore difficult to see how the resulting way can be anything other than a bridleway, although the section does not specifically describe the resulting way as a bridleway.

Thirdly, the order also provides for certain categories of vehicle to be allowed to continue to use the way (subsection (3)).

Advice on use of the section was given in Department of Transport Circular Roads 13/71 on Pedestrianisation. This indicated that the primary use of the section was expected to be for pedestrianisation schemes. The section is often used to close off a short length of side road at a junction with a main road so as to create a cul-de-sac. There appears to be no reason why the section should not be used also in rural areas where exclusion of motor vehicles would, in the view of the local planning authority, improve the amenity of the area.

5.6 How to oppose a path order

The following notes give guidance to anyone who is opposing a public path order on the matters to be considered before an inquiry is held and on the points to be included in an inquiry statement. The form of the inquiry proceedings is dealt with in chapter 5.2.5.

If the objection is dealt with by written representations most of the points below apply. In addition there will be an opportunity to consider, and comment upon, written statements made by the authority in support of the order.

Steps (a),(b),(c) and (d) can be used to decide whether to object to an order. If there is not enough time to make a full assessment before the closing date for objections, a holding objection may be lodged. This can later be withdrawn should a decision be made not to object, but such a decision should not be unduly delayed.

Checking the order The following steps are recommended:
- (a) Check the terms of the order very carefully and ensure that it complies with the legal requirements, eg that facts such as path lengths and directions are correctly stated, and that the section of the Act under which the order is made is correctly cited.
- (b) Obtain a copy of the report considered by the authority's committee when it decided to make the order. From this it will be possible to find out whether the committee was given a proper

5 : CHANGES TO THE NETWORK

assessment of the tests to be applied, under the statute, to the proposal.

(c) Make a full survey of the existing path and prepare a detailed description covering length, width, whether enclosed by hedges, walls or fences, nature of surface, liability to wetness, existence of obstructions, barbed wire, overgrowth, etc. If a diversion is proposed, try, if permission can be obtained from the owner or occupier to walk the new route, to make an assessment of it covering the same points. If confirmation of the order will mean more walking along a bridleway, try to assess its likely condition after wet weather. If it will mean more walking or riding along a road note the distance along the road, assess the width of the road and the existence of a footway or margins, the traffic conditions and sightlines, etc. If it will result in the loss of a view which can only be enjoyed from the existing path, include this in the statement. If the path links with others to form a network, assess the effect the order will have on those links and therefore that network.

(d) Check that notice of the order was published as required by the Act under which it was made and that the requisite time was allowed for objections. If the local newspaper in which the order was published has only a limited circulation in the parish concerned and is not the paper which is best known there, make a point of this in the statement.

(e) Check that the statutory notices and plans were posted at the appropriate points on the path at the proper time and whether they were replaced if damaged or removed during the objection period.

(f) Try to find out whether there are other objectors and discuss the order with them. However, there is no legal requirement which obliges either the order-making authority or the DOE to make available details of the other objectors. If it is the policy of the authority that orders which are opposed are referred back to committee, the objections should be 'background papers' which are open to inspection (see chapter 1.3.7) and details of objectors obtained from them.

(g) Obtain as much information as possible about the use of the path, both by local residents and others. Consult the local council and any local society, residents association, Women's Institutes, etc. The local pub may offer an opportunity to obtain information from the landlord or his customers.

(h) Check whether a map of the public paths in the parish is on public exhibition anywhere locally, or is otherwise readily available for consultation, and that it is accurate. Every local council clerk should have in his possession a copy of the definitive map for his parish.

(i) Find out when the first Ordnance Survey maps at 1:50,000 (or one-inch) and 1:25,000 scale showing the path as a public right of way were published. In many areas rights-of-way information, derived from definitive maps, has become available for the first time within the last five years at 1:25,000 scale, the only scale at which both field boundaries and rights of way are shown.

(j) Try to obtain at least one local witness who can give evidence of use of the path over a considerable period and can be relied upon to give straightforward and relevant answers under examination and cross-examination. An excited, timid or incoherent witness can do more harm than good.

(k) Obtain as much information as possible about the previous history of the path and any complaints of obstruction or intimidation by the landowner or occupier. Check any local guidebooks or path maps, parish histories, inclosure awards, etc for any mention of the path.

Preparing the statement Compose a statement covering the above points, and have it typed and copied. For the inspector and the press, the statement should be one side only of the paper for easy reference. It is also an advantage to use double spacing. Number the paragraphs, do not make them too long, and use paragraph headings where appropriate. Remember that questions may be asked, by the inspector or the representative of the order-making authority, about anything in the statement; every point made must be accurate and capable of substantiation.

The following order is recommended for an objector's statement, equally for an inquiry, hearing or written representation:

(a) Brief introduction identifying the objector and, if he is appearing on behalf of an organisation, giving his position in that organisation, followed by a brief paragraph setting out the objectives of the organisation, the work it undertakes and the number of members. A minute of the committee meeting authorising the objection should be produced. A few details of local activities may be quoted.

(b) Detailed reasons for the objection and a statement, with copies, of any correspondence with the authority about the path and the order.

(c) Reasons why it is considered that the order does not satisfy the grounds or tests or both defined in the Act.

(d) Brief description of the path concerned, saying how it fits into the local network and what is or has been its main use. If the order seeks to close or divert the path and has been prompted by complaints about problems, say so.

(e) Reference to any policy documents which have a bearing on the issue at stage, eg DOE Circulars, local or structure plans.

5 : CHANGES TO THE NETWORK

(f) Request that the inspector recommend or decide that the order be not confirmed or be modified, as appropriate.

If an objector is not the first to be heard, some of his points may already have been covered. If so, he should make clear his support for those, with emphasis on any of importance, but spend most time on matters not previously raised.

He should remember that anything he says or does at an inquiry as a representative of an organisation can help or hinder that body's image. It is essential to remain cool and collected at all times, whatever the provocation, and to put questions to witnesses calmly and politely. When addressing the inspector, it is customary to call him 'Sir' or her 'Madam'.

5.7 Temporary changes

Even a temporary diversion of a path or way must have some statutory authority if illegal obstruction to the public's right of passage is not to be caused. There are several statutes which provide such authority.

5.7.1 Major development

Major development can give rise to a need for temporary changes to rights of way. This need may arise because the construction work requires the existing route to be closed before the permanent replacement can be opened, thereby necessitating a temporary route. Provision for such temporary routes is often found in side roads orders, and in Private Acts of Parliament.

A change may also be temporary because the development is of limited duration. For example, opencast coal mining is followed by restoration of the land, and so the closure of rights of way is referred to in the Act as 'suspension'. There is a similar power under TCPA 90 s 261 to make temporary diversion or closure orders for working of other minerals (see chapter 5.3.7). Land being used for defence purposes for a limited period can also give rise to temporary orders under s 8 of the Land Powers (Defence) Act 1958 (see chapter 5.4.3).

5.7.2 Maintenance

HA 80 s 122 (p 339) authorises the temporary diversion of any highway on to adjoining land to facilitate works to repair or widen it. This section could apply if an eroded path was being restored. The section does not authorise interference with a dwelling or associated land or a tree nursery (subsection (3)). Compensation is payable if damage is caused (subsection (2)).

5.7.3 Animal and plant diseases

Section 23 of the Animal Health Act 1981 (p 377) empowers a Minister, or an inspector acting on his behalf, to make an order prohibiting entry to a place or area which has been notified as 'infected' by an animal disease, such as foot and mouth disease. The section has been supplemented by the Foot and Mouth Disease Order 1983 (p 471). An order under s 23 has the effect of prohibiting use of rights of way across the land.

Such a notification can only be made by the Ministry of Agriculture; there is thus no justification for farmers to take matters into their own hands and seek to exclude users.

Where an area has been declared infected, persons owning or having charge of animals may, under s 27 of the Act, exclude strangers from entering a building or enclosure in which there are animals, but users of rights of way do not count as strangers for this purpose.

Members of the OSS and RA and other users of rights of way have a good record for keeping clear of areas infected with animal diseases. They have often responded also to requests to keep away from areas adjoining those affected, even through they have been perfectly entitled to go there. If there is an outbreak of disease in or near an area in which a walk or ride is planned, the local office of the Ministry of Agriculture should be contacted for details of any orders which may have been made under s 23.

Following an outbreak of sugar-beet rhizomania in Suffolk in 1987 the government realised that it had no proper powers to restrict use of rights of way in such circumstances. As a result Parliament approved the Plant Health (Great Britain) Amendment Order 1989. This amends the Plant Health (Great Britain) Order 1987 to allow entry to 'premises', which includes land, to be prohibited by the Ministry of Agriculture in the event of an outbreak of rhizomania. In a debate on the 1989 order (First Standing Committee on Statutory Instruments, 24 May 1989) the government gave assurances that the powers would be used only to the extent that it was absolutely necessary to do so, and, in particular cases, that it would seek voluntary agreements with landowners for the provision of alternative routes.

5.7.4 Disturbance of a public path over agricultural land

Highway authorities have power under HA 80 s 135, as amended by the Rights of Way Act 1990 (p 342), to order the temporary diversion of a footpath or bridleway for up to three months if necessary to do so to permit an occupier of agricultural land to carry out an excavation or engineering operation which is necessary for the purposes of agriculture.

Such a diversion must be signposted throughout the authorisation period (subsection (4)); additional conditions may be imposed by the

5 : CHANGES TO THE NETWORK

authority to ensure the convenience of the public (subsection (3)(b)). Failure to comply with such conditions is an offence (subsection (6)), but only a local authority or local council may prosecute (subsection (7)).

5.8 Major changes to the network

5.8.1 Rationalisation schemes in Nottinghamshire and West Sussex

In the 1970s, two counties, Nottinghamshire and West Sussex, undertook county-wide rationalisation schemes, ie they sought to review the network of public rights of way in their areas and thereafter propose changes which would, in their view, improve the network. These schemes, sometimes called 'non-statutory reviews' to avoid any confusion with the statutory reviews of definitive maps undertaken under NPACA 49, were given practical effect by the making of creation, diversion and extinguishment orders under HA 80 and earlier legislation. The scale of change has been considerable.

In West Sussex, a 'non-statutory review' was begun in November 1969, before the definitive map had been completed for the whole of the county. The scope of the review included an inspection of all rights of way in the county (which at that time did not include the present Mid-Sussex District), and a listing of the works necessary to bring the paths up to standard with a commitment to carry out those works, except where a path change was proposed. It also included a 'rationalisation' scheme, for 'changes to the path network by way of extinguishments to reduce the total length, creations and diversions both to improve amenity for the public and to improve the use of the land'. Well over 2000 proposals were made for changes to the path network. About half were later the subject of orders, all but two of which were for diversion or extinguishment. A number of orders were abandoned or failed to be confirmed, but many became operative.

In Nottinghamshire, the first orders arising from the review were published in 1978, and many were confirmed, though the scale of change was far less than in West Sussex. The review covered about a quarter of the county and was then abandoned.

Although the courts have never been asked to judge such actions, the Commissioner for Local Administration has, and made the following comments (ref: complaint 1340 H, 7 December 1976): '... I understand that some county councils have undertaken "modification" programmes. The county council will no doubt consider whether or not the resources devoted to the necessary administrative work involved in such schemes would be better devoted to ensuring that the existing network of public paths is well maintained, signposted, waymarked and suitably drawn to the attention of walkers.'

5.8.2 Changing the rights of way network

In 1988 the Countryside Commission published a discussion paper *Changing the rights of way network* including a variety of proposals aimed at making changes to the network easier to obtain. The Commission's stated aim was to encourage 'fine-tuning' of the network rather than large-scale change, although it gave no indication of the scale of the change which it felt was needed. Its proposals were widely criticised by users and local authorities.

In *Managing rights of way: an agenda for action*, published in 1989, the Commission announced that it would not be pursuing the radical options it had floated, although it intended to continue exploring certain ideas with its partners.

6

Obstructions and other nuisances

6.1 What is an obstruction?

An obstruction of the highway is one form of public nuisance. A public nuisance is some matter that materially affects the reasonable comfort and convenience of a class of Her Majesty's subjects who come within the sphere or neighbourhood of its operation. To commit a public nuisance is a crime at common law.

With regard to the definition of an obstruction, in *R v Matthias* (1861) Mr Justice Byles said 'A nuisance to a way is that which prevents the convenient use of the way by passengers', and in *Seekings v Clarke* (1961) Lord Chief Justice Parker said 'It is perfectly clear that anything which substantially prevents the public from having free access over the whole of the highway which is not purely temporary in nature is an unlawful obstruction'. Thus for something to constitute an obstruction there does not have to be a complete blockage of the highway. Anything that impedes the existing legal access is an obstruction. For example, if the legal right of way is over a stile that is four feet high, and the height of the stile is raised to six feet, then there is an obstruction to the extent of the added two feet. (*Bateman v Burge* (1834).) If a fence or wall is erected, or a hedge planted, in such a way that the pre-existing width of a right of way is reduced, the fence, etc, constitutes an obstruction.

In *Durham CC v Scott* (1990) it was held that gates tied by twine to hedges held closed by a loop of twine and barring the entire breadth of a bridleway, being inconvenient to open, were an obstruction. In *Devon CC v Gateway Foodmarkets Ltd* (1990) it was held that supermarket trolleys left for the convenience of shoppers in a pedestrian precinct constituted an obstruction.

Placing barbed wire along the top rail of a stile, locking a gate (or securing it with string or rope so that the fastening cannot easily be undone), placing a post in front of a 'squeezer' stile to prevent sheep getting through, dumping rubbish, putting up an electric fence, erecting a building, extending the boundary of a garden, are all matters that may constitute an obstruction. Whether any matter legally constitutes an obstruction can only be finally determined by the court. In every case it would be for the court to decide whether or not a matter complained of did effectively impede free access along a highway. (*Nagy v Weston* (1965).)

The *de minimis* rule In coming to a conclusion the court would have regard to the maxim '*de minimis non curat lex*': the law is not concerned with trifles — sometimes referred to as the *de minimis* rule (for example, a street trader's stall, predominantly on private land, encroaching on a highway but not obstructing the free passage: *Pugh v Pigden* (1987)). In practice, if it appears to a highway authority that something is an obstruction, it acts on the basis that it is an obstruction. It will be for the person against whom action is taken to show, if he can, that the matter does not constitute an obstruction. (It has sometimes happened that this claim has succeeded on the ground that the matter complained of was too trifling or temporary in nature to be legally an obstruction.)

A crime under statute — section 137 of the Highways Act 1980
In addition to being a crime at common law (ie as a form of public nuisance), obstruction of the highway has been made a crime by statute. Section 137 of the Highways Act 1980 makes it an offence for any person, without lawful authority or excuse, wilfully to obstruct the free passage along a highway. Examples of lawful authority are the powers conferred by statute on a statutory undertaker, eg a water or gas undertaker, to dig up the road to install or repair pipes or cables, and on a highway authority to construct a cattle-grid (HA 80 s 82). Acquiesence by a highway authority in the existence of an obstruction (eg a fruit and vegetable stall) will not prevent the obstruction from being illegal. (*London Borough of Redbridge v Jacques* (1971).) Ignorance of the existence of a highway over the land is no defence. (*Welsh Aggregates Ltd v Clwyd CC* (1988).)

In the event of prosecution for an offence under the section it is necessary to show that each element of the crime as defined in the Act is present (eg that the obstruction was 'wilful'). The various matters that must be proved for a prosecution to succeed are considered in chapter 6.10.

6.2 The highway authority's duty to prevent obstructions

At common law a highway authority is under a duty to seek, prevent and remove obstructions. (*Bagshaw v Buxton Local Board of Health* (1875).) By statute, under s 130 of the Highways Act 1980 (p 339), highway authorities have two general duties:

(a) Under subsection (1) they must protect and assert the rights of the public to the use and enjoyment of the highways for which they are the highway authority.

6 : OBSTRUCTIONS AND OTHER NUISANCES

(b) Under subsection (3) they must prevent as far as possible the stopping-up or obstruction of those highways.

The nature of the duty under s 130 was considered in *R v Surrey CC ex parte Send Parish Council* (1979). While this case was about the special powers of a parish council the general principles concerning the duties under s 130 were considered by the judges.

A path ran behind a number of properties with large gardens. It was not shown on the definitive map but the evidence that it was a public footpath was very strong. Over the years some of the residents had extended their gardens, erected fences and generally obstructed the path so as to make it impossible to walk along unimpeded. Since 1969 various efforts had been made to persuade Surrey CC to exercise its powers under s 116 and s 124 of the Highways Act 1959 (now HA 80 s 130 and s 143) to secure the removal of obstructions. At one stage it seemed that the CC was doing so, as notices under s 124 were issued.

However, in the autumn of 1977, under pressure from landowners who had issued a writ seeking a declaration that the s 124 notices were invalid, the CC changed its mind and put forward proposals to stop up the existing path and replace it with an alternative. The Parish Council had by then exercised its powers under s 116(6) of the 1959 Act (now HA 80 s 130(6)). When the CC failed to take action, the Parish Council applied to the High Court for an order of *mandamus* to require the CC to carry out its obligation under s 116, namely to assert and protect the rights of the public to the use and enjoyment of the highway. The CC's defence was that it had a discretion in its compliance with the duty imposed by s 116 and that its proposals for a replacement path were a reasonable exercise of that discretion.

Lord Justice Lane commented on that argument as follows: 'It seems to me that the use of the word "proper" indicates that the local authority must have a discretion not only as to the form of the proceedings which they choose to take, for example, section 124 or an action in the Chancery Division — that is not in dispute — but also have a further discretion as to the way in which and the extent to which those proceedings ought to be prosecuted ... But then one asks oneself the next question: what are the limits of that discretion? Those limits must be culled from the words of the Act themselves. The local authority must at all times act with the object of protecting the highway and of preventing or removing any obstruction, and, more broadly speaking, of promoting the interests of those who enjoy the highway or should be enjoying the right of way and the county council must likewise operate against the interests of those who seek to interrupt such enjoyment of the highway.'

Mr Justice Ackner agreed that the application should be granted: 'I accept that there must be some discretion arising out of the words "proper proceedings" taken together with the duty of the council under subsection (3) to prevent "as far as possible" the stopping-up or obstruction of highways. So I accept that in a proper case a proper compromise of proceedings may be made. But such a compromise must be intended to promote the policy and the object of the Act. The compromise which was here suggested, on the contrary, would have resulted in the objects of the Act being frustrated. It would have *extinguished* the highway and provided something else in its place — a pathway which is clearly open to the various criticisms that have been referred to in the affidavits.'

The statutory powers reinforce the duty that exists at common law, but do not supersede the common law duty, the latter being confirmed by the Act. (HA 80 s 333(1) — p 358.)

Advice to highway authorities on the carrying out of the duties imposed by s 130 is contained in DOE Circular 1/83, paras 19 & 20 (p 484). In *R v Lancashire County Council, ex p Guyer* (1980) it was held by the Court of Appeal that where a serious dispute existed concerning the legal status of a way, with conflicting evidence as to whether it was public or private, an authority was under no duty under the section to assert the applicant's claim to the use and enjoyment of the path by taking action to secure the removal of the obstruction. From this decision it is clear that the legal status of the path should be established, eg by an application under WCA 1981 s 53 (see chapter 4.6.8), before seeking the removal of an obstruction under s 130(1).

A county council may, under the general power conferred by LGA 72 s 101, enter into an agency agreement with a district council for the district to carry out these duties. But if it does so, it retains a responsibility to see that the duty is carried out.

In addition to the general duties imposed by the Act under s 130, a specific duty is placed on highway authorities by s 150 (p 347) to remove obstructions which arise in a highway, whether from an accumulation of snow, from the falling down of banks, or from any other cause. In *Worcestershire CC v Newman* (1974) the Divisional Court considered the meaning of the words 'from any other cause'. In the opinion of the Lord Chief Justice, Lord Widgery, supported by the other judges, the words 'should be confined to sudden and substantial obstructions occurring without warning and requiring to be removed with equal urgency'.

6.3 The highway authority's powers of enforcement

The following powers are held by highway authorities to enable them to perform their duties for protecting the public's right of free passage over a public highway:

(a) An authority has power under s 130(5) to institute or defend legal proceedings or take such other steps as may be expedient in pursuance of its duties under s 130. A non-metropolitan district council is given similar authority in pursuance of its powers. Authorities also have a general power to institute or defend legal proceedings. (LGA 72 s 222 — p 309.)

6 : OBSTRUCTIONS AND OTHER NUISANCES

(b) Under HA 80 s 143 (p 344) a highway authority (or a non-metropolitan district council exercising maintenance powers under HA 80 ss 42 and 50) has power to require the removal from a highway of any structure (including any machine, pump, post or other object capable of causing obstruction) which has been erected or set up other than under statutory powers. The procedure is simple. The authority serves a notice, requiring the removal of the structure within a specified period, on the person having control or possession of the structure. If the structure is not then removed, the authority may itself remove the structure and recover the reasonable expenses incurred in so doing from the person concerned. There is no requirement to give the person a second notice, but the authority is not allowed to remove the structure until a month after the notice has been served.

(c) Under HA 80 s 149 (p 347) an authority may require the removal forthwith of anything deposited on a highway so as to constitute a nuisance.

(d) If the authority considers that something deposited on a highway should be removed urgently, under HA 80 s 149(2) it may do so itself. It has power to recover the costs of removal, and to seek authority from a magistrates' court for the disposal of things deposited.

(e) As owner of the surface of a publicly-maintainable highway (p 48), an authority has power to remove anything placed on or planted in that surface without its permission or without lawful authority.

(f) Powers to require the removal of specific types of obstruction or other nuisance are conferred by various sections of the 1980 Act. These are considered later when dealing with specific forms of nuisance (see chapter 6.7.10).

(g) The Local Government (Miscellaneous Provisions) Act 1976, s 16 (p 313), confers power on a local authority to serve on an occupier (or manager) of land a notice that requires him to give the authority the name and address of the owner (and, if the land is leased, the name of the tenant) of the land. Failure to comply, or the giving of information known to be false, is an offence. Section 44 defines a 'local authority' as including a local council for the purposes of s 16. A more specific power relating to functions under HA 80 is given by s 297 of that Act (p 352).

6.4 Ploughing and other disturbance or damage

6.4.1 Introduction

Interference with the surface of a path by ploughing is a public nuisance at common law and is illegal. (*Griesly's case* (1669).) However in the

RIGHTS OF WAY

following circumstances it is lawful for a farmer to plough a footpath or bridleway:
- (a) Where there is a common law right to plough in respect of a particular path.
- (b) Where there is a statutory right to plough under HA 80 s 134 as amended by the Rights of Way Act 1990.

Ploughing and associated disturbance, and the subsequent growing of crops which obstructed or encroached on rights of way, were found by the Countryside Commission's 1988 survey to be the most common form of obstruction. This finding led to the passage of amending legislation in the Rights of Way Act 1990.

6.4.2 Common law right to plough

The legal theory is that a common law right to plough is a limitation by the landowner on the dedication of a right of way, which was imposed at the time when the right of way was dedicated. The theory has important practical consequences, for it means that a right to plough cannot be acquired by prescription, ie by ploughing over a period of 20 years or more, since ploughing would not have begun at the time when the path came into existence. Furthermore, the right cannot be claimed over a right of way which has been created by or under a statute, eg in an inclosure award, or by a creation agreement or creation or diversion order.

In the case of *Mercer v Woodgate* (1869) a farmer was prosecuted for destroying the surface of a public footpath by ploughing. It appeared that the path had been ploughed annually from within living memory. The court held that the path must be deemed to be subject to the right of the landowner to plough it and that the public must tread out the path afresh after each ploughing. Lord Chief Justice Cockburn said: 'There is no doubt that as far as living memory goes back, while on the one hand the public has enjoyed this right of way, on the other hand the owner or occupier of the field during the same period has from time to time ploughed up the whole of his field without regard to the particular track over which the footpath passes. The only proper inference to be drawn is, that the exercise of this right of the owner has been coeval with the exercise of the right of way of the public; and again, the proper inference from that is, that the right of the public was granted, or the original dedication of the way was made, subject to this right in the owner to periodically plough up the soil.' The existence of a right to plough should be recorded in the definitive statement. If it is so recorded, that is conclusive evidence of the right. (WCA 81 s 56(1)(e) — p 381.)

The existence since 1949 of a statutory right to plough (see below) has made it more difficult to establish a common law right. Regular ploughing in the past 40 years or so could be evidence of no more than

6 : OBSTRUCTIONS AND OTHER NUISANCES

an exercise of the statutory right. A further difficulty in establishing a common law right is that from September 1940 to September 1945 a farmer could be authorised by the Ministry of Agriculture under the Defence (General) Regulations to plough up a 'public, private or customary way', although any authorisation was without prejudice to a claim that a common law right to plough existed.

It is estimated, therefore, to establish a common law right based on long use, a farmer would have to show regular ploughing prior to 1949, and probably prior to 1940, back to the limit of living memory. If a right to plough is not recorded in the statement accompanying the definitive map, the onus is on the occupier of land to prove that the right exists, either in court or through a definitive map modification order, should he wish to rely on it as a defence against prosecution.

The meaning of 'plough' has never been considered by the courts. But the amendments made by the Rights of Way Act 1990, by providing a statutory right to carry out disturbance other than ploughing, and by making specific provision in relation to crops, have raised the question whether a common law right to plough is a right to use only a plough. If that is so, then any other operations carried out on that way will be subject to s 134. It is submitted that the common law right to plough does not, in any event, carry with it any right to grow crops on the way: s 137A will thus apply in all cases.

6.4.3 Statutory right to plough

The statutory right to plough, or otherwise disturb, a right of way is contained in HA 80 s 134, as amended by the Rights of Way Act 1990 (p 341). Practical guidance on this replacement section, and on the other changes made by the 1990 Act, is to be found in *Guidance Notes for farmers* and *Guidance Notes for highway authorities* (see 'Further Reading').

Ways to which the right applies Section 134 applies to footpaths and bridleways which are not field-edge paths. 'Field-edge path' is defined in s 329 as a footpath or bridleway that follows the sides or headlands of a field or enclosure. In addition the way must pass over agricultural land, or land being brought into use for agriculture (subsection (1)).

What is permitted The right applies if the occupier is ploughing, or otherwise disturbing, the surface of all or part of the field or enclosure in accordance with the rules of good husbandry. The rules of good husbandry are described in the Agriculture Act 1947, s 11. He may then disturb the surface of the path or way if it is not reasonably convenient to avoid disturbing it so as to render it inconvenient for the exercise of the public right of way. Thus, if a path across a field had traditionally been left unploughed when the field was ploughed, but was then ploughed on one occasion, the occupier would have to have good reason to demonstrate that it was not reasonably convenient to leave it unploughed on that occasion.

The 'other disturbance' has to be associated with operations similar to, or connected with, the growing of a crop; subsection (2) makes it clear that the right to disturb does not extend to any excavation or engineering operation.

6.4.4 Making good and marking the line

If the right to disturb is exercised, the occupier becomes liable to two duties (subsection (3)). He must make good the surface of the way to not less than its minimum width so as to make it reasonably convenient for the exercise of the public right of way. He must also indicate the line of the path or way across the field, again to not less than its minimum width, so that it is apparent to members of the public wishing to use it. Failure to comply with these duties is an offence (subsection (4)).

The time allowed for making good and marking the line The time allowed for this work varies. If the disturbance is the first disturbance for the purposes of sowing a particular agricultural crop, the time allowed is 14 days beginning with the day on which the surface of the path or way was first disturbed for those purposes (subsection (7)(a)).

But once that 14-day period has come to an end, the time allowed for work following any further disturbance in connection with that crop is 24 hours beginning when the surface is first disturbed.

This difference in time allowed is intended to allow a succession of operations to be undertaken within the 14 days after first disturbance without restoration work being required after each operation.

Subsection (8) gives the authority power to authorise an extension of up to 28 days to the time allowed for this work, but application for such an extension must be made before the initial time allowed has expired. A farmer may not therefore fail to comply the work in the permitted time and then apply for an extension.

6.4.5 The minimum width

The work of making good and marking the line has to be carried out over an area not less than the 'minimum width' of the path or way. This width is defined in Sch 12A para 1 (p 371) as follows:

(a) If the width of the way is proved, eg by inclusion in the statement accompanying the definitive map, that width is the minimum width.

6 : OBSTRUCTIONS AND OTHER NUISANCES

(b) If it is not proved, the minimum width is:
    (i) if the way is a cross-field footpath, 1 metre;
    (ii) if the way is a field-edge footpath, 1½ metres;
    (iii) if the way is a cross-field bridleway, 2 metres;
    (iv) if the way is a field-edge bridleway or a carriageway (whether cross-field or field-edge), 3 metres.

These minimum widths also have effect in relation to the authorisation of works under s 135 (see chapter 6.4.7) and in relation to interference by crops under s 137A (see chapter 6.5.2). If the occupier fails to comply with his duty to make good and mark the line, and the highway authority carries out work in default under Sch 12A, it must do so to a width not less than the minimum width, and may do so up to a 'maximum width' (see below).

6.4.6 Enforcement and default powers

The duty to enforce Highway authorities are given a specific duty, by subsection (6), to enforce the provisions of section 134. They may do so either by exercising the powers in Sch 12A (see below), or by prosecuting under s 134(4) (see below) or s 131A if the offence is one of disturbing the surface without authority (see chapter 6.4.7). They also have duties to act under s 135(8) and s 137A(5) below.

The powers in Schedule 12A Schedule 12A gives highway authorities, and non-metropolitan district councils exercising claimed maintenance powers under HA 80 ss 42 and 50, various powers to carry out works which may be exercised in default of compliance with the provisions of sections 134, 135 and 137A. The powers may also be exercised if there is disturbance of the surface of a path or way such as to render its use inconvenient.

In relation to section 134 the power to carry out works arises in two ways. Firstly, if the surface has not been made good so as to make it reasonably convenient for the exercise of the right of way, Sch 12A para 3 authorises any necessary works. But, by virtue of sub-paragraph 3(2), the power to carry these out may not be exercised until the time allowed for the occupier to do so has expired.

Secondly, if the occupier fails to carry out his duty under s 134(3)(b) so to indicate the line of the way as to make it apparent to members of the public, Sch 12A para 4 gives the authority to carry out any necessary default works. Again, by virtue of sub-paragraph 4(3), the power to carry these out may not be exercised until the time allowed for the occupier to do so has expired.

The works must be carried out to at least the minimum width (as defined above), and may be carried out over a width not exceeding the

maximum width (para 3(1) and 4(2)). The 'maximum width' is defined in para 1 as follows:
(a) If the width of the way is proved, eg by inclusion in the statement accompanying the definitive map, that width is the maximum width (ie it is the same as the minimum width for that way).
(b) If it is not proved, the maximum width is:
   (i) if the way is a footpath (cross-field or field-edge), 1.8 metres;
   (ii) if the way is a bridleway (cross-field or field-edge), 3 metres;
   (iii) if the way is a carriageway (cross-field or field-edge), 5 metres.

Any authorised person may enter on to the land concerned, or other land reasonably believed to be in the same occupation, for any purpose connected with these default works, and may take vehicles, machinery or equipment with him (para 7). This power allows an authority to take equipment down farm tracks rather than have to lug it over stiles. But, unless the entry is solely to obtain information, 24 hours' notice must be given to the occupier (para 8(1)); the notice must contain the information in para 8(1)(a)-(d). If it proves impossible to identify the occupier the notice can be affixed to objects on the land (para 8(2)). But in either case the notice must not be given before the power has become exercisable.

The authority may, under para 9, recover its reasonable expenses from the occupier, or, where a disturbed surface has been restored by the authority, any other person responsible for the disturbance. But there is a defence under sub-para 9(2) for anyone to show reasonable authority or excuse for the disturbance, or for an occupier to show that the surface was not disturbed by him or with his consent.

Prosecutions The right to prosecute for failure to comply with the duties in section 134(3) to make good and mark the surface is restricted to highway authorities, non-metropolitan district councils and local councils. Individuals may not prosecute.

What if there is ploughing or other disturbance without authority? If there is ploughing or other disturbance of the surface outside the authority conferred by section 134, eg if a field-edge path or a byway is ploughed, action may be taken by an authority as follows, provided the disturbance is such as to render the exercise of the right of way inconvenient:
(a) The default power in Sch 12A para 3 may be exercised.
(b) A prosecution may be undertaken under s 131A.

6.4.7 Other disturbance of the surface

If the surface has been disturbed action may be possible under HA 80 s 131A (p 341). This section, added by the Rights of Way Act 1990,

6 : OBSTRUCTIONS AND OTHER NUISANCES

applies to footpaths, bridleways and carriageways which are not 'made-up carriageways'. 'Made-up carriageway' is defined in HA 80 s 329 (p 357) as a carriageway, or part thereof, which has been metalled or in any other way provided with a surface suitable for the passage of vehicles. The reference to a part of a carriageway means that a carriageway may be separated into two parts: one which is a made-up carriageway and one which is not.

The section applies only if the disturbance is such as to render the highway inconvenient for the exercise of the public right of way. Anyone responsible for causing such a disturbance commits an offence. Subsection (2) limits the right to prosecute to the highway authority, non-metropolitan district or local council. It also places on the highway authority the duty to bring proceedings where desirable in the public interest.

Section 131A was introduced by the Rights of Way Act to ensure that anyone ploughing or disturbing a path outside the authority conferred by s 134 (see below) committed an offence. Examples would be ploughing a field-edge path or a byway open to all traffic, provided that the byway was not surfaced.

But its application is not restricted to ways over agricultural land. It can thus be used, for example, if a developer disturbs the surface of a path across a building site, or cyclists or horses churn up a footpath.

The highway authority, or a non-metropolitan district council exercising maintenance powers under HA 80 s 42, may carry out works to make good the surface of a right of way to which s 131A applies. The power to do so is in Sch 12A para 3(1). A minimum of 24 hours' notice must be given (Sch 12A para 8). For further details of the procedure under Sch 12A see p 177.

In both s 131 and 131A the offence is committed only if the damage or disturbance is carried out without lawful authority or excuse. Such authority will arise under, eg, s 134 for paths across agricultural land; it will also arise when statutory undertakers exercise their powers to carry out works in highways.

Specific provision for the authorisation by the highway authority of excavation or engineering operations on agricultural land is to be found in HA 80 s 135, as amended by the Rights of Way Act 1990 (p 342). Under the section a highway authority may authorise such disturbance for up to 3 months (subsection (1)) and may impose conditions to protect users (subsection (4)). Failure to comply with any conditions is an offence (subsection (6)), but a prosecution may be brought only by the highway authority, or, with its consent, by the district or local council (subsection (7)). The default powers in Sch 12A may also be used where there is a failure to comply with conditions attached to an authorisation.

The authority may also divert the path temporarily — see chapter 5.7.4.

6.4.8 Damaging the surface of a highway

HA 80 s 131 (p 340) creates three offences. The first is to make a ditch or excavation in a highway over which there are vehicular rights, such as a way shown as a byway on a definitive map. The second is to remove any soil or turf from any part of any highway, including a footpath or bridleway, except to improve the highway with the consent of the highway authority. The third is to deposit anything whatever on any highway so as to damage it.

However it is no longer a specific offence to damage a highway. That offence, previously contained in s 117(1)(e) of the Highways Act 1959, was abolished by the Criminal Damage Act 1971. This Act makes it an offence (s 1 — p 304) to destroy or damage property belonging to another person either with the intention of destroying or damaging the property or being reckless as to whether it would be damaged or destroyed.

'Property' is defined by s 10 of the 1971 Act as being property of a tangible nature, and as belonging to any person who has control of it or any proprietary right in it. It follows that the surface of a publicly-maintainable highway, which is vested in the highway authority under HA 80 s 263 (p 352), is to be treated as the property of that authority for the purposes of the section. Anyone damaging the surface of a publicly maintainable highway would be committing an offence under s 1 of the 1971 Act unless he is able to rely on the defences contained in s 5. These specify that it is a lawful excuse under s 1 for a person to have believed that the authority would have agreed to the destruction or damage, or that the act was done in order to protect his property or his right of interest in property where that was in immediate need of protection and that the means of protection adopted were reasonable in the circumstances. It is sufficient under the section to have held the belief honestly, whether or not it was justified.

An authority (or indeed any person) seeking to take action against anyone damaging the surface of a footpath or bridleway may therefore take action under HA 80 s 131(1) if any soil or turf has been removed, or under the Criminal Damage Act 1971.

6.5 Crops and overhanging vegetation

6.5.1 Crops as an obstruction

A crop growing on a public path may be an obstruction under HA 80 s 137. Prior to the passage of the Rights of Way Act 1990, and the introduction of the new s 137A (see below), prosecution under s 137 for obstruction was the only legal action available to deal with crops. In the following cases under s 137 magistrates convicted persons of unlawfully obstructing a path by causing crops to grow on it:

6 : OBSTRUCTIONS AND OTHER NUISANCES

(a) Buckinghamshire : oil-seed rape 3–4 feet high at Emberton (1987)
(b) Buckinghamshire : cereals 4–6 inches high at Emberton (1987)
(c) Hertfordshire : oil-seed rape and cereals at Cotterell (1987)
(d) Humberside : crops at Wetwang (1987)
(e) Lincolnshire : crops at Harlaxton (1987)
(f) Norfolk : crops at Orby (1988)
(g) Oxfordshire : broad beans at Bampton (1988)
(h) Suffolk : oil-seed rape 4 to 5 feet high at Leiston (1988)
(i) Suffolk : peas 18 inches high at Norton Cove (1988)
(j) Kent : crops at Newchurch, Old Romney, St Mary-in-the-Marsh and Dymchurch (1990)
(k) Gloucestershire : cereals and oil-seed rape at Staunton (1990)
(l) Berkshire : oil-seed rape at Oakley Green (1990)
(m) Buckinghamshire : wheat crop 18-inch high at North Crawley (1990)

But although these cases showed that s 137 could be used where the crop could be shown to be an obstruction to the free passage of users, the courts have no power under the section to order the removal of obstructions, and, in any event, the time taken for cases to come to court meant that the crop would have been harvested before the magistrates reached their verdict.

Furthermore, although authorities appear to have a general power to remove obstructions (see HA 80 s 333 and chapter 6.3 above), they were generally reluctant to use it to clear crops, and appeared to have no power to recover their expenses from the occupier of the land. The result was that the growing of crops on or adjacent to paths frequently rendered them inconvenient to use.

6.5.2 Section 137A of the Highways Act 1980

This new section (p 343), inserted by the Rights of Way Act 1990, seeks to tackle these problems. It does so by imposing (subsection (1)) a duty on the occupier of any agricultural land on which a crop other than grass has been sown or planted to take such steps as may be necessary:

(a) To ensure that the line of any 'relevant highway' on the land is so indicated to not less than its minimum width as to be apparent to members of the public wishing to use the way.
(b) To prevent the crop from so encroaching on the way, or any way on adjoining land, as to render the exercise of the public right of way inconvenient. Subsection (2) defines encroachment by a crop as being when any part of a crop grows on, or extends onto or over, the way in such a way as to reduce its apparent width to less than its minimum width.

RIGHTS OF WAY

'Minimum width' has the same meaning as in relation to s 134 (see above). In other words, the section requires an occupier of land where a footpath runs across a field in which a crop other than grass is growing to ensure that at all times a width of not less than 1 metre is kept defined in such a way that the line of the path is clear, and that it is also kept free of crops growing on it, or encroaching on it (eg by falling onto it), in such a way as to render it inconvenient to use, again to a width of not less than 1 metre. If the path runs around the edge of the field, the corresponding minimum width is 1½ metres. If the way in question is a bridleway, the widths are doubled, ie 2 metres if it runs across the field, 3 metres if it is a field-edge bridleway.

The term 'relevant highway' is defined by subsection (6) as including footpaths, bridleways and carriageways which are not made-up carriageways (see chapter 6.4.3 for comment on the analogous definition in s 131A).

'Crops other than grass' For the crop to cause the occupier to be subject to the duty in the section the crop must be other than 'grass' (subsection (1)). Since many crops to which Parliament intended that the duties should apply, eg cereals, are classified botanically as grasses, subsection (3) amplifies this term by providing that a crop shall be treated as grass if, and only if, it is of a variety commonly used for pasture, silage or haymaking, whether or not that particular crop is intended for that use, and if it is not a cereal crop.

The effect of this provision is that a non-cereal grass crop being grown for, or of a variety commonly grown for, pasture, silage or haymaking is not covered by the provisions of s 137A. It is possible that, if it grows in such a way as to cause an obstruction to the free passage, the occupier will commit an offence under s 137. It is also possible that the authority will be able to exercise its powers to remove obstructions, or, if the way is maintainable at public expense, to remove anything planted or growing in the surface, which is vested in the authority. But it will normally be in the interests of the occupier to protect his crop from trampling by keeping a clear way defined through it for the public to follow.

Prosecutions Failure to comply with the duty is an offence (subsection (4)): it renders the occupier liable to prosecution. There is no restriction on prosecution under this section; guidance on conducting such a prosecution is given in chapter 6.11 below.

Default powers The powers in Sch 12A may be used by the authority if the occupier fails to comply with his duty (Sch 12A para 4). The only notice that need be given is the 24 hours' notice of entry required by para 8 of the Schedule, and work may be carried out to any width up to the 'maximum width' of the highway (as defined above) (para 4(2)).

6 : OBSTRUCTIONS AND OTHER NUISANCES

Thus if an occupier carries out his duty in respect of a cross-field footpath, he need do so only to a width of 1 metre (unless the width is proved to be some other figure). But if he fails to do so, the authority may carry out default works to a width of up to 1.8 metres, and may recover from him the cost of so doing.

Enforcement The highway authority has a specific duty to enforce the provisions of the section (subsection (5)).

6.5.3 Overhanging vegetation

Where a hedge, tree, shrub or vegetation of any description overhangs a highway, or any other road or footpath to which the public has access, so as to endanger or obstruct the passage of vehicles or pedestrians, the highway authority or district council has power under HA 80 s 154 (p 348) to require the owner or occupier by notice to lop or cut back the overgrowth. An owner or occupier may appeal to the magistrates to have the notice set aside. If, subject to any appeal, the work is not done within the stated period, the highway authority may do it itself and recover the cost from the owner.

The only uncertainty in this section is how much, in the case of a bridleway, the owner can be required to lop. He can clearly be required to lop up to a height of six feet so as to clear a passage for pedestrians, to whom the section specifically refers. It is not clear whether he can be required to lop up to nine feet or ten feet, which is the necessary comfortable height for a person on horseback. (The section does not mention horse-riders.) There can, of course, be no doubt that the highway authority can lop to this height on a bridleway at its own expense in exercise of its general maintenance powers. In one case, the county council decided, when the owner ignored its s 154 notice, to cut the overgrowth to nine feet and to charge the owner two-thirds of the cost, ie the equivalent of lopping to six feet. This was obviously the safer course, but perhaps a little generous to the owner.

Where vegetation overhanging a highway was set in place intentionally (eg by the sowing of an arable crop, or by the planting of a row of ornamental shrubs), any obstruction or inconvenience caused may be an offence under s 137 or 137A and action taken accordingly. (See above.)

Where vegetation overhanging a highway grew naturally then, if the decision of the court in *Walker v Horner* (1875) is followed (a case that concerned s 72 of the Highways Act 1835, the precursor of HA 80 s 137), the landowner will not be held to have 'wilfully' obstructed the highway and will therefore not be guilty of the offence contained in the section. The fact that no offence is committed under s 137 does not affect the power conferred by s 154 to require the overgrowth to be cut back or lopped.

It should be noted that the power under s 154 relates to vegetation that overhangs a highway from adjoining land. Where vegetation grows *on* a highway, section 154 has no application. (The vegetation may cause the way to be out of repair — see chapter 7.1.)

No means that is satisfactory to both walkers and farmers has so far been found for dealing with the difficulty caused to walkers by oil-seed rape. This crop, when it approaches full height, is about six feet tall. Even if the width of a path is left unsown along the length of a cross-field path, the fully grown rape falls across it, presenting an insuperable obstacle even to the average walker. To prevent the obstruction of the path by the crop, it is generally necessary to leave a strip six feet wide unsown on each side of the path — a total width of about 15 feet. To leave such an area uncultivated is likely to be unwelcome to the farmer; to leave anything less fails to overcome the difficulty met by the walker, and fails to comply with the law. However the crop, as overhanging vegetation, constitutes an obstruction, and the law should be upheld.

6.6 Bulls, dogs and other animals

6.6.1 Bulls

WCA 81 s 59 (p 384) makes it an offence, subject to important exceptions, for the occupier of a field crossed by a right of way to cause or allow a bull to be at large in it. The exceptions are bulls no more than 10 months old, and those not of a recognised dairy breed which are at large with cows or heifers. Dairy breeds are Ayrshire, British Friesian, British Holstein, Dairy Shorthorn, Guernsey, Jersey, Kerry. Any bull over the age of 10 months is prohibited on its own, and any such bull which is of a recognised dairy breed is prohibited even if accompanied by cows or heifers.

Section 59 effectively replaces any byelaws made by county councils (prior to 1 April 1974) or by district councils since that date, as subsection (3) specifies that it takes precedence over a byelaw in case of conflict. However, the section does not affect byelaws which apply in other places such as parks or streets.

The section applies to rights of way which are footpaths, bridleways and byways as defined in WCA 81 s 66. While it does not apply directly to ways shown as RUPPs on definitive maps, they will, for the purposes of s 66, be either byways (if vehicular rights can be proved) or bridleways.

This section in the Wildlife and Countryside Act is controversial, and was hotly debated at all stages of the Act's passage through Parliament, since over most of the country it effectively permits the pasturing of bulls where they were previously banned. However the government defeated all attempts to amend or delete it.

Another statutory provision may be relevant. Section 3 of the Health and Safety at Work Act 1974 (p 312) places an obligation on employers

6 : OBSTRUCTIONS AND OTHER NUISANCES

and self-employed persons not to put at risk the health and safety of persons not in their employment. Breach of the duty is an offence.

Enforcement of the 1974 Act is primarily the responsibility of the Health and Safety Executive, although there is no restriction on who can prosecute. Anyone who thinks that an offence has been committed under the Act should report the matter either to the police or to the Executive. A Guidance Note published by the Executive in 1985 (see 'Further Reading') gives advice on the custody of bulls in fields and areas to which the public have access. In the event of personal injury, liability for damages may be incurred under the general law of negligence or, possibly, under the Occupiers' Liability Act 1957 (see chapter 2.6.6). See also DOE Circular 32/81 (p 480).

6.6.2 *Dogs*

Where a dog effectively prevents use of a way, for example by standing in the middle of a path facing oncomers with snarls and bared teeth, or where it merely frightens users, for example by running round them, barking in a threatening manner, in either case, since the dog impedes the free use of the way, it constitutes a public nuisance at common law and falls to be dealt with accordingly (see chapter 6.7.10).

By statute, under the Town Police Clauses Act 1847 (p 287), it is an offence for any person to allow any unmuzzled ferocious dog to be at large in a 'street' (as defined in s 3 of the Act). The Dogs Act 1871 (p 287), as extended by the Dangerous Dogs Act 1989 (p 418), empowers a magistrates' court to order that a dangerous dog be kept under proper control or destroyed. The court may in addition by order disqualify the owner from keeping a dog for a specified period. Home Office Circular 89/63 (p 509) advises magistrates on 'ferocious' and 'dangerous' dogs.

If a dog causes injury, the keeper of the animal is liable for damages in civil law if it can be shown that the animal's dangerous characteristics were known to the keeper, ie if it can be proved that the dog had previously caused injury or shown a tendency to attack and that the keeper was aware of this. (Animals Act 1971, s 2 — p 302.)

The Guard Dogs Act 1975 (p 312) makes it an offence (s 5) to permit the use of a guard dog at any premises other than a dwelling-house or agricultural land (s 7). The offence is not committed if a person capable of controlling the dog is present on the premises and either the dog is under this person's control or it is tied up (s 1). In addition a notice warning that a guard dog is present must be exhibited at each entrance (s 1(3)).

6.6.3 *Horses*

As noted earlier (p 54) a person who rides a horse on a footpath without the landholder's consent commits trespass. The landholder can order him off or, where appropriate, sue for damages, or do both things. In some cases the harm is caused not so much to the landholder as to walkers lawfully using the path, since riders can, for instance, make a narrow path almost impassable with churned-up mud. A district council has power, under LGA 72 s 235, to make a byelaw prohibiting horse-riding on specified footpaths in its area and, where such a byelaw is in force, riding on that path is an offence. It is also possible to control horse-riding by means of traffic regulation orders, which can be more simply obtained than byelaws. For details of the procedure see chapter 5.5.1.

If a horse injures a person lawfully using the bridleway (eg a walker) the keeper of the horse is liable, provided he knew that the horse was likely to cause the injuries suffered: s 2 of the Animals Act 1971 (p 302). Thus in *R v Dart* (1865) Dart turned his horse, which he knew to be vicious, onto a common over which there was an unfenced public path. An eight-year-old child was kicked by the horse and killed. Dart was prosecuted for manslaughter. He was convicted. Baron Channell said: 'I entertain no doubt that the turning of a horse on to a common across which there is a public path, with a knowledge of its vicious propensities, is an unlawful act, and exposes the person doing it to the charge of culpable negligence.' A rider will be liable if he can be shown to have been negligent in controlling the horse.

6.6.4 Animals generally

Section 2 of the Animals Act 1971 (p 302) makes the keeper of an animal liable for damages if it injures another person, and if the keeper was aware of the animal's tendency to cause injury. Thus if a farmer places an animal that he knew had dangerous characteristics in a field crossed by a public right of way and a walker is attacked, the farmer would be liable to be prosecuted under the Health and Safety at Work Act 1974 (see p 184), and could be sued for damages by the walker under the 1971 Act if there is evidence of the farmer's knowledge. This would apply even, for example, if the animal was a bull not banned under WCA 81 s 59. But, under s 5 of the 1971 Act (p 302), the liability does not arise if the damage is wholly the fault of the injured person. If the injured person was a trespasser, the liability arises only if the animal was unreasonably kept on the premises to protect people or property.

Under s 2, the keeper of an animal belonging to a dangerous species (as defined in s 6 (p 302)) is liable for any injury it causes, except as provided for in s 5.

6.7 Other forms of obstruction or nuisance

6.7.1 Statutory nuisances

Part III of the Environmental Protection Act 1990 contains provisions dealing with what are termed 'statutory nuisances'. Although the Act

6 : OBSTRUCTIONS AND OTHER NUISANCES

does not refer directly to problems on rights of way, it is nevertheless submitted that its provisions can be of benefit to those wishing to see such problems dealt with.

Definition of 'statutory nuisance' Section 79 (p 423) contains a list of matters defined as statutory nuisances for the purposes of Part III of the Act. These include the following:

(a) Any premises in such a state as to be prejudicial to health or a nuisance.
(b) Any accumulation or deposit which is prejudicial to health or a nuisance.
(c) Any animal kept in such a place or manner as to be prejudicial to health or a nuisance.
(d) Any other matter declared by any enactment to be a statutory nuisance.

Among the other enactments declaring a matter to be a statutory nuisance is s 151 of the Mines and Quarries Act 1954 (p 294). This provides that a quarry, whether worked or not, which by reason of its accessibility from a highway constitutes a danger to the public, and which is not provided with an efficient and properly maintained barrier so designed and constructed as to prevent people from accidentally falling into the quarry, constitutes a nuisance for the purposes of the 1990 Act.

'Premises' is defined in s 79 as including land, and 'prejudicial to health' as meaning injurious, or likely to cause injury, to health. For something to be a nuisance within the meaning of the legislation it has been held to be sufficient for it to interfere with personal comfort. (*Bishop Auckland Local Board v Bishop Auckland Iron Co* (1882).) The nuisance may, or may not, be also prejudicial to health. A matter may therefore be a statutory nuisance for the purposes of the 1990 Act without necessarily being a nuisance at common law. As indicated above (p 169), an obstruction to a highway is a nuisance at common law. In *Trevett v Lee* (1955) Lord Evershed said 'a nuisance to a highway consists either in obstructing it or rendering it dangerous'.

The duties of local authorities The local authority responsible for dealing with statutory nuisances is the district or London borough council (s 79(7)). Outside London and the metropolitan counties it is thus a different authority from the highway authority.

The authority is under a duty (s 79(1)) to cause its area to be inspected from time to time to detect any statutory nuisances on which it ought to take action. The Secretary of State has power, under Sch 3 para 4 (p 429), to declare an authority in default of this duty and thereafter to order the authority to carry it out, or, if it fails to do so, to do the work himself at the authority's expense.

RIGHTS OF WAY

If an authority receives a complaint of a statutory nuisance from someone living in its area, it is under a duty to take such steps as are reasonably practicable to deal with the complaint.

The action an authority can take over a statutory nuisance is set out in s 80 (p 424). If it is satisfied that a statutory nuisance exists, or is likely to occur or recur, it must serve an abatement notice on the person prescribed in subsection (2) of that section. That person may, under subsection (3), appeal to the magistrates' court against the notice. Supplementary provisions with regard to such appeals are to be found in Sch 3 to the Act (p 427). Failure to comply with a notice is an offence (subsection (4)). If the notice is not complied with, the authority may abate the nuisance itself (s 81(3)).

If the authority fails to take action, an individual has the right to do so, under s 82. Details of the procedure are in chapters 6.9 and 6.12.

The Act is useful because:

(a) It gives the magistrates' court a power in the nature of an injunction. Section 80 allows a local authority to serve a notice prohibiting or restricting the occurrence or recurrence of the nuisance.

(b) Breach of an order, or failure to comply with a notice, can lead to a high fine, the current maximum being £20,000 in certain cases.

6.7.2 Stiles, gates and barriers

A right of way may be dedicated subject to the right of the landowner to place stiles or gates across it. Any such limitation on the dedication should be recorded in the statement accompanying the definitive map. A stile or gate erected other than upon dedication or by, or with the consent of, the highway authority is a nuisance at common law and an unlawful obstruction. If the width of a gate across a bridleway (measured between the posts) is less than five feet, the highway authority may require the owner to widen or remove it. (HA 80 s 145 — p 345.) For a carriageway, (including a byway open to all traffic), the corresponding width is 10 feet.

A highway authority may, under HA 80 s 147 (p 346), authorise the erection by the owner, lessee or occupier of a stile or gate to prevent the ingress or egress of animals on land which is used, or being brought into use, for agriculture or forestry. The authority may impose conditions for maintenance, and for enabling the right to be exercised without undue inconvenience, eg by specifying measurements to be employed in the design. There is no appeal against an authority's refusal to grant authorisation or its imposition of conditions. If an authorisation is granted, the right of way becomes subject to a condition that the stile or gate may be erected provided any conditions imposed by the authority are complied with. The authorisation, together with any conditions, should be recorded in the statement accompanying the definitive map by means of a modification order.

6 : OBSTRUCTIONS AND OTHER NUISANCES

A highway authority may itself provide and maintain a 'barrier, rail or fence' in a footpath for the purpose of safeguarding users. (HA 80 s 66 — p 330.) It is submitted that this would entitle an authority to erect a stile in a footpath, if necessary, to prevent horse-riders or motorcyclists from using it. See also chapter 7.7.4.

Section 175A of the 1980 Act (p 351) requires that regard must be had to the needs of blind and disabled persons in the execution of works or the placing or permanent obstructions (which term presumably includes stiles or gates) in streets.

For the responsibility to maintain stiles and gates see chapter 7.4.

6.7.3 Unauthorised or misleading notices and signs

Notices containing false or misleading statements It is an offence under NPACA 49 s 57 (p 291) for any person to place or maintain, on or near any way shown on a definitive or revised definitive map as a footpath, bridleway or RUPP, a notice containing any false or misleading statement likely to deter the public from using the way. A fine may be imposed by way of penalty and the magistrates may order the offender to remove the notice on pain of a continuing fine if he does not. It is the duty of the highway authority to enforce the provisions of s 57, ie to initiate prosecutions. Prosecutions under the section can be brought by the highway authority or district council (LGA 72 s 187(3) — p 309), but not by a local council or a private individual. The section applies to rights of way shown on the definitive map, except those shown as byways open to all traffic.

Section 57 appears to cover cases where the owner puts up notices like 'Danger, fierce dogs' and there are either no dogs or they do not have access to the path. If they do have access to the path the notice will not be misleading, see below. A difficulty arises over cases where a bridleway or footpath runs over a private drive or occupation road and the owner erects a notice saying 'Private Road' at the entrance. Whether this is a misleading statement likely to deter walkers or horse-riders has never been decided by the courts. Probably the best way of dealing with the matter is not by prosecution under this section but for the highway authority to erect a signpost near the owner's notice.

Unauthorised and misleading signs The painting, inscribing or affixing without lawful authority or a reasonable excuse of any picture, letter, sign or other mark upon the surface of a highway or upon any tree, structure or works in the highway is an offence under HA 80 s 132 (p 341). The highway authority has power to remove any such sign.

The authority may also require the owner or occupier of any land to remove any object or device for the guidance or direction of persons using the road. (Road Traffic Regulation Act 1984 s 69(1) — p 402.) If he fails to do so the authority may remove the object or device itself and recover the cost (subsection (2)).

RIGHTS OF WAY

6.7.4 Intimidation

It sometimes happens that the right to use a public right of way is challenged by the landowner in such a way that no physical obstruction takes place. For instance, he may tell path-users to keep off his land, or he may keep a fierce dog on his land which effectively deters people from using path. What, if anything, can be done to counter this sort of behaviour?

The duty of the highway authorities under HA 80 s 130 to assert and protect the rights of the public to the use and enjoyment of public rights of way is wide enough for them to take appropriate action to stop intimidatory tactics (as by issuing a warning that continuance of the conduct will be treated as obstruction).

Further, section 4 of the Public Order Act 1986 (p 407) makes it an offence to use towards another person threatening or insulting words or behaviour with intent to cause that person to believe that imminent unlawful violence will be used against him. Section 5 (p 407) makes it an offence for similar behaviour, or the display of any threatening, abusive or insulting sign or writing, to be used to cause harassment, alarm or distress. Under either section the offence is committed only if intent can be proved (s 6).

A person who assaults, or threatens to assault, a path-user could also be prosecuted under the common law. Assault includes any action which causes the victim to fear immediate application of force and thus could encompass the pointing of a gun, whether loaded or not. Another type of proceeding is an application to a magistrates' court for the offending person to be bound over to keep the peace as provided for in the Justice of the Peace Act 1361. The magistrates have the power also to bind over the complainant (the person against whom intimidation was used), so this approach can have its drawbacks. Lastly the user may initiate proceedings for obstruction, under HA 80 s 137 (see chapter 6.10) or possibly under s 28 of the Town Police Clauses Act 1847 (p 287) or the common law (see chapter 6.13.2). For dogs, see chapter 6.6.2.

6.7.5 Motor vehicles

As noted on p 54, s 34 of the Road Traffic Act 1988 (p 416) provides that any person who, without lawful authority, drives a motor vehicle on any footpath or bridleway commits an offence. Even where lawful authority is given, the driver is subject to other provisions in the 1988 Act. Section 2 (p 412) makes it an offence to drive a motor vehicle on a road recklessly, and s 3 (p 412) an offence to do so carelessly or inconsiderately. 'Road' is defined in s 192 (p 417) to include footpaths and bridleways. Clearly a driver using the footpath or bridleway with the consent of the owner must exercise a high standard of care. What

6 : OBSTRUCTIONS AND OTHER NUISANCES

may be permissible when driving on a vehicular road could well be reckless on a footpath or bridleway where ordinary users would not expect to meet a vehicle.

It is an offence under s 72 of the Highways Act 1835 to drive a carriage of any description (which term includes a motor vehicle or pedal cycle) on any footway by the side of a public carriageway.

Promotion or participation in a race or trial of speed between motor vehicles on any public highway is an offence. (RTA 88 s 12 — p 413.) Promotion or participation in a trial other than a race or trial of speed is an offence unless the trial is authorised under regulations. (RTA 88 s 13 — p 413.) Promotion or participation in a trial between motor vehicles on a footpath or bridleway is an offence unless the trial is authorised by the highway authority and the consent of the owner obtained in writing. (RTA 88 s 33 — p 416.) There is no restriction on prosecution under any of the sections.

A highway authority, as owner of the surface of a publicly-maintainable highway (see chapter 2.5.2), is entitled to secure the removal of vehicles or caravans parked, or tents pitched, on a highway (eg on a grass verge) by applying for an order for possession of the land affected. (*Wiltshire County Council v Frazer* (1984).) The fact that the vehicles, etc do not block the highway is of no relevance.

6.7.6 Firearms and fires

It is not a specific offence to shoot across a public right of way, but to do so could amount to a common law nuisance (see chapter 6.7.10), wilful obstruction of the highway under HA 80 s 137 (see chapter 6.10), a breach of the Health and Safety at Work Act 1974 (p 312) or intimidation (see chapter 6.7.4).

It is an offence under HA 80 s 161(2) (p 349) to light any fire, or discharge any firearm or firework, within 50 feet of the centre of a highway which is a carriageway if as a result any user of the highway is injured, interrupted or endangered. The section applies to rights of way over which there are vehicular rights, eg ways shown on the definitive map as byways open to all traffic, but not to footpaths and bridleways. Under s 161A (p 350) it is an offence to light a fire on any land with similar effect as under s 161, but again only applying to users of carriageways. Section 161A was introduced following problems caused to drivers on busy roads by straw- and stubble-burning, but it applies equally to the effects on walkers or riders on quiet unsurfaced byways.

It is also an offence under s 28 of the Town Police Clauses Act 1847 (p 287) to discharge any firearm, or throw or discharge any stone or other missile, in any street so as to obstruct, annoy or endanger residents or passers-by. 'Street' is defined in the Act as including any road, square, court, alley and thoroughfare, or public passage. The Act originally applied only in towns which adopted it, but was extended to apply to all boroughs and urban districts by s 171 of the Public Health Act 1875 and to the whole of England and Wales by LGA 72 Sch 14 paras 23 and 26. However it is not clear that this extension means that 'street' in this context now includes all rural footpaths and bridleways, and the courts have not been asked to decide this point.

Section 19 of the Firearms Act 1968 (p 301) makes it an offence for a person to have a loaded air-weapon, or any other firearm whether loaded or not, together with ammunition, in a public place, unless he can prove lawful authority or reasonable excuse. A public place includes any highway (s 57) and other premises or place to which the public have or are permitted to have access. The section thus applies both to public rights of way and to permissive paths. Section 20 of the same Act makes it an offence for a person to trespass on land with a firearm unless he proves that he has a reasonable excuse.

Generally speaking, a licence or permit is required for the possession of a firearm (except in the case of an air-weapon), and a person could not claim to have lawful authority under s 19 if he had an unlicensed weapon. A reasonable excuse could be claimed by a person who was, for example, shooting vermin on his own land or land of an employer.

6.7.7 Dangerous excavations and erections

It is a nuisance at common law to make excavations and erections on land adjoining a public path, if these make the path unsafe to persons using it with ordinary care. In some cases it is a statutory offence to make any excavations near a public path or leave them unprotected. Thus railways adjoining a highway must be fenced. (Railway Clauses Consolidation Act 1845 s 68.) A quarry which, by virtue of its accessibility to the public, constitutes a danger to the public is a statutory nuisance for the purposes of the Environmental Protection Act 1990. (Mines and Quarries Act 1954 s 151 as amended by the 1990 Act — p 294.) Application may be made to the magistrates' court for an order that the nuisance be abated (see chapters 6.9 and 6.12).

Where there is an unfenced, or inadequately fenced, source of danger on land adjoining a highway a local authority may, by notice, require the owner to execute any necessary work of protection, repair, removal, or enclosure to obviate the danger. (HA 80 s 165 — p 351.) The owner has a right to appeal to a magistrates' court against a notice and, subject to such an appeal, the authority, if he does not comply with the notice, may do the necessary work and recover the costs from the owner.

6.7.8 Barbed wire at the side of highways

HA 80 s 164 (p 350) provides that where there is on any land adjoining a highway barbed wire which is likely to be injurious to persons or

6 : OBSTRUCTIONS AND OTHER NUISANCES

animals lawfully using the highway, the highway authority may serve a notice in writing upon the occupier of the land requiring him to abate the nuisance within a stated time (not less than one month nor more than six months from the date of the notice). If the owner does not comply with the notice, the highway authority may apply to a magistrates' court for an abatement order and may then proceed to do the necessary work itself; it may also recover the expenses incurred.

The only difficulty about this provision is in deciding whether a fence is near enough to the highway to be dangerous to persons or animals. This is a question of fact to be answered after considering all the circumstances, eg width of the path, whether the fence is on the same level, etc. For example, in *Stewart v Wright* (1893) the plaintiff was walking on a windy day along a footpath which had a barbed-wire fence. His coat was blown on to the wire and torn. The court held that the fence was a nuisance to users of the highway and the plaintiff recovered damages for the injury to his clothing. Section 164 refers only to barbed wire at the side of highways: where barbed wire is put across a path it is an obstruction and should be dealt with as such (see chapters 6.8 & 6.10). District councils have concurrent power with highway authorities under this section.

6.7.9 Pesticides

The use of a pesticide on a right of way is not specifically an offence, although it could constitute an offence under s 3 of the Health and Safety at Work Act 1974 (p 312), or possibly under HA 80 s 161(4) (p 349). A code of practice for farmers and growers published by the Health and Safety Executive (see 'Further Reading') advises that rights of way should not be oversprayed, and that, if the product label advises that people and animals should stay out of a crop which has been sprayed, the need for warning notices where rights of way join or cross the treated area should be considered.

Failure to follow the guidance in the code is not in itself an offence, but the code could be used in legal proceedings under the 1974 Act or regulations made under that Act, or under the Food and Environment Protection Act 1985.

6.7.10 Miscellaneous nuisances

At common law An activity that is not a statutory nuisance may nevertheless be a nuisance at common law, as defined in *R v Matthias* (p 44). A common law nuisance may be either private or public. The former is not a crime and must be dealt with under civil law, ie the remedy is to sue for damages or seek an injunction (or both). The latter is both a crime and a tort (a civil wrong), so that a wrongdoer may be both prosecuted and sued.

RIGHTS OF WAY

Activities which have been held to be a public nuisance at common law include the following:
(a) Replacing a two-feet-high stile with a five-barred gate. (*Bateman v Burge* (1834).)
(b) Erecting a gate across a path even if it is not locked or fastened. (*James v Hayward* (1630).)
(c) Placing telegraph posts on the roadside verge without statutory authority so as to interfere with walkers. (*R v United Kingdom Telegraph Co Ltd* (1862).)
(d) Not keeping a garden wall in good repair so that it falls on to the footway. (*Mint v Good* (1951).)
(e) Allowing fat to fall on a paved footway so that a walker slips. (*Dollman v Hillman* (1941).)

The test applied by the courts is whether there is unreasonable interference: if the interference is minimal and the conduct otherwise reasonable, then it does not constitute nuisance, eg 'occasional hitting of cricket ball across a highway may be a minor inconvenience to users but is not a nuisance'. (*Stone v Bolton* (1949).)

The main duty of securing the removal of obstructions and the abatement of nuisances rests with the highway authority under HA 80 s 130. A private individual cannot bring an action to abate a nuisance unless he has suffered personal injury or loss. He can however abate it himself by removing so much of an obstruction as is necessary to enable him to pass on his journey (see chapter 6.8.1). Where he is injured, he can bring an action for damages. *Mint v Good* and *Dollman v Hillman* above are instances where the plaintiffs obtained damages for injuries they received from the nuisances. The common law rights of the individual regarding obstructions and nuisances are expressly protected by HA 80 s 333(1) (p 358).

Under statute The commission of various other acts on the highway renders the offender liable to a fine under HA 80. Such acts include the following:
(a) Depositing, without lawful authority or excuse, anything whatsoever on a highway if as a consequence a user of the highway is interrupted (s 148 — p 346), or injured or endangered (s 161(1) — p 349.)

In *Remet Co Ltd v London Borough of Newham* (1981) the Divisional Court of the Queen's Bench Division held that for an offence to be committed under s 148 the depositing had to be intentional. Accidental deposit is therefore not within the section. But the court indicated that where someone followed a practice that was likely to result in material falling on to the highway, he should be deemed to intend the probable consequences of his action.

In *Puttnam v Colvin* (1984) it was held that the word 'excuse' in s 148

6 : OBSTRUCTIONS AND OTHER NUISANCES

imported the concept of reasonableness as a fact to be determined in each case, and that accordingly it was open to a court to find the offence not committed on the ground of *de minimis* (eg where the interruption was trifling or temporary).

(b) Permitting, without lawful authority, any filth, dirt, lime or other offensive matter to flow on to the highway. (s 161(4) — p 349.)

(c) Placing any rope, wire etc, across a highway so as to be dangerous unless adequate warning is given. (s 162 — p 350.)

(d) Pulling down or obliterating a traffic sign, milestone or direction post, including any sign or waymark. (s 131(2) as applied by CA 68 s 27(6) — p 300 & 340.)

6.8 Getting an obstruction removed

In the first part of the chapter we examined the nature of an obstruction in law and the characteristics of certain particular types of obstructions. We now turn to consider the steps that can be taken to see that an obstruction is removed. There are four courses of action to be considered.
1. Removing the obstruction oneself — the remedy of self-help.
2. Reporting the problem.
3. Prosecution of the person responsible under section 137 or 137A of the Highways Act 1980.
4. Application for an abatement order under the Environmental Protection Act 1990.

6.8.1 Self-help — the remedy of abatement

It is an ancient principle of the common law that a person who suffers damage from the existence of a nuisance is entitled to 'abate' it, ie to remove it. The courts have on a number of occasions pronounced on the nature of the remedy. Thus in *Seaton v Slama* (1932) Mr Justice Maugham said 'If access to a way over which a person has a right is obstructed by an unlocked gate in such circumstances as I have to deal with here, I see no reason sufficient to justify him taking the gate away. If the gate is locked he may be entitled to break the lock. If there is a fence across the entrance to the way he may be justified in removing a sufficient part of the fence to enable him to have free access to the way.'

In *Colchester Corporation v Brooke* (1845) Lord Chief Justice Denman said 'A public nuisance becomes a private one to him who is specially and in some particular way inconvenienced thereby, as in the case of a gate across a highway which prevents a traveller from passing, and which he may therefore throw down: but the ordinary remedy for a public nuisance is itself public, that of indictment; and each individual who is *only* injured as one of the public can no more proceed to abate than he can bring an action.'

And in *Dimes v Petley* (1850) Lord Chief Justice Campbell said 'If there be a nuisance in a public highway, a private individual cannot of his own authority abate it, unless it does him a special injury, and he can only interfere with it as far as is necessary to exercise his right of passing along the highway; we clearly think he cannot justify doing any damage to the property of the person who has improperly placed the nuisance in the highway, if avoiding it he might have passed on with reasonable convenience.'

The 'special injury' referred to in the last judgment is the inconvenience of being prevented by the presence of the obstruction from exercising the right to pass along the highway.

At the present day, when it is common knowledge that many paths are overgrown, and that one's way may be obstructed by overhanging vegetation, it is submitted that it is not unreasonable for a walker to take with him a pair of pocket secateurs, and that he will not be acting unlawfully if he uses these to clear vegetation that impedes his progress along a path, provided always that he does no more than is necessary to enable him to make his way conveniently along the route. If he does anything more than this, for example if he goes out with the express intention of clearing a particular path, equipped with such tools as a saw, a spade or a pick-axe, he risks going beyond what the remedy of abatement allows. (For the correct way to undertake path clearance work, see chapter 8.7.)

The enthusiast who goes beyond what the law allows lays himself open to various penalties. He may be guilty of the criminal offence of damaging property without lawful authority under s 1 of the Criminal Damage Act 1971 (p 304), and he can also be sued for damages by the owner or occupier. There is, however, a defence in s 5 of the 1971 Act (p 304) to a charge of criminal damage if the person concerned destroyed or damaged the property believing that a right, such as a public right of way, was in immediate need of protection and that the means of protection adopted were reasonable having regard to all the circumstances. It is immaterial for the purposes of the section whether or not the belief is justified provided that it is honestly held.

A further matter that should be borne in mind is the provision in s 139 of the Criminal Justice Act 1988 (p 410) that makes it an offence for any person to have with him in any place to which the public have access (thus including public rights of way and concessionary paths) any article that has a blade or is sharply pointed. It is a defence to show 'good reason or lawful authority' for having the article. It will be noted that the conjunction in the last sentence is 'or', not 'and'. Thus it is a defence to show 'good reason' for having the article. Good reasons might, it is suggested, include such matters as taking a pair of scissors to a night-school class on dressmaking, or the carrying of sample tools by a salesman. It is submitted that it would be 'good reason' for having

6 : OBSTRUCTIONS AND OTHER NUISANCES

a pocket-sized pair of garden secateurs to show that they were carried for the purpose of cutting back any undergrowth, met while walking, that impeded progress on a public right of way.

6.8.2 Reporting problems

To the landowner or occupier The direct approach to the landowner or occupier should always be considered. If he is willing to deal with the difficulty, such an approach can often secure a quick solution and at the same time foster good relations.

It can, however, sometimes be difficult for a member of the public to find out who owns the land concerned. (The powers of a local authority to discover details of ownership and tenancy of land were noted earlier, see p 173). There is no public register showing the owner of every plot of land in the country (such as exists in France). A step towards having such a register has been made by the Land Registration Act 1988. For further details see p 101.

If land is known to be part of a particular farm, the name of the occupier of the farm (who may not, of course, be the owner or the tenant of the land) can be found from the electoral register, a copy of which for the area is usually to be found at the nearest post office. An enquiry about land ownership directed to the clerk of the local council can also sometimes be fruitful.

To the local council Although parish and community councils have, as noted on p 36, no duties in respect of rights of way, they do have considerable powers, and a council which takes an interest in its rights of way can do much to assist in getting obstructions and other nuisances dealt with.

To a user organisation It is always useful for an organisation representing the interests of users, whether a local society or a branch of a national body such as the RA, to receive details of problems encountered on paths. If an attempt is made to close the path at a future date, evidence that someone had tried to use it, but had encountered problems, will be helpful in establishing that it is needed for public use. The RA can supply forms for reporting path problems.

To the highway authority Since it is a highway authority that has the legal power to secure the removal of an obstruction (or to deal with kindred matters such as the failure to restore a path after ploughing) it will be by making a report to the highway authority that a member of the public will most commonly seek to have an obstruction removed.

A report made for this purpose should give full details of the exact circumstances of the matter complained of; the nature of the obstruction

RIGHTS OF WAY

(eg a locked gate), its exact location, preferably with a grid reference (if possible with eight figures), and (if known) the number of the footpath concerned. (Vague descriptions such as 'near the church', or 'by the river' merely waste time.) Also given should be the date and time when the obstruction was met; the names and addresses of any witnesses; and, if known, the name and address of the landowner. A sketch-map showing the site of the obstruction can often be helpful.

A sample report form is given on p 243. Alternatively, a report can take the form of a letter setting out the matters mentioned above, addressed to the Chief Executive of the authority in which the obstruction lies, at the address of its principal offices. It will assist in enabling the letter to reach the relevant department and officer if the letter is headed, 'Complaint about obstruction of public path'.

If the report or letter fails to have the desired effect, further action may be needed to induce a response. See chapter 8.2.

6.9 Action in the magistrates' court

6.9.1 Introduction

Action may be taken by any individual or organisation in the magistrates' court under the following provisions:

(a) Prosecution for wilful obstruction of the free passage along the highway. (HA 80 s 137 — chapter 6.10.)

(b) Prosecution for failure to comply with the duty to keep a path clearly defined to its minimum width through crops. (HA 80 s 137A(1)(a) — chapter 6.11.)

(c) Prosecution for failure to comply with the duty to keep a path convenient to use to its minimum width through crops. (HA 80 s 137A(1)(b) — chapter 6.11.)

(d) Application for an order to require that a statutory nuisance be abated. (EPA 90 s 82 — chapter 6.12.)

This chapter gives a description of the proceedings which are common to all provisions, and, in general, also apply to proceedings under HA 80 s 56 (see chapter 7.6).

6.9.2 Before starting proceedings

As a preliminary step efforts should be made to have the problem resolved. The first step is to report the obstruction to the highway authority (see chapter 8.2.1). The authority should be given a reasonable period of time in which to take action, and at least one reminder sent if the first letter brings no response.

The next step is to write to the person believed to be responsible for the problem, keeping a copy of the letter, giving him notice that, unless

6 : OBSTRUCTIONS AND OTHER NUISANCES

he removes the obstruction, proceedings will be brought. The letter should be sent by recorded delivery to give proof if the matter reaches court. Sample letters are given in the separate sections on the different powers. The 'person' may be an individual or a corporation such as a limited company.

Many people fear the cost involved in bringing a private prosecution. If the case is a clear one, money should not enter into the matter. But remember that if the complainant loses his case, costs can be awarded against him. If he wins, and the defendant decides to appeal, the costs could become quite high.

Three things must be borne in mind at all times. First, that anyone issuing such a summons is in the position of a complainant. He is not an advocate and, therefore, must himself give evidence to prove his case (unless there is a plea of guilty). He cannot merely call witnesses and get them to prove his case. Secondly, that this is a criminal prosecution and the magistrates must be satisfied 'beyond reasonable doubt' that the defendant, who is the accused person, is guilty of the offence with which he has been charged. Finally, if advance warning is received that difficult legal problems will be raised by the defendant, a solicitor should be employed.

Before starting proceedings a complainant should be certain of the following:

(a) He can prove his case beyond reasonable doubt. At all times the onus of proof is on him.

(b) He can prove that the path about which complains is a highway (see below).

(c) The offence complained of has truly been committed, eg that the obstruction about which he complains is truly an obstruction to the free passage along the highway, and that it is wilful.

(d) The person who will be the defendant is the correct person. This can be a major difficulty and one which might not be resolved. It might result in losing the case.

(e) The evidence is of sufficient quality. It is useful to produce photographs of the problem with a map marked to show the position or positions from which the photographs were taken. Where photographs are produced as evidence, the person who took them should be present as a witness, to prove that it was he who took the photographs, and to state the day on which they were taken. It is preferable for the photographs to be taken on the day mentioned in the summons, and to contain an identifiable feature. It is also preferable (but not essential) if the photographer can say that he developed the prints. If lengths or widths are important, eg if it is claimed that a path was not clear of crops to the minimum width specified for the purposes of HA 80 s 137A, a measure should be laid on the ground and photographed; the same measure should be produced in court.

6.9.3 Proof of highway status

The definitions of 'footpath' and 'bridleway' in both HA 80 s 329 (p 357) and WCA 81 s 66 (p 384) make it clear that such ways are regarded by the law as highways, to which HA 80 ss 137 and 137A will thus apply.

It is essential to prove that the path is a highway. If it is on the definitive map a copy of the definitive map and statement should be obtained. It should be certified by the surveying authority to be a true copy of the map as amended by subsequent definitive map modification orders. If the authority of the map is challenged the court should be referred to the provisions of WCA 81 s 56(4). It is not sufficient to rely on an Ordnance Survey map or some other map (eg in a guidebook); neither has sufficient authority.

If the path is not on the definitive map it is possible that it may be included in the list of streets maintained by the highway authority (see chapter 4.10). This is more likely to be the case in an urban or suburban area for which no definitive map has yet been prepared. The inclusion of a highway in the statutory list of streets is not conclusive evidence that the highway is a public right of way, but is undoubtedly very strong evidence. It would nevertheless be unwise to rely on the list as sufficient proof of status without actual evidence of user.

In any other case it will be necessary to prove by evidence that the path is a public right of way although it may be preferable first to seek the inclusion of the path on the definitive map by means of the definitive map order procedure (see chapter 4.6.8).

In *R v Ogden, ex parte Long Ashton Rural District Council* (1963) the council prosecuted Ogden (under HA 59 s 121, the predecessor section of HA 80 s 137) for obstructing a footpath. There was no definitive map for the area at the time. Ogden's defence was that the path was not public and claimed that the magistrates had no jurisdiction to determine this issue. The magistrates agreed and refused to hear the case. On appeal by the prosecutor, the High Court held that, since s 269 of the Highways Act 1959 (now HA 80 s 312) expressly provided for summary trial of the offence, the magistrates had jurisdiction to hear and determine the issue raised by Ogden. Accordingly an order of mandamus was issued requiring the magistrates to do so.

6.9.4 Anticipate the defence

A complainant who has made sure of his facts (see above) will probably have already anticipated most of the possible defences. The defendant can raise many defences. Some of them, and the answers, include the following:

(a) 'It wasn't me'. If letters have been written and other investigations carried out, this defence can be met.

6 : OBSTRUCTIONS AND OTHER NUISANCES

(b) 'The offence was committed more than six months before the date on which you issued your summons'. Magistrates' courts can only hear cases if the proceedings are brought within six months of the date of the alleged offence.

6.9.5 *Laying the complaint*

A summons in the magistrates' court is stated by 'laying an information' before a magistrate. The information is a form which must be set out as shown in the separate sections below.

Each magistrates' court has its own clerk, whose office should be consulted for details of the local system for the laying of complaint. Some will send a form which can be filled in with the words of the complaint. In other cases the complaint will have to be typed in duplicate. Some clerks insist upon the complainant attending their office to sign the complaint form in front of them but others will allow the document to be sent in by post. There is no charge for making the complaint.

The clerk to the magistrates will then make out the actual summons. The complainant must attend on the date stated in the summons. It is therefore essential, when making the complaint, to discuss with the clerk the possible hearing dates in order to ensure that a convenient date is fixed. The summons is usually sent to the complainant, who must serve it on the defendant. This can be done by post but if so should be done by recorded delivery with proof of posting. Alternatively it can be served on the defendant personally. Two copies of the summons are sent to the complainant. One should be served on the defendant and the certificate on the back of the second copy should be completed by the complainant. It is a wise precaution for the complainant to make an additional copy for himself, it being useful to be able to refer to it in court.

Before the hearing date contact may be made by the defendant or his solicitor. It is fair for the solicitor to try and talk a complainant out of continuing his prosecution. Listen to him but resist. He will probably want to be told details of the case against his client so that he can think up some grounds for the defence. Be wary. It may be possible to get him to give some details of his case.

6.9.6 *The hearing*

It is useful, for a number of reasons, for the complainant and his witnesses to get to the court well before the hearing begins. If the defendant or his solicitor have not made contact before the date of the hearing, they may want to do so before the hearing starts. Again be wary. Don't tell them too much, but listen for details of their case. It is also useful to try and have a word with the clerk to the magistrates before the court sits. (Most clerks are helpful to unrepresented litigants.) He is there to advise the magistrates on the law, but they alone will decide the facts. Do not be surprised if the defendant asks for an adjournment. Only about one-third of magistrates' court cases are heard on the first occasion.

The first hearing date that is given will not necessarily be the occasion for a full hearing. Most magistrates' courts treat the first hearing as being largely administrative. If the defendant indicates that he is going to plead not guilty the court will almost invariably adjourn the case to a later date when adequate time will be allowed. If the defendant pleads guilty on the first occasion, the case will generally be dealt with immediately.

When the case is called the complainant (but not his witnesses) and the defendant (with his solicitor, but not his witnesses) will go into court. The clerk will read out the charge to the defendant and the defendant will be asked to say whether he pleads guilty or not guilty.

If he pleads guilty, the complainant can give a short explanation of what the case is about but does not need to take an oath or affirmation.

The defendant or his solicitor will then make a speech urging the court to be as lenient as possible. At this stage the complainant may hear strident criticisms of himself or any organisation of which he is a member. He will not normally be allowed to reply, but if there is an unwarranted or untruthful oral attack upon him or his organisation, he can ask the magistrate if he may be allowed to set the record straight.

If the defendant pleads 'not guilty', the complainant must then embark upon the presentation of his case. The case is likely to proceed as follows:

(a) The complainant opens his case. He should describe the facts, but briefly because it will be repetitive of his evidence and that of his witnesses. The opening is not made on oath. He should then refer the court to the law, for instance, by reading out HA 80 s 137 and such quotations from judgments as are relevant to the case. At this stage he should also produce the definitive map and explain the nature and location of the path and the problem.

(b) The complainant goes into the witness-box and gives the facts of his case. He should restrict himself to the following facts:
  (i) That the footpath or bridleway is a highway.
  (ii) Description of the problem.
  (iii) Statement of who caused the problem, if it is in his personal knowledge.
  (iv) Any letters or discussions that he has had with the defendant about the problem. If the defendant has been violent or used bad language, this may be mentioned.
  (v) Any documents, particularly the copies of any letters that

6 : OBSTRUCTIONS AND OTHER NUISANCES

have passed between him and the defendant. Very often the production of documents has a most impressive effect.

(c) The defendant or his solicitor may then cross-examine the complainant. The aim of cross-examination is to obtain admissions which weaken the complainant's case. Most cross-examination is by suggestion, 'Would you agree with me that...?' If the complainant does not agree, he should say so.

(d) When the defendant or his solicitor sits down the complainant can give further evidence to clarify any of the points that have been raised in cross-examination. However, he must deal only with matters raised in cross-examination.

(e) It is always useful to have at least one witness who will corroborate the essential parts of the evidence, particularly that relating to the obstruction itself. That person should have been sitting outside the court until the clerk to the magistrates is told that he is wanted as a witness. He will then be called into court and, after he has taken the oath, the complainant asks him questions even if the only question is 'Will you now give your evidence?' He may then be cross-examined by the defendant or his solicitor in the same way as the complainant was cross-examined. At the end of his cross-examination the complainant may ask him further questions, but only on matters which have been raised in his cross-examination. This procedure will also be adopted with any other witnesses called by the complainant.

(f) When the complainant has called all his witnesses he should tell the magistrates that he has finished his case. The solicitor for the defendant has two alternatives at this stage. He can call the defendant and any witnesses. He can, however make a speech, which is usually known as 'submitting that there is no case to answer'. This may be based on suggestions that there are insufficient allegations of fact to make up proof of the offence. It may be a long technical submission to the effect that there is a legal point which enables his client to be acquitted at this stage. The complainant is entitled to reply to this speech, but no advice can be given as to how this should be done. Each case will depend on its own facts and the legal points that are raised. If the magistrates find that there is 'no case to answer' the complainant has lost and that is the end of the case.

(g) If the magistrates find there is a case to answer, or if there is no such submission, the defendant will give evidence. He will give this in reply to questions by his solicitor. The complainant is then entitled to cross-examine him. Cross-examination is an art beyond the scope of this book. However, remember at all times that cross-examination must be restricted to asking questions. These questions can, however, be to ask the defendant if he agrees with a statement made to him. After the cross-examination has been concluded, his advocate is entitled to ask him further questions but these must be restricted to the matters raised in cross-examination. The procedure will be adopted with any witnesses that the defendant wishes to call.

(h) At this stage, the defendant or his advocate may make a speech commenting on the evidence and raising legal points. The final speech is the defendant's prerogative. The only occasion on which the complainant can make a speech after that is if the defendant raises any legal points and he feels able to answer them, for instance by reading any of the earlier quoted statements of law which are relevant.

The magistrates will then make and announce their decision. If they find the accused guilty, they will decide upon the penalty. It is a matter for them alone. The complainant can ask for an order that the defendant pays his costs. These will be his expenses, the expenses of his witnesses and the cost of providing any documentary evidence. If the court announces a finding of guilty the defendant's solicitor may make a speech in mitigation similar to that mentioned above. It would be better not to reply. By now the court should have heard all the facts.

If the magistrates decide that the defendant is not guilty the defendant's solicitor will almost certainly ask the court that the complainant pays the defendant's costs. He can oppose the request by suggesting, for instance, that he brought the action for the public good and in good faith. The award of costs, and the amount of costs, is within the court's absolute discretion.

6.9.7 Appeals

If the complainant is unsuccessful he can appeal against the decision, but only if he can allege that there has been an error of law. This is most difficult to substantiate, mainly because hardly any magistrates give reasons for their decision.

If he is successful, the defendant can always appeal. An appeal must be commenced by a written notice of appeal, which must be served upon the complainant. If one is received, a solicitor should immediately be consulted. Appeals are almost invariably very expensive, and may be the defendant's strongest weapon.

6.10 Prosecutions for obstruction under the Highways Act 1980

In order to consider the evidence that will be needed to secure a conviction it is necessary to examine carefully each element of the make-up of the offence contained in section 137.

6 : OBSTRUCTIONS AND OTHER NUISANCES

6.10.1 'Without lawful authority or excuse'

The courts have held that 'lawful authority or excuse' means that the person causing the obstruction must be clearly authorised by law, ie by or under an Act of Parliament or as a limitation or condition subject to which the highway was dedicated. Mere convenience to the accused is not a defence. Thus in *Campodonic v Evans* (1966) Evans blocked a public footpath by locking a gate. He pleaded in defence that people left the gate open and he had to lock it to prevent his cattle straying. The magistrates decided that this constituted 'lawful authority or excuse'. The prosecutor appealed. The High Court held that the defendant's excuse was not lawful and sent the case back to the magistrates with a direction to convict. The Court took a similar view in *Durham CC v Scott* (1990).

Nor can the highway authority by its licence or acquiescence make lawful any obstruction which is otherwise unlawful. In *London Borough of Redbridge v Jacques* (1971) Jacques had pitched a stall in a public highway for many years without objection by the authority. On one occasion in 1969 he was prosecuted. The magistrates found that although his stall was an obstruction, the authority, by its acquiescence, must be deemed to have given him lawful authority. The prosecuting authority appealed. The High Court upheld the appeal and Lord Chief Justice Parker put the law succinctly when he said: 'A valid licence cannot be given to perform an unlawful act'. On the other hand, where the action complained of (leaving a pile of stones on the highway) was done by a subcontractor in the course of carrying out road repairs, it was held to have been done with lawful authority. (*King v Page* (1970).)

If the defendant claims statutory authority then the wording of the statute must be specific. (*Hunt v Broome* (1974), right of peaceful picketing in s 134 of the Industrial Relations Act 1971 was not 'lawful authority' for those on picket duty to obstruct the highway.)

By virtue of s 101 of the Magistrates' Courts Act 1980, the burden of proving whether or not he had lawful authority or excuse rests with the accused.

6.10.2 'Wilfully'

The word 'wilfully' does not mean that the accused need have consciously intended to obstruct the way. The offence is committed if he does something which, for whatever reason, has the effect of causing an obstruction. This point was emphasised by Lord Chief Justice Parker in *Arrowsmith v Jenkins* (1963) when he said: 'I am quite satisfied that section 121 (1) of the Act of 1959 (now HA 80 s 137), on its true construction, is providing that if a person, without lawful authority or excuse, intentionally as opposed to accidentally, that is, by an exercise of his of her free will, does something or omits to do something which will cause an obstruction, he or she is guilty of an offence.'

A person is also obstructing wilfully if he fails to remove an obstruction he has caused only indirectly. (*Gully v Smith* (1883).) In that case a badly constructed wall on Gully's property fell into the highway, obstructing it. Smith asked Gully to remove it. He did not do so, and was prosecuted. The magistrates convicted him and the High Court upheld the conviction. Lord Coleridge said: 'It appears to me that the appellant (who had repaired the wall and so afforded evidence of his being the owner of the wall) having, notwithstanding his having been repeatedly requested to remove the obstruction caused by the falling of the wall, failed to remove it, his case, notwithstanding his having done no positive act causing the obstruction, came within the words of s 72 (of the Highway Act 1835) "or shall in any way wilfully obstruct the free passage of any highway". Not fulfilling, after notice, a duty to remove an obstruction, comes, I think, on the true construction of the Act, within the words "wilfully obstruct"'.

6.10.3 'Obstructs the free passage'

In *Seekings v Clarke* (1961), it was held that a blockage projecting 2½ feet over a 17-foot way was an unlawful obstruction. Lord Chief Justice Parker said: 'It is perfectly clear that anything which substantially prevents the public from having free access over the whole of the highway which is not purely temporary in nature is an unlawful obstruction. There is, of course, exception to that. One possible exception would be on the principle of *de minimis*, which would no doubt cover the common case of the newsagent who hangs out a rack of newspapers, which though they project over the highway project only fractionally. Other cases may be where for some purpose or other a use has to be made of the highway, for instance for scaffolding, where the question in every case is whether it was or was not a reasonable user.'

In *Wolverton Urban District Council v Wills* (1962), Mr Justice Slade commented: '(i) that every member of the public is entitled to unrestricted access to the whole of a footway, save in so far as he may be prevented by obstructions lawfully authorised; (ii) that, subject to the *de minimis* principle, any encroachment on the footpath which restricts him in the full exercise of that right and which is not authorised in law, is an unlawful obstruction; and (iii) that every member of the public so restricted in the use of the footway is necessarily obstructed in that, to the extent of the obstruction, he is denied access to the whole of the footway; that is, he is obstructed in his legal right to use the whole of the footway.'

In *Tomkins v Padfield* (1973), Padfield locked a gate across a path and was prosecuted by Tomkins. The magistrates refused to convict since they thought an agile person could climb it. The Queen's Bench Div-

6 : OBSTRUCTIONS AND OTHER NUISANCES

ision allowed an appeal by Tomkins, holding that the gate was undoubtedly an obstruction. Mr Justice Mars-Jones said: 'The respondent had been at all material times in full control of the land on which the gate was situated. Although on a number of occasions he had been asked to remove the chain and padlock by the Urban District Council, he had failed to do so.... The short point that this Court has to consider is whether the locking of a gate approximately three foot nine inches in height which would be climbed by an able bodied adult person constitutes an obstruction within the meaning of section 121 of the Highways Act 1959.... It seems to me that this matter is quite beyond argument; this gate, padlocked as it now is, undoubtedly does obstruct free passage along the highway.'

However a purely temporary obstruction which inconveniences nobody is not a breach of section 137. (*Absalom v Martin* (1974), bill poster parked van on footway for about 10 minutes, no evidence of anyone being obstructed, refusal of magistrates to convict upheld by the High Court.)

6.10.4 A continuing offence

It is clear that the offence of obstruction is a continuing one, ie the obstructor commits the offence by failing to remove the obstruction just as much as by putting it up in the first place. (*Abel v Stone* (1969).) The facts were that a fence in Verwood, Dorset, had been erected in 1963-4 across a path shown on the definitive map. In 1966 the fence had become the property of Stone. In September 1968 Dorset CC ordered Stone to remove the fence. He declined to do so and Abel (Clerk of Dorset CC) prosecuted him. Stone pleaded that the fence had been constructed more than 6 months previously and so the prosecution should not be brought (see chapter 6.9.4). The justices agreed and dismissed the case. Abel appealed.

The Queen's Bench Division was of the opinion that there was an offence, Lord Chief Justice Parker saying: 'The case of *Gully v Smith* (1883) makes it perfectly clear that there can be a wilful obstructing of free passage by an act of omission as well as an act of commission and where, as here, a notice has been given of requiring the obstruction to be removed, then failure to comply with that notice is evidence of a wilful obstruction... for my part I am quite satisfied that a wilful obstruction of this sort is a continuing offence and certainly occurs whenever there is failure to comply with a notice.'

6.10.5 The penalty

The magistrates can impose a fine but cannot order the obstruction to be removed (but see chapter 6.12 for a separate power to make an order requiring a nuisance to be abated). There may well be cases where a person obtains so much benefit from an obstruction that he is prepared to regard the payment of successive fines as a sort of licence fee. This happened in *A-G v Harris* (1961). The facts were that every Sunday Harris put up a stall on the footway outside a cemetery in Manchester and sold flowers from it. He was prosecuted and convicted 70 times for obstructing the footway. At that time the maximum fine was £2 and Harris appeared willing to pay this. The court held that persistent and deliberate flouting of the law was a grave and serious injury to the public and warranted the grant of an injunction to prevent continuation of the offence. The action was brought by local complainants with the Attorney-General's permission, because the injury was to the public at large rather than to one individual.

6.10.6 Before starting proceedings

If efforts to persuade the highway authority to secure the removal of the obstruction are not successful, a letter should be written to the person believed responsible for the obstruction. This might read as follows:

Dear Mr Barnfather,

I recently tried to walk Topsey footpath number 17 over your land at Lower Blackacre Farm and found it to be obstructed. The obstruction took the form of a gate locked with a padlock and chain. I enclose a map showing the path and the location of the obstruction. I believe that this obstruction is a wilful obstruction of the free passage along the highway, within the meaning of section 137 of the Highways Act 1980.

I must ask you to remove the obstruction within 14 days of today's date or, alternatively, I must contemplate bringing proceedings in your local magistrates' court for obstruction of the highway under section 137 of the Highways Act 1980.

Yours sincerely,

6.10.7 The wording of the complaint

The complaint to be used in a prosecution under s 137 should take the following form:

6 : OBSTRUCTIONS AND OTHER NUISANCES

INFORMATION
M.C. ACT 1980 SECTION 1: M.C. RULES 1981, R 4
LOWTOWN MAGISTRATES' COURT

Date of alleged offence:	2 April 1991
Accused:	Harry Barnfather
Address:	Lower Blackacre Farm, Topsey, Barsetshire
Alleged offence:	Without lawful authority or excuse did wilfully obstruct the passage along the highway, namely the public footpath number 17 running from Otley Road at grid reference 696785 to Hewit Road at grid reference 683772, by locking or causing to be locked with a padlock and chain a gate across the highway contrary to section 137 Highways Act 1980.
The information of:	John Smith 25 Whiteacre Lane Lowtown Barsetshire
Telephone number:	Lowtown 12345.
Date of information:	15 April 1991
	Who (upon oath) (after affirmation) states the accused committed the offence of which particulars are given above.
	Taken (and sworn) (and affirmed) before me
	Justice of the Peace/Justices' Clerk.

(M.C. means magistrates' courts)

6.10.8 Particular points

(a) The complainant will need to prove that the obstruction was an obstruction to the free passage along the highway. This does not mean that the obstruction was such that no-one, however agile,

209

was able to use the way — see the quotation in *Tompkins v Padfield* (p 206).

(b) The complainant will also have to prove that the obstruction was 'wilful' (see chapter 6.10.2). This can mean that it had actually been erected by the owner or occupier or that he had allowed it to remain in position for an unreasonable period of time. It is for this reason that a letter should be written to the owner or occupier asking him to clear the obstruction.

(c) It is difficult to know whether the landowner or the occupier, eg the tenant, should be charged. No firm rules can be laid down but knowledge of the path and the obstruction can sometimes help. This is also a particular difficulty where the obstruction is on the boundary between two owners' or occupiers' land. As much information as possible should be obtained before proceedings are started in order to make it as certain as can be that it is the defendant who is responsible for the obstruction. In certain circumstances where there is doubt as to which of two or more persons is responsible, it may be possible to summons them jointly or to summons one for the actual offence and the other for aiding, abetting, counselling or procuring the commission of the offence.

(d) Another problem might well be 'is it the actual owner or occupier who is responsible, or is it his employee?' If the notice mentioned above has been given, then the complainant should be prepared to argue that the employer (in other words the owner or occupier) is responsible for the actions of his employee. The giving of notice allows quotation of the judgment in *Gully v Smith* (p 207).

(e) 'I've a right to obstruct the way'. Remember that the section says that it is only an offence if the path or way is obstructed 'without lawful authority or excuse'. One possible defence is that it was dedicated subject to an obstruction. If possible, before proceedings are begun, find at least one witness who can say that the obstruction has not always been there.

(f) 'The obstruction was caused more than six months before the date of the summons'. In cases where the obstruction remained in place for some time the offence is what is known as 'a continuing offence'. There is judicial authority for this in the case of *Abel v Stone* (p 207). If the obstruction was, for example, caused by a person blocking the way on a particular occasion, there is therefore more urgency to issue the summons than in the case of a barbed-wire fence which remains in place for a year or more.

6.11 Prosecutions for crop interference under the Highways Act 1980

The provisions of s 137A were considered in detail in chapter 6.5.2. Two separate duties are imposed on occupiers of land by the section,

6 : OBSTRUCTIONS AND OTHER NUISANCES

and two separate offences therefore arise as the possible subject of proceedings.

6.11.1 Before starting proceedings

If efforts to persuade the highway authority to secure the removal of the obstruction are not successful, a letter should be written to the person believed responsible for the obstruction. This might read as follows:

Failure to make the line apparent on the ground

> Dear Mr Barnfather,
>
> I recently tried to walk footpath number 17 over land which I believe you to occupy at Lower Blackacre Farm and found that, where the path crosses the field marked 'A' on the enclosed map, it was not clearly indicated on the ground to a width of at least 1 metre, as required by section 137A of the Highways Act 1980.
> That section was added by the Rights of Way Act 1990, and I enclose a copy of *'The Rights of Way Act 1990 : Guidance notes for farmers'*, published by the Ministry of Agriculture and the Countryside Commission, which explains your duties under this legislation.
> I must ask you to take steps to make the line of the path clear within 7 days of today's date or, alternatively, I must contemplate bringing proceedings in your local magistrates' court for your failure to indicate the line of the path across the field in contravention of section 137A of the Highways Act 1980.
>
> Yours sincerely,

Failure to prevent encroachment by crops

> Dear Mr Barnfather,
>
> I recently tried to walk footpath number 17 over land which I believe you to occupy at Lower Blackacre Farm and found that, where the path crosses the field marked 'A' on the enclosed map, it had been encroached upon by crops growing on or

alongside it, so that a width of less than 1 metre was left available for the public to use without being inconvenienced in the exercise of their public right of way. It is a requirement of section 137A of the Highways Act 1980 that that width be left convenient for the public to use.

That section was added by the Rights of Way Act 1990, and I enclose a copy of *'The Rights of Way Act 1990 : Guidance notes for farmers'*, published by the Ministry of Agriculture and the Countryside Commission, which explains your duties under this legislation.

I must ask you to take steps to clear the crops so that the path is convenient to use over a width of at least 1 metre within 7 days of today's date or, alternatively, I must contemplate bringing proceedings in your local magistrates' court for your failure to prevent encroachment by crops on the path in contravention of section 137A of the Highways Act 1980.

Yours sincerely,

6.11.2 *The wording of the complaint*

Failure to make the line apparent on the ground

INFORMATION
M.C. ACT 1980 SECTION 1: M.C. RULES 1981, R 4
LOWTOWN MAGISTRATES' COURT

Date of alleged offence:	2 April 1991
Accused:	Harry Barnfather
Address:	Lower Blackacre Farm, Topsey, Barsetshire
Alleged offence:	Failed to ensure that the line on the ground of the public footpath number 17 running from Otley Road at grid reference 696785 to Hewit Road at grid reference 683772 was, between grid reference 696785 and grid reference 693780, so indicated to not less than its minimum width as to be apparent to members of the public wishing to use it, contrary to section 137A(1)(a) Highways Act 1980.

6 : OBSTRUCTIONS AND OTHER NUISANCES

The information of:	John Smith 25 Whiteacre Lane Lowtown Barsetshire
Telephone number:	Lowtown 12345.
Date of information:	15 April 1991
	Who (upon oath) (after affirmation) states the accused committed the offence of which particulars are given above.
	Taken (and sworn) (and affirmed) before me,
	Justice of the Peace/Justices' Clerk

Failure to prevent encroachment by crops

INFORMATION
M.C. ACT 1980 SECTION 1: M.C. RULES 1981, R 4
LOWTOWN MAGISTRATES' COURT

Date of alleged offence:	2 April 1991
Accused:	Harry Barnfather
Address:	Lower Blackacre Farm, Topsey, Barsetshire
Alleged offence:	Failed to prevent a crop from so encroaching on that part between grid reference 696785 and grid reference 693780 of the public footpath number 17 running from Otley Road at grid reference 696785 to Hewit Road at grid reference 683772 as to render it inconvenient for the exercise of the public right of way, contrary to section 137A(1)(b) Highways Act 1980.
The information of:	John Smith 25 Whiteacre Lane Lowtown Barsetshire

Telephone number:	Lowtown 12345.
Date of information:	15 April 1991
	Who (upon oath) (after affirmation) states the accused committed the offence of which particulars are given above.
	Taken (and sworn) (and affirmed) before me,
	Justice of the Peace/Justices' Clerk

6.11.3 Particular points

The complainant will need to be able to say, and demonstrate in his evidence, that the following apply:

(a) The person alleged to have committed the offence is the occupier of the land. The letters above are drafted to indicate a belief that the addressee is the occupier. It is important to note that an offence under s 137A can only be committed by the occupier.

(b) The offence complained of has been committed. Particular care should be taken with the preparation of the evidence and the taking of photographs, especially to ensure that the width of such path as may be apparent can be identified by reference to a tape measure or scale. The complainant, and his witnesses, will also need to prove to the satisfaction of the court that the path was not apparent to them, as members of the public, or that they were inconvenienced in the exercise of their public right of way, as the case may be.

(c) If the defence claims that the crop was grass (within the meaning given to that term by s 137A), that that claim can be refuted, ie that the crop was in fact a cereal or some other crop which is not grass within the meaning of the section.

6.12 Application for an order to abate a nuisance

Details of the Environmental Protection Act 1990, the duties of district and London borough councils and the definition of 'statutory nuisance' are to be found in chapter 6.7.1.

6.12.1 Before starting proceedings

Efforts should be made to persuade the highway authority to secure the removal of the obstruction, and, if necessary, to persuade the district council (if a different authority) that the matter complained is a statutory

6 : OBSTRUCTIONS AND OTHER NUISANCES

nuisance upon which it has a duty to take action. If these are not successful, a letter should be written to the person believed responsible for the nuisance. This might read as follows:

Dear Mr Barnfather,

I recently tried to walk footpath number 17 over your land at Lower Blackacre Farm and found it to be obstructed. The obstruction took the form of a gate locked with a padlock and chain. I enclose a map showing the path and the location of the obstruction. I believe that this obstruction is a nuisance to users of the highway, and a 'statutory nuisance' within the meaning of section 79 of the Environmental Protection Act 1990.

I must ask you to remove the obstruction within 14 days of today's date or, alternatively, I must contemplate bringing proceedings in your local magistrates' court under section 82 of the Environmental Protection Act for an order requiring you to remove the obstruction.

Yours sincerely,

Subsections (6) and (7) require 21 days' notice to be given to the defendant of the intention to bring proceedings. If the letter above does not have the desired effect, a notice as set out below should be sent by recorded delivery with proof of posting.

NOTICE

Environmental Protection Act 1990 section 82

To: Harry Barnfather

Of: Lower Blackacre Farm, Topsey, Barsetshire

Take notice that I, John Smith of 25 Whiteacre Lane, Lowtown, Barsetshire intend to apply at the expiration of 21 days from the date of this notice to the Lowtown magistrates' court for an order under section 82 of the Environmental Protection Act 1990 requiring you to abate a nuisance, namely a gate locked with a padlock and chain at grid reference 690780 on the public footpath number 17 running from Otley Road at grid reference

RIGHTS OF WAY

696785 to Hewit Road at grid reference 683772, and prohibiting you from causing the nuisance to recur.

This is the notice required by subsections (6) and (7) of the said section 82.

Signed   Date

6.12.2 The wording of the complaint

The information to be used in a case under the Act should take the following form:-

INFORMATION
M.C. ACT 1980 SECTION 1: M.C. RULES 1981, R 4
LOWTOWN MAGISTRATES COURT

Date of alleged offence:	2 April 1991
Accused:	Harry Barnfather
Address:	Lower Blackacre Farm, Topsey, Barsetshire
Alleged offence:	Breach of section 82 Environmental Protection Act 1990.
The information of:	John Smith
25 Whiteacre Lane
Lowtown
Barsetshire
Telephone number:	Lowtown 12345.

Who (upon oath) (after affirmation) states that the public footpath number 17 running from Otley Road at grid reference 696785 to Hewit Road at grid reference 683772 which crosses land at Topsey Barsetshire owned or occupied by you (being 'the said premises') was on the 2nd day of April 1991 obstructed by a gate locked with a padlock and chain at grid reference 690780; and the said obstruction is

6 : OBSTRUCTIONS AND OTHER NUISANCES

> a statutory nuisance, that is to say that by virtue thereof the said premises are in such a state as to be a nuisance; and you have failed to abate or remove the nuisance; and the said John Smith is aggrieved by the said nuisance and seeks an order that you may be required to abate it and be prohibited from causing it to recur.
>
> Date of information: 15 April 1991
>
> Taken (and sworn) (and affirmed) before me,
>
> Justice of the Peace/Justices' Clerk

6.12.3 Further provisions of the section

Subsection (2) of section 82 provides that, if satisfied that the nuisance exists, or that, although it has been abated, it is likely to recur, the magistrates must make an order. The order may require the defendant to abate the nuisance, carrying out any works necessary to do so, or it may prohibit a recurrence of the nuisance, again requiring the defendant to carry out any necessary works, or it may both require an abatement and prohibit a recurrence.

In other words, if the nuisance complained of is a padlocked gate, and by the time the case comes to court the padlock has been removed, the court still has power, if satisfied that it may be put back, to prohibit the defendant from so doing.

The court also has power to impose a fine on the defendant.

If the court finds for the complainant under subsection (2), it has, by subsection (12), to order the defendant to pay to the complainant 'such amount as the court considers reasonably sufficient to compensate him for any expenses properly incurred by him in the proceedings'.

If the court makes an order, and it is not complied with by the defendant, subsection (8) gives the court power to impose a further fine on him, including a daily fine (up to £200 per day) if the non-compliance continues after the conviction. On such a conviction the court also has power, under subsection (11), to direct the local authority to take the action that the defendant should have taken, but before so doing the authority must be given the chance of being heard by the court.

RIGHTS OF WAY

6.13 Other legal action

6.13.1 Applications for judicial review

In some circumstances it may be possible to challenge the decision of the Secretary of State, a local authority or a public body in the courts by means of judicial review. For example, a decision may have been reached without following the correct procedure, or there may have been a breach of natural justice in that both sides of an argument have not been fairly considered.

The *Send* case reported on p 171 was an application by the Parish Council for an order of *mandamus* requiring the CC to carry out its duty under s 116 of the Highways Act 1959 (now HA 80 s 130) to secure the removal of obstructions. Two examples of applications for orders of *certiorari* are *Pearson's* case (p 86) and the *Hood* case (p 86). An example of an application for a *declaration* is *Mason's* case (p 81). All these cases show that judicial review can be a valuable method of seeking clarification of the law. Where the law has been shown to be defective, as in the Hood and Mason cases, it has been possible to persuade Parliament to amend the legislation to remedy the defects. However, any application for judicial review will involve large sums of money, and careful legal advice must therefore be taken before even trying to commence proceedings. The applicant must also be able to show a 'sufficient interest'.

6.13.2 Prosecutions for obstruction under the common law

The obstruction of a highway is a common law misdemeanour and an offender can be prosecuted by way of indictment in the Crown Court. The Crown Court can impose a penalty of imprisonment. It seems that this method of prosecution is rarely used, and then mainly in cases of demonstrations, etc, which block streets.

Anyone contemplating a prosecution by this method should consult a solicitor experienced in Crown Court litigation, a subject which is outside the scope of this book.

6.13.3 Civil proceedings for an injunction

Where an illegal act which is injurious to the public is being committed, an injunction can be sought by the Attorney-General from a civil court (county or High Court) to stop the act complained of. *A-G v Harris* (p 208) is an example.

Again, as with a common law prosecution, a solicitor should be consulted before seeking to initiate civil proceedings for an injunction.

7

Maintenance and improvement

7.1 What constitutes maintenance?

The exact extent to which rights of way should be maintained is not set out in detail in any Act of Parliament. However the courts have considered the question. In *R v High Halden* (1859) it was held that the parish (the highway authority of the day) was under a duty to put a highway in such repair as to be reasonably passable for the ordinary traffic of the neighbourhood at all seasons of the year.

In *Burgess v Northwich Local Board* (1880) Mr Justice Lindley said: 'The duty of the highway surveyors is to repair and keep in repair; which means, I apprehend, to keep the road as dedicated to the public in such a state as to be safe and fit for ordinary traffic.' The Secretary of State's view of the extent of the duties of highway authorities is similar. (DOE Circular 1/83 paras 17 and 18 — p 484.)

What does the word 'maintenance' cover? HA 80 s 329 (p 357) defines it as including repair for the purposes of the Act. Does this include the removal of obstructions? In *Hereford and Worcester CC v Newman* (1975) the Court of Appeal decided that it did not. In that case Mr Newman had applied to his local magistrates' court under s 59 of the Highways Act 1959 (now HA 80 s 56) for orders requiring the then Worcestershire CC to put certain footpaths in proper repair. The problems making the paths, in his view, 'out of repair' were as follows:

(a) A 7-foot-high hawthorn hedge growing in the middle which made passage impossible.
(b) A barbed-wire fence and thick undergrowth across the path. Passage could only be effected by climbing the fence and forcing a way through the undergrowth.
(c) A barbed-wire fence of several strands.
(d) A length of path of at least 6 feet flooded with effluent from a cesspit to a depth of at least 1 foot.

The magistrates granted the orders under s 59. The CC appealed to the Divisional Court, which dismissed the appeals in respect of (a), (b) and (c) but remitted the case of the cesspit outlet to the magistrates for further consideration. The CC appealed against the Divisional Court's decision to the Court of Appeal.

In the Court of Appeal Lord Justice Cairns said that he would give the word 'repair' what he felt to be its natural meaning, and went on: 'I consider that a highway can only be said to be out of repair if the surface of it is defective or disturbed in some way. Not every defect in the surface would constitute being out of repair — eg an icy road would not in my view be out of repair. But if the surface is in a proper condition I do not think it can ever be said that the highway is out of repair. In the present case the path which I feel least doubt about is the one that was obstructed only by a barbed-wire fence. I cannot imagine anybody describing the presence of such a fence as a want of repair of the path. I would allow the appeal ... The other two paths have a substantial growth of vegetation in them. That vegetation no doubt constitutes an obstruction, but it must also interfere with the surface of the paths. If there had merely been branches and thorns overhanging from the sides of the footpaths I should not consider that they were out of repair, but I understand that a hawthorn hedge in one case and thick undergrowth in the other is actually rooted in the surface of the paths. With some hesitation I am of the opinion that this did cause the paths to be out of repair. I would therefore dismiss the appeal in respect of footpaths ...'

In the view of Lord Justice Lawton repair in relation to highways or bridges 'connotes the restoration to a sound or unimpaired condition that which has become unsound or unimpaired by neglect or use. A highway or bridge which had become unusable because of an act of obstruction would not as a matter of the ordinary usage of English be out of repair'.

Mr Justice McKenna thought differently. In his view 'An obstructed highway, pending the removal of the obstruction, can be said to be "out of repair" and to remain out of repair until the obstruction is removed.' However, he was in a minority of one, and the Court allowed the appeal in respect of the path obstructed solely by the barbed-wire fence but dismissed the two other appeals.

The effect of this case, considered further in chapter 7.6, which sets out the procedure to be followed under HA 80 s 56, is to make it clear that there is a distinction between the duty to maintain and repair on the one hand and the duty to protect the public's rights and remove obstructions on the other. From the highway authority's point of view there are adequate powers to take action in furtherance of either duty; from the point of view of a person seeking to enforce the duty the relatively straightforward procedure under s 56 contrasts with the need to apply for judicial review to enforce the duty to remove obstructions.

A further limitation on the meaning of maintenance is that it does not include improvement. The duty to maintain and repair does not confer a power to execute works which would alter the character of the way. Such powers do exist, and are considered in chapter 7.7.

In carrying out any work the authority must have regard to the needs of disabled or blind persons whose mobility might thereby be impaired. (HA 80 s 175A — p 351.)

7 : MAINTENANCE AND IMPROVEMENT
7.2 Whose job is it?

7.2.1 Privately- and publicly-maintainable highways

A highway may be *publicly maintainable*, ie it is maintainable at public expense by the highway authority, or it may be *privately maintainable*, ie an individual or body has the duty of maintaining it. The latter duty can arise by prescription (long-standing custom), by tenure (related to property), by enclosure of a previously-unenclosed highway or under a special enactment. Where a new highway is dedicated, the person dedicating it is responsible for its maintenance unless he comes to an agreement with the highway authority for it to be publicly maintainable (see chapter 3.4.4).

Footpaths and bridleways NPACA 49 s 47 made all footpaths and bridleways in existence at that time or coming into force thereafter publicly maintainable. The section was repealed by the Highways Act 1959, which came into effect on 1 January 1960. It is therefore submitted that any footpath or bridleway that was in existence at that date is publicly maintainable. The position with regard to footpaths and bridleways that have come into being since that date is as follows. If a path or way is constructed by a highway authority, or is created by a public path creation or diversion order under HA 80 or TCPA 90, or a public path creation agreement under HA 80 s 25, it is publicly maintainable. In addition, the normal practice of the Secretary of State, when making side roads orders under HA 80 s 18, is to specify that any new path or way created by the order is maintainable by the highway authority.

Other new paths may not be publicly maintainable. There is, for example, no provision that makes a public path created by a local council under HA 80 s 30 publicly maintainable. Nor will a path expressly dedicated or constructed by a landowner or developer be publicly maintainable unless the highway authority has accepted it as such under the provisions of either HA 80 s 37 or s 38.

A right of way that comes into existence as a result of presumed dedication under HA 80 s 31 (see chapter 3.3) is publicly maintainable if it is shown that the path was legally in existence on 1 January 1960. Whether a path which is presumed to have been dedicated under HA 80 s 31 comes legally into existence at the date of expiry of the 20-year period or, retrospectively, from the date of the commencement of the 20-year period, has not been determined by the courts.

Dual liability Where a way was privately maintainable, but is now, as a result of the provisions mentioned above, also publicly maintainable, the private liability to maintain remains. Where this dual liability exists, HA 80 s 57 (p 328) gives the highway authority power to charge the cost of repairing the way to the person by whom it is privately maintainable should the authority be forced to carry out work by an order under HA 80 s 56.

Ways reclassified from RUPPs The provisions in CA 68 and WCA 81 relating to the reclassification of RUPPs were intended to ensure that the reclassified ways became publicly maintainable, regardless of how they were shown after reclassification. There is no difficulty in relation to WCA 81 s 54: subsection (4) provides for a way shown on a definitive map as a consequence of a confirmed reclassification order to be publicly maintainable.

The position with regard to RUPPs reclassified under CA 68 is more complicated. Paragraph 9(2)(a) of CA 68 Sch 3 provided that a RUPP reclassified under a special review would be publicly maintainable, but only 'as from the date of publication of the definitive map and statement in the special review'. Where such a map has been published (ie if the review has been completed), the provision thus applies.

But if the review was abandoned under the provisions of WCA 81 s 55, it is submitted that it does not do so. The rule as to maintenance liability thus becomes the same as for any other path or way. Where reclassification was as a footpath or bridleway, the definitive map on which the way was first shown is likely to have had a relevant date prior to 1 January 1960: such a date will be sufficient to establish that the way was in existence at that date, and is thus publicly maintainable by virtue of NPACA 49 s 47.

Ways becoming byways under WCA 81 s 53 Under WCA 81 s 53 (p 379) a modification order may be made to add a way directly to the map as a byway, or to upgrade to that status a way previously shown as a footpath or bridleway. Neither type of order has a bearing on the liability to maintain, which will be governed by the provisions applying to vehicular ways described below.

The effect of WCA 81 s 54(7) Section 54(7) of the 1981 Act (p 380) states that nothing in that section, or in s 53, obliges a highway authority to provide, on a way shown on a definitive map as a byway, a metalled carriageway or a carriageway which is by any other means provided with a surface suitable for the passage of vehicles. This provision, derived from a similar one in CA 68 Sch 3, has reportedly been taken by some authorities to mean that depiction of a way as a byway in some way reduces their liability to maintain it. It is submitted that this is an incorrect reading of the section, and that its correct interpretation is that the effect of an order under s 53 or s 54 is to leave unchanged the extent of maintenance liability on a particular way.

Other ways over which there are vehicular rights The maintenance of ways over which there are vehicular rights is not so clearly defined. If such a way was in existence on 31 August 1835, it is publicly

7 : MAINTENANCE AND IMPROVEMENT

maintainable by virtue of s 23 of the Highway Act 1835. If it came into being thereafter, it is publicly maintainable only if a justices' certificate (which should be in the local record office) has been issued or a statutory provision compiled with, eg if it has been constructed by the highway authority. However it should not be necessary to have to ascertain the existence of a way in 1835; the list of streets required by HA 80 s 36(6) (see chapter 4.10) to be made, and kept up to date, by the highway authority should give the required information. In *A-G v Watford Rural District* (1912) Lord Justice Parker took the view that the onus would fall on the highway authority to prove that a way was not publicly maintainable, not on some other party to prove that it was. If a way is not included in the lists of streets, the highway authority should be able to explain why.

Bridges What of bridges over which a footpath or bridleway passes? HA 80 s 328(2) (p 357) provides that where a highway passes over a bridge or through a tunnel, that bridge or tunnel shall be taken for the purposes of the Act to be a part of the highway. The liability of a highway authority to maintain a footpath or bridleway therefore includes the maintenance of any bridge by which the path crosses a natural stream or obstacle. In *R v Southampton* (1852) the parish vestry of Shorwell (Isle of Wight) (the highway authority of the day) was held liable to repair a footbridge by which a path crossed a small stream.

If the bridge is the means by which a path crosses a man-made obstacle such as a canal or railway the probability is that the canal authority or British Rail is liable to maintain the bridge under a special statute. In such a case the authority has to keep the bridge up to date, ie in such a condition as to meet modern needs. In *A-G v Sharpness New Docks Co* (1914) a canal company had by an Act of 1791 to make bridges to take highways over its canal 'and all such bridges shall, from time to time be supported, maintained and kept in sufficient repair' by the company. The canal was built in 1812. Did the company have to maintain the bridges to the standards of 1812 or 1914? Lord Justice Vaughan Williams summarised the position: 'I am of opinion that, for the purpose of maintaining bridges, the standard which the company are bound to observe is not the standard existing at the time of the passing of the Act, but the standard existing at the present time, that is, the standard of the present traffic'.

If a bridge is privately maintainable by reason of tenure, and the person liable to maintain it is also liable to maintain the approaches, that liability extends to 100 yards from each end of the bridge. (HA 80 s 49 — p 326.)

7.2.2 The duties of highway authorities

HA 80 s 41 (p 325) places upon highway authorities the duty to maintain those highways that are maintainable at the public expense. However, a county council will not always carry out the work itself. A non-metropolitan district council has a right to take over the maintenance of footpaths and bridleways (s 42 and below) and can, by agreement, have other functions delegated to it. A parish or community council may undertake certain maintenance powers, either as the agent of the county council or district council or in its own right; its powers are considered in chapter 7.2.4 below. Lastly, much work is undertaken by volunteers, and chapter 8 describes some commonly undertaken tasks. However, if the authority neither undertakes maintenance work itself nor arranges for anyone else to do it, and a highway becomes 'out of repair', there is a procedure, described in chapter 7.6, whereby the authority's duty can be enforced through the courts.

7.2.3 The powers of non-metropolitan district councils

A non-metropolitan district council may undertake maintenance. This power may arise in one of two ways.

Agency agreement under LGA 72 s 101 An agency agreement may be entered into with the county council under LGA 72 s 101. If it is, the highways to be maintained and the financial and other arrangements will be the subject of agreement. It will be up to the county council to ensure that the agreement provides for payment to be made only when work has been carried out.

Such an agreement may be also be made for the performance by the DC of other CC functions, eg the duty to remove obstructions or the duty to review the definitive map.

Claimed maintenance powers under HA 80 s 42 Alternatively, the district council may claim maintenance powers under HA 80 s 42 (p 325). Only publicly-maintainable footpaths and bridleways (in rural areas) may be maintained. Schedule 7 (p 370) sets out procedures for the claiming of the powers, the provision of estimates for the cost of the work and the making of payment thereafter. It also provides (para 9(1)) that the district council must have available for public inspection a list of the highways which it is maintaining under claimed powers. Paragraph 7 requires a district council exercising maintenance powers to indemnify the county council against any liability arising out of work it has undertaken or out of its failure to undertake work.

A district council which claims powers under s 42 thereby acquires the right to exercise other powers. For a list of these see chapter 1.3.3.

However, although these provisions ought to ensure that paths are maintained, whether by the county or by the district, problems have often arisen, with districts claiming that the county council has provided insufficient funding and the county claiming it cannot control the districts.

7 : MAINTENANCE AND IMPROVEMENT

A study of agency agreements and claimed maintenance powers published by the Audit Commission in 1987, although about roads rather than rights of way, came to a similar conclusion. It recommended that s 42 should be repealed and that maintenance agency should be a contractual arrangement.

A non-metropolitan district council may also, under HA 80 s 50 (p 326), undertake the maintenance of any privately-maintainable footpath or bridleway.

Section 61 of the 1980 Act (p 329) allows the Secretary of State to make regulations to supplement the powers under sections 42 and 50, but he has not done so.

7.2.4 The powers of local councils

HA 80 s 43(1) (p 326) permits a local council to undertake the maintenance of any footpath or bridleway within its area which is maintainable at the public expense. There is a proviso in s 43 that nothing in the section affects the duty of the highway authority to maintain the footpath or bridleway. If a local council does exercise its power of maintenance, the county council, or a district council exercising claimed maintenance powers, may, under s 43(2), defray the whole or part of any expenditure so incurred. Some highway authorities enter into agreements with local councils about the work to be done by each and the sharing of costs.

By HA 80 s 50(2) (p 326) the local council may also maintain privately-maintainable footpaths or bridleways in its area.

Sections 43 and 50 confer powers, not duties; whether to exercise them is for the local council to decide. The powers do not extend to footways nor to ways over which there are vehicular rights.

In the experience of the OSS and RA it is useful for local councils to undertake minor repairs, with the highway authority doing more costly and substantial repairs. A local council which is doing minor repairs will be better able to draw the attention of the authority to any substantial work needed.

7.2.5 Waterside paths

Tow-paths of navigable waterways Whose duty is it to repair a tow-path? If the tow-path is a publicly-maintainable highway (p 221), the highway authority must maintain the surface but has no duties regarding the banks. The British Waterways Board has a duty to maintain its commercial and cruising waterways in a suitable condition for use by vessels driven by mechanical power of the size which customarily used the waterway in the nine months prior to 8 December 1967. (Transport Act 1968 s 105.) The Board takes the view that s 105 does not place on it any obligation to maintain tow-paths. In practice the Board will normally restore a tow-path by backfilling piling with dredgings from the channel when it carries out maintenance work. When lengths of hitherto derelict canal are restored, whether by the Board or by volunteers, the tow-path is normally restored as well.

Other navigable waterways are under the control of the National Rivers Authority. There is no duty on the Authority to maintain tow-paths as such (where they exist), but it is subject to section 8 of the Water Act 1989. This provides that the Authority shall be under a general duty to promote the use of its land for recreational purposes and, in considering or formulating any proposals relating to its functions or those of a water undertaker, to have regard to the desirability of preserving for the public any freedom of access to areas of woodland, mountain, moor, heath, down, cliff or foreshore and other places of natural beauty.

A Code of Practice issued under section 10 of the 1989 Act (see 'Further Reading') notes that 'the public rights of way along what was once a working tow-path provide a valuable recreational resource'.

River banks Where a public right of way exists along a river bank that is not a tow-path the highway authority is under a duty to maintain the path, if necessary by repairing the river bank, provided that the way is publicly maintainable.

If a path runs along an embankment, the embankment is repairable by the highway authority if it is part of the path, but not if it is an independent construction. In *A-G v Staffordshire CC* (1905) the court refused a declaration that the highway authority had to repair an embankment along the top of which ran a road. Conversely in *Sandgate Urban District Council v Kent CC* (1898) the court held that a sea-wall was repairable by the authority because it was necessary for the protection of a road.

Erosion of waterside paths What if the line of a path is eroded by a river? So long as any part of the path remains, the duty to repair it continues. Once a path has been completely destroyed (not merely covered by water at certain times), it seems that the authority may be relieved of any obligation to reinstate it. This, at any rate, was held to be the position in a case where the repair 'would cost more than the subject matter of the repair is reasonably worth'. (*R v Greenhow* (1876).) It seems, therefore, that whether the duty to repair has ceased to exist is a matter of fact to be determined by the court according to the circumstances of the case. (For example, where the erosion is gradual, the authority is aware of the damage that is occurring and fails to take remedial action, the court might decline to hold that the authority had ceased to be liable to repair.)

Whether a right of way ceases to exist when the line of a path is totally eroded by a river is undecided. Since the line of a right of way

7 : MAINTENANCE AND IMPROVEMENT

(like a property boundary) is fixed, it is submitted that the right of way remains, with the result that a walker who chose to follow the line of the way by wading through the water would not be a trespasser.

Where a path runs along a coast and its line is destroyed, eg by a fall of cliff, it seems that the right of way ceases to exist, at any rate where the former line passes over what has become sea. The duty to maintain the path also ceases to exist.

In such circumstances it would be open to an authority to create a replacement path either by means of a creation order or agreement or by acquiring the land which now adjoins the coast so as to be able to dedicate a path along its length.

Similar action could be taken by an authority where a path had been eroded by a river.

7.3 How wide should a path be?

The statement accompanying the definitive map prepared under NPACA 49 or modified by WCA 81 sometimes gives the width of a path. If it does, then, by s 56(1) of the latter Act, the statement is conclusive evidence of the width (see chapter 4.6.9).

If the path has been set out by virtue of an inclosure award, its width is usually prescribed in the award. The same applies to paths brought into being by modern public path creation or diversion orders. If such evidence exists, but no width is recorded in the definitive statement, a modification order may be made under WCA 81 s 53 to amend the statement.

If a path runs between fences (or walls etc) the presumption is that the whole area between these has been dedicated to the public provided the fences were laid out by reference to the highway. In *A-G v Benyon* (1969) Lord Justice Goff said: 'It is clear that the mere fact that a road runs between fences, which of course includes hedges, does not *per se* give rise to any presumption. It is necessary to decide the preliminary question whether those fences were put up by reference to the highway or for some other reason. When that has been decided then a rebuttable presumption of law arises, supplying any lack of evidence of dedication in fact, or inferred from user, that the public right of passage, and therefore the highway, extends to the whole space between the fences and is not confined to such part as may have been made up. One has to decide the preliminary question in the sense that the fences do mark the limit of the highway unless there is something in the condition of the road or the circumstances to the contrary.'

If the width of a path is not defined by physical boundaries or by inclusion in the definitive statement or other document, it is that which has been habitually used by the public; this is a matter of evidence.

For certain purposes, statute defines a width for a path of otherwise undefined width. Provisions inserted by the Rights of Way Act 1990 into the Highways Act 1980 (see sections 134, 135, 137A of, and Sch 12A to, that Act) define minimum and, in some cases, maximum widths for paths affected by ploughing and other disturbance and by crops. See chapter 6.4.5. In addition, on a bridleway, a highway authority may require a gate to be at least five feet wide. (HA 80 s 145 — p 345.)

While there is no general statutory minimum width for a footpath or bridleway, a common sense width is that which is sufficient for two walkers or riders to pass.

7.4 Stiles and gates

Any stile or gate across a footpath or bridleway must, under HA 80 s 146 (p 346), be maintained by the landowner in a safe condition and to the standard of repair required to prevent unreasonable interference with the rights of users. This duty applies unless there is a specific agreement or condition to the contrary (eg for a stile erected under HA 80 s 66 or 147).

If the landowner fails in his duty, the highway authority, or a non-metropolitan district council exercising maintenance powers, may, after giving not less than 14 days' notice to both the owner and occupier, do any work necessary and charge the cost to the owner. The owner may also be committing an offence under sections 3 and 33 of the Health and Safety at Work Act 1974. See also chapter 2.6.2 for his potential liability to anyone injured because of a defective stile or gate.

If a landowner incurs expense in complying with his duty, he is entitled to recover at least 25% of this from the authority. This provision was introduced by the Countryside Act 1968 to provide a fair division of expenditure between owners and the highway authority. However, it has not had the desired effect of keeping stiles in good repair, because many highway authorities have failed to compel landowners to carry out their duties and landowners have rarely troubled to claim the grants due to them. In some counties the highway authorities have, as an alternative, provided stile kits for landowners, or volunteers acting on their behalf, to erect.

There is no statutory design to which stiles must comply, although a British Standard was published in 1979 covering post-and-rail stiles, kissing-gates and bridle-gates. Our recommendations on stile design and construction in chapter 8.6 are based upon this Standard. The diversity of stile designs found throughout England and Wales is, in our view, an attractive feature of the path network which should be perpetuated, provided that all stiles are maintained in a safe condition and are easy for all users, including the elderly, to cross.

7.5 The civil liability of highway authorities

Until 1964 authorities were liable only for 'misfeasance', ie for injuries resulting from repairs inadequately carried out. Under a rule of law,

7 : MAINTENANCE AND IMPROVEMENT

known as the 'doctrine of non-feasance', highway authorities were exempt from liability for non-repair of highways. This rule was abolished, as from 4 August 1964, by the Highways (Miscellaneous Provisions) Act 1961 s 1(1). Highway authorities have since then been liable for injury resulting from a highway being in disrepair. Section 1 of the 1961 Act is now HA 80 s 58 (p 329).

Section 58(2) provides that it shall be a defence for a highway authority to prove that it has taken reasonable care to maintain to the standard appropriate for a highway of that character, having regard to the traffic expected to use it. The doctrine of contributory negligence is expressly reserved (HA 80 s 58(1)) so that reduced damages will be awarded if a user has behaved unreasonably and is held partly responsible for his own injury.

In *Whiting v Hillingdon LBC* (1970) the plaintiff stepped into some undergrowth at the side of a path to allow someone to pass. The undergrowth concealed a tree stump, on which she injured her leg. The accident took place in April 1966. The highway authority had inspected the path in July 1965 and carried out a clearance of undergrowth in February 1966. The Court held that the authority had exercised reasonable care in its duty and was not liable.

In *Pridham v Hemel Hempstead Corporation* (1969) the plaintiff was walking along a metalled footpath. She caught her foot in a hole some 10 inches by 7 inches and injured her ankle. The Corporation carried out quarterly inspections. The Court considered the authority could have inspected more frequently and she was awarded damages. The Corporation appealed and the Court of Appeal reversed the High Court decision. Lord Justice Davies commented: 'The Judge had accepted that the system was reasonable and satisfied the test in section 1(2) of the Act and he should not have embarked on a work study exercise and come to the conclusion that an even better system of inspection was possible. The system was reasonable and the fact that it was practicable to do more did not make the system unreasonable.'

In *Haydon v Kent CC* (1978) the plaintiff slipped on a metalled footpath covered with impacted snow and ice and broke her ankle. She sued the county council for breach of its duty under s 44(1) of the Highways Act 1959 (now HA 80 s 41(1)) to maintain the path. The Court of Appeal held by a majority that, since 'maintenance' was defined in s 295 of the 1959 Act (now HA 80 s 329) to include 'repair', the duty under s 44(1) was wider than repairing the surface of the path itself and included removing the snow and ice so as to keep the path safe for those entitled to use it. On the facts, the Court found that the council had not been in breach of its duty. Its policy was to treat main roads first and then those paths which were reported to them as dangerous. It had been told of the condition of the path in the morning and had cleared it in the afternoon, but not in time to prevent the plaintiff's accident.

RIGHTS OF WAY

Although he reached the same conclusion as the other two appeal judges, Lord Denning disagreed with their view that the duty under s 44 included a duty to remove snow and ice. He also opined that failure to remove snow etc from the highway as required by s 129 of the 1959 Act (now HA 80 s 150 — p 347) did not give rise to civil action for damages.

These cases suggest that a highway authority should exercise greater care and attention on a metalled path than on an unmetalled field-path. Walkers on country paths must be expected to look out for uneven surfaces, roots and other minor hazards. However, the cases show that a highway authority cannot ignore its paths. If the authorities had not been able to show a reasonable and workable system of inspection and repair the decisions could well have been in favour of those who were injured.

7.6 Enforcing the duty to maintain

7.6.1 Introduction

As noted above (see chapter 7.2.2) a highway authority is under a duty to maintain those highways which are publicly maintainable. That duty can be enforced by any member of the public using the procedure under HA 80 s 56 (p 327) and described in this section. It is a useful and important procedure, particularly because the initial stages are relatively simple.

The principal limitation upon its use is that it applies only to publicly maintainable highways which are out of repair. Since, as noted on p 221, virtually all footpaths and bridleways are publicly maintainable, the restriction to such ways is not a serious one. However, the interpretation placed by the Court of Appeal on the meaning of 'out of repair' in *Hereford and Worcester CC v Newman* (1975) should be noted. As the judgments in the case, summarised on p 219, indicate, 'repair' must be linked strictly to restoration of the highway surface, or of a bridge forming part of the highway. The procedure cannot be used to secure the removal of obstructions, or of overhanging vegetation, nor can it be employed to require stiles or gates to be maintained. The emphasis placed by the judges was on the need for anything growing in the surface to have 'just grown there'; a tree, or crops, deliberately planted there, even without the permission of the highway authority, will not be covered by s 56. The principal use of the sections is thus to secure the repair of defective surfaces or bridges. The repair secured by use of the section is only to the standard traditional to the way; improvements do not come within the duty to maintain under s 56.

7 : MAINTENANCE AND IMPROVEMENT

7.6.2 Outline of the procedure

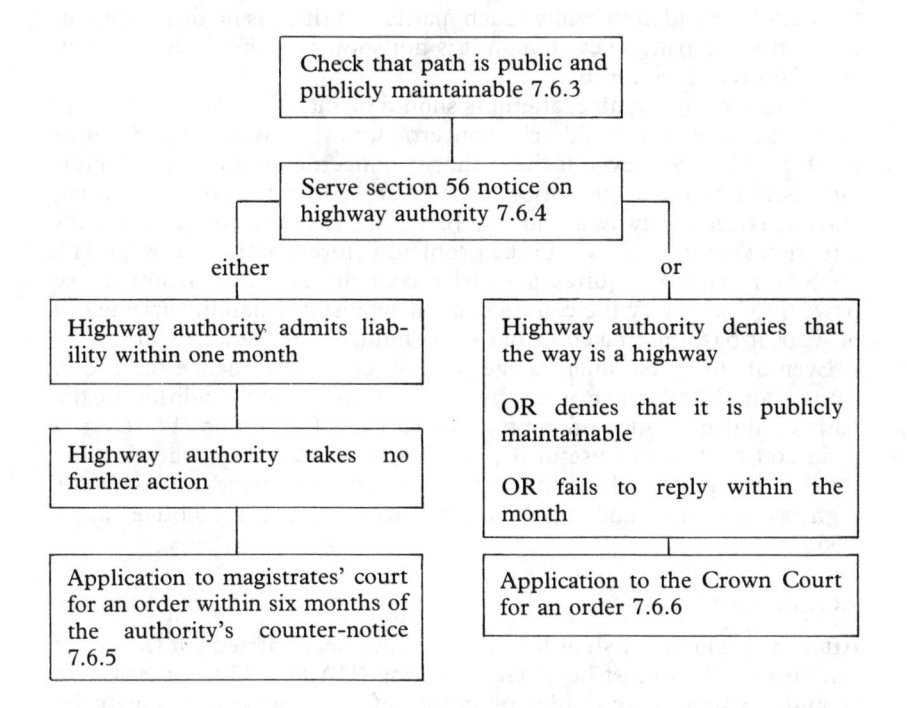

```
          ┌─────────────────────────────┐
          │ Check that path is public and│
          │ publicly maintainable 7.6.3  │
          └──────────────┬──────────────┘
                         │
          ┌──────────────┴──────────────┐
          │ Serve section 56 notice on   │
          │ highway authority 7.6.4      │
          └──────────────┬──────────────┘
        either                        or
```

Highway authority admits liability within one month	Highway authority denies that the way is a highway
Highway authority takes no further action	OR denies that it is publicly maintainable
	OR fails to reply within the month
Application to magistrates' court for an order within six months of the authority's counter-notice 7.6.5	Application to the Crown Court for an order 7.6.6

The chart above summarises the various steps. It is important to note that the first step, the serving of the notice, does not commit the complainant (the person serving the notice) to any further steps. In some cases the service of the notice alone will stir the authority into action, but note the comments below about the preliminary steps to be taken before the notice is served. If court action is needed, whether it will be in the magistrates' court or the Crown Court will depend on the highway authority's reaction, if any, to the notice.

7.6.3 The preliminary steps

The first formal part of the procedure is the service of a notice on the highway authority, but before that step is taken a number of matters must be considered and, if necessary, investigated. The first of these is to be certain that the path is a public right of way. If it is on the definitive map (unless subsequently closed or diverted) then by virtue of WCA 81 s 56 it is a public right of way. If it is not on the definitive map, it could nevertheless be a public right of way. However, use of the s 56 procedure to ascertain the status of a path is not to be recommended. The definitive map order procedure described in chapter 4.6.5 is intended to resolve such matters. If there is no dispute about the status of a path, even though it is not shown on the definitive map, the s 56 procedure can be used.

Before serving a notice, attempts should be made, by correspondence or discussion with the authority concerned, to seek to have the problem resolved. However, even if the authority concerned is a non-metropolitan district council, the notice must be served on the county council, since it is the highway authority. In such a case the county council's attention should be drawn to the problem before a notice is served. HA 80 Sch 7 para 7 requires a district council exercising maintenance powers to indemnify the county council against any liability arising out of work it has undertaken or out of its failure to undertake work.

Even at this preliminary stage the collection of evidence for use in court should be kept in mind. A note describing the condition of the path should be made and kept so that it can, if necessary, be referred to in court. It is also useful if photographs can be taken showing the state of the path both at the time of initial correspondence with the highway authority and immediately before serving the notice under s 56.

7.6.4 *Serving the notice*

After the preliminary steps listed above have been carried out the notice can be served. It must be given in writing (HA 80 s 320 — p 354) and should be sent to the chief executive of the highway authority by recorded delivery post. (HA 80 s 322 — p 355.) A copy of the notice should be retained by the complainant. A specimen notice is given below.

The following points should be borne in mind when preparing the notice:
(a) If action is intended over several paths, a separate notice must be served in respect of each.
(b) To avoid problems over representation in court, the notice should be given by an individual, even if he is acting on behalf of an organisation.
(c) The same individual must make any application to a court.

7 : MAINTENANCE AND IMPROVEMENT

> To Barsetshire County Council, County Hall, Barset.
>
> TAKE NOTICE that I John Smith of 25 Whiteacre Lane, Lowtown, claim that the way described in the Schedule hereto is a highway maintainable at the public expense.
>
> AND TAKE NOTICE that a portion of the said way between the stile at grid reference 695784 and the point at which the said way joins Otley Road at grid reference 696785 and being a distance of one hundred yards or thereabouts is out of repair.
>
> AND TAKE NOTICE that I hereby require you pursuant to sub-section (1) of Section 56 of the Highways Act 1980 to state:
> *(a)* whether you admit that the said portion of way is a highway maintainable at the public expense, and
> *(b)* whether you admit that you are the authority liable to maintain the said portion of way.
>
> Dated 15 February 1991
>
> JOHN SMITH
>
> SCHEDULE
> Footpath number 17 in the parish of Topsey as shown on the definitive map for the county of Barset prepared under the Wildlife and Countryside Act 1981.

7.6.5 *Applying to the magistrates' court*

If the highway authority admits, by formal notice or by letter, within one calendar month of the date of the notice served by the complainant, that the highway is public and that it is the authority liable to maintain it, then, if it does not embark upon and complete the repair work within a period of time which appears reasonable to the complainant, he may apply to the magistrates' court for an order requiring the authority to put the path in proper repair. It is essential that application be made to the court before the expiry of six months from the date of the authority's formal notice, or else the opportunity to do so will pass, and a new notice will have to be served by the complainant.

Before issuing a complaint (making an application) the path should be inspected again. It is a wise precaution to make further notes and take further photographs as previously described. An application to the magistrates' court is made by making a complaint before a magistrate. The complaint takes the following form:

RIGHTS OF WAY

COMPLAINT
M.C. ACT 1980 SECTIONS 51,52 : M.C. RULES 1981, R 4
LOWTOWN MAGISTRATES' COURT

Date of information:	15 April 1991
Defendant:	Barsetshire County Council
Address:	County Hall, Barset
Matter of complaint:	That there was and is a public highway known as footpath 17 in the parish of Topsey leading from Otley Road at grid reference 696785 to Hewit Road at grid reference 683772 maintainable at public expense; and a portion of the said highway lying between the stile at grid reference 695784 and the point at which the said highway joins Otley Road at grid reference 696785 is out of repair; and Barsetshire County Council has admitted that the said highway is a highway and that it is liable to maintain it.
	That the said John Smith applies to this Court pursuant to section 56 of the Highways Act 1980 for an order that Barsetshire County Council may be required to appear and show cause why it should not be ordered, if the court finds that the said portion of highway is out of repair, to put it into proper repair within such period as shall be specified in the order.
The complaint of:	John Smith
Address:	25 Whiteacre, Lowtown
Telephone no:	Lowtown 12345
	Who (upon oath) (after affirmation) states that the defendant is responsible for the matter of complaint of which particulars are given above.
	Taken (and sworn) (and affirmed) before me
	Justice of the Peace/Justices' Clerk

7 : MAINTENANCE AND IMPROVEMENT

For further information about procedure in the magistrates' court see chapter 6.9.

The procedure of the court in hearing the complaint is likely to be straightforward. The complainant only has to prove three matters:

(a) Service of the summons on the highway authority.
(b) That the notice has been served and that the highway authority has admitted its liability. The complainant has to go into the witness-box and produce by way of evidence, on oath, the original notice and the letter or counter-notice received from the authority.
(c) The complainant then gives a description of the state of the path to prove that it is out of repair. He should call another person to corroborate his evidence and to prove that the way is actually out of repair. It is helpful if photographs can be produced demonstrating the disrepair, but it must be possible to 'prove' them, eg by calling the photographer to give evidence. The photographs should show the path as it was immediately before the complaint was made.

The only argument in a case of this nature should be whether the path is out of repair. It is therefore a question of fact. If the case is lost, there is a right of appeal, under HA 80 s 317 (p 354), to the Crown Court. A solicitor should be consulted before proceeding further. There is some doubt whether a member of the public with no special interest in the way, ie no special property interest, is entitled to his costs if the application is successful but there is no harm in asking.

7.6.6 Applying to the Crown Court

If the highway authority fails to reply within one month to a notice, or serves a notice denying either that the way is a public highway or that it is publicly maintainable, any proceedings have to be brought in the Crown Court. An individual complainant has the right of audience in the Crown Court but, as the authority is likely to instruct a barrister to appear for it, consideration should be given by the complainant in such a case to the instruction of a solicitor, who would in turn instruct a barrister. Crown Court proceedings are expensive and time-consuming.

7.6.7 Further application to the magistrates' court

If a magistrates' court or the Crown Court orders a highway authority to put a highway in proper repair and the works have not been carried out by the end of the period specified in the order, the complainant may apply to the magistrates' court for an order authorising him to carry out the works himself (s 56(6)).

If the court is satisfied that the highway has not been put in proper repair, it must either extend the period specified in the original order or make a new order authorising the complainant to do the work. A complainant armed with such an order may, under s 56(7), recover from the highway authority expenses he reasonably incurs in carrying out repair works.

The first such authorisation of which we are aware was obtained in February 1991 by Mrs Zara Bowles from Axminster magistrates' court. The court had in April 1988 ordered Devon CC to put bridleway Axminster 49 and Membury 7 into proper repair by 31 December 1990. The CC failed to do so, and upon application by Mrs Bowles, the court authorised her to carry out the works.

7.7 Improving rights of way

7.7.1 Introduction

Highway authorities have power to effect various improvements to rights of way. The landowner or occupier may be entitled to compensation if his rights are injuriously affected by the improvement.

In carrying out any work the authority must have regard to the needs of disabled or blind persons whose mobility might thereby be impaired. (HA 80 s 175A — p 351.)

7.7.2 Signposting and waymarking

Although the words 'waymark' and 'waymarking' do not appear in legislation, CA 68 s 27(7) defines references to signposts as including references to other signs or notices serving the same purpose. Such 'other signs' can be taken to include waymarks. Whether the cairns traditionally used for mountain or moorland waymarking fall within the definition of 'other signs or notices serving the same purpose' as signposts has not been considered by the courts.

The duty to signpost where a path leaves a metalled road A highway authority's duties and powers to signpost and waymark are to be found in CA 68 s 27 (p 300). Authorities have a duty (subsection (2)) to signpost all footpaths, bridleways and byways where they leave a metalled road. No time limit was placed for compliance with this duty and, over 20 years since it was imposed, it has still not been fully complied with.

Signposts must indicate the nature of the public right, ie whether it is a footpath, bridleway or byway (subsection 2(a)). Authorities have discretion whether signs indicate the destination of the way and the distance to this (subsection 2(b)).

An authority can be relieved of its obligation to signpost a path where it leaves a metalled road if it considers a sign at that point is unnecessary and if the local council, or chairman of a parish meeting where there is

7 : MAINTENANCE AND IMPROVEMENT

no parish council, agrees. By withholding that agreement, a local council can thus require an authority to carry out its duty, but no period is laid down within which this must be done.

Meaning of 'road' and 'byway' 'Road' is not defined in CA 68, and thus the meaning of 'metalled road' in s 27 is not clear. Generally, eg in the Road Traffic Regulation Act 1984 and Road Traffic Act 1988, 'road' is defined as including any highway and any other road to which the public has access.

If 'road' in CA 68 is given a similar interpretation, the term 'metalled road' would cover any metalled way that was a highway or a way to which the public had access: it would not be restricted to metalled carriageways. Thus if a footpath ran along a metalled farm drive, but then diverged from it, there would be a duty to erect a sign at that point. On such an interpretation, it would appear that the duty to erect a signpost extends to locations where a metalled footpath, bridleway or byway meets an unmetalled one.

'Byway' is defined in s 27 as a byway open to all traffic (ie the same definition as in WCA 81 s 66). While this does not in itself mean that signs can only be put on ways shown as byways on a definitive map, this is in practice likely to be the case, since it would be difficult to decide other than by reference to the definitive map that a particular way was a 'byway'.

Signposts, waymarks and the Traffic Signs Regulations The relationship between s 27 and the provisions in Part V of the Road Traffic Regulation Act 1984 relating to traffic signs is not entirely clear. Section 65 of the 1984 Act permits traffic signs to be erected on or near highways only if they are of a design prescribed under regulations or directions given by the Secretary of State. Signs for footpaths and bridleways have not been so prescribed since 1966. There is a sign for byways in the current regulations (Traffic Signs and General Directions 1981 sign 737.1). However, a forthcoming revision of the regulations is expected to remove any doubt by reinstating a prescribed sign, while allowing authorities flexibility to retain the present variety of designs. There is no prescribed sign for waymarking footpaths, bridleways and byways. A sign in the shape of an arrow is recommended by the Countryside Commission, following the report of its Waymarking Study Group. The arrow is shown on p 257, and details of the recommended colours for footpaths, bridleways and byways are given there.

Entry onto land Section 71 of the 1984 Act (p 402) gives authorities power to enter on land for the purpose of erecting signs for footpaths and bridleways, including other signs such as waymarks.

Waymarking along the route: duties and powers The authority's duties under s 27 extend to the placing of signs at points along a path or way where the authority considers it necessary to have a signpost or waymark to assist persons unfamiliar with the locality (subsection (4)). Although the reference to the opinion of the authority gives a measure of discretion, the authority must give some consideration to whether it needs to take action in pursuance of this duty.

The authority also has a general power (subsection (1)) to erect and maintain signposts along a path or way.

Consultation with the owner or occupier This power may be exercised only after consultation with the owner or occupier of the land concerned. The requirement is to consult, not to obtain consent: he cannot refuse to allow waymarking. However, most waymarking is carried out by painted on, or fixing signs to, objects such as gateposts, stiles, trees or walls. Since these will be the property of the landowner, his permission is needed to waymark on them. If that permission is not given, the authority can avail itself of its power to erect signs in the surface of the path.

If an authority proposes to carry out its duty under subsection (2) to erect a signpost where a path leaves a metalled road and the sign is placed on land that forms part of a road which is a publicly-maintainable highway, eg on a grass verge, the highway authority is the owner of the land concerned (see chapter 2.5.2) and the requirement to consult does not apply. If the road is not a publicly-maintainable highway, or the sign is placed along the way, the duty to consult does apply.

Signposting and waymarking of RUPPs The position of RUPPs is anomalous. By definition these are at least of bridleway status and so can be signposted or waymarked as such. However, if the authority is satisfied that vehicular rights exist they can be marked as byways. Once reclassified under WCA 81 s 54 their status should be clear, and they can be signed accordingly.

Waymarking by volunteers An authority can give permission for other persons, eg voluntary workers, to erect and maintain signposts (subsection (5)). In practice much waymarking, and some erection of signposts, is carried out by volunteers. Guidance on the practical aspects of waymarking is in chapter 8.5.

7.7.3 Widening

Section 72(2) of the Highways Act 1980 (p 331) gives a local authority power to enter into a public path creation agreement or make a creation order for the purpose of widening an existing footpath or bridleway in

7 : MAINTENANCE AND IMPROVEMENT

the same way as if it was creating a new path or way. This power could be useful in cases where the use of a path or way has increased.

7.7.4 Aids to passage

Section 66(3) of the Highways Act 1980 (p 330) empowers a highway authority to provide and maintain in a footpath such barriers, rails or fences as it thinks necessary for safeguarding persons using the footpath. This enables the authority to erect, for example, bollards or a stile at the entrance to a wide footpath so as to prevent unlawful use by vehicles or horses, or put a handrail at steep or difficult points along the path. The power does not extend to bridleways but these are covered by the general power to improve highways given by s 62 (p 330).

7.7.5 Footways alongside, subways under and bridges over carriageways

Some improvement powers which apply only to carriageways are nevertheless of interest to walkers.

Section 66(1) of the Highways Act 1980 (p 330) requires a highway authority to make a footway by the side of any carriageway if it considers one necessary. This can be important, for footpaths frequently terminate on carriageways. Walkers can rarely avoid having to make part of their journey along a carriageway and footways are increasingly necessary on rural roads near villages.

Section 69 of the 1980 Act empowers an authority to construct a pedestrian subway under any carriageway; s 70 extends this power to the provision of footbridges over carriageways where these are necessary to make it safer or easier for pedestrians to cross the road. The widening of many main roads and the consequent speeding-up of traffic frequently make such facilities desirable.

7.7.6 Margins for horse-riders

Horse-riders also often find that part of their journey has to be along a carriageway. As this can be both dangerous and unpleasant, HA 80 s 71 (p 331) imposes a duty on the highway authority to provide an adequate grass or other margin for horse-riders or driven livestock by the side of any carriageway where it considers such provision necessary or desirable in the interests of safety.

Whether or not there is a margin, a horse has a right to be on a carriageway (except a motorway) and drivers of motor vehicles must take special care when passing horses. In *Burns v Ellicott* (1969) the plaintiff was riding her horse along a road. The defendant drove a car in the same direction and passed her with only inches to spare. The horse took fright, reared up, struck the car and was seriously injured. The defendant pleaded that he had not been negligent. Mr Justice Paull, awarding the plaintiff the cost of the horse and an extra £20, said

RIGHTS OF WAY

'A car driver must take great care in passing a horse. His duty is to slow down and give the horse a wide berth.'

7.7.7 Other specific improvement powers

The 1980 Act also contains the following powers of improvement which may be usefully applied to rights of way:

- (a) Levelling. (Ss 76,77 — p 331.)
- (b) Constructing a bridge to replace a ford or stepping stones (S 91 — p 332), or reconstructing a bridge. (S 92 — p 332.)
- (c) Planting trees and shrubs. (S 96.)
- (d) Metalling. (S 99.)
- (e) Draining the path and digging a ditch alongside. (S 100 — p 332.)
- (f) Treating the highway to mitigate dust. (S 104.)
- (g) Providing a cattle-grid. (S 82.)
- (h) Protecting against hazards of nature. (S 102 — p 333.)

All these are powers, not duties. Compensation may be payable to the owner or occupier.

7.7.8 The general power of highway authorities

In addition to these specific powers, HA 80 s 62 (p 330) gives highway authorities a general power to carry out any work for the improvement of a highway. This power could be used to authorise making steps on a steep or muddy path, putting stepping-stones in a stream, or laying planks over boggy sections.

7.7.9 Powers of local councils

Lighting The Parish Councils Act 1957 gives local councils powers to improve paths with the consent of the owner and occupier. One of the most important is lighting. (S 3 — p 296.) The number of public paths likely to require lighting is small, but lights can be important on paths leading to, for example, a village hall or a bus stop.

Seats and shelters Section 1 of the 1957 Act (p 296) empowers local councils to erect seats and shelters at the side of public paths.

Notice of danger By s 72 of the Road Traffic Regulation Act 1984 (p 402) a local council may, with the consent of the landowner, erect on or near a footpath or bridleway notice of the existence of any danger.

General power In addition to these specific powers, LGA 72 s 137, as amended, empowers a local council to incur expenditure (to a current maximum of £3.50 per elector) on anything which in its opinion is in the interests of its area, or any part of it, or all or some of its inhabitants.

7 : MAINTENANCE AND IMPROVEMENT

Many small improvements to footpaths or bridleways could come within this definition.

The provision is authority only for spending the money: the landowner's consent to any improvement will normally be needed. In addition it is also necessary that the benefit conferred on the inhabitants is commensurate with the expenditure. The money can be spent directly by the council, or given to another person or body for it to spend.

8
Things you can do

8.1 Introduction

In the previous seven chapters we have explained the law on rights of way. Readers will by now be aware of the duties placed upon highway authorities to look after the public's interests, and of the wide range of powers available to them to carry out those duties.

But what if a right of way has not been maintained, or is obstructed? How can the problem be resolved, and, if necessary, how can the highway authority be obliged to carry out its duty?

The first step is to report the problem. Chapter 8.2 considers to whom that report is best made, and what move to make next if no action results. To gain a general picture of the state of rights of way in an area, a survey may be needed — chapter 8.3 offers advice on its conduct and follow-up.

Practical work The remainder of the chapter deals with further practical action. Chapter 8.4 describes how a map or guide to the local paths may be produced, and chapters 8.5 to 8.7 give information about three types of practical path work which can easily be carried out by volunteers: waymarking, stile building and path clearance.

In most instances, a volunteer doing practical path work is undertaking the statutory duty either of the highway authority, eg clearance of surface vegetation, maintenance of the surface or waymarking, or of the landowner, eg clearance of overhanging vegetation or repair of stiles. Even where the work is not a duty, liabilities can fall on the authority or the owner if it is not properly carried out. It is therefore essential that permission be obtained beforehand for any practical work both from the highway authority and from the landowner, or occupier if he has power to give consent.

There are many other aspects to practical work, all of which are fully dealt with in *Footpaths*, a handbook published by the British Trust for Conservation Volunteers (see 'Further Reading'). The Trust also publishes handbooks on dry-stone walling and fencing which contain further advice on stiles and gates. Affiliation to it brings various benefits to any voluntary organisation planning practical path work.

8 : THINGS YOU CAN DO

8.2 Getting problems dealt with

8.2.1 Reporting problems

To the landowner or occupier In cases of obstruction, the direct approach to a landowner or occupier to resolve a problem should not be ignored. As noted in chapter 6, if he is willing to deal with the matter, this can be the quickest solution. More details of the best way to make such an approach are given in chapter 6.8.2.

To the local council As explained in chapter 1.3.6, although parish and community councils have no duties in respect of rights of way, they do have considerable powers, and a council which takes an interest in its rights of way can do much good work. Whether a particular local council is interested, and likely to act upon a report, is impossible to predict unless one has had previous dealings, but if the council is known to be keen, the report should be sent to it.

To a user organisation User organisations such as the RA are often able to help. They can give advice, supply addresses, make approaches to appropriate bodies and, in certain circumstances, organise practical work on the ground.

To the highway authority Unless it seems that a problem is likely to be resolved by being reported to the owner, occupier or local council, a report should be made to the highway authority. All problems, whether obstructions, ploughing, bulls, or lack of maintenance, should be reported.

If a non-metropolitan district council is known to be exercising powers on behalf of a county council, the report should be sent to it.

A sample report form, giving the details which will be needed by the authority, is set out below.

Status of path — delete as necessary
Footpath/Bridleway/Road used as public path/Byway open to all traffic

Parish/Community	Definitive map number (if known)
Route details From	Name and address of landowner or occupier (if known)

RIGHTS OF WAY

> Grid reference
>
> To
>
> Grid reference
>
> Details of problem, with grid references where possible
>
>
>
> Date when the problem was encountered
>
> Name and address   Signed
>
> Please continue overleaf if necessary

This form is suitable for the submission of individual reports. The RA can supply a free leaflet *Report that path problem* which includes a similar form.

8.2.2 Inducing a highway authority to act

The duties and powers of a highway authority with regard to the removal of obstructions and the carrying out of maintenance work have been considered earlier (see chapters 6.2 and 7.2.2). But what if, having received a report of a problem, an authority fails to act?

Various courses are open. Before considering these a word of warning may be in order. Experience shows that in very many instances failure by an authority to act over a particular obstruction is due not to incompetence, sloth, or any lack of will, but to sheer pressure of work. In a medium-sized English county there can be as many as 9000 paths extending for 3000 miles. The volume of work generated by this kind of network can be prodigious. And dealing with maintenance or obstructions is only one part of an authority's responsibilities for rights of way. Committee briefs must be prepared, diversion orders processed, enquiries from the public answered, and the mammoth task of updating the definitive map tackled. In our experience in all but a small minority of counties the number of staff employed on footpath work bears no

8 : THINGS YOU CAN DO

relation to the number needed if an authority's duties are properly to be carried out.

One reason for this seems to be that since footpaths are rights of way, responsibility for this work rests with a county's surveyor who, being mainly interested in roads, treats footpaths as a minor and insignificant part of his department's duties. This attitude is, however, gradually changing.

But Parliament has given authorities the duties with the intention that they be carried out, and councillors must see that their council obeys the law. So if an authority takes too long to deal with a problem, or if it intimates that it intends to take no action, one or more of the following actions can be taken.

A letter to the committee chairman A letter asking for action can be sent to the chairman of the authority's committee that has responsibility for rights of way. The name of the committee and of its chairman can be obtained from the authority's information office.

A letter to a councillor A letter can be sent to a councillor (either one in whose ward the problem is located or one in whose ward the aggrieved person lives) asking the councillor to press for action and, if the matter is not resolved satisfactorily, to have the matter placed on the agenda for the next meeting of the council committee which has responsibility for public rights of way.

Asking the local council to act An approach can be made to the local council in which the problem is located. If the problem is an obstruction, the council should be requested to instruct the clerk to write to the highway authority giving details of the obstruction and requesting the authority to secure its removal. This step has an important significance since, under HA 80 s 130(6), if such a council, or a meeting in a parish or community where there is no council, represents to the highway authority that a highway has been stopped-up or obstructed, it is the duty of the authority, unless satisfied that the representations are incorrect, to take proper proceedings. If it fails to do so, the local council or meeting may apply to the High Court for an order of *mandamus* (see chapter 6.2 for an example of such action).

A complaint to the Local Ombudsman Part III of the Local Government Act 1974 set up two bodies of commissioners, the Commission for Local Administration in England and the Commission for Local Administration in Wales. Their function is to investigate complaints by members of the public who claim to have suffered injustice through maladministration by certain public bodies. The Commissioners are popularly known as the Local Ombudsmen and are so referred to here. They are distinct from the Parliamentary Commissioner for Administration (see chapter 1.3.9) who investigates complaints against government departments and agencies.

Maladministration is not defined in the 1974 Act, but is taken by the Local Ombudsman to cover administrative action (or inaction) which is in some way improperly based. Excessive delay, neglect, incompetence, failure to observe rules or procedures and failure to carry out statutory duties are examples of improper conduct which may amount to maladministration. But a Local Ombudsman normally may not investigate a matter if the complainant has a right of appeal to a tribunal or a Minister, or has a right of recourse to a court.

The Local Ombudsmen may investigate complaints of maladministration by a county council, a district council, a London borough council, the City of London, a joint board (including national park boards), the exercise by the National Rivers Authority of its land drainage functions, and a police authority (except the Home Secretary who is the police authority for London). A parish or community council may be investigated only if it is acting as agent for a county or district council.

Making a complaint A complaint can be made directly to the Ombudsman, or it may be made to a member of the authority, with a request that he forward the complaint to the Ombudsman. In either event the Ombudsman will ask the chief executive of the authority to comment on the complaint before he decides whether to conduct a formal investigation. This may suffice to resolve the problem.

The procedure for submitting complaints is explained in a free booklet *Your Local Ombudsman* produced by the Commissions and available from them and from council offices.

An authority which has been investigated by the Local Ombudsman must make his report available to the public and the press. If he has found maladministration the authority must consider the report and tell him what action it proposes to take. It is not bound to take any action, but may be forced to do so by adverse publicity. Experience shows that a well-publicised finding of maladministration can be an effective way of securing improvements in the administration by an authority of its responsibilities for public rights of way.

In the period January 1988 — December 1991 Local Ombudsmen found maladministration in the following cases:

(a) Failure to investigate possible existence of a right of way *(Kingswood BC, January 1988)*.

(b) Failure to clear obstructions from a path proposed for extinguishment *(Reigate and Banstead BC, January 1988)*.

(c) Unreasonable delay in dealing effectively with obstructions *(Shepway BC, February 1988)*.

8 : THINGS YOU CAN DO

(d) Unreasonable delay in removing obstructions, failure to reach a decision after two years and inadequate reports to committees *(North Hertfordshire DC, May 1988)*.
(e) Unreasonable delay in removing obstructions *(Rochester upon Medway BC, August 1988)*.
(f) Failure to deal promptly with complaints of obstructed paths *(Warwickshire CC, November 1988)*.
(g) Unreasonable delay in tackling problems caused by fierce dogs intimidating path-users *(Rochester upon Medway BC, March 1989)*.
(h) Failure to include an alternative footpath in a side roads order *(Kent CC, May 1989)*.
(i) Unauthorised development and misleading assurances about access *(Gwynedd CC, August 1989)*.
(j) Unreasonable delay in clearing obstructions from a bridleway *(Wiltshire CC, November 1989)*.
(k) Unreasonable delay in dealing with obstructions on a footpath *(Derbyshire CC, May 1990)*.
(l) Unreasonable delay in clearing obstructions from three bridleways *(Devon CC, February 1991)*.
(m) Failure to take action to resolve uncertainties about the line of a path *(Humberside CC, May 1991)*.
(n) Unreasonable delay in dealing with obstructions and failure to enforce effectively the provisions of the Rights of Way Act 1990 *(North Yorkshire CC, November 1991)*.
(o) Failure to deal effectively with complaints, failure to keep councillors informed and failure to implement confirmed diversions on the ground *(Essex CC, December 1991)*.

In his annual reports for 1987 and 1988 one of the ombudsmen, Mr F G Laws, referred to complaints about paths, saying in the latter report that what he asked of authorities was that complaints about obstructions should be recorded, that cases should be dealt with systematically and that a reasonable allocation of resources should be made to ensure that paths were not lost or totally neglected.

The RA's bulletin *Footpath Worker* (see 'Further Reading') regularly summarises reports by the Local Ombudsmen.

A complaint to the District Auditor Each local authority has its accounts audited by an auditor appointed by the Audit Commission. The Commission has prepared a Code of Audit Practice for local authorities (see 'Further Reading'). The Local Government Finance Act 1982 s 15 requires an auditor to satisfy himself that the authority has made proper arrangements for securing economy, efficiency and effectiveness in its use of resources. The Code (paragraphs 35–39) says that this responsibility should be discharged by including a value-for-money element to the audit. It defines effectiveness as how well a programme or activity is achieving its established goals or other intended effects.

The auditor should pay particular attention to good management practice, for example, by monitoring results against predetermined performance objectives and standards, to ensure that outstanding performance is encouraged and unacceptable performance corrected. Further, although it is not an auditor's functions to question policy, he should consider the effects of policy and examine the arrangements by which policy decisions are reached. There appears therefore to be scope for anyone who considers that the action an authority has taken to fulfil its rights-of-way functions has been lacking in effectiveness to ask the auditor to investigate that alleged lack of effectiveness as part of his audit. The authority, or the Audit Commission, will provide details of the auditor.

A complaint to the magistrates' court A magistrates' court has power to order an authority to take action on a complaint under the following powers:

(a) If the problem is that the path is out of repair, HA 80 s 56 can be used (see chapter 7.6).
(b) If the magistrates can be persuaded that an obstruction is a statutory nuisance, an abatement order can be sought under the Environmental Protection Act 1990 (see chapter 6.12).
(c) If an obstruction is 'sudden and substantial', it may come within HA 80 s 150 (see p 172).

An application to the High Court for *mandamus* The provision in s 130 described in chapter 6.2 clearly gives considerable power to local councils, but would the principles enunciated also apply to an application by an individual? The only case in which such an application has been considered is *R v Lancashire CC, ex parte Guyer* (1980) which was also concerned with obstructions to a path not shown on the definitive map, but, unlike the *Send* case (p 171), the status of the path was hotly disputed. The CC argued that the provision did not require action to be taken to determine the status of a way which was in dispute. The Court of Appeal upheld this view, and refused to grant an order of *mandamus*.

From these cases it seems that the Court would grant an order of *mandamus* if an individual applied in respect of a highway authority's failure to secure the removal of obstructions from a way shown on the definitive map if, and only if, it could be demonstrated to the satisfaction of the Court that the authority had so exercised its discretion as to take no effective action whatsoever, not that it had chosen to adopt one course of action rather than another.

8.3 Path Surveys

The aim of a path survey is to walk the paths and to note their condition and the action needed to remedy any problems.

As the basis for a nationwide sample survey of the rights-of-way network in 1988, the Countryside Commission published a survey manual (see 'Further Reading'). This gives guidance and sample forms to use. If the guidance is followed, it would be possible to compare your results with the results from the Commission's survey (see 'Further Reading').

Benefits The main benefits of a path survey are:
(a) To focus attention on the paths and remind people living in the area of an often neglected local asset.
(b) To get all the paths walked or ridden and obstructions, illegal ploughing, overgrowth, bulls in fields, misleading notices, etc, noted for future action.
(c) To note any gaps in the path network and seek to get them filled by the creation of new paths.
(d) To provide documentary evidence of path use which may be produced at subsequent public inquiries in connection with proposed extinguishments or diversions or definitive map orders.
(e) To provide an invaluable opportunity for ramblers and other organised path users to co-operate with parish councillors, local individuals, schools, Women's Institutes and civic or preservation societies.

Timing and participation Path surveys are good projects for two main reasons: firstly, because almost anybody can do them, secondly, they are flexible in timing and can take place at any time of the year.

The only skill required is the ability to follow a large-scale map accurately. (Where those making the survey are totally inexperienced in rights-of-way work some briefing may be needed.) This means that local people and organisations can be involved. Surveys may prove particularly attractive to schools as they can be spread over a period of time and combined with outdoor teaching (eg local land use-patterns, local history and natural history).

The local council The interest and co-operation of the local council is an important part of a successful path survey.

Even if a local council seems unlikely to be interested, it should be approached about the proposed survey as a matter of courtesy. At the

RIGHTS OF WAY

same time other local bodies should be invited to take part, eg schools, Women's Institutes, local societies.

It is desirable that a map showing the public rights of way should be exhibited in every parish and community at a point where it is always available for reference, eg outside the village hall or church. Where this is not already the case, or if the map is out of date, the local council should be encouraged to arrange for the exhibition of an up-to-date map.

Maps The usual map for survey use is the OS 1:25,000 scale map, which will have public rights of way marked on it (see chapter 4.11). However, a check will need to be made with the surveying authority to ensure that any changes to the definitive map subsequent to OS's publication date are noted. The OS 6″ to the mile or 1:10,000 scale maps are more detailed, and therefore correspondingly more useful, but are also about 20 times as expensive as the 1:25,000 map. Small-scale maps, such as the 1:50,000 Landranger, are not suitable, as they do not show field boundaries.

The surveying authority may be willing to provide a copy of the definitive map for the area.

How to organise a survey Surveying the paths means walking or riding them and reporting on their condition. What this involves will vary considerably from one parish to another. A small parish with a dozen public paths may be dealt with in an afternoon. A large parish with over 100 paths could take several weekends especially if the paths are hard to locate on the ground. The size of the job can be varied to match the availability of people. A local school undertaking a parish survey could spread it over a month or so; a Women's Institute could split a large parish into sections.

The organiser's job is to make sure that every path is walked or ridden, and that the surveyors know what to record. A party can be divided into groups. The leader of a group must be able to read a map. The other important job will be the reporting procedure; provision of a form for all surveyors to use is recommended.

The various steps to be taken are as follows:
(a) Appoint party leaders.
(b) Obtain clearly readable copies of a suitable map for the parish one for each party and one to be kept as a master. Make sure that path numbers are added if necessary and are readable.
(c) Mark on the master copy of the map, in different colours, the paths to be walked by each group. One way of allocating paths is simply to divide the parish into equal portions.
(d) When all paths are allocated, mark up the maps for the groups. Colour in only the paths for that group using different colours for footpaths and bridleways.

8 : THINGS YOU CAN DO

(e) Prepare a master list of the paths to be walked or ridden by each group. The list will allow a check to be made later. Give each group a list of the paths it is to walk or ride.
(f) Give each group leader the marked-up map, list of paths to be walked or ridden and a report form for each path.
(g) Leaders should ask party members to share the jobs, for example, filling in the report forms, following the route on an ordinary map, looking out for stiles, gates and useful landmarks.
(h) Tell leaders to whom the reports, lists and maps should be returned.

The law It is desirable that people surveying paths should have some idea of rights-of-way law, eg what constitutes an obstruction or a misleading notice. If they do not possess this knowledge the written guidance to surveyors may need to be more detailed.

What to look for
(a) Things to be put right, eg obstructions, ploughing and crops, overgrowth and undergrowth, locked gates, faulty, dangerous or missing stiles and footbridges, misleading or deterrent notices, impassable mud, illegal use by vehicles.
(b) Improvements to be made, eg signposts, waymarking, proposals for new linking paths to create round walks or rides, places where walker/rider conflict needs sorting out.
(c) Corrections to existing maps. Physical features are not always shown correctly on maps. Hedges may have been removed, new bridges provided, woodland cut down, old buildings removed or new ones erected. It is useful for these changes to be noted and included in the survey report. Changes since the latest OS map can be reported to Ordnance Survey.

Subsequent action Even if local people take no part, the holding of a survey alone will arouse interest, particularly if it is publicised. But full value comes only with effective subsequent action. A report should be produced containing both a summary of findings, and details of the individual problems. The report should be forwarded to the highway authority (or its agent) with a request for action. Copies should also be sent for information to the other local authorities and to representatives of user groups, and can usefully be sent to the local library and record office.

Publishing the survey A report should be released to the press when the details of the problems are forwarded to the local authorities.

RIGHTS OF WAY

A sure way of ensuring press coverage is to use statistics. Thus the accompanying press release might read:

> The 500-member East Barset Ramblers' Group today demanded action from Barsetshire County Council over the 'deplorable' state of public paths in the north-west of the county.
>
> Launching the findings of a recent survey by the Group, Chairman Mrs Jean Walker said:
>
> 'It is virtually impossible to go for a pleasant walk in the area we surveyed around Scrooby, Henshaw and Hensleyhurst.
>
> 'We looked at 57 paths which the public has a legal right to use, with a total length of nearly 20 miles.
>
> 'We found that over two-thirds of them either had problems serious enough to deter the average walker or were totally impassable.
>
> 'There were no fewer than 47 obstructions, including a house and a cesspit, 33 missing stiles and gates and 23 paths obscured by ploughing and crops.
>
> 'Even if the paths were in better order they would be difficult to find and follow.
>
> 'At least 74 signposts are needed to show where paths leave roads, and 55 of the 57 paths need waymarking with painted or metal arrows to help the public find their way.
>
> 'This is a shocking state of affairs.
>
> 'We have sent details of all the problems we found to the County Council, which has a legal duty to see that all the public paths are kept in good order.
>
> 'We are also asking the parish councils in the area to help up get matters put right.
>
> Mrs Walker concluded:
>
> 'Walking in the countryside is Britain's most popular recreation, with over 10 million people regularly taking a walk of two miles or more.
>
> 'The countryside around Scrooby is particularly attractive, and many local people would undoubtedly go and enjoy a walk there if only the paths were in better shape.
>
> 'We shall be pressing the County Council to take action to see that this happens.'
>
> -ends-

The local press should also be invited to report and photograph the survey while in progress. The best time is at the very beginning.

8.4 Producing a path guide or map

The production of a path guide or map can have several benefits. If produced by a local group or society it will help that body's work locally as well as its membership and finances, and by publicising the paths it will encourage their use, possibly by people who would not otherwise go walking. This in turn will help to keep the paths in good condition and save them from threats of closure.

Contents of the text The greatest care should be taken to ensure that the descriptions of paths are accurate. This should include the checking of each description by at least one person other than the author. Try to base your descriptions on permanent rather than temporary or seasonal landscape features, but bear in mind (and warn readers) that even apparently permanent features may change or disappear during the currency of a book. The inclusion in the guide of information on history, topography or botany will add to the value of the guide and serve as a useful publicity and selling point.

If possible this information should appear with, but be distinguished from, the walk descriptions. It is also useful to include a map showing the location of the walks. Before text is submitted to a publisher or to a printer, the paths need to be walked again and any problems dealt with.

The following should also be included in the guide: details of the publisher and its other publications, the address to which reports of path problems should be sent, information on local public transport services, a list of local Ordnance Survey maps and a note on rights and responsibilities in the countryside. For this last note the Countryside Commission may give permission for its Access Charter to be reproduced.

Who will publish the guide? An individual or organisation can be their own publisher. Alternatively they can try to interest an established publisher in the proposed guide. A variant is to have a series of walks published in a local paper, and then compile a book of the most popular ones.

However the guide is published the preparation of the text will be the responsibility of the individual or organisation. Having done this, many authors of path guides have wanted to retain control and so have published the guide themselves.

The first step should be to decide the area the guide will cover, and how long the walks will be. Some ideas to help in planning can be obtained from other path guides.

Writing for an established publisher The main advantage is that the work is limited. The author provides the text, and possibly the maps. The publisher arranges printing and distribution.

This has advantages if it would be difficult for the author to arrange distribution. But a publisher may not sell a local guide through the small local shops, village post offices, etc that would be willing to stock it.

Some idea of how a book will appear if a publisher takes it up can be judged from looking at some of his other publications. Many publishers have a standard format for walk guides. A publisher will either pay a royalty fee based on the number of copies sold or a fixed sum agreed in advance. A reasonable royalty is 10% of the retail price.

Writing for a newspaper This can be an excellent way of bringing local walking opportunities to the notice of the public. Before approaching a newspaper it is sensible to have a good number of walks planned; if the first few walks featured in the paper are popular there will be a demand to continue the series. Once the walks have been described for a paper it is relatively easy subsequently to prepare them for publication in a book. But if this is a long-term aim the author should agree it with the paper so that there is no misunderstanding. The paper needs to know that copyright is to be retained. If maps based on Ordnance Survey material are provided to a paper it will be liable to OS for royalties.

Being your own publisher The first step is to make a thorough assessment of the proposed publication. Work out how many pages the text and maps will take up, add space for other information and advertisements (if any) and decide the type of cover. A four-colour cover is undoubtedly an eye-catcher in the shops but will add substantially to the cost. A skilfully drawn design in one colour will be a lot cheaper and almost as effective. When calculating the number of pages bear in mind that printers work in multiples of eight.

Having obtained this information, printers can be approached for estimates. As their prices will vary, it is worth obtaining three estimates. Having obtained an estimate of the printing cost, the retail price of the book can be calculated. A bookseller or newsagent stocking the guide will expect a discount of one-third off the cover price. This leaves two-thirds of the cover price, out of which you must pay the printer and meet all the other costs associated with the guide's production. A suggested starting-point is to calculate the unit cost of printing and production and to treble it to obtain the retail price. On this basis, the publisher will retain about one-third of the price as surplus. This can be used to finance other work on the paths and to provide capital for future editions or other publications.

Finding the capital to pay the printer can be an obstacle which needs to be solved at an early stage. Bodies such as the Countryside Commission, the local authority or tourist board may be keen to encourage

8 : THINGS YOU CAN DO

use of the paths and willing to make a grant or an interest-free loan. The printers may be willing to delay payment of part of the bill to allow it to be financed from sales revenue.

If you are an individual or an organisation which is not a charity, tax may be payable on the profits made as a publisher. For a charity, provided that the trading is to further one of its principal aims, there is statutory exemption from taxation. A liability to tax will also arise where an individual receives royalties from a publisher or Public Lending Right.

Maps accompanying the text One approach is for sketch-maps in a book to be detailed enough to enable the reader to follow the walk either from the text or from the map. This has the advantage of enabling the reader to start the walk at any point and also to walk in the reverse direction to that indicated in the text. This is perhaps the ideal to work for, but it needs an artist or draughtsman capable of producing maps of suitable quality.

Alternatively, it may be sufficient merely to provide an outline sketch-map, and to encourage the walker to buy an OS map, preferably at 1:25,000 scale.

Using Ordnance Survey maps OS maps are, like other publications, copyright. To base maps on them OS's permission will have to be obtained prior to publication and a royalty fee paid. The fee will depend on the extent to which the maps in the guide could be used as a substitute for the local OS map. Copyright in OS maps lasts for 50 years. Maps published more than 50 years ago are therefore out of copyright, and can be used for reproduction free of charge. The disadvantage is that such maps are out of date; survey work will be needed to correct the information.

Advertisements As well as bringing in useful revenue, advertisements can be used to fill spaces which would otherwise remain blank, such as the insides of covers. Pubs along the walks, local shops selling ramblers' gear and bus operators are potential advertisers.

Producing a footpath map A footpath map for a relatively large area must inevitably be based on an Ordnance Survey map and the comments above apply. Assuming that this hurdle is overcome, you will then have to decide whether to use one or more colours. Using only one colour saves money but great care with symbols has to be taken to avoid paths and field boundaries being confused. The use of two or more colours gives greater scope, but, in addition to being more expensive, means more work in producing separate drawings for each colour.

If the map is printed on one side only the reverse can be used for walk descriptions, publicity for other publications and information on the public's rights and responsibilities in the countryside.

Distribution Retail outlets such as booksellers and newsagents expect at least 33 ⅓% discount. Wholesalers, who supply retailers, expect even more — up to 50% or more. Members of organisations can usually be found to go round retail outlets to persuade them to stock the publication. Try and avoid placing copies on a sale or return basis, but bear in mind that distribution is not a once and for all task; regular return visits, or telephone calls, are necessary to ensure that outlets are kept well supplied. Space will be needed to store the unsold copies of a guide or map, and these should be insured against damage such as flood or fire.

Publicity The best time to launch a walks publication is generally considered to be the spring, so as to sell the guide at the most popular time for walking. At least two weeks before the actual publication date send a news release to the local papers describing the book and enclosing a review copy. A display featuring the book and the work of the organisation responsible mounted in a local library at the same time will give a useful boost to sales and membership. A poster using the design of the cover may be used in the windows of retail outlets to give extra publicity. It can also be useful to send copies to magazines such as *Country Walking* and *The Great Outdoors* as well as to bodies such as the OSS, the RA and the Youth Hostels Association (addresses in chapter 9.5) for possible review in their journals.

The publication automatically has copyright vested in it. Copyright law requires that a copy be sent within a month of publication to the Superintendent, Copyright Receipt Office, The British Library, Store Street, London WC1E 7DG. If one of the five following libraries requests a copy within a year of publication, it must be sent: Bodleian Library, Cambridge University Library, National Library of Scotland, Trinity College Library Dublin, and National Library of Wales.

Sending your publication to the British Library has the advantage that it will be listed in the British National Bibliography, which is a further source of publicity and orders.

Public Lending Right Where a book has one or more named individuals as author or joint authors, those people will normally be entitled to apply for Public Lending Right (PLR). The amount payable is based on the estimated number of times the publication is lent out from public libraries. Although the right is vested in the individual, the amounts which become payable can be assigned to another person or organisation, including charities such as the RA and OSS. Details and application forms can be obtained from the PLR Office, Bayheath House, Prince Regent Street, Stockton-on-Tees, Cleveland TS18 1DF.

8 : THINGS YOU CAN DO

8.5 Waymarking

8.5.1 Introduction

The legal background to waymarking and signposting is to be found in chapter 7.7.2; the general guidance in chapter 8.1 should also be noted. Before work can be started, the consent of both the highway authority and the owner or occupier must be obtained, not only to the scheme in general but also to the actual locations for the waymarks. A preliminary survey will also be needed to determine these locations. It is essential that the correct line of the right of way should be waymarked.

Regular maintenance of any waymarking scheme is essential. Not only can the waymarks fade, or be removed, but the trees or posts on which they are painted or fixed may be removed, or become obscured by growth of vegetation. When obtaining consents for the initial waymarking ask also for the right to return and renew waymarks as necessary.

8.5.2 The recommended arrow

The shape of the arrow recommended by the Countryside Commission, supported by the OSS and RA, is shown below.

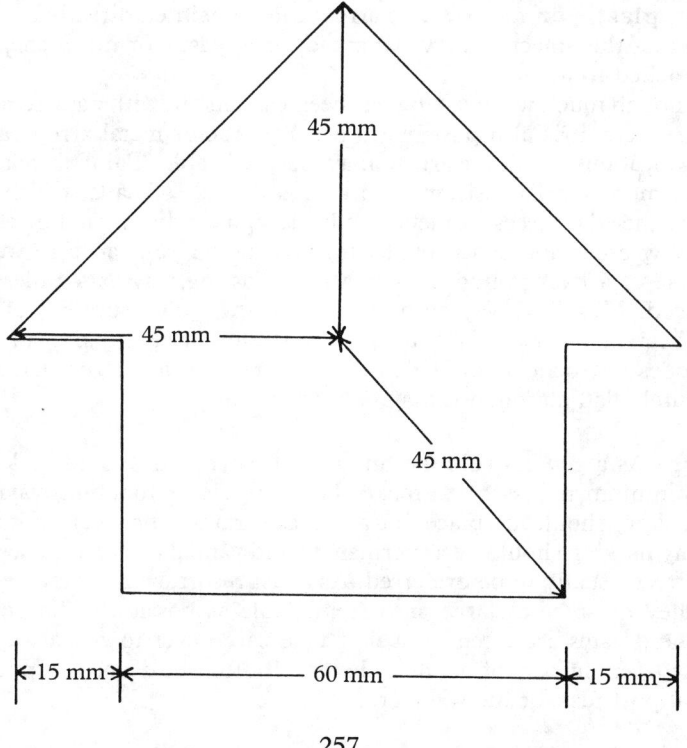

RIGHTS OF WAY

The recommended colours, from British Standard range 4800 or the Munsell range, are as follows (see the Commission's leaflet *Waymarking public rights of way*):
Footpath — Yellow — British Standard 08 E 51: Munsell 3.75Y 8.5/12
Bridleway — Blue — British Standard 20 E 51: Munsell 5P P7/8
Byway — Brick Red — British Standard 06 E 55 (approximate): Munsell 1 OR 5/14

The colour to be used on a way shown on a definitive map as a RUPP will depend on whether or not there appear to be vehicular rights over it. If there are, then it is a byway for the purposes of the Countryside Act and the byway colour should be used. If not, bridleway blue should be used.

Through routes, such as long-distance paths, may require waymarking to be continued along roads through towns and villages. In particular this may be needed to indicate the way out of a town or village. The Commission has not recommended a symbol or colour for such waymarks, but a number of highway authorities have agreed to the standard symbol being used in white for such purposes. The vertical face of curbstones has been used through a built-up area to avoid marking buildings and walls.

Paint, plastic or metal? The arrow can be painted directly on to the surface of the object to be waymarked, or a plastic or metal shape can be attached to it.

Although much waymarking has been carried out with painted arrows on trees, etc, it is also possible to use a plastic or metal arrow, and in some locations, such an arrow may be preferable. Paint is relatively cheap, more vandal resistant and avoids the use of nails, which must never be used on trees. A metal or plastic sign can be erected by anyone in any weather and can provide, through better resistance to weather and use of a background colour, a more lasting waymark unless it is removed. Most highway authorities have their own supplies of signs which can be made available to approved voluntary groups. A solid sign that does not bend is difficult to fix securely on a surface that is not absolutely flat, although it may be more durable.

Siting As a general rule the number of waymarks should be kept to the minimum necessary to make the route clear. Junction waymarks (see below) should be placed at a junction rather than before it. Sites for waymarking should be as permanent and vandal resistant as possible, with trees usually to be preferred. As a last resort, stones may be used, but they must be as large and irremovable as possible. The posts of stiles and gates are often used, but take care never to put a waymark on the opening part of a gate. There will often be a need to put up a special post just for the waymarks.

8 : THINGS YOU CAN DO

Since waymarks have to face the oncoming walker or rider a completely different set of arrows has to be put up for each direction; it is seldom that one arrow will serve for both directions. A turning from a major to a minor path may need more than one arrow if the walker or rider's attention is to be attracted.

Angles The diagrams below give a general indication of how to show the direction taken by a path.

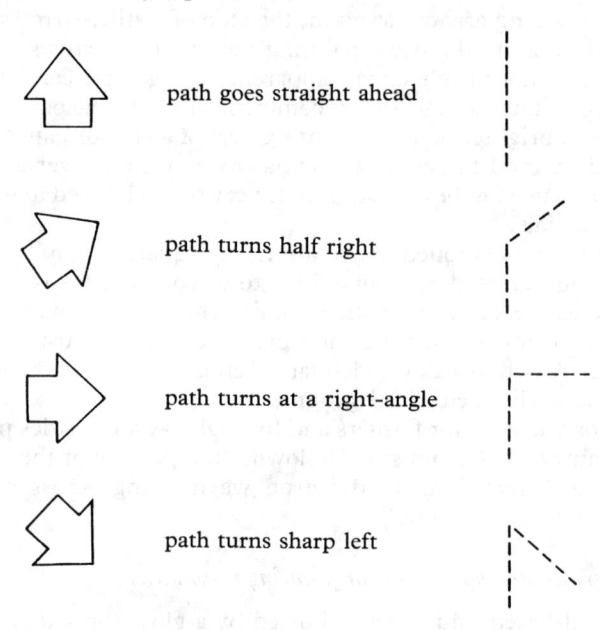

    ⬆   path goes straight ahead

    ⬀   path turns half right

    ➡   path turns at a right-angle

    ⬋   path turns sharp left

If in doubt about the correct angle, experiment by fixing an arrow shape, eg the centre of a stencil, in position temporarily and then stand back at least ten paces to see the arrow as it will appear to the approaching walker or rider. If necessary, adjust it so that it will convey the true change of direction.

Curved surfaces present a particular problem in obtaining the correct angle. Two solutions are flattening the surface or making the arrow smaller, and thereby less ambiguous.

Junctions At junctions of paths several single arrows can be used or they can be combined into a junction arrow in the style of an advance road sign. Such a junction arrow would be too large if it consisted of basic-size arrows, so each arm is reduced in size. The overall width of the object to be marked will usually determine the overall size of a junction arrow, and it will need to be carefully drawn (a carpenter's pencil is recommended) before painting.

Large fields These present special problems, as also do fields where a rise in the ground obscures the view of exit from the field from the point of entry. The solution usually lies in an additional device at the point of entry or exit or both.

The angle of a standard arrow on a gate or stile, seen before going through the gate or across the stile, will be difficult to remember adequately if the path is not visible on the ground and the exit not apparent. A solution is an arrow on the horizontal, eg a metal arrow affixed to, or a long arrow carved in, the step of a stile. Arrows painted on the horizontal need more repainting than vertical arrows.

If the exit is not visible or not apparent, a large disc can be used as a visual target. The Commission recommends that this be painted white, this being the brightest colour. Painting part of a stile or gate white can also provide a good target. If a disc has to be viewed over a hump in the field it will need to be on a stout pole very securely fixed to withstand gales and vandals.

If the devices mentioned above are not adequate it may be possible to use specially-erected posts on which to waymark. This is only likely to be practicable on a permanent basis where the ground is never cultivated or run over with farming machinery. Such posts should be of pressure-treated wood, of adequate section to withstand cattle rubbing, and securely fixed in the ground.

The guidance notes for farmers and for highway authorities produced by the Countryside Commission following the passage of the Rights of Way Act 1990 give further advice on waymarking across cultivated fields (see 'Further Reading').

8.5.3 Materials and equipment for painting waymarks

Paint An oil-based undercoat, followed by a gloss topcoat, will prove more lasting than emulsion paint, which wears badly out of doors. Non-toxic paints should be used so that there is no danger to livestock. Non-drip paint can be easier to use. Waymarking is economical in the use of paint. The smallest quantities can be bought and decanted into a small tin for use on site. Paint spraying is seldom satisfactory as the paint is too thin and invariably runs on vertical surfaces.

Brushes Very small brushes are required, with fine points for the arrow corners. White spirit should be taken in screw-top jars.

Stencils Use of a stencil should be encouraged, either to paint directly through or to give an outline shape. Old vinyl flooring is pliable and easy to cut. The centre piece can be useful for providing a temporary waymark to help decide on the correct angle (see chapter 8.5.2) and for use as a mask over an arrow if a contrasting background colour is to be painted round the arrow.

8 : THINGS YOU CAN DO

Tools Useful tools for surface cleaning and minor clearance associated with a waymarking project are a wire brush, curved Surform, sickle, folding saw and bush pruners.

Kit generally It is worth taking some trouble to get the right containers for paint and white spirit, open pots for stirrer sticks, cleaning tools, brush holders, rags, etc. It is also worth remembering that you are almost certain to get paint on yourself at some stage in the operation, so go suitably dressed.

8.6 Stile Building

8.6.1 Introduction

Building stiles is one of the simplest, but at the same time most useful, tasks regularly undertaken by volunteer footpath workers. The importance of having stiles which are both soundly constructed and easy to climb should not be underestimated, since the deterrent effect, particularly on less agile users, of poorly designed or maintained stiles can be considerable.

The British Standards Institution has published a British Standard for stiles, bridle-gates and kissing-gates (see 'Further Reading'), but this is written for the technical expert rather than the layman. The guidance and design we give below is for a wooden stile built to the measurements contained in the standard and of the type most commonly found in lowland Britain. Where we give a measurement not contained in the standard or suggest a variation it is printed in *italics*. In some areas, different materials and different designs are traditional, and we would wish to see such traditions continue. Designs for other types of stiles may be found in the *Footpaths, Fencing* and *Dry Stone Walling* Handbooks published by the British Trust for Conservation Volunteers. In all cases, stiles should be soundly constructed, easy for all users to climb and effective in preventing the movement of animals between fields.

The stile design Since stile sites vary so much, it is impossible to design one stile which will meet all needs. The design therefore uses maximum and minimum dimensions, and offers a choice of one step or two. A two-step stile allows some variation in the height, and is normally required if the ground is sloping. Where such a stile is built, the steps may be placed either at right angles (British Standard) or parallel to each other. The design also allows for one stile post to be made higher to provide a better hand hold. In such a case the step should be placed closer to the higher post (300 mm between posts — see diagram). Where a two-step stile is required by the site, use of parallel steps and an extended post, with the higher step next to the higher post gives users a better hold on a post while crossing the stile.

RIGHTS OF WAY

8.6.2 Dimensions

	One step	Two step
Height of top of top rail above ground	900mm (36")	900mm min (36" min) 1050mm max (41" max)
Width between uprights	1000mm min (39" min)	1000mm min (39" min)
Step height rise from the ground to the ends of the (bottom) step and between steps	300mm max (12" max)	300mm max (12" max)
Stepover height from the top of the (top) step to the top of the top rail	600mm (24")	450mm max (18" max)
Depth in ground Stile posts Step supports Upper step supports	750mm min (30" min) 500mm min (20" min)	750mm min (30" min) 500mm min (20" min) 600mm min (24" min)
Step overlap from the step support to the front edge of the step	Approx. 40mm (approx 1½")	Approx. 40mm (approx 1½")
Rail spacing	300mm max (12" max)	300mm max (12" max)

Timber sizes
 	
Stile posts
  section
 	
  length — hand-hold post
  length — other posts
	
	100mm x 100mm min (4" x 4" min)
	2350mm (92")
	1750mm min (69" min)
	2350 max (92 max)
		
		100mm x 100mm min (4" x 4" min)
		2500mm (100")
		Height★ + 850mm min
		(Height★ + 33" min)
		Height★ + 1450mm max
		(Height★ + 56" max)
		★of top rail above ground

Rail sections
 	
  British Standard
 	
  Our recommendation
	
	87mm x 38mm
	(3½" x 1½")
	75mm x 50mm
	(3" x 2")
		
		87mm x 38mm
		(3½" x 1½")
		75mm x 50mm
		(3" x 2")

Steps
  section
 	
  length
	
	175mm x 50mm
	(7" x 2")
	900mm (36")
		
		175mm x 50mm
		(7" x 2")
		900mm (36")

8 : THINGS YOU CAN DO

	One step	Two step
Step supports		
section	150mm x 75mm	150mm x 75mm
	(6" x 3")	(6" x 3")
length	750mm (30")	step height above ground
		+ 450mm (18")

8.6.3 Construction and erection

Prior inspection of the site should always be made. This enables the timber to be cut and treated, and the construction of the stile to be carried out in advance, leaving erection of the ready-made stile and construction of the steps as the only operations to be carried out on site.

The British Standard recommends that rails be stub mortised full-size into the posts for a depth of 50 mm (2'). Alternatively it permits skew nailing of the rails with three 100 mm nails at each end, in which case the rails should be housed in the face of the posts to a depth of at

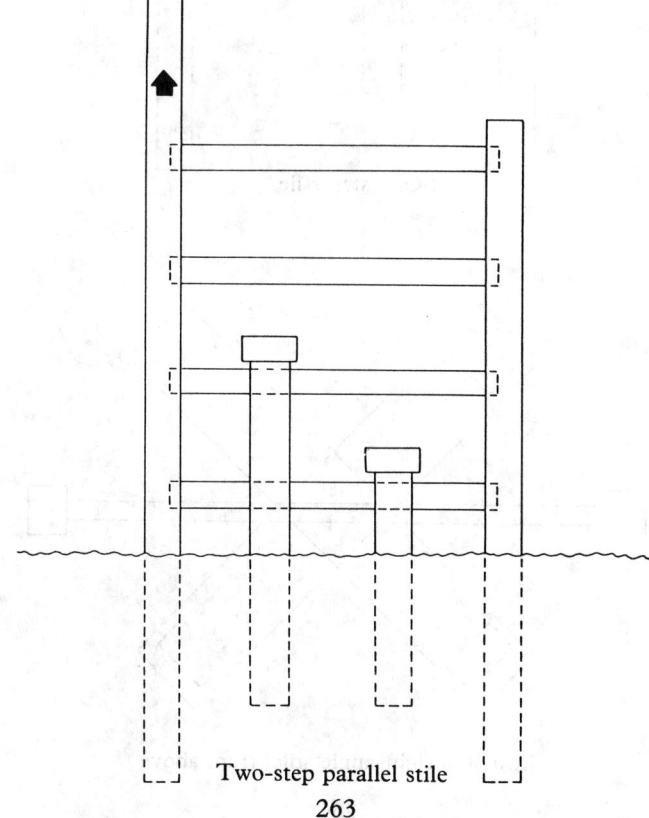

Two-step parallel stile

RIGHTS OF WAY

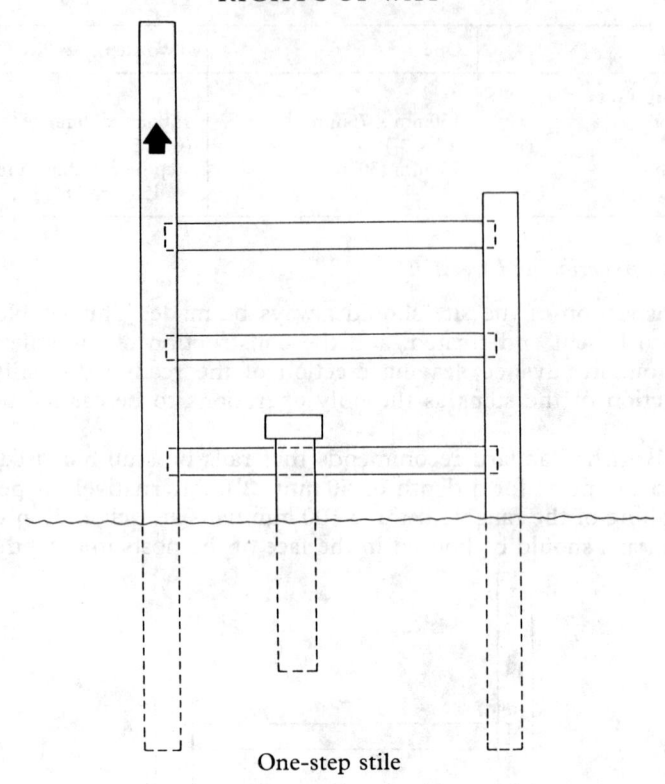

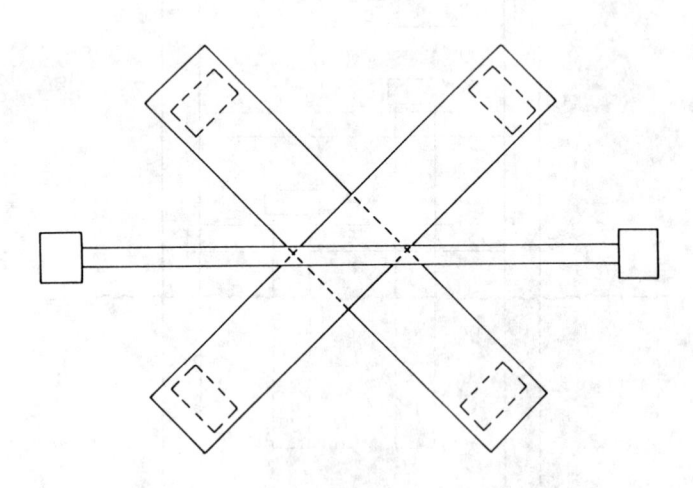

One-step stile

Two-step right-angle stile, from above

8 : THINGS YOU CAN DO

least 10 mm. If mortising is not possible, we recommend bolting rather than nailing the rails to the posts. Steps should be skew nailed to their supports with 125mm (5') nails.

An important point to note in the design and construction is that the steps should never be nailed to the rails, as this would result in a 'see-saw' effect when the earth settles, and the supports become loose in the ground.

On site, the order of construction is as follows:

(a) Assemble the main frame if not prefabricated. If the joints are bolted do not fully tighten the nuts at this stage.

(b) Dig the holes for the stile posts. A rabbiting spade (curved blade and cutting edge) is the most useful spade shape. A post hole borer with a nine-inch diameter plate with two flaps saves time in soft earth. If the ground is at all hard or rocky a crowbar is needed. A short trowel is useful as the hole gets deeper.

(c) Place the soil removed from the holes on to a plastic sheet to assist in finally leaving the site clean. Make the holes just sufficiently oversize to accommodate a rammer all round the post. The best shaped rammer has a semi-circular head of 4" diameter (from 'Drivall'). Home made pipe rammers are made from discarded lengths (e.g. 4½ ft) of heavy gauge water pipe of 1¼" and 1" OD with T-shaped bend fitted at the end.

(d) Set the main frame firmly in the bottom of the holes, and, after tightening nuts where necessary, secure it by progressively filling and ramming in the removed soil. Avoid using loose stones unless they can be firmly wedged in, as it is essential that this back-filling is progressively well compacted. Use a spirit-level to check the positioning of the main frame, especially on a slope.

(e) Set the step supports in and secure as above. You will find that it is quite difficult to get the supports in exactly the right place at the right depth and upright on both sides.

(f) Skew nail the step(s) to the supports, and secure any adjacent wire or fencing. However, if the stile is installed in wire fencing the posts must not be used as straining posts. Remove any sharp corners from the stile steps or elsewhere on the stile.

(g) Where necessary, paint or fix waymarks to the posts.

(h) Carry out any necessary surfacing work to prevent mud and erosion where people will step off the stile, and generally leave the site tidy.

8.7 Path Clearance

Introduction There is no general authority for a member of the public to undertake the clearance of a right of way, and any project of that nature will require permission from the landowner and the highway authority, both generally and in relation to matters such as bonfires. While it is generally considered permissible to carry light cutting-equipment, such as secateurs or small sickles, on a ramble, and clear surplus growth as one goes, the carrying of larger tools such as saws would be open to objection unless consent to undertake clearance has been obtained. A weapon such as a flick-knife must never be carried for this purpose, and if the carrying of any clearance equipment is ever challenged, a reason must immediately be given, otherwise a charge of carrying an offensive weapon in a public place could result.

A further criminal offence relating to knives in public places has been introduced by section 139 of the Criminal Justice Act 1988 (p 410). That section makes it an offence to have in a public place an article which has a blade or is sharply pointed. 'Public place' includes any place to which there is at the time public access, even if only on payment. The only defence relevant to footpath workers is to prove 'good reason' for having it. It is submitted that possession of an article of a kind to which the section refers for the purpose of clearing obstructing vegetation would be possession with 'good reason'.

Checking the route Unless the path or way lies between hedges and is clearly defined, the exact line to be cleared should be carefully checked first on the definitive map and then on the ground with the owner or occupier, or the authorised representative of one or other. Apart from ensuring that the clearance party sticks to the right of way, this may furnish a valuable means of discussing path problems in an amicable way, and also assist future co-operation.

Width and height of clearance If the width of the path is defined, eg in the statement accompanying the definitive map, that is the maximum width that should be cleared. Otherwise, in practice, a good working minimum is 1½ metres for a footpath and 2½ metres for a bridleway. In every case, the width to which a path is to be cleared should be agreed with the owner or occupier and highway authority before the work is started. If the path to be cleared is a long one and manpower and time are limited it will be better to clear the whole path to a width of, say, one metre rather than to clear the ends to a greater width and leave part of the path uncleared. A further working party can be arranged for a later date to complete the work. On a very wide path there will usually be no need to clear a width greater than three metres, as to do more would destroy cover for wild life. For a footpath, clearance to a height of at least two metres will be necessary; for a bridleway a minimum height of three metres will be required.

Trespass and violent entry onto premises Except where permission is given, clearance should only be undertaken from the path itself; there

8 : THINGS YOU CAN DO

is no right to go on to land adjoining the path to undertake clearance or to start a bonfire. In addition, care should be taken not to remove overgrowth or undergrowth not directly on the line of the right of way, or fences or barbed wire. (The removal of fences or barbed wire could lead to the straying of stock.) Any unauthorised clearance could constitute an act of trespass for which damages could be claimed, or could be alleged to be the offence of criminal damage.

Further legal liability could arise under the Criminal Law Act 1977, s 6 of which (p 314) makes entry with violence on to premises an offence. Section 12 of the Act (p 314) defines 'premises' as including land adjacent to buildings and violence as including violence directed against property.

Organisation and supervision The number of people needed for a particular clearance will depend on the nature and condition of the path, the type of overgrowth and undergrowth and the weather. As a rough guide, it will take eight workers a day to clear 200 metres of dense growth (two hedges grown together and intermeshed) to a width of two metres. For this purpose, a day's work would be from, say, 10 am to 5 pm with an hour's break for lunch. More volunteers will be needed if a shorter day is worked or if there is a bonfire to be tended or fed. Every working party must have a leader who will be responsible for ensuring that the following applies:
(a) Every member of the party has proper tools and can use them correctly and safely (this would include any local enthusiasts who wish to join in the work).
(b) The path is cleared to the agreed width throughout its length.
(c) The party sticks to the correct line of the path.
(d) The path is left in a tidy condition and free of litter and spoil.
(e) Dogs and children are kept away from the working area (ideally they should not be present in the working party).

Tools for clearance For minor clearance, reliance may be placed on the tools most readily available, eg secateurs, sickles and shears used for gardening, and a stout walking-stick can be used to subdue nettles and thistles when out walking. For tougher clearance work more specialist tools will be required, such as the following:
(a) Saws. Each participant should have the use of small triangular bow-saw. Larger bow-saws and pruning saws with long handles should also be available.
(b) Sickles. Each participant should have the use of a sickle, together with a pair of welding gloves, generally to protect against scratching, but particularly to protect the hand not holding the sickle.
(c) Slashers or long-handled billhooks are useful for dense or entangled growth, but are much more dangerous to use. They also

require considerable energy, are easily broken through misuse, are more expensive than sickles and are less easily manipulated.
- *(d)* Mattocks or grubbers for uprooting tree-roots.
- *(e)* Long-handled pruners, or toggle loppers, including the ratchet type which allows several movements of the handles for one cut.

When a party regularly undertakes clearance work, responsibility for custody and maintenance of the tools should be placed on one individual. Maintenance will include regular cleaning and sharpening to ensure that the tools are in condition for use at any time.

Use of a machine can substantially reduce the amount of labour needed. Extensive use is made by some groups of petrol brush-cutters, carried on a harness and using either circular-saw blades or nylon-filament heads, not for heavy initial clearance, but for regular maintenance work to prevent the path from becoming overgrown; only two people are needed in such circumstances. Protective clothing is needed by operators, and training is recommended before starting to use such equipment.

Safety precautions Health and safety requirements apply to working party organisers. It is the duty of the party leader to ensure that the members at work are spaced apart at a safe distance, know how to use the tools and are not likely to get in each other's way or cause any injury. He should also ensure that members are properly clothed for rough work and wear suitable leather or heavy gloves for dealing with hawthorn, brambles, nettles, etc.

If bonfires are started to dispose of debris, he should ensure that they are kept under control at all times, and that, when the site is left, they are stamped out or thoroughly damped down and that bare earth areas are cleared around the fires. If bonfires are lit on the path itself, care should be taken to avoid damage to nearby trees or hedges. If permission is obtained for bonfires to be lit in a field adjoining the path, any unburnt logs or sticks which might get wedged into farm machinery or otherwise cause damage should be removed from the field at the end of the day and replaced on the path.

Insurance Possible dangers from path clearance activities are as follows:
- *(a)* Personal injury caused by a member of the clearance party either to himself, to another member of the party or to a spectator.
- *(b)* Damage to clothing or tools.
- *(c)* Damage to trees, shrubs or fences along the line of the cleared path.
- *(d)* Loss or straying of stock caused by gaps left in hedges as a result of clearance.

It is possible to insure against any or all of these eventualities. Where that work is undertaken on behalf of a highway authority or parish

8 : THINGS YOU CAN DO

council, it is not unreasonable to expect that body to arrange for insurance cover for you, as this can often be done through existing arrangements. This should be sorted out before any work begins. The OSS, the RA, and other bodies such as the British Trust for Conservation Volunteers all have policies, but this does not mean that these policies cover all their members or affiliated groups at all times in all the cases mentioned above. For instance, the RA policy is restricted to indemnifying people carrying out work on behalf of the RA against liability claims. It is not a personal accident policy, and it does not automatically apply to organisations affiliated to the RA. The BTCV's policy is the most comprehensive and includes third-party insurance.

Bird nesting Path clearance can cause serious damage to bird life if undertaken at the wrong time of the year or without proper care. Many species nest in hedgerows and the nesting season normally lasts from the beginning of April to the end of August. During that period major clearances involving drastic cutting back of hedgerows or heavy clearance of undergrowth should not be undertaken; such jobs should be reserved for the autumn and winter months. During the summer, the clearance of nettles, thistles and brambles is permissible. The summer months will also be found convenient for obtaining the necessary permission for the clearance programme for the coming autumn and winter.

Publicity Any voluntary work undertaken for the public good is worth publicising in the local press. When a clearance is to take place particulars should be given to the press at least one week in advance, so that reporters and photographers can be notified. Those particulars should include the name of the leader and any special points of interest, eg if the path to be cleared is of historic interest, or if any participant may be 'newsworthy', eg a octogenarian or local personality. If a representative is not sent to the clearance, the press can be told afterwards what has been achieved and given a name and telephone number for further enquiries. Clearance is a photogenic activity, so it will be useful for future publicity for photographs to be taken of the work, for example for display at the next annual general meeting.

Signposting and waymarking after clearance Farmers and landowners have a general fear of trespass and vandalism. It is in their interests that rights of way should be clearly signposted and waymarked so as to minimise the risk of trespass. When a path is cleared it is a good thing to follow this up by waymarking it (see chapter 8.5); the owner's permission for this can be sought when he is approached about the clearance.

9

Further information

9.1 A right to roam — access to open country and commons

Distinct from a right of way — a right to follow a defined route — is a right of the public to roam at will over any part of a certain area of land. Such a right may arise in the following ways.

9.1.1 By permission of the landowner

Access may be by express permission. The right here is concessionary and is revocable at any time. The access may be granted subject to conditions, eg that dogs must be kept on a lead, or that access is to be suspended during specified periods. Failure to comply with any condition on which access is granted makes the entrant a trespasser and liable accordingly (see chapter 2.4).

Certain bodies have a power conferred by statute to make byelaws regulating activities on land owned by them and to which they have allowed the public access. For example, the National Trust has a power to make byelaws conferred by the National Trust Acts 1907-1971, and the Forestry Commission has power so to do under the Forestry Act 1967.

Local authorities have power under NPACA 49 s 90 to make byelaws for the preservation of order and the prevention of damage on land belonging to them in a national park or area of outstanding beauty (established under s 87 of the 1949 Act) or to which the public are given access by agreement or order (see chapter 9.1.2 and 9.1.3 below), or in consequence of acquisition, under Part V of the 1949 Act.

Other byelaw-making powers are conferred on local authorities by, *inter alia*, the Commons Act 1899, ss 1, 10; the Open Spaces Act 1906, s 15; and the Countryside Act 1968, s 41. Infringement of a byelaw is a criminal offence and renders the offender liable to prosecution and to the penalties prescribed in the byelaws concerned.

9.1.2 Access agreements

Part V of the 1949 Act confers power on local planning authorities to conclude agreements with landowners under which land specified in the agreement that is 'open country' should, subject to restrictions, be open to access by the public. 'Open country' is defined by the Act as

9 : FURTHER INFORMATION

meaning any area appearing to the authority to consist wholly or predominantly of mountain, moor, heath, down, cliff or foreshore (including any bank, barrier, dune, beach, flat, or other land adjacent to the foreshore). The definition was extended by the Countryside Act 1968 to include river-banks and woodland.

The Act operates not by conferring a positive right of access, but negatively by providing that where an access agreement has been concluded in respect of a certain area, a member of the public who enters without breaking or damaging any wall or fence and who observes the pertinent restrictions shall not be a trespasser. Those restrictions are of three kinds:

(a) Restrictions set out in the Second Schedule to the 1949 Act. These apply to all land subject to an access agreement (or access order, see below). They prohibit such matters as driving a vehicle, lighting a fire, killing or disturbing livestock, removing or damaging plants or trees, depositing rubbish, and neglecting to shut a gate, and allowing a dog not to be 'under proper control'.

(b) Restrictions agreed between the authority and the landowner and set out in the agreement. A restriction commonly found under this head is one providing that access should be suspended for up to a maximum number of days each year (eg to facilitate shooting). A restriction may also take the form of requiring dogs to be on a lead at all times.

Where a person fails to comply with a restriction under (a) or (b) he becomes a trespasser and is liable accordingly, see chapter 2.4.

(c) Restrictions contained in byelaws made by the authority under s 90 of the 1949 Act (see above) for the regulation of activities on land subject to an access agreement. Such byelaws may, and in practice in some instances do, replicate one or more of the restrictions set out in the Second Schedule to the 1949 Act. Where a matter, eg disturbing wildlife or allowing a dog not to be 'under proper control', appears in the Second Schedule and also is prohibited by a byelaw, then someone who commits the relevant act is liable both in civil law for trespass, and in criminal law for breach of the byelaw.

Restrictions relating to access land do not terminate or in any way limit the rights of the public that exist by virtue of there being a public right of way across the land. For example, the closure of access land under the terms of an agreement during a shooting season does not affect the right of the public to use a public path across the land during this period.

9.1.3 Access orders

It may happen that an authority is minded to conclude an access agreement for certain land but the landowner is unwilling to grant

RIGHTS OF WAY

access. In such a case the authority has power under s 59 of the 1949 Act to make an access order. Appeal against the making of an order lies to the Secretary of State for the Environment, who may direct that an inquiry should be held.

In the event of an order taking effect the rights of the public are those that are enjoyed over land in respect of which an access agreement has been concluded. Failure to comply with the restrictions in the Second Schedule renders the entrant a trespasser; infringement of a byelaw made by the authority in respect of the land constitutes a criminal offence.

Since the order is made without the landowner's consent, there can be no special restrictions of the kind that can be included in an access agreement. The Act (s 70) requires the authority to pay as compensation to the landowner a sum equal to the amount by which the value of the land has been depreciated by reason of the making of the order.

9.1.4 Common land under Law of Property Act 1925 s 193

The Law of Property Act 1925 s 193 confers on members of the public rights of access for air and exercise to certain land, including the following:

(a) Land which is common land and which lay within the Metropolitan Police District in 1866.
(b) Land which is common land which lies within an area which immediately before 1st April 1974 was a borough or urban district.
(c) Land which was common land on 1st January 1926 and in respect of which the landowner has executed a deed declaring that a public right of access exists over the land.

'Common land' is land over which one or more persons have a right, termed a 'right of common', over the land in addition to the landowner. Rights of common are generally annexed to a particular piece of land, eg as where annexed to one or more farms in a valley is the right to graze specified numbers of sheep on the surrounding hills. For further publications on common land see 'Further Reading'.

Access is subject to restrictions set out in the section (eg no vehicles may be driven, or fires lit, on the land) and to byelaws made for the regulation of activities on the land.

9.1.5 Common land owned by the National Trust

The National Trust Act 1907 s 29 imposes on the Trust a duty to keep common land owned by the Trust unenclosed and unbuilt upon as open space for the recreation and enjoyment of the public. The Act permits certain works to be carried out, such as the making and maintaining of footpaths and the erection of temporary enclosures for the purpose of renovating turf and protecting trees and plantations.

9 : FURTHER INFORMATION

The National Trust Act 1971 empowers the Trust to do anything on land to which s 29 of the 1907 Act applies that appears to the Trust to be desirable for the purpose of providing, or improving, opportunities for the enjoyment of the property by the public, and in particular to provide such facilities as parking places, lavatories and shelters, provided that the erection of any building (other than a tool shed) whereby the access of the public is prevented has the consent of the Secretary of State.

9.1.6 *Common law — acquisition by long usage?*

The common law accepts local custom as being capable of giving rise to a valid, legally-enforceable right, provided that the custom is ancient in origin, has been exercised continuously, is certain, and is reasonable. For example, in *New Windsor Corporation v Mellor* (1975) the court upheld the customary right of the inhabitants of a particular parish to indulge in lawful 'sports and pastimes' on certain land in the parish.

Until recently, however, it has always been accepted that long usage is incapable of giving rise to a right for the public at large to roam at will over certain land. (*A-G v Antrobus* (1905).) An indication that this principle may not be absolute was contained in the decision of the court in *R v Doncaster Metropolitan Borough Council* (1986). In this case Mr Justice McCullough accepted, following *Antrobus* (above), that no right could be granted to the public at large to wander at will over an undefined open space and that no such right could be acquired by presumed grant, but that it was nevertheless possible for the public to have a right to take recreation in a defined area. (*Re Hadden* (1932).) If an express grant of such a right had been produced the court would, he said, have recognised its validity.

In the absence of such an express grant, it was open to the court to infer, from the fact that rights of recreation had been long enjoyed, and the fact that these could not be sufficiently explained as arising by mere sufferance or licence, that at some time in the past these rights had been validly granted. From the evidence the court was satisfied that the inference was to be drawn. Thus the public had a legal right to recreation over the land concerned (and since it followed from this that the land was 'open space' within the meaning of TCPA 71 s 290(1) (now TCPA 90 s 336(1)), the local authority that owned the land was not entitled to dispose of any part of it without complying with the requirements of LGA 72 s 123).

The right that was held to exist included, it is safe to assume, a right to wander at will for the purpose of taking exercise. But it is submitted that the decision must be treated with caution. *Re Hadden*, on which the judgment of Mr Justice McCullough hinged, concerned a gift that was construed as creating a trust under which land was held for the purpose, the charitable purpose, of public recreation. It is an ancient principle of the law that the public can be the beneficiary of a charitable trust. (It is of no matter that 'the public' has no *locus standi* to enforce the trust since a charitable trust is never capable of being enforced by a potential beneficiary, this being the duty, and sole responsibility, of the Attorney-General.)

But to create a trust under which land is held *by* trustees *for* the public, as in *Re Hadden*, is a very different thing from making a grant *to* the public (a group that does not constitute a capable grantee), as was inferred to have taken place in the *Doncaster* case. It is submitted, therefore, that the *Doncaster* decision does not establish conclusively that a public right to roam at will over land, whether defined in area or not, is capable of being acquired by long usage. (It is to be noted that the case was heard in the Queen's Bench Division. Had the case gone to Chancery it is possible that the outcome might have been different.)

9.1.7 Information about rights of access to land

There is no equivalent to the definitive map recording land over which there is a right to roam freely. The following sources of information do exist.

National Trust land National Trust land over which the public has free access is often shown on Ordnance Survey maps at 1:25,000 (Pathfinder and Outdoor Leisure) and 1:50,000 (Landranger) scale.

Land subject to access agreements and orders or acquired for access Under NPACA 49 s 78 every local planning authority whose area comprises any land subject to an access agreement or order, or acquired under ss 76 or 77 of the Act for public access, must prepare, and keep up to date, a map showing the land and certain other information. The map must be available for public inspection (subsection (2)). The National Parks and Access to the Countryside Regulations 1950 require the map to be on a scale on not less than 2½ inches to the mile (regulation 11).

Common land subject to a right of access If the land is registered as common land or as a town or village green in the register prepared and maintained under the Commons Registration Act 1965, any public rights of access may be recorded in that register. But failure to note any public rights does not affect their existence. Moreover, certain land was exempt from registration.

Land acquired as open space Land which is owned by a local authority and made available as public open space is not required to be recorded on any map, but the local authority should be able to state which areas it holds as public open space.

9 : FURTHER INFORMATION
9.2 Statistics of recreational activity

Information about people's leisure activities is contained in the General Household Surveys (GHS) 1977, 1980, 1983 and 1986 and the National Surveys of Countryside Recreation (NSCR) 1977 and 1984. The GHS is an annual survey carried out by the government's Office of Population Censuses and Surveys which, in the years listed above, included questions on leisure activities; the NSCR is a special survey carried out for the Countryside Commission, and planned in conjunction with the GHS so that the results could be compared.

In all the surveys 'going for a walk' was defined as a walk of two miles or more, although the distance walked was not ascertained. The percentage of adults interviewed can be compared for the third quarter of the year:

GHS 1980	GHS 1983	NSCR 1984	GHS 1986
22%	23%	21%	23%

Although the GHS questions related to walking anywhere, those in the NSCR related to walking in the countryside, and it seems fair to claim that the GHS figures reflect participation rates for walking in the countryside.

The GHS also asked about participation at different times of the year:

% participating in four weeks prior to interview

January-March	15
April-June	21
July-August	23
October-December	17
Annual average	19.1

These figures indicate a high level of participation throughout the year. Further questions revealed also a high frequency. On average each member of the adult population of England and Wales took a walk of two miles or more 20 times in 1986. Since that population is around 38 million, this gives a total number of days on which such a walk was taken by adults of approximately 750 million in 1986. The comparative figure for horse-riding was 22 million days.

Further questions were asked in the GHS about the age, education, etc, of the interviewees. The answers are included in the GHS Reports (see 'Further Reading') and show that the popularity of walking extends throughout the community, and not confined to one age group, or to a group with a particular educational background, or to a region of the country.

9.3 Long-distance routes

The Committee on Footpaths and Access to the Countryside, appointed in July 1946, and known as the Hobhouse Committee after its Chairman, Sir Arthur Hobhouse, was asked to consider the measures necessary for the provision of long-distance and coastal footpaths.

In its report, published in September 1947 (Cmnd 7207) it recommended the establishment of such routes, setting out proposals for six inland paths in addition to the creation of coastal routes in the areas proposed by the National Parks Committee as either National Parks or Conservation Areas (now known as Areas of Outstanding Natural Beauty).

The six recommended inland paths were: The Pennine Way (as subsequently established), a route from Cambridge to Seaton in East Devon via the Chilterns and the Ridgeway (subsequently established in part as the Ridgeway Path), the Pilgrims Way from Winchester to Canterbury (included in large part in the North Downs Way), a route from Beachy Head along the South Downs Way to Winchester and thence to meet the Cambridge-Seaton route (established in Sussex only as the South Downs Way), an Offa's Dyke Path (as subsequently established) and a Teddington-Cricklade Thames-side Walk (not proceeded with in the 1950s but recently revived — see below).

In the coastal areas of National Parks and Conservation Areas the Committee estimated that about 200 miles of new path would be needed to create complete coastal paths in each area, and that the total length of such paths, if created, would be just under 900 miles, or about 30 per cent of the total coastline of England and Wales.

The statutory mechanism for the establishment of long-distance routes is in NPACA 49 ss 50A–55 (p 288-291). This operates by the Commission (now the Countryside Commission, previously the National Parks Commission) or the Countryside Council for Wales investigating the idea and then submitting to the Secretary of State a report containing its proposals for the route, including proposals for the establishment of new paths and ferries where necessary, and the provision of accommodation and refreshment facilities.

When the Secretary of State has approved the proposals, the Commission or Council works through highway authorities to secure their implementation; it has no powers of its own other than to offer finance, normally as 100% grant. The authorities exercise their powers to create paths by agreement or order, or to divert paths (see Chapters 3.4 and 5.3). The result has been painfully slow progress on some routes, as the table below shows. For most routes, the length of new path to be created has been less than a quarter of the total; much use has been made of existing paths.

Even at the date of official opening of a route, there have often been sections where the original proposals have not been implemented and

9 : FURTHER INFORMATION

temporary alternatives have been substituted. However, if a permanent variation of the proposals is deemed necessary by the Commission or Council, a varying report must be submitted to the Secretary of State under s 55.

Long-distance routes established to date are as follows:

Route	Length (km)	Report approved	Officially opened
Pennine Way *Edale to Kirk Yetholm*	402	6.7.1951	24.4.1965
Cleveland Way *Helmsley to Filey*	150	11.2.1965	24.5.1969
Pembrokeshire Coast Path *Amroth to Cardigan*	269	3.7.1953	16.5.1970
Offa's Dyke Path *Chepstow to Prestatyn*	270	27.10.1955	10.7.1971
South Downs Way *Eastbourne to Buriton extension to Winchester*	129	28.3.1963 7.1988	15.7.1972
North Cornwall Coast Path *Marsland Mouth to Penzance*	217	7.4.1952	19.5.1973
South Cornwall Coast Path *Penzance to Cremyll*	214	3.6.1954	19.5.1973
Ridgeway Path *Overton Hill to Ivinghoe*	137	5.7.1952	29.9.1973
South Devon Coast Path *Plymouth to Lyme Regis*	150	22.6.1959	14.9.1974
Dorset Coast Path *Lyme Regis to Sandbanks*	116	4.4.1963	14.9.1974
Somerset and North Devon Coast Path *Minehead to Marsland Mouth*	132	13.1.1961	20.5.1978
North Downs Way *Farnham to Dover*	227	14.7.1969	30.9.1978
Wolds Way *Filey to Hessle*	115	26.7.1977	2.10.1982
Peddars Way and Norfolk Coast Path *Thetford to Cromer*	138	8.10.1982	7.86
Thames Path *Thames Barrier to Thames Head*	342	28.9.1989	

The South Downs Way is a long-distance bridleway throughout its length. West of the Thames, ie from Streatley to Overton Hill, the Ridgeway Path is a long-distance bridleway.

The five coastal paths in Cornwall, Devon and Dorset together form an 830-km route, the South West Peninsular Coast Path or South West Way, from Minehead via Lands End to Bournemouth.

The routes currently under consideration by the Commission are a Hadrian's Wall route, and a Pennine Bridleway, on each of which project officers are employed.

As well as the routes developed by the Commissions, there are numerous other long-distance walks, some well-defined on the ground, and looked after by both voluntary effort and local authorities, eg the Oxfordshire Way, others existing only through the publication of a guidebook, but nevertheless providing most enjoyable walking. Details of these routes and their guidebooks are contained in a Handbook published by the Long Distance Walkers' Association (see 'Further Reading').

With the transfer on 1 April 1991 of the Commission's functions in Wales to the Countryside Council for Wales, responsibility for Offa's Dyke Path has become shared. (EPA 90 Sch 11 — p 429.)

9.4 Further reading

Journals The RA's magazine *Rambling Today* and the Society's journal *Open Space* contain information about rights-of-way law and practice as well as the general activities of their organisations; in addition the RA publishes a bulletin *Footpath Worker* which reports court cases and decisions on definitive map and public path orders.

Information of interest may also be found in *Countryside Commission News* and *Enjoying the Countryside*, published by the Commission, and in *Byway and Bridleway*, the journal of the Byways and Bridleways Trust.

Legal Acts of Parliament, Statutory Instruments and most government circulars may all be obtained from Her Majesty's Stationery Office (HMSO). The Acts are sold as passed by Parliament and are not annotated to show subsequent amendments or repeals, or to show which sections have not yet been brought into operation. The series of Statutes in Force, also published by HMSO, is designed to meet this problem, although in many cases reference is needed to an updating supplement as well as to the most recent republication of the Act in question.

Equally comprehensive coverage is given by the Encyclopedias in the Local Government Library, published by Sweet and Maxwell, of which the *Encyclopedia of Highway Law and Practice* is most likely to be of interest to readers of this book. The Encyclopedias are produced in a loose-leaf format, kept up to date with regular releases of new material,

9 : FURTHER INFORMATION

and contain annotated Acts of Parliament in addition to the relevant Statutory Instruments and circulars.

The *Rights of Way Law Review*, published by the Byways and Bridleways Trust, is a regular publication in loose-leaf format. The *Journal of Planning and Environmental Law* published monthly by Sweet and Maxwell often contains reports and articles on rights-of-way law.

Two useful single books are *Highway Law* by Stephen Sauvain (Sweet & Maxwell, 1989) and *The law of the countryside: the rights of the public* by Tim Bonyhady (Professional Books, 1987).

The classic textbook of highways was formerly *Pratt and Mackenzie's Law of Highways*, (Butterworths), but as the latest edition (the 21st) was published in 1967 and the last supplement in 1971, it is now almost wholly out of date for statute law.

Historical The publications of the Bedford Square Press (26 Bedford Square, London WC1B 3HU), part of the National Council of Voluntary Organisations, include several which give useful historical background.

Roads and Tracks of Britain by Christopher Taylor (Dent, 1979) deals thoroughly with the historical development of highways generally.

Publications relating to specific chapters A publication with reference CCP is obtainable from the Countryside Commission's publications department; one with reference CCD from the Commission in Cheltenham (for addresses see chapter 9.5).

Chapter 1
Enjoying the countryside: priorities for action (1987) (CCP 235)
Local authorities' involvement with rights of way in England and Wales (1991) (CCD 43)
Managing rights of way: an agenda for action (1989) (CCP 273)
National rights of way condition survey 1988 (1990) (CCP 284)
Out in the country: your rights and responsibilities (1990) (CCP 186)
Paths for People, a guide to public paths for members of parish, town and community councils. Available from the RA in English and Welsh.
Paths, routes and trails: policies and priorities (1989) (CCP 266)
Policies for enjoying the countryside (1987) (CCP 234)
Report of the Committee on Footpaths and Access to the Countryside (Hobhouse Committee) (1947) HMSO
Report of the Committee on the Consolidation of Highway Law (1959) HMSO
Report of the Footpaths Committee (Gosling Committee) (1968) HMSO
Report of the work of the Rights of Way Review Committee 1979-1981 (1982) Available from the RA.
Your Local Ombudsman, available from the Commissions for Local Administration

Chapter 4
A guide to definitive map procedures (1990) (CCP 285)
Definitive map modification and reclassification orders: guidance notes on evidence (1989) Available from PINS 1, Room 13/21, DOE, Tollgate House, Houlton Street, Bristol BS2 9DJ
Definitive map modification orders: digest of decisions (1989) (CCD 42)
Inclosure Acts and Awards (Seminar papers, 1988) Byways and Bridleways Trust
Rights of way : 1st monitoring report (1985) (CCP 202)
Rights of way : 2nd monitoring report (1987) (CCP 242)
The Open Register — a guide to information held by the Land Registry and how to obtain it. Available from HM Land Registry and District Land Registry offices.
The Ordnance Survey and Land-Use Mapping, Dr J B Harley (1979) Geo Abstracts
Valuation Office records created under the 1910 Finance Act (Information sheet 68) (1987) Public Record Office

Chapter 5
Changing the rights of way network: a discussion paper (1988) (CCP 254)
Changing the rights of way network: our consultations (1989) (CCP 277)
'Who needs a hole in the wall?' Available from the RA

Chapter 6
Pesticides: code of practice for the safe use of pesticides on farms and holdings (1990) HMSO
Ploughing footpaths and bridleways: a study of the law and practice (1985) (CCP 190)
Report to the Rights of Way Review Committee by the working party on ploughing and cropping (1989) Available from Countryside Commission in Cheltenham
The Rights of Way Act 1990 : guidance notes for farmers (CCP 299)
The Rights of Way Act 1990 : guidance notes for highway authorities (CCP 301)
Safe custody of bulls on farms and other similar premises: Health and Safety Executive Guidance Note GS 35 (1985) HMSO

Chapter 7
The Water Act 1989: Code of Practice on conservation, access and recreation (1989) DOE
Waymarking for footpath and bridleway (1975) HMSO
Waymarking public rights of way (1992) (CCP 246)

9 : FURTHER INFORMATION

Chapter 8
British Standard for stiles, bridle-gates and kissing-gates (BS 5709:1979 with amendment 3957:1982) British Standards Institution
Code of Audit Practice for local authorities and the National Health Service in England and Wales (1990) Audit Commission
Dry stone walling) Handbooks published by the British Trust for
Fencing   ) Conservation Volunteers
Footpaths   )
National rights of way condition survey 1988 (1990) (CCP 284)
National rights of way condition survey 1988: technical report (1990) (CCD 58)
Rights of way survey manual (1988) (CCP 250)

Chapter 9
Digest of Countryside Recreation Statistics 1978 (CCP 86)
General Household Survey Reports for 1977,1980,1983,1986 HMSO
Long Distance Walker's Handbook by Barbara Blatchford for the Long Distance Walkers' Association (Fourth edition 1990) A & C Black
National countryside recreation survey 1984 (1985) (CCP 201)
Our Common Land, Paul Clayden (1985 with 1992 supplement) OSS
Our common, our village green (1988) OSS
Paths, routes and trails: a consultation paper (1988) (CCP 253)
The Law of Commons, G D Gadsden (1988) Sweet & Maxwell

9.5 Useful addresses

Association of County Councils, Eaton House, 66A Eaton Square, London SW1W 9BH (071-235 1200)
Association of District Councils, 26 Chapter Street, London SW1P 4ND (071-233 6868)
Association of Metropolitan Authorities, 36 Old Queen Street, London SW1H 9JE (071-222 8100)
Audit Commission, 1 Vincent Square, London SW1P 2PN (071-828 1212)
British Horse Society, Stoneleigh, Kenilworth, Warwickshire CV8 2LR (Coventry (0203) 696697)
British Trust for Conservation Volunteers, 36 St Mary's Street, Wallingford, Oxfordshire (Wallingford (0491) 39766)
Byways and Bridleways Trust, The Granary, Charlcutt, Calne, Wilts SN11 9HL (Kellaways (024 974) 273)
Central Council of Physical Recreation, Francis House, Francis Street, London SW1P 1DE (071-828 3163/4)
Commissions for Local Administration (Local Ombudsman)
   England: 21 Queen Anne's Gate, London SW1H 9BU (071-222 5622)

RIGHTS OF WAY

Wales: Derwen House, Court Road, Bridgend, Mid Glamorgan (Bridgend (0656) 61235)

Council for the Protection of Rural England, Warwick House, 25-27 Buckingham Palace Road, London SW1W 0PP (071-976 6433)

Council for the Protection of Rural Wales, 14 Broad Street, Welshpool, Powys SY21 7SD (Welshpool (0938) 2525)

Council on Tribunals, St Dunstan's House, Fetter Lane, London EC4A 1BT (071-404 4954)

Country Landowners Association, 16 Belgrave Square, London SW1X 8PQ (071-235 0511)

Countryside Commission

Headquarters: John Dower House, Crescent Place, Cheltenham, Gloucestershire GL50 3RA (Cheltenham (0242) 521381)

Publications Department: Printworks Lane, Levenshulme, Manchester M19 3JP (061-224 6287)

Regional Offices

Eastern: Terrington House, 13-15 Hills Road, Cambridge CB2 1NL (Cambridge (0223) 354462)

Midlands: Cumberland House, Broad Street, Birmingham B15 1TD (021-632 6503)

Northern: Warwick House, Grantham Road, Newcastle upon Tyne NE2 1QF (091-232 8252)

North West: 2nd Floor, 184 Deansgate, Manchester M3 3WB (061-833 0316)

South East: 4th Floor, 71 Kingsway, London WC2B 6ST (071-831 3510)

South West: Bridge House, Sion Place, Clifton Down, Bristol BS8 4AS (Bristol (0272) 739966)

Yorkshire and Humberside: 8a Otley Road, Headingley, Leeds LS6 2AD (Leeds (0532) 742935)

Countryside Commission for Scotland, Battleby, Redgorton, Perth PH1 3EW (Perth (0738) 27921)

Countryside Council for Wales, Plas Penrhos, Ffordd Penrhos, Bangor, Gwynedd LL57 2LQ (Bangor (0248) 370444)

Cyclists Touring Club, 69 Meadrow, Godalming, Surrey GU7 3HS (Godalming (0483) 417217)

Department of the Environment:

Headquarters, 2 Marsham Street, London SW1P 3EB (071-276 3000)

Directorate of Rural Affairs, Tollgate House, Houlton Street, Bristol BS2 9DJ (Bristol (0272) 218811)

Regional Offices

East Midlands: Cranbrook House, Cranbrook Street, Nottingham NG1 1EY (Nottingham (0602) 476121)

Eastern: Heron House, 49/53 Goldington Road, Bedford MK40 3LL (0234 63161)

9 : FURTHER INFORMATION

Greater London: GLP4, Millbank Tower, 21–24 Millbank, London SW1P 4QV (071-211 0100)
Northern: Wellbar House, Gallowgate, Newcastle upon Tyne NE1 4TD (091-232 7575)
North West: Sunley Tower, Piccadilly Plaza, Manchester M1 4BE (061-832 9111)
South East: Charles House, 375 Kensington High Street, London W14 8QM (071-605 9721)
South West: Tollgate House, Houlton Street, Bristol BS2 9DJ (0272 218811)
West Midlands: Five Ways Tower, Frederick Road, Edgbaston, Birmingham B15 1SJ (021-631 4141)
Yorkshire and Humberside: City House, New Station Street, Leeds LS1 4JD (0532 438232)
Farmers Union of Wales, Llys Amaeth, Queen's Square, Aberystwyth SY23 2EA (Aberystwyth (0970) 2755)
Health and Safety Executive, Baynards House, Chepstow Place, London W2 (071-229 3456)
Her Majesty's Stationery Office, 51 Nine Elms Lane, London SW8 5DR (071-873 0011)
House of Commons, London SW1A 0AA (071-219 3000)
House of Lords Records Office, London SW1A 0PW (071-219 5316)
Land Registry, Lincoln's Inn Fields, London WC2A 3PH (071-405 3488)
National Association of Local Councils, 108 Great Russell Street, London WC1B 3LD (071-636 4066)
National Farmers Union, Agriculture House, Knightsbridge, London SW1X 7NJ (071-235 5077)
Open Spaces Society, 25A Bell Street, Henley-on-Thames, Oxfordshire RG9 2BA (Henley (0491) 573535)
Ordnance Survey, Romsey Road, Maybush, Southampton, SO9 4DH (Southampton (0703) 775555)
Parliamentary Commissioner for Administration, Church House, Great Smith Street, London SW1P 3BW (071-212 7676)
Public Record Office, Ruskin Avenue, Kew, Surrey TW9 4DU (081-876 3444)
Ramblers' Association, 1/5 Wandsworth Road, London SW8 2XX (071-582 6878)
Sports Council, 16 Upper Woburn Place, London WC1H 0QP (071-388 1277)
Sports Council for Wales, Sophia Gardens, Cardiff CF1 9SW (Cardiff (0222) 397571)
Welsh Office, Cathays Park, Cardiff CF1 3NQ (Cardiff (0222) 825111)
Youth Hostels Association, Trevelyan House, St Albans, Herts AL1 2DY (St Albans (0727) 55215)

Acts, Regulations and Circulars

Introduction
In this Part of the book we have included the text of the relevant parts of the Acts of Parliament, Regulations and Government Circulars. The contents of these publications are Parliamentary or Crown Copyright and we are grateful to the Controller of Her Majesty's Stationery Office and to the issuing departments for circulars for permission to include them in this book. Regulations, whilst subordinate to Acts of Parliament, are made by the Statutory Instrument approved by Parliament and have the force of law.

Circulars contain guidance issued on behalf of the Secretary of State; their advice is not mandatory, except where it is backed by an Act or Regulation, and the courts have been known to overrule guidance in a Circular.

Where an Act or Regulation has been amended by subsequent legislation, we have included it as amended, not as originally enacted. We believe that the details included in the following pages represent the legislation in force as at 1 April 1991, the date on which the provisions of the Environmental Protection Act 1990 creating the Countryside Council for Wales came into effect. In each case we have given details of the legislation which brought about the amendments, with one exception. That exception is the Criminal Justice Act 1982, which prescribed a new standard scale of fines for most offences and amended existing legislation to make reference to levels on that standard scale. The current monetary values assigned to the levels were set in 1984 and are as follows:

Level 1 £50 *(£200)*
Level 2 £100 *(£500)*
Level 3 £400 *(£1,000)*
Level 4 £1,000 *(£2,500)*
Level 5 £2,000 *(£5,000)*

They will be increased to the amounts shown in brackets when section 17(1) of the Criminal Justice Act 1991 is brought into operation.

If we have overlooked any amendment, we apologise, but cannot accept liability arising out of an inaccuracy.

By each piece of legislation we have included, by the word *Text*, a reference to the pages(s) on which its interpretation appears in the preceding chapters. Where we have included only part of a section or Schedule, or subsection, paragraph or sub-paragraph, we have indicated the location of omitted parts of the text by (...), and the non-inclusion of certain parts by a reference to the parts concerned in square brackets, eg [(9) not included].

Acts

DEFENCE ACT 1842

16. Power to stop up or divert footpaths and bridleways
It shall be lawful for the principal officers of Her Majesty's ordnance for the time being (...) to stop up or divert any public (...) footpaths or bridleways.

17. Alternative way to be provided
Provided that always that whenever any footpath or bridle road shall be stopped up as aforesaid, another path or road shall be provided in lieu thereof respectively, at the expense of the ordnance department and at such convenient distance therefrom as to the principal officers of Her Majesty's ordnance shall seem proper and necessary.
Text: p 158
Powers of 'the principal officers of Her Majesty's ordnance' now exercised by Secretary of State for Defence.

RAILWAY CLAUSES CONSOLIDATION ACT 1845

61. Company to make sufficient approaches and fences to such highway crossing on the level
If the railway shall cross any highway other than a public carriageway on the level, the company shall at their own expense, make and at all times maintain convenient ascents and descents and other convenient approaches, with handrails or other fences, and shall, if such highway be a bridleway, erect and at all times maintain good and sufficient gates, and if the same shall be a footway, good and sufficient gates or stiles, on each side of the railway, where the railway shall communicate therewith.
Text: p 57

65. Justices to have power to order repair of bridges, etc
Where, under the provisions of this or the special Act, or any Act incorporated therewith, the company are required to maintain or keep in repair any bridge, fence, approach, gate, or other work executed by them, it shall be lawful for two justices on the application of the surveyor of roads or of any two householders of the parish or district where such work may be situate, complaining that any such work is out of repair, after not less than 10 days notice to the company, to order the company to put such work into complete repair, within a period to be limited for that purpose by such justices; and if the company fail to comply with such order they shall forfeit five pounds for every day they fail so to do; and it shall be lawful for the justices by whom any such penalty is imposed to order the whole or any part thereof to be applied in such manner and by such persons as they think fit, in putting such work into repair.
Text: p 57

TOWN POLICE CLAUSES ACT 1847

3. Interpretation
(...)
The word 'street' shall extend to and include any road, square, court, alley and thoroughfare, or public passage (...)
(...)

28. Penalties
Every person who in any street, to the obstruction, annoyance, or danger of the residents or passengers, commits any of the following offences, shall be liable to a penalty not exceeding level 3 on the standard scale for each offence, or, in the discretion of the justice before whom he is convicted, may be committed to prison, there to remain for a period not exceeding fourteen days; that is to say,
(...)
Every person who suffers to be at large any unmuzzled ferocious dog, or sets on or urges any dog or other animal to attack, worry, or put in fear any person or animal:
(...)
Every person who (...) by means of any cart, carriage, sledge, truck or barrow or any animal, or other means (...) wilfully causes any obstruction in any public footpath or other public thoroughfare;
(...)
Every person who wantonly discharges any firearm, or throws or discharges any stone or other missile (...);
Text: p 185, 190, 191
Amended by Police and Criminal Evidence Act 1984 Sch 7 Pt 1.

DEFENCE ACT 1860

40. Stopping up, diversion or alteration of level of highway
It shall be lawful for the said Secretary of State, without any writ being issued or other legal proceedings being adopted, to stop up or divert or alter the level of any highway (...) through under or adjoining any lands comprised in any such declaration as aforesaid; he, if necessary, previously making, opening, or laying down another good and sufficient way (...) in lieu of that stopped or diverted.
Text: p 158
'declaration as aforesaid' — declaration of lands taken under or affected by the Act.

DOGS ACT 1871

2. Control of dangerous dogs
Any court of summary jurisdiction may take cognizance of a complaint that a dog is dangerous, and not kept under proper control, and if it appears to the court having cognizance of such complaint that such dog is dangerous, the court may make an order in a summary way directing the dog to be kept by the owner under proper control or destroyed.

RIGHTS OF WAY

Text: p 185
Amended by Dangerous Dogs Act 1989 s 2.
For additional powers of the court, see the Dangerous Dogs Act 1989 (p 418).

MILITARY LANDS ACT 1892

13. Application of section 116 of the Highways Act 1980
In relation to a footpath crossing on or near to any land leased under this Act, the Highways Act 1980 shall have effect as if in section 116 thereof (...) there were added to the grounds for stopping up or diverting a highway specified in subsection (1) the ground that the highway crosses or runs inconveniently or dangerously near to any such land:
Provided that–
(a) a magistrates court shall not make an order under the said section 116 authorising the stopping up or diversion of the footpath unless it is satisfied that a new footpath convenient to the public will be substituted thereof, or that the footpath as diverted will be convenient to the public, as the case may be, and
(b) if the order is made, an appeal shall not lie therefrom to the Crown Court under section 317 of the said Act of 1980 on the ground that the new footpath, or the footpath as diverted, as the case may be, is not convenient to the public.
In this section 'footpath' has the same meaning as in the said Act of 1980.
Text: p 158
Amended by Highways Act 1959 Sch 22, London Government Act 1963 s 16(2) and HA 80 Sch 24.

BRITISH TRANSPORT COMMISSION ACT 1949

57. As to rights of way over footpaths, etc
As from the passing of this Act no right of way as against the Commission shall be acquired by prescription or user over any road footpath thoroughfare or place now or hereafter the property of the Commission and forming an access or approach to any station goods-yard wharf garage or depot or any dock or harbour premises of the Commission.
Text: p 64

NATIONAL PARKS AND ACCESS TO THE COUNTRYSIDE ACT 1949

50A. Application of Part IV of this Act to Wales
(1) The provisions of this Part of this Act shall, subject to the next following subsection, apply to land in Wales as they apply to land in England.
(2) Where a provision of this Part of this Act confers a function on the Countryside Commission as respects England (or land of any description in England), the Countryside Council for Wales shall have the corresponding function as respects Wales (or land of a similar description in Wales).
Inserted by EPA 90 Sch 8 para 1(6). See also EPA 90 Sch 11 para 5 (p 430).

51. General provisions as to long distance routes

(1) Where it appears to the Commission, as respects any part of England, that the public should be enabled to make extensive journeys on foot or on horseback or on a bicycle not being a motor vehicle along a particular route, being a route which for the whole or greater part of its length does not pass along roads mainly used by vehicles, the Commission may prepare and submit to the Minister a report under this section.

(2) A report under this section shall contain a map showing the route, defining those parts thereof over which there exists a public right of way, and indicating in each case the nature of that right; and the report shall set out such proposals as the Commission may think fit–

(a) for the maintenance or improvement of any public path or road used as a public path along which the route passes;

(b) for the provision and maintenance of such new public paths as may be required for enabling the public to journey along the route;

(c) for the provision and operation of ferries where they are needed for completing the route; and

(d) for the provision of accommodation, meals and refreshments along the route.

(3) A report under this section may also include such recommendations as the Commission may think fit for the restriction of traffic on existing highways along which the route passes.

(4) Before preparing a report under this section the Commission shall consult every joint planning board, county council and district council through whose area the route passes; and it shall be the duty of every such board or council to furnish to the Commission such information as the Commission may reasonably require for the purposes of the report.

(5) A report under this section shall contain an estimate, in such form as the Minister may require, of the capital outlay likely to be incurred in carrying out any such proposals contained therein as are mentioned in subsection (2) of this section, of the annual cost of maintaining any existing public paths or roads used as public paths along which the route passes and any new public paths provided for by the proposals, and of the annual expenditure likely to be incurred by local authorities in connection with the provision and operation of ferries, and the provision of accommodation, meals and refreshments, so far as those matters are provided for by the proposals.

Text: p 276
Amended by CA 68 s 21, LGA 72 Sch 30 and EPA 90 Sch 8 para 1(7).

52. Approval of proposals relating to a long distance route

(1) On the submission to the Minister of a report under the last foregoing section, the Minister shall consider any proposals contained in the report under subsection (2) of that section and may either approve the proposals, with or without modifications, or reject the proposals:

Provided that where the Minister does not propose to approve the proposals as set out in the report he shall, before coming to a determination as to what action to take under this subsection, consult with the Commission and such other authorities and persons as he may think fit.

(2) As soon as may be after the Minister determines under the last foregoing subsection either to approve any proposals, with or without modifications, or

to reject them, he shall notify his determination to the Commission and to every joint planning board, county council and district council whose area is traversed by the route to which the report relates.
(3) Proposals approved by the Minister under subsection (1) of this section, either as originally set out in the report or as modified by the Minister, are hereinafter referred to as 'approved proposals relating to long distance routes'.
Text: p 276

53. Ferries for purposes of long distance routes
(1) Where approved proposals relating to a long distance route include proposals for the provision and operation of a ferry, the authority who are the highway authority for either or both of the highways to be connected by ferry–
(a) shall have power to provide and operate the ferry and to carry out such work and do all such things as appear to them expedient for the purpose of operating the ferry;
(b) may agree with any person or body of persons for the provision and operation of the ferry by him or them and for the making by the highway authority of such contributions as may be specified in the agreements:
Provided that nothing in this subsection shall–
(i) be construed as conferring on such an authority an exclusive right to operate a ferry;
(ii) authorise the doing of anything which, apart from this subsection, would be actionable by any person by virtue of his having an exclusive right to operate a ferry, unless he consents to the doing thereof;
(iii) authorise the doing of anything on land, or as respects water over land, in which any other person has an interest, if apart from this subsection the doing thereof would be actionable at his suit by virtue of that interest and he does not consent to the doing thereof;
and before carrying out any work in the exercise of powers conferred by this subsection, being work on the bank or bed of any waterway, the highway authority shall consult with such authorities having functions relating to the waterway.
(2) A highway authority may acquire land compulsorily for the purpose of any of their functions under paragraph (a) of the last foregoing subsection.
Text: p 60, 276
Amended by Local Government, Planning and Land Act 1980 Sch 7 para 34.

54. Accommodation, meals and refreshments along long distance routes
(1) Where approved proposals relating to a long distance route include proposals for the provision, along any part of the route, of accommodation, meals and refreshments, any local planning authority through whose area, or in the neighbourhood of whose area, that part of the route passes shall have power to make such arrangements under this section as are requisite for giving effect to the last-mentioned proposals.
(2) The arrangements which may be made by an authority under this section are arrangements for securing, at places in their area convenient for persons using the part of the route in question, the provision, whether by the authority or other persons, of accommodation, meals and refreshments (including intoxicating liquor):

Provided that an authority shall not under this section provide accommodation, meals and refreshments except in so far as it appears to them that the facilities therefor are inadequate or unsatisfactory, either generally or as respects any description of accommodation, meals or refreshments, as the case may be.

(3) For the purposes of arrangements under this section a local planning authority may erect such buildings and carry out such work as may appear to them to be necessary or expedient.

(4) The foregoing provisions of this section shall not authorise an authority, on land in which any other person has an interest, without his consent to do anything which apart from this section would be actionable at his suit by virtue of that interest.

(5) A local planning authority may acquire land compulsorily for the purpose of any of their functions under this section.

Text: p 276

The Broads Authority is a local planning authority for the purposes of this section. (s 111A added by Norfolk and Suffolk Broads Act 1988 Sch 3 para 2.)

55. Variation of approved proposals

(1) Where proposals relating to a long distance route have been approved by the Minister under section fifty-two of this Act, the Commission may from time to time prepare and submit to the Minister a report proposing any such variation of the approved proposals as the Commission may think fit.

(2) Where, as respects any proposals approved as aforesaid, it appears to the Minister, after consultation with the Commission, expedient that the proposals should be varied in any respect and the Commission have not submitted to the Minister a report proposing that variation, the Minister may direct that the proposals shall be so varied.

(3) Subsection (4) of section fifty-one of this Act, and subsections (1) and (2) of section fifty-two thereof, shall with the necessary modifications apply to a report or direction under this section; and subsection (5) of the said section fifty-one shall with the necessary modifications apply to any such report.

(4) Where the Minister approves, with or without modifications, any proposals contained in a report under subsection (1) of this section, or gives a direction under subsection (2) of this section, the proposals for the variation of which the report was made or direction given shall thereafter have effect subject to the provisions of the report or direction; and references in this Act to approved proposals relating to a long distance route shall be construed accordingly.

Text: p 276

57. Penalty for displaying on public paths notices deterring public use

(1) If any person places or maintains, on or near any way shown on a definitive map, or on a revised map prepared in definitive form, as a public path or road used as a public path, a notice containing any false or misleading statement likely to deter the public from using the way, he shall be liable on summary conviction to a fine not exceeding level 1 on the standard scale.

(2) The court before whom a person is convicted of an offence under the last foregoing subsection may, in addition to or in substitution for the imposition of a fine, order him to remove the notice in respect of which he is convicted within such period, not being less than four days, as may be specified in the

RIGHTS OF WAY

order; and if he fails to comply with the order he shall be liable on summary conviction to a fine not exceeding two pounds for each day on which the failure continues.

(3) It shall be the duty of a highway authority to enforce the provisions of this section as respects any public path, or road used as a public path, for which they are the highway authority; and no proceedings in respect of an offence under those provisions shall be brought except by the highway authority required by this subsection to enforce those provisions as respects the path or road in question or by the council of the district in which the notice is placed or maintained.

Text: p 189

A district council may also take action. See LGA 1972 s 187(3) (p 309).

101. Crown land

(1) The following provisions of this section shall have effect for applying certain provisions of this Act to Crown land, that is to say land an interest in which belongs to His Majesty in right of the Crown or the Duchy of Lancaster, or to the Duchy of Cornwall, and land an interest in which belongs to a Government department or is held in trust for His Majesty for the purposes of a Government department.

[(2) to (5) not included.]

(6) Part IV (...) of this Act shall apply to Crown land (...).

[(7) to (11) not included.]

Text: p 38, 74

Part IV of the Act includes the provisions in sections 50A to 57 above and also the (now-repealed) provisions relating to the survey of rights of way and the preparation of definitive maps.

114. Interpretation

(1) In this Act the following expressions have the meanings hereby assigned to them respectively, that is to say–

(...)

'interest', in relation to land, includes any estate in land and any right over land, whether the right is exercisable by virtue of the ownership of an interest in land or by virtue of a licence or agreement, and in particular includes sporting rights;

'land' includes land covered by water (...);

(...)

'owner', in relation to any land, means (...) a person other than a mortgagee not in possession, who, whether in his own right or as a trustee or agent for any other person, is entitled to receive the rack rent of the land or, where the land is not let at a rack rent, would be so entitled if it were so let (...);

(...)

DOGS (PROTECTION OF LIVESTOCK) ACT 1953

1. Penalty where dog worries livestock on agricultural land

(1) Subject to the provisions of this section, if a dog worries livestock on any agricultural land, the owner of the dog, and if it is in the charge of a person other than its owner, that person also, shall be guilty of an offence under this Act.

DOGS (PROTECTION OF LIVESTOCK) ACT 1953

(2) For the purposes of this Act worrying livestock means–
(a) attacking livestock, or
(b) chasing livestock in such a way as may reasonably be expected to cause injury or suffering to the livestock or, in the case of females, abortion, or loss of or diminution of their produce;
(c) being at large (that is to say not on a lead or otherwise under close control) in a field or enclosure in which there are sheep.
(2A) Subsection (2)(c) of this section shall not apply in relation to–
(a) a dog owned by, or in the charge of, the occupier of the field or enclosure or the owner of the sheep or a person authorised by either of those persons; or
(b) a police dog, a guide dog, a trained sheep dog, a working gun dog or a pack of hounds.
[(3) not included].
(4) The owner of the dog shall not be convicted of an offence under this Act in respect of the worrying of livestock by the dog if he proves that at the time when the dog worried the livestock it was in the charge of some other person, whom he reasonably believed to be a fit and proper person to be in charge of the dog.
(5) Where the Minister is satisfied that it is inexpedient that subsection (1) of this section should apply to land in any particular area, being an area appearing to him to consist of wholly or mainly of mountain, hill, moor, heath or down land, he may by order direct that the subsection shall not apply to land in that area.
(6) A person guilty of an offence under this Act shall be liable on summary conviction to a fine not exceeding level 3 on the standard scale.

2. Proceedings

(1) As respects an offence under this Act alleged to have been committed in respect of a dog on any agricultural land in England and Wales, no proceedings shall be brought except–
(a) by or with the consent of the chief officer of police for the police area in which the land is situated, or
(b) by the occupier of the land, or
(c) by the owner of any of the livestock in question.
[(2) and (3) not included.]

3. Interpretation and supplementary provisions

(1) In this Act–
'agricultural land' means land used as arable, meadow or grazing land, or for the purpose of poultry farming, pig farming, market gardens, nursery grounds or orchards; and
'livestock' means cattle, sheep, goats, swine, horses, or poultry, and for the purposes of this definition 'cattle' means bulls, cows, oxen, heifers or calves, 'horses' includes asses and mules, and 'poultry' means domestic fowls, turkeys, geese or ducks.
(2) In this Act the expression 'the Minister' as respects England and Wales means the Minister of Agriculture and Fisheries (...)
(3) The power of the Minister to make orders under subsection (5) of section one of this Act shall be exercisable by statutory instrument and shall include power, exercisable in the like manner, to vary or revoke any such order.

RIGHTS OF WAY

Text: p 45
Amended by Criminal Law Act 1977 Sch 6 and WCA 81 Sch 7.

MINES AND QUARRIES ACT 1954

151. Fencing of abandoned and disused mines and of quarries
(1) It shall be the duty of the owner of every abandoned mine and of every mine which, notwithstanding that it has not been abandoned, has not been worked for a period of twelve months to secure that the surface entrance to every shaft or outlet thereof is provided with an efficient enclosure, barrier, plug or other device so designed and constructed as to prevent any person from accidentally falling down the shaft or from accidentally entering the outlet and that every device so provided is properly maintained:
Provided that this subsection shall not apply to mines which have not been worked for the purpose of getting minerals or products thereof since the ninth day of August, eighteen hundred and seventy-two, being mines other than of coal, stratified ironstone, shale or fireclay.
(2) For the purposes of Part III of the Environmental Protection Act 1990, each of the following shall be deemed to be a statutory nuisance that is to say:–
[(a) not included]
(b) a shaft or outlet of a mine to which the proviso to the foregoing subsection applies, being a shaft or outlet with respect to which the following conditions are satisfied, namely,–
(i) that its surface entrance is not provided with a properly maintained device such as is mentioned in that subsection; and
(ii) that, by reason of its accessibility from a highway or a place of public resort, it constitutes a danger to members of the public; and
(c) a quarry (whether in course of being worked or not) which–
(i) is not provided with an efficient and properly maintained barrier so designed and constructed as to prevent any person from accidentally falling into the quarry; and
(ii) by reason of its accessibility from a highway or a place of public resort constitutes a danger to members of the public.
[(3) and (4) not included.]
Text: p 187, 192
Amended by EPA 90 Sch 15 para 5.

OCCUPIERS' LIABILITY ACT 1957

1. Preliminary
(1) The rules enacted by the two next following sections shall have effect, in place of the rules of the common law, to regulate the duty which an occupier of premises owes to his visitors in respect of dangers due to the state of the premises or to things done or omitted to be done on them.
(2) The rules so enacted shall regulate the nature of the duty imposed by law in consequence of a person's occupation or control of premises and of any invitation or permission he gives (or is to be treated as giving) to another to enter or use the premises, but they shall not alter the rules of the common law as to the persons on whom a duty is imposed or to whom it is owed; and accordingly for the purpose of the rules so enacted the persons who are to be

OCCUPIERS' LIABILITY ACT 1957

treated as an occupier and as his visitors are the same (subject to subsection (4) of this section) as the persons who would at common law be treated as an occupier and as his invitees or licensees.

(3) The rules so enacted in relation to an occupier of premises and his visitors shall also apply, in like manner and to the like extent as the principles applicable at common law to an occupier of premises and his invitees or licensees would apply, to regulate–

(a) the obligations of a person occupying or having control over any fixed or moveable structure, including any vessel, vehicle or aircraft; and

(b) the obligations of a person occupying or having control over any premises or structure in respect of damage to property, including the property of persons who are not themselves his visitors.

(4) Any person entering any premises in exercise of rights conferred by virtue of an access agreement or order under the National Parks and Access to the Countryside Act 1949 is not, for the purposes of this Act, a visitor of the occupier of those premises.

2. Extent of occupier's ordinary duty

(1) An occupier of premises owes the same duty, the 'common duty of care', to all his visitors, except in so far as he is free to and does extend, restrict, modify or exclude his duty to any visitor or visitors by agreement or otherwise.

(2) The common duty of care is a duty to take such care as in all the circumstances of the case is reasonable to see that the visitor will be reasonably safe in using the premises for those purposes for which he is invited or permitted by the occupier to be there.

(3) The circumstances relevant for the present purpose include the degree of care, and of want of care, which would ordinarily be looked for in such a visitor, so that (for example) in proper cases–

(a) an occupier must be prepared for children to be less careful than adults; and

(b) an occupier may expect that a person, in the exercise of his calling, will appreciate and guard against any special risks ordinarily incident to it, so far as the occupier leaves him free to do so.

(4) In determining whether the occupier of premises has discharged the common duty of care to a visitor, regard is to be had to all the circumstances, so that (for example)–

(a) where damage is caused to a visitor by a danger of which he had been warned by the occupier, the warning is not to be treated without more as absolving the occupier from liability, unless in all the circumstances it was enough to enable the visitor to be reasonably safe; and

[(b) not included.]

(5) The common duty of care does not impose on an occupier any obligation to a visitor in respect of risks willingly accepted as his by the visitor (the question whether a risk was so accepted to be decided on the same principles as in other cases in which one person owes a duty of care to another).

(6) For the purposes of this section, persons who enter premises for any purpose in the exercise of a right conferred by law are to be treated as permitted by the occupier to be there for that purpose, whether in fact they have his permission or not.

Text: p 52, 185

RIGHTS OF WAY
PARISH COUNCILS ACT 1957

1. Power to provide seats and shelters in roads
(1) Subject to the provisions of section five of this Act, a parish council may provide and maintain seats and shelters for the use of the public, and cause them to be installed or erected in proper and convenient situations in, or on any land abutting on, any road within the parish.
[(2) not included.]
Text: p 240

3. Power to light roads and public places
(1) The council of a parish or community or, in the case of a parish for which there is no parish council, the parish meeting may (subject to the provisions of section five of this Act) for the purpose of lighting the roads and other public places in the parish, or community, or in any part thereof–
(a) provide and maintain such lamps, lamp posts, and other materials and apparatus as they think necessary;
(b) cause such lamps, lamp posts and other materials and apparatus to be erected or installed on or against any premises or in such other places as may be convenient;
[(c) and (d) not included.]
[(10) not included.]
Text: p 240
Amended by LGA 72 Sch 14.

5. Provisions as to consents and access
(1) A parish meeting shall not have power by virtue of the foregoing provisions of this Part of this Act to provide any seat, shelter, clock, lamp or lamp post, or any other material or apparatus–
[(a) not included.]
(b) in any road which is not a highway or in any public path, except with the consent of the owner and the occupier of the land over which the road runs;
[paragraph (c) & subsections (2) to (4) not included.]
Text: p 240

7. Interpretation
In this Part of this Act except so far as the context otherwise requires–
'in' in a context referring to things in a road includes a reference to things under, over, across, along or upon the road;
'public path' has the meaning assigned to it by section twenty-seven of the National Parks and Access to the Countryside Act 1949;
'road' means any highway (including a public path) and any other road, lane, footway, square, court, alley or passage (whether a thoroughfare or not) to which the public has access.
Text: p 240
'public path' was defined in s 27 of the National Parks and Access to the Countryside Act 1949 as meaning a highway which is either a footpath or a bridleway. The definition in WCA 81 s 66 (p 385) is identical.

LAND POWERS (DEFENCE) ACT 1958

8. Stopping up and diversion of highways
(1) The powers conferred on the Minister of Transport by section 49 of the Town and Country Planning Act 1947 (...) shall also be exercisable where–
(a) land is, or is to be, used by a Secretary of State for the purposes of an installation provided or to be provided for defence purposes, or is used by a manufacturer of aircraft as an airfield wholly or mainly in connection with the manufacture of aircraft for defence purposes; and
(b) the Minister of Transport and Civil Aviation is satisfied that, for the land to be so used efficiently without danger to the public, it is necessary that a highway should be stopped up or diverted.
[(2) and (3) not included.]
Text: p 158
Note: Subsections (2) and (3) allow for an order to be temporary, and for anyone originally liable to maintain the highway concerned to be again liable at the end of such temporary closure or diversion.

25. Interpretation
(...)
'defence purposes' includes any purpose of any of Her Majesty's naval, military or air forces, the service of any visiting force within the meaning of Part 1 of the Visiting Forces Act 1952, and any purpose of the Minister of Supply connected with the service of any of the forces aforesaid.
Text: p 158

OPENCAST COAL ACT 1958

15. Suspension of certain public rights of way
(1) Where–
(a) the Corporation apply for opencast planning permission; and
(b) over any part of the land to which the application relates there subsists a public right of way, not being a right enjoyed by vehicular traffic,
the Corporation may also apply to the Secretary of State for an order suspending the public right of way.
(2) The Secretary of State shall not make such an order unless–
(a) opencast planning permission is granted; and
(b) he is satisfied–
(i) that a suitable alternative way will be made available by the Corporation (whether on land comprised in the opencast planning permission or on other land) for use by the public during the period for which the order remains in force; or
(ii) that the provision of such a way is not required.
(3) An order under this section shall specify the date, which shall not be earlier than the making of the order, with effect from which the right of way is suspended.
(4) Where an order has been made under this section the Secretary of State shall revoke it–
(a) if–
(i) no permitted activities have been carried on pursuant to the opencast planning permission on the land over which the right of way subsisted; and

RIGHTS OF WAY

(ii) he is satisfied that there is no early prospect of such activities being so carried on;
or
(b) as soon after such permitted activities have been so carried on as he is satisfied that it is no longer necessary for the purpose of carrying on such permitted activities that the right of way should be suspended.
(5) An order under this section shall include such provisions as may appear to the Secretary of State to be appropriate for securing the reconstruction of the way on the restoration of the land over which the right of way subsisted immediately before the order was made.
(6) Where an order is made under this section then, in connection with the provision of such a suitable alternative way as is referred to in subsection (2) above,–
(a) the order under this section may provide that, in so far as the carrying out of any operations, or any change in the use of land, involved in making the alternative way available or in permitting it to be used by the public, constitutes development within the meaning of the Act of 1990, permission for that development shall be deemed to be granted under Part III of that Act subject to such conditions (if any) as may be specified in the order;
(b) where the order under this section includes provisions in accordance with paragraph (a) above, the Act of 1990 shall have effect as if they were conditions subject to which the opencast planning permission was granted;
[(c) & (d) not included.]
Text: p 150
Amended by Housing and Planning Act 1986 Sch 8, Coal Industry Act 1987 Sch 1 para 7 and Planning (Consequential Provisions) Act 1990 Sch 2 para 5(b).

15A. Suspension of public rights of way — supplementary

(1) Before submitting to the Secretary of State an application for an order under section 15 of this Act, the Corporation shall publish a notice in the prescribed form identifying the right of way and stating–
(a) that the Corporation are proposing to apply for an order suspending it in connection with the working of coal by opencast operations;
(b) that opencast planning permission has been applied for, or, as the case may be, has been granted; and
(c) that objections to the application for the order may be made in writing to the Secretary of State within such time, not being less than 28 days from the publication of the notice, as may be specified.
(2) The duty to publish a notice imposed by subsection (1) above is a duty to publish it–
(a) in two successive weeks in one or more local newspapers circulating in the locality in which the land over which the right of way subsists is situated; and
(b) in the same or any other two successive weeks, in the appropriate Gazette.
(3) The period within which objections may be made expires when the period specified in the last publication of the notice expires; and any period specified in earlier publications is to be treated as extended accordingly.
(4) A notice under subsection (1) above shall name a place in the locality where a copy of the application and of a map showing the right of way can be inspected.

OPENCAST COAL ACT 1958

(5) The Corporation shall also, before submitting such an application to the Secretary of State,–
(a) inform–
(i) in England and Wales, the district council and, except in the case of a metropolitan district, the county council, and any parish or community council or parish meeting;
[(ii) not included.]
(b) send them a map showing the right of way and a copy of their notice under subsection (1) above; and
(c) affix to some conspicuous object at either end of the right of way a notice giving in the prescribed form the prescribed particulars of their proposed application concerning it and of the right to object.
(6) If no objection is made by any such authority, other than a parish or community council or parish meeting, as is mentioned in subsection (5)(a) above, or if all objections which are made by any such authority are withdrawn, the Secretary of State, upon being satisfied that the Corporation have complied with subsections (1) to (5) above, may if he thinks fit make the order.
(7) The Secretary of State may, if he thinks fit, cause a public local inquiry to be held before determining whether to make an order, and shall cause such an inquiry to be held if an objection is made by any such authority and is not withdrawn.
(8) If the Secretary of State causes such an inquiry to be held, he shall consider all objections to the application which are duly made by any person and not withdrawn and the report of the person who held the inquiry before determining whether to make the order.
(9) An order under section 15 of this Act may be made either in accordance with the Corporation's application or subject to such modifications as the Secretary of State may determine.
(10) If the Secretary of State makes an order, the Corporation, as soon as may be after the order is made, shall publish a notice in the prescribed form that the order has been made, describing the right of way which is suspended, stating the date on which the order comes into operation and naming a place in the locality where a copy of the order and of any map to which it refers can be inspected at all reasonable hours, and shall serve a like notice and a copy of the order on any body required under this section to be informed of the application for the order.
(11) The duty to publish a notice imposed by subsection (10) above is a duty to publish it–
(a) in one or more local newspapers such as are mentioned in subsection (1) above; and
(b) in the appropriate Gazette.
(12) In this section 'the appropriate Gazette' means–
(a) the London Gazette in a case where the land over which the right of way subsists is situated in England or Wales;
[(b) not included.]
Text: p 150
Inserted by Housing and Planning Act 1986 Sch 8 and amended by Coal Industry Act 1987 Sch 1 para 7. The form of notices is prescribed by the Opencast Coal (Compulsory Rights and Rights of Way) (Forms) Regulations 1987 SI 1987 No 1915 (p 475).

RIGHTS OF WAY
COUNTRYSIDE ACT 1968

27. Signposting of footpaths and bridleways

(1) A highway authority, after consultation with the owner or occupier of the land concerned, shall have power to erect and maintain signposts along any footpath, bridleway or byway for which they are the highway authority.

(2) Subject to subsection (3) below, at every point where a footpath, bridleway or byway leaves a metalled road the highway authority shall in exercise of their power under subsection (1) above erect and maintain a signpost–
(a) indicating that the footpath, bridleway or byway is a public footpath, bridleway or byway, and
(b) showing, so far as the highway authority consider convenient and appropriate, where the footpath, bridleway or byway leads, and the distance to any place or places named on the signpost.

(3) A highway authority need not erect a signpost in accordance with subsection (2) above at a particular site if the highway authority, after consulting the council of the parish in which the site is situated, or as the case may be the chairman of the parish meeting for the parish, not having a parish council, in which the site is situated, are satisfied that it is not necessary, and if the parish council, or as the case may be the chairman of the parish meeting, agree.

(4) It shall also be the duty of a highway authority in exercise of their powers under subsection (1) above to erect such signposts as may in the opinion of the highway authority be required to assist persons unfamiliar with the locality to follow the course of a footpath, bridleway or byway.

(5) With the consent of the highway authority, any other person may erect and maintain signposts along a footpath, bridleway or byway.

(6) Section 131(2) of the Highways Act 1980 (destruction or defacement of a traffic sign) shall apply to a signpost erected or placed along a footpath, bridleway or byway in pursuance of this section as it applies to a traffic sign placed on or near a highway.

(7) In this section (and in the amendments made by this section in other enactments) references to signposts shall include references to other signs or notices serving the same purpose and references to the erection of a signpost shall include references to positioning any such other sign or notice.

(8) In this section 'byway' means a byway open to all traffic, that is to say, a highway over which the public have a right of way for vehicular and all other kinds of traffic, but which is used by the public mainly for the purposes for which footpaths and bridleways are so used.

Text: p 195, 236
Amended by HA 80 Sch 24, WCA 81 s 65 & Road Traffic Regulation Act 1984 Sch 14. HA 80 s 131: p 340

30. Riding of pedal bicycles on bridleways

(1) Any member of the public shall have, as a right of way, the right to ride a bicycle, not being a motor vehicle, on any bridleway, but in exercising that right cyclists shall give way to pedestrians and persons on horseback.

(2) Subsection (1) above has effect subject to any orders made by a local authority, and to any byelaws.

(3) The rights conferred by this section shall not affect the obligations of the highway authority, or of any other person, as respects the maintenance of the

COUNTRYSIDE ACT 1968

bridleway, and this section shall not create any obligation to do anything to facilitate the use of the bridleway by cyclists.
(4) Subsection (1) above shall not affect any definition of 'bridleway' in this or any other Act.
(5) In this section 'motor vehicle' has the same meaning as in the Road Traffic Act 1988.
Text: p 54
Amended by Road Traffic (Consequential Provisions) Act 1988 Sch 3 para 5. 'Motor vehicle' is defined in RTA 88 s 185 (p 417)

49. Interpretation
[(1) not included.]
(2) In this Act, unless the context otherwise requires–
(...)
'bridleway' and 'footpath' have the meanings given by section 329(1) of the Highways Act 1980;
'land' includes any interest in or right over land;
(...)
Text: p 53
HA 80 s 329(1): p 357

FIREARMS ACT 1968

19. Carrying firearm in a public place
A person commits an offence if, without lawful authority or reasonable excuse (the proof whereof lies on him) he has with him in a public place a loaded shot gun or loaded air weapon, or any other firearm (whether loaded or not) together with ammunition suitable for use in that firearm.

20. Trespassing with firearm
(1) A person commits an offence if, while he has a firearm with him, he enters or is in any building or part of a building as a trespasser and without reasonable excuse (the proof whereof lies on him).
(2) A person commits an offence if, while he has a firearm with him, he enters or is on any land as a trespasser and without reasonable excuse (the proof whereof lies on him).

57. Interpretation
(1) In this Act, the expression 'firearm' means a lethal barrelled weapon of any description from which any shot, bullet or other missile can be discharged (...)
[(2) and (3) not included.]
(4) In this Act:
(...)
'public place' includes any highway and any other premises or place to which at the material time the public have or are permitted to have access, whether on payment or otherwise;
(...)
Text: p 192

RIGHTS OF WAY
ANIMALS ACT 1971

2. Liability for damage done by dangerous animal
(1) Where any damage is caused by an animal which belongs to a dangerous species, any person who is a keeper of the animal is liable for the damage, except as otherwise provided by this Act.
(2) Where damage is caused by an animal which does not belong to a dangerous species, a keeper of the animal is liable for the damage, except as otherwise provided by this Act, if–
(a) the damage is of a kind which the animal, unless restrained, was likely to cause or which, if caused by the animal, was likely to be severe; and
(b) the likelihood of the damage or of its being severe was due to characteristics of the animal which are not normally found in animals of the same species or are not normally so found except at particular times or in particular circumstances; and
(c) those characteristics were known to that keeper or were at any time known to a person who at that time had charge of the animal as that keeper's servant or, where that keeper is the head of a household, were known to another keeper of the animal who is a member of that household and under the age of sixteen.
Text: p 185, 186

5. Exceptions from liability under sections 2 to 4
(1) A person is not liable under sections 2 to 4 of this Act for any damage which is due wholly to the fault of the person suffering it.
(2) A person is not liable under section 2 of this Act for any damage suffered by a person who has voluntarily accepted the risk thereof.
(3) A person is not liable under section 2 of this Act for any damage caused by an animal kept on any premises or structure to a person trespassing there, if it is proved either–
(a) that the animal was not kept there for the protection of persons or property; or
(b) (if the animal was kept there for the protection of persons or property) that keeping it there for that purpose was not unreasonable.
Text: p 186

6. Interpretation of certain expressions used in sections 2 to 5
(1) The following provisions apply to the interpretation of sections 2 to 5 of this Act.
(2) A dangerous species is a species–
(a) which is not commonly domesticated in the British Isles; and
(b) whose fully grown animals normally have such characteristics that they are likely, unless restrained, to cause severe damage or that any damage they may cause is likely to be severe.
(3) Subject to subsection (4) of this section, a person is a keeper of an animal if–
(a) he owns the animal or has it in his possession; or
(b) he is the head of a household of which a member under the age of sixteen owns the animal or has it in his possession;
and if at any time an animal ceases to be owned by or to be in the possession of a person, any person who immediately before that time was a keeper thereof

by virtue of the preceding provisions of this subsection continues to be a keeper of the animal until another person becomes a keeper thereof by virtue of those provisions.
(4) Where an animal is taken into and kept in possession for the purpose of preventing it from causing damage or of restoring it to its owner, a person is not a keeper of it by virtue only of that possession.
(5) Where a person employed as a servant by a keeper of an animal incurs a risk incidental to his employment he shall not be treated as accepting it voluntarily.
Text: p 186

9. Killing of or injury to dogs worrying livestock
(1) In any civil proceedings against a person (in this section referred to as the defendant) for killing or causing injury to a dog it shall be a defence to prove–
(a) that the defendant acted for the protection of any livestock and was a person entitled to act for the protection of that livestock; and
(b) that within forty-eight hours of the killing or injury notice thereof was given by the defendant to the officer in charge of a police station.
(2) For the purposes of this section a person is entitled to act for the protection of any livestock if, and only if–
(a) the livestock or the land on which it is belongs to him or to any person under whose express or implied authority he is acting; and
(b) the circumstances are not such that liability for killing or causing injury to the livestock would be excluded by section 5(4) of this Act.
(3) Subject to subsection (4) of this section, a person killing or causing injury to a dog shall be deemed for the purposes of this section to act for the protection of any livestock if, and only if–
(a) the dog is worrying or is about to worry the livestock and there are no other reasonable means of ending or preventing the worrying; or
(b) the dog has been worrying livestock, has not left the vicinity and is not under the control of any person and there are no practicable means of ascertaining to whom it belongs.
(4) For the purposes of this section the condition stated in either of the paragraphs of the preceding subsection shall be deemed to have been satisfied if the defendant believed that it was satisfied and had reasonable ground for that belief.
(5) For the purposes of this section–
(a) an animal belongs to any person if he owns it or has it in his possession; and
(b) land belongs to any person if he is the occupier thereof.
Text: p 46

11. General interpretation
In this Act–
(...)
'damage' includes the death of, or injury to, any person (including any disease and any impairment of physical or mental condition);
'fault' has the same meaning as in the Law Reform (Contributory Negligence) Act 1945;
(...)

'livestock' means cattle, horses, asses, mules, hinnies, sheep, pigs, goats and poultry, and also deer not in the wild state and, in sections 3 and 9, also, while in captivity, pheasants, partridges and grouse;
'poultry' means the domestic varieties of the following, that is to say, fowls, turkeys, geese, ducks, guinea-fowls, pigeons, peacocks and quails;
(...)
Text: p 186
'Fault' is defined in the 1945 Act as 'negligence, breach of statutory duty or other act or omission which gives rise to a liability in tort or would, apart from this Act, give rise to the defence of contributory negligence'.

CRIMINAL DAMAGE ACT 1971

1. Damaging or destroying property
(1) A person who without lawful excuse destroys or damages any property belonging to another intending to destroy or damage any such property or being reckless as to whether any such property would be destroyed or damaged shall be guilty of an offence.
[Remainder of s 1 not included.]
Text: p 55, 180, 196

5. 'Without lawful excuse'
(1) This section applies to any offence under section 1(1) above (...)
(2) A person charged with an offence to which this section applies, shall, whether or not he would be treated for the purposes of this Act as having a lawful excuse apart from this subsection, be treated for those purposes as having a lawful excuse–
(a) if at the time of the act or acts alleged to constitute the offence he believed that the person or persons whom he believed to be entitled to consent to the destruction of or damage to the property in question had so consented, or would have so consented to it if he or they had known of the destruction or damage and its circumstances; or
(b) if he destroyed or damaged (...) the property in question (...) in order to protect property belonging to himself or another, and at the time of the act or acts alleged to constitute the offence he believed–
(i) that the property, right or interest was in immediate need of protection; and
(ii) that the means of protection adopted or proposed to be adopted were or would be reasonable having regard to all the circumstances.
(3) For the purposes of this section it is immaterial whether a belief is justified or not if it is honestly held.
(4) For the purposes of subsection (2) above a right of interest in property includes any right or privilege in or over land, whether created by grant, licence or otherwise.
[Remainder of s 5 not included.]
Text: p 196

10. Interpretation
(1) In this Act 'property' means property of a tangible nature, whether real or personal (...)

CRIMINAL DAMAGE ACT 1971

(2) Property shall be treated for the purposes of this Act as belonging to any person–
(a) having the custody or control of it;
(b) having in it any proprietary right or interest (...)
[(c) not included.]
[(3) and (4) not included.]
Text: p 196

LOCAL GOVERNMENT ACT 1972

100A. Admission to meetings of principal councils
(1) A meeting of a principal council shall be open to the public except to the extent that they are excluded (whether during the whole or part of the proceedings) under subsection (2) below or by resolution under subsection (4) below.
(2) The public shall be excluded from a meeting of a principal council during an item of business whenever it is likely, in view of the nature of the business to be transacted or the nature of the proceedings, that, if members of the public were present during that item, confidential information would be disclosed to them in breach of the obligation of confidence; and nothing in this Part shall be taken to authorise or require the disclosure of confidential information in breach of the obligation of confidence.
(3) For the purposes of subsection (2) above, 'confidential information' means–
(a) information furnished to the council by a Government department upon terms (however expressed) which forbid the disclosure of information to the public; and
(b) information the disclosure of which to the public is prohibited by or under any enactment or by the order of a court;
and in either case, the reference to the obligation of confidence is to be construed accordingly.
(4) A principal council may by resolution exclude the public from a meeting during an item of business whenever it is likely, in view of the nature of business to be transacted or the nature of the proceedings, that if members of the public were present during that item there would be disclosure to them of exempt information, as defined in section 100I below.
(5) A resolution under subsection (4) above shall–
(a) identify the proceedings, or the part of the proceedings, to which it applies, and
(b) state the description, in terms of Schedule 12A to this Act, of the exempt information giving rise to the exclusion of the public,
and where such a resolution is passed this section does not require the meeting to be open to the public during proceedings to which the resolution applies.
(6) The following provisions shall apply in relation to a meeting of a principal council, that is to say–
(a) public notice of the time and place of the meeting shall be given by posting it at the offices of the council three clear days at least before the meeting or, if the meeting is convened at shorter notice, then at the time it is convened;
(b) while the meeting is open to the public, the council shall not have power to exclude members of the public from the meeting;
[(c) not included]
[(7) and (8) not included.]

RIGHTS OF WAY

Text: p 37
Inserted by Local Government (Access to Information) Act 1985 s 1.

100B. Access to agenda and connected reports
(1) Copies of the agenda for a meeting of a principal council and, subject to subsection (2) below, copies of any report for the meeting shall be open to inspection by members of the public at the offices of the council in accordance with subsection (3) below.
(2) If the proper officer thinks fit, there may be excluded from the copies of reports provided in pursuance of subsection (1) above the whole of any report which, or any part which, relates only to items during which, in his opinion, the meeting is not likely to be open to the public.
(3) Any document which is required by subsection (1) above to be open to inspection shall be so open at least three clear days before the meeting, except that–
(a) where the meeting is convened at shorter notice, the copies of the agenda and reports shall be open to inspection from the time the meeting is convened, and
(b) where an item is added to an agenda copies of which are open to inspection by the public, copies of the item (or of the revised agenda), and the copies of the report for the meeting relating to the item, shall be open to inspection from the time the item is added to the agenda;
but nothing in this subsection requires copies of any agenda, item or report to be open to inspection by the public until copies are available to members of the council.
(4) An item of business may not be considered at a meeting of a principal council unless either–
(a) a copy of the agenda including the item (or a copy of the item) is open to inspection by members of the public in pursuance of subsection (1) above for at least three clear days before the meeting or, where the meeting is convened at shorter notice, from the time the meeting is convened; or
(b) by reason of special circumstances, which shall be specified in the minutes, the chairman of the meeting is of the opinion that the item should be considered at the meeting as a matter of urgency.
(5) Where by virtue of subsection (2) above the whole or any part of a report for a meeting is not open to inspection by the public under subsection (1) above–
(a) every copy of the report or of the part shall be marked 'Not for publication'; and
(b) there shall be stated on every copy of the whole or of any part of the report the description, in terms of Schedule 12A to this Act, of the exempt information by virtue of which the council are likely to exclude the public during the item to which the report relates.
(6) Where a meeting of a principal council is required by section 100A above to be open to the public during the proceedings or any part of them, there shall be made available for the use of members of the public present at the meeting a reasonable number of copies of the agenda and, subject to subsection (8) below, of the reports for the meeting.
[(7) not included.]

LOCAL GOVERNMENT ACT 1972

(8) Subsection (2) above applies in relation to copies of reports provided in pursuance of subsection (6) (...) above as it applies in relation to copies of reports provided in pursuance of subsection (1) above.
Text: p 37
Inserted by Local Government (Access to Information) Act 1985 s 1.

100C. Inspection of minutes and other documents after meeting

(1) After a meeting of a principal council the following documents shall be open to inspection by members of the public at the offices of the council until the expiration of the period of six years beginning with the date of the meeting, namely–
(a) the minutes, or a copy of the minutes, of the meeting, excluding so much of the minutes of proceedings during which the meeting was not open to the public as discloses exempt information;
(b) where applicable, a summary under subsection (2) below;
(c) a copy of the agenda for the meeting; and
(d) a copy of so much of any report for the meeting as relates to any item during which the meeting was open to the public.
(2) Where, in consequence of the exclusion of parts of the minutes which disclose exempt information, the document open to inspection under subsection (1)(a) above does not provide members of the public with a reasonably fair and coherent record of the whole or part of the proceedings, the proper officer shall make a written summary of the proceedings or the part, as the case may be, which provides such a record without disclosing the exempt information.
Text: p 37
Inserted by Local Government (Access to Information) Act 1985 s 1.

100D. Inspection of background papers

(1) Subject, in the case of section 100C(1), to subsection (2) below, if and so long as copies of the whole or part of a report for a meeting of a principal council are required by section 100B(1) or 100C(1) above to be open to inspection by members of the public–
(a) copies of a list, compiled by a proper officer, of the background papers for the report or the part of the report, and
(b) at least one copy of each of the documents included in that list,
shall also be open to their inspection at the offices of the council.
(2) Subsection (1) above does not require a copy of the list, or of any document included in the list, to be open to inspection after the expiration of the period of four years beginning with the date of the meeting.
(3) Where a copy of any of the background papers for a report is required by subsection (1) above to be open to inspection by members of the public, the copy shall be taken for the purposes of this Part to be so open if arrangements exist for its production to members of the public as soon as is reasonably practicable after the making of a request to inspect the copy.
(4) Nothing in this section–
(a) requires any document which discloses exempt information to be included in the list referred to in subsection (1) above; or
(b) without prejudice to the generality of subsection (2) of section 100A above, requires or authorises the inclusion in the list of any document which, if open

to inspection by the public, would disclose confidential information in breach of the obligation of confidence, within the meaning of that subsection.
(5) For the purposes of this section the background papers for a report are those documents relating to the subject matter of the report which–
(a) disclose any facts or matters on which, in the opinion of the proper officer, the report or an important part of the report is based, and
(b) have, in his opinion, been relied on to a material extent in preparing the report,
but do not include any published works.
Text: p 38
Inserted by Local Government (Access to Information) Act 1985 s 1.

100E. Application to committees and sub-committees
(1) Sections 100A to 100D above shall apply in relation to a committee or sub-committee of a principal council as they apply in relation to a principal council.
[(2) to (4) not included.]
Text: p 38
Inserted by Local Government (Access to Information) Act 1985 s 1.

100G. Principal councils to publish additional information
(1) A principal council shall maintain a register stating–
(a) the name and address of every member of the council for the time being and the ward or division which he represents; and
(b) the name and address of every member of each committee or sub-committee of the council for the time being.
(2) A principal council shall maintain a list–
(a) specifying those powers of the council which, for the time being, are exercisable from time to time by officers in pursuance of arrangements made under this Act or any other enactment for their discharge by those officers; and
(b) stating the title of the officer by whom each of the powers so specified is for the time being so exercisable;
but this subsection does not require a power to be specified in a list if the arrangements for its discharge by the officer are made for a specified period not exceeding six months.
(3) There shall be kept at the offices of every principal council a written summary of the rights–
(a) to attend meetings of a principal council and of committees and sub-committees of a principal council; and
(b) to inspect any copy documents and to be furnished with documents,
which are for the time being conferred by this Part, Part XI below and such other enactments as the Secretary of State by order specifies.
(4) The register maintained under subsection (1) above, the list maintained under subsection (2) above and the summary kept under subsection (3) above shall be open to inspection by the public at the offices of the council.
Text: p 38, 126
Inserted by Local Government (Access to Information) Act 1985 s 1. The enactments specified by the Secretary of State for the purpose of subsection (3)(b) are listed in the Local Government (Inspection of Documents) (Summary of Rights) Order 1986 SI 1986 No 854.

LOCAL GOVERNMENT ACT 1972

100H. Supplemental provisions and offences
(1) A document directed by any provision of this Part to be open to inspection shall be so open at all reasonable hours and–
(a) in the case of a document open to inspection by virtue of section 100D(1) above, upon payment of such reasonable fee as may be required for the facility; and
(b) in any other case, without payment.
(2) Where a document is open to inspection by a person under any provision of this Part, the person may, subject to subsection (3) below–
(a) make copies of or extracts from the document, or
(b) require the person having custody of the document to supply to him a photographic copy of or of extracts from the document,
upon payment of such reasonable fee as may be required for the facility.
(3) Subsection (2) above does not require or authorise the doing of any act which infringes the copyright in any work except that, where the owner of the copyright is a principal council, nothing done in pursuance of that subsection shall constitute an infringement of the copyright.
[remainder of section not included.]
Text: p 38
Inserted by Local Government (Access to Information) Act 1985 s 1.

112. Appointment of staff
(1) (...) a local authority shall appoint such officers as they think necessary for the proper discharge by the authority of such of their or another authority's functions as fall to be discharged by them (...)
Text: p 34

187. Local highway authorities and maintenance powers of district councils
(3) With respect to footpaths and bridleways within their area a district council shall have–
(a) the like powers as a highway authority under section 57(3) of the National Parks and Access to the Countryside Act 1949 (prosecution of offences of displaying on footpaths notices deterring public use)
Text: p 189
Amended by HA 80 Sch 25. National Parks and Access to the Countryside Act 1949 s 57(3): p 291

222. Power of local authorities to prosecute or defend legal proceedings
(1) Where a local authority consider it expedient for the promotion or protection of the interests of the inhabitants of their area–
(a) they may prosecute or defend or appear in any legal proceedings and, in the case of civil proceedings, may institute them in their own name; and
(b) they may, in their own name, make representations in the interests of the inhabitants at any public inquiry held by or on behalf of any Minister or public body under any enactment.
(2) In this section 'local authority' includes the Common Council.
Text: p 172

RIGHTS OF WAY

225. Deposit of documents with proper officer of authority, etc
(1) In any case in which a document of any description is deposited with the proper officer of a local authority, or with the chairman of a parish or community council or with the chairman of a parish meeting, pursuant to the standing orders of either House of Parliament or to any enactment or instrument, the proper officer or chairman, as the case may be, shall receive and retain the document in the manner and for the purposes directed by the standing orders or enactment or instrument, and shall make such notes or endorsements on, and give such acknowledgements and receipts in respect of the document as may be so directed.
(2) All documents required by any enactment or instrument to be deposited with the proper officer of a parish or community shall, in the case of a parish or community not having a separate parish or community council, be deposited in England with the chairman of the parish meeting or in Wales with the proper officer of the district council.
Text: p 109

228. Inspection of documents
(1) The minutes of proceedings of a local authority shall be open to the inspection of any local government elector for the area of the authority and any such local government elector may make a copy of or extract from the minutes.
(2) A local government elector for the area of a local authority may inspect and make a copy of or extract from an order for the payment of money made by the local authority.
(3) The accounts of a local authority and of any proper officer of a local authority shall be open to the inspection of any member of the authority, and any such member may make a copy of or extract from the accounts.
(4) Any abstract of the accounts of a body whose accounts are required to be audited in accordance with Part VIII of this Act and of any officer of such a body and any report made by an auditor on those accounts shall be open to the inspection of any local government elector for the area of the body, and any such local government elector may make a copy thereof or extract therefrom, and copies thereof shall be delivered to any such local government elector on payment of a reasonable sum for each copy.
(5) Subject to any provisions to the contrary in any other enactment or instrument, a person interested in any document deposited as mentioned in section 225 above may, at all reasonable hours, inspect and make copies therefrom on payment to the person having custody thereof of the sum of 10p for every such inspection, and of the further sum of 10p for every hour during which such inspection continues after the first hour.
(6) A document directed by this section to be open to inspection shall be so open at all reasonable hours and, except where otherwise expressly provided, without payment.
(7) If a person having the custody of any such document–
(a) obstructs any person entitled to inspect the document or to make a copy thereof or extract therefrom in inspecting the document or making a copy or extract,
(b) refuses to give copies of extracts to any person entitled to obtain copies or extracts,
he shall be liable on summary conviction to a fine not exceeding level 1 on the standard scale.

LOCAL GOVERNMENT ACT 1972

(8) This section shall apply to the minutes of proceedings and to the accounts of a parish meeting as if that meeting were a local authority.
Text: p 109

250. Power to direct inquiries
(1) Where any Minister is authorised by this Act to determine any difference, to make or confirm any order, to frame any scheme, or to give any consent, confirmation, sanction or approval to any matter, or otherwise to act under this Act, and where the Secretary of State is authorised to hold an inquiry, either under this Act or under any enactment relating to the functions of a local authority, he may cause a local inquiry to be held.
(2) For the purpose of any such local inquiry, the person appointed to hold the inquiry may by summons require any person to attend, at a time and place stated in the summons, to give evidence or to produce any documents in his custody which relate to any matter in question at the inquiry, and may take evidence on oath, and for that purpose administer oaths, or may, instead of administering an oath, require the person examined to make a solemn affirmation–
Provided that:
(a) no person shall be required, in obedience of such summons, to attend to give evidence or to produce any such documents, unless the necessary expenses of his attendance are paid or tendered to him; and
(b) nothing in this section shall empower the person holding the inquiry to require the production of the title, or of any instrument relating to the title, of any land not being the property of a local authority.
(3) Every person who refuses or deliberately fails to attend in obedience to a summons issued under this section or to give evidence, or who deliberately alters, suppresses, conceals, destroys, or refuses to produce any book or other document which he is required or is liable to be required to produce for the purposes of this section, shall be liable on summary conviction to a fine not exceeding level 3 on the standard scale or to imprisonment for a term not exceeding six months, or to both.
(4) Where a Minister causes an inquiry to be held under this section, the costs incurred by him in relation to the inquiry shall be paid by such local authority or party to the inquiry as he may direct, and the Minister may cause the amount of the costs so incurred to be certified, and any amount so certified and directed to be paid by any authority or person shall be recoverable from that authority or person by the Minister summarily as a civil debt.
(5) The Minister causing an inquiry to be held under this section may make orders as to the costs of the parties at the inquiry and as to the parties by whom the costs are to be paid, and every such order may be made a rule of the High Court on the application of any party named in the order.
[(6) not included.]
Text: p 129
Amended by Housing and Planning Act 1986 Sch 12 Pt III. The power to recover costs was extended by s 42 of the 1986 Act (p 406).

270. General provisions as to interpretation
(1) In this Act, except where the context otherwise requires, the following expressions have the following meanings respectively, that is to say–
(...)

RIGHTS OF WAY

'land' includes any interest in land and any easement or right in, to or over land;
'local authority' means a county council, a district council, a London borough council or a parish or community council.
(...)
Amended by LGA 85 Sch 16 para 8(b).

HEALTH AND SAFETY AT WORK ACT 1974

3. General duties of employers and self-employed to persons other than their employees
(1) It shall be the duty of every employer to conduct his undertaking in such a way as to ensure, so far as is reasonably practicable, that persons not in his employment who may be affected thereby are not thereby exposed to risks to their health and safety.
(2) It shall be the duty of every self-employed person to conduct his undertaking in such a way as to ensure, so far as is reasonably practicable, that he and other persons (not being his employees) who may be affected thereby are not thereby exposed to risks to their health and safety.
[(3) not included.]
Text: p 184, 191, 193

33. Offences
(1) It is an offence for a person:
(a) to fail to discharge a duty to which he is subject by virtue of sections 2 to 7.
[Remainder of s 33 is not included.]
Text: p 184
The maximum fine is level 5 on the standard scale.

GUARD DOGS ACT 1975

1. Control of guard dogs
(1) A person shall not use or permit the use of a guard dog at any premises unless a person ('the handler') who is capable of controlling the dog is present on the premises and the dog is under the control of the handler at all times while it is being so used except while it is secured so that it is not at liberty to go freely about the premises.
(2) The handler of a guard dog shall keep the dog under his control at all times while it is being used as a guard dog at any premises except–
(a) while another handler has control over the dog; or
(b) while the dog is secured so that it is not at liberty to go freely about the premises.
(3) A person shall not use or permit the use of a guard dog at any premises unless a notice containing a warning that a guard dog is present is clearly exhibited at each entrance to the premises.

5. Offences, penalties and civil liability
(1) A person who contravenes section 1 (...) of this Act shall be guilty of an offence and liable on summary conviction to a fine not exceeding level 5 on the standard scale.

GUARD DOGS ACT 1975

(2) The provisions of this Act shall not be construed as–
(a) conferring a right of action in any civil proceedings (other than proceedings for recovery of a fine or any prescribed fee) in respect of any contravention of this Act or of any regulations made under this Act (...); or
(b) derogating from any right of action or other remedy (whether civil or criminal) in proceedings instituted otherwise than by virtue of this Act.

7. Interpretation
In this Act, unless the context otherwise requires–
'agricultural land' has the same meaning as in the Dogs (Protection of Livestock) Act 1953;
'guard dog' means a dog which is being used to protect–
(a) premises; or
(b) property kept on the premises; or
(c) a person guarding the premises or such property;
(...)
'premises' means land other than agricultural land and land within the curtilage of a dwelling-house, and buildings, including parts of buildings, other than dwelling-houses;
(...)
Text: p 185
Amended by Criminal Justice Act 1982 ss 38,46.

LOCAL GOVERNMENT (MISCELLANEOUS PROVISIONS) ACT 1976

16. Power of local authorities to obtain particulars of persons interested in land
(1) Where, with a view to performing a function conferred on a local authority by any enactment, the authority considers that it ought to have information connected with any land, the authority may serve on one or more of the following persons, namely–
(a) the occupier of the land; and
(b) any person who has an interest in the land either as freeholder, mortgagee or lessee or who directly or indirectly receives rent for the land; and
(c) any person who, in pursuance of an agreement between himself and a person interested in the land, is authorised to manage the land or to arrange the letting of it,
a notice specifying the land and the function and the enactment which confers the function and requiring the recipient of the notice to furnish to the authority, within a period specified in the notice (which shall be not less than fourteen days beginning with the day on which the notice is served), the nature of his interest in the land and the name and address of each person whom he believes is, as respects the land, such a person as is mentioned in the provisions of paragraphs (b) and (c) of this subsection.
(2) A person who–
(a) fails to comply with the requirements of a notice served on him in pursuance of the preceding subsection; or
(b) in furnishing any information in compliance with such a notice makes a statement which he knows to be false in a material particular or recklessly makes a statement which is false in a material particular,

shall be guilty of an offence and liable on summary conviction to a fine not exceeding level 5 on the standard scale.
Text: p 173

44. Interpretation, etc. of Part I
(1) In this part of this Act, except where the contrary intention appears,–
'functions' includes power and duties;
'local authority' means each of the following bodies, namely a county council, a district council, a London borough council, the Common Council and the Council of the Isles of Scilly, and,
[(a) not included.]
(b) in (...) section 16 (...) of this Act, a parish council and a community council.
Text: p 173
Amended by LGA 85 Sch 14 para 55.

CRIMINAL LAW ACT 1977

6. Violence for securing entry
(1) Subject to the following provisions of this section, any person who, without lawful authority, uses or threatens violence for the purpose of securing entry into any premises for himself or for any other person is guilty of an offence, provided that–
(a) there is someone present on those premises at the time who is opposed to the entry which the violence is intended to secure; and
(b) the person using or threatening the violence knows that that is the case.
[(2) and (3) not included.]
(4) It is immaterial for the purposes of this section–
(a) whether the violence in question is directed against the person or against property; and
(b) whether the entry which the violence is intended to secure is for the purpose of acquiring possession of the premises in question or for any other purpose.
(5) A person guilty of an offence under this section shall be liable on summary conviction to imprisonment for a term not exceeding six months or a fine not exceeding level 5 on the standard scale or to both.
(6) A constable in uniform may arrest without warrant anyone who is, or whom he, with reasonable cause, suspects to be, guilty of an offence under this section.
[(7) not included.]
Text: p 267

12. Supplementary provisions
(1) In this Part of this Act–
(a) 'premises' means any building, any part of a building under separate occupation, any land ancillary to a building, the site comprising any building or buildings together with any land ancillary thereto (...)
[(b) not included.]
(2) References in this section to a building shall apply also to any structure other than a moveable one, and to any moveable structure, vehicle or vessel designed or adapted for use by residential purposes; and for the purposes of subsection (1) above–

CRIMINAL LAW ACT 1977

(a) part of a building is under separate occupation if anyone is in occupation or entitled to occupation of that part as distinct from the whole; and
(b) land is ancillary to a building if it is adjacent to it and used (or intended for use) in connection with the occupation of that building or any part of it.
[(3) to (8) not included.]
Text: p 267

HIGHWAYS ACT 1980

1. Highway authorities: general provision
[(1) not included.]
(2) Outside Greater London the council of a county or metropolitan district are the highway authority for all highways in the county or, as the case may be, the district, whether or not maintainable at public expense, which are not highways for which under subsection (1) above the Minister is the highway authority.
(3) The council of a London borough or the Common Council are the highway authority for all highways in the borough or, as the case may be, in the City, whether or not maintainable at the public expense, which are not highways for which under subsection (1) above the Minister is the highway authority.
(4) Subsection (2) above is subject, as respects any highway outside Greater London for which the Minister is not the highway authority under subsection (1) above, to any provision of this Act, or of any order made under this or any other Act, by virtue of which a council other than the council of the county or, as the case may be, the district, in which the highway is situated are the highway authority therefor.
Text: p 32
Amended by LGA 85 Sch 4 para 1 and Sch 17.

3. Highway authority for approaches to and parts of certain bridges
(1) Where a bridge carries a highway for which the Minister is not the highway authority and part of the bridge is situated in one county and part in another the highway authority for the highway carried by the bridge and the approaches thereto is such one of the councils of those counties as may be agreed between them before such a day as the Minister may by order made by statutory instrument appoint or, in default of such agreement, as may be determined by the Minister.
(2) Where the Minister has made a determination under subsection (1) above the determination–
(a) may be varied at the request of the council of either of the counties concerned, and
(b) shall be varied to give effect to any request made jointly to the Minister by those councils,
and any such variation shall take effect on the 1st April falling not less than 3 months, and not more than 15 months, after the date on which the determination is varied.
(3) Where a bridge carries a highway for which the Minister is not the highway authority and subsection (1) above does not apply, but some part of one or more of the approaches to the bridge lies in a county different from the bridge

itself, the highway authority for the whole of that approach or those approaches is the council of the county in which the bridge is situated.
(4) For the purposes of this section, the approaches to a bridge consist of so much of the highway or highways on either side of the bridge as is situated within 100 yards of either end of the bridge.
Text: p 34

14. Powers as respects roads that cross or join trunk or classified roads

(1) Provision may be made by an order under this section in relation to a trunk road or a classified road, not being, in either case, a special road, for any of the following purposes:–
(a) for authorising the highway authority for the road:
(i) to stop up, divert, improve, raise, lower or otherwise alter a highway that crosses or enters the route of the road or is or will be otherwise affected by the construction or improvement of the road;
(ii) to construct a new highway for purposes concerned with any such alteration as aforesaid or for any other purpose connected with the road or its construction, and to close after such period as may be specified in the order any new highway so constructed for temporary purposes;
[(b) not included.]
(c) for any other purpose incidental to the purposes aforesaid;
and references in this section, with respect to an order made thereunder, to 'the road' and 'the highway authority' are references to, respectively, the trunk road or, as the case may be, classified road to which the order relates and the highway authority for that road.
[(2) not included.]
(3) An order under this section–
(a) in relation to a trunk road shall be made by the Minister; and
(b) in relation to a classified road shall be made by the highway authority and confirmed by the Minister.
(4) Parts I and III of Schedule 1 to this Act have effect as to the making of an order under this section; and Schedule 2 to this Act have effect as to the validity and date of operation of any such order.
[(5) not included.]
(6) No order under this section authorising the stopping up of a highway shall be made or confirmed by the Minister unless he is satisfied that another reasonably convenient route is available or will be provided before the highway is stopped up.
Text: p 149

18. Supplementary orders relating to special roads

(1) Provision in relation to a special road may be made by an order under this section for any of the following purposes:–
[(a) and (b) not included.]
(c) for authorising the special road authority–
(i) to stop up, divert, improve, raise, lower or otherwise alter a highway that crosses or enters the route of the special road or is or will be otherwise affected by the construction or improvement of the special road;

HIGHWAYS ACT 1980

(ii) to construct a new highway for purposes connected with any such alteration as aforesaid or for any other purpose connected with the special road or its construction, and to close after such period as may be specified in the order any new highway so constructed for temporary purposes;
[(d) and (e) not included.]
(f) for any other purpose incidental to the purposes aforesaid or otherwise incidental to the construction or maintenance of, or other dealing with, the special road.
[(2) not included.]
(3) An order under this section making provision in connection with a special road shall–
(a) in the case of a special road provided or to be provided by the Minister be made by the Minister; and
(b) in the case of a special road provided or to be provided by a local highway authority, be made by that authority and confirmed by the Minister.
(4) Parts I and III of Schedule 1 to this Act have effect as to the making of an order under this section; and Schedule 2 to this Act has effect as to the validity and date of operation of any such order.
[(5) not included.]
(6) No order providing for the appropriation by or transfer to a special road authority of a highway comprised in the route prescribed by the scheme authorising the special road shall be made or confirmed by the Minister under this section unless either–
(a) he is satisfied that another reasonably convenient route is available for traffic other than traffic of the class authorised by the scheme, or will be provided before the date on which the appropriation or transfer takes effect; or
(b) he is satisfied that no such route is reasonably required for any such other traffic;
and no order authorising the stopping up of a highway shall be made or confirmed by the Minister under this section unless he is satisfied that another reasonably convenient route is available or will be provided before the highway is stopped up.
(8) In this section 'local authority' means the Common Council and the council of a county, district, London borough, parish or community, and includes the parish meeting of a parish not having a separate parish council.
Text: p 149
Amended by LGA 85 Sch 17.

25. Creation of footpath or bridleway by agreement

(1) A local authority may enter into an agreement with any person having the necessary power in that behalf for the dedication by that person of a footpath or bridleway over land in their area.
An agreement under this section is referred to in this Act as a 'public path creation agreement'.
(2) For the purposes of this section 'local authority'–
(a) in relation to land outside Greater London means a county council, a district council or a joint planning board within the meaning of the Town and Country Planning Act 1990, being a board for an area which comprises any part of a National Park; and
(b) in relation to land in Greater London means a London borough council or the Common Council.

(3) Before entering into an agreement under this section a local authority shall consult any other local authority or authorities in whose area the land concerned is situated.
(4) An agreement under this section shall be on such terms as to payment or otherwise as may be specified in the agreement and may, it if is so agreed, provide for the dedication of the footpath or bridleway subject to limitations or conditions affecting the public right of way over it.
(5) Where a public path creation agreement has been made it shall be the duty of the local authority who are a party to it to take all necessary steps for securing that the footpath or bridleway is dedicated in accordance with it.
(6) As soon as may be after the dedication of a footpath or bridleway in accordance with a public path creation agreement, the local authority who are party to the agreement shall give notice of the dedication by publication in at least one local newspaper circulating in the area in which the land to which the agreement relates is situated.
Text: p 71
Amended by WCA 1981 s 64, LGA 85 Sch 17 and Planning (Consequential Provisions) Act 1990 Sch 2 para 45(2).

26. Compulsory powers for creation of footpaths and bridleways
(1) Where it appears to a local authority that there is a need for a footpath or bridleway over land in their area and they are satisfied that, having regard to–
(a) the extent to which the path or way would add to the convenience or enjoyment of a substantial section of the public, or to the convenience of persons resident in the area; and
(b) the effect which the creation of the path or way would have on the rights of persons interested in the land, account being taken of the provisions as to compensation contained in section 28 below,
it is expedient that the path or way should be created, the authority may by order made by them and submitted to and confirmed by the Secretary of State, or confirmed by them as an unopposed order, create a footpath or bridleway over the land.
An order under this section is referred to in this Act as a 'public path creation order'; and for the purposes of this section 'local authority' has the same meaning as in section 25 above.
(2) Where it appears to the Secretary of State in a particular case that there is need for a footpath or bridleway as mentioned in subsection (1) above, and he is satisfied as mentioned in that subsection, he may, after consultation with each body which is a local authority for the purposes of this section in relation to the land concerned, make a public path creation order creating the footpath or bridleway.
(3) A local authority shall, before exercising any power under this section, consult any other local authority or authorities in whose area the land concerned is situated.
(4) A right of way created by a public path creation order may be either unconditional or subject to such limitations or conditions as may be specified in the order.
(5) A public path creation order shall be in such form as may be prescribed by regulations made by the Secretary of State, and shall contain a map, on such scale as may be so prescribed, defining the land over which a footpath or bridleway is thereby created.

(6) Schedule 6 to this Act shall have effect as to the making, confirmation, validity and date of operation of public path creation orders.
Text: p 142

27. Making up of new footpaths and bridleways
(1) On the dedication of a footpath or bridleway in pursuance of a public path creation agreement, or on the coming into operation of a public path creation order, being–
(a) an agreement or order made by a local authority who are not a highway authority for the path in question; or
(b) an order made by the Secretary of State under section 26(2) above in relation to which he directs that this subsection shall apply,
the highway authority shall survey the path or way and shall certify what work (if any) appears to them to be necessary to bring it into a fit condition for use by the public as a footpath or bridleway, as the case may be, and shall serve a copy of the certificate on the local authority mentioned in paragraph (a) above or, where paragraph (b) applies, on such local authority as the Secretary of State may direct.
(2) It shall be the duty of the highway authority to carry out any works specified in a certificate under subsection (1) above, and where the authority have carried out the work they may recover from the authority on whom a copy of the certificate was served any expenses reasonably incurred by them in carrying out that work, including any expenses so incurred in the discharge of any liability for compensation in respect of the carrying out thereof.
(3) Notwithstanding anything in the preceding provisions of this section, where an agreement or order is made as mentioned in subsection (1)(a) above, the local authority making the order may–
(a) with the consent of the highway authority carry out (in place of the highway authority) the duties imposed by that subsection on the highway authority; and
(b) carry out any works which, apart from this subsection, it would be the duty of the highway authority to carry out under subsection (2) above.
(4) Where the Secretary of State makes a public path creation order under section 26(2) above, he may direct that subsection (5) below shall apply.
(5) Where the Secretary of State gives such a direction–
(a) the local authority who, on the coming into force of the order, became the highway authority for the path or way in question shall survey the path or way and shall certify what work (if any) appears to them to be necessary to bring it into a fit condition for use by the public as a footpath or bridleway, as the case may be, and shall furnish the Secretary of State with a copy of the certificate;
(b) if the Secretary of State is not satisfied with a certificate made under the foregoing paragraph, he shall either cause a local inquiry to be held or shall give to the local authority an opportunity of being heard by a person appointed by him for the purpose and, after considering the report of the person appointed to hold the inquiry or the person so appointed as aforesaid, shall make such order either confirming or varying the certificate as he may think fit; and
(c) subject to the provisions of the last foregoing paragraphs, it shall be the duty of the highway authority to carry out the work specified in a certificate made by them under paragraph (a) above.
(6) In this section 'local authority' means any council or any such joint planning board as is mentioned in section 25(2)(a) above.
Text: p 134

28. Compensation for loss caused by path creation order

(1) Subject to the following provisions of this section if, on a claim made in accordance with this section, it is shown that the value of an interest of a person in land is depreciated, or that a person has suffered damage by being disturbed in his enjoyment of land, in consequence of the coming into operation of a public path creation order, the authority by whom the order was made shall pay to that person compensation equal to the amount of the depreciation or damage.

(2) A claim for compensation under this section shall be made within such time and in such manner as may be prescribed by regulations made by the Secretary of State, and shall be made to the authority by whom the order was made.

(3) For the purposes of the application of this section to an order made by the Secretary of State under section 26(2) above, references in this section to the authority by whom the order was made are to be construed as references to such one of the authorities referred to in that subsection as may be nominated by the Secretary of State for the purposes of this subsection.

(4) Nothing in this section confers on any person, in respect of a footpath or bridleway created by a public path creation order, a right to compensation for depreciation of the value of an interest in the land, or for disturbance in his enjoyment of land, not being in either case land over which the path was created or land held therewith, unless the creation of the path or way would have been actionable at his suit if it had been effected otherwise than in the exercise of statutory powers.

(5) In this section 'interest', in relation to land, includes any estate in land and any right over land, whether the right is exercisable by virtue of the ownership of an interest in land or by virtue of a licence or agreement, and in particular includes sporting rights.

Text: p 136

Disputes about compensation are decided by the Lands Tribunal. (S 307 — p 354.) The regulations are the Public Path Orders and Extinguishment of Public Right of Way Regulations 1983 (SI 1983 No 23) (p 460).

29. Protection of agriculture and forestry

In the exercise of their functions under this Part of this Act relating to the making of public path creation agreements and public path creation orders it shall be the duty of councils and joint planning boards to have due regard to the needs of agriculture and forestry.

Text: p 71, 142

30. Dedication of highway by agreement with parish and community council

(1) The council of a parish or community may enter into an agreement with any person having the necessary power in that behalf for the dedication by that person of a highway over land in the parish or community or an adjoining parish or community in any case where such a dedication would in the opinion of the council be beneficial to the inhabitants of the parish or community or any part thereof.

(2) Where the council of a parish or community have entered into an agreement under subsection (1) above for the dedication of a highway they may carry out any works (including works of maintenance or improvement) incidental to or consequential on the making of the agreement or contribute towards the expense

of carrying out such works, and may agree to combine with the council of any other parish or community to carry out such works or to make such a contribution.
Text: p 71

31. Dedication of way as highway presumed after public use of 20 years

(1) Where a way over any land, other than a way of such a character that use of it by the public could not give rise at common law to any presumption of dedication, has been actually enjoyed by the public as of right and without interruption for a full period of 20 years, the way is to be deemed to have been dedicated as a highway unless there is sufficient evidence that there was no intention during that period to dedicate it.

(2) The period of 20 years referred to in subsection (1) above is to be calculated retrospectively from the date when the right of the public to use the way is brought into question, whether by a notice such as is mentioned in subsection (3) below or otherwise.

(3) Where the owner of the land over which any such way as aforesaid passes–
(a) has erected in such manner as to be visible by persons using the way a notice inconsistent with the dedication of the way as a highway; and
(b) has maintained the notice after the 1st January 1934, or any later date on which it was erected,
the notice, in the absence of proof of a contrary intention, is sufficient evidence to negative the intention to dedicate the way as a highway.

(4) In the case of land in the possession of a tenant for a term of years, or from year to year, any person for the time being entitled in reversion to the land shall, notwithstanding the existence of the tenancy, have the right to place and maintain such a notice as is mentioned in subsection (3) above, so, however, that no injury is done thereby to the business or occupation of the tenant.

(5) Where a notice erected as mentioned in subsection (3) above is subsequently torn down or defaced, a notice given by the owner of the land to the appropriate council that the way is not dedicated as a highway is, in the absence of proof of a contrary intention, sufficient evidence to negative the intention of the owner of the land to dedicate the way as a highway.

(6) An owner of land may at any time deposit with the appropriate council–
(a) a map of the land on a scale of not less than 6 inches to 1 mile; and
(b) a statement indicating what ways (if any) over the land he admits to having been dedicated as highways;
and, in any case in which such a deposit has been made, statutory declarations made by that owner or by his successors in title and lodged by him or them with the appropriate council at any time–
(i) within six years from the date of deposit; or
(ii) within six years from the date on which any previous declaration was last lodged under this section,
to the effect that no additional way (other than any specifically indicated in the declaration) over the land delineated on the said map has been dedicated as a highway since the date of the deposit, or since the date of the lodgment of such previous declaration, as the case may be, are, in the absence of proof of a contrary intention, sufficient evidence to negative the intention of the owner or his successors in title to dedicate any such additional way as a highway.

(7) For the purpose of the foregoing provisions of this section, 'owner', in relation to any land, means a person who is for the time being entitled to dispose of the fee simple in the land; and for the purposes of subsections (5) and (6) above 'the appropriate council' means the council of the county, metropolitan district or London borough in which the way (in the case of subsection (5)) or the land (in the case of subsection (6)) is situated or, where the land is situated in the City, the Common Council.
(8) Nothing in this section affects any incapacity of a corporation or other body or person in possession of land for public and statutory purposes to dedicate a way over land as a highway if the existence of a highway would be incompatible with those purposes.
(9) Nothing in this section operates to prevent the dedication of a way as a highway being presumed on proof of user for any less than 20 years, or being presumed or proved in any circumstances in which it might have been presumed or proved immediately before the commencement of this Act.
(10) Nothing in this section or section 32 below affects section 56(1) of the Wildlife and Countryside Act 1981 (which provides that a definitive map and statement are conclusive evidence as to the existence of the highways shown on the map and as to certain particulars contained in the statement).
(11) For the purposes of this section 'land' includes land covered with water.
Text: p 56, 62–71
Amended by WCA 81 s 72 & LGA 85 Sch 4 para 7.

32. Evidence of dedication of way as highway
A court or other tribunal, before determining whether a way has or has not been dedicated as a highway, or the date on which such dedication, if any, took place, shall take into consideration any map, plan or history of the locality or other relevant document which is tendered in evidence, and shall give such weight thereto as the court or tribunal considers justified by the circumstances, including the antiquity of the tendered document, the status of the person by whom and the purpose for which it was made or compiled, and the custody in which it has been kept and from which it is produced.
Text: p 108

33. Protection of rights of reversioners
The person entitled to the remainder or reversion immediately expectant upon the determination of a tenancy for life, or pour autre vie, in land shall have the like remedies by action for trespass or an injunction to prevent the acquisition by the public of a right of way over that land as if he were in possession thereof.

36. Highways maintainable at public expense
(1) All such highways as immediately before the commencement of this Act were highways maintainable at the public expense for the purposes of the Highways Act 1959 continue to be so maintainable (subject to this section and to any order of a magistrates' court under section 47 below) for the purposes of this Act.
(2) Without prejudice to any other enactment (whether contained in this Act or not) whereby a highway may become for the purposes of this Act a highway maintainable at public expense, and subject to this section and section 232(7) below, and to any order of a magistrates' court under section 47 below,

HIGHWAYS ACT 1980

the following highways (not falling within subsection (1) above) shall for the purposes of this Act be highways maintainable at the public expense–
(a) a highway constructed by a highway authority, otherwise than on behalf of some other person who is not a highway authority;
(b) a highway constructed by a council within their own area under Part II of the Housing Act 1985, other than one in respect of which the local highway authority are satisfied that it has not been properly constructed, and a highway constructed by a council outside their own area under the said Part V being, in the latter case, a highway the liability to maintain which is, by virtue of the said Part V, vested in the council who are the local authority for the area in which the highway is situated;
(c) a highway that is a trunk road or a special road; and
(d) a highway, being a footpath or bridleway, created in consequence of a public path creation order or a public path diversion order or in consequence of an order made by the Minister of Transport or the Secretary of State under section 247 of the Town and Country Planning Act 1990 or by a competent authority under section 257 of that Act, or dedicated in pursuance of a public path creation agreement.
[(3) not included.]
(4) Subject to subsection (5) below, where there occurs any event on the occurrence of which, under any rule of law relating to the duty of maintaining a highway by reason of tenure, enclosure or prescription, a highway would, but for the enactment which abrogated the former rule of law under which a duty of maintaining highways fell on the inhabitants at large (section 38(1) of the Highways Act 1959) or any other enactment, become, or cease to be, maintainable by the inhabitants at large of any area, the highway shall become, or cease to be, a highway which for the purposes of this Act is a highway maintainable at the public expense.
(5) A highway shall not by virtue of subsection (4) above become a highway which for the purposes of this Act is a highway maintainable at the public expense unless either–
(a) it was a highway before 31st August 1835; or
(b) it became a highway after that date and has at some time been maintainable by the inhabitants at large of any area or a highway maintainable at the public expense;
and a highway shall not by virtue of that subsection cease to be a highway maintainable at the public expense if it is a highway which under any rule of law would become a highway maintainable by reason of enclosure but is prevented from becoming such a highway by section 51 below.
(6) The council of every county, metropolitan district and London borough and the Common Council shall cause to be made, and shall keep corrected up to date, a list of the streets within their area which are highways maintainable at the public expense.
(7) Every list made under subsection (6) above shall be kept deposited at the offices of the council by whom it was made and may be inspected by any person free of charge at all reasonable hours and in the case of a list made by the council of a county the county council shall supply to the council of each district council in the county an up to date list of the streets within the area of the district that are highways maintainable at the public expense and the list so supplied shall be kept deposited at the office of the district council and may be inspected by any person free of charge at all reasonable hours.

RIGHTS OF WAY

Text: p 71, 117
Amended by LGA 85 Sch 4 para 7, Housing (Consequential Provisions) Act 1985 Sch 2 and Planning (Consequential Provisions) Act 1990 Sch 2 para 45(3).

37. Provisions whereby highway created by dedication may become maintainable at public expense

(1) A person who proposes to dedicate a way as a highway and who desires that the proposed highway shall become maintainable at the public expense by virtue of this section shall give notice of the proposal, not less than 3 months before the date of the proposed dedication, to the council who would, if the way were a highway, be the highway authority therefor, describing the location and width of the proposed highway and the nature of the proposed dedication.

(2) If the council consider that the proposed highway will not be of sufficient utility to the public to justify its being maintained at the public expense, they may make a complaint to a magistrates' court for an order to that effect.

(3) If the council certify that the way has been dedicated in accordance with the terms of the notice and has been made up in a satisfactory manner, and if–
(a) the person by whom the way was dedicated or his successor keeps it in repair for a period of 12 months from the date of the council's certificate, and
(b) the way has been used as a highway during that period,
then unless an order has been made in relation to the highway under subsection (2) above, the highway shall, at the expiration of the period specified in paragraph (a) above, become for the purposes of this Act a highway maintainable at the public expense.

(4) If the council, on being requested by the person by whom the way was dedicated or his successor to issue a certificate under subsection (3) above, refuses to issue the certificate, that person may appeal to a magistrates' court against the refusal, and the court, if satisfied that the certificate ought to have been issued, may make an order to the effect that subsection (3) above shall apply as if the certificate had been issued on a date specified in the order.

(5) Where a certificate has been issued by a council under subsection (3) above, or an order has been made under subsection (4) above, the certificate or a copy of the order, as the case may be, shall be deposited with the proper officer of the council and may be inspected by any person free of charge at all reasonable hours.

Text: p 72

38. Power of highway authorities to adopt by agreement

(1) Subject to subsection (2) below, where any person is liable under a special enactment or by reason of tenure, enclosure or prescription to maintain a highway, the Minister in the case of a trunk road, or a local highway authority, in any other case, may agree with that person to undertake the maintenance of that highway; and where an agreement is made under this subsection the highway to which the agreement relates shall, on such date as may be specified in the agreement, become for the purposes of this Act a highway maintainable at the public expense and the liability of that person to maintain the highway shall be extinguished.

(2) A local highway authority shall not have power to make an agreement under subsection (1) above with respect to a highway with respect to which they or

any other highway authority have power to make an agreement under Part V or Part XII of this Act.

(3) Subject to the following provisions of this section, a local highway authority may agree with any person to undertake the maintenance of–

(a) a private carriage or occupation road which that person is willing, and has the necessary power, to dedicate as a highway; or

(b) a way which is to be constructed by that person, or by a highway authority on his behalf, and which he proposes to dedicate as a highway;

and where an agreement is made under this subsection the road or way to which the agreement relates shall, on such date as may be specified in the agreement, become for the purposes of this Act a highway maintainable at the public expense.

(4) Without prejudice to the provisions of subsection (3) above and subject to the following provisions of this section, a local highway authority may, by agreement with railway, canal or tramway undertakers, undertake to maintain as part of a highway maintainable at the public expense a bridge or viaduct which carries the railway, canal or tramway of the undertakers over such a highway or which is intended to carry such a railway, canal or tramway over such a highway and is to be constructed by the undertakers or by the highway authority on their behalf.

(6) An agreement under this section may contain such provisions as to the dedication as a highway of any road or way to which the agreement relates, the bearing of the expenses of the construction, maintenance or improvement of any highway, road, bridge or viaduct to which the agreement relates and other relevant matters as the authority making the agreement think fit.

Text: p 72

Amended by LGA 85 Sch 17.

41. Duty to maintain highways maintainable at public expense

(1) The authority who are for the time being the highway authority for a highway maintainable at public expense are under a duty (...) to maintain the highway.

[Subsections (2) to (5) not included.]

Text: p 223

42. Power of district councils to maintain certain highways

(1) Subject to Part 1 of Schedule 7 to this Act, the council of a non-metropolitan district may undertake the maintenance of any eligible highway in the district which is a highway maintainable at the public expense.

(2) For the purposes of subsection (1) above the following are eligible highways:–

(a) footpaths,

(b) bridleways, and

(c) roads (referred to in Schedule 7 to this Act as 'urban roads') which are neither trunk roads nor classified roads and which–

(i) are restricted roads for the purposes of section 81 of the Road Traffic Regulation Act 1984 (30 mph speed limit), or

(ii) are subject to an order under section 84 of that Act imposing a special limit not exceeding 40 mph, or

RIGHTS OF WAY

(iii) are otherwise streets in an urban area.
(3) The county council who are the highway authority for a highway which is for the time being maintained by a non-metropolitan district council by virtue of this section shall reimburse to the district council any expense incurred by them in carrying out on the highway any works of maintenance necessary to secure that the duty to maintain the highway is performed, and Part II of Schedule 7 to this Act shall have effect for that purpose.
Text: p 224
Amended by Road Traffic Regulation Act 1984 Sch 13 & LGA 85 Sch 4 para 11.

43. Power of parish and community councils to maintain footpaths and bridleways

(1) The council of a parish or community may undertake the maintenance of any footpath or bridleway within the parish or community which is, in either case, a highway maintainable at the public expense, but nothing in this subsection affects the duty of any highway authority or any other person to maintain any such footpath or bridleway.
(2) The highway authority for any footpath or bridleway which a parish or community council have power to maintain under subsection (1) above, and a non-metropolitan district council for the time being maintaining any such footpath or bridleway by virtue of section 42 above, may undertake to defray the whole or part of any expenditure incurred by the parish or community council in maintaining the footpath or bridleway.
(3) The power of a parish or community council under subsection (1) above is subject to the restrictions for the time being imposed by any enactment on their expenditure, but for the purposes of any enactment imposing such a restriction their expenditure is to be deemed not to include any expenditure falling to be defrayed by a highway authority or district council by virtue of subsection (2) above.
Text: p 225
Amended by LGA 85 Sch 4 para 12.

49. Maintenance of approaches to certain privately maintainable bridges

Where a person is liable to maintain the approaches to a bridge by reason of the fact that he is liable to maintain the bridge by reason of tenure, his liability to maintain the approaches extends to 100 yards from each end of the bridge.
Text: p 223

50. Maintenance of privately maintainable footpaths and bridleways

(1) Where apart from section 41 above a person would under a special enactment or by reason of tenure, enclosure or prescription be under an obligation to maintain a footpath or bridleway, the operation of section 41(1) does not release him from the obligation.
(2) The council of a non-metropolitan district, parish or community may undertake by virtue of this subsection the maintenance of any footpath or bridleway within the district, parish or community (other than a footpath or bridleway the maintenance of which they have power to undertake under section 42 or, as the case may be, section 43 above) whether or not any other

HIGHWAYS ACT 1980

person is under a duty to maintain the footpath or bridleway; but nothing in this subsection affects the duty of any other person to maintain any such footpath or bridleway.

(3) The power of a district council under subsection (2) above is subject to Part I of Schedule 7 to this Act; and the power of a parish or community council under that subsection is subject to the restrictions for the time being imposed by any enactment on their expenditure.

Text: p 225
Amended by LGA 85 Sch 4 para 14.

56. Proceedings for an order to repair highway

(1) A person ('the complainant') who alleges that a way or bridge–
(a) is a highway maintainable at the public expense or a highway which a person is liable to maintain under a special enactment or by reason of tenure, enclosure or prescription; and
(b) is out of repair;
may serve a notice on the highway authority or other person alleged to be liable to maintain the way or bridge ('the respondent') requiring the respondent to state whether he admits that the way or bridge is a highway and that he is liable to maintain it.

(2) If, within one month from the date of service on him of a notice under subsection (1) above, the respondent does not serve on the complainant a notice admitting both that the way or bridge in question is a highway and that the respondent is liable to maintain it, the complainant may apply to the Crown Court for an order requiring the respondent, if the court finds that the way or bridge is a highway which the respondent is liable to maintain and is out of repair, to put it in proper repair within such reasonable period as may be specified in the order.

(3) The complainant for an order under subsection (2) above shall give notice in writing of the application to the appropriate officer of the Crown Court and the notice shall specify–
(a) the situation of the way or bridge to which the application relates;
(b) the name of the respondent;
(c) the part of the way or bridge which is alleged to be out of repair; and
(d) the nature of the alleged disrepair;
and the complainant shall serve a copy of the notice on the respondent.

(4) If, within one month from the date of the service on him of a notice under subsection (1) above, the respondent serves on the complainant a notice admitting both that the way or bridge in question is a highway and that the respondent is liable to maintain it, the complainant may, within six months from the date of service on him of that notice, apply to a magistrates' court for an order requiring the respondent, if the court finds that the highway is out of repair, to put it in proper repair within such reasonable period as may be specified in the order.

(5) A court in determining under this section whether a highway is out of repair shall not be required to view the highway unless it thinks fit, and any such view may be made by any two or more of the members of the court.

(6) If at the expiration of the period specified in an order made under subsection (2) or (4) above a magistrates' court is satisfied that the highway to which the order relates has not been put in proper repair, then, unless the court thinks

RIGHTS OF WAY

fit to extend the period, it shall by order authorise the complainant (if he has not the necessary power in that behalf) to carry out such works as may be necessary to put the highway in proper repair.

(7) Any expenses which a complainant reasonably incurs in carrying out works authorised by an order under subsection (6) above are recoverable from the respondent summarily as a civil debt.

(8) Where any expenses recoverable under subsection (7) above are recovered from the respondent, then, if the respondent would have been entitled to recover from some other person the whole or part of the expenses of repairing the highway in question if he had repaired it himself, he is entitled to recover from that other person the whole or the like part, as the case may be, of the expenses recovered from him.

(9) Where an application is made under this section for an order requiring the respondent to put in proper repair a footpath or bridleway which, in either case, is a highway maintainable at the public expense and some other person is liable to maintain the footpath or bridleway under a special enactment or by reason of tenure, enclosure or prescription, that other person has a right to be heard by the court which hears the application, but only on the question whether the footpath or bridleway is in proper repair.

Text: p 230

57. Default powers of highway authorities in respect of non-repair of privately maintainable highways

(1) Where a person is liable under a special enactment or by reason of tenure, enclosure or prescription to maintain a footpath or bridleway which, in either case, is a highway maintainable at the public expense, and the highway authority for the highway repair it in the performance of their duty to maintain it, they may, subject to subsection (3) below, recover the necessary expenses of doing so from that person in any court of competent jurisdiction.

(2) Where a person is liable as aforesaid to maintain a highway other than such a footpath or bridleway as is referred to in subsection (1) above the highway authority for the highway may, if in their opinion the highway is not in proper repair, repair it and, subject to subsection (3) below, recover the necessary expenses of doing so from that person in any court of competent jurisdiction.

(3) The right of recovery conferred by the foregoing provisions of this section is not exercisable—

(a) in a case where a highway authority repair a footpath or bridleway in obedience to an order of a court under section 56 above, unless not less than 21 days before the date on which the application was heard by the court the authority gave notice to the person liable to maintain the path or way of the making of an application with respect to it and of the time and place at which the application was to be heard by the court (so however that there is no obligation to give notice to him under this paragraph if he was the person on whose application the order of the court was made);

(b) in any other case, unless the highway authority, before repairing the highway, have given notice to the person liable to maintain it that the highway is not in proper repair, specifying a reasonable time within which he may repair it, and he has failed to repair it within that time.

(4) Where a highway authority exercise a right of recovery from any person under the foregoing provisions of this section, then, if that person would have

HIGHWAYS ACT 1980

been entitled to recover from some other person the whole or part of the expenses of repairing the highway if he had repaired it himself, he is entitled to recover from that other person the whole or the like part, as the case may be, of the expenses recovered from him by the highway authority.
Text: p 221

58. Special defence in action against a highway authority for damages for non-repair of highway

(1) In an action against a highway authority in respect of damage resulting from their failure to maintain a highway maintainable at the public expense it is a defence (without prejudice to any other defence or the application of the law relating to contributory negligence) to prove that the authority had taken such care as in all the circumstances was reasonably required to secure that the part of the highway to which the action relates was not dangerous to traffic.

(2) For the purposes of a defence under subsection (1) above, the court shall in particular have regard to the following matters:–
(a) the character of the highway, and the traffic which was reasonably to be expected to use it;
(b) the standard of maintenance appropriate for a highway of that character and used by such traffic;
(c) the state of repair in which a reasonable person would have expected to find the highway;
(d) whether the highway authority knew, or could reasonably have been expected to know, that the condition of the part of the highway to which the action relates was likely to cause danger to users of the highway;
(e) where the highway authority could not reasonably have been expected to repair that part of the highway before the cause of action arose, what warning notices of its condition had been displayed;
but for the purposes of such a defence it is not relevant to prove that the highway authority had arranged for a competent person to carry out or supervise the maintenance of the part of the highway to which the action relates unless it is also proved that the authority had given him proper instructions with regard to the maintenance of the highway and that he had carried out the instructions.

(3) This section binds the Crown.
[(4) not included.]
Text: p 229

61. Regulations supplementing maintenance powers of district councils

The Minister may by regulations empower non-metropolitan district councils, in relation to highways in respect of which their powers of maintenance under sections 42 and 50 above are exercisable, to exercise subject to such terms and conditions as may be specified in the regulations such additional powers as appear to him–
(a) to be appropriate to supplement powers of maintenance; and
(b) to correspond to powers exercisable in relation to highways by highway authorities;
and accordingly in those sections, in Schedule 7 to this Act and in any other enactment 'maintenance' and 'maintain' where used with respect to the powers

RIGHTS OF WAY

of non-metropolitan district councils under those sections, are to be construed as including the carrying out of operations in the exercise of powers conferred on non-metropolitan district councils by regulations under this section.
Text: p 225
Amended by LGA 85 Sch 4. No regulations have been made under this section.

62. General power of improvement
(1) The provisions of this Part of this Act have effect for the purpose of empowering or requiring highway authorities and other persons to improve highways.
(2) Without prejudice to the powers of improvement specifically conferred on highway authorities by the following provisions of this Part of this Act, any such authority may, subject to subsection (3) below, carry out, in relation to a highway maintainable at the public expense by them, any work (including the provision of equipment) for the improvement of the highway.
(3) Notwithstanding subsection (2) above, but without prejudice to any enactment not contained in this Part of this Act, work of any of the following descriptions shall be carried out only under the powers specifically conferred by the following provisions of this Part of this Act, and not under this section–
(a) the division of carriageways, provision of roundabouts and variation of the relative widths of carriageways and footways;
(b) the construction of cycle tracks;
(c) the provision of subways, refuges, pillars, walls, barriers, rails, fences or posts for the use or protection of persons using a highway;
(d) the construction and reconstruction of bridges and alteration of level of highways;
(e) the planting of trees, shrubs and other vegetation and laying out of grass verges;
(f) the provision, maintenance, alteration, improvement or other dealing with cattle-grids, by-passes, gates and other works for use in connection with cattle-grids;
(ff) the construction, maintenance or removal of road humps;
(g) the execution of works for the purpose of draining a highway or of otherwise preventing surface water from flowing on to it;
(h) the provision of barriers or other works for the purpose of affording to a highway protection against hazards of nature.
(4) A highway authority may alter or remove any work executed by them under this section.
Text: p 239, 240
Amended by Transport Act 1981 Sch 10 & LGA 85 Sch 17.

66. Footways and guard-rails etc for publicly maintainable highways
(1) It is the duty of a highway authority to provide in or by the side of a highway maintainable at the public expense by them which consists of or comprises a made-up carriageway, a proper and sufficient footway as part of the highway in any case where they consider the provision of a footway as necessary or desirable for the safety or accommodation of pedestrians; and they may light any footway provided by them under this subsection.
(2) A highway authority may provide and maintain in a highway maintainable at the public expense by them which consists of or comprises a carriageway,

HIGHWAYS ACT 1980

such raised paving, pillars, walls, rails or fences as they think necessary for the purpose of safeguarding persons using the highway.

(3) A highway authority may provide and maintain in a highway maintainable at the public expense by them which consists of a footpath, such barriers, rails or fences as they think necessary for the purpose of safeguarding persons using the highway.

(4) The powers conferred by the foregoing provisions of this section to provide any works include power to alter or remove them.

(5) The power conferred by subsection (3) above, and the power to alter or remove any works provided under that subsection, shall not be exercised so as to obstruct any private access to any premises or interfere with the carrying out of agricultural operations.

[(6) and (7) not included.]

(8) A highway authority or council shall pay compensation to any person who sustains damage by reason of the execution by them of works under subsection (2) or (3) above.

Text: p 189, 239

71. Margins for horses and livestock

(1) It is the duty of a highway authority to provide in or by the side of a highway maintainable at the public expense by them which consists of or comprises a made-up carriageway adequate grass or other margins as part of the highway in any case where they consider the provision of margins necessary or desirable for the safety or accommodation of ridden horses and driven livestock; and a highway authority may light a margin provided by them under this section.

(2) A highway authority may alter or remove a margin provided by them under this section.

Text: p 239

72. Widening of highways

(1) A highway authority may widen any highway for which they are the highway authority and may for that purpose agree with a person having power in that behalf for the dedication of adjoining land as part of a highway.

(2) A council or joint planning board have the like power to enter into a public path creation agreement under section 25 above, or to make a public path creation order under section 26 above, for the purpose of securing the widening of an existing footpath or bridleway as they have for the purpose of securing the creation of a footpath or bridleway, and references in those sections to the dedication or creation of a footpath or bridleway are to be construed accordingly.

(3) The council of a parish or community have the like power to enter into an agreement under section 30 above for the purpose of securing the widening of an existing highway in the parish or community or an adjoining parish or community as they have for the purpose of securing the dedication of a highway, and references in that section to the dedication of a highway are to be construed accordingly.

Text: p 238

76. Levelling of highways

A highway authority may execute works for levelling a highway maintainable at the public expense by them.

Text: p 240

RIGHTS OF WAY

77. Alteration of levels
(1) Without prejudice to section 76 above, a highway authority may raise or lower or otherwise alter, as they think fit, the level of a highway maintainable at the public expense by them.
(2) A highway authority shall pay compensation to any person who sustains damage by reason of the execution by them of works under this section.
Text: p 240

91. Construction of bridge to carry existing highway maintainable at public expense
A highway authority may construct a bridge to carry a highway maintainable at the public expense but the Minister shall not construct such a bridge without the approval of the Treasury.
Text: p 240

92. Reconstruction of bridge maintainable at public expense
Without prejudice to any other powers they have under this Part of this Act, a highway authority may reconstruct a bridge which is a highway maintainable at the public expense by them, either on the same site or on a new site within 200 yards of the old one.
Text: p 240

100. Drainage of highways
(1) The highway authority for a highway may, for the purpose of draining it or of otherwise preventing surface water from flowing on to it, do all or any of the following:–
(a) construct or lay, in the highway or in land adjoining or lying near to the highway, such drains as they consider necessary;
(b) erect barriers in the highway or in such land as aforesaid to divert surface water into or through any existing drain;
(c) scour, cleanse and keep open all drains situated in the highway or in such land as aforesaid.
(2) Where under subsection (1) above a drain is constructed or laid, or barriers are erected, for the purpose of draining surface water from a highway or, as the case may be, diverting it into an existing drain, the water may be discharged into or through that drain and into any inland waters, whether natural or artificial, or any tidal waters.
(3) A highway authority shall pay compensation to the owner or occupier of any land who suffers damage by reason of the exercise by the authority of any power under subsection (1) or (2) above.
(4) If a person, without the consent of the highway authority, alters, obstructs or interferes with a drain or barrier which has been constructed, laid or erected by the authority in exercise of their powers under subsection (1) above, or which is under their control, then–
(a) the authority may carry out any work of repair or reinstatement necessitated by his action and may recover from him the expenses reasonably incurred by them in so doing, and
(b) without prejudice to their right to exercise that power, he is guilty of an offence and liable to a fine not exceeding three times the amount of those expenses.

HIGHWAYS ACT 1980

[(5) and (6) not included.]
(7) A person who is liable to maintain a highway by reason of tenure, enclosure or prescription shall, for the purpose of draining it, have the like powers as are conferred on a highway authority by subsections (1) and (2) above for that purpose (...)
(8) This section is without prejudice to any enactment the purpose of which is to protect water against pollution.
(9) In this section—
'drain' includes a ditch, gutter, watercourse, soak-away, bridge, culvert, tunnel and pipe; and
'owner' in relation to any land, means a person, other than a mortgagee not in possession, who is for the time being entitled to dispose of the fee simple in the land, whether in possession or in reversion, and includes also a person holding or entitled to the rents and profits of the land under a lease the unexpired term of which exceeds three years.
Text: p 240

102. Provision of works for protecting highways against hazards of nature

(1) The highway authority for a highway maintainable at the public expense may provide and maintain such barriers or other works as they consider necessary for the purpose of affording to the highway protection against snow, flood, landslide or other hazards of nature; and those works may be provided on the highway or on land which, or rights over which, has or have been acquired by the highway authority in the exercise of highway land acquisition powers for that purpose.
(2) The owners conferred by subsection (1) above to provide any works shall include power to alter or to remove them.
(3) A highway authority shall pay compensation to any person who suffers damage by reason of the execution by them under this section of any works on a highway.
Text: p 240

116. Power of magistrates' court to authorise stopping up or diversion of highway

(1) Subject to the provisions of this section, if it appears to a magistrates' court, after a view, if the court thinks fit, by any two or more of the justices composing the court, that a highway (other than a trunk road or a special road) as respects which the highway authority have made an application under this section—
(a) is unnecessary; or
(b) can be diverted so as to make it nearer or more commodious to the public; the court may by order authorise it to be stopped up or, as the case may be, to be so diverted.
(3) If an authority propose to make an application under this section for an order relating to any highway (other than a classified road) they shall give notice of the proposal to—
(a) if the highway is in a non-metropolitan district, the council of that district; and
(b) if the highway is in England, the council of the parish (if any) in which the highway is situated or, if the parish does not have a separate parish council, to the chairman of the parish meeting; and

RIGHTS OF WAY

(c) if the highway is in Wales, the council (if any) of the community in which the highway is situated;

and the application shall not be made if within two months from the date of service of the notice by the authority notice is given to the authority by the district council or by the parish or community council or, as the case may be, by the chairman of the parish meeting that the council or meeting have refused to consent to the making of the application.

(4) An application under this section may be made, and an order under it may provide, for the stopping up or diversion of a highway for the purposes of all traffic, or subject to the reservation of a footpath or bridleway.

(5) An application or order under this section may include two or more highways which are connected with each other.

(6) A magistrates' court shall not make an order under this section unless it is satisfied that the applicant authority have given the notices required by Part 1 of Schedule 12 to this Act.

(7) On the hearing of an application under this section the applicant authority, any person to whom notice is required to be given under paragraph 1 of Schedule 12, any person who uses the highway and any other person who would be aggrieved by the making of the order applied for, have a right to be heard.

(8) An order under this section authorising the diversion of a highway–

(a) shall not be made unless the written consent of every person having a legal interest in the land over which the highway is to be diverted is produced to and deposited with the court; and

(b) except in so far as the carrying out of the diversion may necessitate temporary interference with the highway, shall not authorise the stopping up of any part of the highway until the new part to be substituted for the part to be stopped up (including, where a diversion falls to be carried out under orders of two different courts, any necessary continuation of the new part in the area of the other court) has been completed to the satisfaction of two justices of the peace acting for the same petty sessions area as the court by which the order was made and a certificate to that effect signed by them has been transmitted to the clerk of the applicant authority.

(9) Every order under this section shall have annexed to it a plan signed by the chairman of the court and shall be transmitted by the clerk of the court to the proper officer of the applicant authority, together with any written consents produced to the court under subsection (8) above.

[(10) & (11) not included.]

Text: p 153

Amended by LGA 85 Sch 4 para 24 & Sch 17.

117. Application for order under section 116 on behalf of another person

A person who desires a highway to be stopped up or diverted but is not authorised to make an application for that purpose under section 116 above may request the highway authority to make such an application; and if the authority grant the request they may, as a condition of making the application, require him to make such provision for any costs to be incurred by them in connection with the matter as they deem reasonable.

Text: p 153

Amended by LGA 85 Sch 17.

HIGHWAYS ACT 1980

118. Stopping up of footpaths and bridleways
(1) Where it appears to a council as respects a footpath or bridleway in their area (other than one which is a trunk road or a special road) that it is expedient that the path or way should be stopped up on the ground that it is not needed for public use, the council may by order made by them and submitted to and confirmed by the Secretary of State, or confirmed as an unopposed order, extinguish the public right of way over the path or way.
An order under this section is referred to in this Act as a 'public path extinguishment order'.
(2) The Secretary of State shall not confirm a public path extinguishment order, and a council shall not confirm such an order as an unopposed order, unless he or, as the case may be, they are satisfied that it is expedient so to do having regard to the extent (if any) to which it appears to him or, as the case may be, them that the path or way would, apart from the order, be likely to be used by the public, and having regard to the effect which the extinguishment of the right of way would have as respects land served by the path or way, account being taken of the provisions as to compensation contained in section 28 above as applied by section 121(2) below.
(3) A public path extinguishment order shall be in such form as may be prescribed by regulations made by the Secretary of State and shall contain a map, on such scale as may be so prescribed, defining the land over which the public right of way is thereby extinguished.
(4) Schedule 6 to this Act has effect as to the making, confirmation, validity and date of operation of public path extinguishment orders.
(5) Where, in accordance with regulations made under paragraph 3 of the said Schedule 6, proceedings preliminary to the confirmation of the public path extinguishment order are taken concurrently with proceedings preliminary to the confirmation of a public path creation order or public path diversion order made under section 119 below then, in considering–
(a) under subsection (1) above whether the path or way to which the public path extinguishment order relates is needed for public use; or
(b) under subsection (2) above to what extent (if any) that path or way would apart from the order be likely to be used by the public;
the council or the Secretary of State, as the case may be, may have regard to the extent to which the public path creation order or the public path diversion order would provide an alternative path or way.
(6) For the purposes of subsections (1) and (2) above, any temporary circumstances preventing or diminishing the use of a path or way by the public shall be disregarded.
(7) In this section and in sections 119 to 121 below 'council' includes a joint planning board, within the meaning of the Town and Country Planning Act 1990, for an area which comprises any part of a National Park.
Text: p 81, 137
Amended by Planning (Consequential Provisions) Act 1990 Sch 2 para 45(7).

119. Diversion of footpaths and bridleways
(1) Where it appears to a council as respects a footpath or bridleway in their area (other than one that is a trunk road or a special road) that, in the interests of the owner, lessee or occupier of land crossed by the path or way or of the public, it is expedient that the line of the path or way, or part of that line,

should be diverted (whether on to land of the same or of another owner, lessee or occupier), the council may, subject to subsection (2) below, by order made by them and submitted to and confirmed by the Secretary of State, or confirmed as an unopposed order,–

(a) create, as from such date as may be specified in the order, any such new footpath or bridleway as appears to the council requisite for effecting the diversion; and

(b) extinguish, as from such date as may be so specified in accordance with the provisions of subsection (3) below, the public right of way over so much of the path or way as appears to the council requisite as aforesaid.

An order under this section is referred to in this Act as a 'public path diversion order'.

(2) A public path diversion order shall not alter a point of termination of the path or way–

(a) if that point is not on a highway; or

(b) (where it is on a highway) otherwise than to another point which is on the same highway, or a highway connected with it, and which is substantially as convenient to the public.

(3) Where it appears to the council that work requires to be done to provide necessary facilities for the convenient exercise of any such new public right of way as is mentioned in subsection (1)(a) above, the date specified under subsection (1)(b) above shall be later than the date specified under subsection (1)(a) by such time as appears to the council requisite for enabling the work to be carried out.

(4) A right of way created by a public path diversion order may be either unconditional or (whether or not the right of way extinguished by the order was subject to limitations or conditions of any description) subject to such limitations or conditions as may be specified in the order.

(5) Before determining to make a public path diversion order on the representations of an owner, lessee or occupier of land crossed by the path or way, the council may require him to enter into an agreement with them to defray, or to make such contribution as may be specified in the agreement towards,–

(a) any compensation which may become payable under section 28 above as applied by section 121(2) below; or

(b) where the council are the highway authority for the path or way in question, any expenses which they may incur in bringing the new site of the path or way into fit condition for use for the public; or

(c) where the council are not the highway authority, any expenses which may become recoverable from them by the highway authority under the provisions of section 27(2) above as applied by subsection (9) below.

(6) The Secretary of State shall not confirm a public path diversion order, and a council shall not confirm such an order as an unopposed order, unless he or, as the case may be, they are satisfied that the diversion to be effected by it is expedient as mentioned in subsection (1) above, and further that the path or way will not be substantially less convenient to the public in consequence of the diversion and that it is expedient to confirm the order having regard to the effect which–

(a) the diversion would have on public enjoyment of the path or way as a whole;

(b) the coming into operation of the order would have as respects other land served by the existing public right of way; and

(c) any new public right of way created by the order would have as respects the land over which the right is so created and any land held with it;
so, however, that for the purposes of paragraph (b) and (c) above the Secretary of State, or as the case may be, the council shall take into account the provisions as to compensation referred to in subsection (5)(a) above.
(7) A public path diversion order shall be in such form as may be prescribed by regulations made by the Secretary of State and shall contain a map, on such scale as may be so prescribed,–
(a) showing the existing site of so much of the line of the path or way as is to be diverted by the order and the new site to which it is to be diverted;
(b) indicating whether a new right of way is created by the order over the whole of the new site or whether some part of it is already comprised in a footpath or bridleway; and
(c) where some part of the new site is already so comprised, defining that part.
(8) Schedule 6 to this Act has effect as to the making, confirmation, validity and date of operation of public path diversion orders.
(9) Section 27 above (making up of new footpaths and bridleways) applies to a footpath or bridleway created by a public path diversion order with the substitution, for references to a public path creation order, of references to a public path diversion order and, for references to section 26(2) above, of references to section 120(3) below.
Text: p 59, 81, 140
Amended by WCA 1981 Sch 16.

120. Exercise of powers of making public path extinguishment and diversion orders

(1) Where a footpath or bridleway lies partly within and partly outside the area of a council the powers conferred by section 118 and 119 above on the council extend, subject to subsection (2) below, to the whole of the path or way as if it lay wholly within their area.
(2) The powers of making public path extinguishment orders and public path diversion orders conferred by sections 118 and 119 above are not exercisable by a council–
(a) with respect to any part of a footpath or bridleway which is within their area, without prior consultation with the other council in whose area that part of the footpath or bridleway is situated;
(b) with respect to any part of a footpath or bridleway which is outside their area, without the consent of every council in whose area it is; and
(c) with respect to any part of a footpath or bridleway in a National Park, without prior consultation with the Countryside Commission (if the National Park is in England) or the Countryside Council for Wales (if the National Park is in Wales).
(3) Where it appears to the Secretary of State as respects a footpath or bridleway that it is expedient as mentioned in section 118(1) above that the path or way should be stopped up, or where an owner, lessee or occupier of land crossed by a footpath or bridleway satisfies the Secretary of State that a diversion of it is expedient as mentioned in section 119(1) above, then if–
(a) no council having power to do so have made and submitted to him a public path extinguishment order or a public path diversion order, as the case may be, and

(b) the Secretary of State is satisfied that if such an order were made and submitted to him, he would have power to confirm the order in accordance with the provisions in that behalf of sections 118 and 119 above,

he may himself make the order after consultation with the appropriate authority.

(4) A council proposing to make a public path diversion order such that the authority who will be the highway authority for a part of the path or way after the diversion will be a different body from the authority who before the diversion are the highway authority for it shall, before making the order, notify the first mentioned authority.

(5) Where under subsection (3) above the Secretary of State decides to make a public path diversion order, he may require the owner, lessee or occupier on whose representations he is acting to enter into an agreement with such council as he may specify for the owner, lessee or occupier to defray, or to make such contribution as may be specified in the agreement towards any such compensation or expenses as are specified in paragraphs (a), (b) and (c) of section 119(5) above.

Text: p 126
Amended by EPA 90 Sch 8 para 5(3).

121. Supplementary provisions as to public path extinguishment and diversion orders

(1) A public path extinguishment order or a public path diversion order affecting in any way the area of more than one council may contain provisions requiring one of the councils to defray, or contribute towards, expenses incurred in consequence of the order by another one of the councils; and a public path diversion order diverting a part of the line of the path or way from a site in the area of one local highway authority to a site in the area of another may provide that the first mentioned authority are to continue to be the highway authority for the part of the way after the diversion.

(2) Section 28 above (compensation for loss caused by public path creation order) applies in relation to public path extinguishment orders and to public path diversion orders as it applies in relation to public path creation orders but as if the references in it to section 26(2) above were references to section 120(3) above.

(3) Section 29 above (protection for agriculture and forestry) applies in relation to the making of public path extinguishment orders and public path diversion orders as it applies in relation to the making of public path creation agreements and public path creation orders.

(4) The Secretary of State shall not make or confirm a public path extinguishment order or a public path diversion order, and a council shall not confirm such an order as an unopposed order, if the order extinguishes a right of way over land under, in, upon, over, along or across which there is any apparatus belonging to or used by statutory undertakers for the purpose of their undertaking unless the undertakers have consented to the making or, as the case may be, confirmation of the order.

(5) A consent under subsection (4) above may be given subject to the condition that there are included in the order such provisions for the protection of the undertakers as they reasonably require, but a consent under that subsection shall not be unreasonably withheld, and any question whether the withholding of such a consent is unreasonable or whether any requirement is reasonable shall be determined by the appropriate Minister.

HIGHWAYS ACT 1980

(6) In subsection (5) above the 'appropriate Minister' means–
(a) in relation to statutory undertakers carrying on an undertaking for the supply of electricity or hydraulic power, the Secretary of State; and
(b) in relation to any other statutory undertakers, the Minister.
Text: p 136, 137
Amended by Gas Act 1986 Sch 7, Electricity Act 1989 Sch 18 and Water Act 1989 Sch 25 para 62(6).

122. Power to make temporary diversion where highway about to be repaired or widened
(1) A highway authority who are about to repair or widen a highway, and a person who is about to repair or widen a highway maintainable by him by reason of tenure, enclosure or prescription, may, subject to the provisions of this section, construct on adjoining land a temporary highway for use while the work is in progress.
(2) Where any damage is sustained by the owner or occupier of any land in consequence of the construction of a highway on that land in exercise of a power conferred by this section the owner or occupier of the land may recover compensation in respect of that damage from the authority or other person by whom the highway was constructed.
(3) Nothing in this section authorises interference with land which is part of the site of a house, or is a garden, lawn, yard, court, park, paddock, plantation, planted walk or avenue to a house, or is inclosed land set apart for building or as a nursery for trees.
Text: p 165

123. Saving and interpretation
(1) The provisions of any enactment contained in the foregoing provisions of this Part of this Act do not prejudice any power conferred by any other enactment (whether contained in this Part of this Act or not) to stop up or divert a highway, and do not otherwise affect the operation of any enactment not contained in this Part of this Act relating to the extinguishment, suspension, diversion or variation of public rights of way.
(2) Unless the context otherwise requires, expressions in the foregoing provisions of this Part of this Act, other than expressions to which meanings are assigned by sections 328 and 329 below, have the same meanings respectively as in the Town and Country Planning Act 1990.
Amended by Planning (Consequential Provisions) Act 1990 Sch 2.

130. Protection of public rights
(1) It is the duty of the highway authority to assert and protect the rights of the public to the use and enjoyment of any highway for which they are the highway authority, including any roadside waste which forms part of it.
(2) Any council may assert and protect the rights of the public to the use and enjoyment of any highway in their area for which they are not the highway authority, including any roadside waste which forms part of it.
(3) Without prejudice to subsections (1) and (2) above, it is the duty of a council who are a highway authority to prevent, as far as possible, the stopping up or obstruction of–

(a) the highways for which they are the highway authority, and
(b) any highway for which they are not the highway authority, if, in their opinion, the stopping up or obstruction of that highway would be prejudicial to the interests of their area.
(4) Without prejudice to the foregoing provisions of this section, it is the duty of a local highway authority to prevent any unlawful encroachment on any roadside waste comprised in a highway for which they are the highway authority.
(5) Without prejudice to their powers under section 222 of the Local Government Act 1972, a council may, in the performance of their functions under the foregoing provisions of this section, institute legal proceedings in their own name, defend any legal proceedings and generally take such steps as they deem expedient.
(6) If the council of a parish or community or, in the case of a parish or community which does not have a separate parish or community council, the parish meeting or a community meeting, represent to a local highway authority–
(a) that a highway as to which the local highway authority have the duty imposed by subsection (3) above has been unlawfully stopped up or obstructed, or
(b) that an unlawful encroachment has taken place on a roadside waste comprised in a highway for which they are the highway authority,
it is the duty of the local highway authority, unless satisfied that the representations are incorrect, to take proper proceedings accordingly and they may do so in their own name.
(7) Proceedings or steps taken by a council in relation to an alleged right of way are not to be treated as unauthorised by reason only that the alleged right is not found to exist.
Text: p 170

131. Penalty for damaging highway, etc

(1) If a person, without lawful authority or excuse–
(a) makes a ditch or excavation in a highway which consists of or comprises a carriageway, or
(b) removes any soil or turf from any part of a highway, except for the purpose of improving the highway and with the consent of the highway authority for the highway, or
(c) deposits anything whatsoever on a highway so as to damage the highway, or
(d) lights any fire, or discharges any firearm or firework, within 50 feet from the centre of a highway which consists of or comprises a carriageway, and in consequence thereof the highway is damaged,
he is guilty of an offence.
(2) If a person without lawful authority or excuse pulls down or obliterates a traffic sign placed on or over a highway, or a milestone or direction post (not being a traffic sign) so placed, he is guilty of an offence; but it is a defence in any proceedings under this subsection to show that the traffic sign, milestone or post was not lawfully so placed.
(3) A person guilty of an offence under this section is liable to a fine not exceeding level 3 on the standard scale.
Text: p 180, 195
Amended by Criminal Justice Act 1982 ss 35,38,46.

HIGHWAYS ACT 1980

131A. Disturbance of surface of certain highways
(1) A person who, without lawful authority or excuse, so disturbs the surface of–
(a) a footpath,
(b) a bridleway, or
(c) any other highway which consists of or comprises a carriageway other than a made-up carriageway,
as to render it inconvenient for the exercise of the public right of way is guilty of an offence and liable to a fine not exceeding level 3 on the standard scale.
(2) Proceedings under this section shall be brought only by the highway authority or the council of the non-metropolitan district, parish or community in which the offence is committed; and, without prejudice to section 130 (protection of public rights) above, it is the duty of the highway authority to ensure that where desirable in the public interest such proceedings are brought.
Text: p 178
Inserted by Rights of Way Act 1990 s 1(2).

132. Unauthorised marks on highways
(1) A person who, without either the consent of the highway authority for the highway in question or an authorisation given by or under an enactment or a reasonable excuse, paints or otherwise inscribes or affixes any picture, letter, sign or other mark upon the surface of a highway or upon any tree, structure or works on or in a highway is guilty of an offence and liable to a fine not exceeding level 3 on the standard scale or, in the case of a second or subsequent conviction under this subsection, to a fine not exceeding level 4 on the standard scale.
(2) The highway authority for a highway may, without prejudice to their powers apart from this subsection and whether or not proceedings in respect of the matter have been taken in pursuance of subsection (1) above, remove any picture, letter, sign or other mark which has, without either the consent of the authority or an authorisation given by or under an enactment, been painted or otherwise inscribed or affixed upon the surface of the highway or upon any tree, structure or works on or in the highway.
Text: p 189

134. Ploughing, etc. of footpath or bridleway
(1) Where, in the case of any footpath or bridleway (other than a field-edge path) which passes over a field or enclosure consisting of agricultural land, or land which is being brought into use for agriculture–
(a) the occupier of the field or enclosure desires in accordance with the rules of good husbandry to plough, or otherwise disturb the surface of, all or part of the land comprised in the field or enclosure, and
(b) it is not reasonably convenient in ploughing, or otherwise disturbing the surface of, the land to avoid disturbing the surface of the path or way so as to render it inconvenient for the exercise of the public right of way,
the public right of way shall be subject to the condition that the occupier has the right so to plough or otherwise disturb the surface of the path or way.
(2) Subsection (1) above does not apply in relation to any excavation or any engineering operation.

(3) Where the occupier has disturbed the surface of a footpath or bridleway under the right conferred by subsection (1) above he shall within the relevant period, or within an extension of that period granted under subsection (8) below,–
(a) so make good the surface of the path or way to not less than its minimum width as to make it reasonably convenient for the exercise of the right of way; and
(b) so indicate the line of the path or way on the ground to not less than its minimum width that it is apparent to members of the public wishing to use it.
(4) If the occupier fails to comply with the duty imposed by subsection (3) above he is guilty of an offence and liable to a fine not exceeding level 3 on the standard scale.
(5) Proceedings for an offence under this section in relation to a footpath or bridleway shall be brought only by the highway authority or the council of the district, parish or community in which the offence is committed.
(6) Without prejudice to section 130 (protection of public rights) above, it is the duty of the highway authority to enforce the provisions of this section.
(7) For the purposes of this section 'the relevant period' –
(a) where the disturbance of the surface of the path or way is the first disturbance for the purposes of the sowing of a particular agricultural crop, means fourteen days beginning with the day on which the surface of the path or way was first disturbed for those purposes; or
(b) in any other case, means twenty-four hours beginning with the time when it was disturbed.
(8) On an application made to the highway authority before the disturbance or during the relevant period, the authority may grant an extension of that period for an additional period not exceeding twenty-eight days.
(9) In this section 'minimum width', in relation to a highway, has the same meaning as in Schedule 12A to this Act.
Text: p 81, 175
Amended by Rights of Way Act 1990 s 1(3).

135. Authorisation of other works disturbing footpath or bridleway

(1) Where the occupier of any agricultural land, or land which is being brought into use for agriculture, desires to carry out in relation to that land an excavation or engineering operation, and the excavation or operation–
(a) is reasonably necessary for the purposes of agriculture, but
(b) will so disturb the surface of a footpath or bridleway which passes over that land as to render it inconvenient for the exercise of the public right of way,
he may apply to the highway authority for an order that the public right of way shall be subject to the condition that he has the right to disturb the surface by that excavation or operation during such period, not exceeding three months, as is specified in the order ('the authorisation period').
(2) The highway authority shall make an order under subsection (1) above if they are satisfied either–
(a) that it is practicable temporarily to divert the path or way in a manner reasonably convenient to users, or
(b) that it is practicable to take adequate steps to ensure that the path or way remains sufficiently convenient, having regard to the need for the excavation or operation, for temporary use while it is being carried out.

HIGHWAYS ACT 1980

(3) An order made by a highway authority under subsection (1) above–
(a) may provide for the temporary diversion of the path or way during the authorisation period, but shall not divert it on to land not occupied by the applicant unless written consent to the making of the order has been given by the occupier of that land, and by any other person whose consent is needed to obtain access to it;
(b) may include such conditions as the authority reasonably think fit for the provision, either by the applicant or by the authority at the expense of the applicant, of facilities for the convenient use of any such diversion, including signposts and other notices, stiles, bridges and gates;
(c) shall not affect the line of the path or way on land not occupied by the applicant;
and the authority shall cause notices of any such diversion, together with a plan showing the effect of the diversion and the line of the alternative route provided, to be prominently displayed throughout the authorisation period at each end of the diversion.
(4) An order made by a highway authority under subsection (1) above may include such conditions as the authority reasonably think fit–
(a) for the protection and convenience during the authorisation period of users of the path or way;
(b) for making good the surface of the path or way to not more than the minimum width before the expiration of the authorisation period;
(c) for the recovery from the applicant of expenses incurred by the authority in connection with the order.
(5) An order under this section shall not authorise any interference with the apparatus or works of any statutory undertakers.
(6) If the applicant fails to comply with a condition imposed under subsection (3)(b) or (4)(a) or (b) above he is guilty of an offence and liable to a fine not exceeding level 3 on the standard scale.
(7) Proceedings for an offence under this section in relation to a footpath or bridleway shall be brought only by the highway authority or (with the consent of the highway authority) the council of the non-metropolitan district, parish or community in which the offence is committed.
(8) Without prejudice to section 130 (protection of public rights) above, it is the duty of the highway authority to enforce the provisions of this section.
(9) In this section 'minimum width', in relation to a highway, has the same meaning as in Schedule 12A to this Act.
Text: p 166, 179
Amended by Rights of Way Act 1990 s 1(4).

137. Penalty for wilful obstruction
(1) If a person, without lawful authority or excuse, in any way wilfully obstructs the free passage along a highway he is guilty of an offence and liable to a fine not exceeding level 3 on the standard scale.
Text: p 204
Amended by Police and Criminal Evidence Act 1984.

137A. Interference by crops
(1) Where a crop other than grass has been sown or planted on any agricultural land the occupier of the land shall from time to time take such steps as may be necessary–

RIGHTS OF WAY

(a) to ensure that the line on the ground of any relevant highway on the land is so indicated to not less than its minimum width as to be apparent to members of the public wishing to use the highway; and
(b) to prevent the crop from so encroaching on any relevant highway, whether passing over that or adjoining land, as to render it inconvenient for the exercise of the public right of way.
(2) For the purposes of subsection (1) above, a crop shall be treated as encroaching on a highway if, and only if, any part of the crop grows on, or otherwise extends onto or over, the highway in such a way as to reduce the apparent width of the highway to less than its minimum width.
(3) For the purposes of the application of subsection (1) above in the case of a particular crop, the crop shall be treated as grass if, and only if–
(a) it is of a variety or mixture commonly used for pasture, silage or haymaking, whether or not it is intended for such a use in that case; and
(b) it is not a cereal crop.
(4) If the occupier fails to comply with the duty imposed by subsection (1) above he is guilty of an offence and liable to a fine not exceeding level 3 on the standard scale.
(5) Without prejudice to section 130 (protection of public rights) above, it is the duty of the highway authority to enforce the provisions of this section.
(6) In this section–
'minimum width', in relation to a highway, has the same meaning as in Schedule 12A to this Act, and
'relevant highway' means–
(a) a footpath,
(b) a bridleway, or
(c) any other highway which consists of or comprises a carriageway other than a made-up carriageway.
Text: p 181, 210
Inserted by Rights of Way Act 1990 s 1(5).

143. Power to remove structures from highways
(1) Where a structure has been erected or set up on a highway otherwise than under a provision of this Act or some other enactment, a competent authority may by notice require the person having control or possession of the structure to remove it within such time as may be specified in the notice.
For the purposes of this section the following are competent authorities–
(a) in the case of a highway which is for the time being maintained by a non-metropolitan district council by virtue of section 42 or 50 above, that council and also the highway authority, and
(b) in the case of any other highway, the highway authority.
(2) If a structure in respect of which a notice is served under this section is not removed within the time specified in the notice, the competent authority serving the notice may, subject to subsection (3) below, remove the structure and recover the expenses reasonably incurred by them in so doing from the person having control or possession of the structure.
(3) The authority shall not exercise their power under subsection (2) above until the expiration of one month from the date of service of the notice.
(4) In this section 'structure' includes any machine, pump, post or other object of such a nature as to be capable of causing obstruction, and a structure may

HIGHWAYS ACT 1980

be treated for the purposes of this section as having been erected or set up notwithstanding that it is on wheels.
Text: p 173
Amended by LGA 85 Sch 4 para 25.

145. Powers as to gates across highways
(1) Where there is a gate of less than the minimum width across so much of a highway as consists of a carriageway, or across a highway that is a bridleway, the highway authority for the highway may by notice to the owner of the gate require him to enlarge the gate to that width or remove it.
In this subsection 'the minimum width' means, in relation to a gate across so much of a highway as consists of a carriageway, 10 feet and, in relation to a gate across a bridleway, 5 feet, measured in either case between the posts of the gate.
(2) If a person on whom a notice under subsection (1) above is served fails to comply, within 21 days from the date of service of the notice on him, with a requirement of the notice, he is guilty of an offence and liable to a fine not exceeding 50p for each day during which the failure continues.
Text: p 188, 228

146. Duty to maintain stiles, etc on footpaths and bridleways
(1) Any stile, gate or other similar structure across a footpath or bridleway shall be maintained by the owner of the land in a safe condition, and to the standard of repair required to prevent unreasonable interference with the rights of the persons using the footpath or bridleway.
(2) If it appears to the appropriate authority that the duty imposed by subsection (1) above is not being complied with, they may, after giving to the owner and occupier not less than 14 days' notice of their intention, take all necessary steps for repairing and making good the stile, gate or other works.
For the purposes of this section the appropriate authority is–
(a) in the case of a footpath or bridleway which is for the time being maintained by a non-metropolitan district council by virtue of section 42 or 50 above, that council, and
(b) in the case of any other footpath or bridleway, the highway authority.
(3) The appropriate authority may recover from the owner of the land the amount of any expenses reasonably incurred by the authority in and in connection with the exercise of their powers under subsection (2) above, or such part of those expenses as the authority think fit.
(4) The appropriate authority shall contribute not less than a quarter of any expenses shown to their satisfaction to have been reasonably incurred in compliance with subsection (1) above, and may make further contributions of such amount in each case as, having regard to all the circumstances, they consider reasonable.
(5) Subsection (1) above does not apply to any structure–
(a) if any conditions for the maintenance of the structure are for the time being in force under section 147 below, or
(b) if and so long as, under an agreement in writing with any other person, there is a liability to maintain the structure on the part of the appropriate authority or, where the appropriate authority are a non-metropolitan district council, on the part of either the appropriate authority or the highway authority.

RIGHTS OF WAY

Text: p 50, 228
Amended by LGA 85 Sch 4 para 25.

147. Power to authorise erection of stiles, etc on footpath or bridleway

(1) The following provisions of this section apply where the owner, lessee or occupier of agricultural land, or of land which is being brought into use for agriculture, represents to a competent authority, as respects a footpath or bridleway that crosses the land, that for securing that the use, or any particular use, of the land for agriculture shall be efficiently carried on, it is expedient that stiles, gates or other works for preventing the ingress or egress of animals should be erected on the path or way.

For the purposes of this section the following are competent authorities–

(a) in the case of a footpath or bridleway which is for the time being maintained by a non-metropolitan district council by virtue of section 42 or 50 above, that council and also the highway authority, and

(b) in the case of any other footpath or bridleway, the highway authority.

(2) Where such a representation is made the authority to whom it is made may, subject to such conditions as they may impose for maintenance for enabling the right of way to be exercised without undue inconvenience to the public, authorise the erection of the stiles, gates or other works.

(3) Where an authorisation in respect of a footpath or bridleway is granted under this section the public right of way is to be deemed to be subject to a condition that the stiles, gates or works may be erected and maintained in accordance with the authorisation and so long as the conditions attached to it are complied with.

(4) For the purposes of section 143 above, any stile, gate or works erected in pursuance of an authorisation under this section is to be deemed to be erected under this section only if the provisions of the authorisation and any conditions attached to it are complied with.

(5) In this section references to agricultural land and to land being brought into use for agriculture include references to land used or, as the case may be, land being brought into use, for forestry.

(6) Nothing in this section prejudices any limitation or condition having effect apart from this section.

Text: p 188
Amended by LGA 85 Sch 4 para 25.

148. Penalty for depositing things or pitching booths, etc on highway

If, without lawful authority or excuse–

[(a) and (b) not included.]

(c) a person deposits any thing whatsoever on a highway to the interruption of any user of the highway, or,

(d) a hawker or other itinerant trader pitches a booth, stall or stand, or encamps, on a highway,

he is guilty of an offence and liable to a fine not exceeding level 3 on the standard scale.

Text: p 194

HIGHWAYS ACT 1980

149. Removal of things so deposited on highways as to be a nuisance, etc

(1) If any thing is so deposited on a highway as to constitute a nuisance, the highway authority for the highway may by notice require the person who deposited it there to remove it forthwith and if he fails to comply with the notice the authority may make a complaint to a magistrates' court for a removal and disposal order under this section.

(2) If the highway authority for any highway have reasonable grounds for considering–

(a) that any thing unlawfully deposited on the highway constitutes a danger (including a danger caused by obstructing the view) to users of the highway, and

(b) that the thing in question ought to be removed without the delay involved in giving notice or obtaining a removal and disposal order from a magistrates' court under this section,

the authority may remove the thing forthwith.

(3) The highway authority by whom the thing is removed in pursuance of subsection (2) above may either–

(a) recover from the person by whom it was deposited on the highway, or from any person claiming to be entitled to it, any expenses reasonably incurred by the authority in removing it, or

(b) make a complaint to a magistrates' court for a disposal order under this section.

(4) A magistrates' court may, on a complaint made under this section, make an order authorising the complainant authority–

(a) either to remove the thing in question and dispose of it or, as the case may be, to dispose of the thing in question, and

(b) after payment out of any proceeds arising from the disposal of the expenses incurred in the removal and disposal, to apply the balance, if any, of the proceeds to the maintenance of highways maintainable at the public expense by them.

(5) If the thing in question is not of sufficient value to defray the expenses of removing it, the complainant authority may recover from the person who deposited it on the highway the expenses, or the balance of the expenses, reasonably incurred by them in removing it.

(6) A magistrates' court composed of a single justice may hear a complaint under this section.

Text: p 173

150. Duty to remove snow, soil, etc from highway

(1) If an obstruction arises in a highway from accumulation of snow or from the falling down of banks on the side of the highway, or from any other cause, the highway authority shall remove the obstruction.

(2) If a highway authority fail to remove an obstruction which it is their duty under this section to remove, a magistrates' court may, on a complaint made by any person, by order require the authority to remove the obstruction within such period (not being less than 24 hours) from the making of the order as the court thinks reasonable, having regard to all the circumstances in the case.

(3) In considering whether to make an order under this section and, if so, what period to allow for the removal of the obstruction, the court shall in particular have regard to–

RIGHTS OF WAY

(a) the character of the highway to which the complaint relates, and the nature and amount of traffic by which it is ordinarily used,
(b) the nature and extent of the obstruction, and
(c) the resources of manpower, vehicles and equipment for the time being available to the highway authority for work on highways and the extent to which those resources are being, or need to be, employed elsewhere by that authority on such work.
(4) Where they are under a duty to remove an obstruction under subsection (1) above, a highway authority may–
(a) take any reasonable steps (including the placing of lights, signs and fences on the highway) for warning users of the highway of the obstruction;
(b) sell any thing removed in carrying out the duty, unless the thing is claimed by its owner before the expiration of 7 days from the date of its removal;
(c) recover from the owner of the thing which caused or contributed to the obstruction, or where the thing has been sold under paragraph (b) above, from its previous owner, the expenses reasonably incurred as respects the obstruction in carrying out the duty and in exercising any powers conferred by this subsection, but so that no such expenses are recoverable from a person who proves that he took reasonable care to secure that the thing in question did not cause or contribute to the obstruction.
(5) Where a highway authority sell any thing in exercise of their powers under subsection (4) above, then–
(a) if any expenses are recoverable under that subsection by the authority from the previous owner of the thing, they may set off their expenses against the proceeds of sale (without prejudice to the recovery of any balance of the expenses from the previous owner) and shall pay over any balance of the proceeds to the previous owner; and
(b) if no expenses are so recoverable, they shall pay over the whole of the proceeds of sale to the previous owner.
(6) The foregoing provisions of this section apply to a person liable to maintain a highway by reason of tenure, enclosure or prescription as they apply to the highway authority for that highway, and references in those provisions to a highway authority are to be construed accordingly.
Text: p 172, 230, 248

154. Cutting or felling etc trees that overhang or are a danger to roads or footpaths

(1) Where a hedge, tree or shrub overhangs a highway or any other road or footpath to which the public has access so as to endanger or obstruct the passage of vehicles or pedestrians, or obstructs or interferes with the view of drivers of vehicles or the light from a public lamp, a competent authority may, by notice either to the owner of the hedge, tree or shrub or to the occupier of the land on which it is growing, require him within 14 days from the date of service of the notice so to lop or cut it as to remove the cause of the danger, obstruction or interference.
For the purposes of this section the following are competent authorities–
[(a) not included.]
(b) in relation to a highway for which a local highway authority are the highway authority, that authority and also, if the highway is situated in a non-metropolitan district, the council of that district;

(c) in relation to a road or footpath that is not a highway, the local authority in whose area the road or footpath is situated;
and 'hedge, tree or shrub' includes vegetation of any description.
(2) Where it appears to a competent authority for any highway, or for any other road or footpath which the public has access–
(a) that any hedge, tree or shrub is dead, diseased, damaged or insecurely rooted, and
(b) that by reason of its condition it, or part of it, is likely to cause danger by falling on the highway, road or footpath,
the authority may, by notice either to the owner of the hedge, tree or shrub or to the occupier of the land on which it is situated, require him within 14 days from the date of service of the notice so to cut or fell it as to remove the likelihood of danger.
(3) A person aggrieved by a requirement under subsection (1) or (2) may appeal to a magistrates' court.
(4) Subject to any order made on appeal, if a person on whom a notice is served under subsection (1) or (2) above fails to comply with it within the period specified in those subsections, the authority who served the notice may carry out the work required by the notice and recover the expenses reasonably incurred by them in so doing from the person in default.
Text: p 56, 183
Amended by LGA 85 Sch 4 para 26.

160A. Further powers of highway authorities and district councils in relation to highways
Schedule 12A to this Act shall have effect.
Inserted by Rights of Way Act 1990 s 1(6).

161. Penalties for causing certain kinds of danger or annoyance
(1) If a person, without lawful authority or excuse, deposits any thing whatsoever on a highway in consequence of which a user of the highway is injured or endangered, that person is guilty of an offence and liable to a fine not exceeding level 3 on the standard scale.
(2) If a person, without lawful authority or excuse,–
(a) lights any fire on or over a highway which consists of or comprises a carriageway; or
(b) discharges any firearm or firework within 50 feet of the centre of such a highway,
and in consequence a user of the highway is injured, interrupted or endangered, that person is guilty of an offence and liable to a fine not exceeding level 3 on the standard scale.
(3) If a person plays at football or any other game on a highway to the annoyance of a user of the highway he is guilty of an offence and liable to a fine not exceeding level 1 on the standard scale.
(4) If a person, without lawful authority or excuse, allows any filth, dirt, lime or other offensive matter or thing to run or flow on to a highway from any adjoining premises, he is guilty of an offence and liable to a fine not exceeding level 1 on the standard scale.
Text: p 191, 193, 194
Amended by Highways (Amendment) Act 1986.

RIGHTS OF WAY

161A. Danger or annoyance caused by fires lit otherwise than on highways
(1) If a person—
(a) lights a fire on any land not forming part of a highway which consists of or comprises a carriageway; or
(b) directs or permits a fire to be lit on any such land,
and in consequence a user of any highway which consists of or comprises a carriageway is injured, interrupted or endangered by, or by smoke from, that fire or any other fire caused by that fire, that person is guilty of an offence and liable to a fine not exceeding level 5 on the standard scale.
(2) In any proceedings for an offence under this section it shall be a defence for the accused to prove—
(a) that at the time the fire was lit he was satisfied on reasonable grounds that it was unlikely that users of any highway consisting of or comprising a carriageway would be injured, interrupted or endangered by, or by smoke from, that fire or any other fire caused by that fire; and
(b) either—
(i) that both before and after the fire was lit he did all he reasonably could to prevent users of any such highway from being so injured, interrupted or endangered, or
(ii) that he had a reasonable excuse for not doing so.
Text: p 191
Inserted by Highways (Amendment) Act 1986.

162. Penalty for placing rope, etc across a highway
A person who for any purpose places any rope, wire or other apparatus across a highway in such a manner as to be likely to cause danger to persons using the highway is, unless he proves that he had taken all necessary means to give adequate warning of the danger, guilty of an offence and liable to a fine not exceeding level 3 on the standard scale.
Text: p 195

164. Power to require removal of barbed wire
(1) Where on land adjoining a highway there is a fence made with barbed wire, or having barbed wire in or on it, and the wire is a nuisance to the highway, a competent authority may by notice served on the occupier of the land require him to abate the nuisance within such time, not being less than one month nor more than six months from the date of service of the notice, as may be specified in it.
For the purposes of this section—
(a) the competent authorities, in relation to any highway, are the highway authority and also (where they are not the highway authority) the local authority for the area in which the highway is situated;
(b) 'barbed wire' means wire with spikes or jagged projections, and barbed wire is to be deemed to be a nuisance to a highway if it is likely to be injurious to persons or animals lawfully using the highway.
(2) If at the expiration of the time specified in the notice the occupier has failed to comply with the notice, a magistrates' court, if satisfied on complaint made by the authority that the wire is a nuisance to the highway, may order the occupier to abate the nuisance and, if he fails to comply with the order within

a reasonable time, the authority may do whatever may be necessary in execution of the order and recover from him the expenses reasonably incurred by them in so doing.

(3) If the local authority who are a competent authority in relation to the highway concerned are the occupiers of the land in question proceedings under this section may be taken against them by any ratepayer within the area of that local authority and the foregoing provisions apply accordingly in relation to him and to the authority as they apply in relation to an authority and to an occupier of land.

Text: p 192

165. Dangerous land adjoining street

(1) If, in or on any land adjoining a street, there is an unfenced or inadequately fenced source of danger to persons using the street, the local authority in whose area the street is situated may, by notice to the owner or occupier of that land, require him within such time as may be specified in the notice to execute such works of repair, protection, removal or enclosure as will obviate the danger.

(2) A person aggrieved by a requirement under subsection (1) above may appeal to a magistrates' court.

(3) Subject to any order made on appeal, if a person on whom a notice is served under this section fails to comply with the notice within the time specified in it, the authority by whom the notice was served may execute such works as are necessary to comply with the notice and may recover the expenses reasonably incurred by them in so doing from that person.

(4) Where the power conferred by subsection (1) above is exercisable in relation to land adjoining a street and has not been exercised by the local authority empowered to exercise it, then, if that authority are not the highway authority for the street, the highway authority for the street may request the local authority to exercise the power.

(5) If the local authority refuse to comply with a request made under subsection (4) above or fail within a reasonable time after the request is made to them to do so, the highway authority may exercise the power (and where they do so subsections (2) and (3) above apply accordingly).

Text: p 192

175A. Duty to have regard to needs of disabled and blind in executing works, etc.

(1) In executing works in a street which may impede the mobility of disabled persons or blind persons highway authorities, local authorities and any other person exercising a statutory power to execute works on a highway shall have regard to the needs of such persons.

(2) Any such authority or person as is mentioned in subsection (1) above shall have regard to the needs of disabled persons and blind persons when placing lamp-posts, bollards, traffic-signs, apparatus or other permanent obstructions in a street.

(3) Highway authorities shall have regard to the needs of disabled persons when considering the desirability of providing ramps at appropriate places between carriageways and footways.

(4) In executing in a street any such works as are mentioned in subsection (1) above, any such authority or person as is mentioned in that subsection shall

have regard to the needs of blind persons to have any openings, whether temporary or permanent, in the street, properly protected.
(5) Section 28 of the Chronically Sick and Disabled Persons Act 1970 (power to define certain expressions for the purposes of provisions of that Act) shall have effect as if any reference in it to a provision of that Act included a reference to this section.
Text: p 189, 220, 236
Inserted by Disabled Persons Act 1981.

263. Vesting of highways maintainable at public expense
(1) Subject to the provisions of this section, every highway maintainable at the public expense together with the materials and scrapings of it, vests in the authority who are for the time being the highway authority for the highway.
[(2) to (5) not included.]
Text: p 48, 180

293. Powers of entry for purposes connected with certain orders relating to footpaths and bridleways
(1) A person duly authorised in writing by the Secretary of State or other authority having power under this Act to make a public path creation order, a public path extinguishment order or a public path diversion order may enter upon any land for the purpose of surveying it in connection with the making of the order.
(2) For the purpose of surveying land, or of estimating its value, in connection with a claim for compensation payable by an authority in respect of any other land under section 28 above, or under that section as applied by section 121(2) above, a person who is an officer of the Valuation Office or who has been duly authorised in writing by the authority from whom the compensation is claimed may enter upon the land.
(3) A person authorised under this section to enter upon any land shall, if so required, produce evidence of his authority before entering; and a person shall not under this section demand admission as of right to any land which is occupied unless at least 7 days' notice in writing of the intended entry has been given to the occupier.
(4) A person who wilfully obstructs a person acting in the exercise of his powers under this section is guilty of an offence and liable to a fine not exceeding level 3 on the standard scale.
Text: p 126

297. Power of highway authority or council to require information as to ownership of land
(1) A highway authority or a council may, for the purpose of enabling them to discharge or exercise any of their functions under this Act, require the occupier of any premises and any person who, either directly or indirectly, receives rent in respect of any premises, to state in writing the nature of his own interest therein and the name and address of any other person known to him as having an interest therein, whether as freeholder, mortgagee, lessee or otherwise.
(2) Any person who, having been required in pursuance of this section to give any information, fails to give that information is guilty of an offence and liable to a fine not exceeding level 3 on the standard scale.

(3) Any person who, having been so required to give any information, knowingly makes any mis-statement in respect thereof is guilty of an offence and liable–
(a) on summary conviction to a fine not exceeding the prescribed sum within the meaning of section 32(9) of the Magistrates' Court Act 1980 (£1,000 or such other sum as may be fixed by order under section 143(1) of that Act);
(b) on conviction on indictment or imprisonment for a term not exceeding two years or to a fine, or both.
Text: p 173

300. Right of local authorities to use vehicles and appliances on footways and bridleways

(1) No statutory provision prohibiting or restricting the use of footpaths, footways or bridleways shall affect the use by a competent authority of appliances or vehicles, whether mechanically operated or propelled or not, for cleansing, maintaining or improving footpaths, footways or bridleways or their verges, or for maintaining or altering structures or other works situated therein. For the purposes of this section–
(a) the following are competent authorities, namely, the council of any county, district or London borough, the Common Council, the Council of the Isles of Scilly, any parish or community council, or parish meeting, the Sub-Treasurer of the Inner Temple and the Under-Treasurer of the Middle Temple; and
(b) 'statutory provision' means a provision contained in, or having effect under, any enactment.
(2) The Minister of Transport and the Secretary of State acting jointly may make regulations prescribing the conditions under which the rights conferred by this section may be exercised, and such regulations may in particular make provision as to–
(a) the construction of any appliances or vehicles used under this section,
(b) the maximum weight of any such appliances or vehicles, or the maximum weight borne by any wheel or axle,
(c) the maximum speed of any such appliances or vehicles,
(d) the hours during which the appliances or vehicles may be used, and
(e) the giving by the Minister of Transport or the Secretary of State of directions dispensing with or relaxing any requirement of the regulations as it applies in to a particular authority or in any particular case.
Text: p 46, 55
The regulations referred to in subsection (2) are the Vehicles (Conditions of Use on Footpaths) Regulations 1963 SI 1963 No 2126.

307. Disputes as to compensation which are to be determined by Lands Tribunal and related provisions

(1) Any dispute arising on a claim for compensation under any provision of this Act to which this section applies shall be determined by the Lands Tribunal. The provisions of this Act to which this section applies are sections (...),28,(...),121(2),(...)
[Remainder of section not included.]
Text: p 137

311. Continuing offences

(1) Where by virtue of any provision of this Act, or of byelaws made under it, a person convicted of an offence is, if the offence in respect of which he was

RIGHTS OF WAY

convicted is continued after conviction, guilty of a further offence and liable to a fine for each day on which the offence is so continued, the court before whom the person is convicted of the original offence may fix a reasonable period from the date of conviction for compliance by the defendant with any directions given by the court.

(2) Where a court fixes such a period the defendant is not liable to a fine in respect of the further offence for any day before the expiration of that period.

315. Notice to be given of right of appeal

Where an appeal lies under this Act to the Crown Court or a magistrates' court against a requirement, order, refusal or other decision by a highway authority or a council, the notice given by the authority or council to the person concerned of the making of the requirement or order or of the refusal or other decision against which such an appeal lies shall state the right of appeal to the Crown Court or a magistrates' court, as the case may be, and the time within which such an appeal may be brought.

316. Appeals and applications to magistrates' courts

(1) Where any provision of this Act provides–
(a) for an appeal to a magistrates' court against a requirement, order, refusal or other decision of a highway authority or a council, or
(b) for any other matter to be determined by, or an application in respect of any matter to be made to, a magistrates' court,
the procedure shall be by way of complaint for an order.

(2) The time within which an appeal such as is mentioned in subsection (1)(a) above may be brought is 21 days from the date on which notice of the decision of the highway authority or council is served on the person wishing to appeal, and for the purpose of this subsection the making of the complaint is to be deemed to be the bringing of the appeal.

317. Appeals to the Crown Court from decisions of magistrates' courts

(1) Where a person aggrieved by an order, determination or other decision of a magistrates' court under this Act is not by any other enactment authorised to appeal to the Crown Court he may appeal to that court.

(2) The applicant for an order under section 116 above or any person who was entitled under subsection (7) of that section to be, and was, or claimed to be, heard on the application may appeal to the Crown Court against the decision made by the magistrates' court on the application.

Text: p 235

318. Effect of decision of court upon an appeal

Where on an appeal under this Act a court varies or reverses a decision of a highway authority or of a council it shall be the duty of the authority or the council to give effect to the order of the court, and in particular, to grant or issue any necessary consent, certificate or other document, and to make any necessary entry in any register.

320. Form of notices, etc

All notices, consents, approvals, orders, demands, licences, certificates and other documents authorised or required by or under this Act to be given, made

or issued by, or on behalf of, a highway authority or a council, and all notices, consents, requests and applications authorised or required by or under this Act to be given or made to a highway authority or a council, shall be in writing.
Text: p 232

322. Service of notices, etc

(1) Any notice, consent, approval, order, demand, licence, certificate or other document required or authorised by or under this Act to be given or served on a corporation is duly given or served if it is given to or served on the secretary or clerk of the corporation.

(2) Subject to the provisions of this section, any notice, consent, approval, order, demand, licence, certificate or other document required or authorised by or under this Act to be given or served on any person my be given or served either–
(a) by delivering it to that person, or
(b) by leaving it at his proper address, or
(c) by post;
so, however, that where any such document is sent by post otherwise than in a registered letter, or by the recorded delivery service, it shall be deemed not to have been given or served it if is proved that it was not received by the person to whom it was addressed.

(3) For the purposes of this section, and of section 7 of the Interpretation Act 1978 in its application to this section, the proper address of any person to or on whom any such document is to be given or served–
(a) where the person has furnished an address for service in accordance with arrangements agreed to in that behalf, is the address furnished;
(b) where the person has not furnished an address as provided by paragraph (a) above, is–
(i) in the case of the secretary or clerk of a corporation, that of the registered or principal office of the corporation, and
(ii) in any other case, the person's usual or last known place of abode.

(4) If the name or the address of any owner, lessee or occupier of premises to or on whom any such document is to be given or served cannot after reasonable inquiry be ascertained by the person seeking to give or serve the document, the document may be given or served by–
(a) addressing it to the person to whom it is to be given or on whom it is to be served by the description of 'owner', 'lessee', or 'occupier' of the premises (describing them) to which the document relates, and
(b) delivering it to some responsible person resident or appearing to be resident on the premises or if there is no such person to whom it can be delivered, affixing it or a copy of it to some conspicuous part of the premises.

(5) The foregoing provisions of this section do not apply to the service of–
(a) a notice required or authorised to be served under Part II of, or Schedule 1 to, the Acquisition of Land Act 1981 as applied by this Act, or
(b) a summons.
Text: p 232
Amended by Acquisition of Land Act 1981 Sch 4.

323. Reckoning of periods
(1) For the purposes of this Act–
(a) in reckoning any period which is therein expressed to be a period from or before a given date, that date is to be excluded; and

(b) in reckoning any period therein mentioned of eight days or less which apart from this provision would include a Sunday, Christmas Day, Good Friday or a bank holiday, that day is to be excluded.
(2) In this section 'bank holiday' means a day which is a bank holiday under the Banking and Financial Dealings Act 1971.

326. Revocation and variation of schemes and orders
[(1) not included.]
(2) An order made or confirmed by the Minister, or the Secretary of State, under section 14, 18, (...) of (...) this Act (...) may be revoked by a subsequent order made or confirmed in the like manner and subject to the like provisions.
(5) Without prejudice to subsection (2) above, an order to which this subsection applies confirmed by the Minister, or the Secretary of State, or confirmed as an unopposed order by the authority making it, may be revoked or varied by a subsequent order made or confirmed in the like manner and subject to the like provisions, except that an order confirmed in either way may be revoked or varied by an order confirmed in the other way.
This subsection applies to a public path creation order, a public path extinguishment order, a public path diversion order (...)
(6) Subject to the following provisions in this section (...) an order varying or revoking an order made or confirmed under section 14, (...), 18, (...) above may contain such consequential provisions as appear to the Minister to be expedient.
[(7) to (9) not included.]
Text: p 136
Amended by LGA 85 Sch 17.

327. Application of Act to Crown land
(1) The provisions of this section apply in relation to any land belonging to Her Majesty in right of the Crown or of the Duchy of Lancaster, or belonging to the Duchy of Cornwall, or belonging to a government department, or held in trust for Her Majesty for the purposes of a government department.
(2) The appropriate authority in relation to any land and a highway authority may agree that any provisions of this Act specified in the agreement shall apply to that land and, while the agreement is in force, those provisions shall apply to that land accordingly, subject however to the terms of the agreement.
(3) Any such agreement as is mentioned in subsection (2) above may contain such consequential and incidental provisions, including provisions of a financial character, as appear to the appropriate authority to be necessary or equitable, but provisions of a financial character shall not be included in an agreement made by a government department without the approval of the Treasury.
(4) In this section 'the appropriate authority' means–
(a) in the case of land belonging to Her Majesty in right of the Crown, the Crown Estate Commissioners or other government department having the management of the land in question;
(b) in the case of land belonging to Her Majesty in right of the Duchy of Lancaster, the Chancellor to the Duchy;
(c) in the case of land belonging to the Duchy of Cornwall, such person as the Duke of Cornwall, or the possessor for the time being of the Duchy of Cornwall, appoints;

HIGHWAYS ACT 1980

(d) in the case of land belonging to a government department or held in trust for Her Majesty for the purpose of a government department, that department; and, if any question arises as to what authority is the appropriate authority in relation to any land, that question shall be referred to the Treasury, whose decision shall be final.
Text: p 38, 70

328. Meaning of 'highway'
(1) In this Act, except where the context otherwise requires, 'highway' means the whole or part of a highway other than a ferry or waterway.
(2) Where a highway passes over a bridge or through a tunnel, that bridge or tunnel is to be taken for the purposes of this Act to be a part of the highway.
(3) In this Act, 'highway maintainable at the public expense' and any other expression defined by reference to a highway is to be construed in accordance with the foregoing provisions of this section.
Text: p 223

329. Further provision as to interpretation
(1) In this Act, except where the context otherwise requires–
(...)
'adjoining' includes abutting on, and 'adjoins' is to be construed accordingly;
(...)
'agriculture' includes horticulture, fruit growing, seed growing, dairy farming, the breeding and keeping of livestock (including any creature kept for the production of food, wool, skins or fur, or for the purpose of its use in the farming of land), the use of land as grazing land, meadow land, osier land, market gardens and nursery grounds, and the use of land for woodlands where that use is ancillary to the farming of land for other agricultural purposes, and 'agricultural' is to be construed accordingly;
(...)
'bridleway' means a highway over which the public have the following but no other, rights of way, that is to say, a right of way on foot and a right of way on horseback or leading a horse, with or without a right to drive animals of any description along the highway;
(...)
'carriageway' means a way constituting or comprised in a highway, being a way (other than a cycle track) over which the public have a right of way for the passage of vehicles;
(...)
'council' means a county council or a local authority;
'cycle track' means a way constituting or comprised in a highway, being a way over which the public have the following, but no other, rights of way, that is to say, a right of way on pedal cycles (other than pedal cycles which are motor vehicles within the meaning of the Road Traffic Act 1988) with or without a right of way on foot;
(...)
'field-edge path' means a footpath or bridleway that follows the sides or headlands of a field or enclosure;
(...)

RIGHTS OF WAY

'footpath' means a highway over which the public have a right of way on foot only, not being a footway;

'footway' means a way comprised in a highway which also comprises a carriageway, being a way over which the public have a right of way on foot only;

'functions' includes powers and duties;

(...)

'highway maintainable at public expense' means a highway which by virtue of section 36 above or of any other enactment (whether contained in this Act or not) is a highway which for the purposes of this Act is a highway maintainable at the public expense;

'horse' includes pony, ass and mule, and 'horseback' is to be construed accordingly;

(...)

'land' includes land covered by water and any interest or right in it, over or under land;

(...)

'local authority' means the council of a district or London borough or the Common Council;

(...)

'made-up carriageway' means a carriageway, or a part thereof, which has been metalled or in any other way provided with a surface suitable for the passage of vehicles;

'maintenance' includes repair, and 'maintain' and 'maintainable' are to be construed accordingly;

(...)

'public path creation agreement' means an agreement under section 25 above;

'public path creation order' means an order under section 26 above;

'public path diversion order' means an order under section 119 above;

'public path extinguishment order' means an order under section 118 above;

(...)

'street' includes any highway and any road, lane, footpath, square, court, alley or passage, whether a thoroughfare or not, and includes any part of a street;

(...)

(2) A highway at the side of a river, canal or other inland navigation is not excluded from the definition in subsection (1) above of either 'bridleway' or 'footpath', by reason only that the public have a right to use the highway for purposes of navigation, if the highway would fall within that definition if the public had no such right thereover.

[(3) to (5) not included.]

Text: p 55, 58, 81, 117, 179, 200, 219

Amended by Cycle Tracks Act 1984 s 1, LGA 85 Sch 17, Road Traffic (Consequential Provisions) Act 1988 Sch 3 para 21(2) and Rights of Way Act 1990 s 2.

333. Saving for rights and liabilities as to interference with highways

(1) No provision of this Act relating to obstruction of or other interference with highways is to be taken to affect any right of a highway authority or other person under any enactment not contained in this Act, or under any rule of law, to remove an obstruction from a highway, or otherwise abate a nuisance or other interference with the highway, or to affect the liability of any person

HIGHWAYS ACT 1980

under such an enactment or rule to proceedings (whether civil or criminal) in respect of any such obstruction or other interference.

(2) Nothing in section 134 or 135 above relating to disturbance of the surface of a highway in any manner is to be taken as affecting any right existing apart from this Act to disturb its surface in that manner.

Text: p 172, 194

Amended by Rights of Way Act 1990 s 3.

Schedule 1: Procedures for making or confirming certain orders and schemes

Part 1: Orders

1. Where the Minister proposes to make an order under any of the following provisions, that is to say (...), section 18, (...) or an order relating to a trunk road under section 14 of this Act, he shall prepare a draft of the order and shall publish in at least one local newspaper circulating in the area in which any highway, or any proposed highway, to which the order relates is situated, and in the London Gazette, a notice–

(a) stating the general effect of the proposed order;

(b) naming the place in the said area where a copy of the draft order and of any map or plan referred to therein may be inspected by any person free of charge at all reasonable hours during a period specified in the notice, being a period of not less than six weeks from the date of publication of the notice; and

(c) stating that, within the said period, any person may by notice to the Minister object to the making of the order.

2. Where an order under section 18 (...) of this Act, or an order relating to a classified road under section 14 of this Act, is submitted to the Minister by a local highway authority, that authority shall publish, in the manner specified in paragraph 1 above, the notice there referred to, and that paragraph shall have effect in relation to a notice published by any such authority as if, for the references to the draft order and the making of the order, there were substituted references to the order as submitted to the Minister and the confirmation of the order respectively.

3. Not later than the day on which the said notice is published or, if it is published on two or more days, the day on which it is first published, the Minister or the local highway authority, as the case may be, shall serve on each person specified in such head or heads of the Table set out at the end of this paragraph as apply in the case of the order in question–

(a) a copy of the said notice;

(b) a copy of the draft order or of the order, as the case may be; and

(c) a copy of any map or plan referred to in the draft order or the order relating to a matter which, in the opinion of the Minister or of the local highway authority, as the case may be, is likely to affect the said person.

TABLE

Persons to be served with copies of the documents specified in paragraph 3 of this Schedule.

(i) In the case of (...) every order relating to a trunk road proposed to be made under section 14 of this Act–

Every council in whose area any highway or proposed highway to which the proposed order relates is situated.

RIGHTS OF WAY

[(ii) to (v) not included.]
(vi) In the case of an order proposed to be made under section 14 or 18 of this Act which authorises the stopping up or diversion of any highway–
The council or, in the case of a parish not having a separate council, the parish meeting, of every parish in which the highway is situated and the council of every community in which the highway is situated.
(...)
4. Where the proposed order authorises the stopping up or diversion of a highway, the Minister or the local highway authority, as the case may be, shall, not later than the day on which the said notice is published, or, if it is published on two or more days, the day on which it is first published, cause a copy of it to be displayed in a prominent position at the ends of so much of any highway as is proposed to be stopped up or diverted under the order.
5. At any time, whether before or after the expiration of the period specified in the notice in pursuance of paragraph 1(b) above, the Minister or the local highway authority, as the case may be, by whom the notice was published may, by a subsequent notice published in at least one local newspaper circulating in the area in which the highway, or any proposed highway, to which the proposed order relates is situated, and in the London Gazette, substitute for the period specified in the first notice such longer period as may be specified in the subsequent notice.
6. Where the period specified in a notice published by the Minister or a local highway authority under paragraph 1 above is extended by a notice published under paragraph 5 above, paragraph 3 above shall apply as if the notice under paragraph 5 were a notice under paragraph 1, but the foregoing provision shall not be taken as requiring a copy of the proposed order or of any map or plan referred to in that order to be served on a person on whom it was previously served.
7. (1) If any objection to the proposed order is received by the Minister–
(a) from any person on whom a copy of the notice is required to be served under paragraph 3 above within the period specified in the notice in pursuance of paragraph 1(b) above or, if that period has been extended by a subsequent notice under paragraph 5 above, within the period specified in the subsequent notice, or
(b) from any other person appearing to him to be affected within the period specified in the notice or the subsequent notice, as the case may be,
and the objection is not withdrawn, then–
(i) in the case of an order proposed to be made by the Minister, the Minister and the Secretary of State acting jointly, or
(ii) in the case of an order made by a local highway authority and submitted to the Minister, the Minister,
shall subject to sub-paragraph (2) below, cause a local inquiry to be held.
(2) Except where the objection is made by a person entitled to receive a copy of the notice relating to the order in question by virtue of paragraph 3 above and such one or more of the following heads of the Table set out at the end of that paragraph, that is to say, heads (i) (...), as apply in the case of that order, the Minister and the Secretary of State acting jointly or, as the case may be, the Minister may, if satisfied that in the circumstances of the case the holding of an inquiry under this paragraph is unnecessary, dispense with such an inquiry.

8. (1) After any objections to the proposed order which are not withdrawn and, where a local inquiry is held, the report of the person who held the inquiry have been considered–
(a) in the case of an order proposed to be made by the Minister, by the Minister and the Secretary of State acting jointly, or
(b) in the case of an order made by a local highway authority and submitted to the Minister, by the Minister,
the Minister may make or confirm the order without modifications or subject to such modifications as he thinks fit.
(2) The power under this paragraph to make or confirm the order includes power to make or confirm it so far as relating to part of the proposals contained in it (either without modification or subject to such modifications as the Minister thinks fit) while deferring consideration of the remaining part; and where the Minister makes or confirms part of the order, that part and the remaining part are each to be deemed for the purposes of this Act to be a separate order.
(3) Where the Minister proposes to exercise the power to make or confirm the order subject to modifications, and the modifications will in his opinion make a substantial change in the order–
(a) he shall notify any person who appears to him to be likely to be affected by the proposed modifications;
(b) he shall give that person an opportunity of making representations to him with respect to the modifications within such reasonable period as he may specify; and
(c) before he exercises the power, the Minister or, in the case of an order proposed to be made by the Minister, the Minister and the Secretary of State acting jointly shall consider any representations made to the Minister with respect to the proposed modifications within that period.
9. In this Part of this Schedule references to a proposed order or an order proposed to be made include references to an order made by a local highway authority and submitted to the Minister.
[Part II not included.]

Part III: General
17. If, on or after publishing a notice required by Part I or Part II of this Schedule to be published in connection with the making or confirmation of an order or scheme, it appears to the Minister or a local highway authority desirable to do so, he or they shall take such steps, in addition to those required by the said Part I or Part II to be taken, as will in his or their opinion secure that additional publicity is given in the area affected by the order or scheme to the proposals contained in it.
18. (1) Any person who objects to the making or confirmation of an order or scheme pursuant to this Schedule shall include in the notice of objection a statement of the grounds of objection.
(2) If any notice of objection to the making or confirmation of an order or scheme pursuant to this Schedule does not state the grounds of objection the Minister or, in the case of an order or scheme proposed to be made by the Minister, the Minister and the Secretary of State acting jointly may disregard the objection.
19. (1) Where objections to the making or confirmation of an order or scheme pursuant to this Schedule are to be the subject of a local inquiry, the Minister

or, in the case of an order or scheme proposed to be made by the Minister, the Minister and the Secretary of State acting jointly may, by notice served on the persons making such objections or by the notice announcing the holding of the inquiry, direct that any person who intends at the inquiry to submit–

(a) that any highway or proposed highway to which the order or scheme in question relates should follow an alternative route, or

(b) that, instead of improving, diverting or altering a highway in accordance with the order in question, a new highway should be constructed on a particular route,

shall send to the Minister within such period as may be specified in the notice, being a period not less than 14 days and ending not less than 14 days before the date fixed for the holding of the inquiry, sufficient information about the alternative route or the route of the new highway, as the case may be, to enable it to be identified.

(2) Where the Minister or the Minister and the Secretary of State acting jointly have given a direction under sub-paragraph (1) above in relation to an inquiry, the person holding the inquiry and the Minister or, as the case may be, those Ministers may disregard so much of any objection as consists of a submission to which the direction applies unless the person making the objection has complied with the direction.

20. Proceedings required by this Schedule to be taken for the purposes of an order relating to a trunk road under section 14 of this Act or for the purposes of an order relating to a special road under section 18 of this Act may be taken concurrently (so far as practicable) with proceedings required by this Schedule to be taken for the purposes of an order under section 10 of this Act or, as the case may be, for the purposes of a scheme under section 16 of this Act, relating to that road.

21. Where–

(a) proceedings required to be taken for the purposes of an order relating to a trunk road under section 14 of this Act are taken after the making by the Minister of an order relating to that road under section 10 of this Act, or

(b) proceedings required to be taken for the purposes of an order relating to a special road under section 18 of this Act are taken after the making or confirmation by the Minister of a scheme relating to that road under section 16 of this Act,

the Minister or, in the case of an order proposed to be made by the Minister, the Minister and the Secretary of State acting jointly, may disregard any objection to the order under section 14 or 18 which in his or their opinion amounts in substance to an objection to the order under section 10 or, as the case may be, to the scheme under section 16.

Text: p 149

Schedule 2: Validity and date of operation of certain schemes and orders

1. (1) (...) as soon as may be after a scheme or order to which this Schedule applies has been made or confirmed by the Minister, he shall publish in the London Gazette, and in such other manner as he thinks best adapted for informing persons affected, a notice stating that the scheme or order has been made or confirmed, and naming a place where a copy of it may be inspected free of charge at all reasonable hours.

HIGHWAYS ACT 1980

[(2) not included.]

2. If a person aggrieved by a scheme or order to which this Schedule applies desires to question the validity of it, or of any provision contained in it, on the ground that it is not within the powers of this Act or on the ground that any requirement of this Act or of regulations made under this Act has not been complied with in relation to the scheme or order, he may, within six weeks from the date on which the notice required by paragraph 1 above is first published, make an application for the purpose to the High Court.

3. On any such application, the Court–

(a) may by interim order suspend the operation of the scheme or order, or of any provision contained in it, either generally or in so far as it affects any property of the applicant, until the final determination of the proceedings; and

(b) if satisfied that the scheme or order, or any provision contained in it, is not within the powers of this Act or that the interests of the applicant have been substantially prejudiced by a failure to comply with any such requirement as aforesaid, may quash the scheme or order or any provision contained in it, either generally or in so far as it affects any property of the applicant.

4. Subject to paragraph 3 above, a scheme or order to which this Schedule applies shall not, either before or after it has been made or confirmed, be questioned in any legal proceedings whatsoever, and shall become operative on the date on which the notice required by paragraph 1 above is first published, or on such later date, if any, as may be specified in the scheme or order.

[5 not included.]

Text: p 136, 149

Schedule 6: Provisions as to making, confirmation, validity and date of operation of certain orders relating to footpaths and bridleways

Part I: Procedure for making and confirming certain orders relating to footpaths and bridleways

1. (1) Before a public path creation order, a public path extinguishment order or a public path diversion order is submitted to the Secretary of State for confirmation or confirmed as an unopposed order, the authority by whom the order was made shall give notice in the prescribed form–

(a) stating the general effect of the order and that it has been made and is about to be submitted for confirmation or to be confirmed as an unopposed order,

(b) naming a place in the area in which the land to which the order relates is situated where a copy of the order and of the map referred to therein may be inspected free of charge and copies thereof may be obtained at a reasonable charge at all reasonable hours, and

(c) specifying the time (which shall be not less than 28 days from the date of the first publication of the notice) within which, and the manner in which, representations or objections with respect to the order may be made.

(2) Before the Secretary of State makes a public path creation order, a public path extinguishment order or a public path diversion order, he shall prepare a draft of the order and shall give notice–

(a) stating that he proposes to make the order and the general effect of it,

(b) naming a place in the area in which the land to which the draft order relates is situated where a copy of the draft order and of the map referred to in it may be inspected free of charge and copies thereof may be obtained at a reasonable charge at all reasonable hours, and

(c) specifying the time (which shall be not less than 28 days from the date of the first publication of the notice) within which, and the manner in which, representations or objections with respect to the draft order may be made.

(3) The notices to be given under sub-paragraph (1) or (2) above shall be given–

(a) by publication in at least one local newspaper circulating in the area in which the land to which the order relates is situated;

(b) by serving a like notice on–

(i) every owner, occupier and lessee (except tenants for a month or any period less than a month and statutory tenants within the meaning of the Rent (Agriculture) Act 1976 or the Rent Act 1977 and licensees under an assured agricultural occupancy within the meaning of Part I of the Housing Act 1988) of any of that land;

(ii) every council, the council of every parish or community and the parish meeting of every parish not having a separate parish council, being a council, parish or community whose area includes any of that land;

(iii) every person on whom notice is required to be served in pursuance of sub-paragraph (3A) or (3B) below; and

(iv) such other persons as may be prescribed in relation to the area in which that land is situated or as the authority or, as the case may be, the Secretary of State may consider appropriate; and

(c) by causing a copy of the notice to be displayed in a prominent position–

(i) at the ends of so much of any footpath or bridleway as is created, stopped up or diverted by the order;

(ii) at council offices in the locality of the land to which the order relates; and

(iii) at such other places as the authority or, as the case may be, the Secretary of State may consider appropriate.

(3A) Any person may, on payment of such reasonable charges as the authority may consider appropriate, require an authority to give him notice of all such public path creation orders, public path extinguishment orders and public path diversion orders as are made by the authority during a specified period, are of a specified description and relate to land comprised in a specified area; and in this sub-paragraph 'specified' means specified in the requirement.

(3B) Any person may, on payment of such reasonable charge as the Secretary of State may consider appropriate, require the Secretary of State to give him notice of all such draft public path creation orders, draft public path extinguishment orders and draft public path diversion orders as are prepared by the Secretary of State during a specified period, are of a specified description and relate to land comprised in a specified area; and in this sub-paragraph 'specified' means specified in the requirement.

(3C) The Secretary of State may, in any particular case, direct that it shall not be necessary to comply with sub-paragraph (3)(b)(i) above; but if he so directs in the case of any land, then in addition to publication the notice shall be addressed to 'The owners and any occupiers' of the land (describing it) and a copy or copies of the notice shall be affixed to some conspicuous object or objects on the land.

(4) Where under this paragraph a notice is required to be served on an owner of land and the land belongs to an ecclesiastical benefice, a like notice shall be served on the Church Commissioners.

(4A) Sub-paragraphs (3)(b) and (c) and, where applicable, sub-paragraphs (3C) and (4) above shall be complied with not less than 28 days before the expiration of the time specified in the notice.

(4B) A notice required to be served by sub-paragraph (3)(b)(i), (ii) or (iv) above shall be accompanied by a copy of the order.

(4C) A notice required to be displayed by sub-paragraph (3)(c)(i) above at the ends of so much of any way as is affected by the order shall be accompanied by a plan showing the general effect of the order so far as it relates to that way.

(4D) In sub-paragraph (3)(c)(ii) above 'council offices' means offices or buildings acquired or provided by a council or by the council of a parish or community or the parish meeting of a parish not having a separate parish council.

2. (1) If no representations or objections are duly made, or if any so made are withdrawn, then–

(a) the Secretary of State may, if he thinks fit, confirm or make the order, as the case may be, with or without modifications;

(b) the authority by whom the order was made (where not the Secretary of State) may, instead of submitting the order to the Secretary of State, themselves confirm the order (but without any modification).

(2) If any representation or objection duly made is not withdrawn, the Secretary of State shall, before confirming or making the order, as the case may be, if the objection is made by a local authority, cause a local inquiry to be held, and in any other case either–

(a) cause a local inquiry to be held, or

(b) afford to any person by whom any representation or objection has been duly made and not withdrawn an opportunity of being heard by a person appointed by him for the purpose,

and, after considering the report of the person appointed to hold the inquiry or to hear representations or objections, may, subject as provided below, confirm or make the order, as the case may be, with or without modifications.

In the case of a public path creation order or a public path diversion order, if objection is made by statutory undertakers on the ground that the order provides for the creation of a public right of way over land covered by works used for the purposes of their undertaking or the curtilage of such land, and the objection is not withdrawn, the order is subject to special parliamentary procedure.

(3) Notwithstanding anything in the foregoing provisions of this paragraph, the Secretary of State shall not confirm or make an order so as to affect land not affected by the order as submitted to him or the draft order prepared by him, as the case may be, except after–

(a) giving such notice as appears to him requisite of his proposal so to modify the order, specifying the time (which shall be not less than 28 days from the date of the first publication of the notice) within which, and the manner in which, representations or objections with respect to the proposal may be made,

(b) holding a local inquiry or affording to any person by whom any representation or objection has been duly made and not withdrawn an opportunity of being heard by a person appointed by him for the purpose, and

(c) considering the report of the person appointed to hold the inquiry or to hear representations or objections, as the case may be,

and, in the case of a public path creation order or a public path diversion order, if objection is made by statutory undertakers on the ground that the order as modified would provide for the creation of a public right of way over land

RIGHTS OF WAY

covered by works used for the purposes of their undertaking or the curtilage of such land and the objection is not withdrawn, the order is subject to special parliamentary procedure.

2A. (1) A decision of the Secretary of State under paragraph 2 above as respects an order made by an authority other than the Secretary of State shall, except in such classes of case as may for the time being be prescribed or as may be specified in directions given by the Secretary of State, be made by a person appointed by the Secretary of State instead of by the Secretary of State; and a decision made by a person so appointed shall be treated as a decision of the Secretary of State.

(2) The Secretary of State may, if he thinks fit, direct that a decision which, by virtue of sub-paragraph (1) above, and apart from this sub-paragraph, falls to be made by a person appointed by the Secretary of State shall instead be made by the Secretary of State, and a direction under this sub-paragraph shall state the reasons for which it is given and shall be served on the person, if any, so appointed, the authority and any person by whom a representation or objection has been duly made and not withdrawn.

(3) Where the Secretary of State has appointed a person to make a decision under paragraph 2 above the Secretary of State may, at any time before the making of the decision, appoint another person to make it instead of the first person appointed to make it.

(4) Where by virtue of sub-paragraph (2) or (3) above a particular decision falls to be made by the Secretary of State or any other person instead of the person first appointed to make it, anything done by or in relation to the latter shall be treated as having been done by or in relation to the former.

(5) Provision may be made by regulations of the Secretary of State for the giving of publicity to any directions given by the Secretary of State under this paragraph.

3. (1) The Secretary of State may, subject to the provisions of this Part of this Schedule, by regulations make such provisions as to the procedure on the making, submission and confirmation of orders to which this Schedule applies as appears to him to be expedient.

(2) Provision may be made by regulations of the Secretary of State for enabling proceedings preliminary to the confirmation of a public path extinguishment order to be taken concurrently with proceedings preliminary to the confirmation of a public path creation order or a public path diversion order.

(3) In this Part of this Schedule–

(a) 'local authority' means

(i) a charging authority, a precepting authority, a combined police authority or a combined fire authority, as defined in section 144 of the Local Government Finance Act 1988;

(ii) a levying authority within the meaning of section 74 of that Act; and

(iii) a body as regards which section 75 of that Act applies,

and includes any drainage authority and any joint board or joint committee if all the constituent authorities are such local authorities as aforesaid;

(b) 'prescribed' means prescribed by regulations made by the Secretary of State; and for the purposes of this Schedule the Civil Aviation Authority and the Post Office are to be deemed to be statutory undertakers and their undertakings statutory undertakings.

HIGHWAYS ACT 1980

Part II: Validity and date of operation of certain orders relating to footpaths and bridleways

4. (1) As soon as may be after an order to which this Schedule applies has been confirmed or made by the Secretary of State or confirmed as an unopposed order, the authority by whom the order was made or, in the case of an order made by the Secretary of State, the Secretary of State, shall publish, in the manner required in relation to the class of order in question by paragraph 1(3) above, a notice in the prescribed form describing the general effect of the order, stating that it has been confirmed or made, and naming a place where a copy of it as confirmed or made may be inspected free of charge and copies thereof may be obtained at a reasonable charge at all reasonable hours, and–
(a) serve a like notice on any person on whom notices were required to be served under paragraph 1(3)(b), (3C) or (4) above; and
(b) cause like notices to be displayed in the like manner as the notices caused to be displayed under paragraph 1(3)(c) above;
but no such notice or copy need be served on a person unless he has sent to the authority or the Secretary of State (according as the notice or copy would require to be served by an authority or by the Secretary of State) a request in that behalf specifying an address for service.

(2) A notice required to be served by sub-paragraph (1)(a) above, on–
(a) a person on whom notice was required to be served by paragraph 1(3)(b)(i) or (ii) above, or
(b) in the case of an order which has been confirmed or made with modifications, a person on whom notice was required to be served by paragraph 1(3)(b)(iv) above,
shall be accompanied by a copy of the order as confirmed or made.

(3) As soon as may be after a decision not to confirm an order to which this Schedule applies, the authority by whom the order was made shall give notice of the decision by serving a copy of it on any person on whom notices were required to be served under paragraphs 1(3)(b), (3C) or (4) above.

(4) As soon as may be after an order to which this Schedule applies has come into operation otherwise than–
(a) on the date on which it was confirmed or made by the Secretary of State or confirmed as an unopposed order; or
(b) at the expiration of a specified period beginning with that date,
the authority by whom the order was made or, in the case of an order made by the Secretary of State, the Secretary of State shall give notice of its coming into operation by publication in at least one local newspaper circulating in the area in which the land to which the order relates is situated.

5. Schedule 2 to this Act (except paragraph 1 thereof) applies in relation to an order to which this Schedule applies as it applies in relation to a scheme or order to which that Schedule applies, but with the following modifications:–
(a) for references to a scheme or order to which that Schedule applies substitute references to an order to which this Schedule applies;
(b) for the references in paragraphs 2, 4 and 5 thereof to the date on which the notice required by paragraph 1 thereof is first published substitute references to the date on which the notice required by paragraph 4 above is first published; and
(c) paragraph 4 of that Schedule has effect as if the words 'or on such later date, if any, as may be specified in the scheme or order' were omitted.

RIGHTS OF WAY

6. In this Part of this Schedule 'prescribed' means prescribed by regulations made by the Secretary of State.

Text: p 126

Amended by WCA 1981 Sch 16, SI 1988 No 2152 and SI 1990 No 776. The regulations are the Public Path Orders and Extinguishment of Public Right of Way Regulations 1983 (SI 1983 No 23) (p 460).

Schedule 7: Maintenance of certain highways by district councils

Part I: Regulations governing exercise of powers

1. Before exercising the relevant powers in relation to any highway in respect of which those powers are exercisable, the council of a non-metropolitan district shall give notice of their intention to do so to the county council who are the local highway authority, specifying the highway or highways concerned. In this Schedule 'the relevant powers' means the powers of a district council under sections 42, 50(2) and 230(7) of this Act.

2. If the county council are of the opinion that any highway specified in a notice under paragraph 1 above does not fall within the relevant powers, they may, at any time within the period of six weeks beginning with the date on which they receive the notice, serve a counter-notice on the district council disputing the right of the district council to exercise in relation to the highway concerned any of the relevant powers; and if the dispute is not resolved by the county council and the district council within six weeks after the receipt of the counter-notice by the district council the dispute shall be referred to the Minister for his decision.

3. (1) The relevant powers with respect to a highway specified in a notice under paragraph 1 above become exercisable–

(a) where no counter-notice is served in respect of the highway under paragraph 2 above, at the expiry of the period of six weeks first specified in that paragraph; and

(b) where such a counter-notice is served, when the dispute is resolved in favour of the district council by the councils concerned or, as the case may be, when the Minister's decision on the dispute in favour of the district council is received by the district council;

but if a dispute resulting from the service of a counter-notice under paragraph 2 above is resolved or decided by the Minister against the district council, the relevant powers are not exercisable by the district council in respect of the highway concerned and no further notice under paragraph 1 above may be given by the district council in respect of that highway unless its status is changed or there is such a change in the character of the road as to give reasonable ground for believing it has become an urban road.

(2) In the event that a highway in respect of which the relevant powers have become exercisable in accordance with sub-paragraph (1) above or paragraph 4(2) below becomes a trunk road or classified road, the relevant powers thereupon cease with respect to that highway.

4. (1) Without prejudice to paragraph 3(2) above, the relevant powers cease to be exercisable with respect to any highway–

(a) on such day as may be agreed between the district council and the county council who are the local highway authority for the highway; or

(b) six months after the receipt by that county council of a notice from the district council stating the intention of the district council to cease to exercise those powers;

and any such agreement or notice may relate either to such highway or highways as may be specified in the agreement or notice or to all the highways in respect of which the relevant powers are exercisable at the time the agreement is made, or as the case may be, the notice is served.

(2) Where the relevant powers have ceased to be exercisable with respect to a highway by virtue of an agreement or notice under sub-paragraph (1) above, those powers shall not, except with the consent of the county council who are the highway authority for that highway, again become exercisable with respect to that highway at any time within the period of 10 years beginning with the day on which the powers cease to be so exercisable, but if, at any time after the expiry of that period or, with the consent of the county council, before the expiry, the district council intend again to exercise those powers with respect to that highway, paragraphs 2 and 3(1) above do not apply and those powers become exercisable at the expiry of the period of six weeks beginning with the date on which the county council who are the highway authority receive notice of the district council's intention under paragraph 1 above.

(3) If, by virtue of paragraph 3(2) or sub-paragraph (1) above, the relevant powers cease to be exercisable with respect to any highway, the cessation does not affect the continued existence, on and after the day on which the powers cease to be so exercisable, of any rights or liabilities of the district council in respect of the highway which are in existence immediately before that day.

5. (1) Every district council shall prepare and keep up to date a list of the highways in respect of which the relevant powers are for the time being exercisable by them, and the council shall make the list available for public inspection free of charge at all reasonable hours at the offices of the council.

(2) A copy of any list of highways prepared by a district council under sub-paragraph (1) above and of all amendments for the time being made thereto shall be furnished by the district council to the county council who are the highway authority for the highways concerned.

(3) Except in so far as the relevant powers with respect to a highway cease to be exercisable by a district council in accordance with paragraph 3(2) or paragraph 4(1) above, an entry in the list kept under this paragraph is conclusive evidence that the highway specified in the entry is one in respect of which the relevant powers are exercisable by the district council.

6. A statement by or on behalf of the Minister that a highway is or is not a classified road is conclusive for the purposes of sections 42 and 230(7) of this Act and of this Schedule.

7. A district council shall indemnify a county council in respect of any claim made against the county council, as highway authority,–

(a) in respect of a failure to maintain a highway at a time when the relevant powers were exercisable by the district council with respect to the highway; or
(b) arising out of any works of maintenance on a highway carried out by the district council in exercise of those powers.

Part II: Reimbursement by highway authorities of certain expenses of district councils

8. The provisions of this Part of this Schedule apply where a district council are exercising the power under section 42 of this Act in relation to any highways within their district, and references in the following provisions of this Part of this Schedule to a district council and to their maintenance power are to be construed accordingly.

RIGHTS OF WAY

9. On or before 15th December in each year the district council shall submit to the county council for their approval a detailed estimate of the cost for the ensuing financial year of the maintenance of every highway in respect of which their maintenance power is exercisable, and on any such estimate being approved by the county council, either with or without modifications, the amount to be paid by the county council under section 42(3) of this Act is, subject to paragraph 10 below, the amount of that estimate, or of that estimate as amended by any supplementary estimate submitted to and approved by the county council, or such less sum as may have been actually expended by the district council on the highways in question during that financial year.

10. The county council are not liable to make payment towards the cost of the maintenance of any highway until they are satisfied, by a report of such one of their officers or such other person as they may appoint for the purpose, that the works of maintenance are being or have been properly executed.

11. The district council may at any time, and from time to time, submit to the county council for their approval a detailed supplementary estimate.

12. A county council shall not unreasonably withhold approval of an estimate submitted to them under this Part of this Schedule, and any question whether their approval has been unreasonably withheld, or whether any works of maintenance are being or have been properly executed, or as to the liability of a county council to make a payment under section 42(3) of this Act, shall be determined by the Minister.

Text: p 224
Amended by LGA 85 Sch 4 para 42.

Schedule 12

Part I: Notices to be given by the applicant for order under section 116

1. At least 28 days before the day on which an application for an order under section 116 of this Act is made in relation to a highway the applicant authority shall give notice of their intention to apply for the order, specifying the time and place at which the application is to be made and the terms of the order applied for (embodying a plan showing what will be the effect thereof)—
(a) to the owners and occupiers of all lands adjoining the highway;
(b) to any statutory undertakers having apparatus under, in, upon, over, along or across the highway;
(c) if the highway is a classified road, to the Minister;
(d) if the highway is a classified road in a non-metropolitan district, to the district council, and if the highway is a classified road in, or partly in, a parish or community which has a separate parish council or community council, to the parish or community council, as the case may require or, in the case of a parish which does not have a separate parish council, to the chairman of the parish meeting.

2. Not later than 28 days before the day on which the application is made the applicant authority shall cause a copy of the said notice to be displayed in a prominent position at the ends of the highway.

3. At least 28 days before the day on which the application is made the applicant authority shall publish in the London Gazette and in at least one local newspaper circulating in the area in which the highway is situated a notice containing the

HIGHWAYS ACT 1980

particulars specified in paragraph 1 above, except that there may be substituted for the plan a statement of a place in the said area where the plan may be inspected free of charge at all reasonable hours.
[Part II not included.]
Text: p 153
Amended by LGA 85 Sch 4 para 43.

Schedule 12A. Further powers of highway authorities and councils in relation to interference with highways

Interpretation

1. (1) For the purposes of this Schedule the 'minimum width' and 'maximum width' of a highway shall be determined in accordance with sub-paragraphs (2) and (3) below.
(2) In any case where the width of the highway is proved, that width is both the 'minimum width' and the 'maximum width'.
(3) In any other case–
(a) the 'minimum width' is–
(i) as respects a footpath which is not a field-edge path, 1 metre,
(ii) as respects a footpath which is a field-edge path, 1.5 metres,
(iii) as respects a bridleway which is not a field-edge path, 2 metres, or
(iv) as respects any other highway, 3 metres, and
(b) the 'maximum width' is–
(i) as respects a footpath, 1.8 metres,
(ii) as respects a bridleway, 3 metres, or
(iii) as respects any other highway, 5 metres.

Competent authorities

2. For the purposes of this Schedule each of the following shall be a competent authority in relation to a highway–
(a) the highway authority; and
(b) in the case of a highway maintained by a district council under section 42 or 50 of this Act, that council.

Power to carry out works

3. (1) Where the surface of–
(i) a footpath,
(ii) a bridleway, or
(iii) any other highway which consists of or comprises a carriageway other than a made-up carriageway,
has been so disturbed as to render it inconvenient for the exercise of the public right of way, a competent authority may make good the surface to an extent not less than the minimum width nor greater than the maximum width.
(2) Where the surface of a footpath or bridleway was disturbed under the right conferred by section 134(1) of this Act, the power conferred by sub-paragraph (1) above shall not become exercisable until the expiration of the period which is the relevant period for the purposes of section 134, or an extension of that period granted under subsection (8) of that section.
(3) Where the surface of a footpath or bridleway was disturbed under the right conferred by section 135 of this Act, the power conferred by sub-paragraph (1)

RIGHTS OF WAY

above shall not become exercisable until the expiration of the period which is the authorisation period for the purposes of section 135.

4. (1) Where the occupier of any land fails to carry out the duty imposed on him by section 134(3)(b) or 137A(1) of this Act in relation to a highway, a competent authority may carry out such works as may be necessary or expedient for the purpose of rectifying the default.

(2) Sub-paragraph (1) above does not authorise the carrying out of works to an extent greater than the maximum width of the highway.

(3) Where the surface of a footpath or bridleway was disturbed under the right conferred by section 134(1) of this Act, the power conferred by sub-paragraph (1) above shall not become exercisable until the expiration of the period which is the relevant period for the purposes of section 134, or an extension of that period granted under subsection (8) of that section.

5. If the applicant fails to comply with a condition imposed under section 135(3)(b) or (4)(a) or (b) of this Act, a competent authority may carry out such works as may be necessary or expedient for the purpose of rectifying the default.

6. Paragraphs 7 to 9 below have effect in relation to the carrying out by a competent authority of work under paragraphs 3 to 5 above in relation to a highway which passes over any land ('the relevant land').

Entry on land

7. Subject to paragraph 8 below, any person duly authorised in writing by the authority may enter on the relevant land, or any other land the authority reasonably believe to be in the same occupation, for any purpose connected with the carrying out of the work; and may take with him on to the land such vehicles, machinery and other equipment as may be requisite.

8. (1) Except in the case of entry, solely for the purpose of obtaining information, on land other than a building or structure, before entering on any land the authority shall give the occupier not less than twenty-four hours' notice of their intention to do so; and the notice shall–

(a) identify the highway to which it relates; and

(b) specify the work to be carried out and the equipment to be used for that purpose; and

(c) identify the line or lines of passage over the land in question, if any, that may need to be used for access to the site of the work; and

(d) state the date and time when the power to enter on the land becomes exercisable.

(2) Without prejudice to section 322 (service of notices etc.) of this Act, if after reasonable enquiry the authority are satisfied that it is not practicable to ascertain the name and address of the occupier, a notice under this paragraph may be given by addressing it to him as 'The Occupier' of the land (describing it) and affixing copies of the notices to some conspicuous object–

(a) at each end of so much of the highway as is referred to in the notice; and

(b) at such other points in the vicinity of that highway as the authority may consider suitable; and

(c) if appropriate, at a point adjacent to a highway comprising a made-up carriageway from which access is required for equipment.

(3) A notice shall not be given under this paragraph before the power referred to in paragraph 3, 4 or 5 above has become exercisable.

HIGHWAYS ACT 1980

Financial
9. (1) Subject to sub-paragraph (2) below, a competent authority may recover the amount of any expenses reasonably incurred by the authority in, or in connection with, the carrying out of the work–
(a) in a case falling within paragraph 2(1) above, from the occupier of the relevant land or the person who disturbed the surface of the highway, and
(b) in any other case, from the occupier of the relevant land.
(2) A person–
(a) is not liable under sub-paragraph (a) of paragraph (1) above if he shows that he had any lawful authority or excuse for disturbing the surface of the highway, and
(b) is not liable under that paragraph as an occupier of land if he shows that the surface of the highway was not disturbed by him or with his consent.
Text: p 176
Inserted by Rights of Way Act 1990 s 4.

Schedule 23 : Transitional provisions
Private Street Works Code
13. (1) Subject to sub-paragraph (3) below, where a highway in existence on 16th December 1949 (the date of the coming into force of the National Parks and Access to the Countryside Act 1949, referred to below as 'the 1949 Act')–
(a) was immediately before 1st January 1960 a highway repairable by the inhabitants at large by virtue only of section 47(1) of the 1949 Act (which extended to all public paths the then rule of law whereby a highway was repairable by the inhabitants at large), and
(b) would, if the said section 47 had not been enacted, be a private street for the purposes of the private street works code,
the fact that the highway is a highway maintainable at the public expense by virtue of section 36(1) of this Act shall not prevent its being treated for the purposes of the private street works code as a private street.
This paragraph does not apply to a highway in Greater London other than the outer London boroughs.
(2) Subject to sub-paragraph (2) below, where a highway in existence on 3rd August 1968 (the date of the coming into force of the Countryside Act 1968) would, if paragraph 9(2)(a) of Schedule 3 to that Act (which provides that as from the date of publication of the definitive map and statement in a review carried out by an authority under Part III of that Schedule certain ways shown on the map are to be highways maintainable at the public expense) had not been enacted, the fact that a highway is a highway so maintainable by virtue of the said paragraph 9(2) shall not prevent its being treated for the purposes of the private street works code as a private street.
(3) Where the street works authority exercise the powers exercisable by them by virtue of sub-paragraph (1) or (2) above in relation to a highway or part of it, the sub-paragraph in question shall not thereafter apply to that highway or that part, as the case may be, so as to enable the authority to exercise those powers in relation to it on any subsequent occasion.
Likewise, where before the commencement of this Act the street works authority exercised the powers exercisable by them by virtue of–
(a) paragraph 24 of Schedule 24 to the Highways Act 1959 (from which sub-paragraph (1) above is derived) or section 50 of the 1949 Act (from which the said paragraph 24 was derived), or

RIGHTS OF WAY

(b) section 76(1) of the Highways Act 1971 (from which sub-paragraph (2) above is derived),
in relation to a highway or part of it, sub-paragraph (1) or, as the case may be, (2) above shall not apply to that highway or part, as the case may be, so as to enable the authority to exercise the powers exercisable by virtue of sub-paragraph (1) or (2) above in relation to it.

LOCAL GOVERNMENT, PLANNING AND LAND ACT 1980

Schedule 28: Urban development corporations — land

Part III: Land — supplementary : Extinguishment of public rights of way

11. (1) Where any land has been vested in or acquired by an urban development corporation or local highway authority for the purposes of this Act and is for the time being held by that corporation or authority for those purposes, the Secretary of State may by order extinguish any public right of way over the land.
(2) Where the Secretary of State proposes to make an order under this paragraph, he shall publish in such manner as appears to him to be requisite a notice–
(a) stating the effect of the order; and
(b) specifying the time (not being less than 28 days from the publication of the notice) within which, and the manner in which, objections to the proposal may be made,
and shall serve a like notice–
(i) on the district planning authority (...) in whose area the land is situated; and
(ii) on the relevant highway authority.
In this sub-paragraph 'the relevant highway authority' means any authority which is a highway authority in relation to the right of way proposed to be extinguished by the order, other than an authority which has applied for the order to be made.
(3) Where an objection to a proposal to make an order under this paragraph is duly made and not withdrawn, the provisions of paragraph 12 below shall have effect in relation to the proposal.
(4) For the purposes of this paragraph an objection to such a proposal shall not be treated as duly made unless–
(a) it is made within the time and in the manner specified in the notice required by this paragraph; and
(b) a statement in writing of the grounds of the objection is comprised in or submitted with the objection.
[(5) to (7) not included.]
12. (1) In this paragraph any reference to making a final decision, in relation to an order, is a reference to deciding whether to make the order or what modification, if any, ought to be made.
(2) Unless the Secretary of State decides apart from the objection not to make the order, or decides to make a modification which is agreed to by the objector as meeting the objection, the Secretary of State shall, before making a final decision, consider the grounds of the objection as set out in the statement

comprised in or submitted with the objection, and may, if he thinks fit, require the objector to submit within a specified period a further statement in writing as to any of the matters which the objection relates.

(3) In so far as the Secretary of State, after considering the grounds of the objection as set out in the original statement and in any such further statement, is satisfied that the objection relates to a matter which can be dealt with in the assessment of compensation, the Secretary of State may treat the objection as irrelevant for the purpose of making a final decision.

(4) If, after considering the grounds of the objection as set out in the original statement and in any further statement, the Secretary of State is satisfied that, for the purpose of making a final decision, he is sufficiently informed as to the matters to which the objection relates, or if, where a further statement has been required, it is not submitted within the specified period, the Secretary of State may make a final decision without further investigation as to those matters.

(5) Subject to sub-paragraphs (3) and (4) above, the Secretary of State, before making a final decision, shall afford to the objector an opportunity of appearing before, and being heard by, a person appointed for the purpose by the Secretary of State; and if the objector avails himself of that opportunity, the Secretary of State shall afford an opportunity of appearing and being heard on the same occasion to the statutory undertakers, urban development corporation or other person, if any, on whose representation the order is proposed to be made, and to any other persons to whom it appears to the Secretary of State to be expedient to afford such an opportunity.

(6) Notwithstanding anything in the preceding provisions of this paragraph, it appears to the Secretary of State that the matters to which the objection relates are such as to require investigation by public local inquiry before he makes a final decision, he shall cause such an inquiry to be held; and where he determines to cause such an inquiry to be held, any of the requirements of those provisions to which effect has not been given at the time of that determination shall be dispensed with.

Text: p 152

ACQUISITION OF LAND ACT 1981

32. Power to extinguish certain public rights of way

(1) This section applies where land is acquired, or proposed to be acquired–
(a) in pursuance of a compulsory purchase order; or
(b) by agreement for a purpose, and by an authority, such that the compulsory acquisition of the land could be authorised by a compulsory purchase order; and there subsists over any part of the land a public right of way, not being a right enjoyable by vehicular traffic.

(2) If the acquiring authority is satisfied that a suitable alternative right of way has been or will be provided, or that the provision thereof is not required, the acquiring authority may by order extinguish the right of way; and Schedule 6 to the Highways Act 1980 shall have effect as to the making, confirmation, validity and date of operation of any such order.

(3) If the acquiring authority is not the Secretary of State–
(a) the order under subsection (2) above shall not take effect unless confirmed by the Secretary of State, or unless confirmed, as an unopposed order, by the

acquiring authority under paragraph 2(1) of Schedule 6 to the Highways Act 1980 as applied by this section; and
(b) the Secretary of State shall not confirm the order unless satisfied that this section applies, and that a suitable alternative right of way has been or will be provided or that the provision thereof is not required.
(4) The time specified in the order under subsection (2) above as the time from which the right of way is extinguished shall not be earlier than–
(a) confirmation of the order, or if the Secretary of State is the acquiring authority, the making of the order;
(b) if in the exercise of the power conferred by section 11(1) of the Compulsory Purchase Act 1965, or by agreement, the acquiring authority takes possession of the land, the date on which the authority takes possession of the land;
(c) if the acquiring authority does not take possession of the land in exercise of any such power, the date on which the acquisition of the land is completed.
(5) Where a right of way is extinguished under this section at a date before the acquisition of the land is completed, then if at any time thereafter it appears to the acquiring authority that the proposal to acquire the land has been abandoned, the acquiring authority shall by order direct that the right shall revive, without prejudice, however, to the making of a new order extinguishing the right.
[(6) & (6A) not included.]
(7) This section shall not apply where section 251 or 258 of the Town and Country Planning Act 1990 (extinction of public rights of way over land held for planning purposes) applies.
(8) This section applies subject to any provision to the contrary in any other Act and subject in particular to the exclusion of this Part of this Act by:
section 23(3) of the Civil Aviation Act 1949;
section 14(2) of the Civil Aviation Act 1971;
(9) Except as provided in this section nothing in this Act shall be taken to authorise the extinction of any public right of way.
Text: p 152
Amended by Airports Act 1986 Sch 6 and Planning (Consequential Provisions) Act 1990 Sch 2 para 53(3).

33. Land acquired before commencement of this Act

(1) In section 32 above 'compulsory purchase order' includes–
(a) a compulsory purchase order under the Acquisition of Land (Authorisation Procedures) Act 1946; and
(b) an authorisation under section 2 of that Act (which was repealed by the Statute Law Revision Act 1953).
(2) Section 32 above shall apply in relation to land acquired before the commencement of the said Act of 1946 by a local authority, being–
(a) land acquired compulsorily under any public general Act in force immediately before the commencement of the said Act of 1946 other than–
(i) the Light Railways Acts 1896 and 1912;
(ii) Part III of the Housing Act 1936;
(iii) the Town and Country Planning Act 1944; or
(b) land acquired by agreement for a purpose such that the land could have been so acquired compulsorily.

ACQUISITION OF LAND ACT 1981
Text: p 152
The Public Path Orders and Extinguishment of Public Right of Way Orders Regulations 1983 (SI 1983 No 23) (p 460) apply to orders made under s 32.

ANIMAL HEALTH ACT 1981

23. Orders as to infected places and areas
The Ministers may make such orders as they think fit, subject and according to the provisions of this Act, for all or any of the following purposes–
(...)
(b) for prohibiting or regulating the movement of animals and persons into, within, or out of an infected place or area;
(...)

27. Exclusion of strangers
(1) A person owning or having charge of any animals in a place or area declared infected with any disease may affix, at or near the entrance of a building or enclosure in which the animals are, a notice forbidding persons to enter the building or enclosure without the permission mentioned in the notice.
(2) Thereupon it shall not be lawful for any person, not having by law a right of entry or way into, on, or over that building or enclosure, to enter to go into, on, or over the building or enclosure without that permission.
Text: p 166

NEW TOWNS ACT 1981

23. Extinguishment of public rights of way
(1) Where any land–
(a) has been acquired for the purposes of this Act by a development corporation or local highway authority and is for the time being held by that corporation or authority for those purposes, or
(b) has been acquired under this Act by the Secretary of State and is for the time being held for the purposes for which he acquired it,
the Secretary of State may by order extinguish any public right of way over the land.
(2) Where the Secretary of State proposes to make an order under this section, he shall publish in such manner as appears to him to be requisite a notice–
(a) stating the effect of the order, and
(b) specifying the time (not being less than 28 days from the publication of the notice) within which and the manner in which, objections to the proposal may be made,
and shall serve a like notice–
(i) on the district planning authority in whose area the land is situated; and
(ii) on the relevant highway authority.
In this subsection 'the relevant highway authority' means any authority who are a highway authority in relation to the right of way proposed to be extinguished by the order, other than an authority who have applied for the order to be made.
(3) Where an objection to a proposal to make an order under this section is duly made and is not withdrawn, Schedule 8 to this Act shall have effect in relation to the proposal.

RIGHTS OF WAY

(4) For the purposes of this section an objection to such a proposal shall not be treated as duly made unless–
(a) it is made within the time and in the manner specified in the notice required by this section; and
(b) a statement in writing of the grounds of the objection is comprised in or submitted with the objection.
[Subsections (5) to (7) not included.]

Schedule 8
1. In this Schedule, 'the relevant Minister' means–
(a) in relation to an order under section 23 above, the Secretary of State,
[(b) and (c) not included.]
and any reference to making a final decision, in relation to an order, is a reference to deciding whether to make the order or what modification, if any, ought to be made.
2. Unless the relevant Minister decides apart from the objection not to make the order, or decides to make a modification which is agreed to by the objector as meeting the objection, the relevant Minister–
(a) shall, before making a final decision, consider the grounds of the objection as set out in the statement comprised in or submitted with the objection, and
(b) may, if he thinks fit, require the objector to submit within a specified period a further statement in writing as to any of the matters to which the objection relates.
[Paragraph 3 not included.]
4. If–
(a) after considering the grounds of the objection as set out in the original statement and in any such further statement, the relevant Minister is satisfied that, for the purpose of making a final decision, he is sufficiently informed as to the matters to which the objection relates, or
(b) where a further statement has been required, it is not submitted within the specified period,
the relevant Minister may make a final decision without further investigation as to those matters.
5. Subject to paragraphs 3 and 4 above, the relevant Minister–
(a) shall, before making a final decision, afford to the objector an opportunity of appearing before, and being heard by, a person appointed for the purpose by the relevant Minister; and
(b) shall, if the objector avails himself of that opportunity, afford an opportunity of appearing and being heard on the same occasion–
(i) to the statutory undertakers, development corporation or other person, if any, on whose representation the order is proposed to be made; and
(ii) to any other persons to whom it appears to the relevant Minister to be expedient to afford such an opportunity.
6. (1) Notwithstanding anything in the foregoing provisions of this Schedule, if it appears to the relevant Minister that the matters to which the objection relates are such as to require investigation by public local inquiry before he makes a final decision, he shall cause such an inquiry to be held.
(2) Where the relevant Minister determines to cause such an inquiry to be held, any of the requirements of those provisions to which effect has not been given at the time of that determination shall be dispensed with.
Text: p 152

WILDLIFE AND COUNTRYSIDE ACT 1981

53. Duty to keep definitive map and statement under continuous review

(1) In this Part 'definitive map and statement', in relation to any area, means, subject to section 57(3),–
(a) the latest revised map and statement prepared in definitive form for that area under section 33 of the 1949 Act; or
(b) where no such map and statement have been so prepared, the original definitive map and statement prepared for that area under section 32 of that Act; or
(c) where no such map and statement have been so prepared, the map and statement prepared for that area under section 55(3).
(2) As regards every definitive map and statement, the surveying authority shall–
(a) as soon as reasonably practicable after the commencement date, by order make such modifications to the map and statement as appear to them to be requisite in consequence of the occurrence, before that date, of any of the events specified in subsection (3); and
(b) as from that date, keep the map and statement under continuous review and as soon as reasonably practicable after the occurrence on or after that date, of any of those events, by order make such modifications to the map and statement as appear to them to be requisite in consequence of the occurrence of that event.
(3) The events referred to in subsection (2) are as follows–
(a) the coming into operation of any enactment or instrument, or any other event, whereby–
(i) a highway shown or required to be shown in the map and statement has been authorised to be stopped up, diverted, widened or extended;
(ii) a highway shown or required to be shown in the map and statement as a highway of a particular description has ceased to be a highway of that description; or
(iii) a new right of way has been created over land in the area to which the map relates, being a right of way such that the land over which the right subsists is a public path;
(b) the expiration, in relation to any way in the area to which the map relates, of any period such that the enjoyment by the public of the way during that period raises a presumption that the way has been dedicated as a public path;
(c) the discovery by the authority of evidence which (when considered with all other relevant evidence available to them) shows–
(i) that a right of way which is not shown in the map and statement subsists or is reasonably alleged to subsist over land in the area to which the map relates, being a right of way to which this Part applies;
(ii) that a highway shown in the map and statement as a highway of a particular description ought to be there shown as a highway of a different description; or
(iii) that there is no public right of way over land shown in the map and statement as a highway of any description, or any other particulars contained in the map and statement require modification.
(4) The modifications which may be made by an order under subsection (2) shall include the addition to the statement of particulars as to–

RIGHTS OF WAY

(a) the position and width of any public path or byway open to all traffic which is or is to be shown on the map; and
(b) any limitations or conditions affecting the public right of way thereover.
(5) Any person may apply to the authority for an order under subsection (2) which makes such modifications as appear to the authority to be requisite in consequence of the occurrence of one or more events falling within paragraph (b) or (c) of subsection (3); and the provisions of Schedule 14 shall have effect as to the making and determination of applications under this subsection.
(6) Orders under subsection (2) which make only such modifications as appear to the authority to be requisite in consequence of the occurrence of one or more events falling within paragraph (a) of subsection (3) shall take effect on their being made; and the provisions of Schedule 15 shall have effect as to the making, validity and date of coming into operation of other orders under subsection (2).
Text: p 91, 99, 222

54. Duty to reclassify roads used as public paths

(1) As regards every definitive map and statement, the surveying authority shall, as soon as reasonably practicable after the commencement date,–
(a) carry out a review of such of the particulars contained in the map and statement as relate to roads used as public paths; and
(b) by order make such modifications to the map and statement as appear to the authority to be requisite to give effect to subsections (2) and (3);
and the provisions of Schedule 15 shall have effect as to the making, validity and date of coming into operation of orders under the subsection.
(2) A definitive map and statement shall show every road used as a public path by one of the three following descriptions, namely–
(a) a byway open to all traffic;
(b) a bridleway;
(c) a footpath;
and shall not employ the expression 'road used as a public path' to describe any way.
(3) A road used as a public path shall be shown in the definitive map and statement as follows–
(a) if a public right of way for vehicular traffic has been shown to exist, as a byway open to all traffic;
(b) if paragraph (a) does not apply and public bridleway rights have not been shown not to exist, as a bridleway; and
(c) if neither paragraph (a) nor paragraph (b) applies, as a footpath.
(4) Each way which, in pursuance of an order under subsection (1), is shown in the map and statement by any of the three descriptions shall, as from the coming into operation of the order, be a highway maintainable at the public expense; and each way which, in pursuance of paragraph 9 of Part III of Schedule 3 to the 1968 Act, is so shown shall continue to be so maintainable.
(5) In this section 'road used as a public path' means a way which is shown in the definitive map and statement as a road used as a public path.
(6) In subsections (2)(a) and (5) of section 51 of the 1949 Act (long distance routes) references to roads used as public paths shall include references to any way shown in a definitive map and statement as a byway open to all traffic.
(7) Nothing in this section or section 53 shall limit the operation of traffic orders under the Road Traffic Regulation Act 1984 or oblige a highway authority to

WILDLIFE AND COUNTRYSIDE ACT 1981

provide, on a way shown in a definitive map and statement as a byway open to all traffic, a metalled carriage-way or a carriage-way which is by any other means provided with a surface suitable for the passage of vehicles.
Text: p 87, 98, 222
Amended by Road Traffic Regulation Act 1984 Sch 13 para 53.

55. No further surveys or reviews under the 1949 Act
(1) No survey under sections 27 to 32 of the 1949 Act, or review under section 33 of that Act, shall be begun after the commencement date; and where on that date a surveying authority have not completed such a survey or review begun earlier, the Secretary of State may, after consultation with the authority, direct the authority–
(a) to complete the survey or review; or
(b) to abandon the survey or review to such extent as may be specified in the direction.
(2) Where such a survey or review so begun is abandoned, the Secretary of State shall give such notice of the abandonment as appears to him requisite.
(3) Where, in relation to any area, no such survey has been so begun or such a survey so begun is abandoned, the surveying authority shall prepare for that area a map and statement such that, when they have been modified in accordance with the provisions of this Part, they will serve as the definitive map and statement for that area.
(4) Where such a survey so begun is abandoned after a draft map and statement have been prepared and the period for making representations or objections has expired, the authority shall by order modify the map and statement prepared under subsection (3) so as–
(a) to give effect to any determination or decision of the authority under section 29(3) or (4) of the 1949 Act in respect of which either there is no right of appeal or no notice of appeal has been duly served;
(b) to give effect to any decision of the Secretary of State under section 29(6) of that Act; and
(c) to show any particulars shown in the draft map and statement with respect to which no representation or objection has been duly made, or in relation to which all such representations or objections has been withdrawn.
(5) Where such a review so begun is abandoned after a draft map and statement have been prepared and the period for making representations or objections has expired, the authority shall by order modify the map and statement under review so as–
(a) to give effect to any decision of the Secretary of State under paragraph 4(4) of Part II of Schedule 3 to the 1968 Act; and
(b) to show any particulars shown in the draft map and statement but not in the map and statement under review, and to omit any particulars shown in the map and statement under review but not in the draft map and statement, being (in either case) particulars with respect to which no representation or objection has been duly made, or in relation to which all such representations or objections have been withdrawn.
(6) Orders under subsection (4) or (5) shall take effect on their being made.
Text: p 90

56. Effect of definitive map and statement
(1) A definitive map and statement shall be conclusive evidence as to the particulars contained therein to the following extent, namely–

(a) where the map shows a footpath, the map shall be conclusive evidence that there was at the relevant date a highway as shown on the map, and that the public had thereover a right of way on foot, so however that this paragraph shall be without prejudice to any question whether the public had at that date any right of way other than that right;
(b) where the map shows a bridleway, the map shall be conclusive evidence that there was at the relevant date a highway as shown on the map, and that the public had thereover at that date a right of way on foot and a right of way on horseback or leading a horse, so however that this paragraph shall be without prejudice to any question whether the public had at that date any right of way other than those rights;
(c) where the map shows a byway open to all traffic, the map shall be conclusive evidence that there was at the relevant date a highway as shown on the map, and that the public had thereover at that date a right of way for vehicular and all other kinds of traffic;
(d) where the map shows a road used as a public path, the map shall be conclusive evidence that there was at the relevant date a highway as shown on the map, and that the public had thereover at that date a right of way on foot and a right of way on horseback or leading a horse, so however that this paragraph shall be without prejudice to any question whether the public had at that date any right of way other than those rights; and
(e) where by virtue of the foregoing paragraphs the map is conclusive evidence, as at any date, as to a highway shown thereon, any particulars contained in the statement as to the position or width thereof shall be conclusive evidence as to the position or width thereof at that date, and any particulars so contained as to limitations or conditions affecting the public right of way shall be conclusive evidence that at the said date the said right was subject to those limitations or conditions, but without prejudice to any question whether the right was subject to any other limitations or conditions at that date.
(2) For the purposes of this section 'the relevant date'–
(a) in relation to any way which is shown on the map otherwise than in pursuance of an order under the foregoing provisions of this Part, means the date specified in the statement as the relevant date for the purposes of the map;
(b) in relation to any way which is shown on the map in pursuance of such an order, means the date which, in accordance with subsection (3), is specified in the order as the relevant date for the purposes of the order.
(3) Every order under the foregoing provisions of this Part shall specify, as the relevant date for the purposes of the order, such date, not being earlier than six months before the making of the order, as the authority may determine.
(4) A document purporting to be certified on behalf of the surveying authority to be a copy of or of any part of a definitive map or statement as modified in accordance with the provisions of this Part shall be receivable in evidence and shall be deemed, unless the contrary is shown, to be such a copy.
(5) Where it appears to the Secretary of State that paragraph (d) of subsection (1) can have no further application, he may by order made by statutory instrument repeal that paragraph.
Text: p 81, 90, 174

57. Supplementary provisions as to definitive maps and statements
(1) An order under the foregoing provisions of this Part shall be in such form as may be prescribed by regulations made by the Secretary of State, and shall

contain a map, on such scale as may be so prescribed, showing the modifications to which the order relates.

(2) Regulations made by the Secretary of State may prescribe the scale on which maps are to be prepared under section 55(3), and the method of showing in definitive maps and statements anything which is required to be so shown.

(3) Where, in the case of a definitive map and statement for any area which have been modified in accordance with the foregoing provisions of this Part, it appears to the surveying authority expedient to do so, they may prepare a copy of that map and statement as so modified; and where they do so, the map and statement so prepared, and not the map and statement so modified, shall be regarded for the purposes of the foregoing provisions of this Part as the definitive map and statement for that area.

(4) The statement prepared under subsection (3) shall specify, as the relevant date for the purposes of the map, such date, not being earlier than six months before the preparation of the map and statement, as the authority may determine.

(5) As regards every definitive map and statement, the surveying authority shall keep–
(a) a copy of the map and statement; and
(b) copies of all orders under this Part modifying the map and statement,
available for inspection free of charge at all reasonable hours at one or more places in each district comprised in the area to which the map and statement relate and, so far as appears practicable to the surveying authority, a place in each parish so comprised; and the authority shall be deemed to comply with the requirement to keep such copies available for inspection in a district or parish if they keep available for inspection there a copy of so much of the map and statement and copies of so many of the orders as relate to the district or parish.

(6) Notwithstanding anything in subsection (5), an authority shall not be required to keep available for inspection more than one copy of–
(a) any definitive map and statement; or
(b) each order under this Part modifying the map and statement,
if, as respects the area to which that map and statement relate, a subsequent map and statement have been prepared under subsection (3); and the said single copies may be kept in such place in the area of the authority as they may determine.

(7) Every surveying authority shall take such steps as they consider expedient for bringing to the attention of the public the provisions of this Part including, in particular, section 53(5) and subsection (5).

(8) Regulations under this section shall be made by statutory instrument which shall be subject to annulment in pursuance of a resolution of either House of Parliament.

Text: p 104, 135
The regulations are the Wildlife and Countryside (Definitive Maps and Statements) Regulations 1983 SI 1983 No 21 (p 445).

58. Application of ss 52 to 57 to inner London

(1) Subject to subsection (2), the foregoing provisions of this Part shall not apply to any area to which this subsection applies; and this subsection applies to any area which, immediately before 1st April 1965, formed part of the administrative county of London.

RIGHTS OF WAY

(2) A London borough council may by resolution adopt the said foregoing provisions as respects any part of their area specified in the resolution, being a part to which subsection (1) applies, and those provisions shall thereupon apply accordingly.

(3) Where by virtue of a resolution under subsection (2), the said foregoing provisions apply to any area, those provisions shall have effect in relation thereto as if for references to the commencement date there were substituted references to the date on which the resolution comes into operation.

Text: p 36, 91

59. Prohibition on keeping bulls on land crossed by public rights of way

(1) If, in a case not falling within subsection (2), the occupier of a field or enclosure crossed by a right of way to which this Part applies permits a bull to be at large in the field or enclosure, he shall be liable on summary conviction to a fine not exceeding level 3 on the standard scale.

(2) Subsection (1) shall not apply to any bull which—
(a) does not exceed the age of ten months; or
(b) is not of a recognised dairy breed and is at large in any field or enclosure in which cows or heifers are also at large.

(3) Nothing in any byelaws, whenever made, shall make unlawful any act which is, or but for subsection (2) would be, made unlawful by subsection (1).

(4) In this section 'recognised dairy breed' means one of the following breeds, namely, Ayrshire, British Friesian, British Holstein, Dairy Shorthorn, Guernsey, Jersey and Kerry.

(5) The Secretary of State may by order add any breed to, or remove any breed from, subsection (4); and an order under this subsection shall be made by statutory instrument which shall be subject to annulment in pursuance of a resolution of either House of Parliament.

Text: p 184

62. Appointment of wardens for public rights of way

A local authority may appoint such number of persons as appears to the authority to be necessary or expedient to act as wardens as respects a footpath, bridleway or byway open to all traffic which is both in the countryside and in the area of the authority, and the purpose for which the wardens may be so appointed is to advise and assist the public in connection with the use of the path or way.

Text: p 44

66. Interpretation of Part III (sections 53 to 66)

(1) In this Part—
'bridleway' means a highway over which the public have the following, but no other, rights of way, that is to say, a right of way on foot and a right of way on horseback or leading a horse, with or without a right to drive animals of any description along the highway;
'byway open to all traffic' means a highway over which the public have a right of way for vehicular and all other kinds of traffic, but which is used by the public mainly for the purpose for which footpaths and bridleways are so used;
'definitive map and statement' has the meaning given by section 53(1);

WILDLIFE AND COUNTRYSIDE ACT 1981

'footpath' means a highway over which the public have a right of way on foot only, other than such a highway at the side of a public road;
'horse' includes a pony, ass and mule, and 'horseback' shall be construed accordingly;
'public path' means a highway being either a footpath or a bridleway;
'right of way to which this Part applies' means a right of way such that the land over which the right subsists is a public path or a byway open to all traffic;
'surveying authority', in relation to any area, means the county, metropolitan district or London borough council whose area includes that area.
(2) A highway at the side of a river, canal or other inland navigation shall not be excluded from any definition contained in subsection (1) by reason only that the public have a right to use the highway for purposes of navigation, if the highway would fall within that definition if the public had no such right thereover.
(3) The provisions of section 30(1) of the 1968 Act (riding of pedal cycles on bridleways) shall not affect the definition of bridleway in subsection (1) and any rights exercisable by virtue of those provisions shall be disregarded for the purposes of this Part.
Text: p 81, 200
Amended by LGA 85 Sch 3 para 7(6).

70A. Service of notices

(1) Subject to subsection (2), section 329 of the Town and Country Planning Act 1990 (...) (which provide for the service of notices and other documents) shall apply to notices and other documents required or authorised to be served or given under this Act.
(2) Subsections (2) and (3) of the said section 329 shall not apply to a notice required to be served under paragraph 2 of Schedule 14.
(3) This section shall not affect the operation of (...) paragraph 3(4) of Schedule 15.
Inserted by Wildlife and Countryside (Service of Notices) Act 1985 s 1, amended by Planning (Consequential Provisions) Act 1990 Sch 2 para 54(2).
TCPA 90 s 329 : p 439

71. General Interpretation

In this Act:
'the 1949 Act' means the National Parks and Access to the Countryside Act 1949;
'the 1968 Act' means the Countryside Act 1968;
'the commencement date', in relation to any provision of this Act and any area, means the date of the coming into force of that provision in that area;
'modifications' includes additions, alterations and omissions, and cognate expressions shall be construed accordingly;
(...)

Schedule 14: Applications for certain orders under Part III:

Form of applications
1. An application shall be made in the prescribed form and shall be accompanied by:

(a) a map drawn to the prescribed scale and showing the way or ways to which the application relates; and
(b) copies of any documentary evidence (including statements of witnesses) which the applicant wishes to adduce in support of the application.

Notice of applications
2. (1) Subject to sub-paragraph (2), the applicant shall serve a notice stating that the application has been made on every owner and occupier of any land to which the application relates.
(2) If, after reasonable inquiry has been made, the authority are satisfied that it is not practicable to ascertain the name or address of an owner or occupier of any land to which the application relates, the authority may direct that the notice required to be served on him by sub-paragraph (1) may be served by addressing it to him by the description 'owner' or 'occupier' of the land (describing it) and by affixing it to some conspicuous object or objects on the land.
(3) When the requirements of this paragraph have been complied with, the applicant shall certify that fact to the authority.
(4) Every notice or certificate under this paragraph shall be in the prescribed form.

Determination by authority
3. (1) As soon as reasonably practicable after receiving a certificate under paragraph 2(3), the authority shall:
(a) investigate the matters stated in the application; and
(b) after consulting with every local authority whose area includes the land to which the application relates, decide whether to make or not to make the order to which the application relates.
(2) If the authority have not determined the application within twelve months of their receiving a certificate under paragraph 2(3), then, on the applicant making representations to the Secretary of State, the Secretary of State may, after consulting with the authority, direct the authority to determine the application before the expiration of such period as may be specified in the direction.
(3) As soon as practicable after determining the application, the authority shall give notice of their decision by serving a copy of it on the applicant and any person on whom notice of the application was required to be served under paragraph 2(1).

Appeal against a decision not to make an order
4. (1) Where the authority decide not to make an order, the applicant may, at any time within 28 days after service on him of notice of the decision, serve notice of appeal against that decision on the Secretary of State and the authority.
(2) If on considering the appeal the Secretary of State considers that an order should be made, he shall give to the authority such directions as appear to him necessary for the purpose.

Interpretation
5. (1) In this Schedule–
'application' means an application under section 53(5);
'local authority' means a non-metropolitan district council, a parish or com-

munity council or the parish meeting of a parish not having a separate parish council;
'prescribed' means prescribed by regulations made by the Secretary of State.
(2) Regulations under this Schedule shall be made by statutory instrument which shall be subject to annulment in pursuance of a resolution of either House of Parliament.
Text: p 99
Amended by LGA 85 Sch 3 para 7(8). The Regulations are the Wildlife and Countryside (Definitive Maps and Statements) Regulations 1983 SI 1983 No 21 (p 445).

Schedule 15: Procedure in connection with certain orders under Part III
Consultation
1. Before making an order, the authority shall consult with every local authority whose area includes the land to which the order relates.

Coming into operation
2. An order shall not take effect until confirmed either by the authority or the Secretary of State under paragraph 6 or by the Secretary of State under paragraph 7.

Publicity for orders
3. (1) On making an order, the authority shall give notice in the prescribed form–
(a) describing the general effect of the order and stating that it has been made and requires confirmation;
(b) naming a place in the area in which the land to which the order relates is situated where a copy of the order may be inspected free of charge, and copies thereof may be obtained at a reasonable charge, at all reasonable hours; and
(c) specifying the time (not being less than 42 days from the date of the first publication of the notice) within which, and the manner in which, representations or objections with respect to the order may be made.
(2) Subject to sub-paragraph (4), the notice to be given under sub-paragraph (1) shall be given–
(a) by publication in at least one local newspaper circulating in the area in which the land to which the order relates is situated;
(b) by serving a like notice on–
(i) every owner and occupier of any of that land;
(ii) every local authority whose area includes any of that land;
(iii) every person on whom notice is required to be served in pursuance of sub-paragraph (3); and
(iv) such other persons as may be prescribed in relation to the area in which that land is situated or as the authority may consider appropriate; and
(c) by causing a copy of the notice to be displayed in a prominent position–
(i) at the ends of so much of any way as is affected by the order;
(ii) at council offices in the locality of the land to which the order relates; and
(iii) at such other places as the authority may consider appropriate.
(3) Any person may, on payment of such reasonable charge as the authority may consider appropriate, require an authority to give him notice of all such

orders as are made by the authority during a specified period, are of a specified description and relate to land comprised in a specified area; and in this sub-paragraph 'specified' means specified in the requirement.

(4) The Secretary of State may, in any particular case, direct that it shall not be necessary to comply with sub-paragraph (2)(b)(i); but if he so directs in the case of any land, then in addition to publication the notice shall be addressed to 'The owners and any occupiers' of the land (describing it) and a copy or copies of the notice shall be affixed to some conspicuous object or objects on the land.

(5) Sub-paragraph (2)(b) and (c) and, where applicable, sub-paragraph (4) shall be complied with not less than 42 days before the expiration of the time specified in the notice.

(6) A notice required to be served by sub-paragraph 2(b) on the owner or occupier of any land, or on a local authority, shall be accompanied by a copy of so much of the order as relates to that land or, as the case may be, the area of that authority; and a notice required to be served by that sub-paragraph on such other persons as may be prescribed or as the authority may consider appropriate shall be accompanied by a copy of the order.

(7) A notice required to be displayed by sub-paragraph (2)(c) at the ends of so much of any way as is affected by the order shall be accompanied by a plan showing the general effect of the order so far as it relates to that way.

(8) At any time after the publication of a notice under this paragraph and before the expiration of the period specified in the notice for the making of representations and objections, any person may require the authority to inform him what documents (if any) were taken into account in preparing the order and–
(a) as respects any such documents in the possession of the authority, to permit him to inspect them and take copies; and
(b) as respects any such documents not in their possession, to give him any information the authority have as to where the documents can be inspected;
and on any requirement being made under this sub-paragraph the authority shall comply therewith within 14 days of the making of the requirement.

(9) Nothing in sub-paragraph (8) shall be construed as limiting the documentary or other evidence which may be adduced at any local inquiry or hearing held under paragraph 7 or 8.

Representations or objections made with respect to abandoned surveys or reviews

4. (1) This paragraph applies where a survey begun under sections 27 to 32 of the 1949 Act, or a review begun under section 33 of that Act, is abandoned after a draft map and statement have been prepared.

(2) If an order modifies the definitive map and statement so as–
(a) to show any particulars shown in the draft map and statement but not in the definitive map and statement; or
(b) to omit any particulars shown in the definitive map and statement but not in the draft map and statement,
any representation or objection duly made with respect to the showing in or omission from the draft map and statement of those particulars shall be treated for the purposes of paragraphs 6 and 7 as a representation or objection duly made with respect to the corresponding modifications made by the order.

Severance of orders

5. (1) Where at any time representations or objections duly made and not withdrawn relate to some but not all of the modifications made by an order, the authority may, by notice given to the Secretary of State, elect that, for the purposes of the following provisions of this Schedule, the order shall have effect as two separate orders–
(a) the one comprising the modifications to which the objections or representations relate; and
(b) the other comprising the remaining modifications.
(2) Any reference in sub-paragraph (1) to an order includes a reference to any part of an order which, by virtue or one or more previous elections under that sub-paragraph, has effect as a separate order.

Unopposed orders

6. (1) If no representations or objections are duly made, or if any so made are withdrawn, the authority may:
(a) confirm the order without modification; or
(b) if they require any modification to be made, submit the order to the Secretary of State for confirmation by him.
(2) Where an order is submitted to the Secretary of State under sub-paragraph (1), the Secretary of State may confirm the order with or without modifications.

Opposed orders

7. (1) If any representation or objection duly made is not withdrawn the authority shall submit the order to the Secretary of State for confirmation by him.
(2) Where an order is submitted to the Secretary of State under sub-paragraph (1), the Secretary of State shall either–
(a) cause a local inquiry to be held; or
(b) afford any person by whom a representation or objection has been duly made and not withdrawn an opportunity of being heard by a person appointed by the Secretary of State for the purpose.
(3) On considering any representations or objections duly made and the report of the person appointed to hold the inquiry or hear representations or objections, the Secretary of State may confirm the order with or without modifications.

Restriction on power to confirm orders with modifications

8. (1) The Secretary of State shall not confirm an order with modifications so as–
(a) to affect land not affected by the order;
(b) not to show any way shown in the order or to show any way not so shown; or
(c) to show as a highway of one description a way which is shown in the order as a highway of another description,
except after complying with the requirements of sub-paragraph (2).
(2) The said requirements are that the Secretary of State shall–
(a) give such notice as appears to him requisite of his proposal so to modify the order, specifying the time (which shall be not less than 28 days from the date of the first publication of the notice) within which, and the manner in which, representations or objections with respect to the proposals may be made;

(b) hold a local inquiry or afford any person by whom any representation or objection has been duly made and not withdrawn an opportunity of being heard by a person appointed by the Secretary of State for the purpose; and
(c) consider the report of the person appointed to hold the inquiry or to hear representations or objections.

Local inquiries
9. The provisions of subsections (2) to (5) of section 250 of the Local Government Act 1972 (which relate to the giving of evidence at, and defraying the cost of, local inquiries) shall apply in relation to any inquiry held under paragraph 7 or 8 as they apply in relation to a local inquiry which a Minister causes to be held under subsection (1) of that section.

Appointment of inspectors etc.
10. (1) A decision of the Secretary of State under paragraph 6, 7 or 8 shall, except in such classes of case as may for the time being be prescribed or as may be specified in directions given by the Secretary of State, be made by a person appointed by the Secretary of State for the purpose instead of by the Secretary of State; and a decision made by a person so appointed shall be treated as a decision of the Secretary of State.
(2) The Secretary of State may, if he thinks fit, direct that a decision which, by virtue of sub-paragraph (1) and apart from this sub-paragraph, falls to be made by a person appointed by the Secretary of State shall instead be made by the Secretary of State; and a direction under this sub-paragraph shall state the reasons for which it is given and shall be served on the person, if any, so appointed, the authority and any person by whom a representation or objection has been duly made and not withdrawn.
(3) Where the Secretary of State has appointed a person to make a decision under paragraph 6, 7 or 8, the Secretary of State may, at any time before the making of the decision, appoint another person to make it instead of the person first appointed to make it.
(4) Where by virtue of sub-paragraph (2) or (3) a particular decision falls to be made by the Secretary of State or any other person instead of the person first appointed to make it, anything done by or in relation to the latter shall be treated as having been done by or in relation to the former.
(5) Regulations under this paragraph may provide for the giving of publicity to any directions given by the Secretary of State under this paragraph.

Notice of final decisions on orders
11. (1) As soon as practicable after a decision to confirm an order is made or, in the case of a decision by the Secretary of State, as soon as practicable after receiving notice of his decision, the authority shall give notice–
(a) describing the general effect of the order as confirmed and stating that it has been confirmed (with or without modification) and the date on which it took effect; and
(b) naming a place in the area in which the land to which the order relates is situated where a copy of the order as confirmed may be inspected free of charge, and copies thereof may be obtained at a reasonable charge, at all reasonable hours.

WILDLIFE AND COUNTRYSIDE ACT 1981

(2) A notice under sub-paragraph (1) shall be given–
(a) by publication in the manner required by paragraph 3(2)(a);
(b) by serving a like notice on all persons on whom notices were required to be served under paragraph 3(2)(b) or (4); and
(c) by causing like notices to be displayed in the like manner as the notices required to be displayed under paragraph 3(2)(c).
(3) A notice required to be served by sub-paragraph (2)(b) on the owner or occupier of any land, or on a local authority, shall be accompanied by a copy of so much of the order as confirmed as relates to that land or, as the case may be, the area of that authority; and, in the case of an order which has been confirmed with modifications, a notice required to be served by that sub-paragraph on such other persons as may be prescribed or as the authority may consider appropriate shall be accompanied by a copy of the order as confirmed.
(4) As soon as practicable after a decision not to confirm an order or, in the case of a decision by the Secretary of State, as soon as practicable after receiving notice of his decision, the authority shall give notice of the decision by serving a copy of it on any persons on whom notices were required to be served under paragraph 3(2)(b) or (4).

Proceedings for questioning validity of orders
12. (1) If any person is aggrieved by an order which has taken effect and desires to question its validity on the ground that it is not within the powers of section 53 or 54 or that any of the requirements of this Schedule have not been complied with in relation to it, he may within 42 days from the date of publication of the notice under paragraph 11 make an application to the High Court under this paragraph.
(2) On any such application the High Court may, if satisfied that the order is not within those powers or that the interests of the applicant have been substantially prejudiced by a failure to comply with those requirements, quash the order, or any provision of the order, either generally or in so far as it affects the interests of the applicant.
(3) Except as provided by this paragraph, the validity of any order shall not be questioned in any legal proceedings whatsoever.

Supplemental
13. (1) The Secretary of State may, subject to the provisions of this Schedule, by regulations make such provision as to the procedure on the making, submission and confirmation or orders as appears to him to be expedient.
(2) In this Schedule–
'council offices' means offices or buildings acquired or provided by the authority or a local authority;
'local authority' means a non-metropolitan district council, a parish or community council or the parish meeting of a parish not having a separate parish council;
'order' means an order to which the provisions of this Schedule apply;
'prescribed' means prescribed by regulations made by the Secretary of State.
(3) Regulations under this Schedule shall be made by statutory instruments which shall be subject to annulment in pursuance of a resolution of either House of Parliament.
Text: p 91, 94–7

RIGHTS OF WAY

Amended by LGA 85 Sch 3. The Regulations are the Wildlife and Countryside (Definitive Maps and Statements) Regulations 1983 SI 1983 No 21 (p 445).

CIVIL AVIATION ACT 1982

48. Power of Secretary of State to stop up and divert highways, etc in the interests of aviation

(1) (...) the Secretary of State may, if he is satisfied that it is necessary to do so in order to secure the safe and efficient use for civil aviation purposes (including the testing of aircraft designed for civil aviation) of any land vested in the Secretary of State or the CAA, or of any land which the Secretary of State or the CAA proposes to acquire, by order authorise the stopping up or diversion of any highway.
[(2) not included.]
(3) An order under subsection (1) of this section may provide for all or any of the following matters, that is to say:
(a) for securing the provision or improvement of any highway so far as the Secretary of State (...) thinks such provision or improvement necessary or desirable in consequence of any such stopping-up or diversion as aforesaid;
(b) for directing that any highway to be provided or improved in pursuance of the order shall –
(i) in England and Wales, be a highway which for the purposes of the Highways Act 1980 is maintainable at public expense;
[(ii) & (iii) not included.]
[(c)-(g) not included.]
(4) An order under subsection (1) of this section may contain such consequential, incidental and supplemental provisions as appear to the Secretary of State (...) to be necessary or expedient for the purposes of the order.
(5) An order under subsection (1) shall, (...) be subject to special parliamentary procedure; and
(a) if the order was made in respect of land in England and Wales, Schedule 1 to the Statutory Orders (Special Procedure) Act 1945 (which sets out the notices to be given and the other requirements to be complied with before an order is made)
[(b) not included.]
shall apply in relation to the order, but, in their application in relation thereto, shall have effect as if paragraph 1 of the said Schedule 1 (...) included the provisions set out in subsection (6) below.
(6) The said provisions are provisions–
(a) requiring notice of the order as proposed to be made to be displayed in a prominent position at the ends of so much of any highway as is proposed to be stopped up or diverted under the order;
(b) requiring notice of the order as proposed to be made to be sent to every local authority in whose area any highway to be stopped up or diverted under the order, or any highway to be provided or improved under the order, is or will be situated.
[(c) not included.]
(7) In subsection (6) above–
(a) the reference in paragraph (b) to a local authority includes a reference to a parish council in England, to a parish meeting of a parish in England not having

CIVIL AVIATION ACT 1982

a separate council, to a council of a community in Wales and to the community in the case of a community in Wales without a council;
[(b) not included.]
(8) The powers of the Secretary of State (...) under subsection (1) above shall include power to make an order authorising the stopping-up or diversion of any highway which is temporarily stopped up or diverted under any other enactment; and the provisions of this section shall not prejudice any power conferred upon the Secretary of State (...) by any other enactment to authorise the stopping-up or diversion of a highway.
[(9) not included.]
Text: p 151

CYCLE TRACKS ACT 1984

3. Conversion of footpaths into cycle tracks
(1) A local highway may in the case of any footpath for which they are the highway authority by order made by them and either–
(a) submitted to and confirmed by the Secretary of State, or
(b) confirmed by them as an unopposed order,
designate the footpath or any part of it as a cycle track, with the effect that, on such date as the order takes effect in accordance with the following provisions of this section, the footpath or part of the footpath to which the order relates shall become a highway which for the purposes of the 1980 Act is a highway maintainable at public expense and over which the public have a right of way on pedal cycles (other than pedal cycles which are motor vehicles) and a right of way on foot.
(2) A local highway authority shall not make an order under this section designating as a cycle track any footpath or part of a footpath which crosses any agricultural land unless every person having a legal interest in that land has consented in writing to the making of the order.
In this subsection 'agricultural land' has the meaning given by section 1(2) of the Agricultural Holdings Act 1986; and 'legal interest' does not include an interest under a letting of land having effect as a letting for an interest less than a tenancy from year to year.
(3) An order made under this section by a local highway authority–
(a) may be confirmed by the Secretary of State either in the form in which it was made or subject to such modifications as he thinks fit;
(b) may be confirmed by the authority as an unopposed order only in the form in which it was made.
(4) The Secretary of State may make by regulations make provision with respect to the procedure to be followed in connection with the making, submission and confirmation of orders under this section; and the Secretary of State shall by regulations under this subsection make such provision as he considers appropriate with respect to–
(a) the publication of notice of the making of an order under this section and of its effect;
(b) the making and consideration of objections to any such order; and
(c) the publication of notice of the confirmation of any such order by the Secretary of State or by a local highway authority, and of the effect of the order as confirmed.

RIGHTS OF WAY

(5) Without prejudice to the generality of subsection (4) above, regulations under that subsection may in particular make provision–

(a) for enabling the Secretary of State to cause a local inquiry to be held in connection with any order under this section submitted to him for confirmation;

(b) for the decision as to whether any such order should be confirmed, and, if so, as to the modifications (if any) subject to which it should be confirmed, to be made by a person appointed by the Secretary of State for the purpose instead of by the Secretary of State;

(c) for any decision made by any such person in pursuance of paragraph (b) above to be treated, for the purposes of any provision of the regulations or this section, as a decision of the Secretary of State;

and subsections (2) to (5) of section 250 of the Local Government Act 1972 (giving of evidence at, and defraying of costs of, local inquiries) shall apply in relation to any local inquiry held in pursuance of paragraph (a) above as they apply in relation to a local inquiry which a Minister causes to be held under subsection (1) of that section.

(6) If a person aggrieved by an order under this section desires to question its validity on the ground that it is not within the powers of this section or on the ground that any requirement of regulations made under subsection (4) above has not been complied with in relation to the order, he may, within six weeks from the date on which any such notice as is mentioned in subsection (4)(c) above is first published, make an application to the High Court.

(7) On any such application, the High Court–

(a) may by interim order suspend the operation of the order, either wholly or to such extent as it thinks fit, until the final determination of the proceedings; and

(b) if satisfied that the order is not within the powers of the section or that the interests of the applicant have been substantially prejudiced by a failure to comply with any such requirement as aforesaid, may quash the order, either wholly or to such extent as it thinks fit.

(8) Subject to subsection (7) above, an order under this section shall not, either before or after it has been confirmed, be questioned in any legal proceedings whatsoever, and shall take effect on the date on which any such notice as is mentioned in subsection (4)(c) above is first published, or on such later date, if any, as may be specified in the order.

(9) A local highway authority may (subject to and in accordance with the provisions of subsections (3) to (8) above) by order made by them and either–

(a) submitted to and confirmed by the Secretary of State, or

(b) confirmed by them as an unopposed order,

revoke an order made by them under this section with the effect that, on such date as the order takes effect in accordance with those provisions, the way designated by the original order as a cycle track shall revert to being a footpath or a part of a footpath (as the case may be) and, as such, it shall only be maintainable at the public expense for the purposes of the 1980 Act if, prior to the original order taking effect, it constituted a highway so maintainable or, on the order under this subsection taking effect, it forms part of a highway so maintainable.

(10) A local highway authority shall have power to carry out any works necessary for giving effect to an order under this section; and in so far as the carrying out of any such works, or any change in the use of land resulting from any such

order, constitutes development within the meaning of the Town and Country Planning Act 1990, permission for that development shall be deemed to be granted under Part III of that Act.
(11) The power to make regulations under subsection (4) above shall be exercisable by statutory instrument, which shall be subject to annulment in pursuance of a resolution of either House of Parliament.
Text: p 161
Amended by Agricultural Holdings Act 1986 Sch 14 and Planning (Consequential Provisions) Act 1990 Sch 2 para 66. The regulations are the Cycle Tracks Regulations 1984 SI 1984 No 1431 (p 472).

4. Provision of barriers in cycle tracks, etc.
(1) A highway authority may provide and maintain in any cycle track such barriers as they think necessary for the purpose of safeguarding persons using the cycle track.
(2) A highway authority may, in the case of any cycle track which is adjacent to a footpath or footway, provide and maintain such works as they think necessary for the purpose of separating, in the interests of safety, persons using the cycle track from those using the footpath or footway.
(3) A highway authority may alter or remove any works provided by them under subsection (1) or (2) above.
(4) Any reference in this section to a cycle track is a reference to a cycle track constituting or comprised in a highway maintainable at the public expense, and any reference to a footpath or a footway is a reference to a footpath constituting or a footway comprised in such a highway.
Text: p 161

5. Compensation
(1) Where any person suffers damage by reason of the execution by a highway authority of any works under section 3(10) or 4 above, he shall be entitled to recover compensation in respect of that damage from that authority.
(2) Where in consequence of the coming into operation of an order under section 3 above any person suffers damage by the depreciation in value of any interest in land to which he is entitled, he shall be entitled to recover compensation in respect of that damage from the local highway authority which made the order; but a person shall not be entitled to recover any compensation under this subsection in respect of any depreciation–
(a) in respect of which compensation is recoverable by him under subsection (1) above; or
(b) which is attributable to the prospect of the execution of any such works as are referred to in that subsection.
(3) Subsections (1) to (3) of section 307 of the 1980 Act (disputes as to compensation to be referred to Lands Tribunal) shall apply in relation to any dispute arising on a claim for compensation under subsection (1) or (2) above as they apply in relation to any dispute arising as mentioned in subsection (1) of that section.
Text: p 161
HA 80 s 307: p 354

RIGHTS OF WAY

6. Application to Crown land

(1) In the case of any Crown land the appropriate authority and a highway authority may agree that any provisions of sections 3 and 4 above specified in the agreement shall apply to that land and, while the agreement is in force, those provisions shall apply to that land accordingly (subject, however, to the terms of the agreement).

(2) Any such agreement as is referred to in subsection (1) above may contain such consequential and incidental provisions, including provisions of a financial character, as appear to the appropriate authority to be necessary or equitable; but provisions of a financial character shall not be included in an agreement made by a government department without the approval of the Treasury.

(3) In this section 'Crown land' means land belonging to Her Majesty in right of the Crown or of the Duchy of Lancaster, or belonging to the Duchy of Cornwall, or belonging to a government department or held in trust for Her Majesty for the purposes of a government department, and the 'appropriate authority' means–

(a) in the case of land belonging to Her Majesty in right of the Crown, the Crown Estate Commissioners or other government department having the management of the land in question;

(b) in the case of land belonging to Her Majesty in right of the Duchy of Lancaster, the Chancellor of that Duchy;

(c) in the case of land belonging to the Duchy of Cornwall, such person as the Duke of Cornwall, or the possessor for the time being of the Duchy of Cornwall, appoints;

(d) in the case of land belonging to a government department or held in trust for Her Majesty for the purposes of a government department, that department.

(4) If any question arises as to what authority is the appropriate authority in relation to any Crown land that question shall be referred to the Treasury, whose decision shall be final.

Text: p 161

8. Interpretation

(1) In this Act–
'the 1980 Act' means the Highways Act 1980; and
'motor vehicle' means a motor vehicle within the meaning of the Road Traffic Act 1988.

(2) Except where the context otherwise requires, any expression used in this Act which is also used in the 1980 Act has the same meaning as in that Act.

Text: p 161

Amended by Road Traffic (Consequential Provisions) Act 1988 Sch 3 para 26.

OCCUPIERS' LIABILITY ACT 1984

1. Duty of occupier to persons other than his visitors

(1) The rules enacted by this section shall have effect, in place of the rules of the common law, to determine–

(a) whether any duty is owed by a person as occupier of premises to persons other than his visitors in respect of any risk of their suffering injury on the premises by reason of any danger due to the state of the premises or to things done or omitted to be done on them; and

OCCUPIERS' LIABILITY ACT 1984

(b) if so, what that duty is.
(2) For the purposes of this section, the persons who are to be treated respectively as an occupier of any premises (which, for those purposes, include any fixed or moveable structure) and as his visitors are–
(a) any person who owes in relation to the premises the duty referred to in section 2 of the Occupiers' Liability Act 1957 (the common duty of care), and
(b) those who are his visitors for the purposes of that duty.
(3) An occupier of premises owes a duty to another (not being his visitor) in respect of any such risk as is referred to in subsection (1) above if–
(a) he is aware of the danger or has reasonable grounds to believe that it exists;
(b) he knows or has reasonable grounds to believe that the other is in the vicinity of the danger concerned or that he may come into the vicinity of the danger (in either case, whether the other has lawful authority for being in that vicinity or not); and
(c) the risk is one against which, in all the circumstances of the case, he may reasonably be expected to offer the other some protection.
(4) Where, by virtue of this section, an occupier of premises owes a duty to another in respect of such a risk, the duty is to take such care as is reasonable in all the circumstances of the case to give warning of the danger concerned or to discourage persons from incurring the risk.
(5) Any duty owed by virtue of this section in respect of a risk may, in an appropriate case, be discharged by taking such steps as are reasonable in all the circumstances of the case to give warning of the danger concerned or to discourage persons from incurring the risk.
(6) No duty is owed by virtue of this section to any person in respect of risks willingly accepted as his by that person (the question whether a risk was so accepted to be decided on the same principles as in other cases in which one person owes a duty of care to another).
(7) No duty is owed by virtue of this section to persons using the highway, and this section does not affect any duty owed to such persons.
(8) Where a person owes a duty by virtue of this section, he does not, by reason of any breach of the duty, incur any liability in respect of any loss of or danger to property.
(9) In this section–
'highway' means any part of a highway other than a ferry or waterway;
'injury' means anything resulting in death or personal injury, including any disease and any impairment off physical or mental condition; and
'moveable structure' includes any vessel, vehicle or aircraft.
Text: p 51

ROAD TRAFFIC REGULATION ACT 1984

Part I : General provisions for traffic regulation

1. Traffic regulation orders outside Greater London

(1) An order under this section (in this Act referred to as a 'traffic regulation order') may, subject to Parts I to III of Schedule 9 to this Act and to subsection (4) below, be made as respects any road outside Greater London where it appears to the authority making the order that it is expedient to make it–
(a) for avoiding danger to persons or other traffic using the road or any other road or for preventing the likelihood of any such danger arising, or

RIGHTS OF WAY

(b) for preventing damage to the road or to any building on or near the road, or

(c) for facilitating the passage on any road or any other road of any class of traffic (including pedestrians), or

(d) for preventing the use of the road by vehicular traffic of a kind which, or its use by vehicular traffic in a manner which, is unsuitable having regard to the existing character of the road or adjoining property, or

(e) (without prejudice to the generality of paragraph (d) above) for preserving the character of the road in a case where it is specially suitable for use by persons on horseback or on foot, or

(f) for preserving or improving the amenities of the area through which the road runs.

(2) The authority having power to make traffic regulation orders, subject to subsection (3) below, and to section 125 of this Act,–

(a) as respects roads other than trunk roads, shall be the local authority, that is to say, the county council or metropolitan district council in England and Wales (...)

[(b) not included.]

[(3) to (5) not included.]

Text: p 158

Amended by LGA 85 Sch 5 para 4(2).

2. What a traffic regulation order may provide

(1) The provision that may be made by a traffic regulation order is (subject to the following subsections and to sections 3 and 4 of this Act) any provision prohibiting, restricting or regulating the use of a road, or of any part of the width of a road, by vehicular traffic, or by vehicular traffic of any class specified in the order,–

(a) either generally or subject to such exceptions as may be specified in the order or determined in a manner provided for by it, and

(b) subject to such exceptions as may be so specified or determined, either at all times or at times, on days or during periods so specified.

(2) Without prejudice to the generality of subsection (1) above, but subject to section 3 of this Act, the provision that may be made by a traffic regulation order as mentioned in that subsection includes any provision–

(a) requiring vehicular traffic, or vehicular traffic of any class specified in the order, to proceed in a specified direction or prohibiting its so proceeding;

(b) specifying the part of the carriageway to be used by such traffic proceeding in a specified direction;

(c) prohibiting or restricting the waiting of vehicles or the loading and unloading of vehicles;

(d) prohibiting the use of roads by through traffic; or

(e) prohibiting or restricting overtaking.

(3) The provision that may be made by a traffic regulation order also includes provision inhibiting, restricting or regulating the use of a road, or of any part of the width or a road, by, or by any specified class, of pedestrians–

(a) either generally or subject to exceptions specified in the order, and

(b) either at all times or at times, on days or during periods so specified.

[(4) & (5) not included.]

Text: p 159

ROAD TRAFFIC REGULATION ACT 1984

3. Restrictions on traffic regulation orders
(1) Except as provided by subsection (2) below or by section 37 of this Act, a traffic regulation order shall not be made with respect to any road which would have the effect–
(a) of preventing at any time access for pedestrians,
(...)
to any premises situated on or adjacent to the road, or to any other premises accessible for pedestrians, (...) from, and only from, the road.
[(2) & (3) not included.]
Text: p 159

4. Provisions supplementary to ss 2 and 3
(1) A traffic regulation order may make provision for identifying any part of any road to which, or any time at which or period during which, any provision contained in the order is for the time being to apply by means of a traffic sign of a type or character specified in the order (being a type prescribed or character authorised under section 64 of this Act) and for the time being lawfully in place; and for the purposes of any such order so made any such traffic sign placed on and near a road shall be deemed to be lawfully in place unless the contrary is proved.
[(2) & (3) not included.]
Text: p 159

5. Contravention of traffic regulation order
(1) A person who contravenes a traffic regulation order, or who uses a vehicle, or causes or permits a vehicle to be used in contravention of a traffic regulation order, shall be guilty of an offence.
[(2) not included.]
Text: p 159.
Note: maximum penalty is level 3 on the standard scale. (Road Traffic Offenders Act 1988 Sch 2.) A fixed penalty fine may be issued when the offence is committed in respect of a vehicle. (Road Traffic Offenders Act 1988 Pt 3 and Sch 3.)

Part II: Traffic Regulation in Special Cases

14. Temporary prohibition of restriction of traffic on roads
(1) If a highway authority is satisfied that traffic on a road should be restricted or prohibited, by reason that works are being or are proposed to be executed on or near the road, or by reason of the likelihood of danger to the public or of serious damage to the highway, the authority, subject to the following provisions of this section and to sections 15 and 16 of this Act, may by order restrict or prohibit the use of that road, or of any part of it, by vehicles, or by vehicles of any class, or by pedestrians, to such extent and subject to such conditions or exceptions as they may consider necessary.
(2) A highway authority, when considering the question of the making of an order under subsection (1) above, shall have regard to the existence of alternative routes suitable for the traffic which will be affected by the order.
(3) Subject to the following provisions of this section and to sections 15 and 16 of this Act, a highway authority may at any time by notice restrict or prohibit

RIGHTS OF WAY

temporarily the use of a road, or of any part of a road, by vehicles, or by vehicles of any class, or by pedestrians, where, owing to the likelihood of danger to the public or of serious damage to the highway, it appears to them necessary that such a restriction or prohibition should come into force without delay.

(4) The provision that may be made by an order under subsection (1) or a notice under subsection (3) above is–

(a) any such provision as is mentioned in any of subsections (1) to (3) of section 2 of this Act, or

(b) any provision restricting the speed of vehicles;

but no such order or notice shall be made or issued with respect to any road which would have the effect of preventing at any time access for pedestrians to any premises situated on or adjacent to the road, or to any other premises accessible for pedestrians from, and only from, the road.

[(5) & (6) not included.]

(7) An order made or notice issued under this section may suspend any statutory provision of a description which could have been contained in the order or notice, (...) and any such provision (other than one contained in the order or notice) shall have the effect subject to the order or notice.

[(8) not included.]

(9) In this section 'alternative road', in relation to a road as respects which an order is made under subsection (1) or a notice is issued under subsection (3) above, means a road which–

(a) provides an alternative route for traffic diverted from the first-mentioned road or from any other alternative road, or

[(b) not included.]

Text: p 160

15. Duration of orders and notices under s. 14

(1) Subject to subsections (2) to (4) below, an order under section 14 of this Act shall not continue in force for more than three months.

(2) If the Secretary of State gives his consent to any such order continuing in force for a period longer than that authorised under subsection (1) above, the order shall continue in force until the end of such period as may be specified by the Secretary of State in giving his consent.

(3) Where the Secretary of State refuses to give his consent under subsection (2) above, no subsequent order shall, except with the approval of the Secretary of State, be made under section 14 of this Act as respects any length of road to which the previous order related, unless at least three months have expired from the time when the previous order ceased to have effect.

[(4) not included.]

(5) A notice issued under section 14(3) of this Act shall not continue in force for a longer period than 14 days from the date of the notice.

Text: p 160

16. Supplementary provisions as to orders and notices under s. 14

(1) A person who contravenes, or who uses or permits the use of a vehicle in contravention of, a restriction or prohibition imposed under section 14 of this Act shall be guilty of an offence.

(2) The provisions of Schedule 3 to this Act shall have effect as to notifying the exercise or proposed exercise of the powers conferred by section 14 of this Act and otherwise in relation to that section.

ROAD TRAFFIC REGULATION ACT 1984

(3) The functions of a highway authority under section 14 of this Act shall, in the case of a road which includes a length for the maintenance of which no highway authority is responsible, extend to that length as well as to the road for the maintenance of which the highway authority is responsible.
[(4) not included.]
Text: p 160
Note: maximum penalty is level 3 on the standard scale. (Road Traffic Offenders Act 1988 Sch 2.) A fixed penalty fine may be issued when the offence is committed in respect of a vehicle. (Road Traffic Offenders Act 1988 Pt 3 and Sch 3.)

22. Traffic regulation for special areas in the countryside
(1) This section applies to roads of the following descriptions, that is to say–
(a) in the case of England and Wales (other than Greater London) roads in, or forming part of, or adjacent to or contiguous with–
(i) a National Park,
(ii) an area of outstanding natural beauty,
(iii) a country park provided under section 7(1) of the Countryside Act 1968 which in the opinion of the Secretary of State serves the purpose set out in section 6(1) of that Act when the considerations in paragraphs (a) and (b) of that subsection are taken into account, and any park or pleasure ground in the Lee Valley Regional Park which in the opinion of the Secretary of State serves that purpose,
(iv) an area in which the Countryside Commission or the Countryside Council for Wales are conducting a project or scheme under section 4 of that Act,
(v) a nature reserve or an area subject to an agreement under section 15 of that Act,
(vi) a long distance route, or
(vii) land belonging to the National Trust which is held by the Trust inalienably; and
[(b) not included.]
(2) This Act shall have effect as respects roads to which this section applies as if the list of purposes for which a traffic regulation order may be made under section 1 of this Act, as set out in paragraphs of subsection (1) of that section, included the purpose of conserving or enhancing the natural beauty of the area, or of affording better opportunities for the public to enjoy the amenities of the area, or recreation or the study of nature in the area.
(3) Subject to subsection (4) below, in the case of any road to which this section applies which is not a trunk road, the Secretary of State may by order under this subsection make as respects that road for the purpose specified in subsection (2) above any such provision as he might so have made by an order under section 1 of this Act if that road had been a trunk road, and this Act shall apply to an order under this subsection as respects any road, as it applies to an order under section 1 as respects a road which is for the time being a trunk road.
(4) The Countryside Commission, the Countryside Council for Wales (...) may each, if they think fit, make submissions to the Secretary of State as to the desirability of making an order as respects any road under subsection (3) above or, if that road is a trunk road, under section 1 of this Act; and the Secretary of State shall not make an order under subsection (3) as respects any road unless–

RIGHTS OF WAY

(a) he has received such a submission with respect to that road; and
(b) the authority having power to make an order as respects that road under section 1 have notified him that they do not intend to make such an order.
Text: p 159
Amended by EPA 90 Sch 8 para 7.

Part V: Traffic signs

69. General provisions as to removal of signs
(1) The highway authority may by notice in writing require the owner or occupier of any land on which there is an object or device (whether fixed or portable) for the guidance or direction of persons using the roads to remove it.
(2) If a person fails to comply with such a notice, the highway authority may themselves effect the removal, doing as little damage as may be; and the expenses incurred by them in doing so shall be recoverable by them from the person in default, and, in England or Wales, shall be so recoverable summarily as a civil debt.
(3) The Secretary of State may give directions to a highway authority requiring the authority to remove, or cause to be removed, any traffic sign or any such object or device as is mentioned in subsection (1) above.
Text: p 189

71. Power to enter land in connection with traffic signs
(1) A highway authority or an authority to whom section 68 of this Act applies or the Secretary of State may enter any land and exercise such other powers as may be necessary for the purpose of the exercise and performance of their powers and duties of placing, replacing, converting and removing traffic signs or their powers and duties under section 69 of this Act.
(2) In this section 'traffic signs' includes signposts for footpaths (within the meaning of the Highways Act 1980) and bridleways, and 'signposts' includes other signs or notices for the same purpose.
[(3) not included.]
Text: p 237

72. Powers exercisable by parish or community councils
[(1) not included.]
(2) A parish or community council may provide, or may contribute, either wholly or in part, towards the cost of providing, on or near any footpath or bridleway, any object or device (not being a traffic sign) for conveying to users of that footpath or bridleway a warning of the existence of danger.
(3) No traffic sign, object or device provided by a parish or community council in pursuance of this section shall be placed on any land (not being a road or part of a road) without the consent of the owner and occupier of the land.
(4) Nothing in this section shall prejudice the exercise by the highway authority or the Secretary of State of their powers under section 69 of this Act; but where any such object or device as is mentioned in subsection (1) of that section is an object or device–
(a) provided by a parish or community council in pursuance of this section, and
(b) so provided on land which the council neither own nor occupy,
the powers conferred on the highway authority by that subsection shall be

ROAD TRAFFIC REGULATION ACT 1984

exercisable in relation to the council and not in relation to the owner or occupier of the land.

(5) For the purpose of complying with a notice under section 69(1) of this Act which, by virtue of subsection (4) above, requires a parish or community council to remove an object or device, the council may enter any land and exercise such other powers as may be necessary for that purpose.

(6) A parish or community council may warn the public of any danger in or apprehended in their area, subject, however, in the case of a warning given by providing any traffic sign, object or device, to the provisions of subsections (1) and (3) above.

[(7) not included.]
Text: p 240

Part X: General and Supplementary Provisions
122. Exercise of functions by local authorities

(1) It shall be the duty of every local authority upon whom functions are conferred by or under this Act, so to exercise the functions conferred on them by this Act as (...) to secure the expeditious, convenient and safe movement of vehicular and other traffic (including pedestrians) and the provision of suitable and adequate parking facilities on and off the highway.

[(2) not included.]
Text: p 159
Amended by LGA 85 Sch 5 para 4(34).

127. Footpaths, bridleways and byways open to all traffic

(1) In relation to any footpath, bridleway or byway open to all traffic–

(a) any reference in section 2(3) or 14 of this Act to pedestrians shall be construed as including a reference to persons to whom subsection (2) below applies, and

(b) any reference in any provision of this Act (except this section) to traffic shall be construed as including a reference to pedestrians and to persons to whom that subsection applies.

(2) This subsection applies to any person driving, riding or leading a horse or other animal of draught or burden.

(3) In this section–

(a) 'footpath' does not include a highway over which the public have a right of way on foot only which is at the side of a public road; and

(b) 'byway open to all traffic' means a highway over which the public have a right of way for vehicular and all other kinds of traffic, but which is used by the public mainly for the purpose for which footpaths and bridleways are so used.

(4) For the purposes of this section a highway at the side of a river, canal or inland navigation shall not be excluded from the definition of a footpath, bridleway, or byway open to all traffic by reason only that the public have a right to use the highway for purposes of navigation, if the highway would fall within that definition if the public had no such right.

[(5) not included.]
Text: p 159

RIGHTS OF WAY

142. General interpretation of Act
(1) In this Act, except where the context otherwise requires, the following expressions have the meanings hereby assigned to them respectively, that is to say–
(...)
'bridleway' means a way over which the public have the following, but no other, rights of way, that is to say, a right of way on foot and a right of way on horseback or leading a horse, with or without a right to drive animals of any description along the way;
(...)
except in section 71(2) of this Act, 'footpath' means a way over which the public has a right of way on foot only;
'highway authority'–
(a) (...) means (...) the authority being either the council of a county, metropolitan district or London borough (...) which is responsible for the maintenance of the road;
[(b) not included.]
(...)
'road' means any length of highway or of any other road to which the public has access, and includes bridges over which a road passes;
(...)
[(2) not included.]
(3) References in this Act to a class of vehicles or traffic (...) shall be construed as references to a class defined or described by reference to any characteristics of the vehicles or traffic or to any other circumstances whatsoever.
Text: p 46, 159
Amended by LGA 85 Sch 5.

SCHEDULE 3 : Notification of Temporary Traffic Restrictions
1. (1) Subject to the following provisions of this Schedule, not less than seven days before making an order under subsection (1) or subsection (5) of section 14, the highway authority shall cause notice of their intention to make the order to be published in one or more newspapers circulating in the district in which the road or part of a road affected by the order is situated, and shall also, within a period of seven days after making any such order, cause a notice of the making of the order to be published in the like manner.
(2) Every such notice shall contain a statement of the effect of the order and, in so far as it relates to an order under subsection (1) of section 14, shall also contain a description of the alternative route or routes available for traffic.
(3) Where the Secretary of State gives his consent to an order under subsection (1) or subsection (5) of section 14 continuing in force longer than the period limited by section 15, the highway authority shall give such notice of his consent as may be directed by him.
2. So long as any order made under subsection (1) of section 14 is in force, a notice stating the effect of the order and describing the alternative route or routes available for traffic, shall be kept posted in a conspicuous manner at each end of the part of the road to which the order relates, and at the points at which it will be necessary for vehicles or, as the case may be, pedestrians to diverge from the road.
3. (1) A notice issued under subsection (3) of section 14 shall describe the

ROAD TRAFFIC REGULATION ACT 1984

alternative route or routes available for traffic, and shall be kept posted in accordance with the provisions of paragraph 2 above.
(2) Where such a notice has been posted, the highway authority may, before the expiry of the period for which the notice can continue in force, proceed to make an order under subsection (1) of section 14 with respect to the same road or part of a road without causing notice of their intention to make the order to be published in any newspaper.
4. In this Schedule references to section 14 or 15 are references to section 14 or 15 of this Act respectively.
Text: p 160

HOUSING ACT 1985

294. Extinguishment of public rights of way
(1) The local housing authority may, with the approval of the Secretary of State, by order extinguish any public right of way over land acquired by them under section 290 (land acquired for clearance).
(2) Where the authority have resolved to purchase under that section land over which a public right of way exists, an order made by the authority in advance of the purchase and approved by the Secretary of State (whether before or after the purchase) shall extinguish that right as from such date as the Secretary of State in approving the order may direct.
(3) The order shall be published in such manner as may be prescribed and if objection is made to the Secretary of State before the expiration of six weeks from its publication, he shall not approve the order until he has caused a public local inquiry to be held into the matter.
(4) The Secretary of State may dispense with such an inquiry as is referred to in subsection (3) if he is satisfied that in the special circumstances of the case the holding of such an inquiry is unnecessary.
Text: p 153
Amended by Local Government and Housing Act 1989 Sch 9. No regulations have been made under this section prescribing the form of orders — the 1937 orders remain in force (p 153).

AIRPORTS ACT 1986

59. Acquisition of land and rights over land
[(1),(2) not included.]
(3) The provisions of the 1982 Act which are specified in subsection (4) below shall apply in relation to any relevant airport operator as they apply in Great Britain to the CAA (...)
(4) The provisions of the Act mentioned in subsection (3) are–
(...)
section 48 (power to stop up and divert highways), except subsection (9),
(...)
Text: p 151
'the 1982 Act': the Civil Aviation Act 1982 (p 392), the CAA: the Civil Aviation Authority.

RIGHTS OF WAY
HOUSING AND PLANNING ACT 1986

42. Recovery of Minister's costs in connection with inquiries

(1) The following provisions of this section apply where a Minister is authorised under or by virtue of any of the following statutory provisions to recover costs incurred by him in relation to an inquiry–

(a) section 250(4) of the Local Government Act 1972 (general provision as to costs of inquiries),

[remainder of subsection not included]

(2) What may be recovered by the Minister is the entire administrative cost of the inquiry, so that, in particular–

(a) there shall be treated as costs incurred in relation to the inquiry such reasonable sum as the Minister may determine in respect of the general staff costs and overheads of his department, and

(b) there shall be treated as costs incurred by the Minister holding the inquiry any costs incurred in relation to the inquiry by any other Minister or government department and, where appropriate, such reasonable sum as that Minister or department may determine in respect of general staff costs and overheads.

(3) The cost of an inquiry which does not take place may be recovered by the Minister from any person who would have been a party to the inquiry to the same extent, and in the same way, as the cost of an inquiry which does take place.

(4) The Minister may by regulations prescribe for any description of inquiry a standard daily amount and where an inquiry of that description does take place what may be recovered is–

(a) the prescribed standard amount in respect of each day (or an appropriate proportion of that amount in respect of a part of a day) on which the inquiry sits or the person appointed to hold the inquiry is otherwise engaged on work connected with the inquiry,

(b) costs actually incurred in connection with the inquiry on travelling or subsistence allowances or the provision of accommodation or other facilities for the inquiry,

(c) any costs attributable to the appointment of an assessor to assist the person appointed to hold the inquiry, and

(d) any legal costs or disbursements incurred or made by or on behalf of the Minister in connection with the inquiry.

(5) An order or regulations under this section shall be made by statutory instrument which shall be subject to annulment in pursuance of a resolution of either House of Parliament.

(6) An order applying this section to a statutory provision may provide for the consequential repeal of so much of that provision, or any other provision, as restricts the sum recoverable by the Minister in respect of the services of any officer engaged in the inquiry or is otherwise inconsistent with the application of the provisions of this section.

Text: p 132
LGA 72 s 250: p 311

PUBLIC ORDER ACT 1986

4. Fear or provocation of violence

(1) A person is guilty of an offence if he–
(a) uses towards another person threatening, abusive or insulting words or behaviour, or
(b) distributes or displays to another person any writing, sign or other visible representation which is threatening, abusive or insulting,
with intent to cause that person to believe that immediate unlawful violence will be used against him or another by any person, or to provoke the immediate use of unlawful violence by that person or another, or whereby that person is likely to believe that such violence will be used or it is likely that such violence will be provoked.
(2) An offence under this section may be committed in a public or a private place, except that no offence is committed where the words or behaviour are used, or the writing, sign or other visible representation is distributed or displayed, by a person inside a dwelling and the other person is also inside that or another dwelling.
(3) A constable may arrest without warrant anyone he reasonably suspects is committing an offence under this section.
(4) A person guilty of an offence under this section is liable on summary conviction to imprisonment for a term not exceeding 6 months or a fine not exceeding level 5 on the standard scale.
Text: p 190

5. Harassment, alarm or distress

(1) A person is guilty of an offence if he–
(a) uses threatening, abusive or insulting words or behaviour, or disorderly behaviour, or
(b) displays any writing, sign or other visible representation which is threatening, abusive or insulting,
within the hearing or sight of a person likely to be caused harassment, alarm or distress thereby.
(2) An offence under this section may be committed in a public or a private place, except that no offence is committed where the words or behaviour are used, or the writing, sign or other visible representation is displayed, by a person inside a dwelling and the other person is also inside that or another dwelling.
(3) It is a defence for the accused to prove–
(a) that he had no reason to believe that there was any person within hearing or sight who was likely to be caused harassment, alarm or distress, or
(b) that he was inside a dwelling and had no reason to believe that the words or behaviour are used, or the writing, sign or other visible representation displayed, would be heard or seen by a person outside that or any other dwelling, or
(c) that his conduct was reasonable.
(4) A constable may arrest a person without warrant if–
(a) he engages in offensive conduct which the constable warns him to stop, and
(b) he engages in further offensive conduct immediately or shortly after the warning.

RIGHTS OF WAY

(5) In subsection (4) 'offensive conduct' means conduct the constable reasonably suspects to constitute an offence under this section, and the conduct mentioned in paragraph (a) and the further conduct need not be of the same nature.
(6) A person guilty of an offence under this section is liable on summary conviction to a fine not exceeding level 3 on the standard scale.
Text: p 190

6. Mental element: miscellaneous
[(1) and (2) not included.]
(3) A person is guilty of an offence under section 4 only if he intends his words or behaviour, or the writing, sign or other visible representation, to be threatening, abusive or insulting, or is aware that it may be threatening, abusive or insulting.
(4) A person is guilty of an offence under section 5 only if he intends his words or behaviour, or the writing, sign or other visible representation, to be threatening, abusive or insulting, or is aware that it may be threatening, abusive or insulting or (as the case may be) he intends his behaviour to be or is aware that it may be disorderly.
Text: p 190

11. Advance notice of public processions
(1) Written notice shall be given in accordance with this section of any proposal to hold a public procession intended–
(a) to demonstrate support for or opposition to the views or actions of any body of persons,
(b) to publicise a cause or campaign, or
(c) to mark or commemorate an event.
(2) Subsection (1) does not apply where the procession is one commonly or customarily held in the police area (or areas) in which it is proposed to be held or is a funeral procession organised by a funeral director acting in the normal course of his business.
(3) The notice must specify the date when it is intended to hold the procession, the time when it is intended to start it, its proposed route, and the name and address of the person (or of one of the persons) proposing to organise it.
(4) Notice must be delivered to a police station–
(a) in the police area in which it is proposed the procession will start,
[(b) not included.]
(5) If delivered not less than 6 clear days before the date when the procession is intended to be held, the notice may be delivered by post by the recorded delivery service; but section 7 of the Interpretation Act 1978 (under which a document sent by post is deemed to have been served when posted and to have been delivered in the ordinary course of post) does not apply.
(6) If not delivered in accordance with subsection (5), the notice must be delivered by hand not less than 6 clear days before the date when the procession is intended to be held or, if that is not reasonably practicable, as soon as delivery is reasonably practicable.
(7) Where a public procession is held, each of the persons organising it is guilty of an offence if–
(a) the requirements of this section as to notice have not been satisfied, or
(b) the date when it is held, the time when it starts, or its route, differs from the date, time or route specified in the notice.

PUBLIC ORDER ACT 1986

(8) It is a defence for the accused to prove that he did not know of, and neither suspected nor had reason to suspect, the failure to satisfy the requirements or (as the case may be) the difference of date, time or route.
(9) To the extent that an alleged offence turns on a difference of date, time or route, it is a defence for the accused to prove that the difference arose from circumstances beyond his control or from something done with the agreement of a police officer or by his direction.
(10) A person guilty of an offence under subsection (7) is liable on summary conviction to a fine not exceeding level 3 on the standard scale.
Text: p 55

16. Interpretation
In this Part–
(...)
'public place' means–
(a) any highway (...), and
(b) any place to which at the material time the public or any section of the public has access, on payment or otherwise, as of right or by virtue of express or implied permission;
'public procession' means a procession in a public place.
Text: p 55

39. Power to direct trespassers to leave land
(1) If the senior police officer reasonably believes that two or more persons have entered land as trespassers and are present there with the common purpose of residing there for any period, that reasonable steps have been taken by or on behalf of the occupier to ask them to leave and–
(a) that any of those persons has caused damage to property on the land or used threatening, abusive or insulting words or behaviour towards the occupier, a member of his family or an employee or agent of his, or
(b) that those persons have between them brought twelve or more vehicles on to the land,
he may direct those persons, or any of them, to leave the land.
(2) If a person knowing that such a direction has been given which applies to him–
(a) fails to leave the land as soon as reasonably practicable, or
(b) having left again enters the land as a trespasser within the period of three months beginning with the day on which the direction was given,
he commits an offence and is liable on summary conviction to imprisonment for a term not exceeding three months or a fine not exceeding level 4 on the standard scale, or both.
(3) A constable in uniform who reasonably suspects that a person is committing an offence under this section may arrest him without warrant.
(4) In proceedings for an offence under this section it is a defence for the accused to show–
(a) that his original entry on the land was not as a trespasser, or
(b) that he had a reasonable excuse for failing to leave the land as soon as reasonably practicable or, as the case may be, for again entering the land as a trespasser.

(5) In this section–
'land' does not include–
(a) buildings other than–
(i) agricultural buildings within the meaning of section 26(4) of the General Rate Act 1967, or
(ii) scheduled monuments within the meaning of the Ancient Monuments and Archaeological Areas Act 1979;
(b) land forming part of a highway;
'occupier' means the person entitled to possession of the land by virtue of an estate or interest held by him;
'property' means property within the meaning of section 10(1) of the Criminal Damage Act 1971;
'senior police officer' means the most senior in rank of the police officers present at the scene;
'trespasser', in relation to land, means a person who is a trespasser as against the occupier of the land;
'vehicle' includes a caravan as defined in section 29(1) of the Caravan Sites and Control of Development Act 1960;
and a person may be regarded for the purposes of the section as having the purpose of residing in a place notwithstanding that he has a home elsewhere.
Text: p 47

CRIMINAL JUSTICE ACT 1988

139. Offence of having article with blade or point in public place
(1) Subject to subsections (4) and (5) below, any person who has an article to which this section applies with him in a public place shall be guilty of an offence.
(2) Subject to subsection (3) below, this section applies to any article which has a blade or is sharply pointed except a folding pocketknife.
(3) This section applies to a folding pocketknife if the cutting edge of its blade exceeds 3 inches.
(4) It shall be a defence for a person charged with an offence under this section to prove that he had good reason or lawful authority for having the article with him in a public place.
(5) Without prejudice to the generality of subsection (4) above, it shall be a defence for a person charged with an offence under this section to prove that he had the article with him–
(a) for use at work;
(b) for religious reasons; or
(c) as part of any national costume.
(6) A person guilty of an offence under subsection (1) above shall be liable on summary conviction to a fine not exceeding level 3 on the standard scale.
(7) In this section 'public place' includes any place to which at the material time the public have or are permitted access, whether on payment or otherwise.
(8) This section shall not have effect in relation to anything done before it comes into force.
Text: p 196, 266
The section came into force on 29th September 1988.

HOUSING ACT 1988

Schedule 10: Housing action trusts — land

Part II: Land — supplementary: Extinguishment of public rights of way

9. (1) Where any land has been vested in or acquired by a housing action trust for the purposes of Part III of this Act and is for the time being held by that trust for those purposes, the Secretary of State may by order extinguish any public right of way over the land.
(2) Where the Secretary of State proposes to make an order under this paragraph, he shall publish in such manner as appears to him to be requisite a notice–
(a) stating the effect of the order; and
(b) specifying the time (not being less than 28 days from the publication of the notice) within which, and the manner in which, objections to the proposal may be made,
and shall serve a like notice–
(i) on the local planning authority in whose area the land is situated; and
(ii) on the relevant highway authority.
(3) In sub-paragraph (2) above 'the relevant highway authority' means any authority which is a highway authority in relation to the right of way proposed to be extinguished by the order under this paragraph.
(4) Where an objection to a proposal to make an order under this paragraph is duly made and not withdrawn, the provisions of paragraph 10 below shall have effect in relation to the proposal.
(5) For the purposes of this paragraph an objection to such a proposal shall not be treated as duly made unless–
(a) it is made within the time and in the manner specified in the notice required by this paragraph; and
(b) a statement in writing of the grounds of the objection is comprised in or submitted with the objection.
[(6) and (7) not included.]

10. (1) In this paragraph any reference to making a final decision, in relation to an order, is a reference to deciding whether to make the order or what modification, if any, ought to be made.
(2) Unless the Secretary of State decides apart from the objection not to make the order, or decides to make a modification which is agreed to by the objector as meeting the objection, the Secretary of State shall, before making a final decision, consider the grounds of the objection as set out in the statement comprised in or submitted with the objection, and may, if he thinks fit, require the objector to submit within a specified period a further statement in writing as to any of the matters which the objection relates.
(3) In so far as the Secretary of State, after considering the grounds of the objection as set out in the original statement and in any such further statement, is satisfied that the objection relates to a matter which can be dealt with in the assessment of compensation, the Secretary of State may treat the objection as irrelevant for the purpose of making a final decision.
(4) If, after considering the grounds of the objection as set out in the original statement and in any further statement, the Secretary of State is satisfied that,

RIGHTS OF WAY

for the purpose of making a final decision, he is sufficiently informed as to the matters to which the objection relates, or if, where a further statement has been required, it is not submitted within the specified period, the Secretary of State may make a final decision without further investigation as to those matters.
(5) Subject to sub-paragraphs (3) and (4) above, the Secretary of State, before making a final decision, shall afford to the objector an opportunity of appearing before, and being heard by, a person appointed for the purpose by the Secretary of State; and if the objector avails himself of that opportunity, the Secretary of State shall afford an opportunity of appearing and being heard on the same occasion to the housing action trust on whose representation the order is proposed to be made, and to any other persons to whom it appears to the Secretary of State to be expedient to afford such an opportunity.
(6) Notwithstanding anything in the preceding provisions of this paragraph, it appears to the Secretary of State that the matters to which the objection relates are such as to require investigation by public local inquiry before he makes a final decision, he shall cause such an inquiry to be held; and where he determines to cause such an inquiry to be held, any of the requirements of those provisions to which effect has not been given at the time of that determination shall be dispensed with.
Text: p 152

NORFOLK AND SUFFOLK BROADS ACT 1988

Schedule 3 — Functions of Authority — Footpaths and bridleways
47. (1) The Authority shall be treated as a local authority for the purposes of sections 25 to 29 of the Highways Act 1980 (public path creation agreements); and sections 72(2) (widening of footpaths etc.) and 118 to 121 (stopping up of footpaths etc.) of that Act shall have effect in relation to the Authority as if it were a county council.
(2) Without prejudice to the powers of any other body, the Authority shall have power to maintain any public path within the Broads.
Text: p 35
'the Authority': the Norfolk and Suffolk Broads Authority created by the Act.

ROAD TRAFFIC ACT 1988

2. Reckless driving
A person who drives a motor vehicle recklessly on a road is guilty of an offence.
Text: p 190
Note: maximum penalty is 6 months imprisonment or the statutory maximum fine (on summary conviction): 2 years imprisonment or a fine or both on indictment. (Road Traffic Offenders Act 1988 Sch 2.)

3. Careless, and inconsiderate, driving
If a person drives a motor vehicle on a road without due care and attention, or without reasonable consideration for other persons using the road, he is guilty of an offence.
Text: p 190
Note : maximum penalty is level 4 on the standard scale. (Road Traffic Offenders Act 1988 Sch 2.)

ROAD TRAFFIC ACT 1988

12. Motor racing on public ways
(1) A person who promotes or takes part in a race or trial of speed between motor vehicles on a public way is guilty of an offence.
(2) In this section 'public way' means, in England and Wales, a public highway (...)
Text: p 191
Note : maximum penalty is level 4 on the standard scale. (Road Traffic Offenders Act 1988 Sch 2.)

13. Regulation of motoring events on public ways
(1) A person who promotes or takes part in a competition or trial (other than a race or trial of speed) involving the use of motor vehicles on a public way is guilty of an offence unless the competition or trial–
(a) is authorised, and
(b) is conducted in accordance with any conditions imposed,
by or under regulations under this section.
(2) The Secretary of State may by regulations authorise, or provide for authorising, the holding of competitions or trials (other than races or trials of speed) involving the use of motor vehicles on public ways either–
(a) generally, or
(b) as regards any area, or as regards any class or description of competition or trial or any particular competition or trial,
subject to such conditions, including conditions requiring the payment of fees, as may be imposed by or under the regulations.
(3) Regulations under this section may–
(a) prescribe the procedure to be followed, and the particulars to be given, in connection with applications for authorisation under the regulations, and
(b) make different provision for different classes or descriptions of competition or trial.
(4) In this section 'public way' means, in England and Wales, a public highway (...)
Text: p 191
Note : maximum penalty is level 3 on the standard scale. (Road Traffic Offenders Act 1988 Sch 2.)

21. Prohibition of driving or parking on cycle tracks.
(1) Subject to the provisions of this section, any person who, without lawful authority, drives or parks a motor vehicle wholly or partly on a cycle track is guilty of an offence.
(2) A person shall not be convicted of an offence under subsection (1) above if he proves to the satisfaction of the court–
(a) that the vehicle was driven or (as the case may be) parked in contravention of that subsection for the purpose of saving life, or extinguishing fire or meeting any other like emergency, or
(b) that the vehicle was owned or operated by a highway authority or by a person discharging functions on behalf of a highway authority and was driven or (as the case may be) parked in contravention of that subsection in connection with the carrying out by or on behalf of that authority of any of the following,

that is, the cleansing, maintenance or improvement of, or the maintenance or alteration of any structure or other work situated in, the cycle track or its verges, or
[(c) not included]
(3) In this section–
(a) 'cycle track' and other expressions used in this section and in the Highways Act 1980 have the same meaning as in that Act,
[(3)(b) and (4) not included.]
Text: p 55
Note : maximum penalty is level 3 on the standard scale. (Road Traffic Offenders Act 1988 Sch 2.)

27. Control of dogs on roads.

(1) A person who causes or permits a dog to be on a designated road without the dog being held on a lead is guilty of an offence.
(2) In this section 'designated road' means a length of road specified by an order in that behalf of the local authority in whose area the length of road is situated.
(3) The powers which under subsection (2) above are exercisable by a local authority in England and Wales are, in the case of a road part of the width of which is in the area of one local authority and part in the area of another, exercisable by either authority with the consent of the other.
(4) An order under this section may provide that subsection (1) above shall apply subject to such limitations or exceptions as may be specified in the order, and (without prejudice to the generality of this subsection) subsection (1) above does not apply to dogs proved–
(a) to be kept for driving or tending sheep or cattle in the course of a trade or business, or
(b) to have been at the material time in use under proper control for sporting purposes.
(5) An order under this section shall not be made except after consultation with the chief officer of police.
(6) The Secretary of State may make regulations–
(a) prescribing the procedure to be followed in connection with the making of orders under this section, and
(b) requiring the authority making such an order to publish in such manner as may be prescribed by the regulations notice of the making and effect of the order.
(7) In this section 'local authority' means–
(a) in relation to England and Wales, the council of a county, metropolitan district or London borough or the Common Council of the City of London, and
[(b) not included.]
(8) The power conferred by this section to make an order includes power, exercisable in like manner and subject to the like conditions, to vary or revoke it.
Text: p 45
Note : maximum penalty is level 3 on the standard scale. (Road Traffic Offenders

ROAD TRAFFIC ACT 1988

Act 1988 Sch 2.) The regulations are the Control of Dogs on Roads Orders (Procedure) (England and Wales) Regulations 1962 SI 1962 No 2340.

28. Reckless cycling
A person who rides a cycle on a road recklessly is guilty of an offence.
In this section 'road' includes a bridleway.
Text: p 54
Note : maximum penalty is level 3 on the standard scale. (Road Traffic Offenders Act 1988 Sch 2.)

29. Careless, and inconsiderate, cycling
If a person rides a cycle on a road without due care and attention, or without reasonable consideration for other persons using the road, he is guilty of an offence.
In this section 'road' includes a bridleway.
Text: p 54
Note : maximum penalty is level 1 on the standard scale. (Road Traffic Offenders Act 1988 Sch 2.)

31. Regulation of cycle racing on public ways
(1) A person who promotes or takes part in a race or trial of speed on a public way between cycles is guilty of an offence, unless the race or trial–
(a) is authorised, and
(b) is conducted in accordance with any conditions imposed,
by or under regulations under this section.
(2) The Secretary of State may by regulations authorise, or provide for authorising, for the purposes of subsection (1) above, the holding on a public way other than a bridleway–
(a) of races or trials of speed of any class or description, or
(b) of a particular race or trial of speed, in such cases as may be prescribed and subject to such conditions as may be imposed by or under the regulations.
(3) Regulations under this section may–
(a) prescribe the procedure to be followed, and the particulars to be given, in connection with applications for authorisation under the regulations, and
(b) make different provision for different classes or descriptions of race or trial.
(4) Without prejudice to any other powers exercisable in that behalf, the chief officer of police may give directions with respect to the movement of, or the route to be followed by, vehicular traffic during any period, being directions which it is necessary or expedient to give in relation to that period to prevent or mitigate–
(a) congestion or obstruction of traffic, or
(b) danger to or from traffic,
in consequence of the holding of a race or trial of speed authorised by or under regulations under this section.
(5) Directions under subsection (4) above may include a direction that any road or part of a road specified in the direction shall be closed during the period to vehicles or to vehicles of a class so specified.
(6) In this section 'public way' means, in England and Wales, a public highway (...) and includes a bridleway but not a footpath.

RIGHTS OF WAY

Text: p 54
Note : maximum penalty is level 1 on the standard scale. (Road Traffic Offenders Act 1988 Sch 2.)

33. Control of use of footpaths and bridleways for motor vehicle trials

(1) A person must not promote or take part in a trial of any description between motor vehicles on a footpath or bridleway unless the holding of the trial has been authorised under this section by the local authority.

(2) A local authority shall not give an authorisation under this section unless satisfied that consent in writing to the use of any length of footpath or bridleway for the purposes of the trial has been given by the owner and by the occupier of the land over which that length of the footpath or bridleway runs, and any such authorisation may be given subject to compliance with such conditions as the authority think fit.

(3) A person who–
(a) contravenes subsection (1) above, or
(b) fails to comply with any conditions subject to which an authorisation under this section has been granted,
is guilty of an offence.

(4) The holding of a trial authorised under this section is not affected by any statutory provision prohibiting or restricting the use of footpaths or bridleways or a specified footpath or bridleway; but this section does not prejudice any right or remedy of a person as having any interest in land.

(5) In this section 'local authority'–
(a) in relation to England and Wales, means the council of a county, metropolitan district or London borough, and
[(b) not included.]

Text: p 81, 191
Note : maximum penalty is level 3 on the standard scale. (Road Traffic Offenders Act 1988 Sch 2.)

34. Prohibition of driving motor vehicles elsewhere than on roads

(1) Subject to the provisions of this section, if without lawful authority a person drives a motor vehicle–
(a) on to or upon any common land, moorland or land of any other description, not being land forming part of a road, or
(b) on any road being a footpath or bridleway,
he is guilty of an offence.

(2) It is not an offence under this section to drive a motor vehicle on any land within fifteen yards of a road, being a road on which a motor vehicle may lawfully be driven, for the purpose only of parking the vehicle on that land.

(3) A person shall not be convicted of an offence under this section with respect to a vehicle if he proves to the satisfaction of the court that it was driven in contravention of this section for the purpose of saving life or extinguishing fire or meeting any other like emergency.

(4) It is hereby declared that nothing in this section prejudices the operation of–
(a) section 193 of the Law of Property Act 1925 (rights of the public over commons and waste lands), or

ROAD TRAFFIC ACT 1988

(b) any byelaws applying to any land,
or affects the law or trespass to land or any right or remedy to which a person may by law be entitled in respect of any such trespass or in particular confers a right to park a vehicle on any land.
Text: p 54, 69, 81, 190
Note : maximum penalty is level 3 on the standard scale. (Road Traffic Offenders Act 1988 Sch 2.) A fixed penalty fine be imposed by virtue of Road Traffic Offenders Act 1988 Pt 3 and Sch 3.

185. Meaning of 'motor vehicle' and other expressions relating to vehicles
(1) In this Act–
(...)
'motor vehicle' means, subject to section 20 of the Chronically Sick and Disabled Persons Act 1970 (which makes special provisions about invalid carriages, within the meaning of that Act), a mechanically propelled vehicle intended or adapted for use on roads;
(...)
Text: p 54

191. Interpretation of statutory references to carriages
A motor vehicle or trailer–
(a) is to be deemed to be a carriage within the meaning of any Act of Parliament, whether a public general Act or a local Act, and of any rule, regulation or byelaw made under any Act of Parliament, and
(b) if used as a carriage of any particular class shall for the purpose of any enactment relating to carriages of any particular class be deemed to be a carriage of that class.
Text: p 54

192. General interpretation of Act
(1) In this Act–
'bridleway' means a way over which the public have the following, but no other, rights of way: a right of way on foot and a right of way on horseback and leading a horse, with or without a right to drive animals of any description along the way,
(...)
'cycle' means a bicycle, a tricycle, or a cycle having four or more wheels, not being in any case a motor vehicle,
(...)
'footpath', in relation to England and Wales, means a way over which the public have a right of way on foot only,
(...)
'prescribed' means prescribed by regulations made by the Secretary of State,
'road', in relation to England and Wales, means any highway and any other road to which the public has access, and includes bridges over which a road passes,
(...)
'statutory', in relation to any prohibition, restriction, requirement, or provision,

means contained in, or having effect under, any enactment (including any enactment contained in this Act),
(...)
[(2) & (3) not included.]
Text: p 54, 191

DANGEROUS DOGS ACT 1989

1. Additional powers of court on complaint about dangerous dog
(1) Where a magistrates' court makes an order under section 2 of the Dogs Act 1871 directing a dog to be destroyed it may also–
(a) appoint a person to undertake its destruction and require any person having custody of the dog to deliver it up for that purpose; and
(b) if it thinks fit, make an order disqualifying the owner for having custody of a dog for such period as is specified in the order.
(2) An appeal shall lie to the Crown Court against any order under section 2 of that Act or under subsection (1) above; and, unless the owner of a dog which is ordered to be delivered up and destroyed gives notice to the court that made the order that he does not intend to appeal against it, the dog shall not be destroyed pursuant to the order–
(a) until the end of the period within which notice of appeal to the Crown Court against the order can be given; and
(b) if notice of appeal is given within that period, until the appeal is determined or withdrawn.
(3) Any person who fails to comply with an order under section 2 of the said Act of 1871 to keep a dog under proper control or to deliver a dog up for destruction as required by an order under subsection (1)(a) above is guilty of an offence and liable on summary conviction to a fine not exceeding level 3 on the standard scale and the court may, in addition, make an order disqualifying him for having custody of a dog for such period as is specified in the order.
(4) A person who is disqualified for having custody of a dog by virtue of an order made under subsection (1)(b) or (3) above may, at any time after the end of the period of one year beginning with the date of the order, apply to the court that made it (or any magistrates' court acting for the same petty sessions area as that court) for an order terminating the disqualification.
(5) On an application under subsection (4) above the court may–
(a) having regard to the applicant's character, his conduct since the disqualification was imposed and any other circumstances of the case, grant or refuse the application; and
(b) order the applicant to pay all or any part of the costs of the application;
and where an application in respect of an order is refused no further application in respect of that order shall be entertained if made before the end of the period of one year beginning with the date of the refusal.
(6) Any person who has custody of a dog in contravention of an order made under subsection (1)(b) or (3) above is guilty of an offence and liable on summary conviction to a fine not exceeding level 5 on the standard scale.
[(7) not included.].
Text: p 185
Dogs Act 1871 s 2 : p 287

WATER ACT 1989

WATER ACT 1989

155. Compulsory powers for carrying out works

(1) Where the Authority or a water undertaker is proposing, for the purposes of, or in connection with, the carrying out of any of its functions–
(a) to carry out any engineering or building operations, or
(b) to discharge water into any inland water or underground strata,
the Authority, or as the case may be, the undertaker may apply to the appropriate Minister for an order under this section.
(2) Subject to the following provisions of this section, the appropriate Minister may, on an application under subsection (1) above, by order made by statutory instrument confer such compulsory powers and grant such authority as he considers necessary or expedient for the purpose of enabling any engineering or building operations or discharges of water to be carried out or made for the purposes of, or in connection with, the carrying out of functions with respect to which the application was made.
(3) Schedule 20 to this Act shall have effect with respect to applications for orders under this section and with respect to such orders.
(4) Subject to the said Schedule 20, an order under this section may–
(a) without prejudice to section 151 above, confer power to acquire compulsorily any land, including–
(i) power to acquire interests in and rights over land by the creation of new rights and interests; and
(ii) power, by the compulsory acquisition by the Authority or any water undertaker of any rights over land which is to be or has been acquired by the Authority or that undertaker, to extinguish any such rights;
(b) apply for the purposes of the order, either with or without modifications, any of the provisions of this Part of this Act which do not apply for those purposes apart from by virtue of this paragraph;
(c) make any authority granted by the order subject to such conditions as may be specified in the order;
(d) amend or repeal any local statutory provision;
(e) contain such supplemental, consequential and transitional provision as the appropriate Minister considers appropriate.
(5) Nothing in any order under this section shall exempt the Authority or any water undertaker from any restriction imposed by Part IV of the Water Resources Act 1963 (abstraction and impounding of water).
[(6) not included.]
(7) In this section and Schedule 20 to this Act 'the appropriate Minister'–
(a) in relation to an application by the Authority for an order under this section or an order made on such an application, means the Secretary of State or the Minister; and
(b) in relation to an application by a water undertaker for an order under this section or an order made on such an application, means the Secretary of State.
Text: p 150

Schedule 20: orders conferring compulsory works powers

Applications for orders

1. (1) Where the Authority or a water undertaker applies to the appropriate Minister for an order under section 155 of this Act, the Authority or, as the case may be, the undertaker shall–

RIGHTS OF WAY

(a) submit to the appropriate Minister a draft of the order applied for;
(b) publish a notice with respect to the application, at least once in each of two successive weeks, in one or more newspapers circulating in each relevant locality;
(c) not later than the date on which that notice is first published–
(i) serve a copy of the notice on each of the persons specified in relation to the application in sub-paragraph (3) below; and
(ii) in the case of a draft order which would authorise the stopping-up or diversion of a footpath or bridleway, cause such a copy, together with a plan showing the general effect of the draft order so far as it relates to the footpath or bridleway, to be displayed in a prominent position at the ends of the part of the path or way to be stopped up or diverted; and
(d) publish a notice in the London Gazette which–
(i) states that the draft order has been submitted to the appropriate Minister;
(ii) names every local authority on whom a notice is required to be served under this paragraph;
(iii) specifies a place where a copy of the draft order and of any relevant map or plan may be inspected; and
(iv) gives the name of every newspaper in which the notice required by virtue of paragraph (b) above was published and the date of an issue containing the notice.
(2) The notice required by virtue of sub-paragraph (1)(b) above to be published with respect to an application for an order shall–
(a) state the general effect of the order applied for;
[(b) not included.]
(c) specify a place where a copy of the draft order and of any relevant map or plan may be inspected by any person free of charge at all reasonable times during the period of twenty-eight days beginning with the date of the first publication of the notice; and
(d) state that any person may, within that period, by notice to the appropriate Minister object to the making of the order.
(3) The persons mentioned in sub-paragraph (1)(c) above in relation to an application for a draft order submitted to the appropriate Minister are–
(a) every local authority whose area is or includes the whole or any part of a relevant locality and every water undertaker, not being the applicant, whose area is or includes the whole or any part of such a locality:
(b) every navigation authority, harbour authority and conservancy authority which would be affected by, or has functions in relation to any inland water which would be affected by, any provision proposed to be made by the order;
(c) in the case of an application by a water undertaker, the Authority;
(d) every owner, lessee or occupier (except tenants for a month or for any period of less than a month) of any land in relation to which compulsory powers would become exercisable if the order were made in the terms of the draft order;
(e) every person who has given notice to the Authority or, as the case may be, the water undertaker requiring it to notify him of applications for orders under section 155 of this Act and has paid such reasonable charge as the Authority or undertaker may have required him to pay for being notified by virtue of this paragraph;

WATER ACT 1989

(f) such other persons as may be prescribed.
(4) In this paragraph 'relevant locality', in relation to an application for an order a draft of which is submitted to the appropriate Minister, means–
(a) any locality which would be affected by any provision proposed to be made by the order for the purpose of enabling any engineering or building operations to be carried out;
[(b) not included.]

Supply of copies of draft orders
2. The applicant for an order under section 155 of this Act shall, at the request of any person and on payment by that person of such charge (if any) as the applicant may reasonably require, furnish that person with a copy of the draft order submitted to the appropriate Minister under paragraph 1 above and of any relevant map or plan.

Powers on an application
3. (1) On an application for an order under section 155 of this Act, the appropriate Minister may make the order either in the terms of the draft order submitted to him or, subject to sub-paragraphs (2) and (3) below, in those terms as modified in such manner as he thinks fit, or may refuse to make an order.
(2) The appropriate Minister shall not make such a modification of a draft order submitted to him as he considers is likely adversely to affect any persons unless he is satisfied that the applicant for the order has given and published such additional notices, in such manner, as the appropriate Minister may have required.
(3) The appropriate Minister shall not, unless all interested parties consent, make an order under section 155 of this Act so as to confer in relation to any land any powers of compulsory acquisition which would not have been conferred in relation to that land if the order were made in the terms of the draft order submitted to him under paragraph 1 above.
(4) Where, on an application for an order under section 155 of this Act, the appropriate Minister refuses to make an order, the applicant shall, as soon as practicable after the refusal, notify the refusal to every person on whom the applicant was, by virtue of paragraph 1(1)(c)(i) above, required to serve a copy of the notice with respect to the application.
(5) The duty of a water undertaker under sub-paragraph (4) above shall be enforceable under section 20 of this Act by the Secretary of State.

Consideration of objections etc
4. (1) If where an application for an order under section 155 above has been made notice of an objection to it is received by the appropriate Minister before the end of the relevant period from–
(a) any person on whom a notice under paragraph 1 or 3 above is required to be served; or
(b) from any other person appearing to the appropriate Minister to be affected by the order as submitted to him or as proposed to be modified under paragraph 3 above,
then, unless the objection is withdrawn, the appropriate Minister shall, before

making the order, either cause a local inquiry to be held or afford to the objector and to the applicant for the order an opportunity of appearing before, and being heard by, a person appointed by the appropriate Minister for the purpose.

(2) Where any objection received by the appropriate Minister as mentioned in sub-paragraph (1) above relates to any powers of compulsory acquisition, the appropriate Minister may require the objector to state in writing the grounds of his objection; and if the appropriate Minister is satisfied that the objection relates exclusively to matters that can be dealt with in the assessment of compensation, he may disregard the objection for the purposes of that sub-paragraph.

(3) In this paragraph 'the relevant period', in relation to an application for any order, means the period ending with whichever is the later of–

(a) the end of the period of twenty-eight days beginning with the date of the first publication of the notice published with respect to the application for the purposes of paragraph 1(1)(b) above; and

(b) the end of the period of twenty-five days beginning with the date of the publication in the London Gazette of the notice published for the purposes of the application by virtue of paragraph 1(1)(d) above,

together, in the case of an application for an order modifications to which have been proposed by the appropriate Minister, with any further periods specified with respect to the modifications in notices under paragraph 3(2) above.

Notice after making of order

5. (1) As soon as practicable after an order under section 155 of this Act has been made, the applicant for the order shall–

(a) publish a notice of the making of the order, at least once in each of two successive weeks, in one or more newspapers circulating in each relevant locality; and

(b) not later than the date on which that notice is first published–

(i) serve a copy of the notice on every person on whom the applicant was, by virtue of paragraph 1(1)(c)(i) above, required to serve a copy of the notice with respect to the application for the order;

(ii) in the case of an order authorising the stopping-up or diversion of a footpath or bridleway, cause such a copy, together with a plan showing the general effect of the order so far as it relates to the footpath or bridleway, to be displayed in a prominent position at the ends of the part of the path or way.

(2) The notice required by virtue of sub-paragraph (1)(b) above to be published with respect to an order under section 155 of this Act shall–

(a) state the general effect of the order;

[(b) not included.]

(c) specify a place where a copy of the order and of any relevant map or plan may be inspected by any person free of charge at all reasonable times.

(3) Where an order under section 155 of this Act has been made, the applicant for the order shall, at the request of any person and on payment by that person of such charge (if any) as the applicant may reasonably require, furnish that person with a copy of the order and of any relevant map or plan.

(4) The duties of a water undertaker under this paragraph shall be enforceable under section 20 of this Act by the Secretary of State.

(5) In this paragraph 'relevant locality', in relation to an order made under section 155 to this Act, means–

WATER ACT 1989

(a) any locality which is affected by any provision made by the order for the purpose of enabling any engineering or building operations to be carried out;
[(b) not included.]
[Paragraphs 6 to 9 not included.]

Interpretation
10. In this Schedule–
'bridleway' and 'footpath' have the same meaning as in the Highways Act 1980;
(...)
and references to a tenant for a month or for any period of less than a month include references to a statutory tenant, within the meaning of the Landlord and Tenant Act 1985, and to a licensee under an assured agricultural occupancy, within the meaning of Part I of the Housing Act 1988.
Text: p 150
The Water (Compulsory Works Powers) (Notice) Regulations 1991 prescribe for the purposes of para 1(3)(f) bodies which have to be sent notice of application for an order which would authorise the stopping-up or diversion of a footpath or bridleway. See p 150 & 471.

ENVIRONMENTAL PROTECTION ACT 1990

Part III: Statutory nuisances and clean air

79. Statutory nuisances and inspections therefor
(1) Subject to subsections (2) to (6) below, the following matters constitute 'statutory nuisances' for the purposes of this Part, that is to say–
(a) any premises in such a state as to be prejudicial to health or a nuisance;
[(b) to (d) not included.]
(e) any accumulation or deposit which is prejudicial to health or a nuisance;
(f) any animal kept in such a place or manner as to be prejudicial to health or a nuisance;
[(g) not included.]
(h) any other matter declared by any enactment to be a statutory nuisance;
and it shall be the duty of every local authority to cause its area to be inspected from time to time to detect any statutory nuisances which ought to be dealt with under section 80 below and, where a complaint of a statutory nuisance is made to it by a person living within its area, to take such steps as are reasonably practicable to deal with the complaint.
[(2) to (6) not included.]
(7) In this Part–
(...)
'industrial, trade or business premises' means premises used for any industrial, trade or business purposes or premises not so used on which matter is burnt in connection with any industrial, trade or business process, and premises are used for industrial purposes where they are used for the purposes of any treatment or process as well as where they are used for the purposes of manufacturing;
'local authority' means, (...),–

(a) in Greater London, a London borough council, (...);
(b) outside Greater London, a district council; and
(c) the Council of the Isles of Scilly;
(...)
'person responsible', in relation to a statutory nuisance, means the person to whose act, default or sufferance the nuisance is attributable;
'prejudicial to health' means injurious, or likely to cause injury, to health;
'premises' includes land (...);
(...)
[(8) not included.]
(9) In this Part 'best practicable means' is to be interpreted by reference to the following provisions–
(a) 'practicable' means reasonably practicable having regard among other things to local conditions and circumstances, to the current state of technical knowledge and to the financial implications;
(b) the means to be employed include the design, installation, maintenance and manner and periods of operation of plant and machinery, and the design, construction and maintenance of buildings and structures;
(c) the test is to apply only so far as compatible with any duty imposed by law;
(d) the test is to apply only so far as compatible with safety and safe working conditions, and with the exigencies of any emergency or unforeseeable circumstances;
(...)
[(10) to (12) not included.]
Text: p 187

80. Summary proceedings for statutory nuisances

(1) Where a local authority is satisfied that a statutory nuisance exists, or is likely to occur or recur, in the area of the authority, the local authority shall serve a notice ('an abatement notice') imposing all or any of the following requirements–
(a) requiring the abatement of the nuisance or prohibiting or restricting its occurrence or recurrence;
(b) requiring the execution of such works, and the taking of such other steps, as may be necessary for any of those purposes,
and the notice shall specify the time or times within which the requirements of the notice are to be complied with.
(2) The abatement notice shall be served–
(a) except in a case falling within paragraph (b) or (c) below, on the person responsible for the nuisance;
(b) where the nuisance arises from any defect of a structural character, on the owner of the premises;
(c) where the person responsible for the nuisance cannot be found or the nuisance has not yet occurred, on the owner or occupier of the premises.
(3) The person served with the notice may appeal against the notice to a magistrates' court within the period of twenty-one days beginning with the date on which he was served with the notice.
(4) If a person on whom an abatement notice is served, without reasonable excuse, contravenes or fails to comply with any requirement or prohibition imposed by the notice, he shall be guilty of an offence.

ENVIRONMENTAL PROTECTION ACT 1990

(5) Except in a case falling within subsection (6) below, a person who commits an offence under subsection (4) above shall be liable on summary conviction to a fine not exceeding level 5 on the standard scale together with a further fine of an amount equal to one-tenth of that level for each day on which the offence continues after the conviction.

(6) A person who commits an offence under subsection (4) above on industrial, trade or business premises shall be liable on summary conviction to a fine not exceeding £20,000.

(7) Subject to subsection (8) below, in any proceedings for an offence under subsection (4) above in respect of a statutory nuisance it shall be a defence to prove that the best practicable means were used to prevent, or counteract the effects of, the nuisance.

(8) The defence under subsection (7) above is not available–

(a) in the case of a nuisance falling within paragraph (a),(d),(e),(f) or (g) of section 79(1) above except where the nuisance arises on industrial, trade or business premises;

[(b) not included.]

(c) in the case of a nuisance falling within paragraph (c) or (h) of section 79(1) above.

[(9) and (10) not included.]

Text: p 188

81. Supplementary provisions

(1) Where more than one person is responsible for a statutory nuisance section 80 above shall apply to each of those persons whether or not what any one of them is responsible for would by itself amount to a nuisance.

(2) Where a statutory nuisance which exists or has occurred within the area of a local authority, or which has affected any part of that area, appears to the local authority to be wholly or partly caused by some act or default committed or taking place outside the area, the local authority may act under section 80 above as if the act or default were wholly within their area, except that any appeal shall be heard by a magistrates' court having jurisdiction where the act or default is alleged to have taken place.

(3) Where an abatement notice has not been complied with the local authority may, whether or not they take proceedings for an offence under section 80(4) above, abate the nuisance and do whatever may be necessary in execution of the notice.

(4) Any expenses reasonably incurred by a local authority in abating, or preventing the recurrence of, a statutory nuisance under subsection (3) above may be recovered by them from the person by whose act or default the nuisance was caused and, if that person is not the owner of the premises, from any person who is for the time being the owner thereof; and the court may apportion the expenses between persons by whose acts or defaults the nuisance is caused in such manner as the court consider fair and reasonable.

(5) If the local authority is of opinion that proceedings for an offence under section 80(4) above would afford an inadequate remedy in the case of any statutory nuisance, they may, subject to subsection (6) below, take proceedings in the High Court for the purpose of securing the abatement, prohibition or restriction of the nuisance, and the proceedings shall be maintainable notwithstanding the local authority have suffered no damage from the nuisance.

RIGHTS OF WAY

[(6) not included.]
Text: p 188

82. Summary proceedings by persons aggrieved by statutory nuisances

(1) A magistrates' court may act under this section on a complaint made by any person on the ground that he is aggrieved by the existence of a statutory nuisance.

(2) If the magistrates' court is satisfied that the alleged nuisance exists, or that although abated it is likely to recur on the same premises, the court shall make an order for either or both of the following purposes—

(a) requiring the defendant to abate the nuisance, within a time specified in the order, and to execute any works necessary for that purpose;

(b) prohibiting a recurrence of the nuisance, and requiring the defendant, within a time specified in the order, to execute any works necessary to prevent the recurrence;

and may also impose on the defendant a fine not exceeding level 5 on the standard scale.

[(3) not included.]

(4) Proceedings for an order under subsection (2) above shall be brought—

(a) except in a case falling within paragraph (b) or (c) below, against the person responsible for the nuisance;

(b) where the nuisance arises from a defect of any structural character, against the owner of the premises;

(c) where the person responsible for the nuisance cannot be found, against the owner or occupier of the premises.

(5) Where more than one person is responsible for a statutory nuisance, subsections (1) to (4) above shall apply to each of those persons whether or not what any one of them is responsible for would by itself amount to a nuisance.

(6) Before instituting proceedings for an order under subsection (2) above against any person, the person aggrieved by the nuisance shall give to that person such notice in writing of his intention to bring the proceedings as is applicable to proceedings in respect of a nuisance of that description and the notice shall specify the matter complained of.

(7) The notice of the bringing of proceedings in respect of a statutory nuisance required by subsection (6) which is applicable is—

[(a) not included.]

(b) (...) not less than twenty-one days' notice;

but the Secretary of State may, by order, provide that this subsection shall have such effect as if such period as is specified in the order were the minimum period of notice applicable to any description of statutory nuisance specified in the order.

(8) A person who, without reasonable excuse, contravenes any requirement or prohibition imposed by an order under subsection (2) above shall be guilty of an offence and liable on summary conviction to a fine not exceeding level 5 on the standard scale together with a further fine of an amount equal to one-tenth of that level for each day on which the offence continues after that conviction.

(9) Subject to subsection (10) below, in any proceedings for an offence under subsection (8) above in respect of a statutory nuisance it shall be a defence to prove that the best practicable means were used to prevent, or to counteract the effects of, the nuisance.

ENVIRONMENTAL PROTECTION ACT 1990

(10) The defence under subsection (9) is not available–
(a) in the case of a nuisance falling within paragraph (a), (d), (e), (f) or (g) of section 79(1) above except where the nuisance arises on industrial, trade or business premises;
(b) in the case of a nuisance falling within paragraph (b) of section 79(1) above except where the smoke is emitted from a chimney;
(c) in the case of a nuisance falling within paragraph (c) or (h) of section 79(1);
[(d) not included.]
(11) If a person is convicted of an offence under subsection (8) above, a magistrates' court may, after giving the local authority in whose area the nuisance has occurred an opportunity of being heard, direct the authority to do anything which the person convicted was required to do by the order to which the conviction relates.
(12) Where on the hearing of proceedings for an order under subsection (2) above it is proved that the alleged nuisance existed at the date of the making of the complaint, then, whether or not at the date of the hearing it still exists or is likely to recur, the court shall order the defendant (or defendants in such proportions as appears fair and reasonable) to pay to the person bringing such proceedings such amount as the court considers reasonably sufficient to compensate him for any expenses properly incurred by him in the proceedings.
(13) If it appears to the magistrates' court that neither the person responsible for the nuisance nor the owner or occupier of the premises can be found the court may, after giving the local authority in whose area the nuisance has occurred an opportunity of being heard, direct the authority to do anything which the court would have ordered that person to do.
Text: p 188, 214–7

Schedule 3 : Statutory nuisances : supplementary provisions
Appeals to magistrates' court
1. (1) This paragraph applies in relation to appeals under section 80(3) against an abatement notice to a magistrates' court.
(2) An appeal to which this paragraph applies shall be by way of complaint for an order and the Magistrates' Courts Act 1980 shall apply to the proceedings.
(3) An appeal against any decision of the magistrates' court in pursuance of an appeal to which this paragraph applies shall lie to the Crown Court at the instance of any party to the proceedings in which the decision was given.
(4) The Secretary of State may make regulations as to appeals to which this paragraph applies and the regulations may in particular–
(a) include provisions comparable to those in section 290 of the Public Health Act 1936 (appeals against notices requiring execution of works);
(b) prescribe the cases in which an abatement notice is, or is not, to be suspended until the appeal is decided, or until some other stage in the proceedings;
(c) prescribe the cases in which the decision on appeal may in some respects be less favourable to the appellant that the decision from which he is appealing;
(d) prescribe the cases in which the appellant may claim that an abatement notice should have been served on some other person and prescribe the procedure to be followed in those cases.

Powers of entry etc
2. (1) Subject to sub-paragraph (2) below, any person authorised by a local

authority may, on production (if so required) of his authority, enter any premises at any reasonable time–
(a) for the purpose of ascertaining whether or not a statutory nuisance exists; or
(b) for the purpose of taking any action, or executing any work, authorised or required by Part III.
[(2) not included.]
(3) If it is shown to the satisfaction of a justice of the peace on sworn information in writing–
(a) that admission to any premises has been refused, or that refusal is apprehended, or that the premises are unoccupied or the occupier is temporarily absent, or that the case is one of emergency, or that an application for admission would defeat the object of the entry; and
(b) that there is reasonable ground for entry into the premises for the purpose for which entry is required,
the justice may by warrant under his hand authorise the local authority by any authorised person to enter the premises, if need be by force.
(4) An authorised person entering any premises by virtue of sub-paragraph (1) or a warrant under sub-paragraph (3) above may–
(a) take with him such others and such equipment as may be necessary;
(b) carry out such inspections, measurements and tests as he considers necessary for the discharge of any of the local authority's functions under Part III; and
(c) take away such samples or articles as he considers necessary for that purpose.
(5) On leaving any unoccupied premises which he has entered by virtue of sub-paragraph (1) above or a warrant under sub-paragraph (3) above the authorised person shall leave them as effectually secured against trespassers as he found them.
(6) A warrant issued in pursuance of sub-paragraph (3) above shall continue in force until the purpose for which the entry is required has been satisfied.
(7) Any reference in this paragraph to an emergency is a reference to a case where the person requiring entry has reasonable cause to believe that circumstances exist which are likely to endanger life or health and that immediate entry is necessary to verify the existence of those circumstances or to ascertain their cause and to effect a remedy.

Offences relating to entry
3. (1) A person who wilfully obstructs any person acting in the exercise of any powers conferred by paragraph 2 above shall be liable, on summary conviction, to a fine not exceeding level 3 on the standard scale.
[(2) not included.]

Default powers
4. (1) This paragraph applies to the following function of a local authority, that is to say its duty under section 79 to cause its area to be inspected to detect any statutory nuisance which ought to be dealt with under section 80 and its powers under paragraph 2 above.
(2) If the Secretary of State is satisfied that any local authority has failed, in any respect, to discharge the function to which this paragraph applies which it ought to have discharged, he may make an order declaring the authority to be in default.

(3) An order made under sub-paragraph (2) above which declares an authority to be in default may, for the purpose of remedying the default, direct the authority ('the defaulting authority') to perform the function specified in the order and may specify the manner in which and the time or times within which the function is to be performed by the authority.
(4) If the defaulting authority fails to comply with any direction contained in such an order the Secretary of State may, instead of enforcing the order by mandamus, make an order transferring to himself the function of the authority specified in the order.
(5) Where the function of a defaulting authority is transferred under sub-paragraph (4) above, the amount of any expenses which the Secretary of State certifies were incurred by him in performing the function shall on demand be paid to him by the defaulting authority.
(6) Any expenses required to be paid by a defaulting authority under sub-paragraph (5) above shall be defrayed by the authority in like manner, and shall be debited to the like account, as if the function had not been transferred and the expenses had been incurred by the authority in performing them.
(7) The Secretary of State may by order vary or revoke any order previously made by him under this paragraph.
(8) Any order under this paragraph may include such incidental, supplemental and transitional provisions as the Secretary of State considers appropriate.
[5 not included]

Statement of right of appeal in notices
6. Where an appeal against a notice served by a local authority lies to a magistrates' court by virtue of section 80, it shall be the duty of the authority to include in such a notice a statement indicating that such an appeal lies as aforesaid and specifying the time within which it must be brought.
Text: p 187
The regulations are the Statutory Nuisance (Appeals) Regulations 1990 SI 1990 No 2276, as corrected by the Statutory Nuisance (Appeals) (Amendment) Regulations 1990 SI 1990 No 2483.

Schedule 11: Transitional provisions

Part I : Countryside functions

Existing areas of outstanding natural beauty and long distance routes
5. (1) This paragraph applies to–
[(a) not included]
(b) any long distance route under Part IV of that Act of which some parts are in England and other parts in Wales.
[(2) not included.]
(3) On and after the appointed day any route to which this paragraph applies shall not cease, by virtue of this Part of this Act to be a single route for the purposes of Part IV of the 1949 Act; but any function which before that day is exercisable by or in relation to the Commission shall, on and after that day be exercisable by or in relation to the Commission (so far as concerns parts of the route in England) and by or in relation to the Council (so far as concerns parts of the route in Wales).

RIGHTS OF WAY

(4) On or after the appointed day the Commission and the Council shall each exercise any function of theirs in relation to an area or route to which this paragraph applies only after consultation with the other; and the Commission and the Council may make arrangements for discharging any of their functions in relation to such an area or route jointly.
Text: p 278
'the 1949 Act': NPACA 49 (p 288), 'the appointed day': 1 April 1991, the 'Commission': the Countryside Commission, 'the Council': the Countryside Council for Wales.

TOWN AND COUNTRY PLANNING ACT 1990

55. Meaning of 'development' and 'new development'
(1) Subject to the following provisions of this section, in this Act, except where the context otherwise requires, 'development' means the carrying out of building, engineering, mining, or other operations in, on, over or under land, or the making of any material change in the use of any buildings or other land.
(2) The following operations or uses of the land shall not be taken for the purposes of this Act to involve development of the land–
(a) the carrying out for the maintenance, improvement or other alteration of any building of works which–
(i) affect only the interior of the building, or
(ii) do not materially affect the external appearance of the building,
and are not works for making good war damage or works begun after 5th December 1968 for the alteration of a building by providing additional space in it underground;
(b) the carrying out on land within the boundaries of a road by a local highway authority of any works required for the maintenance or improvement of the road;
[(c) not included.]
(d) the use of any buildings or other land within the curtilage of a dwellinghouse for any purpose incidental to the enjoyment of the dwellinghouse as such;
(e) the use of any land for the purposes of agriculture or forestry (including afforestation) and the use for any of those purposes of any building occupied together with land so used;
[(f) not included.]
[remainder of section not included.]
Text: p 144

247. Highways affected by development: orders by Secretary of State
(1) The Secretary of State may by order authorise the stopping up or diversion of any highway if he is satisfied that it is necessary to do so in order to enable development to be carried out–
(a) in accordance with planning permission granted under Part III, or
(b) by a government department.
(2) Such an order may make such provision as appears to the Secretary of State to be necessary or expedient for the provision or improvement of any other highway.
(3) Such an order may direct–
(a) that any highway provided or improved by virtue of it shall for the purposes of the Highways Act 1980 be a highway maintainable at the public expense;

TOWN AND COUNTRY PLANNING ACT 1990

(b) that the Secretary of State, or any county council, metropolitan district council or London borough council specified in the order or, if it is so specified, the Common Council of the City of London, shall be the highway authority for that highway;
(c) in the case of a highway for which the Secretary of State is to be the highway authority, that the highway shall, on such date as may be specified in the order, become a trunk road within the meaning of the Highways Act 1980.
(4) Any order made under this section may contain such incidental and consequential provisions as appear to the Secretary of State to be necessary or expedient, including in particular–
(a) provision for authorising the Secretary of State, or requiring any other authority or person specified in the order–
(i) to pay, or to make contributions in respect of, the cost of doing any work provided for by the order or any increased expenditure to be incurred which is attributable to the doing of any such work; or
[(a(ii)) and (b) not included.]
(5) An order may be made under this section authorising the stopping up or diversion of any highway which is temporarily stopped up or diverted under any other enactment.
(6) The provisions of this section shall have effect without prejudice to–
(a) any power conferred on the Secretary of State by any other enactment to authorise the stopping up or diversion of a highway;
(b) the provisions of Part VI of the Acquisition of Land Act 1981; or
(c) the provisions of section 251(1).
Text: p 146
Part VI of the Acquisition of Land Act 1981 is sections 32 and 33 (p 376). The procedure for orders under s 247 is in s 252 (p 433).

248. Highways crossing or entering route of proposed new highway, etc.

(1) This section applies where–
(a) planning permission is granted under Part III for constructing or improving, or the Secretary of State proposes to construct or improve, a highway ('the main highway'); and
(b) another highway crosses or enters the route of the main highway or is, or will be, otherwise affected by the construction or improvement of the main highway.
(2) Where this section applies, if it appears to the Secretary of State expedient to do so–
(a) in the interests of the safety of users of the main highway; or
(b) to facilitate the movement of traffic on the main highway,
he may by order authorise the stopping up or diversion of the other highway.
(3) Subsections (2) to (6) of section 247 shall apply to an order under this section as they apply to an order under that section, taking the reference in subsection (2) of that section to any other highway as a reference to any highway other than that which is stopped up or diverted under this section and the references in subsection (3) to a highway provided or improved by virtue of an order under that section as including a reference to the main highway.
Text: p 150

RIGHTS OF WAY

249. Order extinguishing right to use vehicles on highway

(1) This section applies where–
(a) a local planning authority by resolution adopt a proposal for improving the amenity of part of their area, and
(b) the proposal involves the public ceasing to have any right of way with vehicles over a highway in that area, being a highway which is neither a trunk road nor a road classified as a principal road.
(2) The Secretary of State may, on an application by the local planning authority who have so resolved, by order provide for the extinguishment of any right which persons may have to use vehicles on that highway.
(3) An order made under subsection (2) may include such provision as the Secretary of State (after consultation with every authority who are a local planning authority for the area in question and the highway authority) thinks fit for permitting the use on the highway of vehicles (whether mechanically propelled or not) in such cases as may be specified in the order, notwithstanding the extinguishment of any such right as is mentioned in that subsection.
(4) Such provision as is mentioned in subsection (3) may be framed by reference to –
(a) particular descriptions of vehicles, or
(b) particular persons by whom, or on whose authority, vehicles may be used, or
(c) the circumstances in which, or the times at which, vehicles may be used for particular purposes.
(5) No provision contained in, or having effect under, any enactment, being a provision prohibiting or restricting the use of footpaths, footways or bridleways shall affect any use of a vehicle on a highway in relation to which an order made under subsection (2) has effect, where the use is permitted in accordance with provisions of the order included by virtue of subsection (3).
(6) If an authority who are a local planning authority for the area in which a highway to which an order under subsection (2) relates is situated apply to the Secretary of State in that behalf, he may by order revoke that order, and, if he does so, any right to use vehicles on the highway in relation to which the order was made which was extinguished by virtue of the order under that subsection shall be reinstated.
[(7) not included.]
(8) Before making an application under subsection (2) or (6) the local planning authority shall consult with the highway authority (if different) and any other authority who are a local planning authority for the area in question.
(9) Subsections (2),(3),(4) and (6) of section 247 shall apply to an order under this section as they apply to an order under that section.
Text: p 161

251. Extinguishment of public rights of way over land held for planning purposes

(1) Where any land has been acquired or appropriated for planning purposes and is for the time being held by a local authority for the purposes for which it was acquired or appropriated, the Secretary of State may by order extinguish any public right of way over the land if he is satisfied –

TOWN AND COUNTRY PLANNING ACT 1990

(a) that an alternative right of way has been or will be provided, or
(b) that the provision of an alternative right of way is not required;
(2) In this section any reference to the acquisition or appropriation of land for planning purposes shall be construed in accordance with section 246(1) as if this section were in Part IX.
(3) Subsection (1) shall also apply (with the substitution of a reference to the Broads Authority for the reference to the local authority) in relation to any land within the Broads which is held by the Broads Authority and which was acquired by, or vested in, the Authority for any purpose connected with the discharge of any of its functions.
Text: p 151
Part IX of the Act deals with the acquisition or appropriation of land for planning purposes by a local authority.

252. Procedure for making of orders

(1) Before making an order under section 247, 248, 249 or 251 the Secretary of State shall publish in at least one local newspaper circulating in the relevant area, and in the London Gazette, a notice–
(a) stating the general effect of the order;
(b) specifying a place in the relevant area where a copy of the draft order and of any relevant map or plan may be inspected by any person free of charge at all reasonable hours during a period of 28 days from the date of the publication of the notice ('the publication date'); and
(c) stating that any person may within that period by notice to the Secretary of State object to the making of the order.
(2) Not later than the publication date, the Secretary of State shall serve a copy of the notice, together with a copy of the draft order and of any relevant map or plan–
(a) on every local authority in whose area any highway or, as the case may be, any land to which the order relates is situated, and
(b) on any water, sewerage, hydraulic power or electricity undertakers or public gas supplier having any cables, mains, sewers, pipes or wires laid along, across, under or over any highway to be stopped up or diverted or, as the case may be, any land over which a right of way is to be extinguished, under the order.
(3) Not later than the publication date, the Secretary of State shall also cause a copy of the notice to be displayed in a prominent position at the ends of so much of the highway as is proposed to be stopped up or diverted or, as the case may be, of the right of way proposed to be extinguished under the order.
(4) If before the end of the said period of 28 days mentioned in subsection (1)(b) an objection is received by the Secretary of State from any local authority or undertakers or public gas supplier on whom a notice is required to be served under subsection (2), or from any other person appearing to him to be affected by the order, and the objection is not withdrawn, then unless subsection (5) applies the Secretary of State shall cause a local inquiry to be held.
(5) If, in a case where the objection is made by a person other than such a local authority or undertakers or supplier, the Secretary of State is satisfied that in the special circumstances of the case the holding of such an inquiry is unnecessary he may dispense with the inquiry.
(6) Subsections (2) to (5) of section 250 of the Local Government Act 1972 (local inquiries: evidence and costs) shall apply in relation to an inquiry caused to be held by the Secretary of State under subsection (4).

(7) Where publication of the notice mentioned in subsection (1) takes place on more than one day, the references in this section to the publication date are references to the latest date on which it is published.
(8) After considering any objections to the order which are not withdrawn, and, where a local inquiry is held, the report of the person who held the inquiry, the Secretary of State may, subject to subsection (9), make the order either without modification or subject to such modifications as he thinks fit.
(9) Where–
(a) the order contains a provision requiring any such payment, repayment or contribution as is mentioned in section 247(4)(a); and
(b) objection to that provision is duly made by an authority or person who would be required thereby to make such a payment, repayment or contribution; and
(c) the objection is not withdrawn,
the order shall be subject to special parliamentary procedure.
(10) Immediately after the order has been made, the Secretary of State shall publish, in the manner specified in subsection (1), a notice stating that the order has been made, and naming a place where a copy of the order may be seen at all reasonable hours.
(11) Subsections (2), (3) and (7) shall have effect in relation to a notice under subsection (10) as they have effect in relation to a notice under subsection (1).
(12) In this section–
'the relevant area', in relation to an order, means the area in which any highway or land to which the order relates is situated;
'local authority' means the council of a county, district or parish or London borough, a joint authority established by Part IV of the Local Government Act 1985, a housing action trust established under Part III of the Housing Act 1988 and the parish meeting of a rural parish not having a separate parish council; and in subsection (2)–
(i) the reference to water undertakers shall be construed as including a reference to the National Rivers Authority, and
(ii) the reference to electricity undertakers shall be construed as a reference to holders of licences under section 6 of the Electricity Act 1989 who are entitled to exercise any power conferred by paragraph 1 of Schedule 4 to that Act.
Text: p 137, 146, 161

253. Procedure in anticipation of planning permission.
(1) Where–
(a) the Secretary of State would, if planning permission for any development had been granted under Part III, have power to make an order under section 247 or 248 authorising the stopping-up or diversion of a highway in order to enable that development to be carried out; and
(b) subsection (2), (3) or (4) applies,
then, notwithstanding that such permission has not been granted, the Secretary of State may publish notice of the draft of such an order in accordance with section 252.
(2) This subsection applies where the relevant development is the subject of an application for planning permission and either–
(a) that application is made by a local authority or statutory undertakers or the British Coal Corporation; or

TOWN AND COUNTRY PLANNING ACT 1990

(b) that application stands referred to the Secretary of State in pursuance of a direction under section 77; or
(c) the applicant has appealed to the Secretary of State under section 78 against a refusal of planning permission or of approval required under a development order, or against a condition of any such permission or approval.
(3) This subsection applies where—
(a) the relevant development is to be carried out by a local authority or statutory undertakers and requires, by virtue of an enactment, the authorisation of a government department; and
(b) the developers have made application to the department for that authorisation and also requested a direction under section 90(1) that planning permission be deemed to be granted for that development.
(4) This subsection applies where the council of a county, metropolitan district or London borough or a joint planning board certify that they have begun to take such steps, in accordance with regulations made by virtue of section 316, as are required to enable them to obtain planning permission for the relevant development.
(5) Section 252(8) shall not be construed as authorising the Secretary of State to make an order under section 247 or 248 of which notice has been published by virtue of subsection (1) until planning permission is granted for the development which occasions the making of the order.
Text: p 147

257. Footpaths and bridleways affected by development: orders by other authorities.

(1) Subject to section 259, a competent authority may by order authorise the stopping up or diversion of any footpath or bridleway if they are satisfied that it is necessary to do so in order to enable development to be carried out—
(a) in accordance with planning permission granted under Part III, or
(b) by a government department.
(2) An order under this section may, if the competent authority are satisfied that it should do so, provide—
(a) for the creation of an alternative highway for use as a replacement for the one authorised by the order to be stopped up or diverted, or for the improvement of an existing highway for such use;
(b) for authorising or requiring works to be carried out in relation to any footpath or bridleway for whose stopping up or diversion, creation or improvement, provision is made by the order;
[(c) not included.]
(d) for requiring any person named in the order to pay, or make contributions in respect of, the cost of carrying out any such works.
(3) An order may be made under this section authorising the stopping up or diversion of a footpath or bridleway which is temporarily stopped up or diverted under any other enactment.
(4) In this section 'competent authority' means—
(a) in the case of development authorised by a planning permission, the local planning authority who granted the permission or, in the case of a permission granted by the Secretary of State, who would have had power to grant it; and
(b) in the case of development carried out by a government department, the local planning authority who would have had power to grant planning per-

mission on an application in respect of the development in question if such an application had fallen to be made.
Text: p 146

258. Extinguishment of public rights of way over land held for planning purposes
(1) Where any land has been acquired or appropriated for planning purposes and is for the time being held by a local authority for the purposes for which it was acquired or appropriated, then, subject to section 259, the local authority may by order extinguish any public right of way over the land, being a footpath or bridleway, if they are satisfied –
(a) that an alternative right of way has been or will be provided, or
(b) that the provision of an alternative right of way is not required.
(2) In this section any reference to the acquisition or appropriation of land for planning purposes shall be construed in accordance with section 246(1) as if this section were in Part IX.
(3) Subsection (1) shall also apply (with the substitution of a reference to the Broads Authority for the reference to the local authority) in relation to any land within the Broads which is held by the Broads Authority and which was acquired by, or vested in, the Authority for any purpose connected with the discharge of any of its functions.
Text: p 151
Part IX of the Act deals with the acquisition or appropriation of land for planning purposes by a local authority.

259. Confirmation of orders made by other authorities
(1) An order made under section 257 or 258 shall not take effect unless confirmed by the Secretary of State, or unless confirmed, as an unopposed order, by the authority who made it.
(2) The Secretary of State shall not confirm any such order unless satisfied as to every matter of which the authority making the order are required under section 257 or, as the case may, section 258 to be satisfied.
(3) The time specified–
(a) in an order under section 257 as the time from which a footpath or bridleway is to be stopped up or diverted; or
(b) in an order under section 258 as the time from which a right of way is to be extinguished,
shall not be earlier than confirmation of the order.
(4) Schedule 14 shall have effect with respect to the confirmation of orders under section 257 or 258 and the publicity for such orders after they are confirmed.

261. Temporary stopping up of highways for mineral workings
(1) Where the Secretary of State is satisfied–
(a) that an order made by him under section 247 for the stopping up or diversion of a highway is required for the purpose of enabling minerals to be worked by surface working; and
(b) that the highway can be restored, after the minerals have been worked, to a condition not substantially less convenient to the public,
the order may provide for the stopping up or diversion of the highway during

TOWN AND COUNTRY PLANNING ACT 1990

such period as may be prescribed by or under the order, and for its restoration at the expiration of that period.
(2) Where a competent authority within the meaning of section 257 are satisfied—
(a) that an order made by them under that section for the stopping up or diversion of a footpath or bridleway is required for the purpose of enabling minerals to be worked by surface working; and
(b) that the footpath or bridleway can be restored, after the minerals have been worked, to a condition not substantially less convenient to the public,
the order may provide for the stopping up or diversion of the footpath or bridleway during such period as may be prescribed by or under the order, and for its restoration at the expiration of that period.
(3) Without prejudice to the provisions of section 247 or 257, any such order as is authorised by subsection (1) or (2) may contain such provisions as appear to the Secretary of State, or, as the case may be, the competent authority, to be expedient—
[(a) not included.]
(b) for the stopping up at the expiry of that period of any highway so provided and for the reconstruction and maintenance of the original highway;
[remainder not included]
[(4) and (5) not included]
Text: p 150

287. Proceedings for questioning validity of development plans and certain schemes and orders

(1) If any person aggrieved by a unitary development plan or a local plan or by any alteration, repeal or replacement of any such plan or structure plan, desires to question the validity of the plan or, as the case may be, the alteration, repeal or replacement on the ground—
(a) that it is not within the powers conferred by Part II, or
(b) that any requirement of that Part or of any regulations made under it has not been complied with in relation to the approval or adoption of the plan or, as the case may be, its alteration, repeal or replacement,
he may make an application to the High Court under this section.
(2) On any application under this section the High Court—
(a) may by interim order wholly or in part suspend the operation of the plan or, as the case may be, the alteration, repeal or replacement, either generally or in so far as it affects any property of the applicant, until the final determination of the proceedings;
(b) if satisfied that the plan or, as the case may be, the alteration, repeal or replacement is wholly or to any extent outside the powers conferred by Part II, or that the interests of the applicant have been substantially prejudiced by the failure to comply with any requirement of that Part or of any regulations made under it, may wholly or in part quash the plan or, as the case may be, the alteration, repeal or replacement either generally or in so far as it affects any property of the applicant.
(3) Subsections (1) and (2) shall apply, subject to any necessary modifications, (...) to an order under section 247, 248, 249, 251, 257, 258 or 277 as they apply to any plan or any alteration, repeal or replacement there mentioned.
(4) An application under this section must be made within six weeks of the relevant date.

RIGHTS OF WAY

(5) For the purposes of subsection (4) the relevant date is–
[(a) and (b) not included.]
(c) in the case of an application by virtue of subsection (3) in respect of an order under section 247, 248, 249 or 251, the date on which the notice required by section 252(10) is first published,
(d) in the case of an application by virtue of subsection (3) in respect of an order under section 257 or 258, the date on which the notice required by paragraph 7 of Schedule 14 is first published in accordance with that paragraph, [remainder of section not included.]
Text: p 135

320. Local inquiries
(1) The Secretary of State may cause a local inquiry to be held for the purposes of the exercise of any of his functions under any of the provisions of this Act.
(2) Subsections (2) to (5) of section 250 of the Local Government Act 1972 (local inquiries: evidence and costs) apply to an inquiry held by virtue of this section.
Text: p 129
LGA 72 s 250: p 311

321. Planning inquiries to be held in public subject to certain exceptions
(1) This section applies to any inquiry held under section 320(1),(...)
(2) Subject to subsection (3), at any such inquiry oral evidence shall be heard in public and documentary evidence shall be open to public inspection.
(3) If the Secretary of State is satisfied in the case of any such inquiry–
(a) that giving evidence of a particular description or, as the case may be, making it available for inspection would be likely to result in the disclosure of information as to any of the matters mentioned in subsection (4); and
(b) that the disclosure of that information would be contrary to the national interest,
he may direct that evidence of the description indicated in the direction shall only be heard or, as the case may be, open to inspection at that inquiry by such persons or persons of such descriptions as he may specify in the direction.
(4) The matters referred to in subsection (3)(a) are–
(a) national security; and
(b) the measures taken or to be taken to ensure the security of any premises or property.
Text: p 129

322. Orders as to costs of parties where no local inquiry held
(1) This section applies to proceedings under this Act where the Secretary of State is required, before reaching a decision, to give any person an opportunity of appearing before and being heard by a person appointed by him.
(2) The Secretary of State has the same power to make orders under section 250(5) of the Local Government Act 1972 (orders with respect to the costs of the parties) in relation to proceedings to which this section applies which do not give rise to a local inquiry as he has in relation to a local inquiry.
Text: p 132

TOWN AND COUNTRY PLANNING ACT 1990

329. Service of notices
(1) Any notice or other document required or authorised to be served or given under this Act may be served or given either–
(a) by delivering it to the person on whom it is to be served or to whom it is to be given; or
(b) by leaving it at the usual or last known place of abode of that person, or, in a case where an address for service has been given by that person, at that address; or
(c) by sending it in a prepaid registered letter, or by the recorded delivery service, addressed to that person at his usual or last known place of abode, or, in a case where an address for service has been given by that person, at that address; or
(d) in the case of an incorporated company or body, by delivering it to the secretary or clerk of the company or body at their registered or principal office, or sending it in a prepaid registered letter, or by the recorded delivery service, addressed to the secretary or clerk of the company or body at that office.
[(2) & (3) not included.]

333. Regulations and orders
[(1) to (6) not included.]
(7) Without prejudice to section 14 of the Interpretation Act 1978, any power conferred by any of the provisions of this Act to make an order, shall include power to vary or revoke any such order by a subsequent order.
Text: p 136

336. Interpretation
(1) In this Act, except in so far as the context otherwise requires, (...)–
(...)
'bridleway' has the same meaning as in the Highways Act 1980;
'the Broads' has the same meaning as in the Norfolk and Suffolk Broads Act 1988;
(...)
'development' has the meaning given in section 55, and 'develop' shall be construed accordingly;
(...)
'footpath' has the same meaning as in the Highways Act 1980;
(...)
'highway' has the same meaning as in the Highways Act 1980;
(...)
'local authority' (except in section 252 (...)) means–
(a) a charging authority, a precepting authority (except the Receiver for the Metropolitan Police District), a combined police authority or a combined fire authority, as those expressions are defined in section 144 of the Local Government Finance Act 1988;
(b) a levying body within the meaning of section 74 of that Act; and
(c) a body as regards which section 75 of that Act applies;
and includes any joint board or joint committee if all the constituent authorities are local authorities within paragraph (a), (b) or (c);
(...)
'minerals' includes all minerals and substances in or under land of a kind

ordinarily worked for removal by underground or surface working, except that it does not include peat cut for purposes other than sale;
(...)
For the definitions in the Highways Act 1980 see HA 80 s 329 (p 357).

Schedule 14: Procedure for footpaths and bridleways orders
Part I: confirmation of orders
1. (1) Before an order under section 257 or 258 is submitted to the Secretary of State for confirmation or confirmed as an unopposed order, the authority by whom the order was made shall give notice in the prescribed form–
(a) stating the general effect of the order and that it has been made and is about to be submitted for confirmation or to be confirmed as an unopposed order;
(b) naming a place in the area in which the land to which the order relates is situated where a copy of the order may be inspected free of charge and copies of it may be obtained at a reasonable charge at all reasonable hours; and
(c) specifying the time (which must not be less than 28 days from the date of the first publication of the notice) within which, and the manner in which, representations or objections with respect to the order may be made.
(2) Subject to sub-paragraphs (6) and (7), the notice to be given under sub-paragraph (1) shall be given–
(a) by publication in at least one local newspaper circulating in the area in which the land to which the order relates is situated; and
(b) by serving a similar notice on–
(i) every owner, occupier and lessee (except tenants for a month or a period less than a month and statutory tenants within the meaning of the Rent Act 1977) of any of that land;
(ii) every council, the council of every rural parish and the parish meeting of every rural parish not having a separate parish council, being a council or parish whose area includes any of that land; and
(iii) any statutory undertakers to whom there belongs, or by whom there is used, for the purposes of their undertakings, any apparatus under, in, on, over, along or across that land; and
(iv) every person on whom notice is required to be served in pursuance of sub-paragraph (4); and
(v) such other persons as may be prescribed in relation to the area in which that land is situated or as the authority may consider appropriate; and
(c) by causing a copy of the notice to be displayed in a prominent position–
(i) at the ends of so much of any footpath or bridleway as is to be stopped up, diverted or extinguished by the order:
(ii) at council offices in the locality of the land to which the order relates; and
(iii) at such other places as the authority may consider appropriate.
(3) In sub-paragraph (2)–
'council' means a county council, a district council, a London borough council or a joint authority established under Part IV of the Local Government Act 1985;
'council offices' means offices or buildings acquired or provided by a council or by the council of a parish or community or the parish meeting of a parish not having a separate parish council.
(4) Any person may, on payment of such reasonable charge as the authority may consider appropriate, require an authority to give him notice of all such

TOWN AND COUNTRY PLANNING ACT 1990

orders under section 257 or 258 as are made by the authority during a specified period, are of a specified description and relate to land comprised in a specified area.

(5) In sub-paragraph (4) 'specified' means specified in the requirement.

(6) Except where an owner, occupier or lessee is a local authority or statutory undertaker, the Secretary of State may in any particular case direct that it shall not be necessary to comply with sub-paragraph (2)(b)(i).

(7) If the Secretary of State gives a direction under sub-paragraph (6) in the case of any land, then–

(a) in addition to publication the notice shall be addressed to 'the owners and any occupiers' of the land (describing it); and

(b) a copy or copies of the notice shall be affixed to some conspicuous object or objects on the land.

(8) Sub-paragraph (2)(b) and (c) and, where applicable, sub-paragraph (7) shall be complied with not less than 28 days before the expiry of the time specified in the notice.

(9) A notice required to be served by sub-paragraph (2)(b)(i), (ii), (iii) or (v) shall be accompanied by a copy of the order.

(10) A notice required to be displayed by sub-paragraph (2)(c)(i) at the ends of so much of any way as is affected by the order shall be accompanied by a plan showing the general effect of the order so far as it relates to that way.

2. If no representations or objections are duly made, or if any so made are withdrawn, the authority by whom the order was made may, instead of submitting the order to the Secretary of State, themselves confirm the order (but without any modification).

3. (1) This paragraph applies where any representation or objection which has been duly made is not withdrawn.

(2) If the objection is made by a local authority the Secretary of State shall, before confirming the order, cause a local inquiry to be held.

(3) If the representation or objection is made by a person other than a local authority the Secretary of State shall, before confirming the order, either–

(a) cause a local inquiry to be held; or

(b) give any person by whom any representation or objection has been duly made and not withdrawn an opportunity of being heard by a person appointed by the Secretary of State for the purpose.

(4) After considering the report of the person appointed under sub-paragraph (2) or (3) to hold the inquiry or to hear representations or objections, the Secretary of State may confirm the order, with or without modifications.

(5) In the case of an order under section 257, if objection is made by statutory undertakers on the ground that the order provides for the creation of a public right of way over land covered by works used for the purpose of their undertaking, or over the curtilage of such land, and the objection is not withdrawn, the order shall be subject to special parliamentary procedure.

(6) Notwithstanding anything in the previous provisions of this paragraph, the Secretary of State shall not confirm an order so as to affect land not affected by the order as submitted to him, except after–

(a) giving such notice as appears to him requisite of his proposal so to modify the order, specifying the time (which must not be less than 28 days from the date of the first publication of the notice) within which, and the manner in which, representations or objections with respect to the proposal may be made;

RIGHTS OF WAY

(b) holding a local inquiry or giving any person by whom any representation or objection has been duly made and not withdrawn an opportunity of being heard by a person appointed by the Secretary of State for the purpose; and
(c) considering the report of the person appointed to hold the inquiry or, as the case may be, to hear representations or objections.

(7) In the case of an order under section 257, if objection is made by statutory undertakers on the ground that the order as modified would provide for the creation of a public right of way over land covered by works used for the purposes of their undertaking, or over the curtilage of such land, and the objection is not withdrawn, the order shall be subject to special parliamentary procedure.

4. (1) A decision of the Secretary of State under paragraph 3 shall, except in such classes of case as may for the time being be prescribed or as may be specified in directions given by the Secretary of State, be made by a person appointed by the Secretary of State for the purpose instead of by the Secretary of State.

(2) A decision made by a person so appointed shall be treated as a decision of the Secretary of State.

(3) The Secretary of State may, if he thinks fit, direct that a decision which, by virtue of sub-paragraph (1) and apart from this sub-paragraph, falls to be made by a person appointed by the Secretary of State shall instead be made by the Secretary of State.

(4) A direction under sub-paragraph (3) shall–
(a) state the reasons for which it is given; and
(b) be served on the person, if any, so appointed, the authority and any person by whom a representation or objection has been duly made and not withdrawn.

(5) Where the Secretary of State has appointed a person to make a decision under paragraph 3 the Secretary of State may, at any time before the making of the decision, appoint another person to make it instead of the person first appointed to make it.

(6) Where by virtue of sub-paragraph (3) or (5) a particular decision falls to be made by the Secretary of State or any other person instead of the person first appointed to make it, anything done by or in relation to the latter shall be treated as having been done by or in relation to the former.

(7) Regulations under this Act may provide for the giving of publicity to any directions given by the Secretary of State under this paragraph.

5. (1) The Secretary of State shall not confirm an order under section 257 which extinguishes a right of way over land under, in, on, over, along or across which there is any apparatus belonging to or used by statutory undertakers for the purposes of their undertaking, unless the undertakers have consented to the confirmation of the order.

(2) Any such consent may be given subject to the condition that there are included in the order such provisions for the protection of the undertakers as they may reasonably require.

(3) The consent of statutory undertakers to any such order shall not be unreasonably withheld.

(4) Any question arising under this paragraph whether the withholding of consent is unreasonable, or whether any requirement is reasonable, shall be determined by whichever Minister is the appropriate Minister in relation to the statutory undertakers concerned.

TOWN AND COUNTRY PLANNING ACT 1990

6. Regulations under this Act may, subject to this Part of this Schedule, make such provision as the Secretary of State thinks expedient as to the procedure on the making, submission and confirmation of orders under sections 257 and 258.

Part II: publicity for orders after confirmation
7. (1) As soon as may be after an order under section 257 or 258 has been confirmed by the Secretary of State or confirmed as an unopposed order, the authority by whom the order was made –
(a) shall publish, in the manner required by paragraph 1(2)(a), a notice in the prescribed form–
(i) describing the general effect of the order,
(ii) stating that it has been confirmed, and
(iii) naming a place in the area in which the land to which the order relates is situated where a copy of the order as confirmed may be inspected free of charge and copies of it may be obtained at a reasonable charge at all reasonable hours;
(b) shall serve a similar notice on any persons on whom notices were required to be served under paragraph 1(2)(b) or (7); and
(c) shall cause similar notices to be displayed in a similar manner as the notices required to be displayed under paragraph 1(2)(c).
(2) No such notice or copy need be served on a person unless he has sent to the authority a request in that behalf, specifying an address for service.
(3) A notice required to be served by sub-paragraph (1)(b) on–
(a) a person on whom notice was required to be served by paragraph 1(2)(b)(i), (ii) or (iii); or
(b) in the case of an order which has been confirmed with modifications, a person on whom notice was required to be served by paragraph 1(2)(b)(v),
shall be accompanied by a copy of the order as confirmed.
(4) As soon as possible after a decision not to confirm an order under section 257 or 258, the authority by whom the order was made shall give notice of the decision by serving a copy of it on any persons on whom notices were required to be served under paragraph 1(2)(b) or (7).
8. Where an order under section 257 or 258 has come into force otherwise than–
(a) on the date on which it was confirmed by the Secretary of State or confirmed as an unopposed order; or
(b) at the expiration of a specified period beginning with that date,
then as soon as possible after it has come into force the authority by whom it was made shall give notice of its coming into force by publication in at least one local newspaper circulating in the area in which the land to which the order relates is situated.
Text: p 126, 135
No regulations have been made under the Act. The Town and Country Planning (Public Path Orders) Regulations 1983 SI 1983 No 22 (p 453) apply to orders under Sch 14 as they applied to orders under Sch 20 to the Town and Country Planning Act 1971.

Regulations

Note: where the regulations prescribe forms of orders and notices, *italics* have been used to indicate optional or alternative text and asterisks to denote the location of names or descriptive text.

CHURCH PROPERTY (MISCELLANEOUS PROVISIONS) MEASURE 1960

11. Power to dedicate land for highways
(1) The incumbent of a benefice may dedicate for the purpose of a highway, either with or without consideration, any such land belonging to the benefice as is hereinafter mentioned, that is to say:–
(a) any land forming part of the garden, orchard or appurtenances of the residence house of the benefice and any land contiguous thereto, and
(b) any land forming part of the glebe of the benefice:
Provided that no land shall be dedicated under this section without the consent of the bishop, the Commissioners, the patron and the diocesan dilapidations board.
[(2) not included]
Text: p 72

THE WILDLIFE AND COUNTRYSIDE (DEFINITIVE MAPS AND STATEMENTS) REGULATIONS 1983 SI 1983 No 21

Citation and commencement
1. These regulations may be cited as the Wildlife and Countryside (Definitive Maps and Statements) Regulations 1983, and shall come into operation on 28th February 1983.

Interpretation
2. In these regulations:
'the Act' means the Wildlife and Countryside Act 1981;
'a modification order' means an order made under section 53(2)(a) or (b), or 55(4) or 55(5) of the Act;
'a reclassification order' means an order made under section 54(1)(b) of the Act.

Scale of definitive maps
3. A definitive map shall be on a scale of not less than two and a half inches to one mile (or 1/25,000); provided that where the surveying authority considers it expedient to show any particulars required to be shown on the map on a larger scale, it may employ an inset map for that purpose.

Notation to be used on definitive maps
4. Rights of way to which Part III of the Act applies shall be shown on a definitive map in the manner specified in Schedule 1 hereto.

RIGHTS OF WAY

Modification orders

5. A modification order shall be in the appropriate form (or substantially in the appropriate form) set out in Schedule 2 hereto with such modifications as the circumstances may require, and shall contain a map.

6. A reclassification order shall be in the appropriate form (or substantially in the appropriate form) set out in Schedule 3 hereto with such modifications as the circumstances may require, and shall contain a map.

Provisions supplementary to regulations 5 and 6

7. Regulation 3 above shall apply in relation to the scale of a definitive map.

8. Regulation 4 above shall apply in relation to the map contained in a modification or reclassification order as it applies in relation to a definitive map.

9. The provisions of Schedule 4 hereto shall apply in relation to the making, submission and confirmation of modification or reclassification orders.

Applications for a modification order

10. (1) An application for a modification order shall be in the appropriate form (or substantially in the appropriate form) set out in Schedule 7 hereto, with such modifications as the circumstances may require, and shall contain a map.

(2) Regulation 3 above shall apply in relation to the scale of the map accompanying an application for a modification order as it applies in relation to the scale of the map contained in a modification or reclassification order.

(3) A notice required by paragraph 2 of Schedule 14 to the Act shall be in the appropriate form (or substantially in the appropriate form) set out in Schedule 8 hereto.

(4) A certificate required by paragraph 2 of Schedule 14 to the Act shall be in the appropriate form (or substantially in the appropriate form) set out in Schedule 9 hereto.

SCHEDULE 1 *Regulation 4*

NOTATION TO BE USED ON DEFINITIVE MAPS

(a) A footpath shall be shown by either a continuous purple line or by a continuous line with short bars at intervals, as thus:

―┴―┴―┴―┴―┴―┴―┴―┴―┴―┴―

or by a broken black line with short intervals, as thus:

― ― ― ― ― ― ― ― ― ―

(b) A bridleway shall be shown by either a continuous green line or by a continuous line with cross bars at intervals, as thus:

―┼―――┼―――┼―――┼―

or by a broken line with cross bars in the intervals, as thus:

―│―│―│―│―│―│―

DEFINITIVE MAPS AND STATEMENTS REGULATIONS

(c) A road used as a public path shall be shown by either a green broken line or by a broken line and small arrowheads as thus:

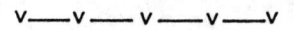

v——v——v——v——v

(d) A byway open to all traffic shall be shown by either a continuous brown line or by a continuous line with arrowheads alternately above and below the line, as thus:

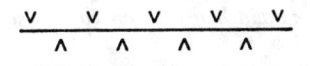

SCHEDULE 2   Regulation 5

FORM OF MODIFICATION ORDER

Wildlife and Countryside Act 1981

[Title of Definitive Map and Statement]

[Title of Order]

Whereas pursuant to section *[53(2)(a)]* *[53(2)(b)]* *[55(5)]* of the Wildlife and Countryside Act 1981 (hereinafter called 'the Act') it appears to the *[insert name of authority]* (hereinafter called 'the surveying authority') that the *[insert title of definitive map and statement]* require modification *[in consequence of the occurrence of an event specified in section 53(3)]* *[specify the appropriate paragraph and sub-paragraph]*, namely, *[specify event]* *[in accordance with the provisions of [section 55(4)] [(a)] [(b)] [(c)]*. i.e.*[specify provision]* *[section 55(5)]* *[(a)]* *[(b)]*, i.e.*[specify provision]* of the Act;
[And whereas the surveying authority have consulted with every local authority whose area includes the land to which the order relates;]

Now, therefore, the surveying authority, in exercise of the power conferred by section *[53(2)(a)]* *[53(2)(b)]* *[55(4)]* *[55(5)]* of the Act, hereby make the following order:
1. For the purposes of this order the relevant date shall be ***** 19**.

2. The *[insert title of definitive map and statement]* shall be modified as described in *[Part I]* *[and]* *[Part II]* of the Schedule hereto and shown on the map annexed hereto.

3. This order shall have effect on the date *[it is made]* *[it is confirmed]*.

RIGHTS OF WAY

4. This order may be cited as the *[insert title of order]* 19**.

Schedule

[Part I]

Modification of *[Definitive]* Map

[Description of path or way to be deleted
Describe position, length and width of path or way in sections, e.g. A-B, B-C, etc., as indicated on map.]
[Description of path or way to be added
Describe position, length and width of path or way in sections, e.g. A-C, B-D, etc., as indicated on map.]
[Description of public right of way to be (upgraded) (downgraded)
Describe position, length and width of public right of way in sections, e.g., A-B, C-D, etc., as indicated on map.]

[Part II]

Modification of *[Definitive]* Statement

Variation of particulars of path or way
[Set out varied description of path or way or additional particulars.]

SCHEDULE 3   Regulation 6

FORM OF RECLASSIFICATION ORDER

Wildlife and Countryside Act 1981

[Title of Definitive Map and Statement]

[Title of Order]

Whereas pursuant to section 54(1)(a) of the Wildlife and Countryside Act 1981 (hereinafter called 'the Act') the *[insert name of authority]* (hereinafter called 'the surveying authority') have carried out a review of such of the particulars contained in the definitive map and statement for their area as relate to roads used as public paths;

And whereas by virtue of section 54(1)(b) of the Act the surveying authority are required by order to make such modifications to the map and statement as appear to them to be requisite to provide for the reclassification of roads used as public paths;

And whereas the surveying authority have consulted with every local authority whose area includes the land to which the order relates;

Now, therefore, the surveying authority, in exercise of the powers conferred by section 54(1) of the Act, hereby make the following order:

1. The relevant date for the purpose of this order shall be ***** 19**.

DEFINITIVE MAPS AND STATEMENTS REGULATIONS

2. The *[insert title of definitive map and statement]* shall be modified by showing as a *[footpath] [bridleway] [byway open to all traffic]* the road(s) used as (a) public path(s) described in the Schedule hereto and shown on the map annexed hereto.

3. This order shall have effect on the date it is confirmed.

4. This order may be cited as the *[name of authority]* Definitive Map (Reclassification) Order 19**.

Schedule

Description of road(s) used as (a) public path(s)	Reclassification

SCHEDULE 4   *Regulation 9*

ADDITIONAL PROVISIONS IN RELATION TO THE MAKING, SUBMISSION AND CONFIRMATION OF MODIFICATION OR RECLASSIFICATION ORDERS

1. A modification or reclassification order shall be made in duplicate.

2. Any notice required to be given, served or displayed by Schedule 15 to the Act shall be in the form set out in Schedule 5 hereto, subject to any necessary modifications, and shall be served on the additional persons specified in Schedule 6 hereto.

3. Any notice or other document to be served on an owner or occupier in accordance with paragraph 3(2)(b)(i) of Schedule 15 to the Act shall at the beginning have clearly and legibly inscribed upon it the words 'IMPORTANT — THIS COMMUNICATION AFFECTS YOUR PROPERTY', and where the notice or document is sent under cover otherwise than in a prepaid registered letter, or by the recorded delivery service, the cover shall in addition be endorsed in like manner.

4. Where a modification or reclassification order is submitted to the Secretary of State for confirmation, it shall be accompanied by:

(a) two copies of the order;
(b) a copy of the notice required by paragraph 3 of Schedule 15 to the Act and a certificate that the requirements of that paragraph have been complied with;
(c) a copy of the relevant section of the definitive map and statement;
(d) a statement of the grounds on which the authority by whom the order was made consider that the order should be confirmed;
(e) any representations or objections which have been duly made with respect to the order and not withdrawn (together with the observations of the authority thereon); and
(f) a certificate that every local authority whose area includes the land to which the order relates has been consulted.

5. After a modification or reclassification order has been confirmed by the Secretary of State, the authority by whom the order was made shall, as soon as the requirements of paragraph 11 of Schedule 15 to the Act have been complied with, furnish to the Secretary of State a certificate to that effect.

RIGHTS OF WAY

6. After a modification or reclassification order has been confirmed, the authority by whom the order was made shall send a copy of the order as confirmed to the Ordnance Survey.

SCHEDULE 5 Regulation 9

FORM OF NOTICE AS RESPECTS MODIFICATION OR RECLASSIFICATION ORDER

NOTICE OF *[MODIFICATION] [RECLASSIFICATION]* ORDER

Wildlife and Countryside Act 1981

[Title of Definitive Map and Statement]

[Title of order]

(1) *[To: ***** of: *****]*

The above named order, made on ***** 19**, is about to be submitted to the (2) *[Secretary of State for the Environment] [Secretary of State for Wales]* for confirmation, or to be confirmed, as an unopposed order, by the (name of authority).

The effect of the order, if confirmed without modification, will be to modify the definitive map and statement for the Area by (2)

*[deleting therefrom the (footpath) (bridleway) (byway open to all traffic) from ***** to *****]*

*[and] [adding thereto the (footpath) (bridleway) (byway open to all traffic) from ***** to *****]*

*[(upgrading) (downgrading) to a (footpath) (bridleway) (byway open to all traffic) the public right of way from ***** to *****]*

*[(varying) (adding to) the particulars relating to the (footpath) (bridleway) (byway open to all traffic) from ***** to ***** by providing that *****]*

*[reclassifying as a (footpath) (bridleway) (byway open to all traffic) the road used as a public path from ***** to *****]*.

A copy of the order and the map contained in it has been deposited and may be inspected free of charge at ***** between ***** a.m. and ***** p.m. on ***** or purchased at a cost of *****.

Any representation or objection with respect to the order may be sent in writing to *[title of appropriate officer and name and address of authority]* before ***** and should state the grounds on which it is made.

If no representations or objections are duly made to the order, or to any part thereof, or if any so made are withdrawn, the *[name of authority]* may, instead of submitting the order (or that part thereof if the authority has by notice to the Secretary of State so elected) themselves confirm the order (or that part of the order). If the order is submitted to the *[Secretary of State for the Environment] [Secretary of State for Wales]* in whole or in part, any representations

DEFINITIVE MAPS AND STATEMENTS REGULATIONS

and objections which have been duly made and not withdrawn will be transmitted therewith.

Dated ***** 19**.

NOTES: (1) Insert only in personal notices.
(2) Omit what is inappropriate.

SCHEDULE 6   Regulation 9

ADDITIONAL PERSONS TO BE SERVED WITH NOTICE OF MODIFICATION OR RECLASSIFICATION ORDER

Area	Name
In England and Wales	Auto-Cycle Union British Horse Society Byways and Bridleways Trust Commons, Open Spaces and Footpaths Preservation Society Ramblers' Association
In the counties of Cheshire, Derbyshire, Greater Manchester, Lancashire, Merseyside, South Yorkshire, Staffordshire and West Yorkshire	Peak and Northern Footpaths Society
Within the county of Buckinghamshire, the districts of Beaconsfield, Chiltern and Wycombe; Within the county of Hertfordshire, the districts of Dacorum and Three Rivers; Within the county of Oxfordshire, the district of South Oxfordshire; and within the district of Aylesbury Vale, the parishes of Aston Clinton, Buckland, Drayton Beauchamp, Eddlesborough, Halton, Ivinghoe, Pitstone and Wendover.	The Chiltern Society
In Wales	Welsh Trail Riders' Association

RIGHTS OF WAY

SCHEDULE 7   *Regulation 10(1)*

FORM OF APPLICATION FOR MODIFICATION ORDER

Wildlife and Countryside Act 1981

[Title of Definitive Map and Statement]

To: *[name of authority]*
of: *[address of authority]*

I/We, *[name of applicant]* of *[address of applicant]* hereby apply for an order under section 53(2) of the Wildlife and Countryside Act 1981 modifying the definitive map and statement for the area by

*[deleting the (footpath) (bridleway) (byway open to all traffic) from ***** to *****]*

*[adding the (footpath) (bridleway) (byway open to all traffic) from ***** to *****]*

*[(upgrading) (downgrading) to a (footpath) (bridleway) (byway open to all traffic) the (footpath) (bridleway) (byway open to all traffic) from ***** to *****]*

*[(varying) (adding to) the particulars relating to the (footpath) (bridleway open to all traffic) from ***** to ***** by providing that *****]*

and shown on the map annexed hereto.

I/We attach copies of the following documentary evidence (including statements of witnesses) in support of this application:

[List of documents]

Dated ***** 19**. Signed *****

SCHEDULE 8   *Regulation 10(3)*

FORM OF NOTICE OF APPLICATION FOR MODIFICATION ORDER

Wildlife and Countryside Act 1981

[Title of Definitive Map and Statement]

To: *****
of: *****

Notice is hereby given that on the ***** 19** I/We ***** of ***** made application to the (name and address of authority) that the definitive map and statement for the area be modified by

DEFINITIVE MAPS AND STATEMENTS REGULATIONS

[deleting the (footpath) (bridleway) (byway open to all traffic) from ***** to *****]

[adding the (footpath) (bridleway) (byway open to all traffic) from ***** to *****]

[(upgrading) (downgrading) to a (footpath) (bridleway) (byway open to all traffic) the (footpath) (bridleway) (byway open to all traffic) from ***** to *****]

[(varying) (adding to) the particulars relating to the (footpath) (bridleway open to all traffic) from ***** to ***** by providing that *****]

Dated ***** 19**. Signed *****

SCHEDULE 9   Regulation 10(4)

FORM OF CERTIFICATE OF SERVICE OF NOTICE OF APPLICATION FOR MODIFICATION ORDER

Wildlife and Countryside Act 1981

[Title of Definitive Map and Statement]

Certificate of service of notice of application for modification order

To: *[name of authority]*
of: *[address of authority]*

I/We, *[name of applicant]* of *[address of applicant]* hereby certify that the requirements of paragraph 2 of Schedule 14 to the Wildlife and Countryside Act 1981 have been complied with.

Dated ***** 19**. Signed *****

Text: p 94

THE TOWN AND COUNTRY PLANNING (PUBLIC PATH ORDERS) REGULATIONS 1983 SI 1983 No 22

Citation, commencement, interpretation and revocation
1. These regulations may be cited as the Town and Country Planning (Public Path Orders) Regulations 1983 and shall come into operation on 28th February 1983.
2. In these regulations, unless the context otherwise requires:
'the Act' means the Town and Country Planning Act 1971; and

'a public path order', means an order made under section 210 or 214(1)(b) of the Act and includes an order revoking or varying any such order.

3. The Town and Country Planning (Public Path Orders) Regulations 1969 are hereby revoked.

Form of order

4. A public path order shall be in the appropriate form (or substantially in the appropriate form) set out in Schedule 1 hereto with such modifications as the circumstances may require.

5. The map required to be contained in a public path order shall be on a scale of not less than twenty-five inches to one mile (or 1/2,500) or on such smaller scale as the Secretary of State may authorise in any particular case.

6. In the case of any conflict between the map and the particulars contained in a schedule to a public path order, the schedule shall prevail.

Procedure

7. (1) A public path order shall be made in duplicate, and where the order is submitted to the Secretary of State for confirmation shall be accompanied by two copies of the order and a copy of any notice published before the submission as required by paragraph 1 of Schedule 20 to the Act, a statement by the authority by whom such order was made of the grounds on which the authority consider that such order should be confirmed, and any representations or objections which have been duly made with respect to such order and not withdrawn together with the observations thereon of the authority.

(2) Where a public path order provides for extinguishing a right of way over land under, in, over, along or across which there is any apparatus belonging to or used by statutory undertakers for the purpose of their undertaking the consent of the undertakers shall also be sent to the Secretary of State when the order is submitted to him for confirmation.

8. After a public path order has been confirmed by the Secretary of State, the authority by whom such order was made shall, as soon as the requirements of paragraph 6(1) of Schedule 20 to the Act have been complied with, furnish to the Secretary of State a certificate to that effect, and a copy of the notice required by that paragraph to be published.

9. After a decision not to confirm a public path order, the authority by whom the order was made shall, as soon as the requirements of paragraph 6(3) of Schedule 20 to the Act have been complied with, furnish to the Secretary of State a certificate to that effect.

10. After a public path order has been confirmed, the authority by whom the order was made shall send a copy of the order as confirmed to the Ordnance Survey.

11. Any notice required to be given, served or displayed under Schedule 20 to the Act authority by whom a public path order is made shall be in the appropriate form (or substantially in the appropriate form) set out in Schedule 2 hereto.

12. The Notice required to be given under paragraphs 1(1) and 6(1)(a) of Schedule 20 to the Act shall be served on the persons specified in Schedule 3 hereto.

TOWN AND COUNTRY PLANNING (PUBLIC PATH ORDERS) REGS.

SCHEDULE 1

Regulation 4

FORMS OF ORDERS

Form No 1

Public Path *[Stopping-Up]* *[Diversion]* Order

Town and Country Planning Act 1971, Section 210

[Title of Order]

Whereas the *[name of order-making authority]* are satisfied that is necessary to *[stop-up]* *[divert]* the *[footpath]* *[bridleway]* to which this order relates in order to enable development to be carried out *[in accordance with planning permission granted under Part III of the Town and Country Planning Act 1971 or the enactments replaced by that Part of that Act]* *[by a government department]*; Now, therefore, the *[name of order-making authority]* in pursuance of the powers in that behalf conferred by section 210 of the Town and Country Planning Act 1971 hereby make the following order:

1. The *[footpath]* *[bridleway]* over the land situate at ***** shown by a bold black line on the map annexed hereto and described in Part I of the Schedule hereto shall be *[stopped-up]* *[diverted]* as provided by this order.

[2. There shall be created to the reasonable satisfaction of [name of order-making authority] an alternative highway for use as a replacement for the [footpath] [bridleway] referred to in Article 1 above as specified in, and over the land described in, Part II of the Schedule hereto and shown by bold black dashes on the map contained in this order.]
or
*[2. The highway over the land situate at ***** described in Part III of the Schedule hereto and shown hatched black on the map contained in this order shall be improved to the reasonable satisfaction of [name of order-making authority] as follows [description of improvement].]*

3. The *[stopping-up]* *[diversion]* of the *[footpath]* *[bridleway]* referred to in Article 1 above shall have effect *[on the date on which it is certified by [name of order-making authority] that the provisions of Article 2 above have been complied with]* *[on the confirmation of this order]*.

[4. The following works [may] [shall] be carried out in relation to the highway described in Part [I] [II] [III] of the Schedule hereto, that is to say: [description of works].]

[5. [Name of person] is hereby required to [pay] [make the following contributions in respect of] the cost of carrying out the above-mentioned works [that is to say; [details of contributions] .]

RIGHTS OF WAY

[6. Where immediately before the date on which a highway is [stopped-up] [diverted] in pursuance of this order there is apparatus under, in, on, along or across that highway belonging to statutory undertakers for the purpose of carrying on their undertaking, the undertakers shall continue to have the same rights in respect of the apparatus as they then had.]

7. This order may be cited as the *[name of order-making authority and name of reference of path or way]* Public Path *[Stopping-Up] [Diversion]* Order 19**.

Schedule

Part I

Description of site of existing path or way

[Describe position and width, where necessary in sections, A-B, B-C, etc, as indicated on map.]

Part II

Description of site of alternative highway

[Describe position and width, where necessary in sections, D-E, E-F, etc., as indicated on map.]

Part III

Description of existing highway to be improved

NOTE: As regards the words in square brackets, insert or omit words as appropriate.

Form No 2

Public Path Extinguishment Order

Town and Country Planning Act 1971, Section 214(1)(b)

[Title of order]

Whereas the *[name of order-making authority]* (hereinafter called 'the Council') *[acquired] [appropriated]* for planning purposes the land situate at ***** described in Part I of the Schedule hereto which is subject to the public right of way to which this order relates and the said land is held by the Council for the purposes for which it was *[acquired][appropriated]*;

And whereas the Council are satisfied that *[an alternative right of way [has been][will be] provided] [the provision of an alternative right of way is not required]*:

TOWN AND COUNTRY PLANNING (PUBLIC PATH ORDERS) REGS.

Now, therefore, the Council in pursuance of the powers in that behalf conferred by section 214(1)(b) of the Town and Country Planning Act 1971 hereby make the following order:

1. The public right of way over the *[footpath]* *[bridleway]* situate at ***** shown by a bold black line on the map annexed hereto and described in the Schedule hereto shall be extinguished *[on the confirmation of this order]* *[at the expiration of ** days from the date of confirmation of this order]*.

2. This order may be cited as the *[name of order-making authority and name or reference of path or way]* Extinguishment Order 19**.

Schedule

Description of site of path or way extinguished

[Describe position and width, where necessary in sections, A-B, B-C, etc., as indicated on map.]

NOTE: As regards the words in square brackets, insert or omit words as appropriate.

SCHEDULE 2   Regulation 11

FORMS OF NOTICES

Form No 1

Notice of Public Path Order

Town and Country Planning Act 1971, Section *[210]* *[214(1)(b)]*

[Name of authority by whom the order is made]

[Title of Order]

(1)*[To: ***** of *****.]*

The above-named order (hereinafter referred to as 'the order') made on the ***** day of ***** 19** is about to be submitted to the Secretary of State *[for the Environment][for Wales]* for confirmation or to be confirmed by the authority as an unopposed order.

The effect of the order, if confirmed without modification, will be to *[extinguish the public right of way running from ***** to ***** [and create an alternative highway in lieu]] [divert the public right of way running from ***** to ***** to a line running from ***** to *****]*.

RIGHTS OF WAY

A copy of the order and the map contained in it has been deposited at ***** and may be inspected free of charge at ***** between the hours of ***** a.m. and ***** p.m. on *****. Copies of the map and order may be purchased.

Any representation or objection with respect to the order may be sent in writing to the *[name and address of order-making authority]* not later than (2) ***** 19** and should state the grounds on which it is made.

If no representations or objections are duly made, or if any so made are withdrawn, the *[name of order-making authority]* may, instead of submitting the order to the Secretary of State for confirmation, themselves confirm the order as an unopposed order. If the order is submitted to the Secretary of State for confirmation any representations and objections which have been duly made and not withdrawn will be sent to the Secretary of State with the order.

Dated ***** 19**.

NOTES: General: As regards the words in square brackets, insert or omit words as appropriate.
(1) Insert only in personal notices.
(2) Insert date not less than 28 days from the date of first publication of this notice.

Form No 2

Notice of Confirmation of Public Path Order

Town and Country Planning Act 1971, Section *[210] [214(1)(b)]*

[Name of authority by whom order was made]

[Title of Order]

(1) *[To: ***** of *****.]*

On ***** 19** *[the Secretary of State] [for the Environment] [for Wales] [name of authority by whom the order was made]* confirmed(2) *[with modifications]* the above-named order.

The effect of the order as confirmed is to *[extinguish the public right of way running from ***** to ***** [and create an alternative highway in lieu]] [divert the public right of way running from ***** to ***** to a line running from ***** to *****]*.

A copy of the confirmed order and the map contained in it has been deposited at ***** and may be inspected free of charge at ***** between ***** a.m. and ***** p.m. on *****. Copies of the order and map may be purchased.

This order becomes operative as from ***** but if any person aggrieved by the order desires to question the validity thereof or of any provision contained therein on the ground that it is not within the powers of the Town and Country Planning Act 1971, or on the ground that any requirement of that Act or any regulation made thereunder has not been complied with in relation to the confirmation of the order, he may under section 244 of the Town and Country

TOWN AND COUNTRY PLANNING (PUBLIC PATH ORDERS) REGS.

Planning Act 1971 within six weeks from [*date on which notice is first published as required by paragraph 6 of Schedule 20 to the Town and Country Planning Act 1971*] make application for the purpose to the High Court.

Dated ***** 19**.

NOTES: General: As regards the words in square brackets, insert or omit words as appropriate.
(1) Insert only in personal notices.
(2) Applicable only to confirmation by the Secretary of state.

SCHEDULE 3 *Regulation 12*

ADDITIONAL PERSONS TO BE SERVED WITH NOTICE OF PUBLIC PATH ORDERS

Area	Name
In England and Wales	Auto-Cycle Union British Horse Society Byways and Bridleways Trust Commons, Open Spaces and Footpaths Preservation Society Ramblers' Association
In the counties of Cheshire, Derbyshire, Greater Manchester, Lancashire, Merseyside, South Yorkshire, Staffordshire and West Yorkshire	Peak and Northern Footpaths Society
Within the county of Buckinghamshire, the districts of Beaconsfield, Chiltern and Wycombe: Within the county of Hertfordshire, the districts of Dacorum and Three Rivers; Within the county of Oxfordshire, the district of South Oxfordshire; and within the district of Aylesbury Vale, the parishes of Aston Clinton, Buckland, Drayton Beauchamp, Edlesborough, Halton, Ivinghoe, Pitstone and Wendover.	Chiltern Society

Text: p 126, 146

RIGHTS OF WAY

THE PUBLIC PATH ORDERS AND EXTINGUISHMENT OF PUBLIC RIGHT OF WAY ORDERS REGULATIONS
1983 SI 1983 No 23

Citation, commencement, interpretation and revocation
1. These regulations may be cited as the Public Path Orders and Extinguishment of Public Right of Way Orders Regulations 1983, and shall come into operation on 28th February 1983.
2. In these regulations:
'the Act' means the Highways Act 1980;
'an extinguishment of public right of way order' means an order extinguishing a public right of way made under section 32(2) of the Acquisition of Land Act 1981;
'a public path creation order' means an order made under section 26 of the Act;
'a public path diversion order' means an order made under section 119 of the Act;
'a public path extinguishment order' means an order made under section 118 of the Act; and
'a public path order' means a public path creation order, a public path diversion order or a public path extinguishment order, and includes an order revoking or varying any such order.
3. The Public Path Orders and Extinguishment of Public Right of Way Orders Regulations 1969 are hereby revoked.

Form of public path orders
4. A public path order shall be in the appropriate form (or substantially in the appropriate form) set in Schedule 1 hereto with such modifications as the circumstances may require.
5. The map required to be contained in a public path order shall be on a scale of not less than twenty-five inches to one mile (or 1/2,500); provided that the Secretary of State may in any particular case authorise a smaller scale.
6. In the case of any conflict between the map and the particulars contained in the schedule to a public path order, the schedule shall prevail.

Procedure for public path orders
7. A public path order shall be made in duplicate and, where the order is submitted to the Secretary of State for confirmation shall be accompanied by two copies of the order, a copy of the notice given before the submission as required by Schedule 6 to the Act, a statement of the grounds on which the authority by whom the order was made consider that the order should be confirmed, any representations and objections duly made with respect to the order and not withdrawn (together with the observations thereon of the authority) and in any case in which the authority is required to obtain the consent of, or to consult with, any other authority or body before the order is made, a certificate that such consent has been obtained or such consultation has taken place.
8. After a public path order has been confirmed by the Secretary of State, the authority by whom the order was made shall, as soon as the requirements of paragraph 4(1) of Schedule 6 to the Act have been complied with, supply the Secretary of State with a certificate to that effect.

PUBLIC PATH ORDERS REGULATIONS

9. After a decision not to confirm a public path order, the authority by whom the order was made shall, as soon as the requirements of paragraph 4(3) of Schedule 6 to the Act have been complied with, supply the Secretary of State with a certificate to that effect.

10. After a public path order has been confirmed, the authority by whom the order was made shall send a copy of the order as confirmed to the Ordnance Survey.

11. Any proceedings required to be taken under the Act for the purposes of a public path extinguishment order may be taken concurrently with any proceedings required to be taken under the Act for the purposes of a public path creation order or public path diversion order.

12. Any notice required to be given, served or displayed under Schedule 6 to the Act by an authority by whom a public path order is made shall be in the appropriate form (or substantially in the appropriate form) set out in Schedule 2 hereto with such modifications as the circumstances require.

13. Where the Secretary of State proposes to make a public path order, any notice required to be given, served or displayed under Schedule 6 to this Act by the Secretary of State shall be in the appropriate form (or substantially in the appropriate form) set out in Schedule 2 hereto, subject to any necessary modifications:

Provided that the authority, who immediately before making the order were the appropriate authority in relation to the making of the order, shall arrange for the deposit of copies of the Secretary of State's draft order in their area, for giving access thereto and for the display of any notices required to be displayed.

14. The notice required to be given under paragraphs 1(1) and (2) and 4(1)(a) of Schedule 6 to the Act shall be served on the persons specified in Schedule 5 hereto.

15. Any notice or other document to be served on an owner, lessee or occupier in accordance with paragraph 1(3) of Schedule 6 to the Act shall at the beginning have clearly legibly inscribed upon it in words

'IMPORTANT — THIS COMMUNICATION AFFECTS YOUR PROPERTY'

and where the notice or document is sent under cover otherwise than in a prepaid registered letter, or by the recorded delivery service, the cover shall in addition be endorsed in like manner.

Claims for compensation as respects public path orders

16.(1) A claim for compensation under section 28 of the Act, or that section as applied by section 121(2) of the Act, in consequence of the coming into operation of a public path order shall be made in writing and shall be served on the authority by whom the order was made (or, in the case of an order made by the Secretary of State, on the appropriate authority referred to in section 28(3) of the Act) by delivering it at the offices of the authority addressed to the Chief Executive thereof or by sending it by prepaid post addressed as aforesaid.

(2) The time within which any such claim shall be served shall be six months from the coming into operation of the order in respect of which the claim is made:

Provided that the period may at any time be extended by the Secretary of State in any particular case.

RIGHTS OF WAY

Form and procedure for extinguishment of public rights of way orders

17. An extinguishment of public right of way order shall be in the form (or substantially in the form) set out in Schedule 3 hereto with such modifications as the circumstances may require, and shall contain a map.

18. Regulations 5,6,7,8,9,10,15 and 16 of these regulations shall apply in relation to an extinguishment of public right of way order as they apply in relation to a public path order.

19. Any notice required to be given, served or displayed under Schedule 6 to the Act by an authority by whom an extinguishment of public right of way order is made shall be in the appropriate form (or substantially in the appropriate form) set out in Schedule 4 hereto with such modifications as the circumstances may require.

20. The council of any county, county district or London Borough comprising the whole or any part of the land in relation to which the Secretary of State proposed to make an extinguishment of public right of way order, or in relation to which such an order is made by another authority, shall arrange for the deposit in their area of copies of the Secretary of State's draft order or, as the case may be, copies of the order may by such other authority, for giving access thereto and for the display of any notices required to be displayed.

SCHEDULE 1   Regulation 4
FORMS OF PUBLIC PATH ORDER

Form No 1

Public Path Creation Order

Highways Act 1980

[Name of authority]

[Title of order]

Whereas it appears to the *[name of authority]* that there is a need for a public *[footpath]* *[bridleway]* over the land to which this order relates;

And whereas the said council are satisfied, having regard to the extent to which the *[path]* *[way]* would add to the *[[convenience]* *[enjoyment]* *of a substantial section of the public]* *[convenience of persons resident in the area]* and to the effect which the creation of the *[path]* *[way]* would have on the rights of persons interested in the land, that the *[path]* *[way]* should be created;

And whereas the *[name of authority or authorities consulted]* have been consulted in pursuance of section 26(3) of the Highways Act 1980 (hereinafter called 'the 1980 Act'):

Now, therefore, the *[name of authority]* in pursuance of the powers in that behalf conferred by the said section 26 of the 1980 Act hereby make the following order:

PUBLIC PATH ORDERS REGULATIONS

1. There shall be at the expiration of ** days from the date of confirmation of this order a public *[footpath]* *[bridleway]* over the land situate at ***** described in the *[first part of the]* schedule here to and shown coloured *[purple]* *[green]* on the map contained in this order.

[2. The rights conferred on the public under this order shall be subject to the limitations and conditions set out in the second part of the schedule hereto.]

3. This order may be cited as the *[name of authority and name or references of path or way]* Public Path Creation Order 19**.

Schedule

[Part I]

Description of land

[Describe position length and width of path or way in sections, eg A-B, B-C.

[Part II]

Limitations and Conditions

Position of path or way to which | Limitations and Conditions
limitations and conditions apply. |

NOTE: As regards the words in square brackets, insert or omit words as appropriate.

Form No 2

Public Path Extinguishment Order

Highways Act 1980

[Name of authority]

[Title of Order]

Whereas it appears to the *[name of authority]* that the public *[footpath]* *[bridleway]* to which this order relates is not needed for public use;

And whereas the *[name of authority consulted]* *[and the Countryside Commission]* have been consulted in pursuance of section 120(2) of the Highways Act 1980 (hereinafter called 'the 1980 Act');

[And whereas the [name of consenting authority or authorities] have consented to the making of this order in pursuance of section 120(2) of the 1980 Act:]

RIGHTS OF WAY

Now, therefore, the *[name of authority]* in pursuance of the powers in that behalf conferred by section 118 of the 1980 Act hereby make the following order:

1. The public right of way over the land situate at ***** shown coloured brown on the map annexed hereto and described in the schedule hereto shall be extinguished at the expiration of ** days from the date of confirmation of this order.

*[2. Notwithstanding anything contained in this order [name of statutory undertakers] shall have the following rights over the land referred to in paragraph 1 hereof, namely: *****.]*

3. This order may be cited as the *[name of authority and name of reference of path or way]* Public Path Extinguishment Order 19**.

Schedule

[Describe position, length and width of path or way in sections, eg A-B, B-C, etc, as indicated (on map.]

NOTE: As regards the words in square brackets, insert or omit words as appropriate.

Form No 3

Public Path Diversion Order

Highways Act 1980

[Name of authority]

[Title of Order]

Whereas it appears to the *[name of authority]* as respects the *[footpath] [bridleway]* referred to in paragraph 1 of this order that in the interests of the *[[owner] [lessee] [occupier]* of the land crossed by the *[path] [way]] [public]* it is expedient that the line of the *[path] [way]* should be diverted.

*[And whereas ***** has agreed to [contribute towards] [defray] [any compensation which becomes payable in consequence of the coming into operation of this order:] [any expenses which are incurred in bringing the new site of the [path] [way] into a fit condition for use by the public:]]*

And whereas the *[name of authority consulted] [and the Countryside Commission]* have been consulted in pursuance of section 120(2) of the Highways Act 1980 (hereinafter called 'the 1980 Act');

[And whereas the [name of consenting authority or authorities] have consented to the making of this order in pursuance of section 120(2) of the 1980 Act:]

PUBLIC PATH ORDERS REGULATIONS

Now, therefore, the *[name of authority]* in pursuance of the powers in that behalf conferred by section 119 of the 1980 Act hereby make the following order:

1. The public right of way over the land situate at ***** shown coloured brown on the map annexed hereto and described in A of the *[first part of the]* schedule hereto shall be extinguished at the expiration of ** days from the date of confirmation of this order.

*[2. Notwithstanding anything contained in paragraph 1 of this order the [name of statutory undertakers] shall have the following rights over the land referred to in the said paragraph, namely: *****.]*

3. There shall be at the expiration of ** days from the date of confirmation of this order a public *[footpath] [bridleway]* over the land situate at ***** described in B of the *[first part of the]* schedule hereto and shown coloured *[purple] [green]* on the map contained in this order.

[4. The rights conferred on the public under this order shall be subject to the limitations and conditions set out in the second part of the schedule hereto.]

5. This order may be cited as the *[name of authority and name or reference of path or way]* Public Path Diversion Order 19**.

Schedule

[Part I]

A

Description of site of existing path or way

[Describe position, length and width of path or way in sections, eg A-B, B-C, etc, as indicated on map.]

B

Description of site of new path or way

[Describe position, length and width of path in sections, eg A-B, D-C, etc, as indicated on map.]

[Part II]

Limitations and conditions

Position of path or way to which limitations and conditions apply.	Limitations and Conditions

NOTE: As regards the words in square brackets, insert or omit words as appropriate.

RIGHTS OF WAY

SCHEDULE 2   Regulation 12

FORMS OF NOTICES AS RESPECTS PUBLIC PATH ORDERS

Form No 1

Notice of Public Path Order

Highways Act 1980

[Name of authority]

[Title of Order]

(1)*[To:* ***** *of:* *****.*]

The above-named order, made on ***** 19**, is about to be submitted to the Secretary of State (2) *[for the Environment] [for Wales]* for confirmation, or to be confirmed, as an unopposed order, by the (2) *[name of authority]*.

The effect of the order, if confirmed without modifications, will be to (2) *[create a public [footpath] [bridleway] from ***** to *****] [extinguish the public right of way running from ***** to *****] [divert the public right of way running from ***** to ***** to a line running from ***** to *****] [revoke] [vary] the ***** Order 19**, so as to *****].*

A copy of the order and the map contained in it has been deposited and may be inspected free of charge at ***** between ***** a.m. and ***** p.m. on *****. Copies of the order and the map may be purchased.

[Compensation for depreciation or damage in consequence of the coming into operation of the order is payable in accordance with section (2)*[28] [121(2)] of the 1980 Act, to which reference should be made.]*

Any representation or objection with respect to the order may be sent in writing to the *[title of appropriate officer and name and address of authority]* before ***** 19**, and should state the grounds on which it is made.

If no representations or objections are duly made, or if any so made are withdrawn, the (2)*[name of authority]* may instead of submitting the order to the Secretary of State (2)*[for the Environment] [for Wales]* confirm the order itself. If the order is submitted to the Secretary of State any representations and objections which have been duly made and withdrawn will be submitted with the order.

Dated ***** 19**.

NOTES: (1) Insert only in personal notices.
(2) Insert or omit words, as appropriate.

PUBLIC PATH ORDERS REGULATIONS

Form No 2

Notice of Confirmation of Public Path Order

Highways Act 1980

[Name of authority]

[Title of Order]

(1)*[To: ***** of: *****.]*

On ***** 19**, (2)*[the Secretary of State] [for the Environment] [for Wales] [name of authority] [confirmed] [confirmed with modifications]* the above-named order.

The effect of the order as confirmed is to (2)*[create a public [footpath] [bridleway] from ***** to *****] [extinguish the public right of way running from ***** to *****] [divert the public right of way running from ***** to ***** to a line running from ***** to *****] [[revoke] [vary] the ***** Order 19**, so as to *****].*

A copy of the order as confirmed and the map contained in it has been deposited and may be inspected free of charge at ***** between ***** a.m. and ***** p.m. on *****. Copies of the order and map may be purchased.

(1)*[Any person who wishes to claim compensation under section* (2)*[28] [121(2)] of the 1980 Act for depreciation or damage in consequence of the coming into operation of the order must make his claim in writing addressed to the Chief Executive* (2)*[name and address of authority], and serve it by delivering it at, or sending it by prepaid post to the above address before ***** 19**.]*

The order becomes operative as from ***** 19**, but if a person aggrieved by the order desires to question the validity thereof, or of any provision contained therein, on the ground that it is not within the powers of the Highways Act 1980, as amended, or on the ground that any requirement of the Act, as amended, or of any regulation made thereunder has not been complied with in relation to the order he may, under paragraph 2 of Schedule 2 to the Act as applied by paragraph 5 of Schedule 6 to the Act, within six weeks from *[date on which notice first published]*, make an application for the purpose to the High Court.

Dated ***** 19**.

NOTES: (1) Insert only in personal notices.

(2) Insert or omit words, as appropriate.

RIGHTS OF WAY

SCHEDULE 3 Regulation 17

FORM OF EXTINGUISHMENT OF PUBLIC RIGHT OF WAY ORDER

Extinguishment of Public Right of Way Order

Acquisition of Land Act 1981

Highways Act 1980

[Name of authority]

[Title of Order]

Whereas the public right of way, not being a right enjoyable by vehicular traffic, to which this order relates subsists over *[land] [part of land]* which *[has been acquired] [is proposed to be acquired]* as mentioned in section 32(1) of the Acquisition of Land Act 1981 (hereinafter called the '1981 Act');

And whereas the *[name of authority]* are satisfied *[a suitable alternative right of way [has been provided] [will be provided over land situate at ***** described in A of the schedule hereto and shown coloured [purple] [green] on the map contained in this order] [an alternative right of way is not required]*:

Now, therefore, the *[name of authority]* in pursuance of the powers in that behalf conferred by section 32 of the 1981 Act hereby make the following order:

1. The public right of way over land situate at ***** described in *[B of]* the schedule hereto and shown coloured brown on the map contained in this order shall be extinguished as from ***** 19**.

2. This order may be cited as the *[name of authority and name or reference of way]* Extinguishment of Public Right of Way Order 19**.

Schedule

[A

Description of site of alternative way

[Describe position, length and width of way in sections, eg A-B, B-C, etc, as indicated on map.]]

[B]

Description of site of way extinguished

[Describe position, length and width of way in sections, eg A-B, B-C, etc, as indicated on map.]

NOTE: As regards the words in square brackets, insert or omit words as appropriate.

PUBLIC PATH ORDERS REGULATIONS

SCHEDULE 4   Regulation 19

FORMS OF NOTICES AS RESPECTS EXTINGUISHMENT OF PUBLIC RIGHT OF WAY ORDER

Form No 1

Notice of Extinguishment of Public Right of Way Order

Acquisition of Land Act 1981

Highways Act 1980

[Name of authority]

[Title of Order]

(1)*[To: ***** of: *****.]*

The above-named order, made on ***** 19**, is about to be submitted to the Secretary of State (2)*[for the Environment] [for Wales]* for confirmation, or to be confirmed, as an unopposed order, by the (2)*[name of authority]*.

The effect of the order, if confirmed without modifications, will be to extinguish the public right of way running from ***** to *****.

The (2)*[name of authority]* is satisfied that (2)*[a suitable alternative right of way [has been provided] [will be provided] over land specified in the order] [an alternative right of way is not required]*.

A copy of the order and the map contained in it has been deposited and may be inspected free of charge at ***** between ***** a.m. and ***** p.m. on *****. Copies of the order and the map may be purchased.

Any representation or objection with respect to the order may be sent in writing to the (2)*[name of appropriate officer and name and address of authority]* before ***** 19**, and should state the grounds on which it is made.
If no representations or objections are duly made, or if any so made are withdrawn, the (2)*[name of authority]* may instead of submitting the order to the Secretary of State (2)*[for the Environment] [for Wales]* confirm the order itself. If the order is submitted to the Secretary of State any representations and objections which have been duly made and withdrawn will be submitted with the order.

Dated ***** 19**.

NOTES: (1) Insert only in personal notices.
  (2) Insert or omit words, as appropriate.

RIGHTS OF WAY

Form No 2

Notice of Confirmation of Extinguishment of Public Right of Way Order

Acquisition of Land Act 1981

Highways Act 1980

[Name of authority]

[Title of Order]

(1)*[To: ***** of: *****.]*

On ***** 19**, (2)*[the Secretary of State] [for the Environment] [for Wales] [name of authority] [confirmed] [confirmed with modifications]* the above-named order.

Its effect is to extinguish the public right of way running from ***** to *****. A copy of the order as confirmed and the map contained in it has been deposited and may be inspected free of charge at ***** between ***** a.m. and ***** p.m. on *****. Copies of the order and map may be purchased.
The order becomes operative as from ***** 19**, but if a person aggrieved by the order desires to question the validity thereof, or of any provision contained therein, on the ground that it is not within the powers of the Acquisition of Land Act 1981 or that any requirement of that Act or the Highways Act 1980, as amended, or of any regulation made thereunder has not been complied with in relation to the order he may, under paragraph 2 of Schedule 2 to the Highways Act 1980, as applied by paragraph 5 of Schedule 6 to the Act, within six weeks from (2)*[date on which notice first published]*, make an application for the purpose to the High Court.

Dated ***** 19**.

NOTES: (1) Insert only in personal notices.
(2) Insert or omit words, as appropriate.

PUBLIC PATH ORDERS REGULATIONS

SCHEDULE 5   Regulation 14

ADDITIONAL PERSONS TO BE SERVED WITH NOTICE OF PUBLIC PATH ORDERS AND EXTINGUISHMENT OF PUBLIC RIGHT OF WAY ORDERS

Area	Name
In England and Wales	Auto-Cycle Union British Horse Society Byways and Bridleways Trust Commons, Open Spaces and Footpaths Preservation Society Ramblers' Association
In counties of Cheshire, Derbyshire, Greater Manchester, Lancashire, Merseyside, South Yorkshire, Staffordshire and West Yorkshire	Peak and Northern Footpaths Society
Within the county of Buckinghamshire, the districts of Beaconsfield, Chiltern and Wycombe; Within the county of Hertfordshire, the districts of Dacorum and Three Rivers; Within the county of Oxfordshire, the district of South Oxfordshire; and within the district of Aylesbury Vale, the parishes of Aston Clinton, Buckland, Drayton Beauchamp, Edlesborough, Halton, Ivinghoe, Pitstone and Wendover.	Chiltern Society

Text: p 126, 137, 140, 142

THE FOOT AND MOUTH DISEASE ORDER 1983 SI 1983 No 1950

27. Power to close footpaths and to prevent entry onto premises in an infected area

(1) Subject to paragraph (2) below, an inspector may, notwithstanding the existence of any public footpath or right of way, prohibit in an infected area the entry of any person–

(a) onto any land (including any common, or any unenclosed or waste land); or

(b) into any agricultural building,
by displaying, or causing to be so displayed, a notice to that effect at every entrance to that land or building.
(2) No person shall enter any land or building in respect of which a notice is displayed under paragraph (1) above, other than–
(a) the owner of any animal on that land or in that building, or the employee of any such owner or any other person yauthorised by him, who enters for the purpose of tending that animal; or
(b) a person entering that land or building under the authority of, and in accordance with any conditions specified in, a licence granted by an inspector.
(3) A notice under paragraph (3) above shall be displayed at every entrance to the land or building to which it relates by the inspector in such manner as will ensure that the restrictions imposed by it are brought to the attention of those persons likely to be affected by them, and shall only be removed by the occupier of the land or building in accordance with the written instructions of the inspector.
Text: p 166

THE CYCLE TRACKS REGULATIONS 1984 SI 1984 NO 1431

Citation and commencement
1. These Regulations may be cited as the Cycle Tracks Regulations 1984 and shall come into operation on 12th September 1984.

Interpretation and application
2. (1) In these Regulations the following expressions have the meanings hereby respectively assigned to them:–
'the Act' means the Cycle Tracks Act 1984;
'the appointed person' means the person appointed by the Secretary of State to hold an inquiry;
'the authority', in relation to any order, means the local highway authority making or proposing to make the order under the Act;
'local authority' means the council of a district or London borough or the Common Council of the City of London;
'the objection period' means the period specified in the notice required by Regulation 4 of the Regulations within which objections to an order may be made;
'operational land' means, in relation to statutory undertakers–
(a) land which is used for the purpose of carrying on their undertaking; and
(b) land in which an interest is held for that purpose,
not being land in which, in respect of its nature and situation, is comparable rather with land in general than with land which is used, or in which interests are held, for the purpose of carrying on of statutory undertakings;
'order' means, in relation to anything occurring or falling to be done before its making, the order as proposed to be made, and in relation to anything occurring or falling to be done on or after its making, the order as made; and
'statutory undertakers' has the same meaning as in section 2(3) of the Act and 'statutory undertakings' shall be construed accordingly.

CYCLE TRACKS REGULATIONS

(2) These Regulations apply to orders made or proposed to be made by a local highway authority under section 3 of the Act.

(3) Regulations 3, 4, 7 and 10 of these Regulations apply to orders made or proposed to be made under section 3(9) of the Act with the substitution for the expression 'footpath' of the expression 'cycle track'.

Procedure before making an order

3. Before making an order the authority shall consult with–

(a) one or more organisations representing persons who use the footpath to which the order relates or are likely to be affected by any provisions of the order, unless it appears to the authority that there is no such organisation which can appropriately be consulted;

(b) any other local authority, parish council or community council within whose area the said footpath is situated;

(c) those statutory undertakers whose operational land is crossed by the said footpath; and

(d) the chief officer of police of any police area in which the said footpath is situated.

Procedure after making an order

4. On making an order the authority shall–

(a) publish once at least in a local newspaper circulating in the locality in which the footpath to which the order relates is situated a notice which

(i) describes the general effect of the order stating that it has been made and requires confirmation;

(ii) names a place in the locality in which the footpath to which the order relates is situated where a copy of the order may be inspected free of charge at all reasonable hours; and

(iii) specifies the period (not being less than 28 days from the date of the first publication of the notice) during which, and the address to which, objections to the order can be made and states that all objections must be made in writing and must specify the grounds thereof,

(b) cause a copy of the said notice to be displayed in a conspicuous position at the ends of so much of the footpath to which the order relates as is affected by the order,

(c) cause a copy of the said notice to be displayed in one or more places where public notices are usually displayed in the locality concerned, and

(d) send a copy of the said notice to all those consulted under Regulation 3 of these Regulations.

Objections

5. (1) Objections to an order may be made during the objection period.

(2) Any person wishing to object to an order shall send within the objection period, and to the address specified in the notice required by Regulation 4 of these Regulations, a written statement of his objection and of the grounds thereof.

Local inquiries

6. (1) Where an order is submitted to the Secretary of State for confirmation he shall, subject to paragraph (2) below, cause a local inquiry to be held.

RIGHTS OF WAY

(2) The Secretary of State may, if satisfied that in the circumstances of the case the holding of an inquiry under this Regulation is unnecessary, dispense with such an inquiry.

Notice of inquiry
7. (1) A date, time and place for the holding of the inquiry shall be fixed and may be varied by the Secretary of State, who shall give not less than 42 days notice in writing of the date, time and place to every objector.
Provided that–
(a) with the consent in writing of the objectors the Secretary of State may give such lesser period of notice as may be agreed with them; and
(b) where it becomes necessary or advisable to vary the time or place fixed for the inquiry, the Secretary of State shall give such notice of the variation as may appear to him to be reasonable in the circumstances.
(2) The authority shall–
(a) not later than 21 days before the date of the inquiry, display a copy of the notice of the inquiry in a conspicuous place near to the footpath to which the order relates and also in one or more places where public notices are usually displayed in the locality concerned; and
(b) if the Secretary of State so directs, publish in one or more newspapers circulating in the locality in which the footpath to which the order relates is situated such notices of the inquiry as he may specify.

Appointment of inspectors etc
8. The Secretary of State may, if he thinks fit, by notice served on the objectors or by the notice announcing the holding of the inquiry, direct that a decision as to whether the order the subject matter of the inquiry should be confirmed and, if so, as to the modifications (if any) subject to which it should be confirmed, may be made by the appointed person instead of by the Secretary of State; and a decision made by the appointed person shall be treated as a decision of the Secretary of State.

Considerations of objections at the inquiry
9. (1) Any person interested in the subject matter of a local inquiry may appear at the inquiry either in person or by counsel, solicitor or other representative.
(2) Any person so interested may, whether or not he proposes to appear at the inquiry, send to the appointed person at the address given in the notice referred to in Regulation 4 of these Regulations such written representations as he may wish to make in relation to the subject matter of the inquiry with a view to their consideration by the appointed person at the inquiry.
(3) The appointed person may–
(a) refuse to hear any person, or to consider any objection or representation made by any person, if he is satisfied that the views of that person or the objection or representation are frivolous, and
(b) refuse to hear any person if he is satisfied that the views of that person have already been adequately stated by some other person at the inquiry.

Notice of final decision on orders
10. (1) As soon as practicable after–
(a) receiving notice of a decision of the Secretary of State to confirm an order in pursuance of his powers under section 3(3)(a) of the Act, or

(b) a decision to confirm an order is made by the authority in pursuance of its powers under section 3(3)(b) of the Act,
the authority shall give notice–
(i) describing the general effect of the order as confirmed and stating that it has been confirmed (with or without modification) and the date on which it took effect; and
(ii) naming a place in the locality in which the footpath to which the order relates is situated where a copy of the order as confirmed may be inspected free of charge at all reasonable hours.
(2) A notice under paragraph (1) above shall be given–
(a) by publication in the manner required by Regulation 4(a) of these Regulations,
(b) by causing a copy of such notice to be displayed in the like manner as the notices required to be displayed under Regulation 4(b) of those Regulations, and
(c) in any case where the order was subject to a local inquiry, by sending a copy to all persons who, having appeared at the inquiry or having submitted written representations in accordance with Regulation 9(2) of these Regulations, asked to be notified of the decision.
Text: p 161

THE OPENCAST COAL (COMPULSORY RIGHTS AND RIGHTS OF WAY) (FORMS) REGULATIONS 1987
SI 1987 NO 1915

Citation and commencement
1.(1) These Regulations may be cited as the Opencast Coal (Compulsory Rights and Rights of Way) (Forms) Regulations 1987.
(2) These Regulations shall come into force on 11th December 1987.

Interpretation
2. In these Regulations–
(a) 'the 1958 Act' means the Opencast Coal Act 1958; and
(b) any reference to a numbered form includes a reference to a document in substantially the same form.

Prescribed forms: suspension of rights of way
3. Forms 1, 2 and 3 in Part I of the Schedule hereto are prescribed forms for the purposes of subsections (1), (5)(c) and (10) respectively of section 15A of the 1958 Act.
[4 not included]

Prescribed particulars
5. The prescribed particulars for the purposes of section 15A(5)(c) of the 1958 Act are the particulars required to be included in a notice in form 2.

Revocation
6. The Opencast Coal (Authorisations and Compulsory Rights Orders) Regulations 1975 are hereby revoked; but any form prescribed by those regulations shall be deemed to be prescribed by these Regulations where an application or

an order as the case may be has been made before the coming into force of these Regulations.

SCHEDULE

Note The singular has been used throughout these forms: where the plural is required it should be used.

PART I   Regulation 3

RIGHTS OF WAY

FORM 1

NEWSPAPER NOTICE OF AN APPLICATION FOR AN ORDER SUSPENDING A PUBLIC RIGHT OF WAY

OPENCAST COAL ACT 1958

***** RIGHT OF WAY APPLICATION 19** *(a)*

1. Notice is hereby given that the British Coal Corporation in connection with the working of coal by opencast operations propose to apply under section 15 of the Opencast Coal Act 1958 to the Secretary of State for an order suspending a non-vehicular right of way as described in Schedule below *(b)*.
2. Opencast planning permission for the working has been *[applied for] [granted] (c)*.
3. A copy of the application and of a map showing the right of way can be inspected at ***** *(d)* between the hours of ***** and ***** *(e)* from ***** to ***** *(f)*.
4. *[An alternative right of way for use by the public during the period for which the order will be in force will be made available as described in the Schedule below.] [No alternative right of way is to be made available.] (c)*
5. Written objections, stating the grounds on which objections are made, may be sent by any person to the Secretary of State before ***** *(g)* at ***** *(h)*. If the *[district council or county council] [local authority] (i)* in whose area any part of the right of way lies objects and do not withdraw their objection the Secretary of State must arrange a public inquiry; if any other person objects and does not withdraw his objection he may arrange a public inquiry if he thinks fit.

SCHEDULE

[PART 1] (j)

RIGHT OF WAY TO BE SUSPENDED *(b)*

OPENCAST COAL REGULATIONS
[PART 2

ALTERNATIVE RIGHT OF WAY] (b) (j)

Dated ***** *[Signature of]* an officer authorised by the British Coal Corporation

Notes

(a) Insert an appropriate name relating to the location of the right of way.
(b) Give sufficient description for the route of the right of way to be identified without reference to a map.
(c) Use whichever version reflects the position.
(d) The Act requires the place to be 'in the locality': it should therefore be within easy reach of people living near the right of way.
(e) Insert reasonable hours during the day.
(f) The dates between which the documents may be inspected should be inserted: it is desirable that the period given should not expire before the end of the period for making objections.
(g) Insert appropriate date: the minimum period is 28 days (ie clear days) from the date of the last newspaper notice, whether in the local newspaper or the appropriate Gazette.
(h) Insert address.
(i) Use the first version if the right of way is in England or Wales omitting reference to a county council if the right of way is wholly within a metropolitan county: the second if it is in Scotland.
(j) Omit where no alternative right of way is to be made available

FORM 2   *Regulations 3 and 5*

NOTICE OF AN APPLICATION FOR AN ORDER SUSPENDING A PUBLIC RIGHT OF WAY TO BE AFFIXED TO A CONSPICUOUS OBJECT AT EITHER END OF RIGHT OF WAY

OPENCAST COAL ACT 1958

***** RIGHT OF WAY APPLICATION 19** *(a)*

1. Notice is hereby given that the British Coal Corporation in connection with the working of coal by opencast operations propose to apply under section 15 of the Opencast Coal Act 1958 to the Secretary of State for an order suspending a non-vehicular right of way as described in the Schedule below *(b)*.
2. Opencast planning permission for the working has been *[applied for] [granted] (c)*.
3. A copy of the application and of a map showing the right of way can be inspected at ***** *(d)* between the hours of ***** and ***** *(e)* from ***** to ***** *(f)*.

RIGHTS OF WAY

4. *[An alternative right of way for use by the public during the period for which the order will be in force will be made available as described in the Schedule below.]* *[No alternative right of way is to be made available.]* (c)

5. Written objections, stating the grounds on which objections are made, may be sent by any person to the Secretary of State before ***** (g) at ***** (h). If the *[district council or county council]* *[local authority]* (i) in whose area any part of the right of way lies objects and do not withdraw their objection the Secretary of State must arrange a public inquiry; if any other person objects and does not withdraw his objection he may arrange a public inquiry if he thinks fit.

SCHEDULE

[PART 1] (j)

RIGHT OF WAY TO BE SUSPENDED (b)

[PART 2

ALTERNATIVE RIGHT OF WAY*]* (b) (j)

Dated ***** *[Signature of]* an officer authorised by the British Coal Corporation

Notes
(a) Insert an appropriate name relating to the location of the right of way.
(b) Give sufficient description for the route of the right of way to be identified without reference to a map.
(c) Use whichever version reflects the position.
(d) The Act requires the place to be 'in the locality': it should therefore be within easy reach of people living near the right of way.
(e) Insert reasonable hours during the day.
(f) The dates between which the documents may be inspected should be inserted: it is desirable that the period given should not expire before the end of the period for making objections.
(g) Insert appropriate date: the minimum period is 28 days (ie clear days) from the date of the last newspaper notice, whether in the local newspaper or the appropriate Gazette.
(h) Insert address.
(i) Use the first version if the right of way is in England or Wales omitting reference to a county council if the right of way is wholly within a metropolitan county: the second if it is in Scotland.
(j) Omit where no alternative right of way is to be made available

OPENCAST COAL REGULATIONS

FORM 3 Regulation 3

NOTICE OF MAKING OF AN ORDER SUSPENDING A RIGHT OF WAY

OPENCAST COAL ACT 1958

***** ORDER 19** *(a)*

1. Notice is given that on ***** *(b)* the Secretary of State in the exercise of his powers under section 15 of the Opencast Coal Act 1958, on the application of the British Coal Corporation, made the ***** *(a)* Order 19** suspending the right of way described below.
2. The order will come into operation on ***** *(c)* and will suspend the right of way until the Secretary of State revokes the order.
[2a. An alternative right of way will be provided as described below.] (d)
3. A copy of the order and of the map to which it refers may be inspected at ***** *(e)* between the hours of ***** and ***** *(f)* from ***** to ***** *(g)*.

SUSPENDED RIGHT OF WAY *(h)*

[ALTERNATIVE RIGHT OF WAY] (d)

Dated ***** *[Signature of]* an officer authorised by the British Coal Corporation

Notes

(a) Insert title of order as made.
(b) Give date on which the order was made.
(c) Give the date specified in the order.
(d) There is no obligation to include this paragraph but it may be included at the option of the British Coal Corporation.
(e) The place must be 'in the locality': it should therefore be within easy reach of people living near the right of way.
(f) Insert reasonable hours during the day.
(g) The dates between which the order may be inspected should be inserted: they should allow a reasonable period for inspection, which period ought not to expire before the operative date of the order.
(h) Give sufficient description for the route of the right of way to be identified without reference to a map. The description need not be as detailed as on the application.
(i) Use the first version if the right of way is in England or Wales omitting reference to a county council if the right of way is wholly within a metropolitan county: the second if it is in Scotland.
(j) Omit where no alternative right of way is to be made available
Text: p 150

Circulars

DOE CIRCULAR 32/81, WELSH OFFICE CIRCULAR 50/81: WILDLIFE AND COUNTRYSIDE ACT 1981

Wardens
14. Section 49 extends the power of local authorities to appoint wardens to patrol any land in a national part or in the countryside generally, provided that the public have access to that land and that the owner and occupier are agreeable to such wardens being appointed. The functions of the wardens are restricted to advising and assisting the public. Similarly, Section 62 extends the power of local authorities to appoint wardens to act on footpaths, bridleways or byways open to all traffic (including any ways shown on definitive maps as Roads used as Public Paths).

Bulls on land crossed by public rights of way
17. Section 59 makes it an offence for an occupier to permit a bull to be at large in a field or enclosure crossed by a public right of way except where a bull (a) does not exceed 10 months, or (b) is not of a recognised dairy breed and is accompanied by cows or heifers. The term 'field or enclosure' excludes open hill areas. Although a road used as a public path (RUPP) is not referred to in the definition in section 66 of a 'right of way to which this Part applies', it is intended that fields crossed by RUPPs should be covered by section 59 since what is shown on the definitive map as a RUPP will, on the ground, be either a public path or a byway open to all traffic. The section 59 provisions replace existing controls by byelaws insofar as these cover bulls in fields crossed by public paths; they do not affect bylaw control over bulls in streets and public places. These provisions do not affect the obligations that employers and others have under the Health and Safety at Work etc. Act 1974 not to put at risk the health and safety of third parties. It is hoped in due course to issue guidance to farmers and path-users on section 59 after consultations with interested bodies.

Regulation of equestrian traffic on public rights of way
18. Under the Road Traffic Regulation Act 1967 traffic orders can be used to prohibit, restrict or regulate the use of highways by vehicles and by pedestrians but not animals. Section 60 of this Act extends the provisions of the 1967 Act so as to bring persons driving, riding or leading horses or other animals of draught or burden within the scope of temporary traffic orders made under section 12 and traffic regulation orders and experimental orders made under sections 1 and 9 respectively which apply outside Greater London (Schedule 1 already provides that orders made by London authorities under section 6 shall apply to animals). The extended provisions have effect only on footpaths, bridleways and byways open to all traffic. Section 12 enables temporary traffic orders to be made for periods of up to three months. In considering such orders highway authorities are required to have regard to the existence of alternative routes suitable for the traffic which would be affected by the order.

Signposting
20. The provisions of section 27 of the Countryside Act 1968 apply only to footpaths and bridleways. Section 65 applies them to byways open to all traffic. Thus, highway authorities now have a duty to signpost such ways wherever they leave metalled roads (except where it is agreed under section 27(3) that such signs are not necessary) and to place signs or waymarks along them to assist persons to follow them. Signposting and waymarking of public rights of way are of considerable benefit to path-users, and also to farmers by helping to prevent trespass. It is hoped that authorities will make greater progress in fulfilling the requirements of section 27 of the 1968 Act, as now amended, and will utilise any assistance offered by voluntary groups for this purpose.

DOE CIRCULAR 1/83, WELSH OFFICE CIRCULAR 1/83: PUBLIC RIGHTS OF WAY

Definitive maps and statements of public rights of way
4. The National Parks and Access to the Countryside Act 1949 required every county council in England and Wales, apart from the former London County Council, to undertake a survey of their area and to prepare and publish a definitive map and statement of the public rights of way, that is footpaths, bridleways and roads used as public paths, within their area. The preparation of the original definitive map and statement for those areas not initially excluded from the requirements of the Act has now been completed. In addition, the Act, as amended by the Countryside Act 1968, provided for the review at not less than five-yearly intervals of all the definitive maps and statements prepared by surveying authorities for their respective areas. The 1968 Act also provided for the review and reclassification of roads used as public paths as byways open to all traffic, bridleways or footpaths on the application of certain prescribed tests.
5. Definitive maps are valuable in two respects: firstly, as a documentary record of public rights of way, which nowadays are themselves a recreational asset in that they enable the public to gain access to and enjoy the countryside; secondly, as conclusive evidence of the existence of certain public rights as at the relevant date assigned to each definitive map. They thus indicate to the public and to landowners where the public may lawfully walk or ride, though they do not exclude the possibility that other rights of may exist. However, in practice the previous system of comprehensive county-wide reviews did not work as well as expected with the result that progress in up-dating definitive maps was uneven. Under the new review procedure introduced by the Wildlife and Countryside Act definitive maps and statements are required to be kept under continuous review and modified by way of orders as and when events of the relevant kind occur. An important feature of the new procedure is the facility for persons to apply to the surveying authority for an order to modify the definitive map and statement and the subsequent right of appeal to the Secretary of State in the event of a refusal.
6. The Secretary of State hopes that the new procedures for the revision of definitive maps will enable continuous progress to be made in keeping them up to date. He recognises however that the work of clearing the present backlog of proposals for amending the definitive map may have to be spread over a number of years. He also recognises that surveying authorities may be faced

with a large number of applications for modification orders in the early years of the new system. It is recommended therefore that wherever possible surveying authorities should periodically publish a statement setting out their priorities for bringing and keeping the definitive map up to date. Potential applicants should have regard to that statement in deciding when to submit their applications for orders. The Secretary of State will take into account the existence of any such statement in considering requests for a direction where no decision has been made within the stipulated 12-month period.

Public path creation agreements
9. Section 64 of the Wildlife and Countryside Act adds a new subsection to section 25 of the Highways Act, the effect of which is that notice of the dedication of footpaths and bridleways, in consequence of a public path creation agreement, must now be given in a local newspaper circulating in the area. Although not mandatory, authorities are also recommended to inform local organisations representing the interests of users of public rights of way of the availability of footpaths and bridleways that derive from creation agreements.

Management of public rights of way
10. Much of the present-day network of public rights of way had its origins in the utilitarian needs of the local community and many rights of way still serve this purpose. The role of public rights of way has however changed dramatically during the present century in that they are now used principally for recreational purposes and constitute a valuable resource at a time of increasing demand for access to the countryside. If the full recreational potential of public rights of way is to be realised it is obviously desirable that they are considered and managed as an integral part of the whole complex of recreational facilities within a given area.
11. There are undoubtedly inadequacies and anomalies in the network of public rights of way in many areas. Moreover the changing use of rights of way has been accompanied by changes in the countryside through which they run as a result of new development and changes in farming practice. In a number of areas the effect of these changes means that the present network is not fully suited to the varying needs of different user groups and may inhibit the effective use of land for agriculture. The Secretary of State believes that the best way of resolving these difficulties and reconciling the increasing demands and pressures on rights of way with the needs of the farming community is by way of local initiatives to modify the existing network, adapting it to the mutual benefit of landowners and users. The Secretary of State recognises however that this can only be achieved and be successful as a result of co-operation between landowners, users and local authorities.

Public rights of way and development
12. Proposals for the development of land affecting public rights of way give rise to two matters of particular concern: the need for adequate consideration of the rights of way before the decision on the planning application is taken and the need, once planning permission has been granted, for the right of way to be kept open and unobstructed until the statutory procedures authorising closure or diversion have been completed.

13. The Secretary of State takes the view that the effect of development on a public right of way is a material consideration in the determination of applications for planning permission and asks local planning authorities to ensure that the effect on the right of way is taken into account whenever such applications are considered. To this end local planning authorities who have not already done so are requested to consider adding to their planning application forms a question about the existence of any public right of way within the site of the proposed development. In addition, in view of the widespread public interest in public rights of way, and as advised in DOE Circular 71/73 (Welsh Office Circular 134/73), planning authorities should consider publicising applications affecting rights of way and take any consequent representations into account. Where it is decided to grant permission for development affecting a right of way consideration should be given at the detailed planning stage to whether a new line for the right of way can be defined which would be generally acceptable to the public. The use of estate roads for this purpose should as far as possible be avoided.

14. The grant of planning permission does not entitle developers to obstruct a public right of way. Development, in so far as it affects a right of way, should not be started, and the right of way should be kept open for public use, until the necessary order under section 209 or 210 of the Town and Country Planning Act 1971 for the diversion or extinguishment of the right of way has been made and confirmed. Nor should it be assumed that an order, once made, will invariably be confirmed. Planning authorities are asked therefore to ensure that applicants whose proposals may affect public rights of way are made aware of the position at the time planning permission is granted. Planning authorities have on occasion granted planning permission on the condition that the right of way should be stopped-up or diverted before the development commences. The Secretary of State takes the view that such a condition is both unnecessary and unreasonable in that it duplicates the separate statutory procedure that exists for diverting or stopping-up the right of way, and would require the developer to do something outside his control.

Powers of the Secretary of State to make orders

15. The Secretary of State is empowered by section 209 of the Town and Country Planning Act 1971 to make orders for the diversion or stopping-up of footpaths and bridleways to enable development to be carried out. The most common circumstance in which this power is exercised is where the application for planning permission is before the Secretary of State either on appeal or following call-in and it is considered expedient to invoke the concurrent procedure under section 216 of the Act in anticipation of planning permission. Such orders can be made only if the application contains sufficient information about the proposed development to enable the Secretary of State to assess the manner in which the development will affect the path or way. Otherwise it is only in exceptional circumstances, for example in relation to development of strategic or national importance, that the Secretary of State would expect to be asked to exercise his power under section 209. It should not be regarded by planning authorities as an alternative to the exercise by them of their order-making powers under section 210 of the Act where they are responsible for granting the planning permission. In such circumstances the Secretary of State expects the authority to make the order.

RIGHTS OF WAY

16. The Secretary of State has similar powers under section 26(2) and 120(3) of the Highways Act 1980 to make orders for the creation, extinguishment and diversion of footpaths and bridleways. As with his powers in the Town and Country Planning Act these powers will be exercised only exceptionally.

Maintenance of public rights of way

17. Most public rights of way are maintainable at public expense. The duty to maintain public rights of way rests with county and London borough councils, as the highway authorities for their areas, by virtue of sections 1, 36 and 41 of the Highways Act 1980. District councils may, nonetheless, assume responsibility for the maintenance of footpaths and bridleways in their area in accordance with section 42 of the Act. They may also undertake the work on behalf of the highway authority on an agency basis under section 101 of the Local Government Act 1972. In addition section 43 of the 1980 Act empowers parish or community councils to maintain footpaths and bridleways within their area without the prior consent or agreement of the highway authority, but the maintenance of footpaths and bridleways by such councils does not absolve highway authorities from discharging their responsibilities. It is hoped that authorities will utilise any assistance which may be available from the Manpower Services Commission, Countryside Commission and voluntary groups.

18. The Secretary of State does not regard it as practicable to recommend specific standards for the maintenance of the different kinds of public right of way. The main consideration in determining the degree of maintenance to be afforded to individual paths or ways is that they should serve the purpose for which they are primarily used and not that they should confirm to an arbitrary standard of construction. Generally speaking they should be capable of meeting the use that is normally made of them throughout the year. In addition whatever work is done should harmonize with the general appearance and character of the surroundings.

Protection of public rights of way

19. By virtue of section 130(1) of the Highways Act 1980 county and London borough councils are responsible, as the appropriate highway authorities, for asserting and protecting the rights of the public to use and enjoy rights of way. They are similarly responsible under section 130(3) of the Act for preventing, as far as possible, the stopping-up or obstruction of public rights of way. District Councils may also assert and protect the public rights but are under no statutory obligation to do so unless they are accepting liability on behalf of the highway authority on an agency basis. In addition highway authorities are required under subsection (6) to take remedial action whenever they receive representations from a parish or community council or meeting that a path or way has been obstructed or stopped-up, or that unlawful encroachment on to roadside waste has taken place, unless satisfied that the representations are incorrect. The Act empowers highway and other authorities to institute legal proceedings or take whatever steps they deem expedient in discharging these duties.

20. The main problem that authorities are likely to encounter in discharging these duties is the obstruction of rights of way. Since it is important that public rights of way should remain unobstructed and open for public use the Secretary of State looks to authorities to ensure that any obstructions they discover or

have reported to them are removed without undue delay. In this connection section 143 enables highway authorities, or district councils acting on their behalf, to secure the removal of obstructions by serving notice on the person responsible and by removing the obstruction themselves at the person's expense should that person fail to comply with the notice. Section 154 empowers both highway authorities and district councils to require owners and occupiers to cut back trees, hedges or shrubs which overhang paths. The Secretary of State considers that authorities should attempt to resolve problems arising from obstruction amicably with the person concerned before resorting to legal proceedings or other statutory action. Clearly where there is uncertainty over the actual status of the path or way alleged to be obstructed, that uncertainty should first be resolved before steps are taken to secure the removal of the obstruction. Where, however, the alleged obstruction is recorded in the definitive map and statement, then, because the statement is conclusive evidence of any recorded limitations or conditions affecting the public right of way, the use of the path or way is subject to the obstruction notwithstanding that it may be inconsistent with the status of the right of way.

Magistrates' court applications
21. Section 116 of the Highways Act 1980 enables an appropriate authority — London borough or county council — to apply to a magistrates' court for an order to stop up or divert a highway of any description, other than a trunk or special road. The provisions apply therefore to footpaths and bridleways notwithstanding that powers are available in Highways and other legislation for securing the extinguishment or diversion of footpaths and bridleways. While it is recognised that there may be circumstances where it is appropriate to use the magistrates' court procedure, for example the extinguishment or diversion of a footpath or bridleway simultaneously with a vehicular right of way, the Secretary of State considers that authorities should make use of the other powers available unless there are good reasons for not doing so.

ANNEX A : REVISION OF DEFINITIVE MAPS AND STATEMENTS OF PUBLIC RIGHTS OF WAY

Modification of definitive maps and statements
6. Section 53 of the Act contains the key feature of the new review procedure, namely the requirement for surveying authorities to keep their definitive maps and statements under continuous review and to modify them by way of orders as events of the relevant kind occur. As indicated earlier the starting point for the implementation of the new procedure is the 'definitive map and statement' for a particular area as defined in section 53(1), until it is replaced by a modified map and statement prepared in accordance with the provisions of section 57(3). Definitive maps and statements for this purpose are:
(a) the latest revised definitive map and statement following the completion of a review carried out under section 33 of the 1949 Act as originally enacted or as amended by the 1968 Act; or
(b) where no review has taken place the original definitive map and statement prepared under section 32 of the 1949 Act; or
(c) for those former county borough and other excluded areas for which the survey provisions were never adopted or for areas where a survey was begun, but abandoned, the map and statement prepared under section 55(3).

RIGHTS OF WAY

7. The reference in section 53(1) to 'any area' stems from the fact that where under section 27(5) of the 1949 Act surveying authorities prepared original definitive maps and statements for different parts of their area at the same or different times they have never been required to amalgamate them into a single definitive map and statement for the whole of their area notwithstanding the requirement in section 34(3) of the 1949 Act to review them concurrently. Thus some surveying authorities may have several definitive maps and statements which together embrace the whole of their area. In practical terms this should make little difference when it come to making orders since statutorily there is no reason why a single order cannot be used to modify more than one definitive map and statement provided that fact is made apparent in the order.

8. Section 53(2) required surveying authorities to modify their definitive maps and statements by order as soon as reasonably practicable after the occurrence of any of the events specified in section 53(3). Section 53(2) is, of necessity, in two parts covering respectively events which occurred before and those which occurred after the commencement date of the new system. The second part also includes the requirement for definitive maps and statements to be kept under continuous review. That the subsection is in two parts does not mean that authorities must complete the modification of their maps and statements for events which preceded the commencement of the new procedure before embarking on modifications relating to subsequent events. It should be a simultaneous process. Moreover, in making orders there is no need for authorities to differentiate between events which preceded and those which succeeded the commencement of the new procedure. It is possible for both to feature in the same order. The modifications to be made to definitive maps and statements are those which the authority consider to be requisite. Consequently the obligation to make orders does not extend to proposals which, in the view of the authority, cannot, on the face of the evidence, be sustained. The procedure for making orders, apart from those which take effect on being made, is set out in Schedule 15 and is explained in greater detail later on in this Annex.

9. The use of an omnibus order (ie one embracing several proposals) has a clear advantage over a single event order in terms of cost and its use, whenever possible, is recommended.

10. It has been suggested that in instances where there is general agreement between the surveying authority, the landowner and path-users that the line of a footpath or bridleway proposed for addition to the definitive map and statement is not the most suitable, a public path order diverting the path or way to the preferred line should be made and considered at the same time as the order adding the right of way to the definitive map. Although in principle the making of concurrent orders is not unacceptable it is not a prerequisite of diversion orders that the footpath or bridleway should first be shown on the definitive map and statement. It is not therefore necessary to add the path or way to the definitive map by means of a definitive map order before considering the diversion order. However the order-making authority must, before proceeding, be satisfied that it is a public footpath or bridleway and that it would be expedient to divert it.

11. The events to be taken into consideration in connection with the modification of definitive maps and statements are set out in section 53(3) of the Act.

12. Subsection 3(a) covers statutory changes to the rights of way network arising from, amongst other things, public path orders under Highways and other

legislation, magistrates' courts orders and private legislation. The modification of the map and statement in consequence of such 'legal events' should not however take place before the order, enactment, etc., has taken effect.

13. Subsection 3(b) concerns the presumed dedication of footpaths and bridleways at common law or by virtue of the provisions of section 31 of the Highways Act 1980. It applies not only to ways not shown on definitive maps and statements but also to footpaths already shown over which bridleway rights are alleged to have been acquired.

14. Subsection 3(c) relates to the discovery by surveying authorities of evidence which shows that a right of way not shown on the map and statement subsists, or is reasonably alleged to subsist, and should therefore be shown; or that a right of way already shown is of a different status and should be up- or downgraded; or that it does not in fact exist and should be taken off; or that the particulars contained in the statement require modification. These provisions apply to footpaths, bridleways and byways open to all traffic.

15. The facility for rights of way not presently shown to be put directly onto definitive maps and statements as byways open to all traffic is new. By definition byways open to all traffic are vehicular rights of way which are used by the public mainly for the purposes for which footpaths and bridleways are used. The principal factor surveying authorities should bear in mind in deciding whether a way ought to be shown on definitive maps and statements as a byway open to all traffic is therefore the purposes for which it is used. Thus if it is used mainly by vehicular traffic as opposed to walkers and horseriders it should as a general rule not be shown. Instances may occur where a way presumed to have been dedicated as a highway for all purposes under section 31 of the Highways Act 1980 also satisfies the definition of a byway open to all traffic. In such circumstances, it would be open to surveying authorities to add the way to the definitive map and statement under section 53(3)(c)(i) of the Act. Section 53(3) also allows for ways presently shown on definitive maps and statements as footpaths and bridleways, but which enjoy vehicular rights, to be up-graded to byways open to all traffic.

16. Surveying authorities, whenever they discover or are presented with evidence which suggests that a definitive map and statement should be modified, are required to take into consideration all other relevant evidence available to them concerning the status of the right of way involved. Moreover before making an order they must be satisfied that the evidence shows on the balance of probability that a right of way of a particular description exists or that a way shown on the map is not in fact a public right of way. The mere assertion, without any supporting evidence, that a right of way does or does not exist would be insufficient to satisfy that test. The limitations on the admissibility of evidence that formerly applied in the case of deletions have been removed thus enabling any evidence that is relevant to be taken into consideration. The conclusive evidential effect of definitive maps and statements means, however, that the evidence must show that no right of way existed as at the relevant date of the definitive map on which the way was first shown. Equally claims of presumed dedication which are based solely on the fact that a way is shown on the definitive map would not be acceptable since the only event that can give rise to a presumption of dedication is user as of right. It would be necessary therefore in the face of evidence which shows that no right of way exists to demonstrate that the path or way has been without interruption and as of right for 20 years for it to remain on the definitive map.

17. As the 'legal events' specified in section 53(3)(a) are matters of fact and therefore beyond doubt there is no need for the order giving effect to them to be publicised. For this reason section 53(6) provides that orders which relate solely to such events shall take effect on being made but that other orders shall be subject to the provisions of Schedule 15. To combine both legal and evidential events in the same order would serve no useful purpose and it is clearly preferable that the former be dealt with separately from the latter. Although definitive maps and statements will not reflect the actual effect of orders immediately, the orders nonetheless effectively modify the definitive map and statement to which they relate on being made or confirmed and are, for the purposes of section 56(1) of the Act, part of the definitive map and statement. In this connection all orders should be accorded a relevant date which must be no earlier than six months before the date on which the order is made.

Procedure for definitive map orders

Forms of Orders

21. The forms of the various orders provided for by the Act, including those which take effect on being made, are prescribed in regulations 5 and 6 and set out respectively in Schedules 2 and 3 of the Regulations. Where appropriate the prescribed form makes provision for separate entries in the schedule to the order for the different modifications that can be made to definitive maps and statements, ie additions, deletions, changes in status and the modification of written statements. The order schedule should include a description of the path or way concerned by reference to the administrative area in which it is located; its position, length and width; nature of the surface; the location of any stiles, gates, fences or other lawful obstructions; particulars of any limitations or conditions pertaining to its use as a public right of way and any other information that would normally be included in the written statement.

Maps

22. The scale of the map referred to in the order is prescribed in the Regulations and must be not less than 1:25,000 although larger scale maps should be used whenever practicable. The scale, orientation and grid references should be clearly shown on the map.

23. Apart from deletions the notation used to depict the various classes or right of way is prescribed in the Regulations for definitive maps and statements. For deletions a continuous bold black line is recommended.

24. Since there is no procedure for the correction of errors once an order has been confirmed, other than as a result of the discovery of evidence, particular attention should be paid to the preparation of orders to ensure that the order map and schedule do not conflict. Moreover since orders effectively modify the definitive map and statement on confirmation and are therefore subject to the provisions of section 56(1) of the Act regarding the conclusive evidential effect of definitive maps and statements the order map and schedule serve the same function respectively as the definitive map and statement.

Severance of Orders

36. The procedure mentioned in paragraph 20 of this Annex whereby omnibus orders may be treated as two separate orders is set out in paragraph 5 or Schedule 15. Surveying authorities who decide to take advantage of this facility are required before doing so to notify the Secretary of State that they propose so to elect. The provision does not enable the order actually to become two separate orders; it provides for the order to be confirmed by the surveying authority in relation to the unopposed proposals before it is submitted to the Secretary of State for confirmation to the extent that it is opposed. The confirmation by the surveying authority would need clearly to identify the proposals to which it relates since statutorily the definitive map and statement is modified by virtue of that confirmation. Furthermore, following confirmation, copies of the order would need to be placed on deposit for public inspection until such time as the details are actually recorded on the map and statement when it is reproduced (see paragraphs 66–68).

37. If the surveying authority secures the withdrawal of objections before submitting an order to the Secretary of State for confirmation, paragraph 5(2) of the Schedule enables the 'separate order' for the opposed proposals then to be treated in the same manner as the (original) order and thus to be confirmed a second time by the surveying authority with respect to the further unopposed proposals. Once the authority is satisfied that it can take the matter no further the order should be submitted to the Secretary of State for confirmation in respect of the opposed proposals. Alternatively authorities may find it simpler to delay notifying the Secretary of State of their intention to use the power of severance until after the completion of any negotiations with objectors notwithstanding that confirmation of the unopposed proposals would be delayed.

Decisions on Orders

40. The different requirements for publicising confirmed orders and the non-confirmation of orders are specified in paragraph 11 of Schedule 15. Orders that are confirmed receive the same publicity as that given to the making of orders and copies of the order as confirmed or extracts therefrom sent to the persons who received copies of the order made. In addition copies of confirmed orders must be sent to the Ordnance Survey (see paragraph 8 of Annex B for the address). Surveying authorities are asked to similarly provide them with copies of 'legal event' orders. As regards decisions not to confirm an order a copy of the decision must be served on the persons on whom notice of the making of the order was served.

Applications for definitive map orders

41. Section 53(5) enables any person to apply to the surveying authority for an order to be made modifying a definitive map and statement as respects any of the 'evidential events' specified in paragraphs (b) and (c) of section 53(3). The procedure for the making and determination of applications is set out in Schedule 14. It includes the right for applicants to appeal to the Secretary of State against the refusal of the surveying authority to make an order.

42. This facility does not extend to the section 53(3)(a) 'legal events', because they relate to matters of fact, or to the reclassification of roads used as public

paths, because surveying authorities have a duty to review and reclassify such rights of way. Persons may nonetheless bring to the notice of surveying authorities any evidence or information which they believe to be relevant. The authority is not, however, statutorily obliged to act on that evidence or information.

Form and Submission of Applications

43. The form of application is prescribed in regulation 10(1) of the Regulations and set out in Schedule 7 thereto. Submitted applications must be accompanied by a map to a scale of not less than 1:25,000 showing the rights of way which are the subject of the application, copies of any supporting documentary evidence, including statements of witnesses and a certificate confirming that notice of the application has been served on the owners and occupiers of the land involved.

Notice of Application

44. Notice that an application for an order has been made must be served by the applicant on every owner and occupier of the land involved. Applicants who are unable to ascertain the name or address of the owner or occupier of the land may apply to the surveying authority for exemption from the requirement to serve a personal notice and for consent to serve notice instead by addressing it to the owner or occupier of the land (as described in the notice) and affixing it to a conspicuous object on the land. Consent should not normally be withheld if the applicant can show that he has made every reasonable effort to identify the owner and occupier of the land. The forms of the notice and certificate are prescribed by the Regulations and are set out in Schedules 8 and 9 thereto.

Consideration and Determination of Applications

45. Surveying authorities are required, as soon as reasonably practicable after receiving the above-mentioned certificate, to investigate the application and, after consulting the relevant district and parish or community councils or meetings, decide whether to make or not to make the order sought. Decisions on applications must be served on the applicant and on the owner and occupier of the land involved, and, in the case of a refusal to make an order, the reasons for the decision should be given. The orders themselves should be made as soon as reasonably practicable after the announcement of the decision to comply with the requirements of section 53(2)(b) of the Act.

46. If after 12 months an application is undecided the applicant may make representations to the Secretary of State for a direction requiring the authority to determine the application by a specified date. The Secretary of State is required to consult the relevant surveying authority before issuing his direction.

Appeals to the Secretary of State

47. In the event of an authority refusing to make an order the applicant has a right of appeal to the Secretary of State against that decision. Appeals must be lodged within 28 days from the date on which the authority issue their decision.

DOE CIRCULAR 1/83 ANNEX A

They should be made in writing, giving the grounds for the appeal, and be accompanied by copies of the application, the map showing the way concerned, the supporting documentation and the authority's decision. A copy of the notice of appeal must also be served on the surveying authority but without the accompaniments. The Secretary of State, on consideration of an appeal, is required to decide on the available information whether an order should be made and if so direct the authority accordingly. He is not empowered to authorise the modification of the definitive map and statement or to make an order himself.

Reclassification of roads used as public paths
48. Section 54 is about the reclassification of roads used as public paths. The need for reclassification stems from the uncertainty about the rights that exist over these ways. The purpose of reclassification is to establish precisely the rights that exist, and the tests regarding suitability and hardship that have applied hitherto have been dropped.
49. Under the provisions of section 54 surveying authorities are required, as soon as reasonably practicable after the commencement of the new procedure, to carry out a review of their roads used as public paths and make orders reclassifying them as byways open to all traffic, bridleways or footpaths. The requirement extends only to ways shown on definitive maps and statements as roads used as public paths. Ways shown as footpaths or bridleways, and over which vehicular rights are alleged to exist, should be considered for upgrading to byways open to all traffic under the general review procedures.
50. The revised criteria to be applied to reclassifications are set out in section 54(3) of the Act. Henceforth, if evidence is available which shows that public vehicular rights exist, the way should be reclassified as a byway open to all traffic; otherwise it should be reclassified as a bridleway unless evidence shows that no bridleway right exist, in which case it should be shown as a footpath.
51. In ascertaining what rights exist over their roads used as public paths authorities should take into account all the evidence at their disposal; that is the evidence which resulted in the way being shown on the definitive map and statement as a road used as a public path in the first place plus any additional evidence discovered in the meantime, including evidence of use by vehicular traffic.
52. Byways open to all traffic, bridleways and footpaths that derive from the reclassification of roads used as public paths are maintainable by highway authorities at public expense, irrespective of whether they were similarly maintainable prior to reclassification, but the Act places highway authorities under no obligation to metal byways open to all traffic or surface them so that they can be used by vehicular traffic.
53. Not all byways open to all traffic will be suitable for present day vehicular traffic. In these circumstances powers are available in the Road Traffic Regulation Act 1967 for highway authorities to make traffic regulation orders to control, regulate or prohibit use by vehicular traffic, or in the Highways Act 1980 to extinguish the vehicular rights whilst preserving the bridleway and footpath rights. The disadvantage of the latter course is that it may expose the way to ploughing with the result that its character and appearance as a landscape feature may be irrevocably destroyed. Highway authorities are asked to have regard to this possibility in deciding what course of action, if any, is appropriate.

Preparation of modified definitive maps and statements
66. From time to time, as orders accumulate to the point at which it is difficult to follow the various changes that have been made, it will be necessary for surveying authorities to replace the modified definitive maps and statement with a consolidated map and statement depicting the actual consequences of the modifications made. Section 57(3) authorises this to be done and further specifies that each time an up to date map and statement is prepared it becomes, for the purposes of the review procedure, the definitive map and statement for that area. On each occasion however the relevant date should be brought forward to a date not more than six months before the updated map and statement is prepared. The date selected should always be later than the relevant date of the latest modification order to be consolidated.

67. In addition section 57(5) requires surveying authorities to make copies of each definitive map and statement and all relevant orders available for public inspection at one or more places within each district in their area and, if practicable, within each parish. In complying with this provision authorities are required to do no more than ensure that the relevant extracts from the map and statement, together with copies of the relevant orders, are available for inspection within each district or parish. Although it is not mandatory, surveying authorities are asked, insofar as it is practicable, to ensure that the documents made available for inspection within each district are deposited at the offices of the district council. The extent to which it is practicable for copies to be made available within parishes will be governed largely by the availability of places to which the public have regular access. Section 57(7) requires surveying authorities to bring to the attention to the public the fact that copies of definitive maps and statements and orders are available for inspection. It is recommended that a notice should be inserted in the local press every time a consolidated map and statement is prepared listing the places where the relevant extracts from that map and statement and any subsequent orders can be inspected free of charge at all reasonable hours. Authorities are requested to send two copies of consolidated maps and statements to the Secretary of State and a copy to the Ordnance Survey.

68. The requirements regarding the availability of definitive maps and statements and copies of orders for public inspection at different places in the surveying authority's area do not extend to maps and statements and orders replaced by consolidated maps and statements. Nonetheless at least one copy of the previous maps and statements together with the orders modifying them is required by section 57(6) to be kept available for public inspection.

Sales of definitive maps and statements
69. It is clearly in the best interests of landowners and the public that the information recorded in definitive maps and statements is readily accessible. The sale of copies of definitive maps and statements is one way of fulfilling this objective. Whilst the Act does not make it mandatory for surveying authorities to place copies on sale those authorities that do not do so at present are asked to make copies available for purchase if there is sufficient demand.

DOE CIRCULAR 1/83 ANNEX B

ANNEX B : PUBLIC PATH ORDERS AND EXTINGUISHMENT OF PUBLIC RIGHTS OF WAY ORDERS

General
3. The statutory provisions relating to the creation, diversion and stopping-up of public rights of way have been framed to secure the protection of both the public rights and the interests of owners and occupiers as well as the interests of bodies such as statutory undertakers. It is essential therefore that authorities who wish to bring an order into effect by a particular date should allow enough time, when making the order, to comply with all the statutory requirements. In particular it should be borne in mind that the closure of a path or way before the right of way over it has been extinguished is unlawful.

Confirmation of Orders

4. Orders to which there are representations or objections require the Secretary of State's confirmation. Consequently, if an authority is satisfied that any representations or objections cannot be met and are unlikely to be withdrawn the order should, if the authority decide to proceed, be submitted to the Secretary of State for confirmation. There has been considerable debate on the question of whether authorities have the discretion not to proceed with opposed orders instead of submitting them to the Secretary of State. Since there is no statutory requirement that opposed orders must be sent to the Secretary of State authorities appear to have such discretion. However, because the statutes do not authorise the withdrawal of orders a formal resolution by the authority not to proceed is considered to be necessary to bring the procedure to an end. The objectors concerned should be notified of any such resolution. Once an order is submitted to the Secretary of State the power of decision passes to him.

5. Orders which are unopposed or to which all the representations and objections have been withdrawn may be confirmed by the promoting authority, but without modification. Thus unopposed orders in need of modification must also be submitted to the Secretary of State for confirmation.

6. Before confirming an order, irrespective of whether it is objected to or not, both the Secretary of State and the order-making authority must be satisfied as to the particular considerations set out in the statutes relating to the different orders. These are described in the sections on the individual Acts.

7. In relation to orders creating new rights of way it is important to allow sufficient time between the date of confirmation and the date on which the order takes effect for the right of way created by the order to be brought into a fit condition for public use and also, in the case of diversion orders, to be made available for public use before the right of way the order extinguishes is stopped up.

8. A copy of confirmed orders must be sent to the Ordnance Survey and should be addressed to the Superintendent, Rights of Way Section, Room C329, Ordnance Survey, Romsey Road, Maybush, Southampton, SO9 4DH. Authorities are asked similarly to send the Ordnance Survey copies of any notices, published under paragraph 7 of Schedule 20 to the 1971 Act or paragraph 4A of Schedule 6 to the 1980 Act, which announce the coming into operation of orders.

RIGHTS OF WAY

Secretary of State's Power of Modification

9. Authorities may care to note that the Secretary of State does not regard the power of modification vested in him as generally available to correct minor errors and defects in orders and certainly never to make good orders which would otherwise be incapable of confirmation because they are defective in a matter of substance. In practice the Secretary of State, in his consideration of orders, normally disregards errors or defects of a minor nature provided they do not, in his view, prejudice the interests of any person or render the order misleading in its purpose. Nonetheless care should be taken in drafting orders to ensure they are correct and free from errors and defects to reduce the possibility of their validity being challenged at a later stage in the procedure.

Forms of Orders

12. The limitations and conditions set out in the schedule to an order should only be limitations and conditions affecting the actual public right, e.g. position and number of stiles and gates. In addition, the description in the schedule of any path or way created by the order should if possible include details of the width of that path or way.

Maps

13. The maps referred to in an order should be on a scale of not less than 1:25,000 or 25 inches to the mile unless the Secretary of State has agreed beforehand to a smaller scale. Extracts from a current edition of an Ordnance Survey map should be used and be endorsed 'Crown Copyright, Reproduced from [or Based on] the Ordnance Survey Map with the sanction of the Controller of HMSO'. The scale and orientation should be clearly shown as well as the grid reference to enable the public to identify the rights of way concerned.

Notices

15. The description in the notice of the general effect of the order should be sufficient to enable the public to understand its fundamental purpose and to identify the rights of way involved.

Town and Country Planning Act 1971

Extinguishment or Diversion of Footpaths and Bridleways to enable Development to be carried out

23. In addition to enabling a footpath or bridleway to be diverted along another route, the Act also enables orders to include provision for the creation of an alternative highway or the improvement of an existing one for use as a replacement for one being stopped up or diverted. Whereas a diversion must either commence or terminate at some point on the line of the original path or way an alternative path or way need not do so and may, for instance, run parallel to the path being stopped up. However, to avoid the creation of a cul-de-sac and to enable the public, where appropriate, to return to that part of the original

path or way not affected by the development, any alternative path provided should link by means of other highways to the original path or way.

24. When the diversion or alternative right of way is proposed to be provided and dedicated over land not owned by the developer, the consent of the landowner(s) to the proposed dedication should be obtained before the order is made.

25. Where development in so far as it affects a path or way is completed before the necessary order to divert or extinguish the path has been made or confirmed, the powers under section 210 and 217 of the Act to make and confirm orders are no longer available since the purpose of the order — to enable development to be carried out — cannot be substantiated. Thus if an order has not been made, it cannot be made, or if made but not confirmed, it cannot be confirmed, irrespective of whether it is opposed or unopposed. In such circumstances authorities must look to other powers, e.g. the Highways Act to secure the diversion or extinguishment of the path or way. In this respect development should be regarded as completed if the work remaining to be carried out is minimal.

Highways Act 1980

Extinguishment of Footpaths and Bridleways

31. The power for local authorities to make orders for the extinguishment of footpaths and bridleways is contained in section 118 of the 1980 Act. Orders can only be made if the authority considers it expedient that the path or way should be stopped-up because it is not needed for public use. In making orders which entail the closure of part only of a path or way care should be taken to avoid creating a cul-de-sac in the remaining part of the path or way.

32. Although the ground for making orders is that the path or way is not needed, when it comes to confirmation the Secretary of State, or order-making authority in the case of unopposed orders, must be satisfied in accordance with section 118(2) that confirmation is expedient having regard to the extent to which the path is likely to be used and the effect that the loss of the path or way would have on the land it serves. It is important therefore that in making orders authorities should give due weight to these considerations. Any temporary circumstances preventing or diminishing the use of the path or way should be disregarded.

33. In addition, the extent to which a creation or diversion order, made in association with the extinguishment order, would provide an alternative path or way to that proposed for closure, may be taken into consideration in the determination of the extinguishment order. Clearly, therefore, where related extinguishment and creation or diversion orders have been made concurrently and representations or objections are duly made to one, but not to the other, and not withdrawn, it is advisable for authorities, if they decide to proceed with the orders, to submit both to the Secretary of State for confirmation.

Diversion of Footpaths and Bridleways

34. The power for local authorities to make orders for the diversion of footpaths or bridleways is contained in section 119 of the Act. As a result of the changes

brought about by the 1981 Act (Schedule 16, paragraph 5) authorities may initiate orders themselves without the prerequisite of an application from the owner, lessee or occupier of the land. The former grounds for making section 119 orders have been replaced by new grounds which enable paths or ways to be diverted if it is considered expedient to do so in the interests of either the owner, lessee or occupier of the land or the public.

35. When making an order on the new grounds, authorities must be prepared to show why they consider the diversion proposed is in the interests of the owner, lessee or occupier, or of the public, since they or the Secretary of State, when considering the confirmation of the order, must be satisfied that the diversion is expedient on the ground(s) stated. They must also be satisfied that the path or way will not be substantially less convenient to the public as a result of the diversion. Other considerations to be taken into account in relation to the question of confirmation are the effect (a) the diversion would have on the public enjoyment of the path or way as a whole; (b) the implementation of the order would have on the land served by the existing right of way; and (c) the new right of way would have on the land it crosses and on other land held with that land.

36. Although the new route provided by a diversion order may in part follow an existing footpath or bridleway, where the whole of the line of the proposed diversion is already a public right of way the path or way to be diverted is in effect being extinguished. In such cases, authorities should make an extinguishment order.

DOE CIRCULAR 1/85; WELSH OFFICE CIRCULAR 1/85: THE USE OF CONDITIONS IN PLANNING PERMISSION

Conditions depending on others' actions

33. It is unreasonable to impose a condition which the developer would be unable to comply with himself, or which he could comply with only with the consent or authorisation of a third party (for example, a condition which requires an aerodrome owner to impose a particular pattern of aircraft flight routeings, when that is a matter for the air traffic control authorities).

34. Although it would be *ultra vires*, however, to require works which the developer has no power to carry out, or which would need the consent or authorisation of a third party, it may be possible to achieve a similar result by a condition worded in a negative form, prohibiting development until a specified action has been taken. The test of whether such a condition is reasonable is strict; it amounts to whether there are least reasonable prospects of the action in question being performed. Thus for example, if it could be shown that, although current sewerage facilities were inadequate for a new housing estate, improvements were under way which would be completed not long after the houses, it might be right to grant permission subject to a condition that houses should not be occupied until the relevant sewerage works were complete. In an appropriate case, too, it might be reasonable to use a condition requiring that the development should not commence until a particular highway had been stopped up or diverted, if there were reason to suppose that the highway authority would be able and willing to take the necessary action. The reasonableness of such a requirement will in all cases depend on the likelihood of the

precondition being fulfilled within such time as to enable the development to be commenced within the time-limit imposed by the permission.

DEPARTMENT OF TRANSPORT CIRCULAR ROADS 1/86; WELSH OFFICE CIRCULAR 3/86 CYCLE TRACKS ACT 1984: THE CYCLE TRACKS REGULATIONS 1984

Introduction
1. This circular refers to the Cycle Tracks Act 1984 (the 1984 Act) and the Cycle Tracks Regulations 1984 (SI 1984 No 1431) (the 1984 Regulations) both of which came into operation on September 12, 1984. It also contains advice on consultation and other matters when a local highway authority proposes to convert all, or part, of a footpath to a cycle track.
2. The 1984 Act removes the right to use mopeds on cycle tracks, makes it an offence to drive or park a motor vehicle on a cycle track; provides a new procedure under which a local highway authority can convert all, or part, of a footpath to a cycle track; and gives highway authorities powers to undertake works to separate a cycle track from an adjacent footway or footpath or to safeguard users of a cycle track.
3. The 1984 Regulations cover the procedure to be followed when a local highway authority proposes to convert all, or part, of a footpath to a cycle track.

Mopeds
4. Section 1(1) of the 1984 Act amends the definition of a cycle track in section 329(1) of the Highways Act 1980 by removing the right to use pedal cycles, which are also motor vehicles within the meaning of the Road Traffic Act 1972, from a cycle track provided on or after September 12 1984.
5. Section 1(2) of the 1984 Act removes the right to use pedal cycles which are also motor vehicles from cycle tracks which were provided before September 12, 1984.
6. The Departments strongly advise against the provision of highways allowing joint use by mopeds and cyclists. The speed difference between mopeds and pedal cycles can make their joint use of such facilities unsafe.
7. Highways which are intended, or provided, for use both by pedal cycles and mopeds cannot be provided as cycle tracks.

Driving and parking of motor vehicles on cycle tracks
8. Section 2(1) of the 1984 Act makes the driving or parking without lawful authority of any motor vehicle on any cycle track an offence subject on conviction to a fine not exceeding the third level of the standard scale (section 37 of the Criminal Justice Act) — as from May 1 1984 £400.
9. Section 2(2) provides a defence if the motor vehicle is being used in certain emergencies, or is engaged in certain work by, or on behalf of, a highway authority or on the apparatus of a statutory undertaker. Section 2(3) defines a statutory undertaker as including any sewerage authorities and the operator of a telecommunications code system.
10. As driving or parking a motor vehicle on a cycle track has by this Act been made a specific offence it will no longer be necessary for highway authorities

to make individual Traffic Regulation Orders under section 1 or 6 of the Road Traffic Regulation Act 1984 to control the use of cycle tracks by motor vehicles.

Electrically Assisted Pedal Cycles

11. Electrically assisted pedal cycles which conform to The Electrically Assisted Pedal Cycles Regulations 1983 (SI 1983 No 1168) are classified as pedal cycles and are not treated as motor vehicles (section 140 of the Road Traffic Regulation Act 1984 and section 193 of the Road Traffic Act 1972). They can be used on cycle tracks without any offence specified in section 2(1) of the 1984 Act. If problems arise through the use of electrically assisted pedal cycles on cycle tracks they can be excluded through a Traffic Regulation Order made under sections 1 or 6 of the Road Traffic Regulation Act 1984.

Conversion of a footpath to a cycle track

General

12. Section 3 of the 1984 Act provides a new procedure under which a local highway authority can convert all, or part, of a footpath to a cycle track. The effect of an order made and confirmed under this section is to convert the footpath, or part thereof, to a cycle track with a right of way on foot. On conversion the cycle track becomes a highway maintainable at public expense (section 36 of the Highways Act 1980) even if the footpath had not previously had that status.

13. A local highway authority can make and confirm an order under section 3 if there are no unwithdrawn objections. If the order is opposed it has to be submitted to the Secretary of State for confirmation. The necessary procedures for the making and confirmation of an order are set down in section 3 and in the 1984 Regulations. For convenience the advice in this Circular follows the general sequence followed when an order is made and confirmed. The advice is cross referenced to the 1984 Act and 1984 Regulations which should be read together with it.

Agricultural Land

14. Section 3(2) of the 1984 Act provides that a local highway authority shall not make an order under section 3(1) converting a footpath which crosses agricultural land unless the written consent of all those having a legal interest in the land has been obtained.

15. Agricultural land is defined as in section 1(2) of the Agricultural Holdings Act 1948; that is, land used for agriculture which is so used for the purpose of a trade or business and land designated by the Minister of Agriculture Fisheries and Food under section 109(1) of the Agriculture Act 1947.

16. Agriculture includes horticulture, fruit growing, seed growing, dairy farming and livestock breeding and keeping, the use of grazing land, meadow land, osier land, market gardens and nursery grounds, and the use of lands as woodlands where that use is ancillary to the farming of the land for other agricultural purposes.

17. Legal interest is defined so as not to include those with an interest in land which amounts to less than a tenancy from year to year.

18. As no order can be made in respect of a footpath or the parts of a footpath that cross agricultural land if the consent(s) required by section 3(2) are withheld, it is advisable for an authority to seek such consent(s) at as early a stage as possible.

Consultation

19. Regulation 3 of the 1984 Regulations specify that a local highway authority proposing to make an order under section 3(1) has, before making the order, to consult:
(a) one or more organisations representing persons who use the footpath involved or who are likely to be affected by any provision of the proposed order;
(b) any other local authority, parish council or community council within whose area the footpath is located;
(c) those statutory undertakers whose operational land is crossed by the footpath; and
(d) the chief officer of police for the area.

20. The Secretaries of State wish to emphasise that it is their view that there should be widespread consultation on any proposal to introduce cyclists onto facilities formerly reserved solely for pedestrian use. Consultation under regulation 3(a) should be as wide as possible including not only organisations representing users of a footpath but also local, and/or national, cycling organisations. It is particularly important to seek the views of organisations representing the interests of disabled people.

21. A list of the National organisations a local authority should consult is at Annex A. The Joint Committee on Mobility of Blind and Partially Sighted People has undertaken to co-ordinate the responses of organisations representing blind and partially sighted people. The Joint Committee on Mobility for the Disabled has agreed to act as a focus for consultation with organisations representing disabled people. Local highway authorities are advised to consult the Joint Committees in the first instance. Authorities should keep in mind the difficulties blind or partially sighted people may have in dealing with written material. These difficulties can also arise with respect to subsequent statutory notices etc.

22. Local highway authorities may also wish to take steps to bring the proposals to the attention of local residents and to explain the implications to them.

23. Though an order made under section 3(1) of the 1984 Act will relate solely to the principle of conversion of all, or part, of a footpath it is considered advisable to ensure that during any consultation exercise, or as part of any explanatory material accompanying any subsequent statutory notice, the fullest practicable details are given on the works of the local highway authority proposes to undertake when providing the cycle track. This is because many of the organisations that a local highway authority consults under regulations 3 are likely to wish to consider the form of segregation it is proposed to provide between a proposed cycle track and an adjacent footpath eg when it is proposed to convert half the width of a footpath. Equally, such organisations may wish to take account of any safety works which a local highway authority proposes to undertake on a cycle track or adjacent footpath.

RIGHTS OF WAY

Making an order

24. When a local highway authority has received any consent(s) required under section 3(2) and undertaken the consultation specified in regulation 3 it can proceed to make an order under section 3(1) to convert all, or part, of a footpath to a cycle track.

25. A copy of a model order is attached (Annex B). The lengths and, when appropriate, width of footpath to be converted should be clearly indicated or specified. If a later date is not specified in the order it takes effect on the date notice of confirmation is published — section 3(8).

Notice of the Making of an Order

26. Regulation 4(a) requires the publication of a notice of the making of an order in at least one local newspaper circulating in the area in which the footpath which the order applies is located. The notice has to:
(a) describe the general effect of the order, stating that it has been made and that it requires confirmation;
(b) indicate where a copy of the order can be inspected free of charge; and
(c) specify the period in which objections can be made to the order (which must be at least 28 days from the first publication of the notice of the making of the order), indicates the address to which objections should be sent and states that an objection should be in writing and should state the grounds for objection.

27. Regulation 4(b) requires a copy of the notice to be displayed at the ends of the length, or lengths, of footpath to which the order applies.

28. Regulations 4(c) requires a copy of the notice to be displayed in at least one of the places where public notices are usually displayed in the locality.

29. Regulation 4(d) requires a copy of the notice to be sent to all those previously consulted under regulation 3.

Objection to an Order

30. Under regulation 5 any person can lodge an objection to an order made under section 3(1) so long as the objection is lodged within the period specified in the notice of the making of the order published under regulation 4(a), is in writing and contains a statement of objection and the grounds of the objection.

Confirmation of an Order

31. If no objections are received to an order, or any objections that have been received are withdrawn, the local highway authority who made the order can proceed to confirm it under section 3(3)(b) of the 1984 Act but only in the form in which it was originally made. A form of endorsement is at Annex B.

32. A local highway authority cannot therefore vary an order it has made under section 3(1). But it can agree to alter any works it proposed to undertake in connection with the provision of the cycle track to meet the concerns of objectors. If any such changes require as a consequence, a variation in the terms of the original order, this would then trigger a fresh consultation and possibly the making of a new order.

33. If there are unwithdrawn objections to an order under section 3(1) the order can only be confirmed by the Secretary of State. Orders requiring the Secretary

of State's confirmation should be submitted to the appropriate Department of Transport Regional Office or the Welsh Office.

Local Inquiries

34. Under regulation 6(1) when an order is submitted by the local highway authority to the Secretary of State for confirmation he shall cause a local inquiry to be held *unless* under the exercise of the discretion given in regulation 6(2) he decides to dispense with an inquiry when he is satisfied that in the circumstances of the case the holding of an inquiry is unnecessary. For example, the Secretary of State will consider exercising his discretion under regulation 6(2) to dispense with an inquiry when the parties to a contested conversion order agree to proceed to his decision on the order on the basis of written representations.

Notice of an Inquiry

35. Under regulation 7(1) the Secretary of State is to fix the time, date and place of the holding of an inquiry and sends written notice to every objector at least 42 days before the opening of the inquiry.
36. If all the objectors agree in writing the Secretary of State can give a lesser period of notice of the inquiry (regulation 7(1)(a)).
37. If it becomes necessary, or advisable, to vary the time or place fixed for an inquiry the Secretary of State can do so giving reasonable notice to the objectors of any change (regulation 7(1)(b)).
38. Under regulation 7(2)(a) the local highway authority must display a copy of the notice of the inquiry issued by the Secretary of State under regulation 7(1) at a conspicuous place near the footpath to which the order relates and in at least one other location in the area where public notices are usually displayed at least 21 days before the inquiry.
39. If directed by the Secretary of State (regulation 7(2)(b)) the local highway authority shall publish in at least one local newspaper circulating in the area such notice of the inquiry as he may specify. Local highway authorities can give additional publicity to the holding of an inquiry beyond that required under the 1984 Regulations should they consider it appropriate.

Inspectors

40. Under regulation 8 the Secretary of State can direct that the inquiry Inspector can make the decision to confirm the order, with or without modifications.
41. A direction by the Secretary of State that the Inspector shall decide the case can be provided either by a separate notice issued to objectors under regulation 8 or as part of the notice of the inquiry.

Consideration of Objections at Inquiry

42. Under regulation 9(1) any person interested in the subject matter of the inquiry can attend it or be represented at it.

43. Under regulation 9(2) any person may submit written representations to the Inspector to be considered by him at the inquiry. Such representations need to be sent to the address referred to or specified under regulation 4(a)(iii). This address should therefore ideally be repeated in the notice of the inquiry issued under regulation 7 where this entitlement can conveniently be set out.

44. Under regulation 9(3)(a) the appointed person can refuse to hear any objection or representation if the views of the person or his objection or representation are frivolous.

45. Under regulation 9(3)(b) the appointed person can refuse to hear any person at the inquiry if his views have been adequately stated by some other person at the inquiry.

46. When considering evidence given at the inquiry or any written representation submitted under regulation 9(2) the appointed person, or the Secretary of State, can take into account any undertakings given by the local highway authority regarding any works it proposes to undertake to separate the proposed cycle track from any adjacent footpath or to increase the safety of users of the cycle track or footpath.

47. Section 3(5) of the 1984 Act applies subsections (2) to (5) of section 250 of the Local Government Act 1972, covering giving of evidence at, and defraying the costs of, local inquiries to inquiries held under section 3.

Secretary of State's Decision

48. Under section 3(3)(a) the Secretary of State may refuse to confirm an order, or confirm it either in the form in which it was made or subject to such modifications as are considered appropriate.

Notice of Final Decision

49. When the local highway authority has been notified of a decision by the Secretary of State, or a duly designated Inspector, to confirm an order under section 3(3)(a) of the 1984 Act, or the local highway authority has itself confirmed an uncontested order under section 3(3)(b), regulation 10(1)(i) requires the local highway authority to give notice of the confirmation of the order.

50. The notice should state the general effect of the order as confirmed and, if confirmed by the Secretary of State or a duly designated inspector, specify whether the order has been confirmed with, or without, modifications. The notice should further state the date on which the order takes effect (regulation 10(1)(i)). Under section 3(8) of the 1984 Act an order can take effect either on the date of publication of the notice of the confirmation of the order or on any later date specified in the order.

51. The notice should also name a place in the general locality of the footpath where the confirmed order can be examined free of charge (regulation 10(1)(ii)).

52. Under regulation 10(2) the notice under 10(1) shall be given:
(a) by publication in at least one local newspaper circulating in the area in which the footpath to which the order applies is located (regulation 10(2)(a));
(b) by a copy of the notice being displayed at the ends of the length, or lengths, of footpath to which the order applies (regulation 10(2)(b)); and
(c) (if a local inquiry was held) by sending a copy of the notice to all those who attended the inquiry, or submitted written representation under regulation 9(2), and who asked to be notified of the decision (regulation 10(2)(c)).

DTp CIRCULAR ROADS 1/86

Challenge to the Legal Validity of an Order

53. Section 3(6) provides that a person aggrieved by a confirmed order has a right to challenge its validity on certain grounds. Any application needs to be made to the High Court within six weeks of the date of publication of the notice of confirmation of the order under regulation 10(2)(a).
54. Section 3(7)(a) provides that the High Court can, by interim order, suspend the operation of a confirmed order either in whole or in part pending final determination of an application made under section 3(6).
55. Section 3(7)(b) provides that the High Court can, on final judgement, quash a defective order, either in whole or in part, if the Court is satisfied that the order is not within the powers in section 3, or that the interests of an applicant have been substantially prejudiced by a failure to comply with any requirement of section 3 of the 1984 Act.
56. Section 3(8) provides that there can be no legal challenge to a confirmed order other than an application to the High Court as provided for in section 3(6) and (7).

Definitive Maps

57. When an order made under section 3(1) comes into effect, the footpath, or part of it, which is covered by the order ceases to be a footpath and becomes a cycle track with a right of way on foot.
58. If the footpath is shown on a definitive map and statement of public rights of way it will have to be deleted from that map and statement if all the footpath has been converted to a cycle track.
59. If only part of the width of the footpath has been converted there will be two distinct but adjacent ways: a cycle track and a footpath. As a footpath remains in existence it can remain on the definitive map; however, any statement describing the footpath may need to be amended to reflect its reduced width.
60. The Departments are consulting the Director General of the Ordnance Survey on the need to show cycle tracks on OS maps and on whether orders confirmed under section 3 should be notified to the Ordnance Survey.

Highways Maintained at Public Expense

61. If the footpath which has been converted, in whole or in part, was not formerly a highway maintainable at public expense the confirmation of an order under section 3 makes the cycle track such a highway (section 3(1)).
62. If the footpath was previously a highway maintainable at public expense the cycle track retains that status.

Work to give Effect to an Order

63. Section 3(10) gives a local highway authority power to undertake any necessary work to give effect to an order made and confirmed under section 3. Any work that would constitute development under Part III of the Town and Country Planning Act 1971 is deemed to have been given planning permission.

RIGHTS OF WAY

Revocation of an Order

64. Section 3(9) allows an order made and confirmed under section 3 to be revoked under the same procedures applied to the making and confirmation of the original order. When such an order is revoked the cycle track reverts to being a footpath, or part of one, and ceases to be a highway maintainable at public expense if the footpath was not previously, or has not itself become, a highway maintainable at public expense.

Works in Cycle Tracks

65. Section 4(1) gives highway authorities power to provide and maintain barriers in any cycle track. Previously, highway authorities only had power to provide barriers in cycle tracks which are included in a highway containing a carriageway — section 66(3) of the Highways Act 1980.
66. Section 4(2) gives highway authorities power to undertake whatever work they think necessary in the interests of safety to separate persons using the cycle track from those using an adjacent footpath or footway.
67. Section 4(3) allows highway authorities to alter or remove any barriers or other works provided under section 4(1) and (2).
68. Section 4(4) restricts a highway authority's power under this section to cycle tracks, footways and footpaths which are highways maintainable at public expense by that highway authority.

Compensation

69. Section 5(1) gives a right to compensation for damage consequent on the undertaking of work to give effect to an order under section 3(10), or the erection of barriers or works under section 4.
70. Section 5(2) gives a right to claim compensation for any reduction in the value of an interest in land arising as a consequence of the coming into operation of an order under section 3, but excludes claims which can be made or anticipated under section 5(1).
71. Section 5(3) refers disputes to the Lands Tribunal linked to section 307 of the Highways Act 1980. Section 307(1) of that Act provides that any dispute arising on a claim for compensation shall be determined by the Lands Tribunal. Subsection (2) of that section applies section 4 of the Land Compensation Act 1961 (costs). Subsection (3) of section 307 applies rules 2 to 4 of the rules in section 5 of the Land Compensation Act 1961 (rules for valuation under compulsory acquisition) to the calculation of compensation, insofar as it is calculated by reference to depreciation of the value of an interest in land.

Application to Crown Land

72. Section 6(1) enables orders to be made and confirmed under section 3, and barriers and works to be provided under section 4 in respect of Crown Land following agreement between the appropriate authority for that land and the highway authority.

DTp CIRCULAR ROADS 1/86

73. Section 6(2) provides that any agreement under subsection (1) may contain provisions of a financial character, but provides that any provisions of such character shall not be included in an agreement made by a Government Department without the Treasury's approval.

74. Section 6(3) defines 'Crown Land' and the 'appropriate authority'. When there is any dispute over what authority is the appropriate authority in relation to any Crown Land the final decision rests with the Treasury.

75. When highway authorities wish to apply the provisions of the 1984 Act to Crown Land the agreement of the appropriate authority for that land should be obtained at an early stage. Such an agreement cannot preclude the highway authority from observing any of the other requirements of the 1984 Act or 1984 Regulations.

Annex A: National Organisations interested in Footpath Conversion Proposals

Organisation	Address
Ramblers' Association) Pedestrians Association)	Ramblers' and Pedestrians Cycle Tracks Unit 1/5 Wandsworth Road London SW8 2XX
Joint Committee on Mobility of Blind and Partially Sighted People	The Secretary Joint Committee on Mobility of Blind and Partially Sighted People 224 Great Portland Street London W1N 6AA
Joint Committee on Mobility for the Disabled	The Hon Secretary Joint Committee on Mobility for the Disabled 9 Moss Close Pinner Middlesex HA5 3AY
Cyclists' Touring Club	The National Secretary Cyclists' Touring Club Cotterell House 69 Meadrow Godalming Surrey GU7 3HS
Friends of the Earth	Friends of the Earth Ltd 377 City Road London EC1V 1NA

RIGHTS OF WAY

Annex B
CYCLE TRACKS ACT 1984: THE COUNTY COUNCIL OF ***** (*****) CYCLE TRACKS ORDER 19**.

The County Council of *****, in exercise of the powers conferred upon them by Section 3(1) of the Cycle Tracks Act 1984 *[having obtained the written consents required by section 3(2) of that Act and]* having undertaken the consultations required by regulation 3 of the Cycle Tracks Regulations 1984, hereby makes the following Order:–

1. The footpath described in the schedule to this Order and shown by zebra hatching on the annexed plan is hereby designated a cycle track.

2. This Order may be cited as the County Council of ***** (*****) Cycle Tracks Order 19** *[shall come into operation at the end of 28 days from the date on which notice of confirmation of this order is first published [1]]*
Given under the Common Seal of the Council the ***** day of ***** 19**
The Common Seal of the Council was hereunto affixed in the presence of:–

*****

Chairman of the Council

*****

Clerk of the Council

*[The foregoing Order is hereby confirmed by the County Council of ***** this ***** day of ***** 19**. The Common Seal of the Council was hereunto affixed in the presence of:–*

*****

Chairman of the Council

*****

Clerk of the Council [2]]

Schedule
The footpath designated a cycle track by this Order is that length of footpath situated at ***** in the ***** of ***** which extends from ***** to ***** (for a maximum width of ***** metres measured from *****).

[1] In the absence of a date being specified the Order comes into operation on first publication of the notice of confirmation.

[2] To be added if Order is confirmed by the Council.

DOE CIRCULAR 2/87

DOE CIRCULAR 2/87: WELSH OFFICE CIRCULAR 5/87: AWARD OF COSTS INCURRED IN PLANNING AND COMPULSORY PURCHASE ORDER PROCEEDINGS

PART II : Costs in respect of compulsory purchase and analogous orders

General principles

30. There is a distinction between cases where appellants take the initiative, such as in applying for planning permission, or undertaking development allegedly without planning permission, and cases where objectors are defending their rights or interests which are the subject of a compulsory purchase order. If a statutory objector to such an order is successful, an award of costs will be made unless there are exceptional reasons for not doing so. To enable an award to be made on grounds of success the claimant must have made a formal objection to the order; the order must have been the subject of a local inquiry which the claimant must have attended (or been represented at) and where the claimant was heard as a statutory objector. (...) In addition the claimant must have had the objection sustained by the Secretary of State's refusal to confirm the order or by his decision to exclude from the order the whole or part of the objector's property. The award will be made against the authority who made the order and does not of itself imply unreasonable behaviour on the part of the authority.

31. No application for costs need be made by a successful statutory objector; the Secretary of State will write to the parties concerned. There are some circumstances in which an award of costs may be made to an unsuccessful objector or to an order-making authority because of unreasonable behaviour by the other party. In practice such an award is likely to relate to procedural matters such as unreasonably causing an adjournment of the inquiry. In these cases an application for costs should be made to the Secretary of State after the inquiry.

Partly successful objectors

32. Where a statutory objector is partly successful in opposing a compulsory purchase order the Secretary of State will normally make a partial award of costs. Such cases arise, for example, where the Secretary of State in confirming an order excludes part of the objector's land, or where a statutory objector to a compulsory purchase order made to clear unfit houses can establish that his home is not unfit or that the property has been wrongly classified as a dwelling house, even though he does not succeed in having it excluded from the order. In the latter case, if this was the only ground on which he objected to the order, he will be treated in the same way as a wholly successful objector.

Analogous orders and proposals

33. The Secretary of State normally awards costs to successful objectors to orders and proposals which he regards as analogous to compulsory purchase orders. In general he will consider an order or proposal to be analogous to a

RIGHTS OF WAY

compulsory purchase order if its making or confirmation takes away from the objector some right or interest in land for which the statute gives him a right to compensation. Some examples of orders and proposals which are considered to be analogous to compulsory purchase orders are set out in the Appendix.

Plural Objections

34. Sometimes a single inquiry is held into two or more proposals, only one of which is a compulsory purchase (or analogous) order, for example an application for planning permission and an order for the compulsory acquisition of land included in the application, or an application for an order under the Water Resources Act 1971 together with an order for the compulsory acquisition of rights in the land concerned. Where a statutory objector to both proposals in either of these examples appears at such an inquiry and is successful in objecting to the compulsory purchase order, the objector will be entitled to an award in respect of the compulsory purchase order only. An objector is not, however, precluded from making an application for the remaining costs on the ground that the authority has acted unreasonably.

Financial and manpower implications
35. This circular is expected to have no immediate financial or manpower implications for local planning authorities. To the extent that the policies set out here are successful in the longer term in discouraging unreasonable behaviour, the result should be a reduction in costs not just for local authorities but for all the parties to planning appeals considered at public inquiries.
36. Ministry of Housing and Local Government Circular 73/65 (WO 35/65 and Department of the Environment Circular 69/71 (WO 149/71) are cancelled.

Appendix: Orders analogous to compulsory purchase orders
(viii) Orders under section 26 of the Highways Act 1980 creating a footpath or bridleway over land;
(ix) Orders under section 65 of the National Parks and Access to the Countryside Act 1949 regarding access to land.

DEPARTMENT OF THE ENVIRONMENT CIRCULAR 25/87; WELSH OFFICE CIRCULAR 50/87 HOUSING AND PLANNING ACT 1986: TOWN AND COUNTRY PLANNING: SIMPLIFIED PLANNING ZONES (SPZs).

Development control
3.2 An SPZ scheme grants planning permission only for the developments it specifies and within the terms is sets out. SPZ schemes cannot grant listed building consent, scheduled ancient monument consent, consent for the display of advertisements or consent for the stopping up or diversion of a right of way. These systems of control will continue to apply in the normal way within the area of an SPZ. Nor can SPZs grant any necessary licences or given any building regulation approval associated with the development.

HOME OFFICE CIRCULAR 63/1989: DANGEROUS DOGS ACT 1989 AND DOGS ACT 1871

[description of the 1989 Act not included.]

Related legislation
The Dangerous Dogs Act 1989 extends and reinforces the powers available to the court under the Dogs Act 1871. Besides the new Act, the provisions which should be particularly noted in respect of the control of ferocious and dangerous dogs are:
(i) section 28 of the Town Police Clauses Act 1847; section 54(2) of the Metropolitan Police Act 1839; section 35(2) of the City of London Police Act 1839. These sections are similarly worded and make it an offence for any person to allow an unmuzzled ferocious dog to be at large in any street (which is interpreted as any street, unfenced ground adjoining or abutting upon any street, or any place of public resort or recreation ground under the control of the local authority). The maximum penalty is a fine at level 3 or 14 days imprisonment.
(ii) section 1(4) of the Dogs Act 1906 provides that where a dog is proved to have injured cattle or poultry, or chased sheep, it may be dealt with under section 2 of the Dogs Act 1871 as a dangerous dog. The effect of the Dangerous Dogs Act 1989 is, therefore, to reinforce the powers available to destroy dogs which have chased sheep and to give the court powers to disqualify their owners from having custody of a dog in future.

'Ferocious' and 'Dangerous' Dogs
It is a matter for the court to decide, in the circumstances of each case. whether a dog might be regarded in law as 'ferocious' or 'dangerous'. In general terms, a dog might be regarded as ferocious if it appears untamed, and dangerous if it is unsafe. It is not necessary for a dog to have bitten or attempted to bite anybody to be 'ferocious'. Nor is it necessary for a 'dangerous' dog to be 'ferocious'. That is to say that a dog with a propensity to attack, even if only in certain circumstances and in respect of certain categories of person, may be considered to be dangerous, although not necessarily ferocious.

The test of whether a dog is dangerous has been held to be
(i) if it has a propensity to do certain acts; and
(ii) if these acts are dangerous.

'Ferocious' applies more to the character or nature of the dog than to its actions. The term 'ferocious' should not, therefore, be interpreted as applying to certain breeds. However, the court may take the view that some breeds are more difficult to tame than others, so that dogs from these breeds are more likely to be 'ferocious' unless the owner has specific reason to believe otherwise.

It may also be, for instance, that dogs of certain breeds, when exercised in twos or threes, are more difficult to keep under control and might, therefore, become more 'ferocious' or more 'dangerous' than when exercised singly by a handler. These are matters to be tested in each case. The important point is that if a dog is 'ferocious', it is an offence to allow it to be at large without a muzzle.

By virtue of section 63(3) of the Magistrates Courts Acts 1980, that Act does not apply to orders made under the Dogs Act 1871. The Dangerous Dogs Act 1989 contains its own provisions for the enforcement of such orders.

RIGHTS OF WAY

It should be noted that, as explained in Home Office Circular 25/89, under the Criminal Justice Act 1988, dogs which have been used in offences may be confiscated as property.

DEPARTMENT OF THE ENVIRONMENT CIRCULAR 18/90, WELSH OFFICE CIRCULAR 45/90 MODIFICATIONS TO THE DEFINITIVE MAP: WILDLIFE AND COUNTRYSIDE ACT 1981

4. However, in making an application for an order to delete or downgrade a right of way, it will be for those who contend that there is no right of way or that a right of way is of a lower status than that shown, to prove that the map is in error by the discovery of evidence, which when considered with all other relevant evidence clearly shows that a mistake was made when the right of way was first recorded. The authority is required, by paragraph 3 of Schedule 14 to the Act, to investigate the matters stated in the application. However it is not for the authority to demonstrate that the map is correct, but for the applicant to show that an error was made. The advice contained in paragraphs 14 and 16 of Annex A to Circular 1/83 (superseded by Circular 21/88) regarding the considerations applicable to the deletion or downgrading of rights of way is again relevant. Authorities may also make orders amending the definitive map and statement where they themselves have discovered evidence of error; the requirement to demonstrate that the map and statement is in error, applies equally to this situation.

6. User groups have expressed concern that the facility to remove rights shown on the definitive map will lead to the widespread loss of rights of way, and to a larger number of spurious applications. However the Secretaries of State do not believe these fears are justified. The Court of Appeal gave careful consideration to the question of the conclusive evidential effect of the definitive map and statement. It concluded that there is no difficulty in reconciling sections 53 and 56 of the Act, once the purpose of the legislation as a whole is understood, namely the preparation and maintenance of an authoritative record in the form of a definitive map and statement showing those highways (namely footpaths, bridleways, roads used as public paths and byways open to all traffic) over which there are public rights. Once prepared, and until subsequently revised, the map and statement is conclusive evidence in rights of way disputes.

7. Authorities will be aware of the need, as emphasised by the Court of Appeal, to maintain an authoritative map and statement of the highest attainable accuracy. The evidence needed to remove a public right from such an authoritative record, will need to be cogent. The procedures for identifying and recording public rights of way have, in successive legislation, been comprehensive and thorough. Whilst they do not preclude errors, particularly where recent research has uncovered previously unknown evidence, or where the review procedures have never been implemented, they would tend to suggest that it is unlikely that a large number of errors would have been perpetuated for up to 40 years, without being questioned earlier.

8. Where an authority is disposed to make an order deleting/downgrading a right of way it should consider, further to the advice in paragraphs 27 and 29 of Annex A to Circular 1/83, the need for additional consultation — for example with local user groups — or publicity to ensure that all the evidence from the public concerning the existence or status of the route, is available.

DOE CIRCULAR 18/90

Roads Used as Public Paths
9. As regards the reclassification of Roads Used as Public Paths (RUPPs), the Court of Appeal's decision similarly confirms the earlier view, that the review procedures in section 54 of the Act are not subject to the provisions in section 56 regarding the conclusive evidential effect of the map and statement. As section 54 indicates, in reclassifying a RUPP the authority should consider the evidence regarding public vehicular rights. If these are shown not to exist then the RUPP should be reclassified as a bridleway, unless there is evidence that bridleway rights do not exist, in which case it may be reclassified as a footpath. If evidence is discovered which demonstrates that the RUPP was put on the map in error (ie that it should not have been shown at all), or that its route is depicted incorrectly, then the authority will need to proceed by way of a modification order under section 53(3)(c)(iii).

Protection of Public Rights of Way
10. Applications to delete or downgrade rights of way should be determined as quickly as possible, to resolve uncertainty. However, because of the nature of the procedures for continuous review of the definitive map and statement introduced by the 1981 Act there is nothing to prevent repeated applications in respect of a single route, if additional evidence is discovered. Authorities will need to consider carefully how best to proceed, where rights of way, on the definitive map, are persistently obstructed. They should seek, in the first instance, to resolve problems amicably. They will need to bear in mind however that the definitive map and statement is conclusive evidence of the rights of way shown thereon, until such time as it is amended by a confirmed order or an order made under section 53(3)(a); and to take such action as is considered necessary, in the particular circumstances, to comply with their statutory duties to protect and assert public rights.

PUBLIC RIGHTS OF WAY AND DEVELOPMENT

Letter dated August 1987 from the Department of the Environment (ref DOE/DRA1/1902/9) and Welsh Office (WO/CC 22/3/1) to county, district and London borough councils.

1. Paragraphs 13 and 14 of DOE Circular 1/83 (WO Circular 1/83) contain advice and guidance on the relationship between public rights of way and development. This letter supplements and amplifies that advice and guidance.

2. Once planning permission has been granted, for a development, commencement of work can often be delayed by the need for any public rights of way affected to be stopped-up or diverted. If such delays are to be avoided, it is important that the proposals for the rights of way are formulated and agreed between the developer and the planning authority and the necessary order made as quickly as possible.

3. It is a statutory requirement that planning permission be granted before the order can be made and the procedure governing its publication, consideration and confirmation commenced. But these stages are invariably preceded by discussion and negotiation on the proposals for the right of way between the developer and the planning authority and quite often by informal non-statutory consultation on those proposals with the organisations representing the interests of users of rights of way. (Separate guidance on such consultation is set out in the Code of Practice drawn up by the Rights of Way Review Committee).

4. Most planning applications do not contain sufficient information to enable the effect on any right of way to be assessed or for proposals for the stopping-up or diversion of such a right of way to be formulated and discussed alongside the consideration and determination of the planning application. Consequently paragraph 13 of the Circular encourages developers and planning authorities to take account of the need for rights of way to be stopped-up or diverted during the consideration of the matters reserved under the planning permission for subsequent approval. There are two advantages if developers submit and discuss with the planning authority their proposals for the right of way at this stage, rather than after approval of the details: first, any potential disadvantages to the public in the alternative arrangements for the right of way can be minimised, so enabling the eventual proposals to gain a wider measure of public acceptance; and second, the statutory procedures associated with the making and confirmation of the necessary order can be put in hand without delay once the details have been approved.

5. However, where the application is for full planning permission, (as for example are mineral extraction applications), the decision on the application may be preceded by lengthy negotiation and discussion between the developer and the planning authority, with the eight week period stipulated in the General Development Order for the determination of planning applications being set aside by mutual consent. If there is a reasonable expectation that planning permission will eventually be forthcoming there is clearly no reason why the proposals for any consequential stopping-up or diversion of public rights of way should not be considered concurrently with, and as part of, discussions on the proposed development rather than await the grant of planning permission. This should include, as far as possible, the preparation in draft of the order, and associated notices, the form of which is prescribed in the Town and Country Planning (Public Path Orders) Regulations 1983.

6. To summarise therefore the Secretary of State looks to developers and planning authorities, whenever practicable, to initiate discussions about the stopping-up or diversion of public rights of way in parallel with the consideration of the application or of the matters reserved for subsequent approval, so that the order may be made as soon as possible, after permission is granted.

PROPOSED CHANGES TO RIGHTS OF WAY AND DEFINITIVE MAPS : A CODE OF PRACTICE ON CONSULTATION FOR LOCAL AUTHORITIES IN ENGLAND AND WALES

[prepared by the Rights of Way Review Committee, revised June 1991]

I. Introduction

1. It is now the view of most authorities with powers to make orders affecting public rights of way that the time and cost involved in processing such orders can be reduced if informal consultation is carried out with interested parties prior to the orders being made.

2. Authorities may find it helpful, therefore, to have guidance on the form of such consultation. To this end, the Rights of Way Review Committee has prepared the following code of practice on consultation. The Committee is chaired by Alan Haselhurst MP and brings together representatives of the

CODE OF PRACTICE ON CONSULTATION

relevant local authority associations, government departments, public agencies, path user groups and farmers' and landowners' organisations.

3. The code is, of course, advisory not mandatory. Failure to comply with the code will not invalidate any subsequent order; and neither does compliance with the code discharge order-making authorities from fulfilling the necessary statutory requirements on the notification of the making and subsequent stages of the orders.

4. The code has been agreed by the Department of the Environment and the Welsh Office and is commended to all relevant authorities by the Association of County Councils, the Association of District Councils and the Association of Metropolitan Authorities.

II. Application of Code

5. The Code should apply to proposals made by local authorities (county and district councils, London borough councils, and national park planning boards) for:

(a) The making of public path creation, diversion and extinguishment orders under sections 26, 118 and 119 of the Highways Act 1980.

(b) The making of an order under section 257 of the Town and Country Planning Act 1990 to divert or extinguish a public footpath or bridleway to enable development to be carried out in accordance with planning permission.

(c) Modification and reclassification orders made by surveying authorities under sections 53 and 54 of the Wildlife and Countryside Act 1981, and to which Schedule 14 and/or Schedule 15 of the Act apply.

(d) Applications by highway authorities to magistrates courts under section 116 of the Highways Act 1980 for the stopping up or diversion of highways.

(e) Creation agreements made under section 25 of the Highways Act 1980, where these are part of a package involving also public path diversion or extinguishment orders.

(f) Side roads orders made under section 14 or 18 of the Highways Act 1980.

(g) Extinguishment of public right of way orders made under section 32 of the Acquisition of Land Act 1981, or section 258 of the Town and Country Planning Act 1990.

(h) Traffic regulation orders made under section 1 of the Road Traffic Regulation Act 1984 to restrict or regulate use of footpaths, bridleways, byways or unsurfaced carriageways (including those shown as byways or RUPPs on definitive maps).

III. Rights of Way affected by planning permission for development

6. Under section 257 of the Town and Country Planning Act 1990, an order can be made to divert or extinguish a public footpath or bridleway to enable development to be carried out in accordance with planning permission. In view of the need to process planning applications quickly and within strictly defined time limits, it is not proposed that the code of practice should apply to planning applications which will, if granted, give rise to such orders. Nevertheless, attention is drawn to paragraphs 12–14 of Department of the Environment Circular 1/83, which stresses 'the need for adequate consideration of the rights of way before the decision on the planning application is taken.'

IV. Consultees

7. The organisations to be consulted will obviously vary, not only from county to county, but within counties and even within districts. It is therefore suggested that a list of consultees be compiled for each district, to be used by both the county and district councils, and that this be sent annually to those included on it, for amendment and updating.

8. Organisations to be included on such a list are:

(a) Other local authorities, including the parish or community council, or chairman of the parish meeting, and national park planning boards.

(b) Statutory undertakers.

(c) Prescribed organisations (as set out in Annex C of DOE Circular 1/83). Details of how, and when, these organisations wish to be consulted are included in Annex A. Authorities should note that the interests of all vehicular users, including four-wheel drive organisations, are being looked after by the ACU which is, in effect, now acting on behalf of MOLARA.

(d) Local organisations. Such local bodies as appear to the authorities to have a sufficient interest in public rights of way in the area concerned.

(e) The Countryside Commission and the Countryside Council for Wales. The Highways Act requires these bodies to be consulted prior to the making of any order with respect to any part of a footpath or bridleway in a national park.

9. The owner and occupier of any land affected by a proposal should be consulted unless the proposal has originated from him or he is otherwise given notice of the proposal, whether under statute or other provision. In cases where such an owner or occupier is not known to the authority representative organisations of farmers and landowners should be contacted and asked to assist. Authorities should bear in mind that a proposal may have an effect on owners and occupiers other than those whose land the path(s) or way(s) in question run(s) or will run as a result of the proposal, and should be prepared to consult accordingly.

10. Regional managers (land use and countryside) of the Ministry of Agriculture are also able to offer independent comment where agricultural interests are affected, and authorities may wish to consult them in appropriate cases.

11. Authorities may not be aware of all the organisations in their area with an interest in public paths (particularly the smaller and newer ones). It would therefore be advisable for authorities to advertise in local newspapers at intervals of, say, four years, to explain that a list of consultees exist and to invite applications for inclusion on the list from any organisation with an interest in public path orders. This should not, of course, preclude local authorities from adding organisations to the list at any time, but it would give authorities the protection of having invited requests and of having responded to all requests so made.

12. In the case of any proposal affecting a statutory long-distance route (national trail), the appropriate regional office of the Countryside Commission or the Countryside Council for Wales should be notified so that they may consider whether it is necessary to make a related order to formally vary the line of the approved route. Any organisation representing users of the route such as Offa's Dyke Association or the South West Way Association should also be consulted.

V. Procedure

13. The letter to consultees requesting comments on a proposed change should include:

CODE OF PRACTICE ON CONSULTATION

(a) A plan, to a scale of not less than 1:10,000 (or 6" to the mile) showing the proposed change, together with a statement of reasons for the change.
(b) Where appropriate, details of any limitations or conditions to which any proposed new route would be subject, or of any works which would be carried out on such a route.
(c) The date by which comments should be received by the authority. This should be not less than 28 days from the date of the letter.
(d) An indication of whether consultees are permitted to inspect the line of any proposed new route without further request, or alternatively the name, address and telephone number of the person or organisation from whom such permission should be sought.
14. The consultees should be requested to acknowledge consultations as they are received from the order-making authorities.

ANNEX A

CONSULTATION WITH INTERESTED ORGANISATIONS

Organisation	Proposals/Orders for which consultation is requested	Person/Address to which pre-order consultation papers should be sent	Person/Address to which the statutory notice etc should be sent on making of order
Auto-Cycle Union	All cases, except those affecting footpaths over which no public vehicular rights are claimed, or suspected, to exist	The appropriate local representative as notified to the authority	Auto-Cycle Union Miller House Corporation Street Rugby Warwickshire CV21 2DN
British Horse Society	All cases	BHS local representative as notified to the authority	BHS British Equestrian Centre Stoneleigh Kenilworth Warwick CV8 2LR
Byways and Bridleways Trust	All cases	BBT local representative as notified to the authority	BBT The Granary Charlcutt Calne Wilts SN11 9HL
Open Spaces Society	All cases, but only in those areas where the Society has notified the authorities concerned of their interest	The appropriate local representative, as notified to the authority	Open Spaces Society 25A Bell Street Henley on Thames Oxon RG9 2BA

RIGHTS OF WAY

Organisation	Proposals/Orders for which consultation is requested	Person/Address to which pre-order consultation papers should be sent	Person/Address to which the statutory notice etc should be sent on making of order
The Ramblers' Association	All cases	RA local representative, as notified to the authority	Ramblers' Association 1/5 Wandsworth Road London SW8 2XX
Peak and Northern Footpath Society	All cases in the area for which the Society is prescribed to receive orders	1 Nelson Street Hazel Grove Stockport SK7 4LR	1 Nelson Street Hazel Grove Stockport SK7 4LR
Chiltern Society	All cases in the area for which the Society is prescribed to receive orders	3 Hither Meadow Lower Road Chalfont St Peter Gerrards Cross Bucks SL9 9AW	3 Hither Meadow Lower Road Chalfont St Peter Gerrards Cross Bucks SL9 9AW
Welsh Trail Riders Association	Cases in Wales only where, claimed or suspected, vehicular rights are affected by any path orders	WTRA Kingcoed Farm Usk Gwent NP5 1DS (except where otherwise notified to the authority)	WTRA Kingcoed Farm Usk Gwent NP5 1DS (except where otherwise notified to the authority)
British Driving Society*	Cases involving reclassifications and for proposals about RUPPs and byways	27 Dugard Place Barford Warwick CV35 8DX	27 Dugard Place Barford Warwick CV35 8DX
Cyclists' Touring Club*	All cases *except* those involving footpaths only	CTC Cotterell House 69 Meadrow Godalming Surrey GU7 3HS (except where otherwise notified to the authority)	CTC Cotterell House 69 Meadrow Godalming Surrey GU7 3HS

Note:
(i)(*) These organisations are not prescribed under the regulations to the relevant Acts.
(ii) Consultation under this code of practice does not obviate the need for compliance with statutory procedures.

Index

For legal cases and legislative provisions see the tables of :-

Cases	12
Statutes (Acts of Parliament)	16
Statutory instruments (Regulations)	23
Circulars issued by government departments	25

For publications referred to under 'Further Reading' see chapter 9.4.

abbreviations used	26	for order to require removal of	
abusive sign or writing	190	obstruction	214, 248
access (right to roam)		assault	190
acquisition of right under		Audit Commission	247
common law	273	aviation purpose, development for	151
agreements	270		
availability of information	274	barbed wire	193
by permission of the landowner	270	barrier, to safeguard user	
orders	271	of footpath	189, 239
to common land	272	bicycle	
to National Trust land	272	all-terrain	54
to open country	270	mountain	54
Acts of Parliament		on bridleway	53
deposited plans	110	on footpath	53
Local and Private	57, 110, 157	on footway	53
petitioning against	157	race	54
agency agreement	224	trial of speed	54
Agriculture, Ministry of *see* Ministry of Agriculture		used recklessly	54
		used while unfit to ride through drink or drugs	54
aid to passage in footpath	239	used without due care and attention	54
air-weapon	192	binding over to keep the peace	190
airport	151	bird nesting	269
airport operator	151	book of reference	
all-terrain bike *see* bicycle		for Ordnance Survey map	112
animal		for Private Act of Parliament	110
as statutory nuisance	187	Bowles, Mrs Zara	236
danger from, to user	186	breach of the peace	190
disease of	166	bridge	
liability for injury caused by	186	construction or reconstruction	240
appeal		joining two counties, responsibility for maintenance	34
against decision of magistrates' court	156, 204, 235	over carriageway	239
against refusal to make modification order	103	bridle-gate, British Standard for	228, 261
application		bridleway	
for change to right of way	136, 153	bicycle on	53
for judicial review	218	creation *see* creation of a highway *and* change to a right of way	
for modification order	99	definition	31
for order to abate a nuisance	214, 248	diversion *see* diversion *and* change to a right of way	
for order to maintain a highway	230, 248		

517

RIGHTS OF WAY

extinguishment *see* extinguishment *and* change to a right of way
  motor vehicle on   54, 190
  width of gate across   228
British Coal Corporation   150
British Library   113, 256
British National Bibliography   256
British Railways Board   56, 57, 157
British Standard for stiles, kissing-gates and bridle-gates   228, 261
British Waterways Board   225
Broads Authority   35
bull   184
byelaw
  to prohibit bull on right of way or in public place   184
  to prohibit cycling on footpath   53
  to prohibit horse-riding on footpath   54
  to regulate access to open country   271
byway open to all traffic
  definition   32
  diversion *see* diversion *and* change to a right of way
  extinguishment *see* extinguishment *and* change to a right of way
  maintenance   222
  restricting vehicular use   153, 158, 161
  signposting   236
  waymarking   236

canal
  bridge over   223
  tow-path   225
capacity to dedicate a right of way   61
carriageway   31, 222
cattle-grid   170, 240
certiorari   218
change to a right of way
  administrative procedure   125
  airport, to permit development of   151
  by private Act of Parliament   157
  charging applicant   136
  closure *see* extinguishment
  coming into operation   134
  compensation for   72, 136, 143
  concurrent orders   143
  confirmation of order   132
  consultation   125
  conversion to cycle track   161
  creation agreement   71
  creation order   142
  decided by an inspector   121
  decision letter on   132
  development, for   144
  diversion
    by magistrates' court order   153
    by public path order   140
    to enable development to take place   146
  extinguishment
    by magistrates' court order   153
    by public path order   137
    to enable development to take place   146
  High Court challenge   135
  housing action trust, for   152
  improved road, caused by   148
  list of powers   123
  magistrates' court, application to   153
  modification of proposal   133
  new road, caused by   148
  New Town, in   152
  notice
    of confirmation   132
    of proposal   126
    of proposed modification   133
  objection to
    consideration of   127
    making of   162
  over military land   158
  prescribed bodies, for receipt of orders   127
  public inquiry into, proceedings at   129
  quarry, to enable development of   150
  rationalisation scheme   167
  revocation of order   136
  Second World War, during   112
  Secretary of State, procedure when order made by   137
  side roads order   149
  slum clearance area, in   153
  statistics of   122
  temporary
    by traffic regulation order   160
    for animal and plant disease   166
    for disturbance of path across agricultural land   166
    for maintenance   165
    for major development   165
  urban development corporation, by   152
  variation of order   136
  vehicular right, extinguishment of   153, 161
Changing the rights of way network   168
Church Commissioners   72
church land, dedication of right of way over   72
Civil Aviation Authority   151
civil law   39
claimed maintenance power   224

INDEX

civil liability *see* liability
clearance
  of crop   181
  of obstruction   172
  of overgrown path   265
Cleveland Way   277
closure of a right of way, *see* change to a right of way, extinguishment *and* change to a right of way, temporary
coal, extraction of   150
code of practice
  for District Auditor   247
  on proposed change to a right of way   126
  on use of pesticides   193
commencement date, for procedures in the Wildlife and Countryside Act 1981   92
Commission for Local Administration   245
Committee on Footpaths and Access to the Countryside (Hobhouse Committee)   31, 73
Committee on the Consolidation of Highway Law   31
common duty of care to visitors   52
common land, access to   272
community council, powers of   36, 154, 240
community meeting, powers of   37
compensation for creation of a right of way   72, 137, 143
conclusive evidence, of definitive map   80, 103
concurrent orders, *see* change to a right of way
condition affecting a right of way
  generally   64
  in definitive statement   77, 81
  in public path order   141, 142
condition attached to planning permission   146
condition of rights of way
  results of Countryside Commission survey   30
confirmation
  of modification order   96
  of public path order   132
  of reclassification order   96
consultation
  before erecting signpost   238
  on proposed change to right of way   125
continuous review *see* review of definitive map and statement
copyright
  of information held by local authorities   38
  of Ordnance Survey map   255

costs
  application for, at public inquiry   132
  of order, charging of applicant   136
Country Landowners Association   31
Countryside Council for Wales   33, 125, 276
Countryside Commission   30, 31, 33, 125, 168, 249, 259, 276
  grants from, for ferries   60
County Agricultural Executive Committee   112
county borough, definitive map of   75, 91, 107
county council *see also* local authority
  functions of, as highway authority   33, 172, 177, 183, 219
  functions of, as surveying authority   34, 89
Court of Appeal   41
creation of a highway *see also* change to a right of way
  by agreement   71
  by dedication   61
  by order   71
criminal damage to property   196, 267
criminal law   39
crop
  obstruction by   180
  removal of   182
Crown Court
  appeal from magistrates' court   156, 204, 235
  application to, for order to to maintain   233, 235
  functions of   40
Crown land
  application of the law to   38
  dedication of paths over   70
  definition   38
cycle track
  conversion of footpath into   161
  definition   31, 161
cycling *see* bicycle

damage
  to property, by user   196
  to property, during path clearance   267
  to surface of highway   180
danger
  arising during practical work   268
  from animal   184
  from excavation   192
  notice of   240
date of review (of definitive map)   82
decision letter   132
declaration, by court   218

RIGHTS OF WAY

dedication of a highway
  express   61
  presumed
    at common law   62
    of one highway over another   68
    under statute   62
defence land   158
defence purposes, definition of   158
definitive map order, see modification order and reclassification order
definitive map and statement see also draft map and provisional map
  amendment to reflect change to a right of way   135
  and local government reorganisation   88, 105
  availability for public inspection   104
  conclusive evidence of the public's rights   80, 103
  conflict between map and statement   81
  continuous review   92
  definition   92
  deletion of way   84, 97
  downgrading of way   84, 97
  geographical extent of survey
    former county boroughs   75, 91, 107
    fully-developed areas   76, 91
    Isles of Scilly   76, 91
    London   75, 89
  information from, on OS map   118
  initial survey
    abandonment under Wildlife and Countryside Act   89
    under Countryside Act   89
    under National Parks and Access to the Countryside Act   74
  Limited Special Review   88
  position at 31 March 1974   105
  position at 28 February 1983   106
  preparation
    of new map under Wildlife and Countryside Act   104
    under National Parks and Access to the Countryside Act   79
  publication   79
  reclassification of roads used as public paths   85, 98
  relevant date   76, 105
  review see review of definitive map
  sale to the public   105
  scale and notation   76, 104
  Special Review   87
delegation of powers to local authority officers   126
de minimis rule   170
Department of the Environment   31

Department of Transport   31
deposit, on highway causing interruption, injury or danger   194
deposited plan for Private Act of Parliament   110
development
  definition   144
  giving rise to a change to a right of way   145
  necessitating temporary closure or diversion   165
  planning application for   144
  planning permission for   145
deviation from a right of way
  injury caused while so doing   50
  right to do so when way obstructed   46
dirt, on highway   194
District Auditor   247
district council see metropolitan district council and non-metropolitan district council
disturbance of surface of right of way see ploughing and other disturbance
ditch
  for drainage   240
  in carriageway   180
diversion, see also change to a right of way
  by magistrates' court order   153
  by public path order   140
  to enable development to take place   146
Divisional Court   40
'doctrine of non-feasance'   229
documentary evidence, see evidence of right of way status
document held by a local authority, right to inspect   109
dog
  and livestock   45
  attack by, on user   185
  control of, on road   45
  giving rise to act of trespass   44
  on a right of way   44
Dorset Coast Path   277
downgrading of a right of way
  amendment of the definitive map   84, 97
  extinguishment of rights by statutory process   153, 161
draft map
  effect of abandonment of survey on   88, 90
  modification to   77
  objection to   77
  preparation of   74
  publication of   76
drainage   240

INDEX

drought, temporary closure during 160
dust, mitigation of 240
duties
  of highway authority
      33, 172, 177, 183, 219
  of surveying authority 34, 89

easement 43
embankment 226
enforcing the duty to maintain 230
enterprise zone 145
entry onto land
  for survey in connection with public path order 126
  to clear crops 182
  to erect sign for footpath or bridleway 237
  to repair disturbed surface 177
Environment, Department of the, *see* Department of the Environment
erosion of path
  by water 226
  temporary diversion to enable restoration 165
estate map 113
estate road
  adoption of, as publicly maintainable 72
event to be considered on review of definitive map 82, 92
evidence of right of way status
  conclusive, of definitive map 80, 103
  documentary 108
  form for collection of 114
  user 114
'evidential' event 93, 94
excluded area *see* fully-developed area
extinguishment, *see also* change to a right of way
  by magistrates' court order 153
  by public path order 137
  to enable development to take place 146

fence, to safeguard user of footpath 189
ferry
  as link between rights of way 60
  grant from Countryside Commission towards 60
field-edge path
  definition 175
  disturbance of 175
  width of 177, 178
filth, flow of, onto highway 194
firearm 191
fire 191
flow of offensive matter, onto highway 194
foot-and-mouth disease 166

footbridge *see* bridge
footpath
  barrier in 189
  bicycle on 53
  creation *see* creation *and* change to a right of way
  definition 31
  diversion see diversion *and* change to a right of way
  extinguishment *see* extinguishment *and* change to a right of way
  horse on 54
  motor vehicle on 54, 190
  width of *see* width
Footpaths Committee (Gosling Committee) 31
Footpath Worker 247
footway 32, 53, 239
ford 240
foreshore 59
fully-developed area
  exclusion ended by Wildlife and Countryside Act 91
  exclusion from definitive map 76

gate
  as limitation on right of way 188
  authorisation for 188
  British Standard for 228, 261
  maintenance of 228
  width of 228
General Development Order 144, 147
General Household Survey 29, 275
golf course, effect on right of way 145
golf tournament, temporary closure during 160
good husbandry, rules of 175
Gosling, Sir Arthur 31
Gosling Committee *see* Footpaths Committee
gravel, extraction of 150
Greater London
  definitive maps in 75
  local authorities in 32, 36
green lane 32, 109
guidebook, production of 253

Hadrian's Wall Path 278
Haselhurst Committee *see* Rights of Way Review Committee
Haselhurst, Mr Alan MP 31
hazard of nature, protection against 240
headland path *see* field-edge path
Hickey, Mr Roy 31
High Court 40
highway *see also* public right of way

521

ceasing to exist due to natural causes 226
definition 31
ownership 48
highway authority
  as owner of surface of publicly-
    maintainable highway 48, 173
  duties of
    summary list 33
    to enforce provisions on crop
      interference 183
    to enforce provisions on disturbance
      of surface 177
    to maintain publicly-maintainable
      highways 219
    to prevent obstruction 170
    to protect and assert the public's
      rights 170
  liability of 50, 228
  obtaining action by 230, 244
highway district record 111
highway order 109
hippy convoy 47
Hobhouse Committee *see* Committee on Footpaths and Access to the Countryside
Hobhouse, Sir Arthur 31
holder, of land
  definition 33
  liability as occupier 50, 52
  trespass against 46
horse
  byelaw to prevent use on footpath 54
  injury caused by 186
  margin for, on carriageway 239
  popularity of riding 29, 275
  traffic regulation order to control
    use of 54
  use on footpath 54
House of Lords
  as court 41
  Record Office 109, 110
housing action trust 145, 152

improvement to a right of way
  general power of highway authority 240
  powers of local council 240
  specific powers 240
inclosure award 110
increment value duty 110
injunction, proceedings for 218
injury to user of a right of way
  arising during practical work 268
  by animal 184
  by nuisance 50

liability for, of highway
  authority 50, 228
liability for, of occupier 50
  when trespassing 51
inspector conducting a public inquiry 130
inquiry *see* public inquiry
insulting behaviour 190
insulting sign or writing 190
insurance, for practical work 268
intention not to dedicate a public right of
  way, evidence of 65
intention to dedicate a public right
  of way 68
interest in land, power to obtain
  details of 173
intimidation 190
Isle of Man 119
Isles of Scilly 76, 91, 119

judicial review 218

kissing-gate, British
  Standard for 228, 261

Lake District national park 35, 125
land held
  for defence purpose 158
  for planning purpose 151
landholder, definition of 33
landowner
  discovering identity of 101
  giving notice to of application for
    modification order 101
    Land Register, access to for land
      ownership details 101
land transfer, and notification of rights
  of way 49
Landranger map 119
Larkhill ranges 158
law of rights of way, development of 30
'legal' event 93, 94
legal proceedings
  by highway authority 172
  by user 204, 210, 214, 230, 248
legal system, rights of way and the 39
levelling 240
liability
  of highway authority 50, 228
  of occupier 50, 52
  of railway undertaking 51, 57
lighting 240
limitation, on right of way
  in definitive statement 77, 81
  in public path order 141, 142
Limited Special Review 88

INDEX

line of right of way
  marking after disturbance of surface 176
  marking through crop 181
list of streets 117
Local Act of Parliament 157
Local Administration,
  Commission for 245
local authority
  access to information held by 37, 109
  definition 32
  deposit of documents with 109
  meeting of, access to by public 37
  register of members 38
local council *see also* community council *and* parish council
  definition 32
  powers of 36, 154, 240
local government reorganisation, effect of
  in 1974 33, 88, 105
  in 1986 33
local government system, rights of way and the 33
Local Ombudsman 245
locus standi, of petitioner against Private Bill 157
London
  borough council, functions of, as highway authority 33, 172, 177, 183, 219
  borough council, functions of, as planning authority 36, 144
  borough council, functions of, as surveying authority 34, 36, 89
  County Council 75
  definitive maps in 75
London Gazette 77, 121, 159
Long Distance Walkers' Association 278
long-distance route 60, 276

magistrates' court
  application to, for closure or diversion order 153
  application to, for order to abate a nuisance 214, 248
  application to, for order to maintain a highway 230, 248
  application to, for order to require removal of obstruction 173, 248
  functions of 40
  proceedings in 198
  prosecution in, for failure to keep path clear of crops 210
  prosecution in, for obstruction 204
making good, of right of way after disturbance 176

maintenance
  agreement by highway authority to undertake 72
  application for enforcement of duty 230
  definition 219
  duty of highway authority 223
  powers of local council 225
  powers of non-metropolitan district council 224
  responsibility for 221
  standard of 219
  temporary diversion in connection with 165
maladministration, investigation of allegation of
  by Local Commissioner for Administration 245
  by Parliamentary Commissioner for Administration 39
Managing rights of way: an agenda for action 168
mandamus 218, 245, 248
map
  as record of rights of way 113
  definitive *see* definitive map and statement
  of admitted rights of way 66, 110
  of estate 113
  Ordnance Survey, showing rights of way 118
  production of 253
margin, for horse-riders on carriageway 239
marking line of right of way
  after disturbance of surface 176
  through crop 181
'maximum width' 178, 228
medium high water
  land above 59
  land below 59
medium low water 59
Menwith Hill 158
metalled road, meaning of 237
metalling 240
metropolitan counties, list of 32
metropolitan district council, *see also* local authority
  functions of, as highway authority 33, 172, 177, 183, 219
  functions of, as planning authority 36, 214
  functions of, as surveying authority 34, 89
mineral extraction 150
'minimum width' 176, 228
Ministry of Agriculture 31, 166
misleading notice 189

mock battle, temporary closure during 160
modification
  of definitive map *see* review of definitive map
    of modification order 96
    of public path order 133
    of reclassification order 96
modification order
  application for 99
  modification of 96
  objection to 95
  prescribed bodies, for receipt of 95
  procedure 94
  statistics of 107
Molesworth airfield 158
motor cycle *see* motor vehicle
motor vehicle
  careless driving 190
  in race or trial of speed 191
  in rally 191
  inconsiderate driving 190
  on cycle track 55
  on footway 191
  on footpath or bridleway 54, 190
  parking of, other than on a road 55
  parking of, on cycle track 55
  reckless driving 190
  removal of, from highway 48
motorway
  effect of, on a right of way 148
  traffic permitted on 149
mountain bike *see* bicycle

National Farmers Union 31
national park (*see also* Broads Authority, Lake District national park *and* Peak District national park) 32, 35
National Parks Commission 276
National Rivers Authority 150, 226
National Survey of Countryside Recreation 275
National Trust, access to common land owned by 272
navigable waterway, tow-path of 225
negativing an intention to dedicate 65
Newman, Mr Peter 219
newspaper, writing a walk description for 254
new road, right of way crossing 148
New Town 152
Norfolk and Suffolk Broads Authority *see* Broads Authority
Norfolk Coast Path 277
non-metropolitan district council
  as planning authority 35, 144

claiming of power to undertake maintenance 34, 224
power to veto application for change to right of way 154
non-statutory review 167
North Cornwall Coast Path 277
North Downs Way 276, 277
notice
  bringing into question existence of a right of way 65
  containing false or misleading statement 189
  deterring public from using a way 189
  of confirmation of order 96, 132
  of danger 240
  of decision not to confirm order 96, 132
  of making of order 94, 126
  of proposed modification to order 96, 133
Nottinghamshire rationalisation scheme 167
nuisance
  abatement notice 188
  at common law 193
  duty of local authority to take action 187
  order to abate 188, 210
  power to require removal of 172
  public 55
  statutory 187

objection, to order *see* change to a right of way, modification order *and* reclassification order
obstruction *see also* problem, reporting of
  crop, as an 47, 180
  definition 169
  duty of highway authority to prevent 170
  effect on diversion order 141
  effect on extinguishment order 138
  effect on magistrates' court application 148
  effect on order to enable development to take place 148
  giving rise to right to deviate 47
  lawful authority for 170
  ploughing, as an 173
  prosecution for
    under common law 218
    under Highways Act 204
  recorded in definitive statement 77
  removal of, by highway authority 173
  removal of, by user 195

INDEX

occupier of land	
discovery of identity	101
liability of	50, 52
Offa's Dyke Path	276, 277
offensive matter on highway	195
Office of Population Censuses and Surveys	275
oil-seed rape	181, 182
Ombudsmen, *see* Commission for Local Administration and Parliamentary Commissioner for Administration	
'once a highway, always a highway'	43
opencast coal mining, effect on right of way	150
open country, access to	270
Open Spaces Society (OSS)	30, 121, 156, 157
Ordnance Survey map	
books of reference	112
copyright in	255
permissive paths on	56, 119
rights of way on	118
use of, for production of guidebook or map	255
'out of repair', meaning of	219, 230
Outdoor Leisure Map	119
overgrown path, clearance of	265
overhanging vegetation	183
owner of land, discovery of	101
ownership	
of land	33
of subsoil under public right of way	48
of surface of public right of way	48
parish council	
involvement with initial survey for definitive map	76
minutes of	113
powers of	36, 154, 240
parish meeting, powers of	37
parking of motor vehicle	
on cycle track	55
other than on a road	55
Parliamentary Commissioner for Administration	39
path clearance	265
path guide or map, production of	253
path survey	249
Pathfinder map	119
Paths for People	37
Peak District national park	35, 125
pedal cycle *see* bicycle	
Peddars Way	277
Pembrokeshire Coast Path	277
Pennine Bridleway	278
Pennine Way	276, 277

permissive path	
nature of	56
occupiers' liability	56
on Ordnance Survey map	56, 119
pesticide	193
Pilgrims Way	276
plan	
deposited, in connection with Private Act of Parliament	110
in modification order	94
in public path order	126
in reclassification order	94
planning application	
for development	144
planning authority	35, 36, 144
planning board in national park, powers of	35
planning permission	
condition attached to	146
effect on right of way	145
grant of	144
planning purposes, land held for	151
plant disease	166
ploughing and other disturbance	
authorisation of, in wartime	112, 175
common law right	174
making good the surface	176
'maximum width'	178
'minimum width'	176
of field-edge path	175
prosecution for	178
statutory right	175
without lawful authority	178
prescribed bodies, for receipt of orders	95, 127
press release	252
Private Act of Parliament	
affecting right of way over railway line	57
containing power to change right of way	157
deposited plan for	110
Private Bill	157
privately-maintainable highway	221
private right of way	43
'Private Road' sign	66, 189
problem, reporting of	
sample form for	243
to a user organisation	197, 243
to the highway authority	197, 243
to the local council	197, 243
to the owner or occupier	197, 243
procession, public, need to give notice	55
prosecution	
for interference by crops	210
for obstruction	204
for ploughing	178, 180

RIGHTS OF WAY

provisional map
    application to Crown Court   78
    publication   78
public inquiry
    inspector conducting   130
    procedure at   129
Public Lending Right   256
public nuisance *see* nuisance
public path order *see* change to a right of way
public procession *see* procession, public
Public Record Office   109, 110, 112
public right of way
    and land transfer   49
    change to *see* change to a right of way
    definition   43
    duty of highway authority to protect   170
    extent of public's rights (*see also* conclusive evidence)   43, 103
    maintenance   219
    obstruction   169
    on OS maps   118
    ownership   48
    survey of   74, 90, 249
    'usual accompaniment'   44
    width of   176, 178, 227
publicly-maintainable highway   221

quarry
    as statutory nuisance   187
    development of, giving rise to change to right of way   150
Queen's Bench Division of the High Court   40

race
    between cycles   54
    between motor vehicles   191
rail, to safeguard user of footpath   189
railway line
    fencing of adjoining highway   57
    liability of railway undertaking   57
    right of way above or below   57
    right of way across on level   56
    trespass on   47
Ramblers' Association (RA)   30, 121, 156, 157, 243
rape, oil-seed   181, 182
rationalisation scheme
    in Nottinghamshire   167
    in West Sussex   167
    Local Ombudsman's views on   167

reclassification order
    modification of   96
    objection to   95
    prescribed bodies, for receipt of   95
    procedure   94
    statistics of   108
reclassification of road used as a public path
    under Countryside Act   85, 98
    under Wildlife and Countryside Act   98
recreational activity, statistics of   275
relevant date, of definitive map   76, 105
reorganisation of local government, *see* local government reorganisation
repair of highway *see* maintenance
Report that path problem   244
reservoir   150
review, date of   82
review of definitive map and statement
    abandonment under Wildlife and Countryside Act   90
    and local government reorganisation   88
    continuous   89
    deletion of right of way under   84, 97
    downgrading of right of way under   84, 97
    Limited Special   88
    non-statutory   167
    reclassification of roads used as public paths   85, 98
    Special   87
    under Countryside Act   83
    under National Parks and Access to the Countryside Act   82
    under Wildlife and Countryside Act   89
rhizomania   166
Ridgeway Path   276, 277
riding
    of bicycle, *see* bicycle
    of horse, *see* horse
right of way, *see* private right of way *and* public right of way
Rights of Way Act (Isle of Man)   119
Rights of Way Review Committee   31, 126
right to roam, *see* access
Riley, Mr Bill   99
river bank
    erosion of   226
    rights over   226
road
    construction of across right of way   148
    definition   32, 56
    restriction or prohibition of traffic over   53, 54, 158
road used as a public path
    definition   31
    maintenance of   222

INDEX

reclassification under Countryside
   Act   85, 98
reclassification under Wildlife and
   Countryside Act   98
rights over   85
signposting   238
rope across highway   195
rules of good husbandry   175
RUPP *see* road used as a public path

safety precaution, for practical work   268
sample path survey   249
search, in connection with land transfer   49
sea-shore
   access to the   59
   rights over the   59
seat   240
Secretary of State   33
self-help in removal of obstruction   195
shelter, erection of   240
shrub, planting of   240
side roads order   149
signpost
   damage to   195
   duty to erect and maintain   236
   pulling down   195
   removal of   195
sign, unauthorised   189
slum clearance area   153
soil, removal of, from highway   180
Somerset and North Devon Coast
   Path   277
South Cornwall Coast Path   277
South Devon Coast Path   277
South Downs Way   276, 277, 278
South West Peninsula Coast Path   278
Special Review   87
special road   148
Spicer Committee *see* Rights of Way
   Review Committee
Spicer, Mr Michael MP   31
staff, appointment of, by local
   authorities   34
Stansted Airport   151
statement
   accompanying definitive map   76
   of priorities for definitive map work   93
statistics
   of changes to right of way   122
   of modification and reclassification
      orders   108
   of recreational activity   275
statutory declaration   116
statutory undertaker   170
stepping stones   240

stile
   as limitation on right of way   188
   authorisation of   188
   British Standard for   228, 261
   construction and design   228, 261
   maintenance   228
stone, throwing of   191
stopping-up *see* extinguishment *and*
   change to a right of way
street
   definition   32
   list of   117
structure on highway, removal of   172
subsoil, under right of way,
   ownership of   48
subway   239
sugar-beet rhizomania   166
surface, of a public right of way
   maintenance of   219
   ownership of   48
surveying authority
   definition   32
   duties of   34, 89
survey of rights of way *see* definitive map
   and path survey

temporary closure and diversion *see* change
   to a right of way
tenant   33
Thames Path   277
This Common Inheritance
   (White Paper)   30
threatening behaviour   190
threatening sign or writing   190
throwing of stone or missile   191
tithe map and apportionment   111
tools, for practical work   265, 267
Tourist Map   119
town council *see* local council
tow-path
   maintenance of   225
   rights over   58
traffic regulation order
   permanent   53, 54, 148, 158
   temporary   160
   to regulate cycling   53
   to regulate horse-riding   54, 159
   to regulate walking   160
traffic sign
   damage to   195
   waymark as   237
Transport, Department of *see* Department
   of Transport
Transport and Works Bill   157
tree, planting of   240

RIGHTS OF WAY

trespass
   as crime 47
   by dogs 45
   by drivers of motor vehicles 54
   by horse-riders 54
   nature of 44, 46
   on highway 44
   resulting from obstruction 46
   with intention to reside 47
trespasser, liability to 51
trial of speed
   involving bicycles 54
   involving motor vehicles 191
trunk road 149
turf, removal of, from highway 180

unauthorised sign or notice 189
unclassified county road 118
unofficial diversion 56
upgrading of a highway
   creation of additional right 71, 72, 142
   improvement to physical condition 240
   recognition of existing right on definitive map 93
Upper Heyford, RAF 158
urban development corporation 145, 152
'usual accompaniment' of a user of a right of way 44

vegetation
   growing in highway 180
   overhanging 183
vehicle on a right of way *see* motor vehicle

walking, popularity of 29, 275
warden, for right of way 44
war
   authorisation of ploughing of right of way 112, 175
   causing change to a right of way 112
War Works Commission 112
water, right of way alongside
   erosion of 226
   maintenance of 225, 226
water, right of way over 63
water undertaker 150
waymarking
   damage to 195
   legal aspects 236
   practical work 238, 257
   recommended design 257
West Sussex rationalisation scheme 167
Who needs a hole in the wall? 146
widening 238
width
   generally 227
   'maximum width' 178, 228
   'minimum width' 176, 228
   of gate 228
   of stile 262
Wolds Way 277

Your Local Ombudsman 246